I'll Take That One Too

Evacuees, the invisible generation

Martin L Parsons

First Published 2013
by DSM
Barmolloch Mhor
Kilmichael Glen
Lochgilphead
PA31 8RJ

British Library Cataloguing in Publication Data A catalogue record of this book is available from the British Library

ISBN 9780954722951

Cover Picture: Jo Parsons. © Jo Parsons. Cover Designed by Hannah Dennis.
Map illustrations by Peter McLure

Picture credits:
The Trustees of the Imperial War Museum, London:
Pages 11, 21, 43, 57, 71, 101, 125, 139, 171, 187, 189, 190, 307
Popperfoto: Pages 40, 66, 187
John Frost Historical Newspapers: Page 45
National Archive: Page 46

Produced by DSM

Printed and bound in the UK by Biddles, part of the MPG Printgroup, Bodmin and King's Lynn

A connective discourse between war-time and present-day generations....

For

Doreen & Irene --

Kimiko & Hannah --

Grace, Hope and Jacob........with love.

Contents

Foreword

It has been 15 years since *'I'll Take That One'* was first published. Considered at the time to be a groundbreaking examination of 'Operation Pied Piper' and the parallel private and CORB evacuations overseas, it remained for some time the main treatise on the topic of civilian evacuation.

Since then, more evidence has become available, more ex-evacuees have been willing to share their stories, and more research has been carried out into the long term consequences of the evacuation of children and the extended separation from their families and home environments.

The aim of this new extended edition is to examine the fresh evidence and shed new light on what took place during the planning stages, the actual implementation of the schemes and the effects post-war. Even today, romantic notions of evacuation abound and the image of working class urchin-like evacuees being taken in by kind middle-class hosts, are difficult to dispel. As will be demonstrated, it was not as simple as merely removing children *et al* from areas of danger to those that were safe....in reality it was more an act of taking children from areas of *perceived* danger to those considered to be *safer*, and there are many instances of evacuees arriving in locations which were in fact more dangerous than the ones they had left.

Operation Pied Piper was interwoven with complex sociological and psychological issues, many of which were not recognised at the time, and if they were, then they were often ignored or 'lost' within the bigger picture.

This account draws upon recently released documents and includes some material only the author has been given access to. Gleaning information from documents not available in 1998, and others which are still officially closed, there is a new appraisal of the complex issues surrounding the evacuation, or non-evacuation, of Belfast and examines why the planning and implementation within the province was too often affected by intransigence and prevarication.

The book will also cover related issues, such as the BBC Schools Broadcasts and Children's Hour which within the bigger picture of wartime Britain may not seem to be that important, but which nonetheless provided an essential link to normality for many children at home, in their receptions areas in the UK, and clandestinely in occupied Europe.

Operation Pied Piper was not the only example of its kind and reference will be made to schemes organised in Germany, where children were evacuated to the 'Greater Reich', and in Finland where 78,000 children were sent to Sweden, 11% of whom never returned home.

In addition, mention will be made of how the research into the children of World War II is having a positive impact on children whose parents are deployed to present-day conflict areas.

The British evacuation schemes remain a contentious episode in British Social History which, although carried out with all the best intentions, has left a legacy of emotional and social fragility on the part of some ex-war children. It is too easy to use statistics to blur the issues.....1.5 million evacuees are too often treated as a whole, whereas they should be seen as 1.5 million individuals with all their attendant emotional and domestic problems; experiences which would have had an influence on how they reacted to the evacuation situation, their return home in 1945 and their lives post-war.

I am greatly indebted to a number of individuals and organisations who have helped me in my quest to seek out the truth; the many ex-war children in the UK, Finland and Germany who have shared their memories and concerns with me; the British evacuees who went overseas both with CORB and privately; the children of collaborators in the Netherlands, particularly Dr Gonda Scheffel-Baars, who thanks to the support and understanding of family, friends and international colleagues, managed to overcome her initial post-war hardship and subsequently committed herself to create opportunities where 'children' of similar backgrounds can find relief; Dr Pertti Kaven who introduced me to many Finnish and Swedish war-children, and when required acted as my interpreter; Prof. Baard Borge in Norway for sharing his research with me; the archivists at the Public Record Office in Northern Ireland and staff in other repositories too numerous to mention. Also I would like to thank my colleagues in the departments of history at the Universities of Reading and Lodz who have supported my research; Jennifer Glanville who runs the Evacuee Archive at the University of Reading and provides informed help and assistance to visiting researchers; Prof. Sidney Brown PhD who gave me unrestricted access to his research material on the Tottenham County School and proof read some of the chapters; and fellow researchers around the world who have kept encouraging me to write again. I would also like to express my gratitude to Sir William and Lady Elizabeth Benyon for providing me with the funds to enable me to continue with my research.

I would like to extend a special word of thanks to Dr Peter Heinl who does outstanding work in alleviating the mental anguish of many ex-war children, and who has patiently guided me through the psychological complexities of war related trauma in children.

Finally, none of this would have been possible without the support of my family and close friends; particularly my wife Jo, the Rev Hugh Ellis who has always been my impartial 'sounding board', Stephen Haley and Jan Hamblin who had the unenviable task of proof reading the manuscript, and Paul Holness who has done so much over the past 15 years to bring the topic of past and present war children into the public domain.

I am very grateful.

Martin Parsons 2013

Preface

In this important book, 'I'll Take That One Too!' Professor Martin Parsons, the founder and director of the as yet only Research Centre for Evacuee and War Child Studies in the UK, traces the history of the UK's evacuee programme that led to the evacuation of an estimated 1.5 million children and mothers; a staggering number representing the greatest population movement in the history of Britain, taking children away from their families and homes to more remote and seemingly safer parts of the country, and some children even across the expanses of oceans to distant shores and continents. By blending the skills of a historian with those of an educationalist, Martin provides penetrating insights into the dynamics and complex tapestry of policy making, administrative planning, bureaucratic hurdles and logistics. Yet, whilst meticulously reconstructing the evacuees' world of experience, he never loses sight of those who were at the receiving end of the evacuation process and whose lives were, often enough, profoundly affected by the evacuation programme.

Designed and implemented by the UK Government in order to protect children living in perceived target areas and densely populated urban areas against the ravages of air attacks, Operation Pied Piper largely achieved its aim in preserving children's lives. However, Martin's painstaking and moving account and analysis of the microcosm of the evacuation experience that includes the testimony of many survivors, breaks down the walls between distant history and the present, and unmasks the often heavy and even tormenting price that had to be paid by former evacuee children and their peers who were subjected to evacuation programmes in several other countries during World War II – a price often, but not only, intimately and seemingly invisibly linked to the profound human experiences of separation, loss and re-bonding aspects of the experience and research which are now being applied to present day 'service children'.

This book represents an exemplary contribution to the history of World War II by providing compelling evidence that the impact of the evacuee experiences did not vanish in May/August 1945, but stayed on in the minds of the survivors to this day – disturbing proof of the long-lasting invidious effects of war. Wars and conflicts do not simply end when the weapons cease firing. The powerful implications of this message for policymakers are all too obvious.

Professor Parsons' thought provoking book highlights yet a further crucial aspect with respect to the future of child care. The preservation of life is crucial. However, Martin recognises that in order to foster and ensure the stable, long-term psychological well-being of children and their development into adulthood, policy making at Government levels has to aspire to absorb and integrate a much more advanced degree of understanding of children's needs, drawing on revolutionary insights gained over the last century in the fields of neuroscience, psychiatry, psychology, psychosomatics and psychotraumatology in order to offer individually tailored, empathetic child-care strategies and programmes, not only in times of war, but also of peace.

I wish Professor Parsons' admirable book the extensive readership it deserves. It will be of interest to a wide range of professionals, including planners in Government departments around the world, and multi-national organisations entrusted to cope with large-scale movements of populations. The humanitarian respect that Professor Parsons extends to the former evacuees and war children of all nationalities and creeds who endured separations from, and even losses of, their childhood homes will ensure that his book will grant them a firm place in the history of World War II and a home in the landscape of memory.

Let us hope that the lessons drawn from this book and the experience of the evacuees will benefit future generations, because children are the most precious 'commodity,' and indeed, the jewels in the crown of any nation.

A most impressive work.

Peter Heinl MD.

Operation Pied Piper

Evacuation in Britain

'To be torn up from the roots of home life, to be sent away from the family circle, in most instances for the first time in a child's life was a painful event.

This was no social experiment; it was a surgical rent only to be contemplated as a last resort ....From the first day of September 1939 evacuation ceased to be a problem of administrative planning. It became instead a multitude of problems in human relationships'.[1]

After a 24 hour trip from the Channel islands an evacuee mother and children wait for a train to take them to the West Country

The evacuation scheme of 1939-45 was not the first official civilian evacuation scheme to be planned in Britain in fact it was the third. The second was planned during the Munich crisis in 1938 but surprisingly the first was organised in Wareham and North Shields[2] in August 1803 when the threat of a French invasion was at its height. This involved the safe dispersal of not only the local population but also their livestock, food, vehicles and anything else likely to be of use to in an emergency.[3]

1 Titmuss. op. cit.

2 People in North Shields were issued with Evacuation permits and instructions:-

That once the alarm had been raised they were to pack blankets and a change of clothes for their family in the 'coverlid' of their bed, and carry meal and meat and potatoes, not exceeding one Peck. They were not allowed to take any article of Furniture, or heavy baggage. They would have only one hour to prepare and then set out'. Dorset Daily Echo. 2nd May 1940

3 Transport was commandeered, drovers were appointed to move cattle and sheep, and overseers were given the task of ensuring that arrangements were carried out. A document issued by the Lord Lieutenant of Dorset on the 17th August 1803, laid down the procedure to be carried out across a wider area. This was to be sub-divided into districts and looked after by persons who between 1939 and 1945 would be identified as billeting officers. A complete list of the inhabitants of each district was compiled, as well as a register of livestock and an inventory of stores. The personnel list included qualifications and experience which could be useful during the emergency. Some people were allocated to civil defence and others were given the role of preparing camps for evacuees!

The third, the Evacuation scheme implemented in 1939, had been planned by an Evacuation sub-Committee of the Imperial Defence Committee as early as 16th February 1931 in order to prevent panic flight and create an orderly exodus from London in the event of war and designed, as Titmuss said, as *'A military expedient, a counter move to the enemy's objective of attacking and demoralising the civilian population'*.[4]

However, these plans were based on assumptions of how any future war might be conducted and were therefore hypothetical strategies based on limited research and conjecture.

On 10th November 1932, in a speech to the House of Commons, Stanley Baldwin, stated:-

> *'I will not pretend that we are not taking precautions in this country. We have done it. We have made our investigations much more quietly and hitherto without any publicity, but considering the years that are required to make our preparations, any government of this country in the present circumstances of the world would have been guilty of criminal negligence had they neglected to make their preparations'*.[5]

Also on 28th November 1934 Churchill addressing his fellow MPs commented:-

> *'...Not less formidable than these material effects are the reactions which will be produced upon the mind of the civil population. We must expect that under pressure of continuous air attack upon London, at least 3,000,000 or 4,000,000 people will be driven out into the open country around the metropolis. This vast amount of human beings, numerically far larger than any armies which have been fed and moved in war, without shelter and without food, without sanitation and without special provision for the maintenance of order would confront the government of the day with an administrative problem of the first magnitude, and would certainly absorb the energies of our small army and our territorial force. Problems of this kind have never been faced before, and although there is no need to exaggerate them, neither, on the other hand, is there any need to shrink from facing the immense, unprecedented difficulties which they involve'*.[6]

The planning and implementation of the evacuation programme was the responsibility of the Sub-Committee for Evacuation of the Imperial Defence Committee, known as the Anderson Committee, which was established after continued interest by MPs requesting an explanation about any proposed evacuation scheme.

The Air Raid Precaution Bill of November 1937 had made no mention of evacuation, although after pressure from some MPs an amendment was tabled to make local authorities responsible for dealing with questions of evacuation; a revision resisted by the Home Secretary who said:-

> *'The Committee for Imperial Defence is actively engaged upon this problem. We already have certain plans in existence. We intend to make them more comprehensive and we shall have them ready for the emergency...we have the question of evacuation firmly in our minds'*.[7]

By the time the Bill had reached the committee stages the Home Secretary had conceded and a new clause was introduced which made it the duty of all local authorities to provide information to the Government for the purpose of assisting the preparation of any evacuation scheme and insisting that the latter should remain as the co-ordinating body.

This policy was reinforced in the Board of Education Circular 1461 issued in January 1938 which stated that:-

> *'...in areas which were so exposed to danger that it would be decided to close schools during the whole period in which raids might be expected, the ideal solution would be evacuation and the difficulties of such a scheme should not prevent its consideration'*.[8]

---

4 Titmuss. op.cit p23
5 House of Commons Debates. 10th Nov.1932 Vol 270 col 633 cited Titmuss op cit p23
6 M. Gilbert Winston S. Churchill Vol V 1922-39 Heinemann 1976 p573
7 House of Commons Debates. 25th November 1937. vol 329 col 1447. cited Titmuss. op cit. p26

Initially, Local Authorities were advised to contact the Home Office for help in preparing plans, but it soon became clear that this shifting of responsibility to local administration was creating a great deal of confusion and a later Circular, No.701262/8, issued by the Home Office on 28th March 1938,[9] instructed Local Authorities not to prepare any plans at all until told to do so by the Home Secretary.[10]

The same circular stated that; *'Authorities will recognise that no single or comprehensive plan for evacuation is practicable. If the necessity arose for evacuation on any large scale, it would be carried out in co-operation between the Government and the Local Authorities. The matter is under examination by the department who will be able, at a later date, to arrange for the subject to be considered in co-operation with the authorities who may be concerned. In the meantime authorities need not take action on this matter in respect of their schemes unless and until specific directions have been issued by the Secretary of State'.*

On 12th May 1938 the Government refused to initiate a billeting survey stating that the problem of evacuation was being studied. Later in the same month, in defiance of Government advice and having received a number of requests to act, including the example below from the Marylebone Labour Party, the London County Council approved the principle of evacuating school children:-

---

8 Exeter Blitz. Box 5. Devon Record Office. Exeter
9 ibid
10 It later became clear after the problems incurred during the mini-evacuation which had taken place during the Munich Crisis in September 1938, that it was vital that the Government remained in overall charge although in close liaison with Local Authorities. Titmuss. Op.cit. p27 Footnote

St. Marylebone Labour Party
Office: 41,
Daventry St.,
London NW1

27th May 1938.

The Home Secretary.
Whitehall,
SW1.

Dear Sir,

I have to inform you that the following resolution was passed unanimously at last night's meeting of the General Committee of this party:-

'That, pending the development of a comprehensive scheme of Air Raid protection for the entire civilian population of London, plans be made by the LCC immediately, so that, upon the first threat of war, the whole school population under the control of the teachers can be transferred at short notice to safer emergency quarters in the Home Counties; such plans to be put to the test before the emergency occurs by means of actual temporary transfers'.

I shall be obliged if you will lay this resolution before the Committee which has just been set up by the Government to consider the question of evacuating civilians in the event of air raids. I have, of course, sent a copy of the Resolution to the LCC.

Yours faithfully,

G.E.M.De Ste.Croix. Secretary.[11]

The Anderson Committee, when established, met in Committee Room 13 of the House of Commons on Friday 27th May 1938 under the Chairmanship of Sir John Anderson. Its terms of reference were:-

> *'To examine the problem of the transfer of persons from areas which might be exposed to continuous air attack and to recommend plans for the purpose'.*[12]

Sir John Anderson

One of its first responsibilities was to divide the country into three categories: Evacuation, Reception and Neutral. According to Titmuss, over 200 Local Authorities in England and Wales designated as reception areas asked for their classification to be changed to neutral and a further 60 Authorities, above those already listed, wanted to be

11 Exeter Blitz. Box 5. Devon Record Office
12 TNA.HO45/17636

classified as evacuation areas. Significantly, no authority on the evacuation list argued with the decision and no authority asked to be a reception area.[13]

This task was not completed until January 1939, by which time the Government had decided to transfer all responsibility for the implementation of any evacuation scheme to the Health Departments. They had taken over officially on 14th November 1938, by which time Sir John Anderson had been appointed to a new role of co-ordinating the Civil Defence.

The Anderson Committee; Priorities

The Anderson Committee made sure that planning precedence was immediately given to London, and elements of specific detailed planning were prioritised as follows:-

- To what extent were there vital activities which must be kept going.
- Conditions under which public order could be controlled.
- Transport.

The necessity to feed and house those evacuated so Government departments concerned i.e. Food, Health, Board of Trade etc. could be consulted.

The Committee felt that it might be necessary to work out two schemes, one for an orderly evacuation and the other for a sudden emergency. Under the former, known as Plan 2, 13 million people were in designated Evacuation areas, 14 million in Neutral areas and 18 million in Reception areas. The Committee also suggested that they should investigate how the French proposed to evacuate Paris should the need arise.[14]

By January 1939, a report to the Home Defence sub-Committee of the Committee of Imperial Defence on 'The State of Readiness of the Civil Defence' concluded that '*Evacuation plans are, at present, very backward*'.[15]

Although this was true in relation to the French planning, the British scheme was in fact in advance of Germany's.[16] The German plans were considered by Sir John Anderson as being irrelevant[17] but, as will be shown in a later chapter, although Germany and Britain had similar priorities when considering initial policies, the decisions made by the Anderson Committee were to have greater impact in terms of practical details and social upheaval.

At the second meeting of the Anderson Committee on the 30th May 1938, W. Eady, Under-Secretary of State at the Home Office, reported that the question of evacuation had been studied over a number of years. According to his figures, 63% of London's population were in essential industries, 35% were classified as being 'not sure' and 2% were classed as non-essential. This was considered by the Committee members to be a very superficial interpretation of the details available.

Basically at this stage the Committee had to consider two important details:-

- Which were the danger zones in London?
- Which were the essential industries that had to continue?

The Committee agreed that the Metropolitan Police District, Potter's Bar to Epsom, could not be regarded as highly vulnerable. So Greater London was divided into three distinct areas:-

---

13 Titmuss. op cit. p32-33

14 In July 1934 Stanley Baldwin had informed the House of Commons that '...so far as I know every country in Europe has carried its work a great deal further than we have carried ours'. House of Commons Debates. 30th July 1934. vol.1292 cols. 2335-6 cited Titmuss op.cit.p33

15 Titmuss op.cit.p33

16 See Chapter. Other European Children.

17 TNA HO45/17636

a. Evacuation, if possible, from an area encompassing Hammersmith to Dagenham and Holloway to Dulwich.

b. A wider area of restricted movement.

c. An outer ring receiving hospital patients.

In order to make this feasible the Committee needed precise information from employers as to the number of men they could do without. They hoped to bring the number needing to be evacuated down to 4,500,000.

The main concerns underlying this plan were as follows:-

a. There was an expectation that a number of people would lose their nerve and stream out of London. Therefore the plans were designed to facilitate this exodus which, to some extent, the Committee felt would take place in any event and therefore ought to be regulated and controlled.

b. It was important that some men who were essential to vital industries would not be lost to the national effort but would be able to continue to work in the safer zones.

c. There would be the need to move between 3 and 4 million people from the city within 72 hours. This would rely heavily on the efficiency and co-operation of the Railway network.

d. There was a need for the Government to implement this plan as soon as tension began. [18]

The third meeting of the Anderson Committee concentrated on the evacuation of children. Although both the members of the Anderson Committee and representatives from the LCC Education Committee, felt that responsibility for this lay with the Government, they did agree that school staff already had a great deal of experience in moving large numbers of pupils to a place at a specific time, and examples such as 100,000 going to the Crystal Palace in 1911, 70,000 for the Silver Jubilee celebrations in London in 1935 and 37,000 to the Coronation in 1937, were cited as positive evidence. In order for the scheme to be effective it was felt necessary for the Committee to liaise closely with the teachers and their professional bodies. The National Union of Teachers had already been approached in January 1938 when Circular 12461 'ARP in Schools' was being considered, so a degree of co-operation had already been established.

On 4th June 1938, the National Union of Teachers executive passed a resolution stating:-

> *'That the executive of the NUT, while not subscribing to any suggestion that war is inevitable, is prepared to co-operate with the Government and Local Authorities in making plans for the safety of school children as effective as possible and to recommend its members in the local areas to consider the desirability of co-operating on a voluntary basis'.*

This then raised the question of the evacuation of teachers. On a number of occasions, Sir Percy Harris asked the members of the NUT present if they felt that teachers would leave their own families. If not, he questioned whether it could be organised so that teachers with family commitments were not employed in the scheme. As it turned out, most teachers from the evacuated areas, with or without families, became involved with the evacuation.

From this point on, teacher representatives were heavily involved in the discussions relating to evacuation. Although according to Professor Sidney Brown, the records of the Teaching Unions[19] show that the National Union of Schoolmasters (NAS) and Union of Women Teachers (UWT) were more critical of Government policies than the National Union of Teachers (NUT) whose members were drawn mainly from the elementary schools.[20] Sir Fred Mander, General Secretary of the NUT, said that it would be impossible to launch a scheme of compulsory evacuation of school children because it was not practical to override parental responsibility, whereas

18 TNA HO45/17636
19 Available in the Modern Records Centre,University of Warwick.
20 Coping with classes during conflict; Education during World War II. Prof. Sidney Brown. Unpub. Paper.

Mrs Parker, President of the NUT, thought that the first reaction of parents would be to refuse unless the whole scheme was properly explained to them. J. Brown, Chairman of the ARP Committee, took a more pragmatic stance and suggested that any plans should be flexible allowing parents, previously against evacuation, to change their minds and send their children with the others.

Anderson himself argued that parents would be inclined to ask a lot of questions about any evacuation scheme and therefore they had to be reassured that adequate attention would be given to the welfare of their children.

Teachers were strongly in favour of billeting children in private houses rather than in camps, hostels or boarding accommodation. Billeting was represented as 'dispersal', and therefore, in theory, it would be possible to put some responsibility upon the host and take some of the daily liability away from the teachers. Under the scheme foster-parents and other hosts were to be given the authority to act *in loco parentis*; Memo Ev.4 Government Evacuation Scheme; Ministry of Health 1939. Clause 72 stated:-

> *'In circumstances in which evacuation would take place, householders in the receiving areas could be relied upon to do everything possible to lighten the lot of the children and mothers compelled suddenly to leave their homes and families and finding themselves in strange surroundings. So far as unaccompanied school children are concerned, the householder will be in loco parentis, and should have no great difficulty in controlling the children and preserving reasonable discipline. The children will be accompanied by their teachers, who will know them and will be able to assist in their control'.*[21]

In the event, some hosts proved to be very effective in taking full responsibility, but teachers in many areas found themselves coping with the 24 hour supervision of charges who were in some cases billeted over hundreds of square miles.

Even for those hosts who took their role of foster parents seriously, it was not always possible for them to control 'difficult' children and some were not willing to impose any means of discipline because of the possible reaction from the child's family and the authorities.

In Circular 1882 issued in October 1939, it was suggested that special arrangements and supervision would be necessary to relieve the individual householder of the unreasonable burden of the small proportion of evacuated children whose behaviour made them unacceptable in ordinary billets, and it was suggested that the Local Authorities should consider whether such cases should not be housed in empty houses which were equipped for the purpose and where accommodation would be of an institutional nature. The Mental Health Emergency Department in London was given the responsibility of compiling a register of workers experienced in dealing with such children and arranging a clearing house of information on cases to which the Medical Officers and Social workers could apply.[22]

In January 1941, concern was expressed by the Ministry of Health officials in Bristol that in a number of areas in Somerset, hostels which had been opened for the reception of unaccompanied evacuees were being used for the permanent accommodation of unbilletable children. Although they agreed that hostels for children in this category were now to be a permanent feature of the scheme, they pointed out that it was not desirable to house every class in the same house and it was hoped that in future separate hostel and clearing hostel accommodation would be available for:-

a. bedwetters, who would only be admitted subject to a medical certificate, otherwise they should be under medical supervision and attend school.

b. difficult children

c. in addition to a Sick bay for minor ailments, including scabies and impetigo and an auxiliary isolation

---

21 Ministry of Health. Government Evacuation Scheme. Memo Ev.4 1939.Clause 72
22 Ministryof Health. Circ.1882 Oct.2nd 1939

hospital if the need arises.[23]

On the 6th May 1941, M.Mann, the Regional Welfare Officer, issued the following memo. to all County Billeting Officers;

> *'At a recent conference in Whitehall, Welfare officers reported that a number of children now being evacuated were unsuitable not only for billets, but for hostels of any normal types. For example children who had been before the courts. I should be most grateful if you could let me know if you consider the problem to be one which is likely to assume dimensions of any size in your County. A distinction is to be made here between children on remand for whom accommodation is not available in Home Office schools, or Remand Homes and children who have been before the courts but now on probation'.* [24]

The issue became a serious one, and in May 1941, the Rural District Councils Association forced questions about it in Parliament.[25] Two months later, on 12th July 1941, the Chief Billeting Officer in Dorchester, wrote the following letter regarding difficult children to the Clerk of the County Council in Dorset expressing concern and offering suggestions:-

> 12 July 1941
>
> From: Dorchester RDC.
>
> Ref. Government Evacuation Scheme. Difficult Children
>
> 1. Cases arise from time to time of children of both sexes who are unruly and with whom the average householder is unable and willing to deal.
>
> 2. It can be understood that where stern measures are indicated, any householder applying them may be proceeded against by parents and guardians in the courts and that is a risk most people will not willingly incur.
>
> 3. The only possible solution is for these children to be placed in Institutions, under competent supervision, where they can be brought under proper discipline until in the opinion of the person in charge, they can be safely sent back to private billets.
>
> 4. The Southampton Authority already run such a home for boys only, evacuated from their area, at Wiverley Park, Lyndhurst. It is always full and additional accommodation is needed. So far as is known, no provision is made for London children or for girls of any evacuated area.
>
> 5. I am unable to give figures for the total number of school children billeted in the County, but in this area the figures are Boys 317 and Girls 279.
>
> 6. I suggest provision should be made for 1% of the total number in the County in assessing the size of the accommodation required.
>
> 7. I therefore recommend:-
>
> a. The County Council be asked to set up two such homes in the County, one for each sex, in suitable houses not in towns, the co-operation of the Evacuation Authorities being asked in provision of higher staff.
>
> b. The administration of each Home to be in the hands of the Local Authority in whose area it is situated.

---

23 Ministry of Health, Bristol. 18th January 1941

24 Memo. 6th May 1941.Letter from Regional Welfare Officer. SRO. Correspondence File

25 Official Circular. May 1941. p137 col.2

c. Administer to the Homes through the Director of Education of the County Council and all applications for the admission of a child be backed by the Head School Teachers of the Parish in which the child is billeted.

Signed W.de. M. Egerton, [26]

Transportation

'After what seemed like hours of stopping and starting we arrived at our final destination. We had expected green fields and trees. What we got was Luton!' [27]

On the 16th June 1938, the Anderson Committee tackled the very difficult problem of transporting an estimated several million adults and 750,000 children from the Metropolitan Police district. In the event 827,000 Primary-school children, 524,000 young children and mothers, 12,700 expectant women and 103,000 teachers and helpers[28] (a pupil-teacher ratio of 8:1)[29] took part.

The Committee, realising that any plan had to be simple, flexible and allow for immediate adjustment to meet conditions which had not been foreseen, recognised that the proportion of inhabitants being evacuated would differ from area to area because of the density of population and their vulnerability.

Reporting to the Committee, Frank Pick, Vice-Chairman of the London Passenger Transport, indicated that the LPT was responsible for an area of 25 miles radius from the centre of London which was in fact 10 miles more than the Metropolitan District. He suggested that the eastern area of the Zone should be considered to be the highest priority, especially the Southwark area south of the Thames, which was very densely populated. Whereas the western area had less population and in his personal opinion there was no risk to the north. His definition of a congested area was one of more than 150 people per acre where bombs would cause great havoc.

Pick pointed out that all motor coaches had already been earmarked for ambulance work and therefore would not be available for evacuation. However, although 50% of the city's 6,000 buses had been assigned to carry on a normal service in the area, and a further 250 had been allotted to work with the Police, it meant that the remaining 2,750 buses could be used to move a limited amount of the population. Depending on the amount of permissible luggage per person, it was estimated that a total of 110,000 people could be taken by bus. This meant that allowing for a three hour return journey to railway stations, 330,000 could be moved per day, increasing to 500,000 per day if the number of buses withheld from the scheme was reduced to below 50%. Many of the Committee had felt that the purpose of the buses would be to transport evacuees to mainline stations but Pick had been adamant that it would be far more prudent to take them out of the city to entrain at smaller stations such as Harrow.[30]

As the carrying capacity of the buses was well below that of the tube, the question arose of whether or not to use the London Underground System. After lengthy discussion it was agreed that the District Line would transport evacuees to join the Great Western Railway at Ealing Broadway and the Southern Line at Wimbledon. The Bakerloo Line would link with the mainline at Willesden, and the Metropolitan Line at Harrow. However, it was decided that the Piccadilly Line would be of limited use because there were no useful connections after Finsbury Park and that the Morden Line was not to be used because it had no mainline connection at all. Though, the Tube system did have a greater passenger capacity and it was estimated that 100,000 people per hour could be moved if 2 trains were full, [31] there were two serious disadvantages. Firstly, the ventilation system, which would have given no protection at all in the event of a gas attack and secondly the risk of flooding from both water and

---

26 W de MEgerton. Chief Billeting Officer.Dorset County Council. Correspondence File.
27 B.Wicks. No Time to Wave Goodbye. Bloomsbury 1988. Reminiscence of Walter Leeds p 49
28 The unpaid helpers were women who had been appointed by the evacuation authorities to accompany the children to their destination where they were usually billeted by the host authority. Around 40,000 were involved in the first evacuation of 1939, but some of them were totally unsuitable and by the middle of 1941 32,000 had been dismissed raising the pupil-helper ratio to 100-1. Titmuss op.cit. p391
29 Ibid p103
30 TNA HO45/17636
31 ibid

sewage, especially if evacuation was taking place during a raid. The area around Bond Street was at particular risk because if the Fleet sewer which passed over Farringdon St. was damaged in any way the District, Metropolitan and Central lines would all be flooded. Likewise any bomb damage near the Embankment would also create serious disruption at Charing Cross Station where three mainline railways converged.[32]

Initially the transportation of so many evacuees was seen as a massive logistical challenge, but the Transport Board worked out a scheme whereby, under Bank-holiday conditions, they would evacuate 100,000 persons per hour by underground, 500,000 per day by bus, or under normal conditions 330-350,000. Their target was 1,000,000 per day for the first two days and then 500,000 thereafter. [33] As these figures were far in excess of the number of passengers who could be processed easily by the main-line stations, the companies concerned were asked to investigate how they could overcome what could potentially become a chaotic situation.

The movement of vast numbers also raised the tangential issue of how to differentiate between genuine evacuees and those who were just entering the underground system for shelter. Although there would not be enough Police on hand, the Committee decided not to use the Army to keep control. The problem remained unresolved.

All the Committee proposals on transportation were sent to the major railway companies and on the 21st June 1938, the Committee invited Sir Ralph Wedgewood, Chief General-Manager of the L.N.E.R., Mr G. S. Szlumper, General-Manager of Southern Rail and Mr V. M. Barrington-Ward, Chairman of the Railway Companies Technical ARP Committee, to respond to the original suggestions.

The Anderson Committee had envisaged a scheme which did not involve long journeys, but instead short ones taking evacuees to a belt of indeterminate width around London, from where they could be de-trained at suitable points within the ring. This was not seen as a problem by the companies. In fact some years before, Southern Rail had been asked to plan an evacuation scheme to take refugees up to 50 miles from the capital from the main-line stations and these papers were still available. The railway companies calculated that they could move 3,600,000 persons in 72 hours if they just ran a skeleton regular service. This was a much higher estimate than the one sent to the Ministry of Transport when the companies said that 60,000 could be moved to a 20-25 mile radius per hour if a skeleton service was used or 115,000 per hour if all trains were utilised.[34]

The companies reassured the Committee that the same capacity could be carried even if main-line stations were damaged. They suggested that should such a situation arise then suburban stations such as Queen's Park or Finsbury Park could be used instead. They also confirmed that carriage sidings would be readily available at most sub-stations and it would be easier to work 'through' platforms than entrain people at passenger bays.

As well as the question of numbers of evacuees, the Committee also had to decide upon safety factors. For instance, was entraining to go on during a raid? Would railway workers be disinclined to work through a raid? What about the transfer of passengers from the tube to the trains? Again in consultation with the rail companies, it was decided that trains actually travelling during a raid should continue their journey but other activities in the station area would stop, thus allowing station workers and others to take shelter. The biggest problem would be the transfer of evacuees from the Underground system. Quite naturally they would be unwilling to come to the surface and it was estimated that a tube train which would normally take 5 minutes to empty might be delayed considerably longer, thus causing problems both in the stations and in the tunnels where trains would be backing up. Therefore, it was suggested that instead of transferring passengers, an alternative would be to take the tube trains to the termini. At least in this way the passengers would be taken out of the city and the evacuees could be distributed by the local buses from these points. In the event, many evacuees were transported from their home areas using a combination of transport networks and systems.

---

32 Even as early as June 1938, a serious debate was taking place within the Anderson Committee as to the actual use of the whole underground transport system. The question of whether or not it should be used as shelters, closed down altogether for safety reasons, or kept going. No decision was made. It was not until 1940 that Londoners themselves made the decision to use the Tubes as shelters. Angus Calder refers to this move as:-'...an heroic assertion of popular rights against a legacy of inept bureaucracy and Tory rule'. Ultimately 80 stations became shelters for 177,000 people.
33 TNA HO45/17636
34 Ibid.

Virtually all archive film depicting the actual movement of evacuees from London, such as the Ministry of Information's 'Westward Ho!' made during the second evacuation in 1940, shows them being transported by bus and over-ground suburban trains to main railway termini, and this does seem to be the most common form of transportation used.

Despite what the propaganda images imply only a small percentage of evacuees actually left from the termini, going instead from stations with through platforms as favoured by the Anderson Committee. For example, most of the children travelling westwards on the Great Western Railway left from Ealing Broadway. Not only did it have a through platform, required to make the entraining and departure of evacuees quicker, but it also had very good links with the Underground system. In the first four days of September 1939, 164 trains carrying evacuees west ran from three stations, Ealing Broadway, Acton and Paddington. The first train, numbered 101, left Ealing at 8.30am on Friday, 1st September 1939 and went to Maidenhead arriving at 9.00am. Others of course went further. The trains, made up of twelve carriages and capable of carrying 800 people per journey, were marshalled at Acton and Old Oak Common[35]. Original estimates suggested that 850 children could leave Paddington per day, 3,200 from Acton and 46,500 from Ealing. In the event these numbers proved to be inflated.[36] On the first day, the Great Western Railway ran 58 trains, rather than 64, carrying a total of 44,032 evacuees, reducing by the fourth and final day to 28 trains carrying 17,796 evacuees.[37]

Evacuees waiting for their train. The girl carrying the doll was very fortunate because some evacuating authorities would not allow children to take dolls or teddies because they took up too much space. Note the different types of luggage

London County Council staff assisted G.W.R personnel in organising the children and adults who had been told to arrive at the station 15 minutes before the departure of the train. Tickets had already been issued at the schools

35 Tim Bryan. Great Western Railway at War. pub. Patrick Stephens Ltd. 1995. p13
36 ibid. pp10-11
37 ibid. p16

where the children had assembled; Yellow tickets to children with teachers, and Pink tickets to children accompanied by their mothers.[38]

The 166 page timetable for evacuation had been printed in early August, but because there was still the Government concern that evacuation might cause panic, a note on the front cover of the timetable warned:-

> *'The Evacuation Train arrangements shewn in this Notice must not be circulated to more members of staff than is necessary for the smooth working of the Programme and information must not be circulated to the General Public'.*[39]

As well as the London evacuation, on the 1st and 2nd of September the G.W.R moved 22,739 evacuees from the Birmingham area in 64 trains to South Wales and Gloucester, and 35,606 evacuees from Liverpool and Birkenhead.[40]

Of course other railway companies were involved. James Roffey recalls travelling from Queens Road Station to Pulborough on the Southern Railway. This embarkation point created its own problems. The station had always been a make-shift place. The railway line itself was high on an embankment and to reach the platform children had to climb up a very steep flight of wooden steps with their bags and cases. Gas-masks were also a problem as the sharp cornered boxes banged against knees and the string cut into the owners' necks. A serious situation almost occurred when a girl tripped over on the stairs causing many others to fall with her.

When the train eventually came into the platform made up of old fashioned carriages with a door to every compartment a melee ensued. Everyone surged forward, brother and sisters and friends struggled to keep together and everyone wanted a window seat.[41] A scene far removed from the orderly entraining shown in the film 'Westward Ho!'.

Some evacuees travelled by an alternative method of transportation not mentioned at all in the Anderson Committee minutes. They did not use trains, buses or the tube, but were taken directly to their reception areas by boat from the Ford Motor Company jetties at Dagenham. Paddle steamers such as the 'Golden Eagle' owned by the General Steam Navigation Company, normally seen on cross-channel routes, had been brought in to pick up evacuees at Dagenham and take them to the east coast ports of Felixstowe, Lowestoft and Great Yarmouth. These steamers were given a destroyer escort.[42] Unfortunately, they were not expected at their destinations and many evacuees spent a few nights sleeping on the floors of schools and church halls in straw filled sacks, before billets could be found.[43]

In total 16,984 children had registered for evacuation by boat but not all turned up. Other vessels used included; The Royal Eagle, The Crested Eagle, The Royal Sovereign, The Royal Daffodil, Queen Charlotte, The Medway Queen and The City of Rochester[44].

The Medway Queen still exists, although in a poor state, and an appeal has been launched to save her.[45]

Transport arrangements also had to be sorted out in the reception areas. On the 3rd February 1939, a memo was sent out to local authorities from the Chief Education Officer in Somerset outlining the basic methods of transport to be used from the Evacuation areas, and the need to consider special provision for certain categories of evacuees such as blind and 'cripples'(*sic*) within the County reception areas.

---

38 ibid. p13
39 Great Western Railway. Circular. London Evacuation Scheme No.2. Also 'Altered working of through passenger trains. August 1939'. cited GWR. op cit.p11
40 GWR at War. op.cit. p16
41 James Roffey. Letter to Author. June 1998
42 J.Rawlins. Private papers.
43 'The Evacuee' Journal of the Evacuee Reunion Association. June 1996
44 ibid. December 1996
45 Having evacuated children from Dagenham on 1st September 1939, she took children from Gravesend on 3rd September and was then taken to Deptford to be fitted out as mine-sweeper and became part of the Royal Navy. In 1940 she earned the title 'Heroine of Dunkirk' having made seven journeys across the Channel to Dunkirk and brought back an estimated 7,000 soldiers. Other ships were involved in both the evacuation of children from London via the Thames and soldiers from Dunkirk. The 'Royal Daffodil' brought 1600 Frenchmen from Dunkirk, but was put out of action when a bomb went through three of her decks. The 'Queen of the Channel' brought 600 from the beaches but was hit the following day by a bomb which broke her back. The 'Royal Sovereign' collected 6,856 men over a period of a few days. The 'Crested Eagle' was hit by a bomb at the Dunkirk mole while transferring 700 men from the 'Fenella' which had also just been hit. The 'Crested Eagle' caught fire and was abandoned on the beach. (the Evacuee. Feb.1997)

'In general it may be assumed that after all the accommodation has been filled up in those residential Special Schools which may be situated in the reception areas, there will be a number of such schools to be evacuated which it will be desired to organise as residential schools in any suitable accommodation that can be found. For example Youth Hostels, small permanent camps, large houses etc.

Blind: The home addresses, circumstances and degree of residual sight of the majority of blind persons in an area will normally be known to the local authority or through blind visitors. The object to be aimed at in their case would presumably therefore be the issue of a ticket attached to either a particular coach at a particular picking up point or to a specified train....

Cripples (sic): The extent to which the cripple population is in touch with organisations varies so widely from area to area that it is impossible to give any guidance as to the methods by which their evacuation might be organised....In general it will probably not be possible to grant evacuation facilities to cripples who are wholly dependent upon others or could not be moved except by ambulance. Apart from the consideration that such cripples might be accommodated in hospital beds earmarked for civilian casualties in the reception areas, chronic, as distinct from self-supporting cripples would probably be happier it they remained in their own homes.....'[46]

46 Chief Education Officer. Somerset. Memo 3rd Feb. 1939. Ref. C/CD/1/6/1

Billets

' ...the general public hardly realises how arduous and how important a service is being rendered by this great army of volunteers. The finding of a billet is only the beginning. The real work starts later'.[47]

Having sorted out the transport problems the Anderson Committee was then faced with the problem of how to demarcate reception areas and how many billets would be required within them.

On the 23rd June 1938, J.C.Wrigley, Director of Housing and Town Planning at the Ministry of Health, attended the meeting to give advice on evacuation accommodation and the provision of water supplies in the reception areas.[48]

His own information came from two sources, both of which were incomplete for the purpose intended. One was the 1931 Census, which gave the numbers of persons living per room, and the numbers of houses erected by local authorities and private companies. There were no statistics on the rates of occupation of these new houses, but it was assumed that it was not higher than the country's average of 4 persons per house. He also used the Ministry of Health Paper EC7 on accommodation in Buckinghamshire as a sample area. Wrigley explained that houses erected by local authorities were usually of the non-parlour type and might be assumed to have 4.5 persons resident in them. Private enterprise houses could be analysed by rateable value:-

- Below £12 per annum would be similar to authority housing.
- £12-£25 per annum could be seen as Lower Middle Class.
- £25+ per annum would be the largest houses.

At this stage it was necessary to have some basic model on which calculations could be made of how many could be billeted per house so the Committee adopted the standard of overcrowding contained in the Housing Act of 1935 and the subsequent Consolidating Act of 1936. However, this represented a very low criterion and so could only be regarded by the committee as a starting point for dealing with overcrowding. It was felt by some that if the recommendations outlined in the Act were adopted in time of war as a standard of billeting, they would produce a social situation of which Britain had no experience. In 1938 the average percentage of houses in the country below the required standard of the 1936 Act was just 1%. Using calculations based on this information, it was estimated that a Lower Middle Class house, comprising 2 reception rooms and 4 bedrooms with an average residency of 4 persons, could take in an extra 10-12 people as evacuees. If children were involved the figure could be higher because those under 12 months did not figure in the equation and those under 10 counted as 0.5.[49]

These figures were unworkable and were amended drastically, and the billeting standard used on all accommodation surveys in England and Wales during the war was one person per habitable room.[50]

Wrigley supplied figures for other counties and a preliminary survey suggested that 1,000,000 evacuees could be accommodated in Berkshire, Buckinghamshire and East and West Sussex, but the Committee still doubted whether the provisions of the Act were too low, and therefore problems would be created if billeting was carried out to its limits. Special consideration was given to the question of coastal towns which had spare capacity outside the holiday season, but no special arrangements were made.

Wrigley was questioned about the increased need for water and the problem of sewage treatment in those areas expecting to receive evacuees. Although it was reckoned that the doubling of the population in the Home Counties would create a 33% rise in water consumption, this increase could be dealt with adequately within a 50

---

47 Ernest Brown. Minister of Health in a pamphlet called 'Government Evacuation Scheme'. (no date). Devon Record Office. Exeter.
48 TNA HO45/17636
49 ibid
50 Titmuss. op. cit. p394

mile radius of London except in a few rural districts. Those areas with a particular need were able to be helped by a £1,000,000 grant for the provision of piped water and the subsequent sewage and drainage disposal.

Later people with a great deal of local knowledge living in small reception areas, informed their local councils of any specific problems relating to water supply and disposal. The following letter was sent to the Clerk of the Dorset County Council on 17th February 1939, and is an indication of some of the localised problems faced by the evacuation planners.

Ashmore Rectory.
Salisbury.
Wilts. 17 Feb. 1939

Dear Sir,

Billeting and Water

A visit from the ARP visitor yesterday reminds me to recall to your notice the irregularity of the water supply here. For at least 7 years to my knowledge, there have been breakdowns in the water supply, insufficient for necessary requirements, on average twice a year, of periods varying from a few days to several weeks.

We have always been assured that it will not happen again but it always has. The next breakdown is due about Easter, if the weather is warm and dry.

Such a lack of water would be much more serious still if Ashmore were filled to capacity with persons evacuated from dangerous areas.

Keeping this in mind, you will, I daresay, either arrange that Ashmore is only moderately used for evacuated persons or that a special watch on the hydrostat, especially washers, be maintained by a competent person, or both. A reservoir is, I understand, not to be finished...'[51]

Similarly, on the 15th March 1939, a confidential letter was sent from the Clerk of the Dorset County Council to the Sherborne reception area in North Dorset, indicating the expected numbers of evacuees which could be supported in the area based on the amount of water available in the villages. The Rural District Council was asked to inform the Clerk if the numbers suggested had to be reduced in line with the availability of water.

The villages in Dorset designated as reception areas, were also divided into three categories. Category 'A': those which could take evacuees immediately, 'B' those which would be considered a second line of billeting should the need arise, and 'C' those which could only be used after work had been carried out on the water supply. When all the details had been collected the following list of the possible numbers of evacuees per village was drawn up:-

Parish	Persons Ordinarily Resident	Children	Helpers	Others	Total	Relatives	Poss. Military Billet	Exc. Empty Houses
C. Ashmore	151	20	11	8	39	18	-	208
C. Bourton	596	72	55	49	176	80	300	1,152
B. Buckhorn Weston	309	44	39	53	136	10	-	355
A. Cann	334	29	52	66	147	32	-	513
A. Compton	165	22	17	16	55	46	-	266
A. East Orchard	93	15	9	12	36	43	-	172
B. East Stour	324	35	23	29	87	37	-	448

51 Dorset County Council. Correspondence File. County Record Office. Dorchester.

Parish	Persons Ordinarily Resident	Children	Helpers	Others	Total	Relatives	Poss. Military Billet	Exc. Empty Houses
A. Fontmell	428	31	66	38	135	78	-	641
B. Gillingham	2,950	420	234	256	910	377	3,000	7,237
A. Iwerne Minster	417	73	33	34	140	66	-	623
C. Kingston Magna	2,553	48	10	18	76	33	-	362
A. Margaret Marsh	38	4	4	10	18	3	-	59
A. Melbury Abbas	262	22	18	19	59	34	-	355
C. Metcombe	572	82	63	61	206	227	-	1,005
C. Stilton	135	14	8	14	36	18	-	189
A. Stour Provost	378	48	46	46	140	64	-	582
C. Sutton Waldron	127	30	12	10	52	21	-	200
A. Todber	99	11	4	2	17	12	-	128
A. West Orchard	60	11	4	8	23	11	-	94
C. West Stour	108	11	16	37	64	15	-	187
Total	**7,797**	**1,042**	**724**	**786**	**2,552**	**1,225**	**3,300**	**1,4876**

Social problems relating to the housing of evacuees were on the agenda as early as 1938, but in the light of what was to transpire, discussions were very cursory and initial measures were ineffective. Wrigley believed that there would be different problems in housing adults and children. In his view the latter could easily be fitted into normal domestic arrangements, albeit at some inconvenience to the householder, but adults were a different matter. He predicted a situation where family members would be divided up among a number of reception households, thus creating problems of transport, communication and mutual family support. He was also uneasy about men being taken from their work in London and having nothing to do in the reception areas although this was not to become a problem as many men not called up for military service or in reserved occupations, tended to stay in the target areas to continue their jobs. Few men were actually evacuated so in 1940, special arrangements were made in some places for husbands to make weekend or longer visits to their wives and families now in the reception areas.

The Final Anderson Committee Recommendations

On the 26th July 1938, the Anderson Committee report was completed and the Home Secretary presented the main principles to Parliament:-

a. That, except in so far as it may be necessary for military or other special reasons to require persons to leave some limited area, evacuation should not be compulsory.

b. That, for the purpose of supporting the national war effort and supplying essential civilian needs, production in the large industrial towns must be maintained, but it is desirable to provide organised facilities for the evacuation of substantial numbers of people from certain industrial areas.

c. That arrangements for the reception of persons who become refugees should be mainly on the basis of accommodation in private houses under powers of compulsory billeting. These arrangements will require very detailed preparation in order to avoid unnecessary hardship either to the refugees or to the persons who receive them.

d. That the initial cost of evacuation arrangements should be borne by the Government, but, that refugees who can afford to contribute towards the cost of their maintenance should be expected to do so.

e. That, to meet the needs of the parents who wish to send their children away, but cannot make their own

> arrangements, special arrangements should be made for school-children to move out in groups from their schools in the charge of their teachers'.[52]

Despite reaching this report stage very quickly, the Committee for Imperial Defence did not even consider the report until 15th September, thus wasting almost two months of precious time. Sir Samuel Hoare, while agreeing that a detailed evacuation plan should be drawn up suggested that *'in existing conditions it was not desirable to publish the Anderson report'*.[53] So it was not issued until 27th October 1938.

This was ten months before the outbreak of war, and one wonders why the general plans and views were not amended during that time to take into account the more social and human side of the evacuation scheme. It is very apparent that little, if any, notice was taken of the views and opinions of parents, and indeed the children and other evacuee groups who were to take part in the process, basically because of the desire to keep the planning and implementation 'secret'. As a result there was a certain dehumanising element inherent in the organisation. These final recommendations came from a bureaucratic procedure which ostensibly ignored the feelings of the individuals concerned, both in the designated reception and evacuated areas, relied on the unquestioning co-operation of teachers, without whom the scheme would have collapsed before it was instigated, and thought fit to create a billeting scheme which required no expert supervision and monitoring from outside agencies both before, and during, the whole evacuation process. The latter responsibility was very much left to the teachers.

It is interesting to note that throughout its deliberations, the Anderson Committee made no reference to, or sought the advice from, members of the community who had actually been involved in an evacuation scheme in Cambridge. Had the committee investigated this in more detail they may have gained some very useful pointers for dealing with the evacuation of children. In 1936, a group of 3,826 Basque Evacuees, refugees from the Spanish Civil War, had arrived in England, 29 of who were housed in a hostel and then billeted in private houses around the Cambridge area. This scheme provides an interesting comparison in many ways, not least the fact that local people raised money to support the hostel in Pampisford Vicarage, and the general supportive attitude they had towards their charges, at least in the beginning, a trait which is not so evident in the Government Scheme from 1939. Members of the local community even got together to decorate the Vicarage before the arrival of the children. Jessie Stewart makes reference in her article 'Recuerdos' in the Cambridge Daily News in 1938 to the work done by the Secretaries in the Hostel and the fact that:-

> *'...they had the support of a large committee including representatives of Societies, Clubs, Laboratories, Syndicates, Schools and Villages which had 'adopted', i.e. made themselves responsible for, the weekly payments for individual children'.*

Although this type of benevolence would not have been possible on the large scale of the Government scheme, there were other community led events which could have been replicated. Within the area, businesses provided funds and there were entertainments which included sports, recreation, taking the children away for holidays, and fund raising events such as fetes, and house to house collections.

However, the group were not to escape the anti-evacuee campaigns that future migrants were to suffer in 1939. The national press criticised the presence of the children and although this was countered by letters from those involved with the Basques, it did have the unfortunate result of putting landlords off having evacuees in their houses, with excuses such as 'the property will deteriorate', 'the neighbourhood will object' being common.[54] The original intention had been to repatriate the Basque children when the situation in Spain improved. However, the alternative was adoption in English homes, and this was the course the Committee took because of the lack of food and employment in Spain at the time made it a better option.

After the Anderson Committee had finalised its proposals, further research and evidence gathering continued. On the 16th September 1938, a month before the publication of the report, and significantly at the time of the Munich

52 House of Commons Debate. 28th July 1938. Vol. 338. col. 3283. cited Titmuss. op.cit.p28
53 ibid. p30
54 Jessie Stewart. 'Recuerdos'. Cambridge Daily News. p23

Crisis, Wrigley sent out a very urgent and confidential circular No. 1742 to the Clerks of all housing authorities in England and Wales asking them to provide him with the information about the amount of accommodation available in the country. For this purpose, as stated above, he defined such accommodation as *'in excess of a standard per house of 1 person per habitable room, a child for this purpose being treated as a whole unit'*.[55]

He gave the Clerks very little guidance beyond stipulating that the return must include all houses and that they should use the material gathered during an Overcrowding Survey carried out under the Housing Act of 1935. Where this information was not available the Clerks were to make an estimate. He realised that the information would not necessarily be totally accurate but the purpose of the return was to provide a broad picture of accommodation in specific districts. Clerks in rural areas were to provide the information parish by parish. In other areas the total could be given as a single figure. The Clerks were given only three days to collect and collate the details and send their replies to the Clerk of the relevant County Council. As this was an emergency interim measure dictated by external events the data would have been of limited use for future evacuations.

By far the most extensive domestic survey was carried out in January 1939, with the object of ascertaining, not only a comprehensive picture of the amount of available accommodation for evacuation purposes, as it was reckoned that at least 90% of places would need to be provided in private houses, but also the numbers of householders who would be willing to take in evacuees. The survey, conducted by 100,000 interviewers, covered 5 million houses. Details of how it was to be conducted and the responsibilities of those collecting the information, were sent to Local Authorities in early January 1939 by the Ministry of Health via a series of Circulars[56] and Memos, and the general public had been informed of the survey and the reasons for it, in a radio broadcast given by Walter Elliot, on 6th January 1939.[57]

The information in both the broadcast and the official documentation was very carefully worded to maintain the element of secrecy surrounding the scheme, yet encouraging people to participate in the collection of data, without creating any panic. The survey was to take account not only of the amount of accommodation but of its suitability, and of the circumstances of individual householders.

The Government asked the local authorities to concentrate primarily on finding accommodation suitable for children, whether school children who came in school units accompanied by their teachers, or younger children who came with their mothers or other adults.

The purpose was to collect detailed information relating to three specific areas of concern:-

a. The amount of surplus accommodation on the standard of one person per habitable room.

b. The amount of surplus to be found in houses which were suitable for the reception of evacuees.

c. The amount to be found in houses where the householder was willing to receive unaccompanied children or teachers.

The study would also provide an opportunity to ascertain and consider the amount and suitability of supplementary provision which could be made in other ways.

Members of the Welsh Nationalist Party complained strongly on cultural and social grounds that Wales should not have been involved in the scheme at all. On 13th January 1939, J. E. Jones, the Organising Secretary of the W.N.P. said in an article to the North Wales Chronicle:-

> *'The indiscriminate transfer of English people into Wales will place the Welsh Language and even the very existence of the Welsh nation, in jeopardy. The national welfare of the Welsh people should be a matter of first consideration by the authorities who are planning evacuation into the countryside. We, as Nationalists, demand that there should be no transfer of population into Wales*

---

55 Circular No. 1742
56 Circular No. 1759
57 For full text see Appendix 6.

that would endanger Welsh nationality. If England cannot make its emergency plans without imperilling the life of our little nation let England renounce war and grant us self-government'.[58]

Although these separatist opinions were held by the Welsh National Party throughout the war, they were a reflection of only a minority of people as the total membership could be numbered in hundreds. They issued another Memorandum in February 1939 expressing further concerns.[59]

The survey itself was a massive undertaking and Government Memo.Ev.1 outlined the need for the careful selection of volunteer interviewers who would take on the role with administrative efficiency.

These volunteers, called 'Visitors', while not being allowed to enter houses for the purpose of obtaining information, would have to satisfy themselves that the home was suitable for children and that their presence would be willingly acceptable. It was suggested that the work of the volunteers would be made easier if the Local Authorities were to send a printed letter signed by the Chairman of the Council, or the Mayor, to all householders appealing for their co-operation with the collection of the data. The content of such a letter was to be left to the discretion of the Council.[60]

In addition to the Visitors, local clergy, women's organisations and other local societies were used to gain the goodwill and cooperation of the people and to add a positive slant to the need for such a survey.

It was the responsibility of the Local Authorities to appoint a responsible officer to oversee the conduct of the survey and choosing sufficient volunteer 'Visitors' to cover the whole district using the Minister of Health's criteria for selection; *Special regard was to be paid to their capacity for dealing in a kindly, tactful and confidential way with the householders, many of whom they would know socially or as neighbours.'*

It was suggested that many people in local government employment such as health visitors, teachers, school attendance officers etc. would be ideally suited for such a role.[61]

According to the Government Memo Ev2. Part IV, their task was to:-

> '...enlist goodwill in time of peace, forming a register of assistance which every humane person would hasten to offer if war came.....The compilation of the register of accommodation is therefore in the interest of the householders, as it is only in this way that difficulties and misfits can be avoided'.

How these words would come back to haunt those who sent children to very poor and sometimes dangerous billets!

In the Amlwch Urban District of Wales concern was expressed by the local Medical Officer about the appointment of female Visitors.

> *'...my main object is to prevent you from too hurriedly appointing lady visitors who, while they may be admirable, say as members of a nursing committee on account of social prestige, may not only be quite incapable of summing up the possibilities of a household from billeting point of view, but partly in a small community like this, may be regarded as unwelcome intruders into the privacy of their neighbours, especially if their qualifications are inadequate'.*[62]

After initial training each Visitor was to be provided with a form of authorisation and a record book for the purpose of making their reports. These were printed by the Ministry and distributed to local authorities in order to save time and provide some semblance of continuity.

---

58 North Wales Chronicle. p13. Cited in North Wales. A Case Study of a Reception Area under the Government Evacuation Scheme. 1939-45. Gillian Wallis. unpub thesis. p63 Flintshire Record Office

59 For full text see Appendix 7

60 For a copy of the letter sent to the residents in Shaftesbury, Dorset. (see Appendix 1).

61 Ministry of Health Circular 1759. 21st January 1939. para. 11

62 North Wales Chronicle. 10th February 1939. cited Wallis op.cit. p19

The Visitors function was to ascertain:-

a. The number of habitable rooms in each dwelling.

b. The number of persons ordinarily resident in the house and, by deduction from the number of habitable rooms, the number of persons who could be accommodated.

c. Where there was a surplus, whether the home conditions would be suitable for unaccompanied children.

d. Where the premises were deemed suitable, whether the householder was prepared in the event of an emergency to receive and care for unaccompanied children up to the maximum on the basis of the Government scheme. Where the householder was unwilling, or willing to take fewer numbers, the facts and reasons were to be noted.[63] The Visitors were to point out to householders that although the acceptance of children should be voluntary, they might be required to take other persons.[64]

'Visitors' in the Shaftesbury area of Dorset[65] had also been asked to note down the Water Supply and Sanitary arrangements available in individual houses under the following codes:-

WATER SUPPLY
W.W. Where the water was obtained from a well.

P.W.C. Where the water was obtained from a piped water supply belonging to the council.

P.W.P. Where the water was obtained from a piped water supply privately owned.

SANITARY ACCOMMODATION

E.C. Where the sanitary accommodation was an earth closet.

W.C. Where the sanitary accommodation was a water closet.[66]

There were of course those persons who, although having space and willingness to take in evacuees, were incapable of doing so. These would include:-

- The aged and infirm living on their own who were barely able to look after themselves.
- Households where there was a confirmed invalid.
- Persons living alone whose employment required them to be absent all day.

In such cases the Visitors were asked to explore the possibility of the householder taking in children if they were accompanied by an adult, or whether some arrangement could be made for the child outside school hours.

Where householders were willing to receive evacuees but were unable to do so because of lack of appropriate beds and bedding, the Visitors were asked to indicate this information on the form.[67]

The Visitors were also asked to report where householders had already made private arrangements to accommodate relatives or others in the event of any emergency. The Government were concerned that 'private evacuation' did not get out of hand and that enough billets would be available for the official scheme.

The Visitors were given some interesting instructions on how to deal with farms in rural areas. In wartime the Government planned to increase home production, therefore under the Evacuation Scheme it wanted to ensure

63. Memo Ev.1 Paragraph 7
64 Memo Ev.1 Paragraph 8.
65 Letter to nominated 'Visitors' 20th January 1939. From J. Stace Macey. Clerk to Shaftesbury RDC.
66 Local water supply was also an important issue during the second evacuation in 1940. On 30th October 1940, the Town Clerk of Chipping Norton, Oxfordshire wrote to the County Clerk, F.G. Scott, describing the difficulties experienced in the town with regard to water levels. The only answer he received was:-
'...the County council were very well aware of the serious strain being put on all public services as a result of evacuation and trusted that some solution to the problems might be found before the winter' Chipping Norton. Doc. 106. Oxfordshire Record Office.
67 Memo.Ev.2 Paragraph 13.

that there was enough flexibility to allow for the housing of additional labour on the farms, but not to the extent that this impeded the farmer's normal activities. They were also to consider the degree of isolation, especially where a farm, or other dwelling, was a distance of more than 2 miles away from a suitable school.[68]

Although these concerns were laudable, in practice many children were billeted on isolated hill and moorland farms in Wales and the West Country, and as a result many teachers had problems keeping in contact with their charges.

Local Authorities were asked to provide information about empty houses and other suitable buildings in their locality, especially large ones, which could house a substantial number of evacuees. The exceptions included local schools, for obvious reasons, but school houses were to be treated as private houses and could be considered when housing any accompanying teachers and helpers. However, when the scheme was implemented, it was found that many local planners had forgotten about the teachers and they were left to find their own accommodation.

The Government laid down detailed guidelines as to how the information was to be collected and recorded. As soon as returns came in from Visitors, the officer in charge of the survey had to examine the book and tabulate the information on a form issued by the Ministry. He then had to make a provisional entry as to the numbers of transferred persons to be accommodated in each house and identify in specific columns the numbers of unaccompanied children, accompanied children with mothers, helpers, teachers and others, including those who had made private arrangements. With the latter he was also asked to work out how much space for extra evacuees was available in the house when these numbers were taken into consideration. He was also given the task of deciding whether reasons given by householders for not having evacuees were valid and could therefore justify exemption. If he thought that exemption was unjustified, he had to note the number of persons, other than unaccompanied children, who could be housed.

It is obvious that those householders who came into this category were not going to be too happy about having evacuees forced upon them. Inadvertently by adopting this policy the Local Officer, under instruction from the Government, was creating a situation where problems and ill-feeling would be inevitable within some billets from the very start of the scheme.

Considering the amount of work which had to be co-ordinated both at regional and local level and then carried out 'in the field', the time scale for the return of the forms was very tight. A summary of the Survey was to be sent to the Ministry of Health by the 28th February 1939, and a copy sent to the Clerk of the County Council by the same date.

Details of the progress of the operation within each local area were kept centrally and a close check was made on the distribution and receipt of relevant information so that all parishes kept to the time allowed. The following is a small extract from the Record of Progress document kept by the Clerk to the Dorset County Council. (RO represents Registration Office).[69]

---

68 Memo. Ev.2 Paragraph 11d. January 1939
69 Dorset County Council Minutes.

Parish	Sent to RO	Return from RO	DO.OC Noted	Form B Noted	Sent to Visitor	Return From Visitor	Sent to RO Decision	Return with Decision	Passed for Reg	Registered
ASHMORE	21.1.39	21.1.39	NIL	27.1.39	1.2.39	20.2.39	20.2.39	21.2.39	21.2.39	24.2.39
BOURTON	23.1.39	4.2.39	9.2.39	9.2.39	9.2.39	16.2.39	16.2.39	18.2.39	21.2.39	24.2.39

'Visitors' books, and the completed register of the survey, were to be kept in a suitable place to be distributed to those operating the Evacuation scheme should the need arise.

The final summary, sent to the Ministry on Form E4, contained all the relevant information collected from all parishes and villages in the designated areas.

The following is an extract from the final submission form E4 from Shaftesbury in Dorset

Government Evacuation Scheme. Form E4

Ministry of Health Circular 1759

(Grand) Summary of Accommodation

County: Dorset Rural District of Shaftesbury

(In rural districts a separate return is required for each parish and a summary of the district as a whole.)[70]

Provisional Declaration of Las as to Nos. To be accom.	Total No Habitable Rooms	Total No additional persons who could be accom.	Unacc Child	Teachers	Others	Private	Total	Add.Matts D	Bedding S	Blankets D	Blankets S
Private Houses	11687	4387	1037	718	776	1076	3607	121	285	435	1020
Hotels B.Houses	177	133	3	4	2	140	149				
Empty Houses Camps Hostels	-	10	-	2	8	10	-	4	2	12	6
TOTAL	11864	4530	1040	724	786	1216	3766	125	287	435	1026
ASHMORE Private H. TOTAL	234	92	20	11	8	8	57	-	1	-	3
BOURTON Private H Total	900	332	70	55	49	80	256	6	7	33	63
ETC ETC											

It is important to note that the figures in the columns headed Mattresses and Blankets were supposed to provide an indication of the shortfall of these articles within the reception areas. This was especially important when the villages were small and yet were required to accept significant numbers of evacuees. It was well known in the reception areas that in the country parishes farm labourers, often on low wages, did not keep a large stock of extra bedding. However, in practice the use made of these figures did not work out in the way everyone expected. In response to the form, the Ministry of Health had arranged to send 2,000 blankets and 800 mattresses to the Dorchester Rural District Council for dispersal as required. However, by the 31st August 1939, only 150 blankets had arrived and there were no extra mattresses. The Chief Billeting Officer sent a telegram to the LCC and the Ministry of Health suggesting that under the circumstances, evacuees should each take their own blanket with them into the reception areas. He simply received a reply stating that this was not possible.

There were also problems with basic furniture. Again, many farm labourers were not able to purchase the extras needed to house evacuees. When this was pointed out at a Council meeting, the Billeting Officer replied that

70 File E3 Shaftesbury RDC. Evacuation of Refugees. General File. 16th September 1939 to 16th March 1939. Dorset Record Office.

there was nothing in the Government's billeting notices that allowed the local areas to purchase extra furniture and charge the expense to the scheme. All they could do was point out the problems and send a letter of protest, which he duly did.[71]

Some blankets did eventually arrive in the Dorset area, and advertisements like the one below appeared in the local newspapers. But the distribution of them was delayed by bureaucracy as people had to apply for them, even though the authorities already knew that some individual hosts and whole reception areas needed them urgently.

> *'Billeting Notice.*
> *Blankets and Bedding*
>
> *A further supply of blankets is now available and householders who have evacuees billeted upon them should send their applications in writing stating:-*
>
> *The number of blankets*
>
> *The number of camp beds needed to make up their requirements for the use of evacuees now in their homes.*
>
> *A limited supply of waterproof sheeting is also ready for issue where needed for younger children. These blankets, beds and sheeting are Government property and will be delivered to the householder against his signature within a few days of application'*[72]

The blankets provided were not usually in very good condition. In an article in the Dorset County Chronicle and Swanage Times on the 9th November 1939 dealing with social conditions in the Dorchester area, the investigative reporter C.K.Young wrote:-

> *'It was with a disgusted gesture that Mr Groombridge, Deputy-Chief Evacuation Officer for Dorchester, threw down the blankets that the Government has provided for refugees whose foster parents have insufficient. 'Feel them', he said. 'How much cold are they going to keep out? You would need six or eight to feel any difference at all'. I felt the thin cotton stuff and prayed for a mild winter in Dorset'.*[73]

The haste in collecting and collating the data meant that mistakes were inevitable, and on the 13th March 1939 the Minister of Health sent the following memo to all Local Authorities.

> 'Not all Local Authorities completed forms E4 correctly. The column 'Others' was meant to be the number of persons, other than unaccompanied children, who the Local Authority considered householders might reasonably be required to receive after allowing for such factors as extreme age or infirmity. Although most Local Authorities did, others have only entered the numbers the householders volunteered to receive'.[74]

The Local Authorities were therefore asked to confirm their final numbers with the Ministry in London as soon as possible.

When all the returns were analysed, the results showed that on a basis on one person per habitable room, there was enough space to house 6,050,000 people[75].

However, for various reasons such as requisition by Government departments, empty houses already earmarked for use by companies leaving London, lack of water supplies and sewage disposal, and proximity to target areas and military installations, not all this space could be used. Some Authorities expressed their concerns even before the survey had taken place as this entry in the Didcot Parish Council Minutes of 19th January 1939 indicates.

---

71 Dorset County Chronicle and Swanage Times. 7th September 1939.
72 Dorset Daily Echo 28th October 1939
73 Dorset County Chronicle and Swanage Times. 9th November 1939
74 Ministry of Health Memo. ref. 99043/101
75 TNA HO45/17636

> 'In relation to the order that a census should be made to ascertain how many places would be available for evacuees within this Parish. The Council still maintains that this area is not suitable for the people evacuated from other areas owing to the undoubted extra number of people such as extra depot workers, railway workers and military who would have to be accommodated in Didcot and, in the circumstances, this Council does not consider any good can be done if this census is taken'.[76]

The 'still' refers to a minute quoted in the Didcot Advertiser on 21st October 1938 when the Council had explained its reasons for not having evacuees.

> 'In the opinion of this Council it is undesirable that Didcot should be used for the billeting of children from other areas owing to the proximity of government stores and the railway junction'.[77]

The problem of who was entitled to accommodation was not one which went away easily. Even after the Evacuation scheme had been fully implemented, some reception areas which were deemed to be in the front line of evacuee billeting, were still having to compete with other agencies for billeting places. On 5th November 1940, the Dorchester Rural District Council discussed this question of billeting at some length. It had been intimated by the Ministry of Health that all suitable empty properties in their area could be requisitioned and now empty furnished houses could also be used for evacuees. The Chief Billeting Officer, Admiral Egerton, informed the Council that a Co-ordinating Officer was to be appointed to liaise between all parties competing for the same accommodation and maintain an overview of the situation. However, it was thought that although this would be useful for the Ministry, it would not help the Billeting Officers in the villages.[78]

Taking all the various reasons for not having evacuees into consideration the final billeting figure was reduced to 4,800,000.[79]

This still remains a remarkable figure and shows a generally favourable response from householders to the Government's request for billets.

One very interesting feature to come out of this 1939 survey was that 18% of the available billeting accommodation in England and Wales, amounting to 1,100,000 rooms, had already been reserved by private evacuees.....seven months before war was declared! In Scotland the figure was 21%, probably due to the number of people making temporary arrangements in Scotland.[80]

Of the accommodation available in Hotels and Boarding Houses, amounting to 207,000 rooms, 8% had been privately reserved by February 1939[81].

A number of the 'domestic' places reserved were in the western and south-western counties of England, but the most significant percentages were in Buckinghamshire, where although 116,245 places were available 27% were reserved by unofficial evacuees, West Sussex (26%), Berkshire, Oxfordshire and Herefordshire (25%), East Sussex (24%) and Dorset and Westmoreland (23%). Generally speaking the private reservations were highest in those counties with the largest proportion of large houses.[82]

The importance of the flight to the West at the outbreak of war can be seen in the figures from Devon where private evacuees out-numbered official evacuees by 700%, and on 7th September 1939 the Cornish Guardian reported that 1370 private evacuees had booked hotel rooms in the St Austell area.

---

76 Didcot Parish Council Minutes. 19th January 1939.
77 Didcot Parish Council Minute quoted in Didcot Advertiser, 21st October 1938.
78 Dorset County Chronicle and Swanage Times. 7th November 1940
79 Titmuss. op. cit. p37
80 ibid. p37 and p102
81 ibid. p38
82 ibid. p38 plus. Wartime Bucks. 1939-1945. Buckinghamshire Record Office. 1995

According to Titmuss, it was not until he had produced his own official analysis on evacuation figures in 1943 that the Government realised that although 1.5 million people had been evacuated under the official scheme, nearly 2 million had made private arrangements[83]. Householders who took in private evacuees were only entitled to billeting allowances if it could be proved that the children's parents were unable to pay an adequate payment direct to the householder.

Titmuss's accommodation analysis was based on his study of the movement of population in six of the larger evacuated areas between mid-summer 1939 and the 29th September 1939, when National Registration was introduced[84]. He found that during the period the loss of population, including both official and private evacuation was:-

Greater London	1,444,000
Liverpool, Bootle and County Boroughs	86,500
Birmingham, Smethwick and County Boroughs	50,000
Manchester, Salford and County Boroughs	123,700
Leeds County Borough	33,000
Sheffield County Borough	13,200
Total	**1,750,400**

Titmuss based his findings on the fact that by 29th September it had been estimated that 22% of evacuees had already returned home. Calculations were then made of the number of official evacuees still away from home. The difference between these figures and those indicating the loss of population represented the number of private evacuees who had not returned by 29th September.

Although the Government was concerned about these private reservations, they could do very little about it beyond appealing to people not to take up this accommodation until the Government scheme had been fully implemented. Unless people went to stay with relatives it was generally the more well-off members of the community who could afford to take themselves into the country for an indeterminate amount of time.

> *'I spent the day at Tadworth, near Epsom Downs, with Pamela Foster who has evacuated her children there'.*[85]

Newspapers contained advertisements from hotels in safer areas where some people stayed for the duration of the war. One actress stopping at a luxury hotel in North Wales in 1940 found it contained:-

> *'...women whose sole occupation seemed to be backgammon, a lot of drinking and a little knitting for the troops'.*[86]

But by 1941 even journalists on the Times were becoming a little sarcastic when describing these hotel guests:-

> *'The hotels are filled with well-to-do refugees, who too often have fled from nothing. They sit and read and knit and eat and drink, and get no nearer the war than the news they read in the newspapers...'* [87]

Owners of Hotels, Boarding Houses, and anyone else providing accommodation for payment, had to inform the police. The following notice appeared in newspapers on the 1st September 1939.

---

83 Titmuss. op. cit. p102
84 This registration excluded all service personnel and those crews on ships, or actually berthed in ports, and totalled 2.2% of the total population in the UK.
85 John Colville. Fringes of Power. Downing Street Diaries.1939-55.Hodder and Stoughton 1985. 28th January 1940. p75
86 Norah Bearing. A Friendly Hearth. pub. Cape 1946 p11. cited A. Calder. The People's War. Panther 1971. p42
87 The Times. 10th January 1941

POLICE NOTICE
ALIENS ORDER

NOTICE IS HEREBY GIVEN that under the Aliens Order, 1920, as now amended,

ALL PERSONS PROVIDING LODGING OR SLEEPING ACCOMMODATION FOR REWARD shall cause a Registration Form AR-E to be completed by all persons, except members of H.M. Forces in UNIFORM, using their premises for lodging and sleeping accommodation.

Any hotel, boarding house, lodging house, apartment-house keeper etc. wishing to obtain further information on the subject is requested to apply to the nearest police station and an initial supply of the form AR-E will be given free. [88]

Some owners of the larger estates and houses also took in 'paying guests' to help the upkeep:-

> *'In order to keep Uppark going, which with its silver plate, its large rooms and its periodical repairs is no light task, they (Meg Fetherstonhaugh and Admiral Sir Herbert Meade-Fetherstonhaugh) have taken in some paying guests for the duration of the war...The PGs (sic) included Lady Mary Glyn, daughter of the 8th Duke of Argyle and widow of the Bishop of Peterborough,..There was also A.Cecil, nephew of the Prime Minister Salisbury, Mr. Charles Mead, whose interests centred on hunting and shooting. Lastly there was Audrey Paget, daughter of Lord Queenborough'.* [89]

In response to an influx of war-workers into the county, from August 7th 1941 restrictions were placed on people in Somerset letting their houses or rooms to any 'guests' who were not there on the night of 6th August 1941 without the written consent of the Evacuation Committee. The order did not apply to inns, licensed premises or lodging house but to all domestic dwellings/rooms whether the habitation was furnished or not. Anyone contravening the order was subject to a fine or imprisonment under the Defence Regulations.[90]

Implementation

> *'It was a problem for me to move from a working class school into an upper class one...In Battersea there was no awareness that there was something on the other side of the fence because all the London children were the same. I had to have elocution lessons when I went to Bromley because I was South London...'ain't ya'and all that'.*[91]

> *'In accordance with the announcement which will be made by radio today, all schools in evacuation areas and neutral areas are to be closed for instruction for at least a week from today. In reception areas schools should be reopened as soon as arrangements for the education of the children evacuated to the locality can be completed'*[92].

For some schools the evacuation of September 1939 was not the first time that they had been affected by such events. A full year before the declaration of war, at the time of the Munich Crisis, the staff and pupils at the Tottenham County School[93] were to hear some vital news. Mr Ware, a teacher at the school wrote in unusually stark terms: *'Then came the last week in September (1938). When we reached school on that Monday morning, we learned that Tottenham had been declared a Priority Area'.*[94] As with other 'Priority Areas' if an emergency should arise it had been decided that all Tottenham's schools would close. Letters were sent home inviting parents to the School to hear the details of the proposed evacuation scheme from the Headteacher.

---

88 Dorset County Chronicle and Swanage Times. 1st September 1939
89 Colville. op.cit. Thursday 15th February. 1940. p86
90 SRO. C/CD/1/6/4
91 Dorothy Lofts. cited in 'Innocents Abroad'. Edward Stokes. Allen and Unwin. 1994 p4
92 Letter from M.G.Holmes. Board of Education. London. 3 September 1939
93 I am indebted to Prof. Sidney Brown PhD a former pupil at Tottenham County School for allowing me access to his personal files and research.
94 Chronicle; Evacuation Number p13

In this procedure Tottenham County School was following a routine replicated by hundreds of other schools in those districts designated as Evacuation areas. Fortunately there were a sizeable number of parents who were not strangers to the School as the pre-war *Chronicles*[95] have revealed. A co-operative team spirit prevailed linking staff, pupils and parents in this difficult quiet period some time before the real evacuation. Such bonding as there was may have been minimal, but it could have provided a basis for subsequent, more marked homogeneity. For months before evacuation it could be argued that some schools revealed the potential for closer teacher-pupil relationships some of which were enhanced by the *in loco parentis* war-time roles.

During the crisis in September 1938, the Home Office had contacted the National Federation of Women's Institutes for help. As Dame Frances Farrer stated, ' *the official evacuation scheme had not been worked out, the tiny department dealing with it at the Home Office ....was so utterly swamped by evacuation enquiries that they accepted with deep gratitude the loan of a typist and a typewriter from NFWI.*[96]

In addition, the Women's Voluntary Service[97], which had only been established in May 1938,[98] was also involved, but required guidance. Dame Frances Farrer recalled that:

> *Lady Reading (the Chairman of WVS) sent me a SOS to help with personnel to organise the scheme locally. I was in the country but luckily had with me the key to no 39* [99]*. I rushed up to London in the car, obtained various papers from the office and then had a long sitting at WVS recommending people who might be roped in within each county to organise the evacuation scheme*[100]

The meeting took place on September the 24th and 26th, after which the NFWI wrote to all the County Federations in the areas to be covered by the evacuation, and formed a 'flying squad' of six existing WI Voluntary organisers to visit the liaison officers and the County Federations.

The next day the Home Office asked if the NFWI could help evacuate children under five years of age as well. The official scheme had made no provision for these younger children, but the mothers were growing desperate when they realised that there were no gas masks for babies. In spite of all the difficulties NFWI agreed, and in the next couple of days improvised a scheme for despatch, transport and billeting of the younger children and babies.

When all had been set up, the Home Office told the NFWI to put all arrangements on hold, and to await Neville Chamberlain's return from Munich. They were able to do this with one exception - 60 children from Bessborough Street, Westminster, had already been taken to Cambridge. The Prime Minister returned with the message *'I believe it is peace for our time'*, and the children who had been taken to Cambridge were returned home.

This whole episode came to be known as 'The Institute war week'. It had shown how an evacuation scheme could work and how willing the village WI members were to co-operate. One institute President explained that within a day of receiving the emergency letter her WI had *arranged a place for a crèche, and for helpers, and got the promise of many cots, mattresses and blankets. Board and lodging was found for 91 children. It was all done in a couple of hours.*[101]

The NFWI had a reputation as a powerful lobbying organisation, so it is not surprising that they subsequently sent a Memorandum to both Sir John Anderson, then Minister of Civilian Defence at the Home Office and to Mr Walter

95 School Magazine.
96 Note from Dame Frances Farrer - Gen Sec NFWI (evacuation file NFWI Archives, Women's Library) cited in Countrywomen in war time - Women's Institutes 1938 – 1945 Anne Stamper. Paper delivered to The Second International Conference on the History of Voluntary Action, held at Roehampton Institute, University of Surrey, 9-11 September 2003.
97 The organisation was to co-operate with Local Authorities and with other voluntary societies but it was very different from other women's organisations with a tradition of voluntary service, such as Women's' Institutes, Towns Women's Guilds or Women's Co-operative Guilds. Whereas the latter were organised to meet the interests of their members, the WVS had been specifically created as a war time service.
98 A Council was formed with Lady Reading in the Chair and included representatives of the National Council of Women, the Family Endowment Society, the Women's Engineering Society and the National Society for Equal Citizenship, but not the NFWI. The brief of this new organisation was:.........to provide a channel through which women could enrol in the Air Raid Precautions Services; bring home to every household in the country what air attack would mean; make known to every household what it could do for its own protection and to help the Community.
99 39 Eccleston Street, Victoria, London, - the Headquarters of NFWI
100 Dame Frances Farrer. op cit.
101 Home and Country, November 1938, p.451, NFWI Archives, The Women's Library

Eliot, Minister of Health, containing detailed practical suggestions on how future evacuation procedures might be improved.[102]

As it happened, the proposed evacuation during the Munich Crisis came to nought apart from in a few selected areas, but during the remainder of 1938 through to evacuation in 1939, notwithstanding Chamberlain's post-Munich assurances, preparations for the worst were being made in many educational establishments, and something of the atmosphere of the time comes through in this account written for the Tottenham County School *Chronicle*, again by Mr. Ware:

> *'A hectic time ensued. Staff meeting followed Staff meeting. The ordinary school routine was relegated to the limbo of things forgotten ... Pupils were told what articles to bring with them. They printed their names and addresses on labels: during the exodus these would be tied on to outer garments and would form some kind of identification disc'.*[103]

Mr Ware's choice of such words as '*hectic*' and phrases such as *'relegated to the limbo of things forgotten'* captures perfectly the changed atmosphere which was pervading. Although the source was the 'official' publication of the School, there is in this an implicit note of urgency and an awareness of priorities which were not merely educational. There seems to be little evidence of 'formality' and the situation became one in which many lessons were simply not conducted and children appear to have been left to their own devices for much of the day. Presumably, statutory regulations such as registration and assembly were followed, but it seems that it was not until the School had settled in the town of March in the Fens that normal teaching was resumed. How far this interlude affected subsequent practice is difficult to ascertain accurately, but the staff no doubt would have entertained understandable anxieties about restoring a degree of order, notwithstanding their extended pastoral role. Like the children in their charge, the teachers were to have no idea of where they were going to escape the anticipated Blitz on London, or of the attitude of their future hosts in the reception areas. Sadly, the official sources at local government level in Cambridgeshire reveal little of substance. The Co-ordination of the evacuation arrangements had been assigned by the Clerk to the County Council to the Public Assistance Officer in 1938. In accordance with the regulations of the Ministry of Health the responsibility for *'the reception of evacuees at the railhead and their transport ... to certain pre-determined distribution centres'* was confirmed and encouragingly *'with the assistance of the WVS light refreshments would be provided at the district centres'.*[104] It was noted that *'particulars had been received from the Traffic Controller of the arrival times of the trains and their approximate load of evacuees consisting of children unaccompanied except by schoolteachers, and later, infants under five and their mothers and other persons'*. At this stage everything appeared to be under control.

But just months before the outbreak of hostilities, the local authority minutes indicated that there was growing worry about 'congestion at March Station' yet this paled into insignificance when it was suggested that not only the quantity but the quality (at least in the health sense) of the London children was a source of anxiety. A request was received from the March area committee '*for sanction to be given to the formation of an additional Decontamination Squad at March*' which, eventually, was passed up to the Home Office where, it seems, it disappeared![105]

Throughout the country, local authorities were discussing the evacuation process in Council and Evacuation sub-committee meetings. Documents and correspondence available in the Somerset Record Office reveal how one such committee was dealing with the planning issues surrounding the scheme.

> *'An organisation can be devised very quickly which would be capable of functioning effectively at short notice, but preparatory action is essential. Local authorities should at once complete their*

102 Copies of these memoranda are in the Evacuation file in the NFWI archives at the Women's Library
103 Chronicle; Evacuation Number p13op cit
104 Isle of Ely Executive Sub Committee A.R.P. Minutes of 21 April 1939 in Council of the Isle of Ely Minutes of the Proceedings of the County Council for the Year 1939-40, p.63, County Record Office, Cambridgeshire County Council, Cambridge.
105 ibid 24 May 1939 p151

arrangements to the last and smallest detail....in order that each individual worker at the business end of the affair knows precisely what he has to do'[106]

On the 3rd February 1939, the County Education officer commented on the plans from his perspective and was keen to point out that there was an essential difference between the evacuation scheme being organised and that which had been contemplated during the Munich crisis of September 1938. This difference being that the '*present plan was driven by the need to move certain priority classes and priority areas, and not for the whole of that proportion of the population, whether adult or juvenile, which is not indispensable*'[107].

Correspondence from the Clerk of Somerset County Council, Harold King, to Local Authorities puts the planning of evacuation at County level into perspective. On June 16th 1939 he sent memo. stating that;

> '*While it appears that the majority of local authorities in this County have the preparation of their organisation for dealing with the reception of evacuees well in hand, there are still a number who have not yet been able to send me even an outline of their proposals. May I make it quite clear that the County Council do not desire in any way to intrude on what is admittedly the function of the Local Authorities.....However, it was the express wish of the Regional Commissioner, General Sir Hugh Elles, that the County Council should be aware of the general arrangements which are being made by the local authorities.....I am instructed to ask that the organisation for putting into execution the Government Evacuation Scheme shall be completed in detail and lodged with me before the August holidays.....*'.[108]

It is interesting to note that in his opinion the County Council had no definite functions with regard to the actual organisation for receiving and billeting evacuees, other than coordinating traffic arrangements and acting as the welfare authority for certain priority classes of evacuees.

The County Council was aware that the reception areas would have to depend largely on voluntary workers, possibly at short notice. One important issue in Somerset was that they also recognised the fact that as their work might be carried out at inconvenient times and they would be dealing with a transient population who would be uncertain and harassed, the volunteers might be subject to psychological pressure. A subject, which bearing in mind the time these issues were being discussed, indicates an insightful and caring attitude on the part of the council.

It was deemed necessary to contact voluntary workers as soon as possible because when any emergency arose it would be too late. As a consequence, local authorities were asked to make sure they had the holiday addresses of all their staff and the latter were to be told to remain in close proximity to a wireless through which announcements regarding the evacuation would be made. This might then necessitate an early return from their vacation.

In some areas rehearsals were organised. In Dorset the official memorandum relating to the billeting of children was submitted to the Dorchester Rural District Council, stating that there would be evacuation rehearsal and that the railway company would make the entire arrangements for the transport of evacuees from London to the local detraining stations, in this case Dorchester. The Council's responsibility would be to undertake the reception and it was expected that children would be marched as quickly as possible to a central place where sanitation, first aid facilities and rough sleeping accommodation in case trains were delayed, would be available. From here they would be dispersed to outlying villages. The Ministry of Transport would provide sufficient vehicles to transport the children to a central 'de-bussing' station in each village and the Rural District Councils would then take charge of the children at each of these points. [109]

---

106 Somerset Record Office. File C/CD/1/6/1/ Evacuee Correspondence. 1938-39
107 ibid.
108 ibid.
109 Dorchester Rural District Council Minutes. 31st May 1939.

During the week immediately before the Evacuation scheme was implemented, hosts in some of the designated reception areas were given an indication of their responsibilities and the amount of money they would receive and how they could claim it. In Weymouth a loud speaker van was organised to tour the streets telling hosts of the time their charges were arriving and also any other important details they should know, [110] such as the expectation that they should *'control and care for evacuees as if they were their own children and should any difficulty arise they were to inform the Billeting Officer'.*[111] They were also asked to look out for those children suffering from home-sickness and to report cases when they were particularly concerned.

The payment to hosts of 10/6 per week for the first child and 8/6 for the subsequent children was to cover *'full board and all the care that would be given to a child in their own home'*[112]. The money was not meant to cover the cost of clothes or medical expenses, which hosts were under no obligation to meet, although a teacher evacuated with his school from Liverpool described how some hosts took on the extra financial burden of providing evacuees with extra clothes and shoes despite not having to do so.

> *'The billeting money they, the foster parents, drew from the Post Office each week would barely cover the cost of a child's board and lodging. It has never been generally known what personal sacrifices were made by the humble cottagers. They willingly accepted responsibility for an evacuee, provided it with food and a bed and then saved every spare penny to buy it something new to wear for Chapel on Sunday. In Wales I have soon learnt that one must go to Chapel suitably attired. This was one reason, maybe the main reason, why the villagers wanted their evacuees to look respectable on one day at least, during the week'.*[113]

Local Pub used as a Billeting Office

Using a form which was available from the local billeting officer, disbursements were to be made weekly in advance, usually at the local Post Office; but not always as the following advertisement would suggest.

110 Dorset Daily Echo. 25th August 1939.
111 Dorset County Chronicle and Swanage Times. 31st August 1939.
112 ibid.
113 From 'Welsh Rarebits' the anonymous and unpublished account of a Liverpool teacher evacuated to North Wales. 1939-45. cited in Wallis op.cit. p131

'BILLETING PAY DAYS

Payments to persons who have received evacuated children and mothers in the Wareham and Purbeck area are made as follows:-

Wareham. 17, West St Wednesdays. 9 - 1 and 2 - 5

Winfrith. Village Hall. Tuesdays. 9 - 12.30

West Lulworth. Conservative Rooms. Tuesdays. 2 - 5

Bere Regis. Women's Institute. Wednesdays. 2 - 5

Morden. Village Hall. Wednesdays. 9.30 - 12.30

Corfe Castle. Room at Mrs Thomas's, West St. Mondays. 9.30 - 12.30

Steeple. Blackmanston Farm. Mondays. 2 - 4.'[114]

Although hosts were informed that the children would arrive with rations to last them for 48 hours they were advised to buy and store an additional week's requirement of staple foods.[115] Supplies of these 'evacuee' ration bags had been arranged as early as the 28th April 1939, [116] and were the overall responsibility of the Food (Defence Plans) Department. The department had acquired the necessary stocks of emergency rations which were initially held centrally. They were then sent to the relevant detraining stations in the reception areas where an authorised representative of the receiving Local Authority had to take general charge and assume responsibility for their distribution. The amount of emergency rations sent to each area had been calculated in accordance with the number of people actually deposited at the stations and the original consignments were sent to the relevant Station Masters. Sometimes, for convenience, the bags were moved to somewhere more central for example in the case of Shaftesbury, to the Guildhall.

The paper carrier bag given to the children generally contained:-

> *'Child...1 can of meat, 2 cans of milk (1 sweet/1 unsweet), 2 packets or 1 pound of tea, a quarter of a pound or 2 x 2d Chocolate biscuits.*
>
> *Adults...exactly the same plus one extra can of meat'.*

In some areas children received some fruit and a triangle of processed cheese.

The whole process was not exempt from the usual bureaucracy. When the rations were issued notice ER1 had to be handed to each adult. This ER1 stated:-

> *'The food in this bag is provided free of cost.*
>
> *It is an emergency ration for your consumption during the next 48 hours. After that interval, the retail food shops will, it is anticipated, have received sufficient supplies to meet the requirements of an additional population in the area you are to be billeted. You are asked to make as few purchases as possible during the first 48 hours'.*

At the end of the day Form ER2 had to be completed by the Distribution Officer.

```
'ER2
Daily return or Emergency Rations Issued.

1.    Name of Detraining Station.

2.    Name of Reception Area.
```

114 ibid. 21st September 1939
115 Dorset County Chronicle and Swanage Times. 21st September 1939
116 Food Defence.1839/38.

3. Number of Evacuee persons to whom rations were issued.

4. Signature of Officer i/c distribution.

Date.....'

In some areas the bags were given to the children as they got *on* the trains and the contents were eaten on the journey sometimes with devastating results!

> *'Each of the children, apart from their pathetic bundles, had a large carrier bag and in that there were iron rations. They included a tin of bully beef and a tin of pears. We were in the carriage for four and a half hours during which time the kids ate their pears and were sick'.*[117]

It is evident from other documents that any unissued or spare rations were sold. A letter from the Town Clerk of Chipping Norton to the Ministry of Food on 20th January 1940 provides an account of the food originally supplied under the Evacuation Scheme which had not been used and an indication that cheques totalling £16.15s were being forwarded to the Ministry.[118]

Now all the planning had been done, the Councils, officials and volunteers in both the Evacuation and Reception areas were in a state of readiness. Under the *Pied Piper* instructions there were to be two warnings. On the first, the Evacuation Officer would satisfy himself that the organisation which he had prepared was ready to be implemented, that the necessary information had either been given in advance, or was to be disseminated immediately via parents' meetings, posters or loud speaker vans. The Evacuating Officer would also verify that the transport authorities had received the preliminary warning and were taking appropriate action.

At the Second Warning, Head-teachers in the evacuation areas would be instructed to arrange for pupils to bring to school the luggage they required, and that no parties of children should be dispersed to handicraft, domestic subjects, swimming baths or education visits. Identity cards and labels would be prepared and teachers would remain on call over the weekend. If evacuation was decided upon, final notices in the form of a simple code word followed by each day of the week.....e.g. *Pied Piper. Monday*, would be prepared by the Evacuating Officer to be ready for delivery to every school in his area.

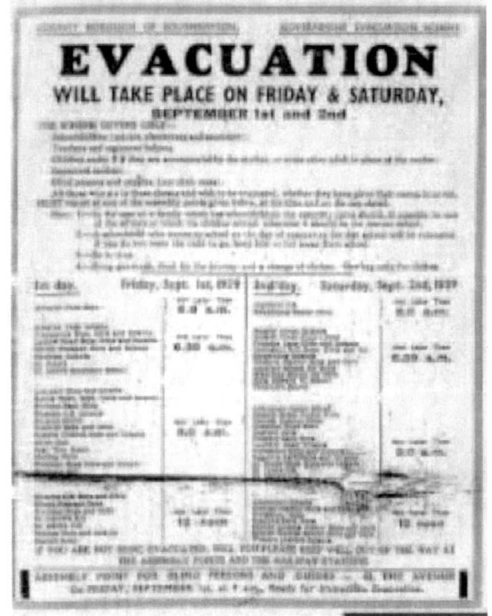

Evacuation Poster showing timetable of evacuation

117 Ben Wicks. No Time to Wave Goodbye. Bloomsbury. 1990. Reminiscence of a teacher.

118 Chipping Norton Borough Council. Doc.28. 20th January 1940.

After a summer of uncertainty Operation Pied Piper was finally implemented on Friday September 1st 1939. For the next four days approximately 1.5 million mothers and children, unaccompanied school children, teachers, helpers, pregnant women and 'special cases' embarked on trains, buses and paddle steamers and left some of Britain's major cities, vulnerable locations and other perceived target areas to those considered to be relatively safer.

During the previous week, teachers had prepared their classes for the possibility of war and the need for evacuation while at the same time insisting that the practices that many of them carried out each day were just a precaution, so as not to instil any sort of panic in the minds of pupils or parents.

On the same day thousands of hospital patients were moved to safer areas or sent home to free-up hospital beds; 2,200 doctors and 15,000 nurses were posted to casualty hospitals. Private vehicles, coaches and trucks were sent as auxiliary ambulances to various areas of the country and thirty civilian casualty trains were sent to specific locations.[119]

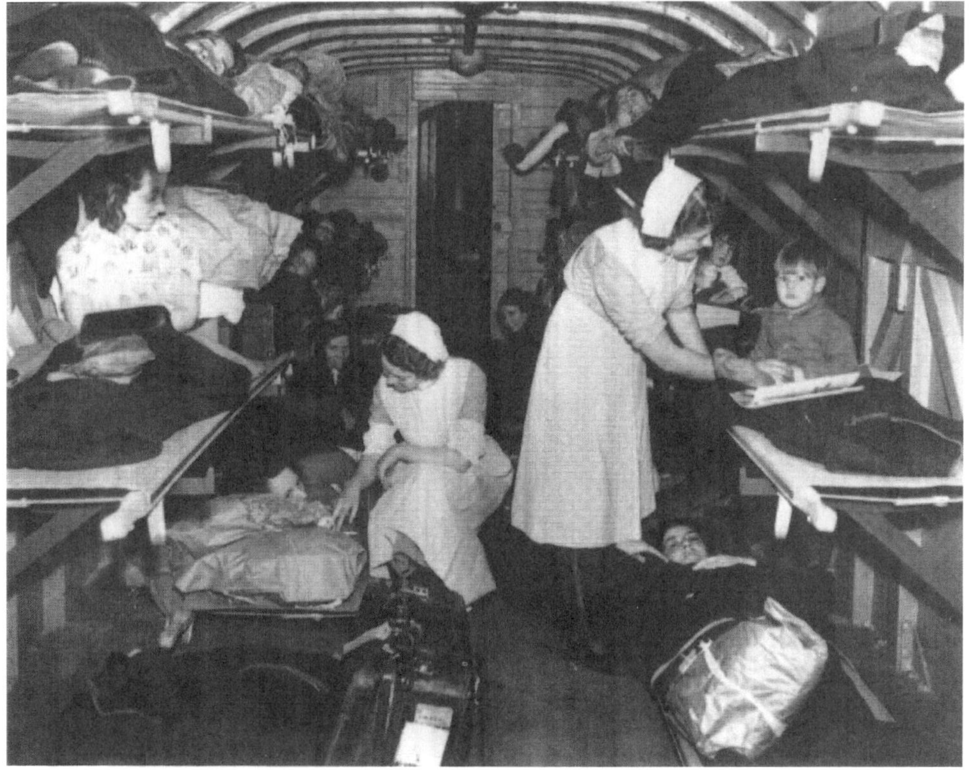

Special arrangements were made to evacuate patients from London hospitals.
Some went by coaches and others, like these, on hospital trains.

On the 31st August the London Passenger Transport Board had announced:-

> *'From about 9 a.m. tomorrow until 6pm the scheme for evacuating school children and others under Government direction will begin.*

119 T.L.Crosby. Impact of Civilian Evacuation in the Second World War.. Croom Helm. 1986. p28p97

> *Both rail and road services for ordinary passengers will be severely curtailed between these hours for the next three to four days.... as necessary stations will be closed altogether to traffic other than official evacuation traffic.*
>
> *It is felt that the public will co-operate so that the organisation may run smoothly. They are advised that they should travel only if compelled.*
>
> *From approximately 7 o'clock tonight London Transport Green Line coach services will be curtailed or withdrawn'.*[120]

All advertised L.M.S railway excursions were cancelled throughout the weekend. [121]

The evacuation of Tottenham County School began on the first day. The scene on that Friday remains clearly etched on the mind of former pupil Tom Farmer:

> *'On that day we assembled at School, tied labels to our luggage and persons and marched off in double file to Stamford Hill Station'.*[122]

Although other contacts thought the station was West Green it was, to be precise, Seven Sisters Station that was to be the point of departure. Significantly, despite differences over such detail, all ex-evacuees from the school had a similar view of the atmosphere. Tom Farmer recalled the parents following 'the crocodiles' of children while Cyril Goodwin spoke of 'heart-wrenching' partings intensified by the fact that many older children were accompanied by siblings 'adding to the parents' anguish'.[123] It was left to the resilient Mr Ware to record the departure in a more upbeat manner:

> *'... about four hundred members of the School headed by Mr Ware bearing a banner and a load of embarrassment, marched to West Green Station. The streets were lined with relations and friends come to say goodbye to us ... On the platform we divided into groups of ten with a member of staff or helper to each group'.*[124]

It amounted to the greatest evacuation of civilians in British history and ushered in a period of immense difficulty for those responsible for children's health, education and social well-being.

Some newspaper headlines described the extent of the organisation and planning in biblical terms:-

---

120 Dorset Daily Echo. 31st August 1939.
121 ibid
122 Tom Farmer, 20 July 2000. Letter.
123 Cyril Goodwin, 18 November 2000. Letter to Prof. Brown.
124 Chronicle Evacuation Number, p.16.

GREATEST EVACUATION IN HISTORY HAS BEGUN

EXODUS OF THE BIBLE DWARFED; THREE MILLION PEOPLE ON THE MOVE

EVEN THE EXODUS OF THE BIBLE...THE FLIGHT OF THE ISRAELITES FROM EGYPT....IS DWARFED INTO INSIGNIFICANCE. [125]

NO NEED TO WONDER

Evening Despatch

PIANOS of QUALITY

EVACUATION OF SCHOOLCHILDREN TO BEGIN TO-MORROW — *Official*

SUDDEN DECISION IS "ONLY A PRECAUTION"

Birmingham And Smethwick Affected

WOMAN SAID TO HAVE HAD 4 REVOLVERS

BRITAIN'S DEFENCE

DIARY OF TO-DAY'S EVENTS

Newspaper headlines – Evening Despatch

By mid-September 1939, the plans made specifically for London were adapted and extended beyond the Capital to other areas regarded as potential targets. By the end of the month 35% of those eligible for evacuation from the LCC, 66% of those from Merseyside, 33% from Portsmouth and Southampton and 20% from Coventry had left for the reception areas, the majority during the weekend of the 1st-4th.

These variations in numbers may be explained by the amount and intensity of poverty or hardship within particular evacuated areas. Parents with few material possessions and perhaps ill-educated may have been more easily persuaded by local government officials, or were simply more compliant and followed instructions issued by the local Authorities to evacuate. They might also have been persuaded by the fact that the Government implied that they would look after all their needs if they left home. It was also unlikely that families in poor areas were able to make their own arrangements to travel to safety and the figures seen here are an indication of only those in the scheme who could not evacuate themselves. It is also worth remembering that some of those eligible did not want to go. It is unfortunate that the figures for this group of people are not available. If they were, they would provide an interesting indication of the acceptance of the scheme by the general population at whom it was aimed.

To be absolutely successful the scheme demanded a high degree of parental confidence in the efficiency of Government arrangements. Asking parents to send children away for an indefinite period, to an unknown destination and to the care of strangers was not a decision that would be taken lightly. It also meant that the local preparations in the reception areas had to be equally efficient and required a great deal of co-operation between the agencies involved.

Travis Crosby has suggested that the authorities in areas such as Manchester, where the planning was carried out very effectively, created a confidence which led to an overall success rate of 70% of those eligible for evacuation, whereas areas inadequately prepared, fraught with bureaucratic red-tape or where the administrators were remote from the people, were less successful.[126] Other areas were simply handicapped by lack of time.

---

125 Dorset Daily Echo 1st September 1939
126 Crosby. op. cit.

EVACUATION
FROM LONDON

SCHOOL CHILDREN
MOTHERS with CHILDREN
living in the London evacuation area

MOTHERS with CHILDREN
AGED and BLIND PEOPLE
INFIRM and INVALIDS
living in evacuation area who have made arrangements with relatives or friends for accommodation in a safer area

Evacuation from London notice

There were also other factors which dissuaded families from sending their children away. Some older children were needed at home to look after younger siblings while the mother was out at work. Some were ill and could not travel. Some were caught up in a certain amount of family fatalism, some of which was reported in some local press:-

'If one of us is going to die, it would be better if we all died together'[127] ; sentiments which are often referred to by evacuees when interviewed.

Joan Faulkner stated that:-

> *'My mother, in her wisdom, decided that if we were going to die then we should die together as a family. That meant all the aunts and cousins as well'.* [128]

But such attitudes were not confined to the beginning of the war and in some cases later decisions to remove evacuees because of the bombing created a conflict of interests between family and evacuee. Lyn Mendlson, recalls that while living in Weston-Super-Mare in 1941 the town was bombed on many occasions, and although she did not want to go, her parents decided to take her back to London 'to die together'. She lived with a kind family, loved the sea and enjoyed walking along the causeway to Anchor Head. The train line to Paddington went along the bottom of the garden and she remembers leaning out of the window waving and sobbing and taking the last look at a plot of land which she had been allowed to cultivate. This desire to stay made her feel very guilty at the time. (Even now when she regularly visits Weston she always looks out of the train window at the garden.)[129]

The initial evacuation plans did not apply to the cities of Bristol, Nottingham, Plymouth or South Wales These were designated by the Government as 'Neutral Evacuation Areas' and it was difficult to get children out of these areas unless the parents had the money to do so[130]. But, in the case of Bristol, some people made their own arrangements when the raids started. At the time of the Bristol Blitz inAugust 1940, W.R.Strickland, Assistant Coordinating Officer for Somerset, was sent information on the movement of the population of the city by an Inspector White in the Chief Constable's office. He reported that people left Bristol in four different stages.

---

127 Dorset Daily Echo. 25th August 1939.
128 Joan Faulkner. Letter to author and oral testimony. Nov. 1996. MERL Archive
129 Lyn Mendlson. Letter to author 29th January 1997. MERL Archive
130 Angus Calder. The People's War.. Panther. 1971 p42

> 'First Stage: A large number of people who can afford to keep more or less two establishments going and have supplementary petrol allowances. These people travel as far as Clevedon and Weston-Super-Mare. No figures can be given.
>
> Second Stage: Between 300 and 400 come out on buses and spend the evening in the public houses etc. If the Alert is sounded in Bristol they remain the night, but otherwise they return late in the evening.
>
> Third Stage: After the Alert has sounded in Bristol about 1000 leave the city for Somerset, a large proportion of which have, no doubt, made some arrangements for a bed.
>
> Fourth Stage: About 1000, not more, who leave the city after a raid has started when it looks as though it is going to be heavy'[131]

The Welsh Nationalist Party protested in a memorandum issued in February 1939, against the 'neutral' classification for South Wales, stating that the increased industrial activities in the seaport towns and dense industrial districts would make the area an important military objective in a time of war. They also suggested that children should be evacuated from these areas and have first rights to be moved to the Welsh rural areas.[132] The Nottingham City Council also objected strongly to the city's classification but nothing is available to indicate the views of Plymouth, even though there had been a definite change in policy. On 22nd December 1938 a confidential report which had been sent to the Lord Privy Seal by a Ministry of Health Committee containing a list of 'Areas from which evacuation is desirable' included Plymouth, and local areas such as Stonehouse and Devonport. A map also clearly indicated the city as an area of evacuation. But within ten days there had been a dramatic change in policy and Plymouth found itself classified as a neutral area, not listed for either evacuation or reception. This change was to have serious unforeseen consequences on Plymouth.[133]

Had the original designation stood, the area around Plymouth would have avoided the influx of evacuees from other parts of the country. As it was, it became saturated with evacuees. Again there was the additional problem of those who could afford to do so evacuating themselves to the area and taking up accommodation initially reserved for official evacuees, thereby putting a great deal of pressure on the local planning and support services.[134] However, the whole situation raises the question of how many people in the central planning groups realised the significance of Plymouth as a major naval base, and indeed Bristol as a port and industrial area. Surely both would have been considered by an enemy as a potential target, and later actions by the Luftwaffe were unfortunately to prove this to be a correct assumption. Fortunately Plymouth had its designation changed to an evacuation area, but figures relating to the bombing raids on Bristol show that between August 1940 and June 1941, it was the fifth most heavily bombed city in Britain with 89,000 properties destroyed or damaged, 1,378 deaths[135] and 3,240 persons injured[136]. Local historian John Penny's register of deaths as a result of the Bristol Blitz, names 175 children ranging in age from 1month -15 years old before an official evacuation policy was implemented[137]. When Winston Churchill visited Bristol on Easter Saturday in 1942, he described a *'battered Bristol'...... 'we walked and motored through devastation such as I had never thought possible.'*[138]

In January 1941, Mrs Faulk, a WVS group leader in Bristol, wrote a report entitled 'Public Evacuation Scheme for mothers and children'. She was of the opinion that there would be enough people in the city who would take advantage of such a scheme which should be applied not only to those families who had been bombed out of their

131 Somerset Record Office C/CD/1/6/4. Correspondence File.
132 Welsh Nationalist Party. Memorandum. February 1939. cited Wallis. op. cit. p265
133 Gerald Wasley 'Blitz. An account of Hitler's aerial war over Plymouth in March 1941 and the events that followed'.. Devon Books. 1991. p49
134 One reason given for this 'privatisation' was that some hosts thought that the private evacuees were a better sort of person and were therefore willing to take them in preference to the official evacuees.
135 After major bombings whole families were often buried together in communal graves, such as those in Greensbank Cemetery
136 Penny, J., 'Bristol at War, (Breedon Books Publishing Company LTD 2002), p.181
137 Penny, J., (March 2007) 'The Bristol & District War Memorial: A register of those who lost their lives due to enemy action in Bristol and surrounding districts, 1940-1944', URL: http://fishponds.org.uk/bristolmem.html
138 Churchill, W., in: Gardiner, J., 'The Blitz: The British under attack', (Harper Press 2010 London), p. 282

homes, but others who would like to leave the city. She indicated that the Civic League committee in Knowle West strongly supported the idea of evacuation, and a Miss Bean at the National Council of Social Service, stated that they too were in favour of evacuation from the city because they were having difficulties in dealing with would-be evacuees on a daily basis because of lack of funding, apart from a very small grant available to those who had lost their homes. She suggested that any scheme should involve all children and anyone who wished to take advantage of it.[139]

On the same day Miss Cashmore, who was the district service organiser for WVS Housewives and assistant secretary at the Bristol Council for Refugees based in Stapleton wrote;

> *'......regarding the crisis that has arisen since the recent air attacks on Bristol. It raises the question whether our position as a neutral area is tenable any longer. I myself, and other social workers with whom I have conferred, feel that the city will be well advised to schedule it as a danger area and make a limited evacuation scheme at the earliest possible moment....I am convinced that the absence of an evacuation scheme is causing great unrest in Bristol, because a percentage of those who should be evacuated and are entirely willing to go, cannot because Bristol is still scheduled as a neutral area.'*[140]

A few days later another report indicated that after the heavy raid of the 16th January, 1941 people in the area of Shirehampton who had been reluctant to leave before, particularly those in Barrow Hill Crescent where there were large families in small houses, would now welcome the opportunity to be evacuated.[141]

These concerns were backed up by C.M.MacInnes who in a memorandum on evacuation drew up a damning indictment on the conditions of both personal and public air raid shelters in the city. He reported that Anderson shelters were often unusable because they were wet and sometimes flooded to a depth of 18 inches and even when the Andersons were satisfactory people tended to prefer the public shelters where despite the disadvantages, there was more company. He stated that many preferred *'the noise of these places to the comparative quiet of their own shelters where they have nothing to do but sit shivering and lonely, listening to the thunder of exploding bombs and the noise of burning houses.'* However, he described the conditions in these surface shelters as atrocious and he was concerned that the unhealthy environment in the communal shelters was having a long-term detrimental effect on those using them. There was also the additional hazard of actually getting to them when this could involve a long walk or an expensive bus ride. In addition he highlighted the problems where *'young boys and girls frequently relieved of parental control are beginning to behave in a manner which will soon constitute a serious problem'*. His most significant statement came in the conclusion where he wrote; *'There has, it seems, been too general a tendency on the part of us all to persist in thinking in terms of peacetime conditions, whereas in fact Bristol is concerned today with a situation which more nearly resembles that of a siege.'*[142]

Despite its vulnerability and the bombing raids it had suffered, and all the concerns expressed by various bodies, it was not until 5th May 1941 that Bristol was declared an 'evacuated area'. A rare letter from the Clerk of the County Council to council members of existing reception areas in Somerset, simply eludes to a communication with someone in the Ministry of Health, yet in terms of the welfare of the inhabitants of Bristol, primarily the children, it was a momentous decision.[143]

> 'City of Bristol.
>
> Dear Sir
>
> I wish to confirm my recent telephone conversation with you when I

139 BRO File 11757/1. Report from Mrs. Faulk. Group Leader WVS. 15th January 1941

140 ibid. Report from Miss Cashmore. 15th January 1941

141 ibid.Report from Miss Clay 20th January 1941

142 BRO 11757/1. Appendix B. Assessment of conditions of shelters in Bristol. Memo on evacuation. C.M.McInnes. 18th January 1941.

143 Somerset Record Office. 5th May 1941. WARS/CMW. This is a very rare letter and it has taken years of research in the SRO and Bristol Record Office to find official notification of the change of Bristol's status from neutral to Evacuation. Nevertheless, the official and original communication from the MoH to Somerset CC still remains illusive.

> informed you that the whole of the City of Bristol has now been declared an evacuation area for unaccompanied children. The Ministry of Health wish Somerset to accommodate all remaining children in Bristol whose parents register them for evacuation. The registration is now taking place. I shall be glad if you will put preliminary arrangements in hand at once to receive unaccompanied children.
>
> I understand from the Ministry of Health that, subject to enemy action, the movement is not likely to take place before the end of next week, so this will give you time to complete your preparations. The County Council will, of course, use their best endeavours to arrange for the parties to be sent out as small as possible, but I am sure you will realise that the question of transport will have to be taken into consideration.
>
> Harold King. Clerk to the County Council'[144]

This change in designation meant that the combined total of children and teachers evacuated from Bristol in May, and later in August, 1941 amounted to 20,085[145], including 6671 that were evacuated privately.[146]

This eventual evacuation of the city was not without its problems. Although many evacuees suffered, and were to suffer, from the distress of separation and other psychological problems, the late exodus of Bristol meant that those who already had experienced trauma as a result of the exposure to the heavy bombing, would have their problems compounded by the additional impact of the evacuation procedures; a process known as 'sequential traumatisation'.[147] This was confirmed by the contemporary research carried out by W.E.R.Mons, who stated that *'the effects of their inner experiences appear much more clearly when the strain of evacuation is added to them'*.[148]

Despite the opportunity to evacuate, many children either remained in the city or returned after a very short period of time. As early as June 1941, just a month after the implementation, almost 30% of the evacuees had returned home.[149] The reasons for the latter can be attributed to parental pressure, homesickness, the proximity of some of the reception areas to the city which made the return or collection of children easier to do, and simpler matters such as bringing back older children who were reaching 'employment age' and could therefore add to the family income.[150]

---

144 ibid
145 Although later reports put the total at 21646. BRO. 21131/EC/Adm/12/1 31st March 1942
146 Irvine. Max. To what extent did the designation of Bristol as a 'Neutral Evacuation Zone' damage the lives of its children. Dissertation. 2012
147 This relates to the research carried out by Dr Hans Keilson who studied the long-term effects on Jewish children separated from their parents and who spent much of their time in hiding. Parsons. M. War Child. History Press. p224. See later chapter on Long Term Effects.
148 Mons.W.E.R. 'Air Raids and the child'. British Medical Journal Vol 2. No 4217 1st November 1941.
149 BRO 11757/1 Chief Education Officer to MacInnes 30th June 1941
150 ibid

Education

Wartime School Staffing

Bearing in mind the impact that war was to have on teaching and staffing levels it is worth looking at the situation brought about by the pressures placed on Local Education Authorities (LEAs) and individual schools during wartime conditions.

Before 1926, the Code of Regulations for Public Elementary Schools specified a minimum standard of staffing under which each teacher counted for not more than a prescribed number of children in average attendance, a certified Assistant counted for 60, a student for 20. In 1926, these standards were removed and each LEA had to maintain a cohort of teachers and satisfy the Board of Education that the distribution of them was suitable and adequate.

Between 1926 and 1933, the basis for the Board's examination of this LEA distribution was simply the general impressions provided by His Majesty's Inspectors (HMI) as no attempt was made to evaluate the staffing issues in individual establishments. In 1932, when financial constraints during the depression hit education as well as other sectors of the community, an attempt was made to compare one area with another by means of the Richardson Formula which only took into account the total number of children and the average size of the schools in a given area. This was of very limited use and it was not until 1933, with the introduction of the Kerslake Scales, which took into account the organisation as well as the size of each individual school, that an acceptable measurement of staffing standards became available. They were applied to every school in each area and modifications were made to suit their individual circumstances such as the size and number of rooms etc. However, these scales were never published and the Board did not regard them as a firm standard of staffing, but merely as an indication of where staffing concerns might require further investigation. Although Kerslake was used by HMI and Directors of Education as a peacetime standard of staffing they were strongly criticised on two counts.

1. The scales allowed a school in a rural area controlled by one teacher, to have as many as 35 juniors and infants, or 30 children of all ages. It was felt that these figures were too high and a second teacher was needed before these numbers were reached.
2. There was a problem in Wales where in some areas the bilingual nature of the school population required that younger children had to be taught in separate classes until they had become proficient in the second language i.e English. As many of the schools in Wales were rural and small this made the Kerslake Scales unworkable and led to the introduction of the Shrewsbury Scales, which were applied to all Welsh schools.

Between 1933 and 1939 there was a steady decline in the school population, but the authorities were slow to adjust their staffing levels accordingly, so the general standard of staffing across the country was higher than the Kerslake and Shrewsbury Scales indicated. In consequence, figures available before the war show a level of staffing more generous than that considered necessary when peacetime conditions existed in the schools.

In 1941, the Board of Education carried out a survey of school staffing and compared it to the figures available for 1938.[151] On the 1st April 1941, there were 152,135 teachers in England and Wales actually at the 'chalk-face' teaching 4,595,014 Elementary School children.[152] Out of this figure 118,726 were receiving less than full-time education and 40,749 no teaching at all. As the staff-pupil ratio for April 1941 (30.2), 31st March 1938 (30.27)

151The latter was chosen because the survey in 1939 was never completed due to the outbreak of war and the 1938 figures for the staff-pupil ratio were nearer to that of the 1st April 1941 than to the 31st March 1939.

152 This compares with the figures for 1937-38 when the total school population was 5,396,000. There were 4,755,105 in Elementary Schools , 243,390 in grant-aided secondary schools and 6,561 in Junior Technical Schools. 390,944 were presumed to be attending independent schools. Education in 1938. HMSO 1939 Table 2. p91. Cited in Education and the Social Order 1940-1990. Brian Simon. pub. Lawrence and Wishart 1991. p79

and March 1939 (30.05) were very similar; it would seem at first sight that the decline in the number of teachers had been offset by an increasing fall in the number of children, and that the general level of staffing was very much as it had been pre-war. However, this was not the case and two important factors need to be borne in mind.

1. The evacuation in 1939 and 1940 of children, both privately and under the Government Scheme, resulted in the movement of large numbers of pupils from cities to outlying and rural areas. Pupil-staff ratios in many city schools, working to the Kerslake Scales, were often high. However, in many of the reception areas the schools were much smaller and often organised in an old-fashioned way. Consequently the Kerslake Scales required a much smaller average number of pupils per teacher, so the application of these scales in April 1941 would have required a much higher proportion of teachers than was needed in March 1938.
2. The Kerslake Scales were based on the premise that a stable condition existed in the school. It was expected that the schools would maintain their size and composition throughout the school year and provide a continuity and progression within the teaching.

In 1941 many schools were not in the least bit stable. The September 1939 evacuation, the drift back from reception areas during the phoney-war period, [153] the re-evacuation in 1940, the movement of administrative offices and of workers etc. created a continual ebb and flow of children.

Many school buildings in the 'target areas' had been taken over for use by Air Raid, Fire Service and Medical personnel and were no longer available to serve the educational needs of the returning evacuees and children who remained in the locality. Significantly, at a meeting in January 1940 the President of the Board of Education, when reviewing the first evacuation scheme, stated that any format which was not made compulsory necessarily left a number of children in the evacuation areas for whom education had to be provided, and in order even to achieve a half-time arrangement many authorities would need to recover, wholly or partly, some of the school accommodation which had been diverted to civil defence use. [154] In some 'evacuated' areas this resulted in many returnees getting their education either through official and unofficial home tuition or double-shifting in partially opened schools.[155] so creating a wide range of age distribution within the classes. For example, the area of West Ham in London had been badly hit by the air raids, but the constant movement back and forth of evacuees resulted in some teachers having to teach 6-14 year olds in the same class. However, these arrangements were optional and attendance was generally disappointing. It is worth noting that the same situation was often apparent in small rural schools in the reception areas where teachers also had to deal with a wide diversity of age and ability.[156]

By the beginning of January 1940, in order to accommodate some of the returnees from the September '39 evacuation, 74 emergency schools had been opened in London with a 'double-shift' enrolment limit of 22,000. Fifty-four of these schools, with accommodation for 16,000, received only 6,332 children. In one establishment in Bethnal Green the attendance had dropped by a further 33% after the children had been medically inspected. [157] At an Evacuation conference in January 1940, concerns were expressed about the fact that attendance at these schools was only voluntary, and also about the general medical and moral advantages of attending school causing Earl de la Warr to comment that;

> *'...the children who were in most need of the civilising influence of school life were precisely those who would not attend school without compulsion'.*[158]

153 An estimated 177,000 by December 1939.
154 TNA.ED136/125
155 There were no plans to reopen the schools in the London docklands and there were a lot of children who had not, for a number of reasons, been evacuated. At an evacuation conference in January 1940, Mrs Parker of the NUT wanted the evacuation plans in this area to be 'pushed forward' as she was concerned that these children would receive no education whatsoever for the duration of the war.
156 For visual evidence of this see 'Village School' 1940. Available on the Imperial War Museum Video 'Keep the Wheels Turning'.
157TNA.ED136/125
158 ibid.

The non-availability of education was not only confined to London. Six towns on the South East and East coasts; Deal, Dover, Folkstone, Lowestoft, Margate and Ramsgate had closed all their schools and there was not one single teacher working in the area, as most had gone to the Reception areas. As a result there were 4,577 children within the towns who had not received any education for more than a year. In Hastings the pupil teacher ratio was 260 to 1. In April 1941 only 33 pupils were receiving full time education and 377 less than full-time with 7 teachers. 1,411 children were receiving no education at all.[159] By 1941, pressure was being applied by the Board of Education to reopen these schools on the grounds that they felt the area was no longer in a danger zone because the threat of invasion along this particular stretch of the coast had diminished.

In the reception areas the official and unofficial evacuation resulted in children from many areas coming together into a single school or class.[160] Alternatively pupils from a single evacuated school, especially one with a large number on roll, could be dispersed among smaller reception schools across a large geographical area, a particular problem in Wales. As an example, one teacher, evacuated with a large school from London to mid-Wales, had her children dispersed among schools over 400 square miles of central Wales. She was given a bicycle in order to maintain contact with her charges! [161]

The actual number of teachers available in schools also has to be considered. Male teachers were called up and some, both male and female had been seconded to 'war-work'. In April 1941 it was estimated that of the teachers still on the pay-roll 9,705 were in the forces (86 of whom were women), 2,784 were working for Civil Defence, meal-centres or non-education work and 18,636 were now teaching in reception areas having gone with their schools under the evacuation scheme. Large numbers of teachers had also been used to staff emergency rest centres and feeding centres. Some had been so successful that they had been persuaded to stay on and were consequently not available for teaching duties for months.[162] The shortfall in teacher numbers meant that married women who had been required to leave the profession on marriage[163]and some retired teachers were brought back to fill the vacancies, but these measures created their own problems as will be discussed later. In addition, one has to remember that there were many teachers, including some Great War veterans who should have retired but because of the circumstances were unable to do so, who remained in the classroom performing below their optimum levels.

In Gateshead the LEA employed as many married women as they could get and also tried to secure as many new teachers as possible from those leaving training colleges. But even this source was drying up. It had been proposed to reduce the age of teaching training for men from 18 to 17 years and to shorten teaching practice, but this came to nothing.[164]

Taking all these things into consideration the Kerslake Scale of staff-pupil ratios was no longer appropriate. The prevalent conditions meant that staffing needed to be higher in those schools that had been dislocated by the war. In addition, more teachers were needed to react to conditions as they arose and this often resulted in a time delay between the increased needs of a specific LEA/geographical area and the adjustments of staff to meet them. It was also apparent that more teachers were required to deal with children in an area containing small, scattered schools than those needed to provide adequate provision for the same number of children where schools were large and could be organised into more convenient units.

---

159. TNA.ED 11/243.

160 An example of this is the school at Ashley Green in Bucks. which was the location for a film made by the MOI in 1940 entitled 'Village School'. This two roomed school, staffed by a Head teacher and one other part-time member of staff took in pupils from 29 other schools which had been evacuated to the area. Although some only stayed a few days others remained for the duration of the war.

161 Interview with the author. 1999.

162.TNA. ED 11/243

163 The removal of the marriage bar was proposed in an amendment to the 1944 Education Bill. It was opposed by the Secretary of the Board of Education , but after discussion with the Government it was agreed to accept it. According to H.L.Smith in his essay 'The Effect on the Status of Women' there is no indication that the war record of married women teachers affected this decision. The factors that did have a bearing on it was the expectation that there would be a shortage of teachers after the war and an awareness that the Education Bill would increase the problem.

'The effect on the status of women'. H.L.Smith in 'War and Social Change' ed. Harold L. Smith. Pub. Manchester University Press. p219

164 Memo to LEAs 28th November 1939. TNA.ED 138/148

The survey of 1941 provides a very good insight into the problems of providing an education for children, maintaining a supply of teachers and the migrant nature of the profession in war time. It is obvious that many teachers had to be prepared to move around and in some cases this had a serious impact on their own domestic and family arrangements. Some teachers had been promised that they would be kept in their reception areas to provide some sort of continuity for their pupils and on the basis of this pledge some moved their homes and families to the reception areas, only to find that they were moved soon after to another location. This also caused problems where few of the children they had originally accompanied actually remained in the area. These assurances that teachers could stay with their schools also caused some concern in reception areas where in some cases there was an over-abundance of evacuated teachers. This often led to a great deal of frustration and ill-feeling as the following example illustrates.

In a letter, dated October 9th 1940 addressed to Bertram Bligh at the Board of Education, John Newsom, Chief Education Officer in Hertfordshire complained that:

> '.........*A paradoxical situation has developed during the last few months, in which, while this Authority is finding increasing difficulty in filling vacancies to its permanent staff, there is a superabundance of evacuated teachers for who there is no work here and, particularly in south coast towns, nothing for them if they return to the vulnerable areas. Not only is it a waste of public funds and skilled labour to maintain teachers in idleness but the juxtaposition of local schools with a staffing ration (sic) of approximately one teacher to thirty five children, to an evacuated group of six teachers for the same number, creates a situation which is by no means easy. The recent influx of refugees from London has involved the admission of many hundreds of children to both local and evacuated schools and it is quite impossible to guarantee that the teachers from one Authority will teach children exclusively or even in part evacuated from that area, although some evacuating Authorities are naïve enough to assume that this can be done. A reasonable method of solution would appear to be to look on the problem in one administrative area as a whole; x children and y teachers, and the best arrangements made for full time education....*'[165]

Although Newsom's suggestion would seem to be a practical one and would have alleviated some of the staffing pressures, it would also have created obvious difficulties, notably the divided loyalty of teachers to the reception Authority that made the arrangements and to the evacuation Authority which paid their salaries.

In fairness, some areas such as Hertfordshire did try to overcome this by seconding 'redundant' teachers from the evacuating Authority to their own for the duration of the war, or for however long they were needed, whichever was the shorter. But even this simple solution presented a problem; which authority would be responsible for making up the teachers pay if he or she were called up?

Some schools found themselves in the target areas and were not able to evacuate all their pupils thereby putting considerable pressure on the educational infrastructure. In January 1940, there were 8000 children in London who had registered for evacuation but could not go because of the lack of billets in reception areas.[166] In Gillingham, the ratio was 42 pupils per teacher and all children under the age of 6 were excluded from school. In order to restore full-time education for all children of school age in the area it was estimated that a large number of air-raid shelters would have to be built, which under the financial constraints of the time was unlikely, and 48 extra teachers would be needed in the first instance to replace male teachers being called up. Portsmouth had suffered heavy bombing and although the pupil teacher ratio was 43 –1 many schools were not in use and 5,300 children were getting no education at all. Of the remaining children, 6,528 were receiving part-time education and 3,715 full-time. This was being given by 365 teachers working under very difficult and in some cases extreme conditions. 296 teachers had been evacuated with around 12-13,000 Portsmouth children at a ratio of c1- 40 but it

165 TNA/ED/11/243
166 ibid.

was unlikely that any of these could have been recalled to the city to teach the 'returnees' or those who had remained.

In some target areas the raids and subsequent evacuation had tipped the balance in the other direction. For example Wallasey, at 1-17 had by far the lowest ratio in England and Wales. This was because heavy raids had caused the speedy evacuation of children from the area and the delay of the outward movement of teachers meant that for a while the figures were distorted. HMI cited this as an example of overstaffing, but had not considered that 14 teachers were due for call up and the demands for teachers in the reception area had not been met. By the end of April the ratio had increased to 1-22.8

When the survey was carried out, Wales stood out as an anomaly. Taken at face value one would assume that the pupil teacher ratio in the country appeared to be unfair when compared with LEAs in England. Not one of the Welsh LEAs had a ratio above 1-31, while 18 of their authorities had less than 1– 25 However, there were inherent issues that need to be considered.

1. The majority of schools in Wales were usually smaller than in any English authority, due mainly to two factors;
    - the distribution of population and the denominational designation of some schools.
    - the school buildings and general facilities did not lend themselves to economic use of staffing.
2. Some Welsh LEAs had a very high proportion of male teachers and would therefore be affected by call-up at a later date.
3. Difficulties of language prevented the merger of evacuated parties with the local schools in some parts of Wales. Although it has to be said that this did not always apply as many evacuees from Merseyside were sent to schools in Welsh speaking areas without any language support at all.
4. Out of 18 areas investigated in a preliminary survey only Swansea, Llanelli, Abertillery, Ebbw Vale and Pontypridd had fewer pupils per teacher than before the war. By the time of the actual survey Swansea had been heavily bombed and many children had been privately evacuated. In 5 areas, Anglesey, Caernarvonshire, Carmarthenshire, Carmarthen and Monmouthshire, the ratio was exactly the same as it had been before the war despite the arrival of evacuees. In a further 8 areas the pupil-teacher ratio was higher than before the war.

Even so, despite these factors being taken into consideration there was not one English county, even in the most rural of areas, which could compare with the lowest ratio, Cardiganshire at 1-21, and only Westmoreland could compete with the next 5 lowest Welsh areas which had ratios of 1-22/23. (This does not take into account the situation in Wallasey, see above). It is interesting to note that in their report the HMIs did not consider these areas to be over-staffed, in fact some of them felt that extra teachers were needed.

There were other factors that influenced the ratios. In some cases assurances had been given by the LEAs that specific schools would retain their separate identity when moved to the reception area. As children began to drift home during the 'Phoney War' it became very difficult to honour these agreements without the use of very extravagant staffing. There were also concerns in designated 'neutral zones' which had suffered heavy bombing and as the movement of children from these areas was often uncontrolled it was very difficult to maintain any semblance of full schooling.

By April 1941, these shortages in staff had been somewhat masked by the general decline of the number of children in schools and partly by the use of supply teachers to fill the gaps. The situation was not improved by the decline of students applying for teacher training, preferring in the first instance, to take jobs in war work or join the forces. Even in the least disturbed 'neutral zones' where the pre-war status quo was almost unaffected, the number of teachers available was stretched to the limit and some areas, such as Wolverhampton, which had been able to paper the cracks by using supply staff, had vacancies which they could not fill. The author of the survey report concluded that by the end of 1941…

> ' *….it will be impossible to preserve, even in the least disturbed areas, a standard of staffing comparable with the pre-war standard'.*

The problems of teacher shortages and teacher – pupil ratios did not go away and indeed were exacerbated by the decision taken in 1945 to raise the school leaving age to 15 by April 1st 1947.[167] Not only did this place a tremendous pressure on school buildings especially in war-time target areas where schools had been bombed, but it also required an increase in the number of teachers.

One area, which stands out as the exception to the norm, is Manchester. In total 66,848 children, including those under 5 whether in school or not, and 19,794 mothers and other adults, including teachers, were evacuated between the 1st and 2nd September 1939. Another 1,985 were moved over the next few days but even so, by the 16th September almost 40,000 children still remained in the city.

On the 3rd September the Board of Education had ruled that all schools in the evacuation areas, day or evening, were to remain closed for instruction until further notice.

By mid-September a large number of schools within the city had been requisitioned for ARP and military purposes and a total of 102 buildings were occupied. This raised the serious issue of cost and a great deal of Education Committee time was spent dealing with problems of caretaking, heating, lighting and the employment of caretaking and cleaning staff rather than the implications on the education of the children…both those in the city and those who had been evacuated. So to all intents and purposes nothing was different between the situation in Manchester and other cities around the country. By September 18th most schools in the reception areas were working a double-shift system and consumable stock and equipment was being dispatched to the evacuated schools. However, not all was as it seemed. On October 16th the Emergency Committee of the Council received a deputation asking for the reopening of the Manchester Grammar School. The same matter had also been discussed at a conference of the South Manchester District Women's Cooperative Guild where the delegates passed unanimously an Emergency Resolution;

> *'This conference representing 2561 working class Mothers protest strongly about the lack of educational and welfare facilities for the 50000 children of school age, who remain in, or have returned to Manchester owing to the partial failure of the evacuation scheme….'*

The result was that Manchester Grammar School was reopened.

The situation did not get any better for the authorities when, on the 21st November 1939, the Parents Society of Burnage High School for Boys sent a petition to the Director of Education outlining their concern for their sons' education and at the same time pointing out that their arguments were as valid as those used for the opening of Manchester Grammar. As a result, the school reopened on January 8th 1940. It was also agreed on the 27th November to reopen a few Primary schools, while at the same time informing parents, via Head Teachers, of the *'desire that evacuated children should not return from the reception areas'*.[168]

On the 15th January 1940, the General Purposes sub-Committee reported that there were 15,000 children in the reception areas and a further 20 schools would reopen on January 20th. Safety measures had been completed by a further 19 elementary schools and 3 Municipal schools. On the 19th February it was reported that 82 schools were scheduled to be reopened as soon as the necessary structural changes had been made and in total 142 would be ready to receive children for full time education. By this time only 13,433 Manchester children remained in the reception areas, a number which fell to 11,292 by the end of March.

---

167 This should have happened September 1939 but was delayed because of the war.
168 Government Circular 1483. paras 3-5

As schools were returning, it became obvious that some teachers in the reception areas were now superfluous to requirements. Throughout January and February arrangements were made for the orderly recall of Principal Teachers and Assistant teachers to staff the Manchester schools as they came 'on stream'. By the 19th February, 1,493 teachers, including 309 principals, remained in the reception areas while 1,566 teachers, including 51 principals were working in the city. Even during the evacuation in 1940, after the Phoney War, only 18,500 children registered. Nowhere near the number evacuated in September 1939.[169]

Education Provision

> *'Not the least of the problems placed on the shoulders of the education authorities is the provision of accommodation for children in rural areas. In one case there is a complete school divided among four villages, while in another only half the school came to the Dorset area and the other half went to Somerset'.*[170]

Many rural areas 'did their bit' and accepted their fair share of official evacuees. However, by doing so they put the local administrative infrastructure under some considerable pressure, especially with regard to education. The local community of Purley-on-Thames became a reception area for two distinct groups of people, those who had been officially evacuated and those who owned plots of land along the bank of the river and came to live there for the duration of the war. The former group of 50 children and accompanying mothers came from Islington and Holloway and were found billets within the community. The latter group brought with them a further 100 children of school age. Together this number of evacuee children put considerable pressure on the school, so much so that a second teacher had to be appointed to cope with the pressure. Some of these pupils left during the 'phoney war' period but when the bombing of London began in 1940 the Rural District Council of Bradfield was asked to accommodate 700 children of whom 20 went to Purley. [171]

The entries in the school log book of Bradfield Primary School, situated in the small rural village of Bradfield Southend, in Berkshire, which usually had a constant 110 pupils on the school roll, provide a fair indication of the difficulties faced by Headteachers:-

> *Oct.4th 1939. On instructions from the LEA the children evacuated from the LCC were admitted to school this morning. 57 children were admitted bringing the number on roll up to 206. There is insufficient seating for all the children and some are sitting three to a dual desk.*

This had been the second group of evacuees to arrive at the school. The first children had been privately evacuated.

> *Nov. 1st 1939. Received from the LCC 25 tables and 50 chairs for the use of the evacuees'.*
>
> *Dec. 1st 1939. Several of the evacuated children have returned to London.*
>
> *June 17th 1940. Admitted 11 further evacuated children, mostly from Page Green School, in Tottenham. Mrs Murpitt, a teacher, accompanied them and commenced duties in the school.*
>
> *Oct. 11th 1940. 184 children have been admitted since September 22nd 1939 of whom 82 have left. These consisted mainly of evacuated children'.*[172]

At least this village had sufficient, albeit cramped, accommodation. The lack of communication between central and local government resulted in a great deal of confusion as regards reception areas with suitable education facilities for evacuees. It is also apparent that some Local Education Authorities were not entirely blameless and a lack of local knowledge did not help the situation. For example the West Sussex authority allocated 50 evacuated

169 See Manchester the Exception to the Rule. Parsons M. DSM
170 Dorset Daily Echo. 9th September 1939.
171 Rural District Council Minutes. September 1940
172 Bradfield C.of E. Primary School. Log Book. Berkshire Record Office. D/P/22/28/3

children to the village of Nutborne which had school facilities for only the 20 children already taught there by one teacher. 140 children were sent to Thakeham which also had a resident school population of only 20, and 90 were allocated to Coldwaltham which had a tiny two room school with a staff of two who taught everyone between the ages of 5-14.[173] These teachers would have been overwhelmed had not two staff come with the evacuees.

There were also difficulties in some parts of North Wales where children from Liverpool were sent to schools which had their lessons in Welsh.[174] The Welsh National Party had expressed serious concerns suggesting that English speaking evacuees attending Welsh speaking Schools would harm Welsh Nationalism and Item 7 of the Memo issued by the Party in February 1939 in response to central government's Wartime Evacuation Policy is worth noting:-

> 'We propose that Welsh reception areas should be classified for any further reception purposes…..namely (a) 70% Welsh speaking areas. (b) areas less than 70% Welsh speaking and that mono-glot English school populations shall not be drafted into division (a) under any circumstances since to do so will destroy the continuity of Welsh Education, of Welsh religious life and Welsh rural and social traditions. It will overwhelm the religious organisation of Welsh rural life as well as its linguistic and cultural tradition'.

Despite the fears of the WNP many Liverpool children learnt Welsh very quickly and some even competed successfully in local Eisteddfods.[175]

Children from London being taught Welsh

When the second group of evacuees arrived in Caernarfon in 1940 they were even called derogatory names in Welsh by those who had been evacuated in September 1939![176]

173 James Roffey. op.cit. Personal papers
174 E.O.Humphreys. Education Officer. Anglesey. Report The Education of Evacuated Children. University College of N orth Wales. Archives. V.4594
175 Wallis op.cit.p173

The problems inherent in dealing with this ever changing migrant child population in village schools were so serious that in 1940 the Ministry of Information made a ten-minute propaganda film called 'The Village School' [177] which illustrated some of the problems that teachers, and indeed school buildings, faced during the time of evacuation. It was released in 1941. However, as in similar films portraying a positive message, the producer was intent on showing that despite the vagaries of the war and the pressures put on the local community and the school, everything was working out well, everybody was coping and any problems could be easily overcome. This was not always the case, and there are many examples of the system breaking down under pressure of numbers and conflict of personalities where school communities of sometimes totally different social backgrounds, were trying to co-exist.

The film was in fact pure propaganda and the content had been arranged to suit the needs of the producers who had obviously been given the brief to put across as many positive aspects of the school as possible in nine minutes. In the school log book of the Ashley Green Church of England Primary School where the film was made, there are three significant entries which prove that the film was actually made in the school holidays and the content of the film had been pre-planned.

> *July 5th 1940. End of Summer term.*
>
> *July 29th 1940. For the Ministry of Information and by kind permission of the Board of Education, the Strand Film Company of London this morning began to make a film of the work done in this school. Various and considerable changes had to be made to the school time-table.*
>
> *August 9th 1940. The children's part of the film is now completed and the school is closed for a fortnight's holiday.*[178]

The school was closed on the 16th June 1941, so that the pupils could see the finished film. However, although it was made for propaganda purposes, it has to be said that the head teacher in the film, Mrs James, who was depicted as overcoming all the problems she was confronted with, both educationally and socially, was not entirely a figment of the film maker's imagination. Mrs James ran a two-roomed village school, and research in the registers for the years 1939-45 reveals that she received evacuees from 29 different schools. Although some of them stayed only for a few days they nonetheless put a great deal of pressure onto Mrs James' workload and her management of the school. She did all the teaching herself with the exception of one other helper who worked with the infants.[179].

Other teachers fought tirelessly in order to provide any semblance of education for their charges. Bill Granger recalled that having been evacuated from Walthamstowe with his school, he started off by using a wooden shed at the bottom of someone's garden, before being appointed head-teacher of the local village school while the incumbent was on extended leave. Like Mrs James, Bill divided the school into three groups, seniors, juniors and infants, but unlike Mrs James he was only afforded the luxury of one classroom where all groups had to be taught at the same time.[180]

There were similar problems with school buildings and accommodation throughout the war. In June 1944, Mr G.T. Giles, President of the National Union of Teachers, visited Dorset as part of a fact finding tour. He is quoted as saying that:-

> *'...he had learnt more about conditions within the teaching service than he had learnt for years.....However work was done in schools by only two teachers with children of varying ages was beyond his understanding and yet good work was being done'.*

---

176 P.E.Owen. The Development of the Bilateral System of Education in Caernarvonshire 1903- to date (1961) University College of North Wales. 15234.

177 Imperial War Museum. Compiliation Video. Keep the Wheels Turning. 'The Village School'. Ministry of Information 1941.

178 Ashley Green C.of E. Primary School Log Book. Buckinghamshire Record Office. E/LB/6/3.

179 For a full list of the schools see Appendix 8

180 .'The Evacuee' Journal of the Evacuee Reunion Association. October 1996. MERL Archive

He went on to say that during his trip he had visited about 40 schools in the county. He had seen some of the new senior council schools, which he admired, but of the remainder, the school buildings, except for a few *'were now only fit for the scrap heap'*.... He had seen schools with no water available and where water closets were a rarity. Many of the outsides of the buildings were presentable but the insides were never designed for schools. *'Here is picturesque poverty. Dorset has the children and the teachers but money is not being spent on the buildings'.* [181]

It was not only schools evacuated to Dorset which faced these problems. The following account from a teacher describes the problems he faced when wishing to move into larger accommodation. He and his school had been evacuated to a small village in Berkshire where the existing village school buildings had been adequate, although cramped. When extra families arrived it was necessary to move to bigger premises and he sought the permission of the local Rector to move into the semi-derelict, wooden, church hall at the opposite end of the village to the school. It was not until the spring of 1940 that the evacuees were able to move and one afternoon the older boys carried the desks along the main street followed by the juniors carrying books and chairs. Over the weekend the pupils cut down the hedges, tidied the paths, put up temporary notice boards and hung pictures and maps on the wall to make them a little more presentable. On the Monday the teacher sat the class according to size....smallest at the front, largest at the back. The rest is worth describing in his own words:-

> *"I gave the order to stand, with the idea of marking the occasion of the move with a little ceremony.*
>
> *'Well school,' I began, ' here we are in our new home...'*
>
> *Suddenly the floor began gently to subside and rows of children sank before my eyes like little ships going down. A few books slid off desks and one or two children sat down, standing up quickly again as though they had done something wrong; the smaller ones clung to their desks and everyone stood a little lopsidedly, but they were calm and left it to the stupidest senior to state the obvious.*
>
> *'Please sir,' he said, ' the floor's guv away.'*
>
> *So we all went home."* [182]

Other evacuees tell of similar situations. For example, the Peckham Central Girls School, which had strict rules about the wearing of uniforms, turned up for their first day of schooling in the old Corn Exchange in Pulborough to find that everything was covered in dust, the floor was rotting and there was little furniture suitable for a temporary school. It was not long before the impeccable uniforms became dusty and dirty as the girls were expected to sort out the furniture and clean up the building.[183]

In May 1940, the Education Officer in Somerset informed head-teachers that they should ask the owners of any halls or outside premises which were being considered as potential classrooms for evacuees whether they would be prepared to accept a rent not exceeding that approved by the District Valuer. If necessary, any such building could be requisitioned by the Local Authority under Regulation 51 of the Civil Defence Act 1939. Once an understanding had been made, a representative from the Education Committee would inspect the premises and make further arrangements as and when necessary. This would only apply where numbers of evacuees in an area actually necessitated extra accommodation. [184]

As noted above, many evacuated schools were simply imposed on existing classes and classrooms in the reception areas and even LEAs complained that they received no information directly from the Boards of Education, either as to the numbers of teachers and pupils expected, or the particular schools where they were

181 Dorset County Chronicle and Swanage Times. 29th June 1944.
182 Anon account lent by P.Farley-Rutter from family papers.
183 J.Roffey. Letter to the author. 9th June 98. MERL Archive
184 Education Committee Circ. E281

coming from. This lack of information led to some evacuated schools and existing classes being 'farmed out' to other establishments in order to find space in which to work.

Entries from school log books in Berkshire, such as these...

> *'Feb.26th ...classes in the Junior Department are still receiving instructions in the afternoon sessions at Park Institute (a local church hall), Anderson Baptist Chapel and the Primitive Methodist Chapel'.*
>
> *'March 4th...The remaining London schools:- All Saints, St. Peter's Vauxhall, St. Joseph's RC and Lawn Lane Infants, Vauxhall are to be accommodated at St. Bartholomew's and Anderson Baptist Hall'.*[185]

are commonplace in many school log books of the period.

In some areas there was a certain amount of resentment that evacuees had taken over local facilities. In Pulborough the recently built village hall, the centre of all village activities, was turned into a school. The necessary equipment was sent to the area from Peckham and the rooms changed their purpose. The projection room became the typing class, the room beneath the stage was used for current affairs and had pictures of German and British aircraft plus propaganda posters stuck to the walls. The main hall was used by eight different classes. Trestle tables were formed into a square with a blackboard and easel placed in the middle and lessons on different subjects were delivered in adjacent 'squares' which made it very difficult for children to concentrate.[186]

Some evacuees were not afforded the luxury of remaining in one building. Sylvia Rose, (née Eden) recalls that as a member of the Walworth Central Girls School evacuated to Sturminster Newton in Dorset, she had her lessons all over the town:-

> *'Our schooling was exactly the same as in London but we had to walk to different parts of the town for our lessons. We used to go to the Senior School for our cookery lessons where there was a domestic science room. Other lessons were in the school room of the Wesleyan Chapel....and the Bridge Chapel room. Games lessons were on the recreation ground and there were other lessons in the Royal British Legion Comrades Hut. This is also where we had our communal dinners'.*[187]

It was after some negotiation that the school was eventually housed under the one roof at the Tithe Barn.

Even some London schools which had previously been evacuated in 1939 to their own premises found they were imposed upon by newly evacuated schools without notice. The following extract comes from the school log book of the Commercial Street LCC Junior, Mixed and Infants which had been evacuated to Aston Clinton .... then Anthony Hall .... then to very small premises in Buckland:-

> 'Imposition of New Schools
>
> 25th September 1940.
>
> Miss B.M.K. Knight of Hillbrook Demonstration Infants School, came this afternoon with 14 London school children to join our school. I was given no official notice of this event. They had been evacuated on the 21st September to Drayton Beauchamp and then to us. They come chiefly from Battersea and Tooting. This brings the total number on roll to 38'.[188]

In one instance the pressure on accommodation was so great that there was obviously nowhere for the children to go at all and their classroom during the day became their sleeping quarters at night, as his comment from the minutes of the Didcot Parish Council indicates:-

185 Alfred Sutton Primary School. Wokingham Rd. Reading. Log Book. 1934-62
186 J.Roffey. Letter to the author. 9th June 1998 MERL Archive
187 Sylvia Rose. Letter to the author. 29th Jan. 1998.
188 Commercial Street. London County Council School. Log Book. Bucks. Record Office. E/LB/6/3

> 'It is unfair for classrooms to be used as classrooms during the daytime and as a common lodging house at nightfall....I am anxious that the school should not cease to be used as a school but, if no accommodation can be found then it was their duty to insist the school should be closed as a school'.[189]

This problem of dispersal was not restricted to those evacuated to urban areas. Some schools found themselves billeted in a number of small villages covering many miles. The pupils of one school evacuated to Norfolk were spread over an area of 400 square miles. [190]

In some areas the pressure on buildings and existing classes resulted in the removal of the evacuee children to other premises. In his paper entitled 'The Shipton Saga', John Rawlins highlights a situation which stands as an example of how things could break down. Using evidence from log books and personal diaries one can trace the problems which this particular school, the Upton Cross Junior from West Ham, faced during the first few months of the war. The party of 63 children arrived in early September with two teachers and five assistants and started their lessons in the local Shipton School on the 13th using a double shift system; 9.00 -1.00 for the local children and 1.30 - 4.00 for the West Ham pupils. Within two days alternative accommodation had been found at the YMCA Red Triangle Hut which meant that the school buildings could be used for written work and the hut for any oral work.

On the 18th September the Headmaster had secured the use of the local Beaconsfield Hall for the children of Upton Cross in order to cut down on transfers between other buildings. However, within ten days, the Head of the local school had received a letter from the County accusing him of refusing to allow the Upton Cross children to use his school. The answer to which was quite simply that this had not been the case and the new arrangements were much more convenient. The local school Inspector asked whether or not it would be possible to pool accommodation and on the 2nd October it was decided that the School and Hut would be used alternatively, morning and afternoon, with opposite arrangements every week. On the 4th October the schools were told that the Beaconsfield Hall had been taken over by the LEA because the lighting and ventilation in the Red Triangle Hut was considered to be poor. The situation became even more confusing when on 23rd October, the Head-teacher received a letter from the LEA stating that the Red Triangle Hut and Beaconsfield Hall had been commandeered by the military, the former for canteen purposes where, from Monday to Friday, evacuee children and mothers were required to have their lunches [191] and in consequence, all the children now had to be accommodated in the existing school buildings. This resulted in a great deal of reorganisation in terms of pupils, personnel and equipment, a situation which continued until January 1940 when an entry in the log-book states simply:-

> *'The Upton Cross children assembled here this morning in order to be conveyed to Launton village school near Bicester. They took all their registers of attendance with them and each child was supplied with pencils and stationery......The reason given for the move was the unsuitable and unsanitary conditions pertaining to this old building....'* [192]

This whole saga raises some important questions. First, if the reason for moving the children from the school was because of unsuitable and unsanitary conditions why was this decision made in January 1940 and not before? And, more importantly, why were the local children expected to put up with these conditions and the evacuee children not? Presumably they had had to suffer them long before the arrival of the Upton Cross pupils and had to continue to do so after the latter had left. According to the log-book, it was not until April 1941 that there was an inspection to investigate the re-siting of new *'offices'*, and these were not built until fourteen months later. It is

---

189 Mr. Foster, Didcot Parish Council, in response to a report that a Domestic Science Laboratory in a local school was being used as accommodation for evacuees. The Minute was undated but would be around September to October 1939.
190 Titmuss. op.cit. p112
191 One ex-evacuee recalls that the diet consisted entirely of minced rabbit and vegetables. The rabbits were skinned each morning by a Dr. Scott but the meals were considered to be rather dangerous because they contained slithers of bone. Dr. Scott also served up Rook. Letter to the author from John O'Connor. March 1998. MERL Archive
192 John Rawlins. Private Papers. 1989.

odd that the evacuee children were removed for this reason, when other village schools in the area had bucket toilets and one, Idbury, had no piped water at all until 1944!

Second, why was the YMCA Red Triangle Hut considered suitable for canteen purposes but not for education? Some children were being taught in a Church room in nearby Milton without any toilet facilities at all and worse lighting and ventilation than the YMCA.

Third, log-book entries for Launton school would suggest that there were no problems at this school. Could this whole scenario simply have been a clash of personalities between the resident and visiting head teachers and the unsanitary conditions purely an excuse?

Situations such as these were not uncommon, and resulted in a breakdown in school organisation and communications which caused a great deal of confusion, especially when school children who were to return home in the official scheme of 1945 could not be located. This particular problem was identified by a number of ex-evacuees during recorded interviews.

Some school administrators and Head-teachers, having made the effort to find out about their host areas for planning reasons, were even given incorrect information:-

> Whitehorse Manor School
> Senior Boys School
> Thornton Heath
> Surrey.
>
> June 11th 1940
>
> Dear Sir,
>
> I am the leader of a party of evacuees from Croydon (N1 and N2) which should entrain here for Exeter next Tuesday and arrive somewhere in the neighbourhood of 6 o'clock. I fully appreciate how busy you are preparing for our invasion but it would help me considerably if you could find time to send me a post card just to intimate to me the nature of the district we are likely to reside in for the next part of our earthly pilgrimage. If you simply write on the enclosed card 'urban' , 'semi-urban', 'rural' or 'coastal' the information will be most helpful in planning the necessary limited clothing each child must bring.
>
> Yours faithfully
>
> Sam. J. Cook.

Although the school was evacuated to the city centre the answer sent back was rural! [193]

Other evacuated schools had to find their own accommodation which in itself created problems. The trials and tribulations of one such teacher can be found in the diaries of Eric Gadd who was a teacher in Southampton. His diary entries highlight the problems he faced when attempting to establish a part-time school for evacuees.

> *'June 30th 1940*
> *During the past month I have been conducting a private war with the County Education Officer on a matter which I regard as of vital importance, the grave risks which are being run by the children attending the Gore Road Junior School there. I have put forward these points:-*
>
> *1. The building is an ex-army hut, a relic of the last war. Having been in use continuously for about twenty years, it is in a dilapidated condition.*

193 Exeter Blitz. Box 12. ARP/Evacuation. Devon Record Office.

2. It is constructed entirely of wood, with the exception of the roof; the walls are of thin matchboarding and weatherboard of a combined thickness of about one inch and in no way reinforced.

3. The lighting system is of gas.

4. The roof is low, solid and heavy.

5. The building is less than 400 yards from the main Southern railway line.Leaving aside the effect of a direct hit, this building would be vulnerable even to the effect of a bomb dropped anywhere within half a mile, while an incendiary could have unthinkable results'.[194]

Despite his protestations Gadd was only able to convince the authorities to build air-raid shelters in the corner of the playground.

Later he was to have problems with his pupils as well as the local authorities as this entry for the 3rd January 1941, concerning some newly arrived evacuees, indicates:-

'Within a few hours of their arrival a number of the younger members of the party broke into the fowl-house and killed the fowls, which were consumed by some of the Furzie Close (address of the hostel) guests. The police were called in.

- Contrary to instructions their people light fires in the wards and cook what they fancy there.

- Most of the men come in drunk each night. At Christmas the doctor was called in to deal with a number of boys of 12 and 13 who had been sick. He pronounced them drunk'.[195]

Some schools were not even afforded air-raid protection. In May 1940, the Board of Education sent out a circular which advised that not all schools in rural areas need be provided with shelters in the same way as urban schools. Instead the pupils were to be instructed in how to take shelter within the school if bombs were falling in the area. They were to practise lying on the floor and keeping away from windows, and they were to be told that under no circumstances should they leave the school buildings and go into the open!![196]

The safety of some schools was even affected by the personal decisions of local figures. In 1940, the Rector of Purley-on-Thames rigorously opposed the suggestion made by neighbouring ratepayers that a shelter should be provided for the pupils of the Primary school. He claimed that as the village had been declared a reception area it was obviously considered safe from attack and a shelter would be a waste of money. He went on to say that he had called in experts to inspect the arrangements made at the school and they were found to be satisfactory. On the 16th July 1940, the Parish Council agreed with the Rector but did supply five stirrup pumps[197] and in April 1941 the Berkshire County Council agreed to spend £307 on a shelter in Pangbourne, more than a mile from Purley, to accommodate 110 people.[198] As it turned out the Rev. Skuse's predictions were correct and Purley was not hit, however, this does not excuse the original decision. In 1940 he was not to know with any degree of certainty that the inhabitants would be safe.

The Rector was not alone in his belief that schools did not need shelters. At the Berkshire County Council Meeting on 29th September 1939, the General purposes Sub-Committee reported:-

'Air Raid Precautions' Para. 1 subsection a. As a general principle, children should be kept under cover in school buildings during an air raid. In each school therefore a room, or rooms, should be set apart in which, when an air-raid warning has been given, children should be congregated under the supervision of their teachers. The rooms selected

---

194 Hampshire Evacuees. The Wartime Diary of Eric Wyeth Gadd. cited in 'The Children's War.' Ruth Inglis op.cit.p57
195 Ruth Inglis. The Children's War. op.cit.p79
196 Berkshire County Council Minutes. May 1940.
197 Purley-on-Thames. Parish Council Minutes. July 1940
198 Berkshire County Council Minutes. April 1941.

> for the purpose should be those in which the walls are of substantial thickness and where the amount of window space is relatively small. In such rooms, all windows should be protected by half inch wire mesh netting and, if the walls are not of sufficient thickness, they should be strengthened to a height of about 3 feet 6 inches with suitable material.
>
> Subsection b. In accordance with the general policy outlined in the preceding paragraph it was not considered expedient to provide outside trenches or shelters but, in certain schools additional protective measures might be necessary in view of the large amount of window space which exists and also because of the light type of construction which is to be found in some schools'.[199]

The same policy was apparent in Dorset. On 7th September 1939, the Weymouth Town Council agreed that in the event of an air raid those schoolchildren who lived nearby could go home. But protection in the form of trenches and revetments would be provided for those who could not. This decision was based on parents' wishes. The Town Clerk stated that 799 held the view that children should be kept at school, 963 wanted them sent home immediately and 1,400 wanted them to remain in school until collected.[200]

Also at a meeting of Dorset's Education Committee in July 1940, the Chairman, Councillor Le Berton, stated that a number of petitions had been received asking for covered trenches to be provided for schools in rural areas. But, in his opinion, he felt that such people were under a misapprehension. He suggested that there was not the same amount of danger in remote villages as in areas which were defended by anti-aircraft guns where there was also a danger of falling shrapnel. He thought it not practical to provide cement coverings in all rural districts because the material could not be obtained and he had been told, and agreed, that there was no danger in rural areas from shrapnel. He went on to say that the whole scheme would cost £40,000 and he did not think that the ARP committee would think it necessary or desirable. He suggested that the committee followed the instructions detailed in the Circular; that in the event of a bomb dropping in the vicinity the children were to lie under their desks.[201]

Provision for expenditure on items such as sandbags and wire netting for schools was made in the Berkshire Education Committee accounts of 1939:-

> 'Item 4. Air Raid Precautions: The Committee recommend that the under-mentioned expenditure be approved for the protection of schools on the lines indicated previously.
>
> Elementary Schools: Sandbagging, Wire Netting etc. and obscuration of lights. £1500
>
> Maintained and Aided Schools for wire netting and obscuration of lights. £650'.[202]

Financial implications rather than safety and saving lives seemed to be the prime concern of some Councils. Complaints were made at the Dorchester Town Council meeting on the 13th February 1940, that there were no air-raid shelters in the town and that something should be done about it. Alderman, Mr Rossiter, asked that, *'as there was nowhere that the town's children or evacuees could go in the event of a raid was it possible to bring pressure on the County Council to provide them'*. The answer, from the Town Clerk:-

> *'...It is not part of the County Council measures. This sort of thing costs money'.*[203]

199 Berkshire County Council Minutes. November 1939
200 Dorset Daily Echo. 7th September.1939
201 Dorset County Chronicle &Swanage Times. 1st August.1940
202 Berkshire County Council Education Sub-Committee Minutes. November 1939.
203 Dorset County Chronicle & Swanage Times. 15th February 1940

A search through school log books for village schools in North Wales suggests that air-raid shelters were not provided until September 1940, by which time the area had received numerous air raid warnings; a situation which created serious problems for some of the teachers. On 17th November 1939, the Head-teacher of St. Matthew's Infants School Buckley, North Wales had to send children home during a potential raid:-

> *'An air raid warning was given this morning about 11.15. As we have no shelters and deployment into wet fields is not conducive to good health, I dispersed them to their homes. The school was evacuated in a very short time. Some of the children live 20 minutes walk away. Long distance children are a problem in this respect and something must be done to cater for them'.*

This action did initiate some response:-

> *'Monday 20th September. There have been several complaints over Friday's dispersal of the children. A manager's meeting is to be held tonight'.*

There is no further indication of when, or if, shelters were provided.[204]

Prior to June 1940, the Education Committee in Somerset had at various times considered the question of air-raid protection in their schools and concluded that

a. Trench shelters should only be provided in those parts of the county which had been designated as a neutral area, such as Portishead.

b. That in the reception areas, for protection against blast and the danger of splintering glass in the event of an air raid, pupils should, if possible, be dispersed in the school grounds or the playing fields. However, where this was impracticable, all windows should be opened and all pupils should be instructed to lie on the floor as near as possible to the walls in which the windows were situated.

However, on the 7th June 1940 these instructions were amended in the light of new developments in aerial attacks such as machine-gunning from the air[205], and the witnessing of recent events on the continent. There was no change in the trench shelter provision in the neutral zones, but it was advised that the policy of scattering children in an open space should be reviewed and that as far as possible, consistent with the safeguards against other dangers such as flying glass etc., the children should be found shelter within the existing building. This included pupils presently housed in temporary accommodation. Schools were to be advised by the County Architect on the best procedures to follow and the provision of close-mesh wire screens as protection against flying glass. The Education Committee was not prepared to provide paper or other adhesive material to put directly onto the windows, but they would pay for fitments in both Council and Voluntary aided schools. It was recognised that the problems would be more apparent in newly built schools in the urban areas, rather than many of the older village ones, because of the amount of glass used in the construction of the former. Therefore, it was stipulated that no more than 50 children should be collected in any one room, unless suitable blast-proof partitions were erected. The alternative was fraught with potential danger as it was suggested that older children would either have to scatter over open ground or go, by arrangement, to neighbouring householders (with written permission of the parents and local ARP authorities), or in small groups in private houses near the school, on the understanding that the children could take cover before they can be seen by enemy aircraft! It was thought that unless circumstances were very exceptional, it would mean that children would have to gain cover within 5 minutes of leaving their desks.[206]

It had been thought before the war, that some schools might have to be closed for a short period of time but that such closure would be restricted to those schools where teachers were preoccupied with reception of evacuees.

---

204 St. Matthews Infants School. Log Book. Hawarden R.O E/LB/11/5.
205 Witness account. D.Parsons. Sept. 2012 who recounted German planes machine gunning the Filton area of Bristol in 1940.
206 W.J.Deacon Chief Education Officer. Somerset. Circ. E288 Air Raid Protection in School. 7th June 1940

So, the Somerset Education Committee decided that as there had been no general closure on account of evacuation, there would be no closure on account of air-raids.[207]

Other authorities were also considering the question of air-raid protection and school closures. On the 19th July 1939 Coventry City Council had noted the need to provide air raid precautions for those schools in the city which were not to be evacuated. [208] In most cases such protection would come in the form of Trench Shelters of a least six feet in height, which were to have duckboard floors, sloped to ensure drainage from one side to the other, with seating arranged along one or both walls. There was also to be a gas-curtain over the entrance to make them reasonably gas-proof. In addition they were to have secure roofs to *'provide immunity from splinters, anti-aircraft fragments and shell-fire'*. There was no indication as to how effective these shelters would be if they received a direct hit. [209]

Evacuated Nurseries

Children from the WVS Nursery at Holland Park, West London, get a ride on a station barrow at Euston

In October 1939 an article appeared in the British Journal of Nursing on the topic of 'Hostels Sick Bays and Nurseries', referring to a statement issued previously by the Ministry of Health[210] relating to special residential arrangements required for dealing with 'particular classes of children or mothers' who could not be billeted in an ordinary household.

One suggestion was the use of 'sick-bay' accommodation in separate houses for those children suffering from minor ailments, or convalescing from more serious illnesses. A trained nurse would be in attendance and children would be visited on a regular basis by the local doctor. Hostel-type accommodation with a staff experienced in

---

207 ibid

208 Coventry City Council Minutes. Education Committee. 19th July 1939. Cited in Daniel Bate. A Necessary Evil? Education within Coventry during World War II. Children in War Journal DSM. 2011

209 S.Hussey. 'The School Air Raid Shelter' Re-thinking wartime pedagogies. History of Education Quarterly Vol 43. No4. Winter 2003 p519

210 Circ. 1871. Sept 17th 1939

child-guidance could be provided for 'problem children' who were deemed unacceptable in ordinary billets, and short-stay nurseries could be provided for young children who had to be temporarily separated from their mothers during illness or pregnancy. These nurseries would be properly staffed and be under the charge of a Matron qualified as a State Registered Nurse. The Minister had suggested that there was also a need for long-term residential nurseries for young children separated from their mothers for longer periods, and even for day nurseries in some of the more populated areas. The author commented that any such schemes would take years, to say nothing of them costing millions to carry out.[211]

On the 1st March 1940, the Ministry of Health sent out another memo[212] to Secretaries of voluntary day nurseries and those evacuated from London and to Matrons, Superintendents and Teachers in charge of evacuated parties. This set out the measures needed to deal with the children who became ineligible to remain with the Nursery party that they have had been evacuated with, either because they had reached the age of 5, or because the parents no longer lived in the evacuation area; and how vacancies arising in the parties could be filled.

Before the evacuation began in September 1939, every mother in the evacuation zones with a child under the age of 5 had been given the opportunity of either taking it away themselves, or to arrange for it to be taken by a responsible adult. For those children in this priority group who could not be evacuated for some reason, such as the death or illness of the mother, or could not be accompanied by another member of the family, it was intended that the day nurseries should be used.[213] However, in some cases nurseries took responsibility for the children on their registers without investigating whether they could have been evacuated with their mothers instead. By March 1940, nursery places were both limited in number and costly to maintain, so it was thought necessary that such vacancies that now arose should be used to the best advantage and in the best interest of the whole Evacuation scheme.

The Minister of Health made a decision on three issues:

First, that as places became available in the nursery schools and day nurseries, they should be used to remove those children from the evacuation areas who, in the event of heavy and sustained bombing, could not for some very good reason be taken out of the immediate danger by their mothers, and who were likely to be at a disadvantage in this respect, compared to other children, for some considerable time.

Second, that since the number of such cases was likely to be at least equivalent to the number of vacancies occurring in the country nurseries, some central administration should be established for considering applications, formulating a priority list, overseeing the admission of cases to receiving homes in London and their transport to join nursery parties in the Receptions Areas.

Third, that the LCC, the Evacuation Authorities, the Public Assistance Authorities, the Metropolitan Borough Councils and Welfare Authorities should be made aware of the administrative body in order that any vacancies could be used to the best advantage.

From the outbreak of war, the Evacuation Department of the WVS had received numerous applications from various individuals such as Medical Officers of Health, Welfare Workers, and organisations like Citizens Advice Bureaux, Divisional Dispersal Officers of the LCC, and Care Committee Organisers for the evacuation of children under 5 to residential nurseries, The WVS had managed to use a small 'receiving' home at Bedford College which was maintained by voluntary effort, and, in addition, had been able to transport around 400 nursery age evacuees to the reception areas. During the same time the LCC, as a Public Assistance Authority, also dealt with hundreds of cases which fell within the remit of the Poor Law provision.

The Minister established a link between the various interested parties and the WVS so that the investigation into any case could be done by a member of the LCC's Care Committee, an officer of the Public Assistance

211 British Journal of Nursing. October 1939 .p257

212 Ministry of Health. 1st March 1940. Ref.....99043/676/205/ID. Somerset RO....C/CD/1/6/2

213 Memo Ev4 May 1st 1939. Appendix D. P24 para 9 and 11

Department, and a representative of the standing joint committee of the Metropolitan Borough Councils. Such a group had at its disposal the facilities in every part of the administrative area of London for dealing with individual applications to join a nursery and for arranging for the admission of a child to fill a vacancy. The latter took place after an initial period of observation in a receiving home, during which time the child was medically examined to eliminate the possibility of infectious ailments. If they had been in contact with infected people, or displayed signs of illness, many of them were separated for a period of time before being allowed to mix with the other children. This period of isolation could be extended to the receiving nursery. Every effort was made to ensure that the child was placed in a nursery which, before evacuation, had served the area in which he or she lived.

Unfortunately, the establishment and subsequent responsibilities for ensuring the success of nurseries in the Reception Areas was often very complicated, and the bureaucratic procedures were usually carried out by the administrative staff of the County Councils who now had to fulfil extra duties imposed on them by Central and Regional Government.

As an example, a conference[214] was held at the County Hall in Taunton on the 29th March 1940, to discuss a request from the Ministry of Health that the County Council, as the Welfare Authority for the County[215] should take over the financial and administrative running of two evacuated Day Nurseries; the Westminster Health Society's Day Nurseries at Doulting Vicarage and Pixton Park, Dulverton, and The Princess Christian Day Nursery (Hammersmith) at North Cadbury Court. After a great deal of discussion, during which time the Ministry Representatives were asked to leave the meeting so that specific matters could be discussed in private, the following conclusions were reached. They provide an indication of the depth of concern and the complex nature of the bureaucracy involved.

With regard to Doulting Vicarage five suggestions were put to the Ministry officials:-

a. The County Council would take over the financial and administrative responsibility, subject to the actual management remaining with the Westminster Society, and to the deficiency being charged to the Evacuation Account.

b. Accounts to be paid out of imprest in the first instance, and come to the County Council monthly for certification by the County Medical Officer of Health, who would pass them on to the County Treasurer for re-imbursement.

c. Accounts for items of a capital nature would be referred to the County Council for sanction and passed to the Regional Office of the Ministry, at Bristol, for prior approval.

d. Medical supervision, as distinguished from local medical attendance on sick children, was to be under the control of the County Medical Officer of Health who would make whatever arrangements necessary.

e. The supply of clothing for the children would remain the obligation of the parents, but the County Council must be able to supply clothing where necessary, and charge it to the Evacuation Account.

With regard to Pixton Park and North Cadbury Court, the Council considered that no good reason would be served by making alterations in the existing arrangements at the two Nurseries, which were functioning quite satisfactorily.[216]

But not all young children could be housed in Nurseries. On April 13th 1940, the Ministry of Health in London sent a letter to Mr H. King at the County Council in Taunton expressing some concerns about the plight of some city children. A number of organisations dealing with children under 5 were worried that in the event of air-raids

---

214 Included Chairman of the Public Health and Housing Committee (Mr S.C.Morland),Chairman of the Midwifery and Child Welfare Sub-Committee (Mrs Cooke Hurle),Deputy Clerk to the Council, the County Medical Officer of Health and the County Treasurer. There were also representatives from the Ministry of Health Regional Staff at Bristol. (Dr W.D.Brunyate and Mr C.R.Gove)

215 Excluding the Boroughs of Taunton, Weston-Super-Mare and Yeovil.

216 Somerset County Council. Clerk's Dept. Memo. From Mr S. Strickland. March 1940.

on London there would be a considerable number of small children whose home circumstances would make it desirable for them to be evacuated in groups not with their mothers, but with a responsible adult who they were acquainted with, and who had been trained in the management of young children. It was suggested that under these circumstances rather than putting them into nurseries, billets should be found with householders who were not at present looking after school-children. Although the Minister did not want to put an extra administrative burden on those in the reception areas dealing with the older age range of evacuees, he was happy to accept an offer from the WVS who would employ volunteers to work in close liaison with any County Council and Reception Authority willing to test the possibility of finding billets for the under-5s. So he suggested that the WVS should approach householders and seek answers to the following questions:-

a. Is the householder willing to care for a small child on the basis of the billeting allowance?

b. Is the householder already caring for, or has the householder offered to care for, school children?

c. How far could unwillingness be converted into willingness by the establishment of nursery centres?[217]

d. Has the householder been notified of any other billeting liability? For example for Civil Servants or the Military.

To begin with only three reception counties, Huntingdonshire, Northamptonshire and Somerset would be asked to test the response of householders to the idea. [218]

Nursery provision remained an issue throughout the war, and images of day nurseries were even included in the propaganda film Living With Strangers in 1941 to demonstrate that the younger children were being well looked after.

Education Reform

> *'Any day now the senior boys will take in hand a piece of national work, the cultivation of a large piece of waste ground offered to them by Major Stilwell. After clearing the site it will be trenched in readiness for the growing of root crops. All boys will have to take a turn at gardening'.*[219]

Boys Gardening. This group of boys have cleared and are now cultivating a large area of land near their school.

217 As envisaged in the Min. of Health Circ. 1936. Jan. 9th 1940
218 Letter from J.C.Wrigley. Ministry of Health. London. 12th April 1940
219 Dorset Daily Echo .23rd September 1939

Some educationalists believed that evacuation broke the traditional methods of educational practices and prepared the way for change and those teachers who were absorbed in the scheme were seen by some of their contemporaries as leading the movement for educational reform.[220]

There was a firm belief that city children could now be introduced to new first hand pedagogic experiences such as real nature study, agriculture, horticulture and first hand history and geography. In November 1939, the Board of Education commented:-

> *'Evacuation gave schools a chance for personal initiatives and resourcefulness by challenging them to jettison unreal teaching to look outside at real things rather than at apparatus indoors'.*[221]

As an example of this, on 6th June 1940, the Education Officer in Somerset issued a memo to all teachers in the County;

> 'The committee wish to call attention of teachers at the present time to the importance of devoting some of the Nature Study Lesson in every school to the injurious effects of certain weeds on the food supply of the country.
>
> They desire that the children should be taught to recognise them at different times of the year, to know of their modes of propagation, their harmful effects as exhausting the soil of plant food and moisture, and of their serving as breeding places for certain crop pests. The need of cutting down or otherwise destroying such weeds before they seed should be emphasised.
>
> Attention should be particularly called to the following notifiable injurious weeds:-
>
> Spear Thistle, Creeping or Field Thistle, Curled Dock, Broad-leaved Dock, Raggwort
>
> And in addition to:-
>
> Charlock, Couch Grass, Convolvulus, Nettles, Horse-Tail (Equisetum), Bracken and Brambles.[222]

Brian Simon, in his book 'Education and the Social Order 1940-41', suggests that:-'Primary School teachers, thrown on their own resources in the chaos of evacuation, learnt how much younger children could gain from work with improvised apparatus, pioneering group and informal methods of working and forays into the countryside'.[223]

However, such new methodology presupposed that the teachers could, and would, take advantage of the new experiences on offer. Of the total number of teachers in primary and secondary schools in England and Wales in January 1946, 9,458 were aged over 60, and 33,159 were married women.[224] These, together with previously retired schoolmasters, had been recalled to the profession, some after many years away from the classroom, to fill the places of between 20,000-22,000 teachers[225] who had been called up into the armed forces or carrying out other war work[226] and one would suggest that neither group would necessarily have made the development of new methodologies their highest priority, certainly not during the first wave of evacuation. On 27th November 1939, the Director of Education in Anglesey wrote:-

---

220 H.C.Dent.Education in Transition. London 1944 cited. P.H.J.H. Godsen. Education in the Second World War. 1976.
221 TNA.ED 136/205
222 SCC. County Ed Comm. Ref Circ E.287
223 Brian Simon. Education and the Social Order 1940-1990. Lawrence and Wishart. 1991.p35
224 Ministry of Education estimate. February 1946. cited Titmuss op.cit. p406
225 House of Commons Debates. 19th October 1944 vol.403 col.2511 cited Titmuss op.cit. p407
226 Between 1939 and 1944, the number of male teachers in grant-aided elementary and secondary schools in the UK fell by over 30%. The Impact of War on Civilian Consumption. HMSO 1945. p63

> '...the educational needs of the evacuated children had certainly not been the first concern of either the Evacuation or Billeting Authorities, or indeed the Government departments concerned. For not only were large schools evacuated into rural districts and the pupils scattered over a wide area, but also the billeting arrangements had been more concerned with family units than with school units'.[227]

Investigation into school log books in many of the reception areas, yields very little evidence of any new curriculum initiatives beyond numerous references to 'Nature Study Trail', 'Nature Talks', 'Nature Walks' and 'Gardening' which seemed to be put on at the end of the afternoon and were often cancelled because of bad weather. However, a report in the Dorset Daily Echo on 13th October 1939, did describe the efforts of Mr. G.W. Greening, the Headmaster of the Evershot village school who used 'Agricultural studies' as a basis for what would now be called cross-curricular or integrated studies.[228] As well as cultivating flowers and vegetables the children also raised poultry and kept bees.

These boys from Canning Town in London are being given a gardening lesson at St.Arvans village school in Monmouthshire.

The Caernarvonshire Education Authorities did initiate new courses for evacuated teachers on 'Nature Study' (7th November 1941) and 'The Historical Background of Caernarvonshire' (February 1942) to help them get the most from their surroundings.[229]

However, although curriculum content initiatives were not necessarily a high priority, there had to be a change in actual teaching methodologies, and it is perhaps this experience which led to more child-centred learning taking place in post-war classrooms. Having to teach a large number of children of various ages and abilities, some of whom were there for only a short time, in cramped conditions with few resources, meant that teachers had to draw upon new ideas and methods to cope with the situation. In some areas such an environment gave rise to

---

227 E.O.Humphreys. Education Officer Anglesey. Report. The Education of Evacuated Children. 27th Nov 39. University College North Wales. Archives V4594.
228 Dorset Daily Echo. 13th October 1939
229 Evacuation Group. Prince Rupert School. Liverpool 1941. Log Book Caernarfon RO.

learning programmes and schemes of work suited to individual pupils. By implementing such plans, even on a limited basis, one could argue that some basic curriculum changes were forced upon some teachers, as the following Inspection report for the Ely Market Street School, September 1944, illustrates;

> Report by H.M.I. Mr. S.N.Godfrey
>
> Owing to the limitations and inconvenience of the premise the children attending this school are denied much of the movement and activity that are essential to development. The inadequate provision for washing and the limitations of the office accommodation simply deprive them of the opportunities for social training which should form part of their education. The conditions of heating, lighting and ventilation are unsatisfactory for some of the classes. The inadequate accommodation necessitates promotion of children to the Junior School every 6 months instead of annually and gives rise to considerable difficulty in the Junior and Senior Schools. By the careful planning of work along individual lines and the keeping of detailed records, the head-teacher and her staff have tried to ensure a continuous course for each child. Much of the work done however needs to be reviewed in the light of modern teaching practice.[230]

These changes took place in 1944 when the situation on the Home Front was relatively stable and the pastoral side of the teachers' role was perhaps less of a priority and more time could be spent on developing the school curriculum. It is useful to compare this with the experience of teachers Win Elliott and Sylvia Lewis who were evacuated in 1939. It is obvious from the description of their experience teaching in a small school in the village of Leiston that curriculum initiatives were very low in their list of priorities.

> *'At Leiston school, for one session each day, we had the use of one small room which we and our evacuees shared with a Dagenham headmistress. We had no apparatus, no guidance as to what to do or teach.....we gradually acquired a small collection of reading books, paper, pencils and crayons etc. No high-faluting syllabus, or structured curriculum, but the children learned to read and write and calculate with enjoyment.....The rest of the school day we had to play in the park, or walk the children around the lanes and go to the woods'.*[231]

One teacher, keen to do something new with her pupils, inadvertently created an invasion scare when she organised a Treasure Hunt for her class in the local area. They had been given strict instructions to destroy all the clues, but one was found by a villager. It simply said 'Go forward 500 yards to a gatepost near the cottage. Look for Oxo tin and follow instructions inside'. The locals thought it was the work of Fifth Columnists![232]

Reception

It is important to recognise that some teachers, particularly those in the reception areas, often had other duties imposed on them by local authorities even before the war had started, and some, having taken on the role of the proposed billeting officer, took their duties very seriously. In July 1939, Mr M.T. Perks, the Head-teacher of the Grammar School, in Gillingham, Dorset, organised a full Evacuation rehearsal in meticulous detail using pupils and staff from his own school, in order that all people involved in the reception area could evaluate and amend procedures they were to use when called upon to do so officially. He was keen to ensure the Clerk of the Shaftesbury Council that he proposed:- '......... *on Monday to treat the children as if they were strangers for the purpose of rehearsal and shall treat the member of my staff in charge of the bus as the evacuated Head Teacher, I shall not acquaint him with the suggested routine as arranged'.*[233] It is worth quoting his schedule in full

230 'Cambridge County Records. CES/66C/3. Ely Market Street School.
231 Letter to the author from W. Elliott and Sylvia Lewis. June 1998. MERL Archive.
232 Wallis. op.cit. p147
233 M.T.Perks. letter to J. Stace-Masey. 21st July 1939. Shaftesbury File DC/SYR Dorset Record Office.

because it is an extremely rare example of how local plans were implemented. Note, than even in this document Mr Perks was keen to imply that Evacuation was not a foregone conclusion.

In the event of Evacuation taking place.

PROCEDURE provisionally fixed for Semley Station.

(For trains containing evacuees for Shaftesbury Borough, Shaftesbury RDC areas.)

Evacuees will be either

(a) Unaccompanied children. i.e. School Parties in charge of teachers.

(b) Mothers and children under school age.

The procedure in most details will be similar for (a) and (b) but * indicates alternative arrangements according to the nature of the party.

EVACUEES on ARRIVAL

Detrain on platform.

Lead off over bridge across road into Room allotted for Assembling guided by Marshals.

(The First Aid Room will not be on the station, but possibly some First Aid personnel might be on the platform in case of any evacuees needing immediate attention or assistance in getting to the Assembly Room.)

ENTER Assembly Room. Evacuees are arranged by Marshals in rows and told to sit down.

NB. Walk up to far end of the room first.

Rows parallel to long side of room and fill right hand side of the room first (i.e. side furthest from the Ration Room.)

Leave space between rows.

One gangway in middle of row.

Doorways clear.

Enclosure, near door left-hand side at top of room, clear.

When all are in Assembling Room [Marshal reports to R.O. (Reception Officer) Whistle blows and R.O. gives short explanation of what is going to happen, e.g. First Aid facilities etc.]

R.O. requests Head Teacher or Leader (leaders) of party to accompany him to R.O's. office to exchange necessary information. Deputy R.O. takes charge in the room.

* In a (b) party, if there is no leader, list or roll of party is required for the R.O's. office.

Deputy R.O. asks all who wish to visit the lavatory to stand up.

Those requiring this are escorted out in batches by Marshals, and by teachers in an (a) party.

If all boys, or all girls, or Mothers and children, use the United Dairies Lavatories.

If Mixed School Girls; United Dairies lavatories
Boys; Lavatory on Semley Station platform.

Children are returned to their original places as far as possible and they sit down.

R.O. has now made billeting allocations as between RDC and others and returns with Head teachers or Leader to Assembly Room.

Check that no one is left in lavatories or outside. Marshal to report.

R.O. Instructs.

(i) Half will now go to Shaftesbury direct where they will receive Rations and Milk. Remainder will receive Milk or Water in room and Rations.

(ii) Shaftesbury section to prepare to leave.

Stand Up and make sure they have all Baggage, Gas Masks etc.

(Detail either certain classes on information of Head Teacher or if a (b) party those occupying part of the room. Count roughly by Marshal and Deputy R.O.)

Milk distribution now begins among the remainder.

R.O. Calculates such as to be sent to debussing point.

R.O. to Leader of the Party, 'Send into enclosure e.g. 45 children and 5 teachers or helpers'.

Leader of the party, who will know their names, details this number from those nearest the 'enclosure'.

R.O. sends warning message to be telephoned to Billeting Officers.

*R.O. to Deputy R.O. and Marshals, 'Send in e.g. 20 mothers and 30 children'.

Evacuees enter enclosure.

Deputy R.O. or Marshal counts them and checks. Have all got Baggage complete?

* If (b) party, check also that no incomplete family is included in 'enclosure'.

After check, R.O. gives Deputy R.O. the order to transport Officer and Driver. Deputy R.O. takes party through Ration Room where they will receive rations,... except first of Shaftesbury section when Deputy R.O. will instruct the Ration Officials 'No rations' and go out and load on the bus.

Deputy R.O. hands orders to the transport officer and returns to report to R.O. 'Bus Loaded'.

On the 24th July, Mr. Perks sent a detailed critical evaluation to the Clerk of the Council outlining the events of the day and making some suggestions as to how the initial reception could have been made more effective.

Dear Mr. Stace-Masey,

The 'refugees' arrived 16.35 hrs. were allocated to billets and the Billeting forms completed by 17.10. They were not dispatched to billets which would have taken at least another hour.

It was found that 3 helpers, in addition to the 2 Billeting Officers, were necessary to deal with the clerical work and the handing over to the local transport drivers and foot guides.

The instructions and forms issued worked quite satisfactorily. The words 'Billeting Orders' should be struck out in Form Ev. JSM/9.

Billeting Officers would like to have a Local Transport list of local car transport they can draw on, also have information available about extra blankets and bedding.

At Semley; I think Mr Perks, will find it difficult to deal with the whole 500 in the one room and some 'waiting accommodation' is necessary.

With regard to my suggestion to form a committee in each Parish, I now think it will be sufficient to inform the Senior Billeting Officers that, as a result of the test, it has been found advisable to have additional help when billeting, and to suggest that the Billeting Officers concerned, together with the 'helpers', should constitute a small permanent Committee who would also deal with the after care and 'supervision' as decided in the penultimate paragraph of your draft.

This will avoid any overlapping which might occur if we ask someone who is not appointed as Billeting Officer to form a Committee'.[234]

Even after 'practices' and thorough local planning there were still problems, and in some ways Mr. Perks was quite correct in assuming that the smooth running of any evacuation scheme was not a foregone conclusion. For example, after the results of the accommodation census were made known to local councils the billeting officer in the parish of Bradfield, West Berkshire, was told to expect 300 evacuees in two consignments on the 3rd and 4th of September 1939. Three weeks before these dates he was sent more details about the party which would consist of 270 children and 30 teachers and helpers. Blankets and mattresses were to be made available. The billeting officer and his helpers then re-canvassed the whole parish to make sure that this division of expected evacuees could be housed. They were to arrive at the nearest train station, Theale, at 5.30pm where they were to be taken by bus to the local men's club for distribution to the billets. The local representative of the WVS had set up a committee to distribute the blankets and mattresses and to help with the administration and distribution of the evacuees throughout the parish.

By 1st September neither the blankets nor mattresses had arrived, although everything else was now ready. The billeting officer had every household's voucher already filled in with details about the numbers of children and the money due, and only the names of the children remained to be added. It was planned that all 300 people would be at their billets within an hour of arriving. This being the case they decided not to provide refreshments other than water which had to be fetched from a nearby farm, and agreed that the existing toilet facilities in the club would be sufficient. Everyone was in a state of readiness.

On the evening of Saturday 2nd September a telegram arrived stating that the evacuees would not now arrive until the Monday.

On Monday, at 11 am, another telegram arrived which simply stated '*expect children this afternoon*'. At 3pm a third telegram was received with the message... '*arrangements cancelled*' so the billeting officer told all the helpers to go home until he contacted them again. At 5.30pm on the same day a fourth telegram came... '*children arriving at 6 pm*'. The billeting officer's daughter was then sent out on her bicycle around the parish to search for her father who had gone back to work. By 6.30 he had been found and the WVS reception committee had been

234 M.T.Perks to J.Stace-Masey. 24th July 1939. DC/SYR. Dorset Record Office

reassembled. At 7.30 the buses arrived and deposited 35 school children and 220 mothers and infants. Totally unexpected! All the billeting arrangements that had been made had to be completely reorganised.[235]

A contemporary eye-witness account describes in some detail the problems that this unexpected group created and one can sense the frustration of those in the evacuation 'front line' who had done their best to organise suitable accommodation from the information they had been supplied with.

> *'The evacuees straggle into the clubroom laden with babies, toddlers, parcels and gas masks. The overcrowding, confusion, noise and squalor is unbelievable. Some cannot speak English, many have lost their parcels or their toddlers. Ventilation is inadequate because of the darkened windows. We sort out the unaccompanied children first and without undue delay despatch them to their new homes.*
>
> *Now for these mothers. Next billet has room for mother and one child. 'You mother and young baby, come this way please'.*
>
> *'Oh, I can't go without my friend here. I'd rather spend the night where I am'.*
>
> *'Well you there with the little girl then'.*
>
> *'Oh those other five belong to me'.*
>
> *Hasty search through the books for accommodation for six.*
>
> *So it goes slowly on. The first carloads begin to come back with such messages as 'Mrs Hodge says she can't possibly take the mother and four children because her sister has just arrived from Manchester with six', or 'Mrs Brown wouldn't let us in because she said she had asked for two little girls and would not take in a Polish family instead'.*
>
> *Meanwhile the countryside has grown dark. The mothers and babies in the hut are tired and less reasonable than ever. An Irishwoman stands up and declaims in eloquent but unprintable language against all of us and all our race and all our ancestors. Some eight or nine women refuse to part from each other and we agree to bed them down for the night in the clubroom. Our transport driver reports that the householders have gone to bed and billets can be found for no more. We bed up the residue as comfortably as we can in the hut on sacks of straw and retire to our respective homes for the night'.*[236]

When one reads an account such as this, one realises where some of the innate dissatisfaction with the scheme and the anti-evacuee propaganda emanates from. This seeming lack of organisation was not the fault of either the evacuees or the reception authorities, but both sides tended to level the blame at each other in terms of intransigence and lack of sympathy for the situation everybody found themselves in.

In many of the other designated reception areas most teachers had returned early from their school holidays and 'were holding themselves in readiness to carry out any instructions which may have been given to them and also to assist locally in the reception and billeting of evacuated children'.[237]

An intriguing insight into another teacher's experience, Mr Henschel of Tottenham Country School, has been provided by his son David who was to leave his boarding school to accompany his father's school to March. As a thirteen year-old he recalled the Summer of 1939 clearly:

> *'When my Father ... was summoned by telegram back to school in emergency readiness for a planned evacuation ... the obviously sensible thing was for me to accompany my Father when he reported back to TCS...'.*[238]

235 Miriam Ward. Evacuation. A Reception Area in Berkshire. unpublished account. Undated
236 Miriam Ward. op cit.
237 Berkshire County Council Minutes. August. 1939

In late August 1939 the pupils of Tottenham County School were instructed by Mr Thomas to report to their teachers almost two weeks before the official start of term. David remembered that the hot last days of peace were spent mainly in the playground playing a '*rowdy, potentially lethal game called Jimmy, Jimmy Jump ... and cards – rummy, whist, pontoon*'. It seems that the staff, busy planning the evacuation, left the children unsupervised. David noted: '*I don't remember any lessons, any attempt to teach us anything at all. It was great fun and very jolly*'.[239]

Mavis Cordery, then a newly qualified teacher in the Caversham Senior School in Harley Rd., Reading, recalled in an interview that:-

> *'Staff in school reported to the billeting officer*[240] *in our own school to be allocated.*
>
> *.....Prospective hosts had been told to arrive at the school at a specific time. It was our job to check these people and their assessments and to help calm them down as some were extremely nervous at the prospect of meeting and then housing children from London. There were rumours that the evacuees were coming from the dock and 'slummy' (sic) areas of London and there were all sorts of stories circulating about poor personal hygiene, revolting eating habits, dreadful social habits and low morals. By the time the bus turned up with the children hours later, most people were a bit jumpy to say the least!' Other staff had spent their holiday participating in courses on first aid and anti-gas measures'.*[241]

It was not only the schools in the towns that were taking measures to receive evacuees. Those in small villages, with few children and basic facilities had to do the same. The log-book entries for the East Chinnock School in Somerset, provides a brief insight into how things had to be organised in the first month of evacuation.

> *August 31st Re-opened the school this morning 39 on books*
>
> *September 1st Assembled at school this morning but dismissed the children, having received instructions to close owing to evacuation of children and this being a Reception Area.*
>
> *September 12th School reopened this morning on the advice of the Correspondent and the information being sent to the LEA. The usual full time instruction is being given, while proposals are being made with regards the evacuees.*
>
> *September 18th 6 children belonging to Evacuee mothers were admitted today. Numbers are 32 in the top group.*
>
> *September 22nd Miss Peake, HMI called this afternoon to make inquiries re accommodation of evacuees.*[242]

However, as in other establishments around the country, not all evacuees decided to stay....

> *October 26th 2 more evacuees withdrawn today leaving 2 unofficial and 1 official.*

Although it would seem that the arrival of evacuees was an *ad hoc* process, in reality this was not the case. A great deal of informative correspondence often took place both within the reception areas, and between the Reception and Evacuating authorities, but problems arose when this was not acted on.

---

238 David Henschel, 12 July 2000. Letter.
239 ibid
240 Billeting Officers were appointed under Regulation 22 of the Defence (General) Regulations 1939 by Mayors of Boroughs and County Boroughs, and by Chairmen of the Rural and District Councils. The Ministry of Health had delegated the power of appointment but local authorities were able to appoint anyone who was a person of tact, judgement and had common sense Titmuss op.cit. p391
241 The late Mavis Cordery. Retired Headmistress of Alfred Sutton Girls School. Green Rd. Reading. One-time Billeting Officer. From an interview recorded March 1996. MERL Archive
242 Somerset Record Office E/4 Bx80 263 1-3 1939

'Board of Ed.

Alexandra House

Kingsway London WC2

3 September 1939

Sir

In accordance with the announcement which will be made by radio today, all schools in evacuation areas and neutral areas are to be closed for instruction for at least a week from today. In reception areas schools should be reopened as soon as arrangements for the education of the children evacuated to the locality can be completed. The date at which this stage will be reached will naturally vary as between one area and another, and accordingly the precise date of reopening will be decided by the authorities of the schools.

The reference in this letter to the closure of schools should be taken as applying not only to day schools and classes but also to evening classes in whatever types of institution they are held.

A separate communication is being addressed to the authorities of Training Colleges.

M.G.Holmes [243]

This one was sent to the reception and neutral areas a few days later;

7th Sept. 1939

Sir,

I am directed to state for the information of the Authorities that all schools in evacuation areas will remain closed for instruction until further notice.

Schools in neutral areas may be reopened for instruction on or after Monday, September 11th at the discretion of the authorities of the schools.

An important factor in determining whether schools in neutral areas shall be reopened is the degree of protection available for the children while in school. Authorities have already been given guidance in Circ.1467 on the subject of air raid precautions in schools and where such protection for children in neutral areas has not yet been afforded the authorities concerned are urged to complete the necessary measures with the least possible delay.

It is hoped that schools in reception areas which have not already reopened will do so as soon as possible.

M.G.Holmes.[244]

And, as promised, the situation of Training Colleges was also dealt with.

---

243 Letter from M.G.Holmes. op cit 3rd September 1939

244 Letter from M.G.Holmes. Board of Education. London 7th September 1939

'Dear Sir or Madam

Training College Authorities will wish to know what action to take in regard to reassembling next term.

Training Colleges in evacuation areas should not reopen in those areas for the Autumn Term.

Training Colleges in neutral or reception areas should reopen for the Autumn Term as usual, unless in the case of men students instructions are given to the contrary.

Women's Training colleges in evacuation areas which are to move to premises other than Men's Training Colleges should re-assemble in those premises as soon as they are available.

Women's training colleges in evacuation areas which are to transfer to Men's TC in reception areas should re-assemble in those colleges as soon as they have been vacated by the men students, but as to when this may be no advice can be given at present.

The suggestions in 2/3/4 above are subject to the discretion of the College Authorities in the light of local circumstances. In particular regard should be had to the extent to which the College premises have been provided with adequate air raid protection where this is necessary

S.H.Wood'[245]

As Bristol had been declared a neutral evacuation area, the schools in the city remained open during the Phoney War and throughout the subsequent blitz. Some parents exploited this, and there were cases of children being deliberately sent from surrounding areas to Bristol Grammar School, which remained open throughout the period[246].

Figures for school attendance (see Appendix 2) during this period demonstrate that somewhat perversely this had the positive effect of providing uninterrupted education to the children in Bristol, unlike their peers in other parts of the country.[247] However, as many of the lessons took place in school air-raid shelters, not a conducive environment for teaching and learning because of lack of light and teaching materials, there was tremendous disruption, not helped by the fact that a significant amount of time was spent both in, and going to and from, the shelters. There were a total of 584 air raid warnings from August 1940 to June 1941,[248] so the cumulative amount of time spent in the shelters seriously disrupted the education of Bristol children. In addition, the bomb-damage to school buildings meant that teaching materials and equipment was destroyed and many children were often required to go home because of safety issues. In some areas where schools were open there could be an interesting and unforeseen influence on the number of pupils who actually attended. In some instances it became the norm for the local population to 'trek' to areas of safety at night to escape the raids. These nightly excursions onto the moors in Devon and the countryside around Merseyside meant that many pupils did not return home in time for the start of school in the morning and then left early in the afternoon to escape the cities before the raids began.

Minutes from Council meetings across the country during the latter part of 1938 and throughout 1939 provide an indication as to how much time and effort was being spent by Evacuation committees and Head-teachers in an effort to get reception matters organised. In Cornwall a document was distributed to head- teachers of all Secondary and Elementary schools on 13th July 1939 indicating that:-

245 Letter from S.H.Wood. Board of Education. 3rd September 1939
246 Bradley, A., Personal Interview, 9th September 2011 cited in To what extent did the designation of Bristol as a 'Neutral' evacuation zone, damage the lives of it children. Dissertation. Max Irving. MERL Archive. 2012
247 Irvine op cit.
248 Penny, J., 'Bristol at War', Breedon Book p. 185

> 'We have been told that at present the initial number of evacuees to be expected in the Administrative county is 4,000 and that the eventual total of school children and teachers may reach the figure of 34,000 which means doubling our existing school population'[249]

The question of school size was one which arose on more than one occasion across the whole of the reception areas. For example, most of the London schools were larger than their Somerset counterparts so although agreeing with the principle that evacuated schools should be retained as whole units, it was unlikely that they could ever be accommodated in a single establishment.

The same applied in Cornwall where the LEA commented that;

> 'It is the hope of the evacuating authorities that as far as possible a school will be able to retain its identity within the reception area, but the billeting difficulties already referred to (small villages and settlements) and the very much smaller schools of Cornwall compared with London make this very difficult'[250]

Council members in Somerset suggested that measures should be put in place for a London school to be shared among a maximum of 5 schools in the local vicinity so allowing the London Head Teacher to remain in contact with all the pupils, help retain its identity and maintain some form of continuity. It was also agreed that it would be undesirable to adopt a billeting plan which would spread a complete train load of school children over the whole or greater part of the County. Instead the number of children allocated to various parishes would be commensurate with the available school accommodation. In order to make this process easier, it was proposed that all schools would be closed once an emergency had been declared, or on the first day of evacuation whichever was earlier. This would free-up both the teachers, and the premises. Schools would only reopen when instructed to do so after all the billeting of evacuees had been completed.[251]

All the reception areas had been given a list of 'detraining' stations in a Memo of April 1939 and these were used in planning dispersal from the rail-heads, although some changes had been made between April and September which necessitated alternative arrangements. Some of this information was reported in local newspapers. In May 1939 the West Briton published an article about the arrival of evacuees to Cornwall should the scheme be implemented; 'The schedule of the Government Evacuation Scheme to Cornwall showing the allocations for reception areas and the districts to be served provided for 81,000 children. The detraining stations are Bude (2,500), Launceston (4,300), Wadebridge (12,800), Bodmin (1,500), Camelford (2,600), St Austell (8,200), Camborne (15,700), Truro (9,500), Falmouth (5,000), St Ives (8,100), Penzance (6,000) and Liskeard (5,500).[252]

Detraining stations had already been agreed by the Somerset committee in April 1939, and the County Clerk had pointed out the need for sufficient toilet accommodation to be made available on the stations, an important requirement as many of the children would travel in 3rd class carriages with no access to facilities, and that in rural areas a number of private cars should be on hand to transport evacuees direct to their billets.[253] It was agreed that there was to be no rationing of petrol until all the children had been housed. According to the Clerk to the Somerset Council:-

> '...an organisation can be devised very quickly which would be capable of functioning effectively at short notice, but preparatory action is essential.....Local Authorities should at once complete their arrangements to the last and smallest detail....in order that each individual worker at the business end of the affair knows precisely what he has to do'[254]

---

249 Cornwall Record Office. SRU/SAM/1/77
250 ibid
251 Somerset Record Office C/CD/1/6/1 Evacuee Correspondence 1938-39
252 West Briton. 8th May 1939.
253 Petrol rationing was not introduced until after evacuation was complete.
254 ibid

He also pointed out that Mrs Orr-Ewing of the WVS was *'most anxious that full advantage should be taken of their organisation'*.

Teachers

> *We all thought it was great fun as we wouldn't be sent home … and would be having a nice long holiday............Not a thought for our parents who had waved us off only two days before and for our teachers who had also left their relatives behind'.*[255]

The increased demands on the teaching profession were becoming abundantly clear from the outset of Operation Pied Piper. Many schoolchildren had travelled previously with their teachers on school day-trips, but evacuation to an unknown destination for an indeterminate amount of time was different for both parties and threw up new challenges, not least of which was the fact that some teachers were out of their comfort zones in terms of pastoral care and academic expectations; in the same way that many teachers in the reception areas used to teaching rural children found it hard to manage children from the cities who were a little more 'street-wise'. In addition, it is often forgotten that there was a lot of additional pressure placed on the many married women teachers separated from their own children who in many cases were evacuated with their own schools to a different part of the country. Teachers in general now had to re-adjust to the new circumstances without revealing any outward signs to the children of the anxiety and sense of dislocation they would have understandably felt.

Professor Sidney Brown sheds some interesting light on the role of teachers on the journey and subsequent arrival of the Tottenham County School in March, Lincolnshire. Teacher's son David Henschel wrote of *'a pervading sense of helplessness'* as the train left Tottenham lightened with some *'chatter and jokes to subdue and make the best of it'* orchestrated by *'kindly teachers seeing if all was well.'*[256] Adrienne Waters recalled the kindly attitude of the teachers towards the smaller children on the journey [257] who, as in many other evacuations around the country, were not even allowed personal comforts such as Teddy bears or dolls, which were often confiscated prior to the trains setting off. She also remembered a Mrs Bedding, renowned for her discipline, who on the journey spent her time comforting and handing out sweets and *'little refreshing pads called Quickies.. '* to help the children freshen up.[258]

Teachers looking after some of the less resilient children also had their work cut out. Cyril Goodwin recalled that without warning his younger brother Keith *'jumped up and tried to open the carriage door'*[259] but was calmed down by the teacher.

According to David Henschel the train carrying the children from the TCS eventually pulled into 'a long platform … hot, shadowed and sunlit' where 'awaiting adults, some with their own children' were assembled below 'the nameplate – MARCH – wherever that was no one knew' .[260] On arrival the pupils were to witness an adult confrontation between the Tottenham Headmaster and the 'welcoming' party. Tom Farmer noted:

> *'Dr Thomas had a heated discussion with the billeting officers who wanted to break up the school and disperse the pupils to the surrounding villages. Dr (then Mr) Thomas won the day and we stayed in March.'*[261]

An overwhelming impression running through the testimony sent to Professor Brown is the feeling of unity and identity which the March experience gave the pupil, a sentiment which has endured with some to this day. Ironically, Tottenham was to remain relatively unscathed during the first part of the war whereas it transpired that

255 Doreen Jaques, 7 April 2002. Letter.
256 David Henschel, 12 July 2000. Letter.
257 Adrienne Waters, 13 February 2002. Letter.
258 Adrienne Waters op cit
259 Cyril Goodwin, 14 May 2002. Letter
260 David Henschel, op cit
261 Tom Farmer, 20 July 2000. Letter.

March was a major railway marshalling yard originally built to plans drawn up by German consultants and as a result was to prove an early favourite target for the Luftwaffe![262]

In early 1940 the Government recognised the extra work that teachers were doing and addressed the issue of providing additional allowances to those teachers within the Government Evacuation Scheme. It was agreed by the Ministry of Health that from the 29th January 1940, teachers employed within the State Education sector would receive extra funds payable by the LEA or the body responsible for teachers' salaries. The existing billeting procedures would not be changed, i.e. where a teacher was officially billeted by a householder the entitlement of the latter of 5/- per week would remain the same.

A teacher, who had already obtained alternative accommodation for themselves or, in some cases their families, in or in close proximity to the Reception Area, would not be entitled to receive any housing payments. However, from the end of January, teachers who made private arrangements of this kind would in every case be eligible for a weekly allowance of 5/- or more, according to circumstances, from the authority which employed them. This was dependent on the Chief Billeting Officer of the local reception authority giving his consent to the actual accommodation selected, and in the case of furnished accommodation, that the house had not been designated for other purposes. The teacher(s) concerned had to send a certificate of consent, together with their application for allowances, to their employers.

A teacher wishing to take advantage of the scheme simply had to apply to the Chief Billeting Officer in writing for the certificate and the latter were asked to reply, again in writing, to the teacher concerned as soon as possible after receipt. The Ministry of Health informed the reception areas that such consent should not be unreasonably withheld; but where, for example, the accommodation had been earmarked for the billeting of other personnel a short time scale would enable the teacher to find an alternative.

The scheme also applied to other staff employed by the LEAs and other authorities who had been transferred in a semi-permanent capacity to the reception areas under the Evacuation process, such as nurses and midwives. In the case of the latter, where the salaries were paid by the reception areas on 'transfer', the actual monies allocated for accommodation were to be determined by the Evacuating authority which would then arrange the periodical payment of the additional sum with the Reception Areas.[263]

Although there may have been little curriculum change, what the war did bring about was a shift in the relationship between the teacher and pupil. There was a significant move towards a more pastoral role which was to become a significant part of a teacher's job after the war and has been ever since. One major reason for this was that both teacher and pupil were experiencing the evacuation process together and as a result had a common bond. This has been supported by evidence gathered from oral history sources by Peter Cunningham and Philip Gardner.[264]

Some teachers were dealing with social problems way above the call of duty and their expertise. The following entry in the log book of the 'Boys Evacuated School', Aston Clinton, Buckinghamshire, is significant in two respects. First, it shows that some of the problems dealt with *in loco parentis* were very serious. Second, some of the fears parents have today regarding child safety were just as apparent in the 1940s.

It is often overlooked that crime still existed despite the war and there were paedophiles.

> '11th December 1939. Joseph Mack d.o.b. 5.12.31
> London Address. 111 Nathaniel Buildings. Flower and Dean Street.
> Billeting Address. 6 Buckland Wharf, Aylesbury.
>
> I have today received official information from the Aston Clinton Police officer, in relation to the indecent assault of Joseph Mack, aged 8 years,

262 Trevor Bevis, 24 July 2000. Letter
263 Ref. Circular 1977 MoH and 14th March 1940. J.C.Wrigley C/CD/1/6/2 Somerset Record Office
264 see Oral History and Teachers' Professional Practice: a wartime turning point?. Camb. Journal of Education, Vol 27 No 3 1997 pp 331-341.

on Saturday afternoon 18th November 1939 at 3pm in a wood beside the main road in Aston Clinton. The matter came to Police notice about 14 days after the event and within two days an Aylesbury man named ****** was arrested in Aston Clinton and has since been identified by the children concerned.

The papers concerning the matter have been placed in the hands of the Director of Public Prosecutions. A copy of the above entry is being sent to the LCC Divisional Officer, No. 6 District and to the Community Secretary at 37, Stepney Green. E1.

Children have been repeatedly warned about walking about singly in lonely places at anytime, though of course no details of what to fear have been given'.[265]

Another example was reported in the Dorset County Chronicle and Swanage Times on the 23rd October 1941:-

A 34 year old man from Swanage was gaoled for '12 months imprisonment in the Second Division' for indecently assaulting three evacuees in his care. His claims of using them as 'human hot water bottles' were not accepted by the jury.[266]

Teachers were also responsible for those pupils who, for any reason, decided to run away and paper-work involved in reporting such incidents put an additional strain onto an already overworked profession. As today, the Head-teacher concerned in this episode was keen to write down all the actions that took place so that no accusation of negligence could be levelled at him.

'22nd January 1940.

It was reported to the Head-teacher by Mrs Webb at 5.30pm tonight, that a pupil of Commercial Street LCC Junior, Mixed and Infants School one Bernard Saunders aged 11, billeted at 36, London Rd., Aston Clinton, had left his billet between 9 and 10am after a quarrel with another child billeted at the same address.

Action Taken:

(a) Head. visited Mrs McWhal the foster parent.

(b) Head. visited Mr Delamonte, Head-teacher's assistant, to whom absence was reported by Aaron Saunders, during registration.

23rd January. Head. 'stood by' all night and kept in contact with the Police. No news received from any source since yesterday morning. Head. phoned Chief Dispersal Officer D.O.6 reference the case. Was asked to wait until 2pm for any news. In the event waited until 4pm and then phoned CDO.

Mr Butcher, CDO, then informed the parents who told him that the child had arrived home on the previous day. The CDO wired the Head-teacher to this effect'.[267]

The boy returned to school on the 29th January[268].

There is no indication of what the head-teacher thought about the outcome, but the whole incident does raise a series of questions: Why did the hosts take so long to report the boy missing? How did he manage to return to London unchallenged? Why did the parents not report that he had returned home? They could have given little thought to the emotional state of the teachers involved, especially the Head-teacher. Had it not been for the action

265 The Boys Evacuated School. Aston Clinton. Bucks. School Diary. Bucks Record Office E/LB/8/1
266 Dorset County Chronicle & Swanage Times 23rd October 1941.
267 Commercial Street. LCC School. Log Book. Bucks. Record Office E/LB/8/1
268 .ibid

taken by Aaron Saunders in telling his teacher Mrs Webb, the whole incident could have gone entirely unreported.

In spite of their efforts, teacher help was not well received in all areas. The Billeting Officer in Exeter wrote to the Town Clerk in November 1940:-

> 'Ref. Rumbold Case.
>
> I would like to point out that the responsibility for billeting evacuated children in suitable billets rests with the billeting officer and NOT with the teachers. While at the same time fully agreeing that any assistance that can be given by the teachers in arranging necessary transfers is very welcome and of great assistance, I am also bound to add that from my own personal knowledge many quite unnecessary transfers have been suggested by teachers, which, if they had been acted upon by the billeting officer would have caused unsettlement in both children and householders, who are entitled to consideration as well as evacuated children'.[269]

Another example comes from the Director of West Sussex Education. On the 23rd September 1939, three weeks after the London schools had been evacuated to his area he held a conference which was attended by seventeen liaison officers, two Government inspectors and three LCC inspectors. The Head-teachers from the evacuated schools were not invited or represented. He is quoted as saying:-

> *'Whilst they are teaching in West Sussex, all London County Council teachers are to be regarded as being on the staff of West Sussex Education Authority, whose decision would be final in any matters affecting staff. Any cases of 'friction' caused by 'difficult' teachers should be reported to the Director who will consult the LCC on the matter'.*[270]

No mention was made of any local teachers being considered 'difficult'.

Discrimination of evacuee teachers was not always the norm. In some areas such as Buckinghamshire, Head-teachers from evacuated schools were invited to attend regular meetings of the Local Education office to discuss general and specific issues relating to evacuation.[271]

In January 1941, the Executive of the National Union of Teachers issued a manifesto which stated that they had under review the impact of the existing war conditions on the educational system within the country and they wished to highlight specific observations for the consideration of all the people responsible for, and interested in, the welfare of schools, both in the evacuated and reception areas. They were particularly concerned with the wide ranging demands now being made:-

> *'...upon the public spirit and voluntary services of the teachers. The care of the children outside school, and the delicate work of billeting, the rest centre and registration office, the National Savings Movement and the ARP and Auxiliary Fire Service and the special police, the Home Guard and the nursing services and many other forms of national effort, have already filled the daily programme of the teacher to overflowing'.*[272]

By 1942, the same concerns were being expressed at local level. There were specific worries about the additional tasks having to be carried out by teachers to the detriment of their actual roles in the classroom. At a meeting of the Dorset Education Committee on Monday 26th January 1942, the teachers' representative, Mr J. M. Warren, was reported as being very outspoken on his views regarding the role of teachers within the County. He asserted

269 Exeter Blitz. Box 76. Devon Record Office.
270 James Roffey. op.cit.
271 E/LB/8/1 op.cit.
272 Quoted in the Dorset County Chronicle & Swanage Times. 2nd January 1941.

that they were becoming *'Honorary Clerks to the Treasury, Assistants to Milk Purveyors, Housemaids, Cooks and Bottle Washers'*.[273]

He directed the attention of the committee to an administrative memorandum which referred to the anxiety of the Board of Education that teachers were being taken from their primary duty of teaching in order to attend to all sorts of things in school hours and the classes which suffered the most were those in the charge of head teachers. Another member of the committee suggested that the WVS might undertake some of the administrative roles in school in order to release the teachers for other duties, but there was no reply to this suggestion. However, it is perhaps significant that when in July 1942, the Government issued a circular requesting that the Local Education Authorities made special arrangements for the care of school children during the holidays to enable mothers to continue in work, the Dorset Education Committee rejected it, albeit by the smallest of majorities. It was argued that teachers were already doing enough to assist the war effort and even if they attended schools during the holidays there was no guarantee that many, if any, of the children would be there.[274]

The problem of time off or holidays for teachers and coverage during pupil holidays had been recognised in 1940. In March of that year Circular 1500 entitled 'Holidays in Reception Areas', reminded local authorities of their responsibilities.

> '........*Authorities are reminded of the suggestion contained in Circular 1482 that the teachers should be released for their holidays in rotation, either before or after the set holiday period, so as to enable a sufficient proportion of them to be available for duty during the period while the schools are closed. It will of course be understood that this course would involve no curtailment of the length of holiday which the teachers would otherwise enjoy.....*'

Teachers Billets

Despite all their help and concern for the billeting of their pupils, there is evidence to suggest that in some areas teachers were responsible for finding their own accommodation after all the children had been housed. The suggestion made in January 1939 that empty school houses could be used for evacuated teachers was not taken up, and in many instances teachers found themselves homeless. Three arrived at Aldeburgh on 1st September 1939, and had housed all the children by 10pm. They then found no billets had been allocated to them. The billeting officer duly employed the Town Crier who went through the town shouting out 'Anyone take in a teacher!' By 11.30 they were given lodgings.[275]

A Head-teacher and his wife described three attempts to find a billet when they were first evacuated. The first time they were somewhat disconcerted when, trying to find a billet on a Sunday, they were met by an irate gentleman who came to the door and fiercely announced...*'I am a Christian, and I am not going to take in Evacuees on a Sunday'* ...and he didn't.

The second attempt was at a very large house standing in its own grounds. They were ushered in by the butler... but half an hour later they were on their way again. They had been given a room and were quietly unpacking when a voice shouted..... '*What's all the noise up there?*' The butler reappeared to tell them that '*Madam requires quiet at all times*'. They decided to leave.

Their third attempt was in a farm cottage where the Head remained but his wife returned home. The cottage had no bathroom and everybody had to wash in the sink.[276]

Teachers billeted in some aristocratic houses were not highly thought of:-

---

273 ibid. 29th January 1942
274 ibid. 9th July 1942.
275 Letter to the author from Win Elliott and Sylvia Lewis. April 1998. MERL Archive
276 WRO/F2/850/1-12. Wiltshire Record Office

'Mr. P. asked Mrs W. the housekeeper, if she had a cloth to put on the teachers' table. When the Lady of the house was approached the Gentleman replied, 'Surely a bloody newspaper is good enough for them!'[277].

Some 'digs' were found on a very ad hoc basis. After five hours of walking around in the rain finding billets for the children a teacher quoted in her diary for Mass-Observation:-

'I was fortunate in securing a billet that night with people who passed us in their car when we were leaving the distribution depot .....These kind people followed us around in their car and relieved the kiddies of their belongings whilst waiting to be fixed up with a billet.. It seemed incredible to me that no arrangements had been made for teachers and we had to depend on people's kindness of heart to supply us with accommodation for the night'.[278]

One teacher describes her plight vividly:-

'Two of us were dumped at 6.30pm at an ancient cottage; its condition and contents shouted of extreme poverty.....We were greeted by our hostess who told us that, the house being near a river and mouldy all through, she had done her best to ensure well-aired beds by keeping them in the garden all day, it had been raining since 11am!

The railway lay nearby but she knew that we should soon get used to waking up at 5am when the milk train thundered by.

We sat on the bed in the 'sitting room', spreading a mackintosh first, to have some rations, our hostess meanwhile entertaining us. It appeared that she was disappointed at receiving only two teachers; she had hoped for a third, as there was another spare bedroom, 'Too cold to sleep in' and therefore used for storing apples; but it 'would have been so nice to put a teacher in there'.

A bottle of milk was placed on the table. Later, considerably later, a cup and saucer followed. But...'Don't use that cup till I get a cloth and wipe it out. I'm not much of a housewife and nothing in this house is over clean'.

Next, a cat was brought in, with the comment... 'I'm sorry to say this animal has been distributing fleas all over the place, and the worst of it is my eyes are so bad. Of course when they jump on me, I can catch them...like that, suddenly slapping her shin. Lest the beds should need nocturnal slapping, however, she produced a tin of 'Flit'.

The curtain fell on our first billet. At 7pm we flitted'.[279]

Religious Considerations

Some schools from London contained a significant number of Jewish children which meant that some of their school holidays were different to take account of the Feast of the Weeks (May-June) and Feast of the Passover (March-April) and The Feast of the Trumpets, Yom Kippur and Feast of the Tabernacles (September-October). This was acceptable in London but caused some administrative problems in the reception areas. The teacher concerned with a group who went to Buckinghamshire was very annoyed at the short notice she was given in September 1940 to move the holiday from October 3rd, authorised by Buckinghamshire's LEA, to the 30th September. Despite seeking permission earlier in the month she was not given permission until Saturday 28th

277 ibid
278 Evacuation Box 1. File E. Mass-Observation Archive and cited in Wartime Women ed. Dorothy Sheridan. 1990 p65
279 WRO/F2/850/1-12

September which meant she had to notify all the children and foster parents by visiting their billets and cancelling the weekly milk.[280]

Day to day organisation within schools was also affected by other religious denominations. In Cornwall, which was predominantly Methodist, there was a concerted effort to accommodate all religious beliefs.[281] The Wynford Bellin Baptist Church in Truro sent an open letter to the West Briton on the 4th September 1939 asking host families to check whether or not their evacuees had attended a Baptist Sunday School or church and if so to contact them, or if not, to ensure they attended a Sunday School of some kind.[282] In St Austell a man was sent around the streets with a sandwich board bearing the names of all the Sunday Schools in the area.[283]

The log-book for the Idbury and Fifield C of E school in Oxfordshire indicates that on a number of occasions Roman Catholic children did not attend assembly and the children from St. Anthony's School, Forest Gate were not allowed to attend. This is another example of an administrative oversight which begs the question.... why evacuate a complete Roman Catholic school to a small Church of England village school.[284]

Seventeen Roman Catholic evacuees stayed at Panhydrock House near Bodmin, Cornwall from September 1940. The Agar-Robartes family set up a small chapel in their Gatehouse and arranged for a Catholic Priest to visit to give religious instruction to the children. However, they had to get special dispensation from the Pope to allow the priest to eat and drink before all his services were completed in his parish, because the extra journey to the house resulted in a 30 mile trip on his bicycle.[285]

For one particular evacuee being a Roman Catholic had an advantage. He was the only one at the village school in Shipton and was exempt from attending morning assembly. As a result, he had a lie-in every morning and did not have to attend school until 9.40am.[286]

One particular Council, Cricklade and Wootten Bassett RDC, wrote to the Ministry of Health in March 1940 expressing serious concerns about the wisdom of sending Roman Catholic children to mainly Protestant areas, or to Protestant families, with the comment that *'Roman Catholic children and Protestant householders do not harmonise'*[287]

This difference in religion created serious problems in North Wales where many children from Catholic backgrounds were billeted with Calvinist Methodists. Many local people objected to Priests and teachers from Catholic schools trying to impose restrictions on how they treated their evacuees, and a great deal of correspondence was sent to local councils in an attempt to rectify the situation. This disharmony was particularly difficult to overcome in some areas where the authorities had been forced to initiate compulsory billeting. The Evacuation Officer in the Aled Rural District reported:-

> *'The Billeting Officers generally, whilst disliking the task, are prepared to carry out these duties and to use compulsory powers, providing that Protestant children are the only ones sent to the district. They all explain that householders will not, under any circumstances, receive Catholic children into their homes again, and the Billeting Officers have threatened to resign rather than use these compulsory powers as their sympathies are all with the householders. They all emphasise that this attitude is not the result of religious bigotry, but because of the interference and religious intolerance of the Catholic priests and teachers accompanying the children'.*[288]

In some areas Protestant hosts in Wales were chastised by Catholic priests if their charges did not attend mass. This in itself created problems as there were few Catholic churches in the Principality, and often, where they

280 ibid. 30th September 1939.
281 For a detailed account of Jewish children evacuated to Cornwall see....From East End to Lands End. Susan Soynika.
282 West Briton. 4th September 1939
283 'Evacuation Sidelights'. Cornish Guardian. 7th September 1939. Dormer. C. Evacuation to Cornwall. Dissertation. MERL Archive
284 Idbury and Fifield C.of E. Primary School. Log Book. Oxford Record Office.
285 Dormer. Op cit.
286 Letter to author from John William O'Connor. MERL Archive
287 WRO/F2/850 1-12.
288Denbighshire County Council File 35/4. Letter to W. Brookes Parry to William Jones. 24th Jan 1941.

were available, they were many miles away. If hosts complied with the Priest's requests this often meant them foregoing their own Chapel attendance on a Sunday. In April 1940, the Clerk of the Nant Conway RDC reported:-

> *'...during the last evacuation, children were made to walk as much as eight miles to attend Mass on Sunday mornings and I consider this a hardship on the younger children to have to do this in all weathers'.*[289]

One priest in Liverpool went so far as instructing the parents in his parish whose children had been evacuated to North Wales to bring them home alleging that:-

> *'...any physical danger they might incur in Liverpool was trifling when compared with the spiritual danger they ran by remaining'.*[290]

Sometimes attempts were made to transfer evacuees on religious grounds, but in November 1939 the Clerk to the Denbighshire County Council wrote to Evan Evans, Evacuation Officer for Wales stating:-

> *'I am tired of these attempts to move children simply because they belong to one particular faith and intend to take as firm a stand as I can against any further nonsense of this kind. I hope I can have your support'.*[291]

During the second evacuation in 1940, slightly more care was taken to place Roman Catholics in areas where facilities were available for them. A memorandum simply entitled Plan IV. was issued by E.M.Rich of the London County Council in May 1940 with a specific paragraph relating to Roman Catholic children; *'The Roman Catholic authorities have asked that RC (sic) children may be kept together and billeted in areas where there are Catholic communities. For this reason RC children are being assembled at particular points in London, and are being entrained for places named by me as being suitable by the RC authorities'.*[292]

But, in truth, the situation should not have arisen during the first scheme. On 2nd May 1939 a representative from Liverpool Council, H.W. Lowe, addressed a conference in Caernarfon where he told the evacuating authorities in the reception areas to expect 30% Catholics in the total of 24,000 evacuees allocated to the area.[293]

Organisation and Extra-Curricular

In Dorset the two shift system had been introduced at the very beginning of the war, but by the end of October pupils had been absorbed into the existing system and less than 20 Dorset schools were providing full time education.[294]

In districts where the number of evacuees under the Government scheme was substantial, such as in Berkshire where there were 89 schools involved, and where there were teachers to take charge of these children, the Head teachers of the reception schools were asked to get in touch with their evacuated colleagues and arrange for the reopening of schools on a double-shift system.[295] This shift system resulted in local children attending school from 8.30am to 12.30pm while the schools from Greater London were given the afternoon period from 1.00pm to 4.30pm. This plan was to start on the 12th September, after schools had reopened after the delayed summer break. Later, the time of 1.00 was changed to 1.30 to allow for mid-day meal arrangements in the children's billets. The only other time changes were made during the winter when afternoon school finished earlier at 3.30, or when staff with particular expertise, were recalled to London to help out in schools there thus reducing the number of staff in the evacuated schools.

---

289 Clerk of Nant Conway RDC to C.F.Mott. Evacuation File. 23rd April 1940 Caernarvon Record Office. cited Wallis p165.
290 Padley & Cole. Evacuation Survey. London. 1940. p236-7.
291 Denbighshire County Council.File 8/1. Letter from W.Jones to E. Evans 13th November. 1939. Caernarvon Record Office.
292 E.M.Rich.LCC. May 15th 1940
293 North Wales Chronicle 12th May 1939.
294 Dorset County Council. Education Committee 31st October 1939.
295 TNA.ED.138/34

As an example, the following timetable was drawn up by staff at the Aston Clinton evacuated school just a few days after their arrival in Buckinghamshire in 1939. They were to have the afternoon shift. It is interesting to note that despite their new countryside environment there is little evidence here of the pedagogic enlightenment suggested by educationalists at the time.

1.00 - 1.05	Registration
1.05 - 1.35	Scripture or Religious Instruction*
1.35 - 2.15	Arithmetic
2.15 - 2.45	Geography or History or English
2.45 - 3.00	Recreation
3.00 - 3.30	English or History or Geography
3.30 - 4.00	Physical Training
4.00 - 4.30	English or Nature Study or Art

The host school had a very similar morning timetable from 9.00 - 12.30.

*There were many Jewish children in this party of evacuees, Party 941, so later in the term permission was sought from the Governors to provide Hebrew lessons during the day instead of Scripture.[296]

There were unforeseen difficulties in operating a 'double-shift' pattern. A resident teacher in Wales working this system wrote in a log book on 19th February 1940:-

> *'Working the afternoon shift this week. The children arrive in school tired out after playing all morning and in no frame of mind for schoolwork'.*[297]

The following account from Mavis Cordery provides an interesting insight into the problems such school sharing could create:-

> *'...some children were billeted in the Lower Caversham area. Most of these were from the Rays Central Boys School. We were told that the Headteacher, Mr Fabian, his six staff and the boys, were to share our school. There were too many to absorb into the school and they wanted to stay as one unit, so we had to work out a sharing system. Basically, we had the school premises for the morning and they had the afternoon. This did not mean that we had half-day schooling. We were told that we had to fit in wherever we could and run informal club sessions if normal teaching was impossible. The first week I remember one afternoon having to occupy more than 60 girls under the shelter of the bicycle sheds....we also got round the problem by having large organised games sessions in the afternoon'.*[298]

Mavis went on to say that despite the pressure on the buildings, the schools eventually got on well together and began to do joint ventures such as school plays. She recalled that one of the biggest problems throughout the whole war was the lack of coal and consequently, having to teach in school buildings which were freezing cold during the winter. The head-teacher drew up a staff rota to lead the whole pupil cohort in ten minutes of physical exercise every morning before school, in order to warm up.[299]

---

296 E/LB/8/1. op. cit. 17th October 1939.
297 Caernarfon British School. Log Book 1910-1942. 19th February. 1940. CRO.
298 Mavis Cordery op.cit.
299 ibid

Heating schools was always a problem. The log book of the Commercial Street School contains many entries made during the winters of 1940 and 1941 about lack of coal. On some occasions the school was closed because they had no coal at all and the fire had gone out.[300]

Some small one or two- room village schools relied entirely on open coal fires for their heat. Entries in the log book of St. Matthew's Infant School, Buckley, indicate that the school was always cold and coal was not being delivered. On 22nd January 1940, the thermometer registered 30 degrees of frost...inside the school! The heating boiler cracked...but school continued.[301]

An anonymous ex-teacher, evacuated with his school to a small village north of Newbury in Berkshire, describes the problems he had to face when sharing the facilities of the existing village primary school with only 19 on roll:-

> *'A muddy path led up past the churchyard to a brick Gothic school-house, with narrow pointed windows and an immensely high-pitched roof. There was a tiny dirt yard, divided by a fence into Boys and Girls, with rudimentary lavatories. The school had no water supply and every morning the bigger boys fetched buckets of water from a horse tough outside the church......It was to be one of the coldest winters of the century and even the autumn chills presented difficulties. The winter practice had been to gather the nineteen village children around the stoves, sending boys out 'sticking' to keep up the blaze, but with 50 children now in the school the outer rings were fated to shiver, though they sat in overcoats and gloves. Early in the new year an extended cold spell cut off the village for ten days. Every pump and many of the wells froze and food had to be brought from Newbury by sledge. School was impossible; the boys could find no wood for the fires and even the ink froze in the inkwells. We gave up and took the children out for snow fights and sledging'.*[302]

Despite Mavis Cordery's example of her own school and the evacuated school working together, the general lack of cohesion between establishments was seen as a problem in Berkshire as early as October 1939 and the County Council issued the following statement about their education policy and billeting of evacuated schools:-

> *'Various adjustments have been made since the schools were originally reopened and efforts are now being made to arrange for full-time instruction wherever possible. For this system to be worked effectively there must be a willingness on the part of the Berkshire and evacuated teachers to work together and so bring about the ultimate absorption of the London school children within our own school organisation. In this way, identity of the evacuated schools must disappear and this will be the logical outcome of the impossibility of retaining these schools as separate units'.*[303]

The authorities in Buckinghamshire took this one stage further and appointed evacuated teachers to their own county schools. The authority's own girls' school in Aston Clinton lost a teacher, Mrs Staples, in November 1939 and it was suggested that because the evacuated boys' school had fewer numbers, they could ask one of their staff to apply for the vacancy. This was agreed and a Mrs Webb joined the staff of the girls' school on the 11th December 1939, though, technically, she remained a member of the LCC Evacuee Party.[304]

All these basic administrative and physical arrangements took precedence over everything else and allowed little time for educational reform to take place. Also it needs to be remembered that opportunities for change in curriculum areas such as science and nature study were already predetermined by the local environment and in many rural areas science would have been agriculturally biased.

---

300 E/LB/8/1. op cit. 31st March 1941
301 E/LB11/5 Flintshire Record Office. Hawarden.
302 Anonymous Account. Lent by P. Farley-Rutter from family papers.
303 Berkshire County Council. C/CL/C1/1/42
304 1941LCC Evacuee Party 941.Aston Clinton Girls School. Log Book. Bucks.Record Office. E/LB/8/1. 28th November 1939.

Some schools actually encouraged pupils to work on farms in the local area but not necessarily from an academic or educational motive, more one of economics and giving the pupils something to do. Some of this extra work was 'suggested' by local authorities:-

> '19th June 1940. Following instructions, enquiries were made at the farms in the neighbourhood, whether children can help with the work in the fields. One farmer accepted and a dozen older children went this morning to weed.
>
> 20th June 1940. 10 children worked in the garden of Buckland Vicarage weeding.[305]
>
> 6th June 1941. The senior children spent all week on the local farm planting potatoes.[306]
>
> 30th September 1941. The senior children spent a lot of time this month on the local farm picking and bagging potatoes.[307]
>
> 18th June 1942. The First team of 6 children over the age of 12 began work in agriculture. 3 hours per day every four days'.[308]

This introduction to agriculture must have been of benefit to some evacuees as this newspaper snippet would indicate:-

EVACUEES CHOOSE FARM LIFE

Five evacuees from the London area who left school at Christmas are taking up farm work in the Okehampton district and have abandoned all intention of returning to city life.[309]

This link between the evacuees and the land was an important one and even resulted in a propaganda film called '*Spring Offensive*'[310] which although ostensibly focussed on getting redundant farmland into production, included the bi-line of an evacuee who is shown taking a very serious interest in farming matters. At the beginning of the war even *'The Farmers Weekly'* got involved. In January 1940, it ran a 'Children's Competition' where country children had to describe an evacuee they had got to know, and explain what they thought of the countryside. (At the same time 'town' children were asked to describe their country hosts.) Some of the replies to a fictitious 'Mrs Day' were interesting and in the February 1940 edition she replied through her regular column in the magazine;

> *'The descriptions of your city and country friends have almost all been good, some of them have been very lively and entertaining indeed. It has been interesting to discover the way you think about one another, and the sort of things you notice; and it is especially interesting to learn from these competition entries of yours that so many of the children who war has sent into the countryside are liking it so much that they have no wish ever to live in the town again. Most of the country children say that the town visitors are very quick to learn new things such as looking after animals, even how to drive cattle, and milk and feed cows and clean rabbits and so on.....'*[311]

Some evacuees were also allowed to work on farms, usually during the harvest period, but sometimes throughout the whole year.

---

305 E/LB/8/1 19th & 20th June 1940
306 ibid. 6th June 1940
307 E/LB/6/3 Bucks.Record Office. 30th September 1941.
308 ibid. 18th June 1942.
309 Dorset County Chronicle & Swanage Times. 15th January 1942.
310 Ministry of Information 1941. It deals with the ploughing up of non-productive land and how some local farmers and officials were given powers to confiscate land not being used effectively
311 Farmers Weekly. February 2nd 1940 p47

'The children are helping magnificently with the wartime harvest. The high-school girl on holiday leads the wagon and the evacuee children are all doing their bit; all helping somehow'.[312]

In 1940, because of difficulty in finding people to work on the land, one county council decided to give 'sympathetic consideration' to all reasonable applications for permission to withdraw children from school to undertake agricultural and similar work immediately they reached the age of 14.[313] In February 1940, the Westmoreland County Education Committee drew up a register of evacuees who had arrived in the county from Newcastle and South Shields and shown such an interest in farming that they had expressed a wish to remain in the area as farm workers when they reached school leaving age, rather than return home.[314] A number of the evacuees who went to live on farms actually became very interested in all aspects of agriculture. After they reached school leaving age some returned to work as paid farm labourers and as a result a few actually inherited the farm from their hosts.[315]

It was not only the children who were wanted for work. As early as 8th September 1939, the following advertisement paid for by various manufacturers in the area was placed in the Dorset Daily Echo asking evacuee adults to consider local work.

'NOTICE TO EVACUATED PEOPLE

The Bridport Manufacturers Association feel that it would be the desire of all those capable of working to be given the opportunity to render service of National Importance rather than do nothing at this time of emergency. Work of National Importance is available for all able-bodied workers willing to learn. Will the general public please make this fact as widely known as possible?'[316]

City Schools

While many city school children and teachers were being sent to the country, the school buildings they left behind were closed and remained so until November 1939, but even then 50% of the children in London were not to receive full time education until mid-1940. In the designated evacuation and neutral areas of England and Wales approximately 2000 schools were either requisitioned totally or used by various organisations at different times of the day; 1692 were used by the Civil Defence, the Auxiliary Fire Service had taken over 250, a further 100 were designated as Wardens' posts, and 213 by the military authorities. The remaining 70 were taken over by groups such as the Red Cross for first aid posts, decontamination centres, or in some cases, allocated as temporary mortuaries.[317]

The figures were obtained in December 1939 when a survey of education provision was carried out in all areas of the country and according to Titmuss, are not totally reliable hence the approximation.[318]

The effect of the government's decision to keep some schools closed within the designated evacuated areas during the evacuation process did not only affect the capital. The situation was also of some concern to the Coventry[319] authorities, especially as the actual number of those taking advantage of the evacuation scheme was very low. On the 29th September 1939, the Director of Education in the city, Frank Harrod, sent the following letter to the Board of Education in London.

312 Mrs Frank Carling in Farmers Weekly September 13th 1940 p45
313 Farmers Weekly February 2nd 1940 p25
314 Farmers Weekly February 23rd 1940 p26
315 Personal interviews. This usually happened when the host children were not interested in farming and the business was passed on to the evacuee (now a paid farm-worker) instead.
316 Dorset Daily Echo. 8th September 1939
317 T.L.Crosby. op.cit p93
318 ibid. p94
319 I am indebted to Daniel Bate for allowing me unrestricted access to his research notes on wartime Coventry

'Sir,

My authority is gravely concerned about the education position with regard to public elementary schools within the evacuable area of the city.

As a result of the first evacuation carried out on September 10th and 11th, 2547 children were evacuated from this area under the government scheme and 1035 have been evacuated under private arrangements. Consequently, nearly 6000 children are still in the evacuable area and there are also nearly 3000 that previously attended schools within this area, but reside outside.

My authority would like to know whether there is likely to be any change in the policy of the Board that no schools inside the evacuable area shall be opened for the duration of the war and, if this policy is to remain, what advice the Board can give as to the provision of education facilities for these 6000 children.

I am further instructed to point out that the majority of schools in the evacuable area could be made reasonably safe by the provision of ARP trenches or shelters for use by the children during school hours, and it would be a very serious matter if these 6000 are to be deprived of any form of education for the whole duration of the war.

My authority would be glad if the Board would give their approval to the provision of the necessary protection in these schools...where it is possible, in order that educational facilities may be re-started for some of these children'[320]

No such approval was forthcoming, but the Council had made arrangements for tutorial systems to be in place in two schools, John Gulson and Wheatley Street, and the establishment of a boys club at another, Broad Street Senior Boys. The Stoke Park Senior Girls School planned to open on a group system basis allowing 50 pupils to be in the building at any one time, but even with such good intentions the girls would only receive about 50 minutes of teaching per day.[321]

Thirty-seven school departments had opened in the neutral areas of the city on a voluntary basis with 8,319 out of 11,137 on the registers. By the 31st October 1939, 33 halls and other buildings, as well as 83 private houses, were being used for educational purposes.[322]

Compulsory education was not restored in Coventry until 12th February 1940 when 33 full-time schools and 8 half-time schools were opened in the neutral area, together with 7 full-time and 2 half-time in the evacuation areas.

In March 1940, Coventry's Education Committee reported on the numbers in schools on the 19th February 1940 and the projected figures for 1st April 1940.

Number of Coventry children receiving:	19th February 1940	1st April 1940
Full-time instruction	11076	20660
Part-time instruction	4837	2885
Less than half-time instruction	5317	230
Home Service	316	50
No instruction	2420	150
TOTAL	**23966**	**23975**
Evacuees in Government Scheme	950	927
Private Evacuees	250	230

320 TNA ED 134/153
321 D.Bate op cit
322 Coventry City Minutes. Education Committee 13th December 1939.

Number of Coventry children receiving:	19th February 1940	1st April 1940
TOTAL	**1200**	**1157**
OVERALL TOTAL	**25166**	**25132**

In April 1941, it was estimated that 290,000 children in England and Wales were not receiving full time education, though some areas, such as Coventry, had some success in ensuring that all children had at least a semblance of education provision. As the table above would indicate members of the Education Committee in the city set themselves the target of increasing the number in full-time and part-time education. In reality, they did not achieve their target of 20660, but did completely eradicate the numbers of those receiving no education at all.

Number of children receiving	By report issued on the 17th April 1940	(Provisional Targets set in March 1940)
Full-time	17822	(20660)
Part-time	4637	(2885)
Less than half-time	503	(230)
Home Service	178	(50)
No Education	0	(150)
Total	**23140**	**(23975)** [323]

Coventry was also able to report that 81 of their schools were now open; 63 on a full-time basis and 9 half-time. By July these numbers had increased to 68 full-time, 4 half-time and 9 partly full-time and the number of children now receiving education of some kind rose to 24,614. [324]

Unfortunately, all the work that went into providing an education for the city children, came to an abrupt halt when Coventry was bombed on 14th November 1940 when 25 schools were damaged, 9 of them severely.[325]

According to Daniel Bate it is very difficult to gauge the effect of the measures initiated by the Coventry City Council on the education of the children remaining in the area. However, a report on *'The incidence of backwardness in Coventry Schools'* delivered to the Education Committee in January 1944, indicated that there were around 3000 'backward' (*sic*) children in the city, equating to around 13.5% of the school population at that time. Although the term 'backward' is not defined, and there are no accompanying statistics, the reasons given included; low intelligence, social and war conditions, emotional maladjustment and irregular schooling.[326]

There had been a great deal of confusion over how many children attended school during the winter of 1940-41 and, according to Titmuss, the Ministry of Health, Board of Education and the LCC could not agree to an accurate figure.[327] The LCC put the figure at 81,000 which was considered too low by the Minister of Health.

But, as has been suggested earlier, where education *was* available, both in the cities and the reception areas, the question of class sizes became important and although, in general, they were considered by some of the host schools to be large, they were usually no bigger than the pre-war classes which, in many inner-city schools had numbered more than 40 pupils. But there were of course exceptions. By October 1943, Liverpool had 600 classes in elementary schools with more than 50 children in each, compared with 293 classes of the same size in 1938. Sheffield, which had had 2 classes containing more than 50 in 1938, reported 406 in September 1944, 60 of which continued with more than 60 pupils[328].

Further evidence of the pressure of numbers can be found in Coventry where teachers were divided between the City and the reception areas.

323 ibid 17th April. 1940
324.ibid 17th July 1940
325 Bate op cit.
326 ibid.
327 Titmuss op.cit.p58
328 ibid. p406

POSITION IN COVENTRY				
	1939	1942	August 1943	December 1943
No.of children on roll.	25842	20794	22172	22541
No.of Assistant Teachers	661	518	543	546
No.of Head Teachers	82	80	79	80
Total No. of Teachers	743	598	622	626
Pupil/Teacher Ratio	39.1	40.1	40.8	41.3
Pupil/Teacher Ratio, including Heads.	34.7	34.8	35.6	36.0
No. of classes over 50	45	62	55	75
POSITION IN RECEPTION AREAS, including CAMP SCHOOLS				
No on Roll	-	1300	809	720
No. of Coventry teachers	-	56	33	29
Pupil/Teacher ratio, including heads.	-	24.5	24.5	24.8 [329]

In the light of this evidence, and the present debates on school class sizes, it is worth considering the recommendations made by the members of the Barnett House Study Group in 1947, who researched a group of London children billeted in Oxford. They suggested that *'the educational value of small classes was confirmed beyond a shadow of a doubt by the experience of evacuated schools'*.[330]

It is also important to note that because of the general dislocation of the educational structures and practices, it was generally the less able pupils who suffered. This was due in no small measure to the fact that the 320 special classes in London County Council schools, which had been established to deal with those pupils with special needs, were abandoned during the war years.[331]

Also many more able pupils, such as the author Bob Holman, failed their examinations for the grammar schools because they were so far behind in their studies and in some cases were kept down a year in the Primary School in order to catch up with some of their contemporaries.[332]

Others, including James Roffey and his brother John, returned to an education system in London sadly lacking in the basic necessities in terms of buildings, equipment and teachers. What teachers in the city were faced with was the additional task of bringing children from various ranges of experience up to a common level. No concessions were made to the pre-war examination system and pupils who had been away for some years now found themselves having to sit the examinations for the 'Central' school where they could stay until 16, or if they failed, leave school at 14.

Unsurprisingly, for many the examination was a waste of time. In most cases the authorities refused to agree to the re-examination of those who had failed, and the children were forced to leave school and find work. This had a very serious effect on the future lives of many evacuees. These children had been uprooted from their homes and schools, had their education disrupted through no fault of their own because in many areas no suitable provision had been made, and yet were expected to compete on equal terms with those who had not had their education interrupted and against examination criteria which had been established pre-war. The Board of Education would not compromise standards during wartime. In a document 'Syllabuses and Examination Questions' it stated that *'no general reduction in the standard of difficulty of questions is called for.....'*.[333]. However, in a Circular from the Ministry of Health to the LEAs, it was said that *'.....In the event of invasion, schools in the immediate area of operations and in areas immediately adjacent, will be closed'*.[334]

In a report to the Education (General) Sub-Committee on 13th September 1943, the Chief Inspector of Schools summed up the effect of four years of war on London schools. Although much of what he reported could easily have been said about many schools across the country he stated that:-

---

329 Coventry City Council Minutes. Education Committee 12 Jan. 1944.
330 Barnett House Study Group. London Children in Wartime Oxford. pub. Oxford University Press. London. 1947. p112. For more forward looking educational recommendations from this group see Appendix 9.
331 Titmuss. op.cit. p409
332 Bob Holman. Former Professor of Social Administration. University of Bath. Lecture at the Imperial War Museum. 18th October 1996.
333 S. Brown. Op cit
334 Circ.2319. Ministry of Health to LEAs 22 March 1941. TNA.ED138/148

'Many schools had lost their identity. Re-evacuation, the lack of continuity in school buildings, school staff and syllabuses had made educating the child very difficult'.[335]

Under the circumstances it came as no surprise to the Inspectorate when a test given to a representative sample of 3,000, 13 and 14 year olds in 1943 when compared with results of a 1924 cohort, indicated that:-

'...while children could still write lively and intelligent compositions, spelling was definitely worse than corresponding pupils in 1924'[336]

Education: The Extras

' The Development in the provision of meals and milk at school expressed something very close to a revolution in the attitude of parents, teachers and children to a scheme which only a few years earlier had not been regarded with much respect or sympathy. In place of a relief measure, tainted with the poor law, it became a social service, fused into school life, and making its own contribution to the physical nuture of the children and to their social education...'.[337]

SWANAGE

THE COMMUNAL FEEDING CENTRE FOR EVACUATED CHILDREN

'Voluntary help is urgently needed at the above centre opening on June 19th at the Congregational Schoolroom, High Street, Swanage. Any person willing to help with this war work please write to the County Canteens Organiser, Dorchester'.[338]

School closure in the cities had other effects not often considered by social historians, and certainly not referred to in text books and other resources available in schools. Those with jobs outside the classroom such as dinner ladies, caretakers and cleaners, were no longer required within the school system and this led to job losses, although in time many were re-employed in war related industries. Also the social services linked to the schools in effect ceased to exist and, during the initial stages of evacuation there was no school meal provision which many of the poorer children remaining in, and returning to, London relied on for their daily nourishment.

In 1939, approximately 10,000 children in the London County Council elementary schools had school dinners and 60% of these were provided free. After some of the children were beginning to return during the 'Phoney War' period, school domestic science classes were used to provide meals. In September 1940, 1,700 daily meals were delivered by central kitchens to those schools which remained open, or had not been damaged or requisitioned, and were now delivering lessons. However, because of the second phase of evacuation which took place during the Blitz on London, the numbers of dinners required had fallen to approximately 500 by November 1940.

During the early part of the war the attitude of both central and local government towards school meal provision altered drastically. Before the war, school dinners were provided for those who were genuinely undernourished and who were thought to be in greatest need. Pre-war research carried out by Sir John Boyd Orr, had shown that the diet of the poorest 10% of the population was deficient in nearly all the known vitamins.[339]

In 1941, the Vitamin Welfare Scheme provided either, free orange juice and cod-liver oil to expectant mothers and young children, or Vitamins A and D as alternatives. There was also a concerted advertising campaign throughout the war under *'BBC: The Kitchen Front'*, which was broadcast on the radio Tuesday-Friday at

335 Report to Education (General) Sub-Committee. Ed. No. 208 (addendum) 13th September 1943. cited. Titmuss. op.cit. p408
336 ibid. p408
337 Titmuss. R. Problems of Social Policy. HMSO 1951 p510
338 Dorset Daily Echo. 15th June 1940.
339 Bob Holman. The Evacuation. A Very British Revolution. Lion.1995.p117

8.15am, and *'Food Facts'* which appeared in the newspapers. Both extolled the virtues of Orange Juice and Cod Liver Oil and explained to parents where they could get such commodities.

FOOD FACTS
MUM! MY ORANGE JUICE. MY COD LIVER OIL.
MEMO FOR MUM!

You can buy continued health for your child at any welfare centre or distributing centre. In exchange for a few pence and the coupons in your child's ration book you can get his orange juice and cod liver oil.

Don't get just the orange juice and forget about the cod liver oil - one is just as necessary as the other. Think of Orange Juice and Cod Liver Oil together as you think of pepper and salt, oil and vinegar, mustard and cress. Think of them as the two-part health scheme which your baby needs.'[340]

This practice of issuing Orange Juice was eventually banned in the early 1960s because there was thought to be too much emphasis on Vitamin D, and many doctors were worried about too much absorption of calcium which could lead to hardening of the arteries.[341]

After the first evacuation, during which they had provided those evacuees without food with packed lunches for the journey, the main school-meals kitchens closed until January 1940. Four others opened later and by June 1940, 2,000 school meals were being supplied in 70 centres located in schools. Later, in 1941, the School Meals Service was taken over by the Londoners' Meals Service[342] This had been established by the Ministry of Agriculture and Food (MAF) in September 1940 following the heavy air raids in London, to control emergency feeding centres and to provide school meals for the non-evacuated children who needed them. 2,160 Centres had opened by September 1943, a long way short of the intended 10,000 but nonetheless they served approximately 6,000 meals a day[343].

The service started a successful campaign to persuade as many children as possible to eat at school. It is not an insignificant fact that the Londoners' Meals Service also ran the 'British Restaurants'[344] where a three course meal, including soup, braised tongue and a pudding, cost 9d.[345] Lord Woolton, Minister of Food, was photographed eating such a meal and the caption read *'Those who want luxury feeding in these days are outsiders.'* Prices tended to vary slightly so dinner tickets were issued to those having school dinners which could then be exchanged for a meal at any of the British restaurants. By February 1941, more than 2,000 meals per day were being provided to children. Every child was now entitled to a school meal and, if parents were unable to pay, the whole, or part of the cost was returned to them.[346]

Figures for the period October 1941-February 1945 indicate the overall success of the scheme. Note that % is that of the total on roll.[347]

Date	Meals	inc. Free	Number of Roll
Oct. 1941	9,644 (7.25%)	350 (0,02%)	133,000
Oct. 1942	39,836 (17.9%)	2,355 (1.06%)	221,000
Oct. 1943	62,673 (25%)	3,951 (1.58%)	249,800
Feb. 1944	65,941 (26.5%)	4,415 (1.77%)	248,400
Feb. 1945	51,512 (27%)	3,279 (1,72%)	190,600

340 Dorset County Chronicle & Swanage Times. 27th January 1944.
341 Interview with Dr. Robin Borthwick. General Practitioner. Theale Medical Centre. 21st September 1996. MERL Archive
342 LCC/RC/GEN. London Metropolitan Archive.
343 A. Calder. People's War. op. cit. p446
344 The Civic Restaurants Act, 1947 allowed local authorities to continue the provision of this service under normal peace-time conditions provided it was not run at a loss.
345 Philip Ziegler. 'London at War' Sinclair-Stevenson. 1995. p90
346 Samways. We think you ought to go!. GLRO. 1995 p39
347 ibid.

The significance of October 1941 lies in the fact that this is when it was decided that rest centres where meals were provided, should also be used as much as possible for the provision of *school* meals. At the same time the Londoner's Meals Service took over the central kitchen which meant that the education authorities were only responsible for the collection of dinner moneys and the supervising of pupils during meal times. Also the grant from central government for the provision of school meals increased to between 70-90% over the country, London receiving 70%. This resulted in a rapid extension of the service, helped additionally by the fact that all school meals equipment was provided free of charge.

In January 1942, the service was extended when a 'family rate' was introduced. This meant that for those families in need, the first child would eat for 4d, the second for 3d and any subsequent children for 2d. In April 1942, all these prices were increased by 1d to cover the additional costs of specific ingredients within the meals.[348]

By 1944, almost 66,000 children were having school meals and the role of the teachers became a supervisory one, a role which incidentally was not relinquished until the change of teachers pay and conditions in the 1990s. The pressure on working mothers to be out of the house during the school holidays, resulted in a limited school meals service in the London area during the recess. During the period 1940-45, the numbers of those children having free or subsidised meals rose and this could possibly be used as an indicator of positive social change whereby those in the community who were in need of help now received it.[349]

However, concerns were expressed in the Dorset County Chronicle and Swanage Times on 20th November 1941, about the anomaly of unaccompanied children not getting free meals and, inadvertently pointing out the fact, that the poorer hosts were still bearing most of the responsibility for looking after evacuees. Under the headline 'End this Anomaly of Evacuee Payments' the correspondent, Frank Lloyd, questioned the scheme.

> 'Sir, I want to call the attention of your wide awake paper to the plight of a class of children who are getting a raw deal in the evacuation scheme.
>
> In the hundreds of community feeding centres which are springing up all over the country with up to 90% of Government grant, children who are evacuated with their parents are given free meals if they cannot afford to pay. These children also get free milk in schools on the same basis.
>
> Why then the strange anomaly in Government orders which expressly excludes the child evacuated without a parent from free meals and free milk?
>
> The unaccompanied child, often lonely, and in many cases unwanted in its new home, is made inevitably unpopular and unwelcome by bringing with it a Government allowance as low as 8s 6d/10s 6d for a single child. Parents remain responsible for clothing this war-waif, but everything else it needs is supposed to be found out of 8s 6d a week. Moreover, the Government claims that 3 shillings of this sum is a lodging allowance to put the child on par with the accompanied child for whom 3 shillings is drawn. We are thus left with the astonishing Government attitude that a child who is supposed to be fed on as little as 5s 6d a week must not receive free meals and school milk, however poor they might be.
>
> The Government order says it is assumed that the householder who takes in such a child can afford to provide it with midday meals and milk. Why? The assumption in many cases is false and the 8s 6d child is a burden to many homes.
>
> The child's food, washing and wear and tear of bedding and furniture, cannot be met out of such a mean allowance in these days.

---

348 ibid.p40

349 Health of the School Child: report of the Chief Medical Officer at the Ministry of Education, for the years 1939 - 45. HMSO. London. 1947. p23

> And this is the child who must not get a free meal at the community centre, although a child next door who may have a mother to see to its welfare can be fed for nothing, if there is poverty.
>
> Surely, all Government-evacuated children should be entitled to free midday meals at a time when it is declared policy to augment the rations of the poorer people by community feeding. At least if some of the poor are entitled to free food, all should be. Free meals and milk would bring that miserly 8s 6d to a more reasonable figure. It is well known to billeting officers that evacuees tend to congregate in poor homes. Many well to do people are able to evade their obligations, others deliberately make the evacuees so uncomfortable that they leave. I can quote cases of both.
>
> The evacuee child is therefore often in a home where it is difficult to make ends meet before he came. And such a child, with no one to stand up for him, is supposed to be fed on 5s 6d a week'.[350]

Communal Feeding Centre Officials in some areas took their responsibility for providing meals for evacuees very seriously. As early as November 1939, the Dorset Education Committee established communal feeding centres in Dorchester and other villages in the County. The planning and implementation was the responsibility of the County's Communal Feeding Centres; Canteen organiser Miss A.M.Anderson, who had been appointed on the 18th September at an annual salary of £200 plus travel. The idea behind the scheme was that those children whose foster parents were out at work all day, or had other reasons for being unable to provide a mid-day meal during the week, should be able to have a lunch at a communal dining room. By November approximately 200 evacuees living locally had used the centres. The cost per child was 4d a day or 1s 8d a week which came out of the allowance paid to hosts. For their money each child could receive two helpings of each course which included at least four ounces of meat per helping and, because the meals were done on a three week rota basis, there was not much chance of them getting tired of the same meals. The local paper did a special feature on the Mill Street Mission feeding centre in Dorchester, which was used in the main by Infant aged children, and listed the menu for one particular day. It included: Topside Beef, Potatoes, Cabbage, Gravy, Rice and Raisin pudding.[351]

A similar communal meal scheme was established in January 1940 at Bridport where 100 children ate their midday meal at the Technical Institute in Chancery Lane, again at 4d a meal.[352]

In Shaftesbury the head-teacher of the Senior School provided a midday meal for the evacuee children attending that school. This worked well except that it deprived the local children attending there of the meal formerly provided for them. It had been the intention of the London Education Authority to provide the equipment needed to enable a midday meal to be cooked at St. James' Church Hall, but the equipment was delayed so initially the evacuated children who were having their meal at the Senior School now had to have their meal in their billets, inevitably causing a great deal of annoyance on the part of many hosts, especially those who worked during the day. The provision of midday meals at St. James' was eventually organised from Tuesday 16th January 1940, when the equipment was put in place. Later, on the 24th September 1942, a British restaurant was opened in the town and run by the WVS. Here, children under 15 could have a two course meal for 8d.

The school milk requirement also changed over the period of the war. Like school dinners, milk was provided pre-war to those children who would benefit from it, but after the war started there was an aim to prevent infant under-nourishment by making it available to all. From 1941 it was free to those children whose parents could not afford the cost. The distribution of school milk was problematic during the initial stages of evacuation, but throughout 1940 there was a gradual improvement until every elementary school in London, still open, was

350 Dorset County Chronicle and Swanage Times. 20th November 1941.
351 Dorset County Chronicle & Swanage Times 23rd November 1939
352 Dorset Daily Echo 12th January 1940.

having milk delivered. In addition the Government decided in July 1940 to give free or cheap milk to mothers and small children.[353]

The following advertisement, issued by the Ministry of Food, appeared in local newspapers from the middle of July 1940, but the content is confusing. It initially gives the impression that free milk was available to all expectant and nursing mothers and children under five, but careful reading reveals that this was not the case and such provision depended on income. The information regarding individual applications is another good example of the bureaucratic procedures involved in obtaining what was due to these categories of people. Unwittingly, it also reveals the numbers of bureaucrats which were needed to implement such a scheme.

CHEAP MILK
For Mothers and Children

The National Milk Scheme provides one pint of milk a day at a reduced price or free, for every expectant or nursing mother and every child under five not attending school.

* Get an Application Form from the Milk Officer at your local Food Office, the Post Office will give you the address, and through any Child Welfare Centre, Health Visitor or District Nurse.

* Fill in the top half of the Application Form and have it signed by a responsible person, such as a teacher or clergyman, who knows you well.

* In the case of an expectant mother, the form must also be signed by a Doctor, Certified Midwife or Health Visitor.

* Post the form to the local Food Office. It will be about ten days before you receive your Milk Permit.

MILK AT 2d PER PINT.

* All expectant and nursing mothers and children under five not attending school, will be able to get milk at 2d per pint.

MILK FREE OF CHARGE

* Mothers and children are entitled to free milk if the incomes of both parents together are less than 40 shillings a week, or if an only parent's income is less than 27 shillings and 6 pence a week. These limits are increased by 6 shillings for each non-earning dependant.
* Free milk will also be supplied to mothers and children in households where the householder is receiving public or unemployment assistance, or supplementary old-age pension.
* When applying for free milk you must also fill in the lower half of the Application Form, after the top half has been filled in and signed as explained above.

KEEP THIS ANNOUNCEMENT TO HELP YOU FILL IN THE APPLICATION FORM [354]

The provision of free milk had not always been available in all reception areas. The following announcement appeared in the Isle of Ely and Wisbech Advertiser in September 1939:-

NO FREE MEALS FOR EVACUATED CHILDREN

The Board of Education consider that the payment of 10/6 or 8/6 to the billeting householder

353 Angus Calder. PeoplesWar. op.cit. p132
354 Dorset Daily Echo. 16th July.1940

> sufficient to provide adequate food. Also no free milk will be available except for special dietary cases.[355]

In December 1940, when the Ministry of Health had suggested that a subsidy might be required in order to prevent an inevitable rise in milk prices being passed on to those who already could not afford it, the Treasury had reacted against it, but new economic initiatives, brought about by a reappraisal of food policy, made significant changes so that... 'A social reform of the first magnitude, that at one time looked like languishing for months, if not years, was put into effect almost within days'.[356]

When, in 1943, milk to the general public was rationed, the school milk measure was cut to one-third of a pint, except for pupils getting free milk. They received two-thirds of a pint a day, whereas normal householders received two pints per week in winter, and three to four per week in the summer. This was supplemented by National Dried Milk.[357]

London children in reception areas also received their milk. Those who had got it free of charge when in London continued to get it free, the cost being paid by the London County Council.

> '2nd September 1939. We adopted the Milk scheme today. The milk is supplied by the Tring Co-operative Society. The distribution, pending a medical examination, is on the London County Council basis; granting it free to those who had it free in London. Every child will have two bottles of milk a day. Four of the group were paying and nine were free'.[358]

Rather than have their daily allocation of milk in bottles, these children in Wales get theirs straight from the churn.

Mary Nickerson (née Caw), remembers that in her reception school, Tenbury Elementary, near Ludlow, a crate of a third of a pint bottles of milk were brought into her classroom. Each bottle had a cardboard top with an

355 The Evacuee. October 97.p6 MERL Archive
356 Angus Calder. op.cit. p132
357 ibid. p440
358 E/L/8/1. Bucks Record Office. 2nd September 1940.

indentation in the centre where pupils had to push with their thumb in order to get a straw through. As many of the children hated milk they bribed others to drink it for them because they were not allowed out into the playground until the crate was full of empty bottles.[359]

However, some evacuated schools in the reception areas were not to receive milk until a year after the war had started.

In 1941, the only requirement for free milk was the inability to pay for it, so the Government introduced a scheme of reappraisal to check that no child was precluded from having school milk through the inability to pay. The only way to do this was to use the parents' weekly contribution towards the billeting costs in the reception area as a guide to the *'ability to pay'*. This scheme was not only bureaucratically cumbersome, but also financially unviable as the amount of money collected did not cover the cost of the administration. In consequence, the Government decided to ease the bureaucracy by allowing free milk to all unaccompanied evacuees who were in official billets, whether they could afford it or not.[360]

Number of children who received milk daily: (% of total on roll).[361]

Date	Number	Free	Roll
1939	263,186 (62.6%)	41,596 (9.9%)	420,000
Oct. 1941	83,743 (62.9%)	2,887 (2.1%)	133,000
Oct. 1942	136,065 (61.4%)	5,755 (2.59%)	221,600
Feb. 1944	151,821 (61.1%)	8,081 (3.22%)	248,000
Feb. 1945	113,869 (59.7%)	6,329 (3.32%)	190,600

In some areas the local authorities and general population became aware of the need to provide extra support and care for impoverished evacuees. The specific concern of the residents of Shaftesbury related to clothing. Some of the children who had gone to the town had come from poor areas and some of their parents had become unemployed because of the general upheaval in London. To help alleviate the problem the Town Clerk established an after-care committee with a Mrs Tutin as the Chairwoman and Miss Dewey acting as Secretary who, as far as possible, carried out their work in co-operation with the Head-teachers. When cases of insufficient clothing and footwear were reported to the Committee, members contacted after-care workers in the relevant areas of London to ascertain the financial position of the parents. Where the parents were able to supply clothing all was well, but there were a number of cases where they were unable to do so. Some money had been raised locally and the Head-teachers had access to some small funds of their own but there was still a significant problem and in the second week of November 1939, an appeal was put in the Western Gazette asking for clothing of any description and/or monetary help. An office in the Town Hall, formerly used by the Borough Surveyor, was designated as the depot for the clothing and voluntary helpers were appointed to make up the clothes received into suitable garments for the evacuee children. It was pointed out to critics of the scheme that such clothes were only issued in really necessitous cases and only then after parents had done what they could to help. Foster parents were informed that when they felt there was a need for their charges to be issued with clothing they were to inform the relevant teachers but under no circumstances were they to supply the clothing themselves and claim a refund for the cost retrospectively, as any such payment would not be made. Reference is made to the replacement of an evacuee's shoes in the film 'Village School', so it was a recognised problem nationally.

There were also concerns about the state of attire of many Liverpool evacuees in North Wales as many had travelled with clothes which were unsuitable for the rugged countryside they found themselves in. The WVS organised a door to door collection and also established *'make do and mend'* groups to make sure that at least some of the children had suitable clothing.[362]

359 Mary Nickerson. unpublished account entitled 'Happy Evacuee' sent to Author. May 1996. MERL Archive
360 Samways. op.cit. p41
361 ibid. p53
362 Wallis op cit. p130.

Medical Provision

> *'Who pays for an enjoyed conception in London resulting in an expensive confinement in Dorset?!'*[363]

School closure in the evacuated areas also brought about a decline in school medical services which for some pupils was the only form of treatment they received. This was taken up by the Minister of Health, Walter Elliott, who stated quite categorically that:-

> *'....the Government had no wish to undermine the welfare of future generations. They were determined that the school medical service should survive intact'*[364].

It was not only the school medical service that was required. A Ministry of Health Circular, No. 1882, dated 2nd October 1939, stated that *all* categories of evacuees were to have access to the local medical services. Questions about medical provision and payment were asked by the Councillors at the Wareham and Purbeck Rural District Council on the 26th October 1939.

> *'Who was responsible for payment to local doctors called when evacuees were ill and which doctors could be summoned? The Chief Billeting Officer said that in the case of unaccompanied children, a private Doctor could be called in, but in the case of others the Public Assistance Doctor should be sent for. It was pointed out that a local emergency committee comprising of Doctors, which met at Dorchester, arranged for payment of Doctors through a central fund'.*[365]

In October 1939, a memo from the Ministry of Health stated that;

> 'Mothers with young children below school age who require domiciliary medical treatment for themselves or their children and who are able to pay for the attendance should do so. When medical attention is required at home where the mother is without sufficient means to provide it, the District Medical Officer should be called in. The normal channel for obtaining this assistance is by application to the local Relieving Officer. Necessitous persons who are in their home areas would have no difficulty in knowing where and how to obtain assistance available through the officers of the Public Assistance Authority may be at a loss in new surroundings. It is therefore important to ensure that the health visitors and district nurses who will be in touch with the mothers and children should be familiar with the situation of the offices and residences of the relieving officers so that they may be able to advise the mothers on the matter.....'

The following year in a letter dated 15th July 1940, the Minister of Health stated that when evacuees became sick and were nursed in their billets the host was to be granted an extra five shillings a week if a doctor certified it.

This was not always the recommended practice. In some areas such as Shaftesbury, the local doctors stipulated that unless there was a good reason for doing so, evacuees were not to be cared for at home if a place was available in the local hospital, in this case Vine House, in Sturminster Newton.

One of the greatest misconceptions surrounding the first evacuation in September 1939 was the fact that all evacuees were malnourished, ill-clad, unhygienic, and in some way responsible for taking disease and other complaints into the countryside. Opinions not helped by comments made in reputable professional journals. This stereotypical account was written in the British Journal of Nursing in October 1939;

363 Dorset County Council. Minutes. Sept.1939. Unattributed statement.
364 TNA.ED 50/207. 26th October 1939
365 Dorset County Chronicle & Swanage Times. 2nd November 1939.

'The indignation of persons compelled to admit lousy children - totally uneducated, masterful mothers - bumptious teachers, their " lady " wives and " helpers " to look after their children, but who refuse to take part in the domestic work of the house, can be well imagined. The lady of the house and perhaps her one maid, are expected to slave from morning to night housekeeping, cooking, washing up, cleaning and tidying-up at 6.30,and then to bed worn out.'[366]

And there are numerous examples of complaints about the state of evacuees arriving in various localities across the country. Many were based on hearsay and generalisations, but nonetheless have remained in the public domain.

'Sir,

That, it having been proved that during the recent Government evacuation scheme children suffering from impetigo and in a verminous condition were billeted in the village, this meeting protests against this as an avoidable and grave injustice to the householders concerned. In forwarding this, I beg to add the following observations as expressed at the meeting : That this experience of the village regarding the condition of the evacuated children is not an isolated one, but appears to have been widespread in the area ; and, further, that as the evacuation was organised after many months of preparation, during which the necessity for these particular safeguards was consistently urged, it is difficult to believe that the requirements of the moment justified such a disregard of precautions against infection on the part of a Ministry charged with the safeguarding of the public health.

Yours, etc.,

A. W. CARTER (Honorary Clerk, Acklarn Parish Meeting)[367]

It is true that some of them came from domestic situations in the cities which were less than salubrious and way below the levels acceptable to a civilised society, but this was not true in the great majority of cases.

There is even evidence that many of the diseases that were supposedly brought into the reception areas by evacuees had been prevalent months before they had arrived. The County Medical Officer in Dorset reported in May 1938 that the

'Total number of children in the county excluded from school because of medical conditions: 255 Impetigo, 70 Ringworm, 13 Scabies and 98 are in a verminous condition.'

And a report of June 1940 relating to the welfare of evacuee children stated that:-

'Out of 4 schools in the Shepherd's Bush area of London sending 670 pupils to Pontypridd, there were only one or two with nits. Out of 300 children from the Northwold Rd. Public Elementary School in the East End of London in June 1940, only 8% were considered to be in need of special attention. 1 child had scabies, 5 had nits, 8 suffered from enuresis and 11 with other conditions. Of 1211 children from the Stretford Schools in Manchester, only 80 suffered from 'vermin or nits' and 14 from enuresis.' [368]

Despite the implication made in the statement by Mr Carter, it also has to be remembered that many of the evacuees were not fostered by middle and upper class families in the reception areas, but by agricultural labourers whose own standard of living could also be very basic. So one has to put the social questions surrounding evacuation into context and consider that the plight of each child has to be viewed on an individual basis. Those who left poor homes and arrived in better off surroundings could well have been surprised by what confronted

366 British Journal of Nursing Oct 1939 op cit. p257
367 Resolution passed at the Acklarn Parish Council Meeting. Acklarn, Malton, Yorkshire, October 27th 1939 and reported in the Yorkshire Post.
368 TNA.ED 50/206

them, likewise those from the cities who had been used to indoor sanitation and electricity would have found it difficult to come to terms with earth privies and tallow candles.

In reception areas where the medical practice was rural, the arrival of evacuees put an extra burden onto an already stretched service. This was particularly true of expectant mothers who were evacuated in the first groups. Some hospital beds in Maternity units in the cities had been kept empty to allow space for the expected vast numbers of air-raid casualties which had been projected before the war. However, because these figures were inaccurate and over inflated, fewer beds were actually required. In August 1939, the Dorset County Councillors were told to expect around 800 expectant mothers and that arrangements were to be made to house them. In actual fact only 244 were evacuated to the county, excluding the Poole area.[369]

In Somerset, a memo dated 30th Aug. 1939 entitled the 'Evacuation of Expectant mothers' was sent out from the County Council and listed a few establishments which could be used as maternity homes, together with the names of the women who were to be in charge of them. The Combe Down Convalescent Home in Bath under the charge of Mrs Allingham would take in 40 urgent maternity cases which may be evacuated with midwives. Cranmore Hall in Shepton Mallett, run by Lady Paget, would have 32 beds with 12 additional staff to serve cases among the evacuee population, and the Mary Stanley Home in Castle St., Bridgwater, run by Mrs Butler, would have 20 emergency beds.

Beds would also be made available in various Public Assistance Institutions notably in Dulverton where the Girls Training Home was to be adapted to house 20, and in Chard, Williton, Axbridge and Keynsham. [370]

Notes of a telephone conversation reveal that Mr Brown at the Regional Office in Bristol had contacted Local Authorities in Somerset indicating the number of the 1080 expectant mothers arriving from London who would be allocated to their area; Bridgwater Borough (140), Combe Down (240), Shepton Mallett (100), Kingston (Taunton) (220), Minehead (100) Dulverton (80), Clevedon (140) and Weston Super Mare (60).

They were asked to find billets adjacent to maternity homes in the district which should not be used for any other purpose.[371] This was obviously not an easy task to carry out, as a week later Mr Brown contacted the Local Reception Authorities which had experienced difficulty in finding such billets and considered asking them to requisition empty houses or other suitable buildings to be used as hostels prior to the removal of the mother to a maternity home. After the birth, the mother and child would return to the hostel for a short time prior to going back to London, or else be billeted out in the usual way.

Brown suggested the WVS could find the staff and costs would be refunded by Government, although he hoped that the hostels would be self-supporting as London would try to get the husband to provide for the wife's maintenance so far as possible while in the County. Nothing would be done until the recommendations were received in writing[372].

The October 1939 edition of the British Journal of Nursing contained an article entitled 'Arrangements for expectant mothers in Reception Areas' in which the author described the plans as outlined by the Minister of Health[373]. He had emphasised that under the general direction of the Local Authority Medical Officer of Health, the maternity work involved should be under the clinical supervision of a specialist in Obstetrics who, if circumstances allowed, would be in charge of a maternity unit overseeing complicated cases, and together with other doctors act as consultants in all difficult ante-natal cases, complicated confinements and the treatment of puerperal sepsis.[374]

---

369 Dorset County Council. Public Health Minutes October 1939.
370 REF. File. C/CD/1/6/1. Evacuee Correspondence. 1938-39
371 ibid. Notes from telephone conversation. 20th Oct 1939.
372 30th Oct 1939. REF. File. C/CD/1/6/1. Evacuee Correspondence. 1938-39 Wars/Em Ref. Memo
373 Circ.1871 12th Sept.1939
374 British Journal of Nursing. October 1939. p268

During the evacuation of 1940, expectant mothers sent to emergency maternity units in the reception areas were to be partly accommodated in the unit and partly billeted by the Reception Authorities, both before and after their confinement. Interestingly, it was pointed out by Central Government that as some of these women might be refugees (aliens) the local authority had to ensure that they complied with the Aliens Order of 1920 and the Aliens (Protected Areas) Order.[375]

'Who Pays?' seemed to be the most frequent question asked, especially where pregnancy was involved. In Oxfordshire the County Evacuation controller wrote to the Town Clerk in Chipping Norton:-

> *'I am informed by the City Almoner that a Mrs Phillips, an evacuee expectant mother.....is to be admitted to the Ruskin College Maternity Hospital on the 16th instant. I shall be glad if you will make the necessary transport arrangements and let me know when this has been done'.*

The reply read:

> *'I think it should be suggested that Mrs. Phillips uses the 'bus service to Oxford'.!*

This was agreed by the Controller.[376] Did the reception area pay for the confinement, or did the evacuating authority? No issue seemed to promote such anger as an *'enjoyed conception in London leading to an expensive confinement in Dorset'.*[377]

Alderman Oliver, in the Weymouth Council meeting in September 1939, noted that the Greenhill residence of Captain Hamblin had been requisitioned as a home for one hundred evacuee expectant mothers at a cost of £1,300 per year, excluding rent and rates. He wanted to know if this expense would be met by the Ministry of Health.....the Town Clerk assumed that it would.[378]

The information had obviously taken time to reach the reception areas as this issue of cost had been resolved in late August 1939 when the Ministry of Health agreed to guarantee any payment. Once this had been approved, the reception areas were able to find an extra 1,003 maternity beds by the 2nd September and a further 2,679 by October, in 137 Maternity homes. During which time 2,881 confinements took place[379].

Having found the extra accommodation, the biggest problem was where to find the much needed staff. Of greater concern was that once the babies had been born, the mothers and children needed extra welfare care. This was even more important under their new circumstances because they were away from their extended families which would in a normal situation, have been around to help, either with the new baby or with other dependant siblings. There were other attendant problems. Between 1939-45, illegitimate births had risen by 300% and billeting officers found it very difficult to house such mothers and children on moral grounds. This resulted in many of them being sent to local workhouses where their 'public assistance' costs had to be paid for by the evacuating authority. Some areas were adamant that the costs should not be borne by them and Holman cites one case where the Public Assistance Department in Somerset put two young unmarried mothers back on the train to London.[380]

This whole issue does raise the questions of confidentiality, the rights of the individual and the social mores of the time. Why did the Billeting Officer have to tell the hosts about anyone's personal circumstances? Surely a mother and child were simply a mother and child. The fact that the child was illegitimate should not have been a significant factor.

Some areas were a little more sympathetic and, realising that the Workhouse was not always the best place, appointed social workers to help the mothers. This created a worthwhile service which had not been readily available before the war and is one of the more positive 'spin-offs' of the evacuation scheme.

---

375 Government Evac. Scheme. Memo. June 25th 1940
376 Chipping Norton Borough Council. Doc. 113/4
377 Anonymous Quote. Dorset County Council Minutes. September 1939.
378 John Murphy. Dorset at War. pub. DForest Pub. Co. 1979. p32.
379 Holman 'Evacuation' op.cit. p124
380 ibid. p125

Problems of Social Class and Billeting

'I had settled down quite well in my billet until my mother came......Once she had met my mother, my friend was cool to me because she realised that I was from a different class. My foster mother told me that the parents of my friend were paying extra for her keep so I was not to be too disappointed if she received more treats that I did....I think that was the worst thing that ever happened to me'.[381]

It is reasonable to state that although evacuation relieved the urban areas, it did place extreme burdens on the host localities and all too often it was a case of the poor and underprivileged housing the same from the cities. Even Titmuss remarked that the wealthier classes had evaded their responsibilities quite effectively.[382]

Crosby reinforces this when reporting the findings of the Women's Voluntary Service:-

'We find over and over again that it is the really poor people who are willing to take evacuees and that the sort of bridge-playing set who live at places such as Chorley Wood are very difficult about it all'.[383]

In 1939, one clergyman in charge of a small country parish outside Warwick offered to find billets for child evacuees in the local village and *'tramped many weary miles over muddy fields, getting refusal after refusal, especially from many of the richer people'.*[384]

A teacher from Sheffield wrote to the Times Education Supplement in 1941:-

'....Evacuees were willing to stay in pleasant billets. These were mostly in smaller houses. Larger houses, well known to have plenty of rooms consistently refused to help. Until the well-to-do can be induced to take their responsibility seriously and accept the billeting of children of all kinds as a war time duty or an essential form of National Service, parents could not be expected to participate whole-heartedly in the evacuation programme'.[385]

A letter to The Times on the 15th September 1939 provides an indication of disagreement with some aspects of the evacuation scheme by this particular correspondent who, from other evidence, was not alone in his, or her, beliefs. It also demonstrates the problems of simple Public Relations faced by the authorities:-

'Sir,

As an emergency plan for a few weeks the evacuation of all city children to country homes would be beyond criticism. As a scheme to be carried through several years it simply bristles with difficulties.

Take the middle-class home where the income largely disappeared from the moment war was declared. Here the billeted children have meals with the kitchen staff if we are fortunate enough to have one. But we cannot feed our maids on 8s 6d a week per head. The children must have some food, and they eat more.

But our kitchen staff has probably gone home, either because their own mothers have children billeted on them, or they do not like the extra work in our homes. Many of us are either elderly, not over strong, or busy with our own small children, and unable to do the extra work of cooking, cleaning, washing and mending, unable to afford the extra expenses and the wear and tear to our homes and gardens for more than a short time.

---

381 Edith Green. Taped Interview. June 1995. Edith was evacuated from Walthamstow to Wellingborough in September 1939. MERL Archive
382 Titmuss. op.cit. p372 et al.
383 Crosby. op.cit.p56
384 Norman Longmate. Air Raid. Hutchinson. 1976 p20
385 Crosby. op.cit. p56

Yet many fathers of evacuated children are in good jobs and the mothers are now free to go out to work. Might not the broadcast appeals to the charitable public for clothing also remind parents to do their share at any rate in this respect?

Then, where the mothers are billeted with smaller children, in some cases they do not lift a finger to help, and expect to have everything done for them, and the women naturally dislike being in other people's houses. The teachers, too, are not at all easy or contented.

Now that the children are safely out of the cities, is it not possible to organise empty houses or camps, with teachers, mothers and children running them themselves with voluntary helpers? Happy billets could be left undisturbed, but a heavy burden would be lifted from many homes where the strain of living is already great.

Yours &c E.M.Curtis'[386]

In some areas of the country this action by the upper and middle classes was actively supported by local regulations. An area in Wiltshire refused to take evacuees because:-

'...the servant problem in the large houses is so acute that it would be unfair to billet children on the owners'.[387]

This lack of servants seemed to be a common concern with some of the correspondents to The Times:-

'...my own and other local experience suggests that the evacuation authorities should explain to parents that good manners are the least return they can make for the very real effort and unselfishness on the part of the householders of all conditions, especially in houses where there is a trained and often reduced domestic staff and where the extra work has been cheerfully undertaken and where children live on a scale above the 8s 6d and generally above their own home standard...'[388]

Before the war this lack of cohesion between the classes would not have been a problem worth considering by the voluntary services hierarchy. When asked to appear before the Anderson Committee on the 21st July 1938 to give her opinion on evacuation planning, Lady Reading, head of the Women's Voluntary Service, stated:-

'Evacuees would be quite happy to live in barns or garages in the countryside, especially if they were next door to a middle class house'.[389]

A handwritten note below this comment in the minutes says:-

'...this view was fully endorsed by the Chairman of the Women's Institute, Lady Denman'.

The National Federation of Women's Institutes represented 338,000 countrywomen and in total approximately 148,000 members of the Women's Voluntary Service helped with the organising and implementation of the evacuation and its aftermath.[390]

However, they were not the only interested groups. (For full list see Appendix 3).

To her credit, Lady Reading did change her opinion and told Mass Observation in 1940 that:

'....Evacuation had been a terrible fiasco.....not nearly enough use had been made of the big houses of England'.[391]

---

386 Alton House. Redhill'The Times. 16th September 1939
387 Crosby. op.cit. p50
388Letter to The Times from Beatrix Crofton. Berwick St. John Manor. Wiltshire. 5th October 1939
389 TNA.HO/45 17635
390 Holman. Evacuation op.cit. p143.

This had also been noted by the Ministry of Health in a Circular issued in September 1939, in which regional officers were informed that certain local authorities had not included the really '*good class*' residences in the billeting lists.[392]

Even when the use of such houses was shown in propaganda and feature films the unwillingness of the film characters to welcome evacuees was often apparent. In 'Cottage To Let', made in 1941 and distributed by Gainsborough Pictures, one of the central characters, 'Lady Barrington', when informed by a billeting officer that she was to have evacuees, told her Butler to '*get the spare blankets and eiderdown from the attic...you know, the one with the holes in it'*, implying that this was good enough for an evacuee.

Some housekeepers looking after country properties for absentee or weekend owners were sometimes put in very difficult situations. One evacuee describes the general conversations when arriving at his first billet with his sister:-

> *'Soon we were being driven along a lane that took us right out of the village and then along a bumpy track. The driver didn't say very much except to tell us he was not the billeting officer. The car stopped near a cottage that looked like a picture on a chocolate box, except the garden was overgrown and weedy. When a woman opened the door our driver said 'I've brought you two temporary foster children'.*
>
> *To which she replied...'Well you can just take them away again. I never said I would have any evacuees'.*
>
> *Undeterred he pushed us into the house saying....'According to our lists you have a spare room with a double bed. By law you cannot refuse to take them'.*
>
> *With that he ran to his car and drove away quickly leaving us standing there miserable.*
>
> *The woman was very angry... 'They have no right to dump you on me. I have no food and the shops are miles away. What he will say when he finds out I don't know!*[393]

In fairness this unwelcoming experience, although difficult to comprehend by young children, was not necessarily the fault of the housekeeper. Many in similar circumstances reacted in the same way. This housekeeper obviously had no authority to accommodate evacuees. True, billets in this area at the time were hard to find but surely the billeting officers could have gone about their task in a manner which was a little less authoritarian. As it happened, the children were in the cottage only a short time and the owner did in fact do a lot to make their stay enjoyable. However, one could imagine a similar situation where the housekeeper's job could have been put in serious jeopardy!

But it was not always just the upper classes that were unhappy to provide billets for evacuees. As late in the evacuation process as July 1941, the Incorporated Association of Head Masters had gathered evidence from Head-teachers of evacuated grammar schools that the more well-to-do people, superior artisan and the clerk class had tended to shirk their responsibilities.[394]

It was reported in the Dorset County Chronicle and Swanage Times on 1st August 1940, that a man from Owermoigne was fined £5 for refusing to take evacuees. This was a great deal of money, but the courts also had the power to imprison people for non-compliance. In this particular case the defendant told the court that he preferred to go to gaol rather than pay what he considered to be an excessive fine.[395] Unfortunately, the final outcome of the case was not reported.

---

391 Mass Observation. Topic Collection 5. Evacuation Folder 2/A. 20th February 1940. cited Crosby op.cit p66
392 Titmuss op.cit. p392
393 James Roffey. Letter to Author. 9th June 1998. MERL Archive
394 Titmuss op.cit.p393
395 Dorset County Chronicle and Swanage Times. 1st August 1940.

Some of the upper classes of course took in evacuees and were looked after extremely well. But this was not always the case elsewhere; this diary entry from John Colville, would suggest that in some instances they were tolerated as long as they did not upset the status quo:-

> *'Saturday. September 23rd: After lunch I went by train to Stansted to spend the week-end with the Bessboroughs.....There were also sixty or more orphans, who played cricket happily on the lawn in front of the house and who were carefully excluded from the main part of the house itself, which remains as cheerful and comfortable as ever'.*[396]

Some evacuees were not even allowed in the house. A visit by a host and her evacuees to a friend resulted in the following situation:-

> *'We had been shown the grounds by a girl of 15. Then we were taken to the house, but before we went in we met the girl's mother who asked...'Where are you taking them?*
>
> *'To meet Daddy,' was the reply.*
>
> *'Oh darling! I don't think that is a good idea. I'm sure your little friends are very nice but we do not want them in the house do we? I'll have the buns and barley-water sent out'.*[397]

Others obviously took their responsibilities more seriously and either made over their whole house to the evacuees or made their stay as comfortable as possible.

> *'Sunday September 17th: After lunch and a game of billiards I motored Philip to Middleton via Stoney Stratford and Banbury. The house is occupied by a horde of Roman Catholic children, in the charge of a dozen nuns, and the family are living in cottages'.*[398]

Joan Faulkner, described her first placement with a Mrs Sayers, an American, who was a daughter of a Woolworth magnate and who owned a large house in Wentworth. Joan was given a bedroom which contained full size models of Snow White and the Seven Dwarfs and was chauffeured to school in a limousine[399]. Her second placement was not so luxurious. Joan and her family were billeted on a family in a small council house where she had to share a bed...four children of both sexes sleeping width ways![400]

The 23 children who were billeted at Parham House, Sussex were all given their own dressing gowns with their initials on and had two servants allocated to look after them. At a recent reunion, they all said how happy they had been during their time at the house, and some even returned with their childhood dressing gowns which they had kept.

It has to be recognised that in some cases it was the parents who resented the good treatment that their children were receiving from wealthier hosts. There were fears that they would get 'thoughts above the station' and enjoy the 'high-life' too much. 'Dolly' (pseudonym) remembers in a letter to her first host, Nella Hughes-Smith, how her billets were at either ends of the social scale both in terms of care and experience. It has been reproduced in full as an excellent example of where evacuation had a significant influence on a child's life. It illustrates what a different carefree experience 'Dolly', her 14 year old sister Mary and 5 year old brother 'Tiddler' had until they were taken away by their stepmother because *'they were too comfortable'*. (Two other brothers had been billeted with another family.) One can only speculate how life might have changed for 'Dolly' and her siblings had they been allowed to stay in the billet.

> *'We drove down the long drive and the door was opened by a maid in uniform. As we went in I tripped on the step and fell into the hall. Instead of the expected clip around the ear for being clumsy, you and Mona, the maid, were very concerned. Thus started the only happy memories of*

---

396 Colville op.cit. p27
397 James Roffey. 'Is he being a good boy?' The Evacuee. August 1996.MERL Archive
398 Colville op.cit. p23
399 Joan Faulkner. Letter to the Author. December 1996. MERL Archive
400 ibid

childhood and I have treasured them all my life. I remember you always bathed Tiddler and me yourself although you had two maids. We were bathed, put to bed and you read to us until the dinner gong went.

We had a delightful bedroom, very clean and comfortable, a complete contrast to our home where we slept 'top and tail', 6 in a bed with no sheets and pillow cases. The place was infested with bugs and we had paraffin sprayed on the walls each night, no windows open; you can imagine the smell!

I have many happy memories of playing in the woods near the house, the local hunt, the Garth, scrumping apples from the austere looking house up the lane, in fact not scrumping but openly taking your gardener's wheelbarrow and stripping a whole tree. I came back triumphant to Sallie the cook and presented them to her. I remember when we threw porridge out of the nursery window onto the nectarines, and when Albert the gardener complained you did not punish us but you set up a little plot of our own. You bought us Wellingtons and a fork and trowel and we spent happy times digging in our own garden. When Christmas came we had toys for the first time ever and we were surrounded by love and happiness.

When we heard we were leaving I remember going down the lane and lying in a field of cowslips and crying. Apart from a few months spent in a children's home where life was quite pleasant, my time with you and your family was like a wonderland and a happy release from a very traumatic and unhappy childhood.

You said you thought we went back to London but in fact I went to a couple called Roberts in a bungalow. My stepmother told me years later that she had asked for us to be moved as we were too comfortable. Later I went to a children's home in Maidenhead. I went back to London when I was 13 as my stepmother had had a baby and I was needed to queue for food. When the Blitz started in earnest my father, stepmother and the baby went into the country and left me there alone, having turned off the water and electricity. I wasn't afraid, just glad to be free and I just went into the Anderson shelter when the sirens went and to a neighbour's house for a wash.

I left at 16 and went to Cornwall to work in a children's home. I didn't see my brothers and sisters again'.

It was only by chance that Dolly was billeted with Nella Hughes -Smith. When Nella collected Mary she found her cutting a piece of soap in half to give to Dolly because they were being separated. Nella did not want this to happen so took Dolly as well. [401]

It would be wrong to assume that although in some areas the responsibility for housing evacuees fell on the poorer classes they would offer a more caring environment for evacuees from similar deprived backgrounds. Lilian Evans has made a collection of reminiscences of ex-evacuees from a poor area of Liverpool. They were all evacuated to Wales and it would seem from their comments that there had been a significant amount of anti-evacuee propaganda to warrant the same measures being taken by hosts when their evacuees arrived. Out of 35 evacuees 15 of them, mostly girls, had had their heads shaved.

The man had a chair ready. He said 'Sit here Julie'. He cut and cut and my hair fell on the floor. He then got hair clippers and shaved my head.'

'You're next', he told Ann. She was crying. The lady brought a tin from under the sink with a bottle of purple Gentian Violet and started to paint my head with a little brush. I now had a bald head with purple dots all over and so did Ann.'[402]

Many of the hosts, when asked by the evacuees who were having their heads shaved replied:

---

401 Letter to Author. June 1997. MERL Archive

402 'Aliens'. Anonymous extract from Yesterday's Children. compiled by Lilian Evans.

'Children from Liverpool bring lice, scabies and sores' [403]

Those who were not shaved had their hair washed in disinfectant and many had their clothes burned. Some of them were wearing new clothes!

> *Blodwyn, (the daughter of the house) said to me 'Come on, take your clothes off'.*
>
> *I said 'No!'*
>
> *'Mama, she won't take her clothes off'.*
>
> *Mrs Davis came and told me to undress. She look at me with staring eyes, so slowly I started to take my clothes off. Then I was put in a bath.....The lady got a poker and started to throw my clothes into the back garden. She said to the girls, 'Whatever you do don't touch them!'*
>
> *I felt dirty, the girls kept looking at me as I got out of the bath. I was glad, it smelled awful. Then I was told to kneel on the floor. The woman came with scissors and cut off all my hair then she got some clippers and went over my head. I was bald. I had been in the house twenty minutes.*
>
> *She passed me with the pillowslip with all my clothes in. She threw them in the garden and set them alight'.*
>
> *'You have burnt my dad!'* [404] (referring to a photo in her pocket)
>
> *'First let's get you undressed'.*
>
> *I went to sit on a chair. There was a scream so loud that I jumped. I thought I had sat on the cat. It was the lady.*
>
> *'Go in the back and take all your clothes off ready for a bath'.*
>
> *I know why she screamed....'I had sat on a chair and not had a bath first. Evacuees were alive with lice bugs and I don't know what else she said they had been told. We were washed in Dettol and our hair was shaved off'.* [405]

Julie, Hilda and the others were seven years old. One can only imagine the trauma that she and their peers went through.

These incidents raise an important question. Why did these hosts assume that the evacuees coming to their area would be dirty and lice-ridden!? One can only speculate that such assumptions had been gleaned from someone in authority because so many of the hosts in this small area of Wales adopted exactly the same policy. However, detailed research in the documents relating to this area resulted in very little concrete evidence[406] except a comment stating that:-

> *'...While some voiced their disgust at the condition of the children some hosts chose rather to accept the situation and apply themselves zealously to the task of cleaning up their charges'.* [407]

If the hosts were rather 'zealous', where were the billeting officers when all this was going on? Why did they not do something to stop it? However, any blame for allowing such situations to arise cannot be directed entirely at them. It may be that they simply did not have, or were not given, enough time by the organising authorities to check what was going on. The following statement would suggest that some local councils were unaware of the responsibilities of Billeting Officers and the amount of time needed for them to do their job effectively despite having been sent various Ministry of Health Circulars, including No. 1857 on 27th August 1939, which stipulated

---

403 ibid.
404 Anonymous account Yesterday's Children op.cit.
405 I thought I had sat on the cat....'Hilda'. Lilian Evans. op.cit.
406 Although, in one particular Record Office I was not permitted to view some of the 'open' files dealing with the local evacuation, despite having had access to them the previous day.
407 Wallis op.cit. p84

the frequency of visits to evacuees in their billets. The Clerks of the Amlwch RDC and Nant Conway RDC told their respective councils that the 'Billeting Officers will be able to complete their work in 2-3 hours' and the Billeting Officer in Penmachno was informed that:-

> *'...should occasion arise it is not anticipated that this particular work will involve more than one day release from your duties while ensuring this defence'.*[408]

No consideration was given to follow up work or visits. Such ignorance of the amount of time involved in doing the job properly could only lead to some billeting officers having to pay lip-service to their role, especially if they were responsible for a large geographical area. Under such circumstances, any host wishing to take advantage of their situation in terms of abuse, using evacuees as servants or generally ill-treating them, was in an ideal situation to do so.

Finally, why were there no complaints from the evacuated teachers? One wonders why in school the following morning, the teachers did not question the arrival of their charges with shaven heads? Even today many of the group ask why they did nothing to help. A quote from a teacher, mentioned by some of the group, would suggest that she was not too sympathetic:-

> *'Just be thankful that these nice people took you into their homes. You could be in Liverpool with all the bombs'.*[409]

In fairness, it has to be said that despite this initial treatment a number of this group of evacuees were then well looked after in their billets and did enjoy the remainder of their stay.

Not all people were prepared to countenance the billeting of evacuees on private householders. An anonymous correspondent to the Windsor Express on the 25th October 1940, seriously suggested the building of Concentration Camps in order to house evacuees and some town councils in reception areas discussed the possibility of putting evacuees in segregated communities.[410]

The use of the words concentration camp could have been forgiven as merely identifying some sort of holding area for evacuees, similar to the use of such camps in the Boer War for prisoners. However, even in local papers, journalists were writing articles describing life in the German camps. In August 1939, under the title 'Concentration Camp for Women' the reporter described the Ravensbrueck as having:-

> *'...the usual drastic measures to prevent escape. The whole camp is surrounded by a barricade of high-tension wire and a detachment of S.S. men is always on guard. At their work the inmates are perpetually watched by women warders, who are most strictly forbidden to exchange a single word of private conversation, with their charges...'* [411]

Although, when in October 1939, the Government had produced and published a White Paper on German Concentration Camps, it was obviously not taken too seriously by John Colville, who, in his diary, described the Paper as:-

> *'...a sordid document calculated to appeal to people's lowest instincts, and reminiscent of the 'Corpse factory' propaganda in the last war. It does shed a lurid glow on the bestial sadism of the Germans at their worst; but after all, most evidence is produced from prejudiced sources, and it is in any case undesirable to arouse passions before the war has begun in earnest'.*[412]

Although the concentration camp suggestion was an isolated one, there were communities which objected to having evacuees billeted in their area. The following letter was sent by members of the Lychett Minster Parish Council to the Chairman of the Dorset Civil Defence Emergency Committee on the 24th November 1939:-

---

408 Nant Conway RDC. Letterbook Evac 1939-41 letters 17th and 26th May. Also Amlwch RDC Evac. File 1939-41 letter sent 28th July 1939.
409 Lilian Evans. Letter to Author. July 1998. MERL Archive
410 Crosby op.cit. p53
411 Dorset Daily Echo. 8th August 1939.
412 Colville op.cit. p46

'Sir,

We strongly protest against the billeting scheme for evacuated families who have been sent unexpectedly to this area and billeted upon country families regardless of the differences in the standards of living and of the insurmountable difficulties occasioned by forcibly overcrowding country homes, with the result that many families have returned to London. We suggest an alternative scheme that the Authority responsible take over empty houses and buildings and recondition them to take these families'.

The reply from the Chairman implied that it was a Government and not a County matter. However, later in the war Dorset County Council did in fact refurbish houses for use by evacuee families at its own expense.

These statements and actions tend to contradict the comments made on class by the Canadian diplomat Charles Ritchie in August 1940;

'English men and women of different classes, localities, sets and tastes are for the first time talking to each other', [413]

and Angus Calder made the comment that:-

'...the bombing mixed classes together. Well-off travellers in the London Underground could not miss the thousands of poor people sleeping on the platform'.[414]

It is true that in this situation they could not help seeing each other, but evidence would suggest that in many reception areas the 'classes' did not necessarily get on, nor in many cases did they tolerate each other. To a certain extent this was brought about by a notable condescension of the voluntary services in some of the reception areas and ignorance and misunderstanding on the part of both evacuees and hosts. Despite legislation appearing before war broke out, few authorities had thought enough about the social consequences of such an evacuation scheme. Therefore, in hindsight, it is not surprising that problems relating to mutual suspicion and disregard occurred. Local authorities did not help the situation by using billets that were unsuitable, either from the inadequacy of the building or of the hosts. Also, in some cases the reception areas were expecting either large numbers of people or a preponderance of a specific category. Berkshire County Council were told to expect evacuees as follows; 50% schoolchildren, 30% mothers with children under school age, and 20% cripples (sic), blind helpers, teachers and expectant mothers. As it turned out these figures were not adhered to and in East Berkshire a considerably larger number of women and children arrived than anticipated with the result that many host families who had volunteered to take a school child were called upon to provide lodging for a category of person they had previously declined. This obviously created great difficulties for the reception and billeting officers. In other examples whole company workforces were moved *en bloc* to safer areas and this caused great problems to all aspects of evacuee administration.

'21st March 1941. The staff and families of Folland Aircraft were moved to Exeter from Hamble near Southampton today'.[415]

There is a great deal of evidence to support Crosby's view that the poor took the brunt of housing evacuees.[416] It must also be said that some agreed to take evacuees either through ignorance or a naive sense of well-being. The following letter was written to the billeting officer in Exeter by an 80 year old man and one can detect the apologetic and humble in its tone.

'Our evacuees, a woman and 2 children under 3 years of age, have been with us since November 11th. During all that time my wife has been ill on account of her severe heart trouble. (Angina

---

413 Charles Ritchie. The Siren Years. Macmillan. 1974
414 Angus Calder. The Myth of the Blitz. Cape. 1991. p34
415 Exeter Blitz. Box.16. Devon Record Office.
416 Crosby op.cit. p56

Pectoris). I shall be glad if you will be good enough to give permission to move them as soon as possible....[417]

There was no evidence of any reply or outcome. But the letter does beg the question why did the authorities use 80 year old hosts who were ill?

An article in the November 1939 edition of the British Journal of Nursing drew attention to the case of a Mrs Hatfield, an 83 year old widow living in Malton, who was prosecuted for alleged non-compliance with an order requiring her to take in two evacuees.

In spite of the fact that this woman was in indifferent health and that her housekeeper, aged 55, had also been receiving medical attention, the Evacuation Tribunal stated that they had no other alternative but to uphold the Government's regulations. Although the Tribunal informed her that they would deal with her case as sympathetically as possible, it still went to court. However, the Magistrates threw it out and Mrs Hatfield was awarded the sum of 1 Guinea in costs. The decision to prosecute was made by just one or two people and members of the Malton Urban Council were adamant that had her case been heard by the whole Council a summons would not have been issued. The Chairman of the Evacuation Committee, Councillor F.S.H.Ward was unrepentant and replied that Mrs Hatfield was just one of 235 cases considered by the Committee which was made up of voluntary workers '*doing their best*' under almost impossible circumstances, and explained that they had not taken the decision out of '*a vindictive spirit*'. The public feeling arising from this case obviously became personal and anger was aimed at both Cllr. Ward and his committee as this quote would suggest:

' I am not going to stand reproaches and people cutting me dead in the street or lose my friends and business. The Committee has been cursed up hill and down by people who ought to have known better. All the publicity sought by the other side was simply to make me and my Committee appear as big blackguards as possible'.[418]

Some people did their utmost to avoid having evacuees and used all manner of means and excuses to do so:-

1.12.40

From Doctor.

With reference to Lady Davy: On medical grounds it is not good for her to have ten evacuees in a house with only five bedrooms and 2 living rooms. Because of her public duties Lady Davy requires more than just her bedroom.

This request was turned down by the evacuation authorities on two separate occasions. But the fact that the letter was sent and worded in this fashion does suggest that Lady Davy did have ten evacuees in her house.[419].

There was a certain amount of abuse concerning the issue of medical certificates to help people avoid having evacuees. These could be easily obtained from some Doctors, and in some cases could be purchased for 2/6d.[420]

However, some excuses may have backfired, as this letter would imply:-

28th October. 1940

Dear Madam,

I understand that in response to the billeting notice served upon you, you stated as a reason for being unable to receive evacuees that your daughter has been in bed for three years with Tuberculosis.

---

417 ' Exeter Blitz. Wartime Correspondence. Devon Record Office.
418 The British Journal of Nursing. November 1939. p277
419 ibid
420 Titmuss op.cit. p393

I am unable to trace any record of this in the City Health Department so I would be glad if you will inform me of the name of your medical practitioner in order that I may ascertain further particulars which will enable me to consider whether you can be exempted from billeting or not.

Yours faithfully

C.J.Newman[421]

And, as this letter from the billeting officer in Chipping Norton to the Town Clerk indicates, even senior personnel in the local authorities were becoming very frustrated by some people's lack of co-operation:-

'Dear Mr. Morris,

Mrs.....of....will be in, I expect, with an appeal. She has no reason to appeal, she is actually a miserable, wicked old woman, and if the people are moved it should be stressed that it is for their sakes and not for hers. She absolutely abused them last night so much that Mrs Watts was trying at a late hour to find alternative accommodation for a very nice superior sort of woman and her two small children.

Please give it to the old girl hot and strong, as a witness I can say she deserves it. In fact, could we but direct the bombs, some would do good.

Yours sincerely... [422]

There was an appeal procedure, Ministry of Health Regulation 22. Defence Regulations 1939, through which hosts could go if they had any grievance about the evacuation process. But others relied on the good will and sympathy of neighbours and some local politicians to inform the authorities of problems.

'21.2.41

5.35pm. Councillor Pedlar 'phoned.

One of his van drivers, Moore, lives at 16 Hazel Road. Man, wife, 4 children of his own and two evacuee children. Billeting Officer has called today and says that two more evacuated boys will be billeted upon him tomorrow. The house is a non parlour type.

Mr Pedlar thinks this is damnable as one class of person seems to be carrying all the burden. He does not wish to mention the matter in Council if possible, but points out that houses on his own road and in other roads of similar class do not appear to be taking their share.

He also says that he knows of a case where the husband is on service and his wife has eight children, some of her own and some evacuees'.[423]

This anonymous letter was sent to the Town Clerk's Office in Exeter in mid-1940:-

'...It has come to my notice that childless women resident in Beacon Lane, Whipton, retire to their back rooms when the evacuation authorities are in the district. Alternatively, they go out of their houses.

Is this equality or sacrifice? What do you propose to do about it? What chance does this country stand of pulling through if this is permitted?

Signed. JUSTICE' [424]

The Clerk of the Bradford-on-Avon UDC reported the same problem in 1941:-

421 C.J.Newman. Exeter Blitz. Wartime Correspondence. Devon Record Office.
422 'Chipping Norton Borough Council Doc 78.
423 Exeter Blitz. Wartime Correspondence.
424 ibid.

'...Occupiers have deliberately left their homes during the period of Billeting in an attempt to avoid having to provide accommodation'.[425]

After the Council in St. Ives, Cornwall, had introduced compulsory measures to house evacuees, the editor of the St. Ives Times wrote in June 1940 under the headline 'It occurs to me'...

'Tonight loyal inhabitants of this ancient borough will extend a welcome to little evacuee children driven from their homes and their parents' side as a result of war. Others will look on and do nothing.

I gather that those who have had the task of finding volunteers to house these children have had no light job. A number of people who a short while ago were moaning that they had no seasonal bookings this year were apparently full up immediately the question of evacuees arose. Perhaps we are to have a season after all. I hear that the number of people who have developed heart trouble and kindred ailments this week is staggering. I suppose we must expect to see these poor souls wheeled along the Wharf Road in bath chairs.

One man is alleged to have said he would as soon house Hitler as evacuee children. If this attitude was general he would probably have Hitler and the Gestapo with him sooner than he expected. Perhaps he anticipates becoming a local dictator under the Nazi regime. As I said last week, I consider the fact that the Council had to adopt compulsory measures a serious reflection on the Borough.

I hope that adequate measures will be taken by the authorities to see that children billeted compulsorily are properly and kindly treated...' [426]

This problem of non-compliance with the scheme was recognised as early as September 1939. The Revd. R.W. Sorensen, Labour M.P. for Leighton West, agreed that the behaviour of evacuees in reception areas was a psychological problem, ignorance of the other lifestyles and withdrawal from a stable home life. Also '*working class women used to their own homes and practices would naturally find it difficult to share the home of a stranger*'. [427]

However, the problem of billeting did not go away. At a meeting of the Wareham and Purbeck Rural District Council on 30th October 1940, the Chief Billeting Officer, Mr A.T. Selvey, asked the Council if they were prepared to authorise action being taken against those persons who refused to comply with the requirements of the billeting. Supporting the proposition, a fellow councillor, Mr. I.S. MacDonald was quoted as saying that *'those people who had definitely refused to take evacuees were sitting back laughing at those who had taken them'*. The Mayor, Councillor A.T. Moss, *warned that there was a statutory duty on the part of householders to comply with billeting notices and that in the event of further people coming we shall exercise our powers if we encounter difficulties'*.[428]

As suggested earlier, there were particular problems with housing expectant mothers and one example from Wiltshire where such an evacuee, described as 'a lady of very superior type' was not allowed to stay in her 'superior type of billet' generated an interesting response from the Clerk of the Bradford-on-Avon UDC. He raised the very important issue that if the 'well-to-do' were infringing the Defence Regulations and could be so easily relieved of their obligation to house evacuees, this would put undue pressure on those who were willing to take in evacuees. Also it would make the whole scheme very difficult to manage because he would have no response to any other householder refusing to comply with the regulations.[429]

425 WRO F2/850/1-12.
426 The Evacuee. October 1997 p9.
427 Hansard. Vol 351 14 September. cited Crosby. op. cit. p88
428 Dorset County Chronicle & Swanage Times 31 October 1940.
429 WRO F2/850/1-12. For full text of the letter see Appendix 16.

But even MPs and members of the church had misconceptions about the type of person being evacuated. The M.P for Caenarvonshire, R. Owen, stated:-

> *'It is ludicrous that evacuees should be sent to the beautiful Welsh valleys which only have quiet country pubs'.* [430]

In February 1942, the Vicar of St. Mary's Church, Dorchester commented on the 'heathen' upbringing of many evacuated children.

> *'We have witnessed the return, unwise as it has seemed to many of us, of many of the evacuee children to their homes. Many of them have been brought up in a manner one could call anything but heathen. They had never been to any place of worship or Sunday School and had never been taught to say their prayers...'* [431]

However, despite this concern for the lack of religious practices and morals, in some areas the locals, well known for their religious enthusiasm, did not extend their own Christian values towards the evacuees. On 8th September 1939 the following article appeared in the North Wales Chronicle under the headline 'Something I shall never forget'.

> *'Last Sunday evening (the day war was declared) I saw something I shall never forget. A little crowd of homeless schoolboys evacuated from Liverpool, sat huddled on the pavement in one of the most well-to-do roads in Bangor, outside the house of a married couple who refused to take them. The Billeting Officer had argued and begged. You have seven empty rooms and no responsibilities. You are only taking one grown up. Can't you manage even two of these tired children?*
>
> *'No I can't!', snapped the woman, and closed the door.*
>
> *While the Billeting Officer discussed what to do with the children the garden gate opened and the 'lady' of the house emerged followed by her husband. They were going to Church!*
>
> *They stepped daintily through the pathetic little bundles, the haversacks and gas masks and the children watched them....saying nothing'.* [432]

Despite obvious problems in accepting evacuees in rural areas, some individuals took in more than their fair share. It was reported in February 1940 that a Mrs Price, of Oxford House, Abbotsbury Road, Weymouth, mother of nine children, also had seventeen evacuees. Also a Mrs Allard, 6 Verne Road, Weymouth, mother of three, had sixteen evacuees.[433]

Mrs Dine of the Grosvenor Hotel, Weymouth had 24 evacuees from the Notre Dame Convent High School, Southwark.[434]

Some people who had accepted the proposal of having evacuees, recognised potential problems early in the scheme and were genuinely concerned that some screening should have taken place in order to put the correct combination of evacuees into suitable households. A correspondent to the Bedfordshire Times and Standard in September 1939 is only one example of concerns expressed by a number of responsible hosts.

> *'Sir,*
>
> *After reading your account of the arrangements made for the reception of evacuees in Bedford I was resolved that we must meet our obligations and take them in whether we wanted to or not.*

---

430 Hansard. op.cit.
431 Dorset County Chronicle & Swanage Times.5 February 1942.
432 North Wales Chronicle. 8 September 1939.
433 Dorset County Chronicle & Swanage Times 29 February 1940 & 14 March 1940.
434 Dorset Daily Echo. 15 July 1940

Therefore, on Friday, I felt that common humanity demanded I should take these people under my roof and make them as happy as possible, but I could not live up to my ideals when the Billeting Officer brought me a mother and two children. To have taken them in would have been disloyal to my wife and children. Why were these people not graded?' [435]

However, it did work both ways. One interviewee from a reasonably well-off family was indignant that she was billeted with a very poor couple who had no bathroom and she had to wash in a tin bath in the kitchen with people, including neighbours, walking through.[436]

Teachers must have found the situation arising from poor or ineffectual billeting procedures just as frustrating, as the following entry in a school log book, dated 28th July 1941, would indicate:-

'When every pressure is brought to bear on parents to leave their children in the reception areas, it seems a great pity that billets cannot be found. I wish to quote the case of Arnold Cohen, aged 8, whose parents came to report to me yesterday that they were obliged to take him home as they had been told by the billeting officer that there was no other billet and he suggested that they took him home. The reason given for his being sent from his billet here was that his head was dirty. This may be true but his head was quite clean on June 26th when he was inspected by the school nurse. If his head is infected now, it has happened only during these last four weeks and surely the foster parents could have found it out quickly!'[437]

Any unwillingness on the part of a householder to take in an evacuee and then be forced to do so could only have had a detrimental effect on the relationship between the two. A number of correspondents have described the cattle market situation which occurred in many areas. The fact that so many remember this aspect of the scheme suggests that it had a traumatic effect on their initial, and perhaps later, well-being:-

'There were some seats but many of us had to sit on the floor or stand with our belongings until we were chosen by a foster parent. ....With the foster parent standing in front, the billeting officer would call out 'two girls' or 'one boy'. Sometimes he might say 'Which boy would like to live on a farm?' or 'Is there a girl here who likes horses?'

Each time a forest of hands would go up and it quickly developed into a competitive situation in which the children vied with each other to be chosen'.[438]

Some people in authority also managed to use this system to their own advantage. A teacher from Liverpool reported the following incident in his anonymous memoirs which occurred when he had first been evacuated to North Wales with his school:-

'The billeting officer drew me to one side and asked if I could recommend one nice, clean little girl as his wife would be pleased to take one evacuee....I selected a victim....the 'market' was then declared open'.

He went on to describe the rest of the billeting procedure:-

'To my fellow teacher and I the procedure of adoption was just guesswork, as neither of us could understand a word that was being said. The local helper stood at the door allowing the foster parents in one at a time. She was armed with a 3ft blackboard ruler which she held 'at the slope' considering this an appropriate attitude to adopt in a state of national emergency. When a new customer was admitted the sound of high words and a scuffle came from the waiting room. Obviously, there was a common desire to be the first in the queue and 'bag' the cleanest child'.[439]

---

435 Bedford Times and Standard. September 1939.
436 Jane Macauley. The Evacuee. September 1996. MERL Archive
437 'E/LB/8/1 op.cit.
438 James Roffey. Letter to the Author. 9 June 1998.
439 Extract from Welsh Rarebits. unpub. memoirs of a Liverpool Teacher evacuated to Caernarvon . cited Wallis. p82

However, there were cases where willing hosts having taking in evacuees, then found that they were unable to accommodate their own families. A statement entitled

The Tyranny of the Evacuation Scheme; No Room for Her Own Children at Christmas appeared in the British Journal of Nursing in December 1939.

> *A woman said recently at the Eastbourne Billeting Tribunal, 'My son, who is serving, and my daughter, who is a nurse wish to come home for Christmas, and I cannot accommodate them unless you move the two children billeted on me.'*
>
> *The chairman, Mr. R. A. Gordon, KC stated, 'There are many people in Eastbourne who will not be able to have their relatives with them this Christmas owing to evacuees.'*
>
> *The woman, who said her health was suffering, was advised to produce a medical certificate......*

This situation obviously angered the author who asked,

> *'How about the liberty of the nation for which we are informed we are at war? A 'new Europe' as projected by the Prime Minister is hardly a tempting proposition, failing the sanctity of the home.*[440]

Parental Visits

Travel for evacuees, their teachers and visiting parents was a problem throughout the war and not only during peak times like the Christmas period. Demands were made early in the evacuation process for cheap train fares to allow parents to visit their children. There was a great deal of concern over the amount of money such a journey could take out of the family budget, especially as one of the first acts of the railway companies after war was declared, was to abolish cheap day returns for long distance journeys. Meetings were held between the LCC and the rail companies where the former argued that a flat rate fare to any destination in the reception areas should be introduced. It was agreed that since parents had no say in the final destinations of their children they should not be expected to bear disproportionate costs, especially as some had been evacuated to areas within a short distance of the capital and others to the rural villages of Wales and the North. However, the railway companies found the proposal unacceptable and it was not until November 1939 that the Minister of War Transport announced a programme of limited concessions whereby day trips on Sundays at reduced rates were to be provided to a limited number of destinations, none of which was to be more than 160 miles from the centre of London.[441] This concession was later extended to further distances.

Between 1941 and 1945 the Ministry of War Transport made reduced rate tickets available to parents and relatives wishing to visit evacuated women and children. However, these were usually only allowed to be used for one journey a month for each person, and they could not be used at certain times including Christmas, holiday periods and during troop movements. The following Circular issued jointly by the Ministry of Health and the Board of Education in November 1943, indicates that there was often a need for curtailment of travel facilities.

> 'Government Evacuation Scheme: Travel facilities for teachers, helpers and other transferred staff.
>
> The Ministry of War Transport has stated that it is of paramount importance that passenger traffic on railways during the coming winter should be reduced to a minimum. It is accordingly necessary, as part of the general reduction, to apply the same restrictions as were in operation last winter to free and partly-free journeys allowed to evacuated teachers, helpers and other transferred staff during the period 1st

440 British Journal of Nursing. Op cit. December 1939 p300
441 ibid. p178

> October 1943 and 31st March 1944 ....
>
> Full or partial reimbursement of travelling expenses may therefore not be made in respect of more than 2 journeys in all undertaken by an individual teacher or helper during this period....'[442]

A memorandum had also been issued the previous Easter from the Ministry of Health stipulating that there was to be no cheap travel on the trains between the 22nd and 27th of April 1943

As children were increasingly being sent to the more remote areas of the country, the cost of visits became prohibitive for some people, and a number of ex-evacuees have suggested that it was for this reason they received very few visits from parents and as a result had lost physical and emotional contact with their families; contact which for some, took a long time to re-establish after the war. [443]

Others were a little more fortunate. Some reception areas took the initiative and arranged parental visits. An appeal was launched in the Weymouth area in December 1939 to persuade people with spare accommodation but who could not take evacuees on a permanent basis, to volunteer to house the parents of evacuees over the Christmas break.[444]

On 11th December it was reported that over 300 parents of evacuees arrived in Weymouth by special train. They were either met at the station by their children and hosts, or were taken on by car to the outlying villages or to Portland where they were entertained and fed. This had been arranged by the WVS. The same happened in the Isle of Purbeck just before Christmas and again on the 28th January 1940, when special evacuee trains arrived at Swanage.[445].

These arrangements were so successful that it was announced locally in February 1940, that further trips at special reduced fares for friends and relatives of evacuees in West Country reception areas, were to be organised for the 25th February and 3rd March, with onward connections arranged with local bus companies to isolated villages. Other evidence suggests that there were further trips planned for May, when hosts were advised not to share their Sunday roast with the visitors as meat rationing had come into force by then. The parents had in fact already been informed of this and were told to make their own arrangements by taking sandwiches.

Not all these visits went according to plan. Just one example to illustrate the problems of many is recounted by Margaret Harrod, who had been evacuated to Sway in Hampshire. She was visited by her parents who were not impressed by the fact that she had moved billets and nobody, including Margaret, had told them. They therefore spent a great deal of time searching for her! However the situation was resolved and her mother managed to visit every six weeks.[446]

There was a hidden agenda to these visits as it was the intention that parents should relieve the hosts of the responsibility of looking after the children at least for the day, and that no hosts should feel duty bound to incur any additional expense, although implementing this was not very easy[447].

In August 1940, a certain amount of apprehension was expressed in the Dorset Emergency Committee about parental visits. A letter had been received from the Centre Leader of the WVS for the Wareham District referring to arrangements made for the frequent visits from parents to evacuated children. Whilst she thoroughly appreciated reasons for them, she did point out that they often had an unsettling effect on the children. She indicated that foster parents felt duty bound to offer hospitality which, in many cases, they could ill afford. It was

442 'Exeter Blitz. Box 12. Ministry of Health Circular. November 1943. Devon Record Office.
443 Assorted letters to the Author. MERL Archive.
444 Letter from A.T.Grubb. Dorset Daily Echo .6 December 1939.
445 Dorset Daily Echo. 29. January 1940.
446 Letter to author from Margaret Harrod. 1 March 1997. MERL Archive
447 Dorset Daily Echo 15 February 1940 & 9 April 1940.

suggested therefore that the Committee should write to the Southampton Education Committee, where the majority of the evacuees had come from, explaining the situation in the hope of restricting the visits.[448]

These visits also had an effect on some evacuees. James Roffey recalls that he and his brother and sister were to receive a visit from their mother who had booked a place on one of the fleet of coaches organised to take parents down to Sussex from South London:-

> *'After what seemed a lifetime the convoy of Argosy coaches came slowly down Church Hill and stopped outside the Swan Hotel. All the children were cheering and pushing forward, trying to see which coach their parents were on so that they could be at the right doorway. ....Our mother could only stay at Pulborough for a few hours before she had to rejoin the coach and go on to Shoreham to visit our brother Ernest....We sadly watched the coach leaving and then wandered off feeling very despondent and homesick'.*[449]

For many evacuees these visits were a disappointment and an emotional wrench. Parents and children tried to relate to each other in sometimes very difficult circumstances, and in many ways the situation was false. There was a hope on the part of some evacuees that the relationship between them and their parents would be the same as it had been at home, but of course this was often impossible.

It has to be said that some parents treated these visits as an excursion and an excuse for a visit to the coast or countryside, where seeing their children was of low priority. Not all parents went off to visit their children's foster parents. Some got straight off the coaches and into the local pubs leaving their children outside. This must have been particularly difficult for the evacuees and foster parents to comprehend, and in a way added to the anti-evacuee feeling and the thought that such children were just being dumped in the country to be looked after by others. In some cases, seeing their charges treated in this way by their parents strengthened the bond between the hosts and the children.

On the 17th November 1939 the Ministry of Health issued a Circular, authorising evacuation authorities to pay the fares for parents and husbands wishing to visit any member of their evacuated family who was sick. However, in order to be eligible for the ticket, the person travelling had to produce a Doctor's Certificate, had to be means tested and the money for the fare, wherever and whenever possible, had to be recoverable.[450]

This was not a great deal of help to those families already struggling with their domestic finances.

448 Dorset County Chronicle & Swanage Times 8 August 1940.
449 Letter to Author from James Roffey. June 1998.MERL Archive
450 Ministry of Health Circulars. 1913 & Ev.6. 17 November 1939. cited in Titmuss op.cit. p178 and Exeter Blitz. Box.

The Drift Back

'Many of them, evacuee mothers and children, have drifted back to London. Much ill-feeling has been caused. But the interesting thing is that this feeling is not between the rich and the poor but between the urban and rural poor. This is a perplexing social event. One thing that they say is that these children were evacuated at the end of the holidays and were therefore more verminous and undisciplined than if they had been taken in the middle of the term. But the effect will be to demonstrate to people how deplorable is the standard of life and civilisation among the urban proletariat'.[451]

The Government was very concerned about the rise in discontent and the return of evacuees to the cities at the end of 1939. At a meeting of the Dorchester Council in early December, the Chief Billeting Officer, Admiral W de M. Egerton stated that 600 evacuees had returned to London. This created problems as many of the parents had removed their children without informing the authorities. As a result the Council sent a formal complaint to the Minister of Health about this practice but the reply simply informed them that the letter would receive consideration. However, evacuees had already been returning home from all parts of the country earlier in the year.

By the 5th December 1939, 30% of previously evacuated unaccompanied children and 49 % of accompanied children, together with 50% of the mothers had returned to London.[452]

Figures for January 1940 show that only 55% of unaccompanied children and 12% of mothers with children remained in the reception areas. (See Appendix 4)

All the time they were returning, some reticent hosts were becoming more frustrated at having to retain their charges in line with Government policy but against the wishes of the children and adults. However, some of the blame for the return has to be apportioned to the billeting authorities. The tone of the content of the following letter from the Secretary for Education in Exeter to his colleagues responsible for billeting, would suggest that in some areas there was even severe disagreement between local government departments in the same authority!

Dippas-Wadden Evacuation Party
Mount Pleasant Hall,
Exeter,

28th March 1941

Dear Sir,

I am concerned over the rather large numbers of children who have ventured to Croydon from this Unit during the past week or two. I have continually impressed upon the children the advisability of remaining in this reception area and realising that satisfactory billeting is one of the most vital factors in children's lives here, I have paid very special attention to that and in most cases have obtained alternative billets for the children.

Unfortunately, the billeting authorities have either refused to re-billet children or their action has been so tardy that their parents have withdrawn them from this area. I know quite definitely that practically all the children who have returned from this school have done so because their billets have been unsatisfactory.

If something could be done to ensure greater co-operation between the billeting authorities and ourselves, who are better acquainted with the

451 Harold Nicolson. Diaries and Letters. Vol.2 1939-45. 14 September 1939. Collins. 1967 p33
452 Titmuss. op.cit. p544

> needs of the children, I am confident that the evacuation scheme would operate better than it is now....'.[453]

It was estimated that 98,500 of all unaccompanied children, 408,930 of mothers with children and 154,167 accompanied children had returned home by the end of September 1940.[454]

Teachers, concerned that a lot of these children were now walking the streets, reacted vociferously and suggested that the Board of Education should either close the schools in the home areas or open them up and admit that the scheme was not working. According to a national evacuation count taken in the reception areas in England and Wales on 8th January, a total of 44% of all unaccompanied children, 88% of the mothers, 86% of the accompanied children, 81% of other designated groups and 55% of teachers and helpers, had returned home.[455]

In December 1939, a head-teacher evacuated to Haslemere in Surrey wrote:-

> *'We should be glad to be informed whether the Government really considers education of any importance whatsoever and whether they really intend the evacuation of schools to continue or not. The action of almost all their officials right through this business leads me to suppose that neither matters very much either way'.*[456]

His comments were echoed in many quarters and there was a genuine concern that the problems in the education system, highlighted by evacuation, were simply a continuation of the education policies and general apathy of the 1920s and 1930s during which time expenditure on education was cut, free grammar school places were reduced and, despite advice from educationalists, the leaving age remained the same. The raising of the school leaving age to 15 had first been discussed in 1918. Ironically, its implementation had been timed to take effect from the 1st September 1939, but was of course postponed and not introduced for another eight years.

It is fair to say that in some areas there was a compromise. Some London schools were reopened during the latter end of 1939 but with limited hours and usually with a severely curtailed curriculum. Initially schooling was made available to children of over 11 who lived within a mile of a specific neighbourhood school, but as war progressed and some pupils returned from the reception areas, other ages were catered for as the following timetable from a West London school illustrates:

Date	Notes	No. On Roll	No. Of Classes
29.1.40	Opened for Seniors only	12 half-time	1
29.3.40	After Easter all ages	177 half-time	6
7.4.40	Before Evacuation	383 half-time	12
21.4.40	After Evacuation	352 half-time	10
27.9.40	During Battle of Britain	289 full-time	9
6.12.40	After intensive bombing	137 full-time	5
7.3.41	Return of children from reception areas	237 full-time	6
4.7.41	Return of children from reception areas	342 full-time	9
10.10.41	Return of children from reception areas	400 full-time	10
24.10.41	Reorganised as Mixed and Infants	433 full-time	10[457]

453 J.M.N.Francis.Exeter Blitz. Box 12. Devon Record Office.
454 Titmuss. op.cit. p545
455 ibid. p544
456 TNA.ED 134/74
457 Samways. op.cit. p35

Three returning Evacuees in April 1940 reading a notice about the reopening of a school in their area. Unfortunately, they were all refused admission because it was full.

Once schools did open in target areas the pupils were in danger, not only from raids but from structural defects in some buildings as a result of earlier raids. Despite attempts to get the returning children into school, poor attendance was very common and was as low as 2% in some areas of London. Although these figures rose considerably from the end of 1940, the overall decline in numbers attending school was not as low as one would suppose considering the circumstances. Attendance statistics show how the percentage of full attendance at school fluctuated during the period December 1940-1941, and again from March 1942-45. Unfortunately, no figures indicating the percentage of attendance are available before July 1941, but there are significant factors which are worth highlighting: that few months were drastically lower than the pre-war average attendance of 87%; hop-picking was still a popular pastime which affected school attendance, despite the rigours of war; the drastic decline in attendance during the V1/V2 attacks on London when, coincidentally, there were a high number of schools open to receive pupils. (See Appendix 5)

As early as October 1939 it was estimated that in the Dorchester area twenty per cent of the 1,642 evacuees had left and that billeting officers were dealing with the problems their absence had created. One was the question of debts which the evacuees had left behind and it was suggested that where the billeting officers had the home address of such people they should be contacted and asked for any moneys outstanding.[458]

It was reported on 2nd November 1939 that:-

> *'....evacuees are fast leaving the Wareham Rural District area'.*[459]

Christmas of that year, 1939, was seen by many as the watershed of the scheme *'unless Hitler played up with a bomb'.*[460]

458 Dorset County Chronicle & Swanage Times. 5 October 1939.
459 ibid. 2 November 1939
460 TNA/ED 136/125

In the small village of Ashley Green, 15 out of 20 evacuees registered from the 12th September had returned by the 4th December 1939.[461]

It was somewhat different in Cornwall where it appears that the majority of people felt themselves well received by the Cornish and they did not feel ostracised as much as elsewhere in the country. This is supported by the fact that during the period of Phoney War fewer evacuees seem to have left than in other parts of the country:

> *'From all over England has come the not unexpected news that the evacuated mothers are returning to London in large numbers, and Cornwall is not a little proud that a lower percentage of its evacuees have left than in any other county.... On October 21st there were 500"unaccompanied" children in the [St Austell] Urban District, and since then about 50 children and grown-ups have gone back.'*[462]

It is difficult to ascertain exact numbers and figures for how many evacuees returned home from Cornwall, but it is clear that by this point in the war when across the country '30% of previously evacuated unaccompanied children and 49% of accompanied children, together with 50% of the mothers had returned to London'[463] at least in St Austell, the number returning to the capital does seem to have been much lower than the national average.

It was reported that Parliament was to discuss the question of '*What kind of Christmas are the evacuated children to be given?*' in a debate on 14th November 1939. There was never any suggestion that children should be sent home for the holidays so the debate was to centre on what could be provided in the reception areas. 'Santa Claus' trains and coaches taking parents to visit their children were considered along with home-grown entertainments.' [464]

Programmes of special events such as film shows, Pantomimes and concerts were set up in reception areas in an attempt to keep children in the country. A total of £15,000 was raised in London, £5,000 from the general public, to provide the finance for these Christmas parties in some of the reception areas, and in Liverpool £2000 was allocated to providing Christmas gifts for evacuees.[465]

The Shaftesbury Council laid on a party on the 29th December organised by the Mayor, Deputy Mayor and the billeting officers, assisted by the teachers. The party was also attended by the Mayor of Southwark, Mr Gates, who had travelled down from London at the invitation of the Mayor of Shaftesbury. *'The children were given tea, a paper hat and a cracker in the Guildhall at 4pm and while the tables were being cleared the children remained in their areas and took part in community singing led by a Mr Cliff. The tables were then removed and a number of party games were organised. After these the evacuees were taken upstairs to see the Christmas tree loaded with presents before a Father Christmas arrived to distribute a gift to each child. When the children eventually left they were each given an orange and a bag of sweets'.*

Mr Gates participated in all the games and spoke to the children, many of whom he had known from his visits to the English Martyrs and Penrose Street schools while they had been in London.

The total cost was £15 15s 6d of which £13 was given by the London County Council and the small shortfall was met from local funds. Similar Christmas events, again the responsibility of the Mayor, were repeated in 1941 for those evacuees remaining in the area at that time. However, despite travel restrictions and attempts made to make them stay, some evacuees left Shaftesbury for this Christmas period. It was reported by the Billeting Officer that this created some relief on both sides as in most cases the children were able to stay with their own families for a week or more and their absence gave a certain respite to the hosts who wanted to have their own families with them over the holiday.

---

461 E/AR/6/2 Bucks.Record Office
462 West Briton, 7/12/1939, p.10
463 Parsons, M. 'I'll take that one', (1998) p.111
464 Dorset Daily Echo. 11 November 1939.
465 Titmuss op.cit. p144

Some evacuees organised their own Christmas entertainment as a report from the Retford Times of 15th December 1939 indicates:-

'TOWN HALL CROWDED FOR CONCERT

Since they became Retford's guests the evacuee children from Leeds have won a well deserved reputation in the staging of public entertainment. The Town Hall was packed on Thursday evening for another of their concerts during which the senior boys sang a special song...

'When Retford was invaded by troops of evacuees,

the good folk of Retford were somewhat ill at ease.

But now the invasion's over

and the troops have settled down,

they're as happy as bees in clover,

living in Retford Town'

West Leeds High School for Boys gave a detective sketch and there were items from Patrick Behan, a senior boy, after which a vote of thanks was given by the Mayor on behalf of the people of Retford'.[466]

There is evidence to suggest that some evacuated schools provided entertainment for their hosts very early in the scheme. A newspaper article of 21st September 1939 in the Dorset County Chronicle reported that the local villages around Stratton had been entertained by Section 4 of the Haberdashers School billeted in the area. The headline '*Evacuees entertain Again*' suggests that this was not the first time they had done this.

In Dorset, the County Council's Chief Billeting Officer considered that there were only three parishes which needed any sort of organised Christmas events and he was very concerned that many visiting teachers had had a very hard time working on the evacuation scheme since July and many had either not had a holiday at all, or had been recalled from them in the summer. He felt that under the circumstances it was important that they should have a break over Christmas. In order to do this he suggested that some voluntary arrangements should be made in the parishes concerned whereby the teachers could rest and that instead of parties, the evacuees could be taken to the cinema in Weymouth or Dorchester.[467]

In Buckinghamshire, the County Education Board was not so benevolent towards the evacuee teachers. They requested that evacuated school staff should carry out duties in their host schools over the Christmas period, including Christmas Day and Boxing Day, so that even one child who was unable to stay at their billet during the holiday period could go to the school where there would be some connection with someone from London. Head teachers of evacuated schools were therefore asked to draw up rotas to cover the Christmas break.[468]

The same arrangements were made in Weymouth:-

'There was a great deal of heated debate at the town's Education Committee meeting when it refused to allow evacuated teachers to have an extra half-day's holiday on 22 December for travelling home. It was reported that the Chairman and Clerk had met with teacher's representatives with whom it had already been agreed that schools should close for instruction during the Christmas holidays, but that schools would remain open and a sufficient number of

466 The Evacuee. October 1997. p6.
467 Dorset County Chronicle & Swanage Times. 7 December 1939.
468 E/LB/8/1. Log book entry. 25 December 1939.

evacuated teachers would arrange activities for schoolchildren from other districts as well as their own, and teachers remaining on duty would stagger their holidays before and after Christmas. It was pointed out by one Councillor that non-evacuated teachers were getting the extra half day!'.[469]

The Christmas holiday was not the only 'personal' time that teachers had to give up. There are numerous accounts of teachers losing their holiday to provide recreational facilities for children in the billets and to find the time to deal with social and pastoral aspects with foster parents. The following can be found in the Commercial Rd. School log-book:-

'8th August 1940.

Although the school is officially closed I am attending at school in the mornings to supervise the children who attend. I am also taking the opportunity of dealing with the clothes problem, reporting on it and taking measurements in necessitous cases. I have visited foster parents for the purpose of enquiry before reporting to the Secretary of the Care Committee in Stepney Green East'.[470]

And at the Ashley Green School:-

'10th August to 7th September 1940.

During the summer closure their doors were opened each morning at the customary time. About 30 children arrived each day and stayed in the charge of two members of staff until 4pm. Sometimes the children played organised games in the playground, or painted pictures or played with various toys or in the sand pit. They all had a jolly holiday. At the same time 30 seniors worked in the fields harvesting for the farmers'.[471]

In a deliberate attempt to keep evacuees in the reception areas in December 1939, no special trains were laid on to take the children back home for Christmas, and in Scotland the school holidays were shortened to relieve the pressure on hosts.[472]

However, according to the analysis of the national evacuee return estimates of 5th December 1939, and the actual count made on 8th January 1940, 16% of evacuees still remaining in the reception areas returned home and there was a greater rate of return of mothers with children.

Christmas seemed to be a very important influence on the rate of return.[473]

Between January and February 1940, the Civil Defence Committee held a number of meetings in order to devise a new policy which would redirect propaganda away from the evacuee and more towards the rural householder.[474]

This view was supported by delegates at the Headmasters' and Headmistresses' Conference in January 1940, when they recommended that:-

'...the Government should call upon householders in the reception areas for a generally wider spirit of forbearance and understanding in their acceptance of the children's presence'.[475]

In January 1940 the Civil Defence Committee, under the Chairmanship of Sir John Anderson, held an evacuation conference which took evidence from Government Ministers, representatives from local authorities, including the LCC, and members of the National Union of Teachers. [476]

---

469 Dorset Daily Echo. 30 November 1939
470 E/LB/8/1 Commercial St. School. op.cit. 8 August 1940.
471 E/LB/6/3. Ashley Green School. op.cit. Log Book. 10 August - 7 September. 1940
472 Titmuss. op.cit. p144
473 ibid. p544
474 Crosby. op.cit. p96
475 GLRO EO/WAR/1/65. 22 January 1940 cited Crosby op.cit. p96

After considerable debate, the advisory committee to the Minister of Health came up with three broad strategies.

a. A new evacuation scheme to be brought in when raids actually started, but it would not include the aged, crippled, and mothers with young children because it was thought that these latter categories were more easily housed.

b. A new propaganda campaign in the reception areas.[477]

c. Measures to deal with the growing number of children within the reception areas.

Walter Elliot, Minister of Health, said in Cabinet on the 21st February 1940:-

> *'A persistent stream of propaganda was being maintained and almost every householder was getting something through the letterbox'.*[478]

And, on the 7th February, the President of the Board of Education, Earl De la Warr, had announced that compulsory education would be imposed as soon as the necessary buildings in the cities were available or made safe.[479]

The second strategy included the announcement of increased billeting allowances for all evacuees over 14 years of age to 10/6d per week. In 1939 hosts had received 10/6d for the first child and 8/6d for every subsequent child, and 5/- for teachers. Parents who could afford it, were asked to pay 9/- but the Government were prepared to take 6/-, and those receiving unemployment benefit were not asked to contribute but instead, deductions were made from their assistance benefits, if any of their children were evacuated. All these figures and categories were based on the Poor Law provisions.[480]

These figures had been calculated on the cost of the services provided by evacuation, excluding travel which had been paid for by the Government. In return for these allowances the hosts were expected to *'provide lodging, access to water and sanitary arrangements and, if required, cooking facilities'*.

A further increase was announced on 14th May 1940 by the Minister of Health, Walter Elliott that with effect from 31st May, children aged between 10 and 14 would receive 10/6d per week, 14-16 12/6d per week and 16+ 15/-.

Even in the beginning hosts felt that the first allowances had been inadequate and as early as 4th October 1939, a group of fifteen Weymouth householders who had evacuees billeted on them, got together to press for an increase in payment, especially for evacuees over the age of 10. The Secretary of the group, Mr. Winter, stated that:-

> *'...it was unanimously felt that the allowances are inadequate, especially in the cases of boys and girls of ten years old and over. Some people seem to think that you can provide food for children at a ridiculously low figure, but these growing children between 10 and 17 eat as much in many cases as a full grown man'.*

They all claimed that they had to subsidise the scheme in order to provide the children with proper meals.[481]

The responsibility for assessment and for the collection of money was placed on the County Councils.[482] The Poor Law authorities would collect the money from parents and pass it on to the evacuating authorities who in turn would pass it on to the Government. Despite the administrative procedures, the amount of money collected was a small percentage of that spent by the Government. Government expenditure on unaccompanied evacuees for the financial year 1939 was £6.7 million, of which £559,950 was collected from parents. From 1939 to 1941

---

476 ibid.
477 TNA.CAB 73/1. 21 February 1940. Ministry of Health Circular 1965. 15 February 1940.
478 TNA.CAB.73/1/ 21 February 1940
479 Crosby op.cit. p98
480 Defence Regulations 22(5), 31(A), 32 (6) Section 56. Civil Defence Act.1939. cited as Footnote. Titmuss. op cit. p157.
481 Dorset Daily Echo.4 October 1939.
482 Titmuss. op cit. p157 (Footnote)

local authorities were able to deduct 1/6d per child per year (1/9d after March 1940) for administrative expenses, plus 7.5% for collection fees (8.75% after March 1940).[483]

The average amount of money collected from parents throughout the war was 2/3d per child per week. 2% offered more than the acceptable 6/-, 40% gave 6/-, 11% were on unemployment assistance and 14% were unable to pay and were therefore given a zero assessment. This 'nil payment' differed geographically, 18% in Birmingham, 27% in London, 40% in both Sunderland and Liverpool.[484]

Specific arrangements were made for those people who could not afford the 6 shillings. The householder had to complete a form providing details of income and normal expenditure plus exceptional expenditure. Rent, travelling expenses to work and statutory insurance contributions were deducted from the family income, and allowances were given for the personal needs of the family remaining at home:-

25/- per week for a father and a mother or:
15/- per week for one parent
10/- per week for a dependent adult aged 16 or over
6/- per week for a dependent child under the age of 16.

When these deductions had been made, half of the remaining sum was regarded as available for the repayment of billeting charges. If these figures came to less than 6/- per week, the people concerned were permitted to pay the sum lower than 6/-.[485]

There was also anxiety in some quarters about how money earned from housing evacuees affected those hosts who were receiving outdoor relief. In February 1942, the Dorset Public Assistance Committee was asked to clarify the matter by the Dorchester Rural District Council. The County Public Assistance Officer explained that when the evacuation scheme started a lot of evacuees were billeted on relief recipients. The Committee maintained that there were two forms of billeting. In one, a householder was required to provide accommodation for which a rental allowance was paid, and the other in which the householder was required to billet and maintain the evacuee, for instance in the case of unaccompanied children. In the case where the billeted person was maintained, the amount received was not taken into account for the assessment of relief. In the case where rent was paid it was regarded as sub-letting and the usual course was taken of disregarding the first 2/6d and one third of the remainder and taking the balance into consideration. The District Council considered this to be grossly unfair and that the rental should not be taken into account at all. The Public Assistance Officer explained that out of the 5/- rental the householder would get 3/4d and they took into account the remaining 1/8d as additional income and the reduction in relief was for this amount. However, the Rural District Council's concern must have been listened to because the Public Assistance Committee did agree to disregard the 5/- rent allowance when assessing relief.[486]

Payment for housing evacuees was considered to be one of the setbacks as to why hosts were not coming forward in the numbers expected. This was an ongoing problem throughout the war and there are many examples of local concerns such as the points from a letter dated 20th November 1941, from Frank Lloyd of Spetisbury, Dorset referred to earlier.

General unease about the effect lack of payment was having nationally was also highlighted in a letter sent to all reception areas by the Town Clerk of Carmarthen in 1943:-

'22 November 1943

To all Reception areas.

Billeting allowances are considered to be totally inadequate therefore the

---

483 ibid. p160
484 ibid.
485 ibid. Footnote p158.
486 Dorset County Chronicle & Swanage Times. February 19.1942.

Town Council has passed the following resolution:-

That the Council, in recording its grave concern at the meagre and totally inadequate billeting allowances paid by the Government for the accommodation of evacuees, feels that this is one of the root causes of the immeasurable difficulties which have arisen and are still arising in billeting, particularly in relation to unaccompanied children, as the allowances are insufficient to meet the financial burden thrown upon the householders by the presence of such evacuation, and with a view to alleviating the distress thus caused this council urges HMG in the strongest possible terms to increase the present billeting allowances to such amounts as are adequate to maintain the unfortunate billetees....

Howard White.

Town Clerk'[487]

Despite protests from many quarters payments were not revised again until June 1944, under an Amendment to the Defence Regulations:-

Defence Regs. AGD (B1)24

Amendment to Form E. Incentives to Occupiers.

As from the first pay day in the week commencing Saturday 1st July 1944, the weekly rates of billeting allowances for unaccompanied children are as follows:-

Under 5 years of age 10/6 per week.
5 & Under 10   11/6 per week
10-12   12/- per week
12-14   13/- per week
14-16   14/- per week
16   16/6 per week
17+   17/6 per week [488]

Other methods were used to appeal to hosts and evacuees alike. Throughout March and April 1940, there was an intense programme of newspaper propaganda in the reception areas to persuade more hosts to volunteer and a series of advertisements appeared in local newspapers under various headlines:-

'Thankyou, Mrs Ruggles...we want more like you!'	*14th March 1940.*
'Who'll give a promise to keep this child safe?'	*21st March 1940.*
'Who'll help Mrs Harrison?'	*28th March 1940.*
'Someone here is going to need your help.'	*4th April 1940.*
'Will you share a small burden with your neighbour?'	*11th April 1940.*
'You've been splendid, Mrs Johnson, and you deserve to have some help.'	*18th April 1940.*

487 Exeter Blitz. Box 12. C51945. Devon Record Office.
488 ibid

Who'll give a promise to keep this child safe?

This child's home is in the city. Up to the present his home has been safe. But let us face it: one of these days his home may be a ruin. There is no excuse for feeling falsely secure because nothing has happened yet. The danger of air-raids is as great now as it has ever been.

The Government is arranging to send this child, and some hundred thousands of others, to safety if raiders come. Each will need a home. Only one household in five is caring for these children now. Volunteers are urgently needed. Plans must be made well ahead. There must be no hitch, no delay, in settling the children in safety. Here is *your* chance to help.

You can if you wish make an immediate contribution to this safety scheme. Many households have been looking after evacuated children for six months now. They will be grateful for a rest. If you can take over one of these children, you will be doing a very neighbourly deed and helping greatly in the nation's defence.

To enrol as a host of a child now or in the future, or to ask any questions about the scheme, please get in touch with your local Authority.

The Minister of Health, who has been entrusted by the Government with the conduct of evacuation, asks you urgently to join the Roll of those who are willing to receive children. Please apply to your local Council.

Newspaper appeal for hosts

All these pictorial appeals showed smiling children in the foreground, and in the background silhouettes of bombers, hinting at the danger that could confront them if they stayed in the cities.

There was also an intense poster campaign suggesting that taking in evacuees was 'a national service'.

In 1941, the Ministry of Information released a film called 'Living With Strangers' , in which they attempted to address the issue of conflict between the evacuees and their host families and for once looked at the problems from both sides.[489]

Unfortunately, it is not possible to ascertain how well the film was received at the time because it was not researched by Mass-Observation. But audiences today comprised of people who were evacuated find the content both very amusing and extremely patronising. The film, made by the 'Realist Film Unit', is so obviously staged that it loses much of its credibility and the script still portrays a distorted image of the evacuees. For example the commentator on the film talks about:-

489 Living With Strangers 1941. Made by the Realist Film Unit and produced by the Ministry of Information.

'They will now have to do without their fish and chip shops and cinema and rely on their own entertainment' and *'The adults drink in pubs, we don't do so much of that down here'*

It also creates the impression that the host families are better educated and more socially adjusted than their guests:-

'...the local WI set up needlework classes to show the women evacuees how to make clothes for themselves and their children'.

Implying that they had never done this before, which of course was not true in most cases. In reality, some mothers found it difficult to buy the material required to make these clothes out of their income, as this transcript of a telephone message from a reception area trying to establish such a sewing circle would suggest:-

'8.2.41. Miss Jenkinson telephoned.

I told her about the £5 5s. She suggests that she be allowed to lend mothers money out of this sum to buy materials to make clothes for their children. Mothers will repay if and when they can.

Does the town Clerk agree?

(Answer.Yes)*'* [490]

The film is also useful for another reason. It has an excellent example of how women were treated at the time and considering this film would have been shown in the cinemas, what women were prepared to accept. A rather authoritarian billeting officer, who nonetheless is portrayed as being sympathetic, has to deal with two women, host and guest, over a problem of the ownership of a child's toy. At the end of a long conversation, in which he basically tells them off and suggests there is more to worry about than *'a kiddie's toy'* he sends them away saying:-

'...I have more to do with my time than standing around listening to you all day....... Be off with you before I set about you both!!!!' [491]

Some evacuees, when interviewed, are still rather upset by comparable patronising attitudes of some of their hosts. One, Maureen Stephens, describes how she and her mother who although from the East End prided herself on her general manners and her standards of dress, '*always wearing hats and gloves'*, were taken to a large detached house in St.Albans where the host immediately produced a list of rules and regulations about behaviour and cleanliness. She had preconceived ideas about East Enders. The host made things so difficult for the family that they were prepared to risk the bombing in London and they returned home.[492]

The contemporary Ministry of Information films created an unrealistic image of evacuation. The film 'Westward Ho!', produced in 1940, was an attempt to persuade parents to evacuate their children. It reinforces an atmosphere of romantic adventure when dealing with the journey of evacuees '*through smiling fields'*. There '*were only a few tears in sight'* and everyone, children, billeting officers and foster parents are seen in a relaxed, jovial and genial manner. This was pure propaganda issued at a time when the Government was attempting to persuade people to leave the cities in the second evacuation in 1940. However, this image is one which has been perpetuated until very recently and has contributed to the mistaken belief that all was well with the scheme. Significantly, at the very end of the film there is evidence of a hidden agenda when a soldier says; *'....and for those of us in the forces, we will fight better if we know our children are safe'.*

It is difficult to evaluate objectively the value of this propaganda, but the movement back home would suggest that it had limited success. It can be said that the failure of these visual tactics, first of all to ensure people left the target areas and later to stay in their reception areas, was due partly to the misunderstanding on the part of the

490 Exeter Blitz. Box 76.
491 Extract from soundtrack. Living with Strangers. op.cit.
492 Maureen Stephens. Taped interview. November 1996. MERL Archive

film makers and the Ministry of Information about the depth of antagonism in some areas and, more importantly, the pull of family and community ties.

As an estimated 900,000 of the original 1.5 million evacuees returned during the 'Phoney War' period,[493] the Government Scheme was being undermined, and it received a great deal of criticism from many quarters, including the Press and the Teachers Unions. The Joint Consultative Committee of the NUT in Weymouth, and Evacuated teachers, sent a resolution to the Government in April 1940, stating that they could not stop the drift back to the evacuated areas and the collapse of the scheme. They also expressed their opinion that the proposed new evacuation plans would only add chaos to the existing arrangements, and they were dismayed about 'the lack of any progressive facilities for rationalising the existing evacuation scheme before bombing begins'. Councillor Ronald Gould, of the NUT National Executive, highlighted the three main aspects of evacuation...transport, billeting and education which were of serious concern to teachers and he suggested that Education had been forgotten, despite warnings from the NUT. He thought that the main issue was the fact that in many cases the billeting authorities and the education authorities were not identical, and often there was little co-operation or co-ordination between them. He urged the Government that when the next phase of evacuation was introduced no place should be called upon to take evacuees unless it 'possessed adequate billeting and educational facilities'.[494]

Changes of Billets

The host-evacuee conflict became a serious problem in some areas. Had there not been a 'Phoney War' period perhaps the evacuees would have been tolerated in the spirit of 'doing one's bit'; however, as this period of relative 'inaction' continued, tolerance was replaced by intolerance, resentment and ill-feeling in many of the reception areas. This, in turn, led to countless requests from both guests and hosts, for evacuees to be relocated. Some parents demanded that their children should be moved. The Town Clerk in Chipping Norton, Oxfordshire, was sent the following letter by a Mrs Reading from Plaistow after she had visited her children in their new foster homes during the first weekend of the war.

> *'I went to see my two children today, (Sunday September 10th), and I found Ethel very comfortable and happy with Mrs Webb at No 3 Spring Place, but I am sorry to say I could not say the same for Johnny, he did not complain but I cannot leave him where he is, so I am asking you if you could find somewhere else for him.*
>
> *I know Mrs Pickett of No.4 Spring Place would have him and he would have better care taken of him. His father has been called up for the Navy so I haven't him at home to speak about it, and if he isn't found somewhere better I shall have to bring him back to London......'* [495]

This example is typical of the sort of correspondence received by billeting officers in the reception areas. Other moves were requested on medical grounds although some were very confusing. One can assume that the writer of the following letter was trying to secure accommodation for herself because of her son's illness. (The letter is transcribed verbatim, hence the spelling and grammar errors. It was addressed to the Town Clerk. Chipping Norton.)

> *'3/1/40*
>
> *Dear Mr. Morris,*
>
> *I should have written you Before But have been waiting to see if I could possibly manage to get Back. But I find I cannot do so as Mr Benham is having a run of Bad Luck he is in shipping and there is not much Doing in His Line, and I cannot afford to Be in Chipping without the Allowance he has been making me. If I make enquiries this end could you Keep me on the List of Helpers, as I*

493 Titmuss op.cit. p17

494 Dorset Daily Echo. 20April 1940.

495 Doc. 10 Chipping Norton Borough Council papers. Town Clerks Office. There are no reference numbers except the number of the Document.

want to see if under the circumstances I can get any Pay as I am very worried as it means Keeping my Boy at home here with me and he is Delicate Has Congenital Heart, and I could not expect any one in Chippy Norton to take the risk of having him without I were there. That was my reason For coming with the School But as you know I did all I possibly could to Help in whatever way. If you can Keep me on your List Whilst I make enquiries I can Be Alright for a Billet.

Trusting you will Understand My Position.

Yours sincerely

J. Benham. (Mrs)'[496].

During the first six months of the war in the reception areas of Berkshire, there were fifty transfers of billet per week in Newbury and two hundred and fifty a month in Maidenhead.[497]

Transfers from one area to another were usually allowed provided that both local authorities agreed. The cost of the transfer had to be paid by the parents unless the move took place for educational reasons, when the costs were charged to the evacuation account.[498]

Under the law, it was the local Mayor's duty to appoint three people to act as a tribunal to hear complaints, so that a householder had the right to make a complaint in writing to him and if necessary go before the panel. Evacuees also had the right to put their case. The Town Clerk in Dorchester, speaking at a special meeting of the Town Council on 7th September 1939, was very concerned even at this very early stage of the war, about changes of Billets. He made it known that he was the Chief Billeting Officer with a very able team of billeting officers under him, and only these people were allowed by law to interfere in any billeting whatever. He went on to say:-

'I am not going to stand any interference over unnecessary transfers. I want to make it clear to people who are changing billets in the town or 'swapping' children and that sort of thing that they are guilty of an offence. Although I have been patient up till now the time may come when I have to prosecute, and that will mean a fine or imprisonment. Unless a householder desires, no one other than a billeting officer has authority to go into a house. I have come across cases where the people who would like to get out of their commitments have taken children around the town trying to find billets for them. For this they render themselves liable to prosecution'.[499]

The Chief Billeting Officer in Weymouth, Mr Warren, officially announced on 26th September that all billeted persons in the town had to remain in their present billets without exception until 7th October:-

'The authorities have been very tolerant and have made great efforts to assist the evacuees to settle down. A tremendous amount of work has been done to try and correct the more obvious misfits. But there must be a limit to the unrestricted movement which appears at present to be taken for granted.

Billeting cannot be changed at will by people who profess to be satisfied with what has been provided for them at the Government's expense. Cases of real necessity will still be dealt with by me, but I am determined to put a stop to unnecessary movement amongst the evacuated population and for that reason 'standstill' must be maintained.

People who, after this warning, take the responsibility of leaving the billets which have been allocated to them and seek accommodation elsewhere without the consent of the Chief Billeting Officer run the risk of having to pay for their lodgings from their own resources. If for no other

496 ibid. Letter to Town Clerk from Mrs J. Benham 3 January 1940
497 Crosby op.cit. p32
498 Guide for Billeting Officers. Exeter Blitz. Box 5. Devon Record Office.
499 Dorset County Chronicle & Swanage Times. 14 September 1939.

reason than the National Register is in process of being taken, the standstill order would appear to be entirely justified'.[500]

In support of this, the following notice was placed in the Weymouth local newspapers on 28th October:-

'CHANGE OF BILLETS

The attention of evacuees and others is again drawn to the necessity for obtaining official sanction BEFORE removing from the billets in which the former have been placed.

Failure to observe this will deprive both evacuees and householders of the benefit of a billeting allowance. No change will be sanctioned in future, unless fully warranted by some exceptional circumstance.

Any person aggrieved by a refusal of resettlement may appeal to the Billeting Tribunal'.[501]

This annoyance and frustration was also evident in other areas. In a letter to the Town Clerk of Chipping Norton dated 18th November 1939 a billeting officer, Mr. R.J. Brandum, wrote:-

'Dear Mr Morris,

...Lastly - it is no use any more people requesting transfers even if they have 20 Doctor's Certificates. We have come to the end of our tether. They must produce the necessary accommodation if they wish for a transfer. We have no more willing (sic) householders with accommodation. Mrs Benham and Mrs Nelms have walked and walked. We have not yet moved the boys from Pembridge Terrace, but that will be done this week. King's have gone and the Mayor's. And still I can name many deserving cases which cannot be moved'[502]

Some transfers were deemed unnecessary and some evacuees played the system. Town Councillors in Dorchester, in October 1941, were of the opinion that some of the adult evacuees were 'not playing fair' and they were using the billeting scheme for their own purposes, changing from area to area as their 'private conveniences directed'. The abuse of the scheme in Dorset was halted when the authorities were given the power to withhold billeting notices. This meant that if evacuees wanted to leave their temporary homes they had to satisfy the billeting officers that their reasons were good. If they moved without such authorisation they became ineligible for financial assistance.[503]

Some evacuee mothers with children moved from place to place and chose the areas they wished to go to. These were called 'twicers' and they were in effect getting a 'guided tour' of the best reception areas in the country.

On the 18th September 1939, the Dorset Echo reported:-

EVACUATED WOMEN GOING HOME
A CHEAP FORTNIGHT'S HOLIDAY

Women evacuated from London appear to be returning home in increasing numbers from the south coast although they are not being encouraged to do so by local authorities.

Many of the women were in excellent billets and expressed themselves well satisfied with their reception, but stated that they were returning home with the consent of their husbands.

500 Dorset Daily Echo. 26 September 1939.
501 ibid. 28 October 1939.
502 Doc. 24. Chipping Norton Borough council. Town Clerks papers. No reference numbers.
503 Dorset County Chronicle & Swanage Times. 2 October 1941

It appears that a number of them have treated the evacuation scheme as an opportunity for obtaining a fortnight's holiday at very, very little expense.[504]

The attitude of the evacuees in one area was considered to be having such a detrimental effect on the morals and behaviour of the local children that an article in a local church magazine asked:-

'Is there any necessity for the spoliation of decent homes and furniture, the corruption of speech and the moral standards of our own children?' [505]

Not a very Christian attitude considering the state of the war!

In a memorandum for Wales entitled 'Problem after evacuation is completed' the Deputy Regional Commissioner wrote:-

'...a number of evacuees from Liverpool and Birkenhead would appear to be of a very undesirable type and it is anticipated that their habits and customs will be resented by Welsh householders, especially in rural areas. For example, some of these women are in the habit of frequenting public houses and several cases of drunkenness have already been reported. Today the County Council has been notified that a number of Irish women from Birkenhead, billeted in Eglwysbach in the Urban District of Hiraethog, applied to be billeted in an institution adjoining a public house, or in Llannwst where there are public houses available, and stated that otherwise they would return home. Permission has been refused and it is hoped that they will carry out their threat'.[506].

There was absolute disbelief in some reception areas that the deplorable accounts of the living conditions, morals and social behaviour in the areas evacuated were true, and surprise that such poor physical and moral well being of some of the evacuees could exist in a seemingly well off and modern society. This incredulity may also have been a result of simply not wanting to admit that such a situation could arise in a 'caring society'. One letter to The Times on 22nd September 1939, suggests that not all people were so uncaring that they did not see the benefits of evacuation for the poorer classes, and felt that something needed to be done to relieve the plight of the children from the poorer areas. But the text and tone of the letter is patronising in the extreme and is further evidence of the upper classes dictating the terms:-

'Sir,

While from all my friends in the country comes praise of many town-children evacuees, and, without exception, praise of all the secondary schoolchildren, complaints are pouring in about the half-savage, verminous and wholly illiterate children from some slums who have been billeted on clean homes. Stories with which one cannot but sympathise are told of mattresses and carpets polluted, of wilful despoliation and dirt that one would associate with untrained animals. The authorities, with plenty of time to prepare, seemed to have failed both in the physical and psychological examination of the evacuees, although the mechanics of the great trek have been so well ordered. Now one hears that both women and children of the roughest and uncleanest types are going back to their own homes. At present time, when Britain is fighting for liberty, no Briton would suggest dictatorship methods, but surely something short of these can be evolved to prevent these unfortunate children from being allowed to return to the appalling conditions whence they have been rescued. It is not fair that they should disrupt small houses; but is it not possible to cause, to coin a phrase, grass orphanages under the care of skilled and sympathetic teachers, to come into being? Let the mothers go back if they will. It does not matter so much what happens to

504 Dorset Daily Echo. 18 September
505 Crosby op.cit. p35
506 Denbighshire County Council. File 36 Ruthin R.O Z1352

adults, but surely children should not be allowed to go back to conditions which shame a nation fighting for civilisation....'

Yours faithfully,
F.Tennyson Jesse.
11 Melina Place. NW8[507]

After the Government conferences in early 1940 had introduced incentives for evacuees to stay in the reception areas, a second official evacuation started in 1940 which required the registration of potential evacuees. However, by April 1940, only 95,000 had registered, 220,000 had refused to do so and 842,000 had not replied. This apathy, combined with the local difficulties such as finding host families and the resignation of many billeting officers, put a great deal of pressure on the evacuation scheme. It was not until May 1940, when Malcolm MacDonald was appointed as Minister of Health and Herwald Ramsbotham to the Board of Education that the situation changed.

On the 31st May, MacDonald stated that:-

'...in the light of the latest war developments the Government regard the danger of air attack in the near future as so real that we should have plans for the evacuation of schoolchildren as complete as possible by the beginning of next week. Parents who do not register their children by Monday evening run the risk of not having them taken away'.[508]

They devised several experimental schemes which removed children and non-essential persons from within 10 miles of the Norfolk coast southwards towards Sussex, re-evacuated some of the children who had returned from the original scheme of 1939 to South Wales and the Midlands, persuaded people to move inland from all eastern and south-eastern coastal areas[509], and implemented a 'special' evacuation scheme between 13th-18th June 1940, when 103,000 children left London.[510]

This number was less than expected as throughout the week the Minister and various Ministry spokesmen had been talking in terms of 120,000 leaving on 180 trains. An L.C.C. official at Paddington Station simply stated that about 25% of the children who had registered under the new scheme had not turned up and was quoted as saying *'Probably the parents changed their minds'.*[511]

During each of the six days an average of 15 trains ran on the Great Western and Southern Railway. This time there was 1 teacher or helper for every 15 children. It is interesting to note that this scheme, although lower key than the first, still attracted the same jingoistic reporting as September 1939:-

'...As the trains drew out of the stations there were wild cheers from the children. Boys leaned out of the windows waving their caps and the girls blew kisses to the porters'.[512]

LONDON EVACUATION

Going Like Clockwork

Everything is going like clockwork and the children are behaving admirably. This was how one official of the L.C.C. described the working of the great six-day evacuation scheme from London.........

'I have not heard of a single case of a child forgetting either gas-mask, identity card or ration book,' said the official [513].

---

507 Livesey. Are we at War? op.cit. pp28-29.
508 ibid. 1 June 1940.
509 47,000, 60% of these were children and according to MacDonald 97 trains were to be used to transport them.
510 Angus Calder. People's War. op cit. p148
511 ibid
512 Dorset Daily Echo. 13 June 1940.
513 ibid. 15 June 1940.

Others left the cities voluntarily, but at a slower rate of exit. This was referred to as the 'trickle evacuation' although in some areas the exodus was more like a flood. Unlike the first phase in 1939, this was not an evacuation before the event, and some evacuations took place throughout the Blitz and, in consequence, some panic did occur. After the Blitz had started, many Londoners crowded into the main-line railway stations to catch a train to anywhere, just to get away from the city. As a result, so many East-Enders arrived in the city of Oxford, around 6,000, that the authorities had to take over the Majestic Cinema, (which ironically was showing 'Babes in the Wood'), in order to house them.[514]

Evacuees leaving London in 1940 for billets in the West Country

The following account from the Mayor of Stepney, Councillor Frank. R. Lewey, describes in some detail the problems faced in the target areas.

> *'We resolved to occupy the People's Palace , the theatre in the Mile End Road....this place was big enough to give us elbow room in handling the masses of homeless who were already tramping in like a retreating army, seeking our assistance...When we first set up business at the People's Palace...our very first task was to arrange for the evacuation of mothers and small children who had been rendered homeless, and, after those, for the mothers and children who wished to leave London....*
>
> *I myself, dog tired after a terrific day's work, dragging wearily out of the People's Palace and saw in front of me a great area of deserted prams in the evening light, with the drifting smoke of nearby burning houses dimming them....The mothers had brought their babies in prams, and, of course, we had not foreseen that, and, as they could not take the prams with them on the overcrowded trains, they just had to leave them there in front of the building, so that it was by evening, hardly possible to get in or out except by climbing over a great expanse of them...'* [515]

514 Holman 'The Evacuation' op.cit. p48
515 Ruth Inglis. Children's War. op.cit. p77

The Mayor of Stepney was very concerned to visit the reception areas and thank people for looking after evacuees from his area. The following log book entry supports this:-

> *'7th November 1939. The Mayor and Mayoress of Stepney visited the Aston Clinton Evacuee Boys School after being received, at his request, at the Head-teacher's billet in Buckland. Arrangements were made by the Head-teacher whereby the Mayor met the principal people of Buckland who had been instrumental in welcoming in schools from London'.*[516]

There is evidence to suggest that this second evacuation phase was much better organised. Although the overall arrangements remained the responsibility of local authorities, the Ministry of Health had provided advisers to help local officers. In some cases this came down to simple 'trouble-shooting' as this description by Lucy Faithfull, who was a regional welfare officer in the West Country from 1941, would indicate:-

> *'...I also had problems in Ilfracombe where people just refused to take any foster children. The children had arrived and were staying in schools looked after by teachers and volunteers. I had to live in Ilfracombe for three months and eventually, by visiting and persuasion got them to change their minds.'* [517]

This second evacuation did provide a necessary link between central and local government which was to become very useful in the post-war development of social services. However, even within the scheme there was a continual flow of evacuees returning home and this became such a problem that in June 1940 the Minister of Health, Ernest Brown, sent a copy of a hand-written letter to parents of evacuated children advising them to keep their children in the reception areas:-

A MESSAGE FROM THE MINISTER OF HEALTH TO PARENTS WHO HAVE EVACUATED THEIR CHILDREN.

> *'You are among the many fathers and mothers who wisely took advantage of the Government's Scheme to send their children to the Country. I am sorry to learn that some parents are now bringing their children back.*
>
> *I am writing to ask you not to do this. This is not easy for family life has always been the strength and pride of Britain. But I feel it my duty to remind you that to bring children back to the congested towns is to put them in danger of death or, what is perhaps worse, maiming for life. You will have noticed that the enemy is changing his tactics.*
>
> *He is now concentrating heavier air raids on one or two towns at a time, leaving others alone for the moment.*
>
> *Nobody knows which town he will attack next so don't be lulled into a false sense of security if your home district has been having a quieter time lately.*
>
> *Remember that in April over 600 children under the age of sixteen were killed and over 500 seriously injured in air raids. So keep your children where they are in the reception areas.*
>
> *Don't bring them back even for a little while. This is your duty to the children themselves, to the ARP services in your home town, to those who are working so hard for them in the country, and to the nation.*
>
> *Please read the message as the sincere words of a friend, both to you and the little ones.*
>
> *Yours sincerely*
> *Ernest Brown'* [518]

It is impossible to calculate what effect this letter had on keeping evacuees in the reception areas.

---

516 Aston Clinton School. Log book. 7 November 1939.
517 Holman. op.cit. p51
518 WRO F2/850/1-12.

Conclusion

The concluding comments in this chapter are best expressed by a retrospective report dated 21st June 1941 written by the Clerk to the County Council in Somerset entitled *'Government Evacuation Scheme. Functions of the County Council'*[519] which not only sheds some light on the processes that the Council had gone through over the previous two years but also highlights where there were failings in the system. Although specifically related to Somerset, these observations would have applied to many reception areas across the country where administrators in the reception authorities could have recorded similar information.

> *'In May 1939, the County Council convened its first conference of billeting authorities etc. and assumed general coordination of reception arrangements. A model scheme was prepared for the billeting authorities before the end of July. The Government's Evacuation scheme was first operated on the 1st September 1939 when a total of 44,956 persons were received. The scheme did not go according to plan inasmuch as far greater numbers of mothers with children than unaccompanied children arrived in the County. The County Council had to deal with a very difficult situation. Somerset took a prominent part in obtaining a satisfactory settlement of financial questions.*
>
> *After Dunkirk, there was the hurried evacuation of the South East Coast. The County Council only received 6 hours notice to the effect that Somerset was expected to receive nearly the whole of the population of Hastings. The reception went on through the following 2 days and 2 nights without a stop, and the official of the County Council played an important part in this most difficult operation. Families were separated on entraining and lost their luggage, and the County officials at once acted as a central bureau for uniting families. This bureau has been operating ever since and at least 75% of all the enquiries have been satisfactorily dealt with.*
>
> *After the bombing of London the Government plans broke down. Refugees poured into the County at a rate of 700-1000 a day and the problem began to reach grave proportions. Mr Cooper immediately went to Bristol and interviewed Mr Titherley, the Senior Reception Officer in the Ministry of Health and other responsible officials, when it was agreed that the County Council should assume the general powers of the management with regard to the reception of evacuees. This proved to be so successful that at a conference in October 1940, convened by the Reception Commissioner of the County and Coordinating Billeting Officer of the region, the Somerset scheme was generally adopted and Mr Cooper was appointed coordinating officer for Somerset and Mr Strickland his assistant.*
>
> *Liaison was established with the military, first to assist with defence measures and later to coordinate military and civilian billeting, including the requisitioning and release of properties.*
>
> *The Government policies of dispersal of industry for war work have presented another major problem in the billeting of war workers. The available accommodation is kept constantly under review and action can and has been taken at short notice, many times at night. There has been a good deal of work on the schemes of crash evacuation, shelter, feeding and billeting of war workers. The Ministry of Health will rely on the Coordinating Billeting Officer and his assistant in arranging for any organised transfer of population. The social welfare is under the immediate supervision of Mr Cooper and Mr Strickland.*

The billeting of expectant mothers has always been a very difficult problem and on the suggestion of the County Council a scheme for earmarking billets was suggested to the Ministry. The whole plan was adopted and it is understood is being extended to other counties.

---

519 SRO. Ex/Gen/1

The present total number of evacuees and war workers in the County stands at 127,000.

There are many other aspects of evacuation which have not been covered, but it is pointed out that all this additional work has been undertaken at some time during the 24 hours of the day by Messrs. Cooper and Strickland without any additional assistance apart from Welfare Workers.'

As stated at the beginning, evacuation was not simply a case of moving children and non-combatants from one area to another; instead it was a myriad of complex physical, emotional and psychological issues which to a large extent had not even been considered by those planning the scheme. The complexities of the return home of the evacuees at the end of the war, and the long-term effect that their experiences would have on their post-war lives, are dealt with in later chapters.

Wartime Camp Schools

'I can remember this gorgeous autumn day, beautiful sun and the fields all sort of mellow from the end of summer and I could see this lovely school with all the open air gardens, and the best thing was I could see all these girls there all these girls there all looking so happy and relaxed and enjoying life. And coming from the back streets of Birmingham and the bombing it was like moving to another world. And as we went through the gates I thought, in my own little way as an eleven year old, "Thank you God, this is going to be wonderful", and it was'[1]

Generally speaking, British evacuees who were sent to one of the 31 Camp Schools[2] built in various locations across the UK, fared better in terms of education, care and overall discipline than their counterparts who were evacuated to other parts of the country who were sometimes sharing educational facilities. Many of the ex-camp-school evacuees consider that they were fortunate in where they were sent, but the experience could be rather traumatic for those who not only had to cope with evacuation but also with an unfamiliar boarding school environment.

'I had one year when I was extremely homesick. There was a terrific pain, I had never been away from my people before, although I had stayed with several relatives due to my mother's illness, and my father being in the forces. But I had never had this experience before, this terrible longing, this gnawing feeling inside of me.....In fact at one time I was so homesick and so unhappy that the dormitory master had special permission for me to be taken into the school hospital to be looked after for a week or two to see if they could get me over this terrible crying and feeling of being so lonely'.[3]

The majority of the schools were built to a similar pattern and the daily schedule was often the same. Jim Bartley, a former pupil of a camp-school near Hemel Hempstead, described his usual routine:-

'We were wakened in the morning to walk to the ablution block to wash, return to the dormitory to fold blankets and make bed area tidy, then in dormitory order went to the dining area for breakfast, then morning school, lunch, afternoon school, tea. After tea there was free time but there were many organised activities especially between the hours of 8.00-9.00pm. Each dormitory was looked after by two teachers who took it in turns to read stories to the boys at bedtime which was usually 9.00pm.'[4].

The National Camps Corporation Ltd for England and Wales had been established under the Camps Act, 25th May 1939, and by July 1939 the Chairman of the committee had inspected a total of 155 possible locations, of which 30 were originally chosen[5]. The camps were designed in collaboration with the Royal Institute of British Architects and built from Canadian Maple with shingle roofs. At this time the estimated cost was £17,350 per camp, made up from:

- 15acre site @ £40 per acre....£600
- Layout-roads, drains, central buildings, sleeping quarters....£15,000
- Equipment and furniture.....£1,750

By November 1939 these estimates had risen to a total cost of between £26,000-£37,000.

1 Irene Gladys Jones. Written account. Children on the Move. Staffs. Archive and Heritage. p71
2 See Appendix 11
3 Brian Winch. Taped interview. MERL Archive
4 Jim Bartley. Former evacuee. Taped Interview. November 1996.
5 This later rose to 31

The first camp was completed by October 1939, a further nine by January 1940 and all but three of the final 31 by March 1940.

Once the camps had been constructed the Local Education Authorities designated to use them now had to convince parents that this form of evacuation was a suitable one. They also needed to consider that for some parents and children the residential nature of the schooling could be more stressful than evacuation to hosts in domestic billets.

Very few documents survive which indicate this how this 'persuasion' was carried out, but a rare document from the City of Rochester (Kent) Education Committee does provide an insight into how parents were encouraged to send their children away to the Wrens Warren Residential School, in Sussex[6].

> *'The problem of what to do for the best with regard to evacuating their children is ever with parents in these days of stress and anxiety….The suggestion put before you is easy to carry out into practice. The cost is the same as if your children were evacuated in the usual way, and is paid in exactly the same manner. There are no tiresome conditions, except that the youngsters must be medically fit, and that there is room for them.*
>
> *The advantages are worth examination. In brief they amount to the following:-*
>
> 1. *The children, boys and girls, go to a quiet, healthy spot miles from any town or city, but only 40 miles from their homes.*
> 2. *They are educated and cared for by specially selected staff.*
> 3. *They receive full-time education, with the fullest opportunities for outdoor work, in addition to the usual school lessons.*
> 4. *Games, physical training and sports of all kinds are provided in a way which is impossible in towns under war-time conditions.*
> 5. *Regular medical supervision is afforded free of any extra costs to parents, and there need be no cause for worry on the score of health.*[7]
> 6. *Once a month parents are able to visit their children, being conveyed at a reasonable charge, to and from the school, by buses chartered for the purpose.*
> 7. *The extraordinary character of the school itself……*
>
> *One proviso and one alone is made when admitting a child to the school, namely, that he or she remains there as long as possible whilst the war lasts, and the assistance of the parents in not changing their minds without real reason must be insisted upon from the onset…..'*[8]

Irene Jones can remember being told about the possibility of going to Pipewood by her headmistress;

> *'…..I remember the headmistress standing up and saying that the children could be evacuated to Staffordshire to a boarding school run by Birmingham Education Committee. I want you all to take these forms home and get your mother and father to fill them in to say whether they agree for you to be sent to this school……I took the form home and the only daunting thing was, we had to have blouses and long trousers, which of course most girls didn't wear then, and a thing called a windcheater. Well I had no idea what a windcheater was…..'*[9]

6 I am indebted to John Bell, a former pupil at Wrens Warren, for allowing me access to his personal files.

7 Despite their reassurances there was a serious incident at the camp in the summer of 1941 when some evacuees came across an anti-tank mine left after a Canadian forces military exercise. It was thrown into a stream and retrieved a few days later by another boy who examined the device with a penknife. The fuse exploded. One boy died in hospital of stomach wounds, one lost a number of fingers and the third remained in hospital for nine months suffering from stomach and hand wounds.

8 City of Rochester Education Committee. Letter to parents from Edward H.Webb Education Secretary. 1940

9 Children on the Move. Op cit. p71

The camps were not restricted to England and Wales and the Secretary of State for Scotland, John Colville, formerly opened one at Bromlee, near Edinburgh, comprising 6 dormitory huts, each with teachers' rooms and a common room for teaching purposes, an administrative building, an assembly hall and hospital and sanitary units, to accommodate a total of 350 children and teachers.[10] Under the Camps Act, the Scottish Special Housing Association had already chosen sites in Scotland for four additional camps which would serve two purposes; in peace-time holiday and school camps for children who would be sent there for periods of up to a fortnight, and in war-time provide suitable accommodation for evacuated children from the cities.

In the late 1930s and early 40s the whole question of Camp Schools had led to heated debates between the educationalists on the one side and local and national politicians on the other. Many of these arguments took place within the letter pages of the journal '*Education*'.

Letter from Charles Robertson London Education Committee re Camp Schools dated January 23rd 1940:

> Sir,- In the course of an article on Camps in the issue of Education of January 19, Sir Percival Sharp repeats the suggestion made elsewhere in the Press that the 'hold up' in using the Government's evacuation camps has been due to the unwillingness of London teachers to accept the duties associated with camp life in addition to their ordinary duties as teachers. He goes on to say that I have denied the unwillingness of London teachers, but he does not say that at the same time I have also explained why the LCC was unable to make immediate use of the camps. The fact is that, as at present designed, they are admirably suited for short occupation by parties of school children. For this purpose, with their central heating and electric lighting, their season could be extended somewhat beyond the usual summer months. It is, however, quite a different question to use the camps for permanent and continuous occupation by evacuated schools.........
>
> The only classroom facilities consist of a block of four rooms each capable of holding one form, a hall in which another form might be accommodated, together with two small rooms that might be used for sixth form work. One form could be accommodated during the part of the day in the dining hall. That is to say, there is classroom accommodation for six forms, in addition to the 6th Form an insufficient provision even for a small secondary school that admits only two forms a year. Most London secondary schools admit three forms a year so that, even when allowance has been made for amalgamating some forms because only 60% of the children have been evacuated it is obvious that the school is woefully short of bare class-room accommodation.
>
> ....We are told that the purpose of the Camps Bill was twofold–evacuation in war-time and education in peace-time. This succinct statement makes no reference to education in war-time. When children have been evacuated it is still necessary to educate them, and camp facilities that are adequate for supplementing peace-time education that is given for the greater part of the year in permanent school buildings are not adequate for giving war-time education all the year round, with no access to permanent school buildings.
>
> Signed Charles Robertson
> County Hall London.
> January. 1940 [11]

---

10 Education Journal VOL LXXIV NO 1911. August 25th 1939 p.176
11 Education Journal Vol LXXV No1934 Feb 2nd 1940 p.88.

Sir Percival Sharp replied in his weekly column 'Week by Week':

> *'I am not greatly perturbed by criticism as to the unsuitability in limited respects of the camps for any particular purpose proposed by the government. They were provided, according to Mr Lindsay, for evacuation purposes in war-time and for education in peace-time. I am perturbed by the failure of the government to make reasonable and prompt use of the accommodation provided at so great a cost.*
>
> *Mr Robertson, Chairman of the London Education Committee....takes exception to my suggestion that the camps should be used for the purpose of residential secondary schools on the grounds that the camps are not suitable in all respects for the purpose. I take comfort from the fact that in a circular issued by the Board of Education immediately after my notes were in type, the use of these camps for the purposes I indicated is commended to local authorities.*
>
> *It is true that modifications and additions which can quickly be made may be necessary if conditions approaching the ideal are to be secured, but it is to be remembered that secondary and other schools broken and scattered are now working under conditions far worse than those obtaining in the camps.'*

In May 1940, the Chairman of the National Association of Labour Teachers , J.V.Strudwick, commented;

> *'.....Assuming that private billeting can successfully account for half a million child evacuees and that the occupation of large mansions and other suitable buildings might dispose of another half a million, there would still remain well over a million from the danger zones who should be accommodated in the safer areas. Where are they to be put? The obvious answer is School Camps.*
>
> *This has been advocated previously in your columns and it is indeed more than five months since the Association of Architects, Surveyors and Technical assistants published their plan for school camps for all evacuable children. Is it not high time that such a plan was being put into execution by the government?* [12]

By the time this latter article appeared in the journal some camp-schools had already been completed.

One of them had been planned in advance of the war by the West Ham Council who, because of the areas close proximity to the London docks and therefore a prime target for any enemy bombing, had purchased 38 acres of land in Pixie's Hill in Boxmoor near Hemel Hempstead. They erected a camp school designed to take 200 boys aged 11-13 from various schools in the West Ham area together with teachers, catering staff and a resident nursing sister. The school opened in July 1940 under the headship of Mr Moon who had toured the schools in the area explaining to both boys and parents about the school and its merits.[13]

Another, established in Oxfordshire as early as February 1940, was considered at the time to be an educational experiment. On the 19th February 1940, The Beal Modern School, from Ley Street, Essex, a Central School which had originally been evacuated to Ipswich, became the first 'camp school' when seven coaches containing 182 pupils and 12 teachers arrived at Kennylands Camp, Sonning Common near Reading. The school was divided up into 5 houses; Wolfe, Drake, Clive, Blake and Scott and they competed against each other in all their activities including School work, Gardening, Games and the cleanliness of their dormitories.[14]

The camp, built in 20 acres of ground at a cost of £20,000, had central heating so it could be used throughout the year, its own hospital and sewage disposal plant, an assembly hall with stage and dressing rooms, a dining hall, shower baths and a tuck shop.

An account by John Gould, an ex-Kennylands pupil provides a usual description of the site;

---

12 Education Journal. Vol LXXV No 1947 May 3rd 1940. P377
13 Taped interview with James Barclay. op.cit. November 1996.
14 Kennylands School Log Book. 26th February 1940.

'It consisted of a collection of wooden buildings on either side of a drive…with dormitories on one side and administrative buildings on the other. On the left hand side of the drive were the administration buildings which consisted of a dining room and a kitchen, there was an assembly hall, a hospital, staff quarters, lavatory blocks, a camp manager's house, a boiler house and classrooms. On the right hand side there were 6 dormitories which were 3 one end and 3 the other end of a development with a splendid cricket ground dividing them. My first day memories are of being shown our dormitory with its rows of bunk beds along each side and the whole housed 36 boys in double bunks. Great store was set about being self-sufficient and it was all a question of making your own bed and darning your socks. Cleaning the dormitory was considered most important and I can remember on Saturdays the floor used to be polished and a boy was pulled up and down on a carpet whilst polishing the floor!' [15]

Not all camp-school pupils had to clean their own huts. Audrey Hemming who attended the Pipewood Camp[16] near Blithbury, described her early mornings;

'We got up round 7 o'clock….there used to be something on the radio, exercises, and some of us would do exercises down the middle of the dormitory, and then we'd have to go outside and across to what we called the wash block for showers and a wash. We'd all go to the school hall for assembly, morning prayers, and then over to the dining room for breakfast. We made our own beds, but there were cleaners to clean the dormitories, and after breakfast we started school just after 9 o'clock.'[17]

In Kennylands, the boys received four meals a day prepared by the camp chef who was described as *'a great big man, very tall, white hair and honey eyes'*[18]. As well as a Headteacher, Mr W.L.Norman, the school also had a Camp Manager, Captain F. Mee, who had once been a secondary schoolmaster. When interviewed in 1940, he explained the ethos behind the school:-

'Whatever the boys show a desire to learn we shall be glad to teach them. We are planting an orchard and ploughing up some land for the boys to work…..This kind of school is what I have been urging for years. It will make the boys self reliant and teach them the value of co-operation and the responsibilities of citizenship'.[19]

There would also have been a House Matron, and although there are no specific details for Kennylands, an advertisement for a camp school in Cheshire provides an indication of her basic duties and the remuneration:

'Applications are invited for the post of House Matron at Marton Camp. The matron will act as foster mother to the boys at the camp, and will be responsible for the repair of children's clothing etc. Suitable assistance will be provided. The salary for the appointment, which is subject to one month's notice on either side, will be fixed at a figure between £55 and £90 per annum, plus board, lodging and laundry, in accordance with the qualifications of the candidate appointed…'[20]

Many of the boys studied for the School Certificate or the Royal Society of Arts but their academic studies were balanced by having non-academic activities for part of the day. These included not only sports but also such pursuits as bee-keeping and pig-rearing.[21] Being the first of its kind, the school was visited by the King and Queen on 30th September 1940. They spent some time viewing all areas of the camp including the dormitories, classrooms and other facilities, before going on to look at the piggeries and chicken houses.

---

15 From an interview with John Gould.
16 Pipewood Camp School for girls and Shooting Butts for boys opened in May 1940. They contained c240 pupils from Birmingham and surrounding area.
17 Audrey Hemming. Children on the Move. Evacuation in Staffordshire . Staffs Archive & Heritage. p77
18 B. Winch. Taped interview MERL Archive
19 Dorset Daily Echo. 19th February 1940.
20 Education Journal. Vol LXXVII No 2008 Friday 4th July 1941
21 From a report by R.L.Arkell. Home and Country. September 1942. p138. cited in London Children in Wartime Oxford. op.cit. p50

'This has been a red-letter day in the history of the school. At short notice their Majesties King George VI and Queen Elizabeth, accompanied by Commander and Mrs Campbell and Sir Alan Lascelles, arrived on a visit to the camp.....A visit was made to the pigsty and poultry enclosures and the boys who are mainly responsible for the care of the livestock were honoured by being conversed with by both the King and Queen....'[22]

As well as describing such highlights, the log-book contains entries which are more poignant and reflect the dangers that some of the boys and their families were in;

'I have to record the distressing fact that Peter Gillingham, aged 12 of Form 1a, has lost his whole family consisting of father and mother and five young children by enemy action on the night of the 10th May.'[23]

'I regret to have to record that one of our boys, William Gouldstone, who left school on December 15th last (1944), was killed by enemy action in his home in Ilford on the morning of March 6th. His mother, too, was killed'.[24]

The area was obviously popular for Camp Schools because just 2 miles down the road situated between the villages of Peppard and Gallowstree Common, was another one, Bishopswood Farm, which housed the Senior Boys and Girls from Bedford School who moved in on the 26th February 1940. Doug Dielhenn, an ex-pupil, remembered the layout of the area vividly;

'As one entered the camp by the main gate, on the left was the Headmaster's house and office and on the right a small infirmary run by the school matron. There were 3 boys dormitories, in each 40 boys sleeping on 2-tiered beds. There was a master's room in each dormitory.

On the far side of the camp there were also 3 huts, but only two of them were used as dormitories for about 60 girls. The third hut was used as a classroom for teaching such things as cookery and woodwork. The main assembly hall, complete with stage, also doubled as a classroom for the older boys only who had no teacher but sat and did revision of past work, liable to be asked for the work to be shown at any time.....

Back in London boys and girls never mixed. We saw the girls in chapel every morning where they sat at the centre pews and we boys on either side and at the back. We also saw them at meal times where they were the strange creatures who sat on the other side of the central serving table....At the camp things changed and we had mixed classes, a thing unheard of before. We still sat separately 2 rows of 12 boys and 2 rows of girls. At last we began to realise the girls were human as we were, if you could call us human. The fact that woods surrounded the camp also helped some of us understand more about girls!.....'[25]

There was also an 'ablution' block containing only twelve toilets which served almost 150 boys. Interviewees remember that these facilities were stretched to the limit every other Saturday when the school nurses gave each pupil a dose of laxative. Two showers a week were an important part of the routine as a great deal of emphasis was placed on personal cleanliness. The buildings were arranged in a semi-circle which surrounded a large circular lawn with a flag-pole in the middle, an area which was out of bounds except when used for specific events such as Sports day. As well as the woods described by Doug, there was an also an area of cultivated land where the children participated in the national 'Dig for Victory' campaign. As in Kennylands, there were a number of outdoor pursuits and extra-curricular activities which in some cases initiated life-long interests.

---

22 Beal School for Boys Log Book entry. 30th September 1940
23 ibid 13th May 1941
24 ibid March 9th 1945
25 Interview with Doug Dielhenn

Another pupil was allocated to Bishopwood later in the war. Having already been evacuated to a number of billets, Tony Towner, together with his younger sister, arrived at the camp in 1943 and was to stay there until his mother remarried in 1947. When he was there the school housed the Alexandra Orphanage, which was to amalgamate with another one to become the Royal Alexandra and Albert School. He remembers the school having a 'holiday camp' appearance, but for Tony the experience was not always a happy one. Up until his move to the camp, his life as an evacuee had been somewhat liberal. Now he found himself in what he describes as '*...a strict regime, rigidly controlled along military lines, with one of the house masters known only as Sergeant'*.[26]

The system of control, which required a certain amount of self-regulation by a Prefect and Monitorial system, did lead to some bullying. The inhabitants of the three boys dormitories were divided up according to age, 8-10, 10-12, 12-15, and the progression from one to the other depended on the number of boys leaving at 15 and although this 'promotion' was seen as necessary, many, including Tony, did not look forward to the initiation ceremonies that went with it. His personal account gives very detailed picture of what life was like in Bishopswood, and it is interesting to note the similarities between his description and those of pupils in other camps, such as Jim Bartley. Each day followed the same schedule. The pupils got up at 6.30 and then had to strip their beds completely from the two-tiered bunks. The mattress was folded in half and the folded blankets and sheet, in the form of a sleeping bag, together with a pillow-case, was placed on top. [27] At 6.45 they were marched to the toilet block in pyjamas and dressing gowns and then returned to the dormitories to change their clothes, clean their shoes and have a kit inspection at 7.30. This was a competitive process as marks were awarded for neatness and precision. The time before breakfast at 8.00 (9.00 on Sunday) was spent standing around outside, unless it was raining. Tony recalls breakfast being the highlight of his day. It comprised of porridge, crispy fried bread, baked beans, fried or scrambled powered egg. But he was not as complimentary about the lunches which he simple describes as 'awful'. Fatty mince, or meat stew with cabbage, turnip, swede and lumpy mashed potato, followed by a milk pudding of some kind. Everything had to be eaten. Tea was simply bread and jam, and supper a slice of bread and Marmite.[28] In addition, once a week they were all given their 2 ounces of sweet rations, which became the unofficial currency for bartering.

During their spare time they listened to the wireless and worked on their hobbies. Tony remembers the first Sunday in every month as 'visiting day'. Parents would normally travel in hired coaches from London, or by train and then the local bus service from Reading, and arrive after the Sunday morning church service, which was usually led by the Head-teacher. After spending time with the children they would then leave before afternoon tea for the journey home.

Barbara Hewitt described the parental visits to Pipewood;

> *'Every month we were there, looking out for the coaches to come. 'Here they are!' We used to shout, and we used to see what they'd brought us! They always used to come with something, well of course sweets and chocolates were rationed and we had a little shop at Pipewood, but you couldn't get much unless you'd got the sweet coupons.....They both came and they had to get a coach in Birmingham and all the other parents as well, and they came together, always came together and sometimes they would bring my little sister with them as well, because she was still at home...'*[29]

Ivy Field recalls a visit from her mother;

> *' I do remember my mother bringing me a Bible and she noted various details inside the cover and said, 'If anything happens to us, these are the numbers you need to know'.*[30]

---

26 An Evacuees War. Tony Towner. Evacuee Archive. MERL University of Reading.
27 One can see why many of the pupils from camp schools found the transition to the services, either during the war or as part of national service, easy. The same 'boxing of beds' and inspection routines would have been very familiar to new recruits.
28 Tony Towner. op cit
29 Barbara Hewitt. Children on the Move. Op cit p75
30 Ibid p78

For some this was always a heart-wrenching experience as home-sickness was a problem especially among the younger and more insecure pupils. A number of ex-camp children have described how after such visits many children found their own space to shed a few tears, and it was an unwritten rule that they were left to their own thoughts.

As well as individual reminiscences, which of course can be subjected to memory distortion, some Local Education administrators and Head-teachers of schools kept detailed notes about the process of moving children to the camps. The following example relates to Manchester and provides historians with a very rare opportunity to see a case-study of how one particular area dealt with the planning and implementation of such an enterprise.

The camp school assigned to the Manchester LEA was Somerford Hall in Congelton. It stood on a large site two miles from the town and had been designed for 350 pupils. It was described as having 'excellent facilities for physical training and games'. As with other camps the buildings were made of Canadian Maple, and in a pattern similar to the others, consisted of an education block of four classrooms, a hall with stage and an ante-room. It also had a residential block containing 6 dormitories, large dining room, kitchens, a staff room, two lavatory blocks with WCs, baths and showers and a drying room. There was also a small hospital block, quarters for 8 teachers and separate living quarters for the Head Teacher and the Camp Manager. It was much bigger than the camps at Kennylands and Bishopswood even though it was designed to house almost the same number of pupils. It had been suggested that, if necessary, minor alterations could be made to accommodate extra classes by adapting a dormitory block and using the dining room.

The Board of Education had previously requested that the number of children transferred to the camp should not be less than 150 and the should be organised to receive senior boys drawn from Manchester Schools and other children, either at home or evacuated, whose parents specifically wanted them to move to the camp. The financial liability to parents would be the same as those allocated to billets, i.e. they would make a weekly contribution of 6 shillings.

The Head Teacher and the male teaching staff were to be recruited from teachers already on the Manchester LEA's payroll. They would live on-site and in return for residential duties would receive free board and lodging. The Education committee would be responsible for equipping the classrooms, laboratories and workshops with portable equipment, much of which would be provided out of existing stocks, and all the necessary supplies of stationery, books and other school materials. Any other expenditure would be set against the Evacuee account and would be met in full by central government.

Although there was some delay in using the school because of bad weather conditions affecting the progress of the work, by March the Committee reported that all was in hand. A leaflet had been published giving information to parents, and Head Teachers had been invited to submit lists of senior boys whose parents wished them to transfer to Somerford. Although every effort was being made to get the school open by Easter the committee still had to appoint a Head Teacher and the required staff. The first batch of boys arrived on the 23rd April with more arriving on the 25th. A total of 163 boys were then in residence and it was expected that admissions would continue until such time as the full complement of 350 was reached. The number of teachers had been raised from the initial 6 to 8 and the Head Teacher's wife had agreed to take up the role of School Matron. (Considering the projected number of pupils this is rather a small teaching staff. Had the school reached its full potential the pupil teacher ratio would have been 46 – 1, which even in war-time was rather large. This had been noticed by the head-teacher who commented on staffing issues on a number of occasions ....often to no avail. Luckily, the numbers on roll were usually around the 160 mark.)

From December 1942, the Head Teacher wrote regular reports for the Education Committee. They provide an interesting indication of what life was like in the camp and the facilities available to the boys. It is worth remembering that this type of education was alien to all those who went to Somerford because until this time they had been used to attending day schools and therefore going home in the evenings. The boarding scenario, and all that entailed, was very new and some of the boys, especially the younger ones, took some time to settle down to the routine.

On 21st December 1942, the Head Teacher reported that there had been one case of chicken pox but the boy concerned had been isolated. The time table had been changed to allow the boys the opportunity to go outside in the afternoon and the afternoon lessons had been moved to the evening. Fourteen boys had been confirmed in the Church of England and a Catholic Guild had also been established. The Head had introduced a monthly Prefects supper. In order to stimulate interest in the United States, ten boys had joined the American Foster Parents Plan, and were communicating with 'foster parents' in the USA. Almost all the boys over 12 had been out and about for ten days helping local farmers bring in the potato crop and as a result had earned £80, but there was no mention of whether the boys or the school fund received the money! Preparations were being made for the Christmas pantomime.

18th January 1943. The Dick Whittington production was reported as a great success. Two boys were listed as having scabies and another with an abscess in his ear. Two of the dormitories had been painted in house colours. During the Christmas holidays 123 pupils had gone home leaving only 40 in the camp. Those who remained had had a good time. For Christmas dinner they had Roast Beef, baked and mashed potatoes, sprouts, and Christmas pudding. They had seen films on Christmas night and on the 27th, and on Boxing Day had had a party. On the 28th a local farmer had taken them to the cinema. As the weather had been so mild they spent a lot of time outside.

It is interesting that Christmas was an important time in all the camps, especially for those children who were unable to go home. The school staff made sure that the children had a good a time as possible under the circumstances. Tony Towner described his Christmas at Bishopswood with some fondness. He recalled a large tree without any decorations, but the highlight was the dinner which included a pudding where each portion contained a sixpenny piece. Presents and parcels which had been sent to the children for Christmas had been stored away to be handed out on the day, and those pupils who did not have a parcel, were given one from the schools emergency gifts so that no child missed out. [31] Barbara Hewitt remembers her first Christmas at Pipewood for different reasons; *'Ah, that Christmas was wonderful. With snow on the ground, we all got up Christmas morning and had to put on our woolly dressing gowns and go down to the dining room and fetch a cup of cocoa and take it back to bed with us, oh, that was wonderful'*[32] Each girl had a Christmas stocking filled by a teacher and there was a Carol Concert which parents could attend. They were transported on special buses from Birmingham and offered lunch for 6d.[33]

15th February 1943. The Head Teacher informed the committee that there had been no reoccurrence of the serious cases of chilblains which had been the case the previous year. The main path to the dormitories had been widened and asphalted. In total 123 boys had returned to the school immediately after Christmas although 70 had not attended by the 11th January and 6 by the 31st. He had since been notified that 3 boys would not be returning. Those members of staff who had left were not being replaced and this was putting a great deal of pressure on those who remained. The school urgently needed a sewing maid (this had been resolved by the March report). A branch of the Young Farmers Club had been established and it was reported that the boys were already keeping bees and rabbits and it was hoped that they would have some geese by the summer. (Irene Jones, Pipewood Camp, recalls having to kill and pluck a duck for the Lord Mayors dinner; '*....I can remember I was thinking I can't do that and I remember the teacher said 'Oh yes you can. You clutch it and hold it by its legs, hang it upside down with its neck on the ground, put a bar across its neck and step on it.....*')[34]

15th March 1943. The Head Teacher reported a clean bill of health. Although the play hut had not been completed there was now an oak cabinet to display trophies. Out-of-school clubs now comprised of Handicraft, Gymnastics, Drama, Stamps, Hiking (with rucksacks), Modelling, Aeroplane modelling, Rabbit and Young Farmers, Art, Gardening, Debating and the Somerford Times, the camps own newspaper. It was his aim to get each boy interested in at least one extra-curricular activity. Also, as shoes wore out quickly and repairs were very difficult because of lack of local cobblers, he proposed introducing a cobbling club. During the month, Lieutenant Baum

31 ibid
32 Barbara Hewitt. Children on the Move. Op cit. p74
33 ibid p70
34 Children on the Move op cit p75

from the US Army visited the school and gave a talk and Captain Campbell, the inspector for the National Camps Corporation (NCC), made a visit and deemed everything to be 'satisfactory'.

Like many other camp schools, Somerford received gifts and grants from various organisations both in the UK and from overseas. It had received £5 from the American Foster Parents Plan, and had been promised clothing which could be used for *'necessitous cases'*. In addition, 100 boxes of toffees and games had been sent from the USA under the British War Relief Fund and they had also acquired enough radios for each dormitory to have its own. In addition the school was maintaining a certain amount of self-sufficiency, motivated to some extent by awards from the National Camps Corporation. As a result members of the Gardening club at Somerford constructed a 16 foot greenhouse, 14 garden frames and a set of garden seats to be placed around the quadrangle.

A Mr Body from the Committee had obviously made a visit to the school. Although he said that his general impression was favourable and the members of staff were doing well, he tabled a number of concerns at the Education Committee meeting. The recruitment of teaching staff had always been a problem and it was accentuated both by the shortage of men under 35 and by the fact that the accommodation for residential staff was very restricted. On the day of his visit there were nine assistant teachers with 160 pupils. Although this staff pupil ratio could be considered generous for a day school it was at least two, if not three, short of the level required for boarding school requirements. There were two vacancies that needed filling urgently and advertisements had been sent out. However, he notified the committee that the number of assistant staff should not fall below 12. He spoke of the general complaints about the school dinners. The breakfasts were fine but the Medical Officer had stated that *'the dinner lacks quantity and variety. Boys who ought to be improving in weight were not doing so* (though this was directed at only a few individuals). *The meals needed more meat'*. It was agreed that bread and butter should be available at the evening meal and boys should be encouraged to have seconds if the opportunity arose. He was concerned to point out that Somerford was a *'little community leading a rather limited life and problems are apt to be magnified'*.

By the 19th April, the Head reported that the teacher's cubicles had been enlarged and there was now space for a sitting room as well as a bedroom. Pupil activities included Football and Gardening and he brought the committees attention to the fact that the erection of the greenhouse had involved cross-curricular input from the Maths, technical drawing and handicrafts staff. The newspaper, science and boot mending clubs continued to flourish. The 'Wings for Victory' week had raised the sum of £33.8.0 well beyond the target of £25.

Unfortunately, in May it was reported that the greenhouse had been blown off its base during a gale! However the school had had a successful Sports Day. 80 boys had gone home during the holidays leaving 50 on site. In June this shortfall in numbers had been made up with a new intake of 32 boys, although one was immediately taken home because of homesickness. Eleven boys and 2 teachers had been invested into the Air Scouts and the food was improving!

In July, the school purchased 6 goslings and there was a promise of a cricket square. In September it was reported that the boys had enjoyed swimming in the River Dane. Although there were obviously still problems with staffing, especially over the school holidays when there were only three relief teachers available, the Head was able to overcome this to some extent by spreading staff holidays over a longer period of time.

In October, the boys received 20 pounds of sugar for their bee-hives and they had harvested a heavy crop of tomatoes. The Junior boys had collected '1 hundred-weight of rose hips' for the Women's Voluntary Service to be made into syrup. They had also raised £1.14.6 by making and selling coat posies. This money was sent to Captain Pinnell on the school's adopted 'Ship', together with a batch of letters and a large parcel of knitted comforts made by the typing department in the Education Office.

During December it was reported that 1 pupil had Scarlet Fever and 36 others had tonsillitis. As in the previous year evening school was introduced to make better use of the light afternoons. A weather station had been established and it was hoped that the Young Farmers Club would include poultry among their other interests.

There was no Christmas pantomime in 1943 but a variety show instead. A hundred boys went home and those who stayed had Roast Goose for Xmas dinner. The school received a large parcel of small gifts from the USA which were given to those boys who had had no letter or parcel from home. Several members of staff volunteered to forego their holiday to remain at the school over the vacation, but unfortunately the boiler burst and there was no heating. Consequently those boys and staff who were going home went a few days earlier than expected.

The reports continued into 1944 with the Head Teacher commenting on the day to day running of the school. There were no great alarms throughout this time although there were intermittent problems with the central heating system and a boiler that seemed to be an ongoing cause for concern. The clubs continued to be popular and the staffing issues took up a lot of the Head's time. One problem had been the lack of a school matron since August 1943. As the war progressed and evacuation became a less important issue for parents, the number of boys at the school gradually declined until all of them had either left, because of having reached the school leaving age, or returned to day schools in their own locality.[35]

There are no reports hinting about its success, or lack of it, but personal research into other camp schools would suggest that most of the boys at Somerton would have received a more consistent and wide ranging education than their peers. The activities offered combined academic studies with practical and vocational training. Hobbies were encouraged and there was an awareness of the wider implications of the war. They helped with salvage work, they adopted 'Ships', made comforts for the troops, dug for victory and established school savings clubs. It is also interesting to note that many of the camps schools introduced a Prefectorial system which meant that to some extent the older boys and girls looked after the welfare of the younger pupils. Research would suggest that like any other boarding school institutions of the time, there was an element of bullying but nothing that required reporting in the Head-teachers accounts and it was obvious from entries in the log-books that the welfare and education of the individual children within the school was paramount.

Despite the obvious initial problems of putting state-school 'day' children into a boarding school situation, the Camps scheme was reasonably successful. For some pupils the experience has had a long-term effect on the rest of their lives. Many formed friendships which have remained unbroken, one even became the 'Batman' for a member of staff when they both joined the Army, and a group of ex-camp school scholars still meet every year at the Sayers Croft school in Reigate, Surrey for a reunion weekend. Margaret Hancock (Pipewood) now 74, still sees her school friend Thelma every week.[36]

Others gained a real 'taste' for the countryside through the various agricultural and horticultural activities they had taken part in. Although some of the experiences such as bee-keeping were very much part of a camp school extra-curricular activities, others such as 'Digging for Victory' were used across the country. Many non-camp schools grew vegetables and other crops, and kept chickens and other small animals in order to supplement the rationing.

In many camps, the children were not only working on their own, sometimes extended plots, but also on local estates.....

> *'3rd-6th October 1941. Boys from the school (Kennylands) went to work on the farm each day[37]'*
>
> *'15th September 1943. Boys from 3A spent the afternoon picking up potatoes grown in the camp.*
>
> *'October 11th 1943 24 boys in 4A are potato picking at Harrison's Farm, Peppard today.'*

Reports from the Head Teachers would suggest that the curriculum was not only designed to meet the academic needs of the pupils but also provide opportunities that they perhaps would not otherwise have had. The useful and important extra-curricular activities, created to occupy as much of the child's time as possible, were wide ranging and encompassed many activities not often available to 'day' schools.

---

35 From Parsons M. 'Manchester the Exception to the Rule'. DSM 2003
36 Children on the Move op cit p82
37 Beal School for Boys Log Book. October 31st 1941. P189

There is a tendency to look at the success of the Camp Schools from the pupil's perspective and consequently it is easy to forget that the experience could be just as difficult for the members of staff who were not used to a boarding school environment and were not necessarily trained to look after pupils all day, every day. Pastoral care became an important and serious issue, especially where some of the children were very homesick and where they had lost parents, and it was essential that some form of one-to-one support was provided in such circumstances. It is apparent from oral and written testimonies, that both the teaching and domestic staff became surrogate parents for many of the children and as such the whole situation was a learning curve for all who took part. Olga Harvey commented that the*'....teachers were absolutely first rate and Miss Evans-Rose our headmistress, she was the same. She was a Quaker and she made sure we were well educated. And we were!'*[38]

Despite considerable financial investment during the war, the school buildings were not used to their full potential once the war had finished and all of the children had gone home. In 1945, after the return and demobilisation of the armed forces, many of the female personnel in the camps left to spend more time with their husbands and families, and as the wages were low it was difficult to find suitable replacements for them. Although some camps continued to provide rural accommodation for city children, others changed their roles. Sayers Croft is still owned by Westminster City Council and provides outdoor pursuit experiences for city children, Finnamore Camp became a Borstal housing 366 youths, but is now derelict, Wrens Warren was used to house Dutch children and some displaced French children (it eventually closed in 1953), and Horesleys Green, a camp school specifically designed for disabled children, remains the home of the Wycliffe Bible Translation Society. Some simply disappeared. The Bishopswood Camp is now a playing field, and the only clues to the Kennylands site, are found in the local street names. In March 1946, the 'Beal' boys had left Kennylands and returned to Ilford, but the Education Authority continued to rent the property from the National Camp Corporation and groups of children from all over Essex were sent there for short periods of time. Eventually it became a full-time boarding school until it was closed down in 1980. [39] Pipewood School closed in 1945, and an ex-teacher described her regret as she had envisaged it as *'having a great future and able to offer its pupils a really comprehensive education, and one which recognised the equal importance of each individual'.*[40]

A Comparison .....Life in the German Youth Camps

> *'These camps provided the intensive political and ideological education thought necessary to maintain the national socialist state. However, it is impossible to overlook the fact that a war that had been started by the Nazi regime was the very same one it now wanted to protect its children from; a policy which in the end was doomed to fail.'*[41]

The German regime considered youth camps to be an important part of their domestic strategy, but unlike the British Camp schools which were all purpose built to a similar design, the Kinderlandverschickung (KLV) camps took on many guises. Some had been hotels or boarding houses, others had been youth hostels, convents and schools. In some of the country areas the facilities were very primitive whereas in others, especially those which had formally been popular areas for tourists, they could be considered luxurious. However, some hoteliers and resort owners opposed the requisition of their premises because they were concerned about potential damage, and whether or not they could be used in their original state in the future. Some boys were sent to work on the local farms, as in the district of Swabia. Conditions in the camps varied. In his autobiography, 'A Hitler Youth in Poland', Jost Hermand described the different camps he was sent to during the war. One was a brick-built school in a small village with no electricity or running water and no access to a shop or post-office, one was a luxurious villa in San Remo where they were served by waiters, and the other was a skiing camp where he received winter-war training.

38 Olga Harvey. Children on the Move op cit. p76
39 Letter to the author from Joyce Goddard who taught at Kennylands until 1950.
40 Children on the Move. Op cit. p70
41 Parsons. Lecture 2012

The everyday life in the camps was strictly regulated even down to the amount of allocated dormitory space for each individual, reckoned to be about three cubic metres per person. Each room had to contain at least three beds. The children were to either swim or have a shower once a week and they were to wash their hair every fortnight. During their stay in the camps, they were to receive instruction and take part in recreational facilities. But there were also punishments for those who stepped out of line, usually in the form of beatings or extra drill, even though the former was officially banned within the camps. One boy commented later that *'.....all four pairs of shoes had erupted insoles, because of the marching and the penalty drill'*. [42] In fact, over time many of the punishments on the 'banned' list were used more frequently and it very much depended on the camp ethos as to how the children were dealt with. In some, the teachers and Hitler Jugend leaders were much more liberal in their approach, whereas others were run by Nazi 'hard-liners' who maintained a harsh regime.

One aspect of the camps which was never discussed was the length of stay. This caused a great deal of anxiety for the parents who wanted to be given some indication of how long their children would be away. Eventually the duration was technically limited to six months, but in practice the KLV authorities could extend the length of time at will by simply saying that 'war conditions' made it necessary.

Although most camps had cooks, housekeepers and medical staff, the management of the school was the responsibility of the teachers who, where possible, would come from the same area as the pupils. Although the teachers were technically in charge of the education, the responsibility for delivering it was that of the Camp Leaders (Lagerleiter), who in some cases were teachers themselves. However, the overall coordination of all the other elements of camp life was carried out by a member of the Hitler Youth with the title of '*Lagermannschaftesfuhrer*'. This boy, or girl, would have been previously trained in a special school where they were prepared to take responsibility for introducing Hitler Youth activities and supervising children during their free-time. He, or she, insisted that the qualities of discipline, comradeship, honour, hard work, expected from all German boys and girls, were maintained. However, as more and more of the older HJ members were called up, those left in charge of the KLV were now much younger and lacking the maturity and experience to not only organise the activities but liaise with the teaching staff. As a result, the latter were gradually able to assert their authority. However, teaching staff were also subject to call up, so many of them were replaced by those returning from retirement. Again, a similar situation to that witnessed in the UK.

Von Shirach stated that camp life was the *'ideal form of life for the boys where community was worth everything and the individual nothing'*.

Hitler himself had introduced the pedagogic strategies of the Hitler Youth stating that, *'I want my youth strong and ready. I want an athletic youth. I don't want any intellectual education. With knowing, I spoil my youth.'*[43]

In another speech he commented:

> *'My pedagogy is harsh. Weakness must be chipped away. The youth that will grow up in my fortresses will frighten the world. I want a brutal, authoritarian, fearless, cruel youth. Youth must be all of this. It must be able to bear pain. It must not have anything weak and gentle The light of the free, marvellous beast of prey must once again shine from their eyes. I want my youth to be strong and beautiful....then I will be able to create the new'.*[44]

The life of the girls was determined by his desire to make them good German mothers.

As the philosophy was one of the survival of the fittest, those children who were weaker in terms of sport and physical prowess etc., found the life in the camps very hard. The insistent military drill and 'physical hardening' did not suit all.

---

42 ibid
43 A.Hitler. Mein Kampf
44 Peter Sichrovsky. Born Guilty. Basic Books. New York. 1988 p169

The hierarchical 'pecking' order meant that the strong could dominate the weak, often in a brutal way. Everyone knew their place…those who were forced to clean the shoes of their stronger peers, or do the academic work for those who could not be bothered, those who were sexually abused or in some cases forced to be the abusers. For those at the bottom of the pile, life could be intensely hard. [45] According to Hermand, gaining the approval of ones peers governed ones behaviour. He describes an incident in which he was forced to take part; '*Even when the local Party leader, with whom we normally had little to do, ordered us to chop the heads of chickens, twist off the heads of pigeons with our hands or clobber little rabbits behind the ears with a stick and then cut their throats, we did it without the blinking of an eye. After all, none of us wanted to be called a 'sissy'.*[46]

Added to all of this pressure was the uncertainty of what was going on at home. Were their relatives safe, what was happening at the front? Despite outwardly displaying confidence, many of them suffered from home-sickness, considered to be a sign of weakness, a condition not helped by the irritant diseases such as lice, scabies and impetigo inherent in some of the camps. One of the worst things that could happen to a boy was to have a visit from his mother. Although some women moved to be near their children this was considered to be disruptive and was publically condemned in a speech by Artur Axmann, who had become leader of the Hitler Youth in July 1940. In some camps there was no contact with life beyond the gates at all. There were no radios, letters were often censored and few had any idea what was going on in the war. This was particularly the case of those camps situated in Poland.[47]

However, as in any other situation the experiences of the KLV children depended very much on individual circumstances, and despite the problems, it is apparent that the KLV scheme did save lives. One ex-evacuee, now in her seventies, but then aged eleven, the daughter of a merchant, was sent to a KLV camp. She described how life in the camp had been tough, but her presence there had possibly saved her life. Her home town had been bombed, and she had to wait weeks to get any message from her mother. Her fears for her mother's safety were not helped by the teachers comments that she was certainly now an orphan. Both the mother and the child survived. Another girl was sent to a camp where the teachers were a little more liberal in their regime. She only had to wear her uniform when she left the camp, her mail remained uncensored and racial/ethnic study was not on the curriculum. Whereas a boy sent to Hungary, initially for six months but extended to a year, describes how he was harassed by the teachers and that little sympathy was given to him when he developed epilepsy.

Some parents were becoming increasingly concerned about their children and despite the moral pressure and the threat of sanctions, such as withdrawal of food cards, some parents tried to get them back, and in some cases even offered money for them to stay at home.

As the allied land forces drew nearer, the KLV camps in the East were becoming particularly vulnerable and camp leaders were sent a communiqué by their Hitler Youth superiors stating:-

> *'The enemy threatens your camp. I am compelled by the present situation of the war to put the destiny of the children entrusted to your care into your hands and to leave all responsibility to you. In this hour of need use all your willpower. The most difficult task of your life is imminent. The existence of our nation through our German children is decidedly in your hands! The youth of Germany has got to exist! The time will come that they will erect the banner and will avenge our dead comrades!'*[48]

A memo entitled, '*In Case of Invasion*' contained lists of clothes and food that was to be taken with them, and illustrations on how to make haversacks out of blankets and BDM skirts if there were not enough available. Before leaving they were to destroy all documents which might give away any information about the KLV, and then move from one KLV camp to another, preferably at night. If there was no transport, they were to march. They were also given specific instructions about what to do if confronted by the enemy. If the English or

45 Jost Hermand. 'A Hitler Youth in Poland - Erwiterte KLV 1940-45.
46 ibid p49
47 ibid
48 Lynn H. Nicholas. Cruel World. The Children of Europe in the Nazi Web. Vintage. New York 2005 p60

American forces arrived they were to keep the children in the camp, making sure that all Nazi insignia, camp names and personal badges were removed and the camp itself was to be referred to simply as a residential school. However, if the Russians arrived first they were to remember the motto '*No child in the hands of the barbarous Soviets'* and leave quickly.

The leaders and the children were now left to their own devices; the central organisation had cast them adrift and how they survived, if at all, depended very much on their own resilience and adaptability. As a result, many of the children sent to so-called safety now found themselves facing the onslaught of the advancing armies. Many were killed, many were raped and many of those captured were sent back east and never saw their homeland again until the 'Wall' came down in 1989.

Overseas Evacuation

'The Captain read the Naval Burial Service. The little bodies, wrapped in sailcloth covered with a Union Flag, were committed to the deep. It was an experience I will never forget'.[1]

Some of those who had the money to do so sent their children to safety overseas, and by the beginning of the war thousands of evacuees had taken refuge in the USA and other countries.[2] In total around 19,000 Children were sent abroad, either privately, through sponsorship proposals, or under the Children's Overseas Reception Board (CORB) scheme organised by the Government in 1940. Many of the former who went to the USA pre-war and during the first few weeks, were generally from the middle and upper classes As the original cost of travel was set at £15, more than a month's salary for three-quarters of the British population, it put the scheme way beyond the financial means of the majority of residents in the UK[3]. In addition, British families with friends or relatives in the USA made their own arrangements to leave and it was estimated that 5000 people, mainly women and children, left Southampton for the USA on the 30-31st August 1939.[4]

America was not the only area of respite. Offers of help had also come from other quarters during the early months of 1939, especially from some of the Dominion countries. The Government of Southern Rhodesia and the Canadian Women's Organisations offered to host under-16s and over 60s, and the Australian authorities invited orphans for the duration of the war. However, all these proposals had been rejected on the grounds that the Government did not see the need for any evacuation overseas. One government spokesman responded to the offers by stating that '*...the idea is good hearted, but impracticable'*.[5]

By Spring of 1940 a number of Labour MPs, and others, were becoming concerned about the elitist nature of the private exodus as any voluntary evacuation by those who could afford it would create resentment among those who could not. It was also contrary to the notion of supporting each other in a time of crisis, the immeasurable war-spirit.

After some lobbying the Government was persuaded to introduce a scheme which would increase the availability of overseas evacuation to other sectors of the population. Elspeth Huxley[6] commented on why they were anxious that any proposals should be seen to be egalitarian. In June 1940, she wrote, *'In England, as the papers filled with pictures of the children of the well-to-do posing happily on the country estates of Long Island and Quebec, feeling grew that the safety of the nation's children was too vital and too sacred a thing to be bought with gold. Why should the son of a rich man sleep in security in New York's gay lighted towers, the roar of traffic bound on peaceful errands in his ears, while the son of a poor man dozed in the crowded shelters below our dangerous cities, menaced by the bombers drone? It was unfair; and something ought to be done'*.

However, although agreeing in principle, the Government genuinely recognised that any evacuation overseas could be seen as a panic and defeatist measure far greater than the 'internal' evacuation scheme, and many factors had to be thought through and resolved before any plan could be seriously contemplated. For example any proposed Government initiatives could not compete with privately sponsored ones because there would be fewer ships available to transport those supported by the administration. In addition, what would happen if the allies gained the upper hand in the war, yet were unable to win it outright? Some of the children might never be able to return home a fear which prompted lengthy discussions at Cabinet level, after which it was agreed that the threat of invasion outweighed these negative concerns.

1 Frank Brookshaw. op cit p150
2 Angus Calder. People's War. op.cit. p36
3 TNA.DO131/29
4 The Times. September 1st 1939
5 TNA.DO 35/259/B277/4: TNA.DO 35/529/B305/8: TNA.DO 35/529/B305/4
6 Elspeth Joscelin Huxley (née Grant) 1907-1997 was a writer, journalist, broadcaster, colonial officer, environmentalist and government advisor. She married Gervas Huxley, grandson of Thomas Huxley and cousin of Aldous Huxley.

Geoffrey Shakespeare, MP for Norwich and Parliamentary Under-Secretary at the Dominions Office, was asked to chair an inter-departmental committee including among others Miss Florence Horsbrugh (Conservative), Ministry of Health, and Mr J. Chuter Ede, (Labour) Board of Education.[7] Their brief was to' *consider offers made from overseas to house and care for children, whether accompanied or unaccompanied, from the European war zone, residing in Great Britain, including those orphaned by the war, and to make recommendations thereon'*.[8]

After consultation Shakespeare presented the Committee's final report to the War Cabinet on the 17th June 1940. His recommendations were that:-

- Children should be between the ages of 5-15 and attending school.
- A minimum of 90% of those selected for evacuation had to be attending grant-aided schools.
- Parents of those children selected would be required to pay the normal rate of 6/- per week for maintenance, the same amount applicable to British based evacuees, but the fare for the overseas transportation would be free.
- Parents of children attending independent schools would be required to pay £1 per week maintenance and £15 towards travel costs.
- Preference would be given to children from areas considered to be in most danger from enemy action.
- Preference would be given to children from less affluent families.
- Children would be fostered by Host families or relatives in the overseas reception areas
- As part of their responsibilities, parents had to accept the warnings that children were to be evacuated for the duration of the war. They would only return to Britain as soon as possible after the cessation of hostilities.[9]

While presenting his report Shakespeare was interrupted by a messenger informing Churchill that France was about to surrender. Although entries in the Cabinet Minutes show that the scheme had been endorsed, Churchill himself was so preoccupied with the situation in France that he had not realised a decision had been taken. Had he done so, it would seem from comments he made in later Cabinet meetings and in the Commons, that he would have opposed it.[10] On the 21st June 1940, he told the Cabinet that:-

> *'...a large movement of this kind encourages a defeatist spirit, which is entirely contrary to the true facts of the position and should be sternly discouraged. It is one thing to allow a limited number of children to be sent to North America, but the idea of a large scale evacuation stands on a different footing and was attended by grave difficulties'.*[11]

Once he had the Cabinet's endorsement, Shakespeare established the Children's Overseas Reception Board (CORB)[12] to oversee an evacuation scheme which was to include participants from all strata of society. This egalitarianism not only won the support of many Labour MPs but also from those with other motives, for example, Colonel Josiah Wedgwood who wrote to Churchill, suggesting that, '....*He should approach the United States and get them to take our useless mouths. Their conscience would make them consent; at worst the race*

7 There were also a number of Civil Servants representing all the interested Government departments; A further 16 members. R.A.Wiseman and C.W.Dixon (Dominions Office),L.G.Duke and H.A.Montmerency (Ministry of Health),E.A.Hogan (Scottish Ministry of Health),A.P.Sharman (Board of Education), J.W.Parker (Scottish Board of Education), B.W.Gilbert (Treasury), F.J.Ralfe (Home Office), T.M.Snow and Prof. T.N.Whitbread (Foreign Office), P.H.Brind (Ministry of Labour and National Service), Miss M.S.Cox (Ministry of Pensions), The Hon. J.G.Simon and F.H.Norman (Ministry of Shipping, J.P.Dodds and G.Kimber (Dominions Office Secretaries)

8 Report on Inter-Departmental Committee on the reception of children overseas. Cmd.6213: TNA. CAB.67/7/172. Minutes 15 June 1940: Official CORB History. TNA.DO 131/43.

9 TNA.CAB.65/7/170. 17 June.1940.

10 Ralph Barker. Children of the Benares. A War Crime and its Victims. Methuen. 1987. p28

11 TNA.CAB. 65/7/174. 21 June 1940. Sir Martin Gilbert. Churchill War Papers. Heinemann.p 391

12 Other members included: Arthur Mullins, Permanent Secretary to the Dept of Overseas Trade; Miss Marjorie Maxse, Vice-Chairman of the WVS; G.Hinde, Director of Thomas Cook; George Gibsone, later Chairman of the TUC, Tom Henderson, Scottish Educationalist....both Labour Party Advisors to the Board; Sir Thomas Dunlop, Organiser of CORB evacuation plans to the USA.....plus 7 others.

would survive; they would be by far the best propaganda for armed help',[13] and others who thought... *'the soldiers would fight more happily if they knew that their wives and children were safe'*.[14]

On the 17th June, Circular 1515 outlining the CORB proposals was sent to Local Education Authorities in secret with instructions that they had to be distributed to grant aided schools attended by the less well off. It was also sent to private schools.

On 19th June, Clement Attlee, as Lord President of the Council, tabled the CORB recommendations and report in the House of Commons. On the 20th, the written information reached those parents who might possibly become involved at the same time that it was announced on the radio and in the Press. By mid-morning the response was so great that more than 3,000 people were queuing outside the CORB offices in Berkeley St. London and on the following day over 7000 letters arrived, 94% of them from working class families. Despite having done a 'dress rehearsal' on the previous day, and the reception desk being looked after by two ladies, Thelma Cazalet MP and later Lady Cheetham both very capable of dealing with the public, the clerical team of thirty was totally overwhelmed.[15] Within a few weeks the staff, including such names as Vera Brittain, and the wife of Hugh Dalton, the former Chancellor, increased to 500, reaching a peak of 650 by September 1940 Before helping with the administration, Vera Brittain had already registered her own children, Shirley and John;

> *'Went along to CORB after getting a certificate of evacuation from Cook's. She fixed everything up for me quickly, including the 66 coupons which I am allowed for clothes for each child and of which I am the first recipient. But total value of all parcels sent during the year, including birthday gifts must not exceed £10 per child.'* [16]

Some, such as Lord Lothian the British Ambassador in Washington, were in favour of the scheme and thought that witnessing the need to evacuate children from Britain would persuade host countries remaining neutral to join the war on the allied side. Personally he felt that the USA was out of touch with British war aims and as a result, reluctant to make contributions of weapons or other materiel. He hoped that the arrival of these children would help influence United States public opinion concerning the country's policy of neutrality. In April 1940, he had commented that 'the United States is 95% anti-Hitler, is 95% determined to keep out of the war if it can, and will only enter the war when its own vital interests are challenged, though these vital interests include its ideals'[17]. Another influential supporter was Eleanor Roosevelt, America's First Lady, who immediately after her election as Chairman of the US Committee for the Care of European Children received more than 2000 offers from people wishing to adopt children. Other offers were made directly to the administration in Washington and to other city authorities. In addiction specific companies like Kodak-Eastman, Ford, Hoover and Warner Brothers got involved and offered to take the children of their employees in Britain.

The American Press also generated interest. The Herald Tribune referred to invited evacuees as 'guests of the nation' and the New York Daily Mirror wrote a leader under the heading 'This nation's duty to England's future….' stating that it would be a duty and privilege to give them a home.

Even as late as 1941, Elspeth Huxley wrote 'All over Canada and the United States, from the bustling seaboard cities to the flat and sun-soaked prairie towns, from the mansions of millionaires to the cramped framed houses of the poor, men and women offered the safety of their homes to children from the battle zones'.[18]

At the end of June 1940, articles appeared in some local British newspapers outlining the rationale behind the Overseas Scheme and explaining to parents what their responsibilities would be should they wish to consider the option This one relates to Weymouth in Dorset but they were replicated across the country.

---

13 Parliamentary Debates. Commons 5th Series. Vol.363.1939-40 col. 358. 17 June 1940: TNA.CAB. 65/7/170 17 June 1940: TNA.CAB. 65/8/179 1 July 1940.
14 Parliamentary Debates Commons 5th Series vol.362. 1939-40 cols. 5-6. 18 June 1940. and Westward Ho!. Ministry of Information Film soundtrack. 1940.
15 Sir Geoffrey Shakespeare. Let Candles be Brought In. MacDonald. 1949 p249
16 Vera Brittain's Diary. 1939-45. 25 June 1940. pub. Thorpe 1993. p167
17Michael Henderson. See you after the duration . Britannica 2004 p28
18 ibid p34

PROBLEMS FOR PARENTS

Very soon all Weymouth mothers and fathers will be confronted with perhaps the biggest problem of their lives. Should they keep their youngsters by their sides in Weymouth, a so-called safe area, or send them overseas to a safe land?

They must decide whether they will face the pain of not seeing their own children for perhaps years when at the most important stage in their young lives, but knowing that they are growing up safe from Nazi bombers, from death, injury, and that the youthful minds will not be forever contaminated by total warfare.

All parents in Weymouth are to be sent two forms, dealing with the evacuation of Weymouth children from five to 16 years of age to Canada, USA, Australia, New Zealand and South Africa.

Parents with children attending grant maintained schools should send their replies to the Local Education Authority, Municipal Offices, Weymouth. Those with children attending secondary schools to the Director of Education, Dorchester...and other schools to the Secretary of the Overseas Reception Board c/o Thomas Cook and Sons Ltd., Berkeley St., London W1.

It is explained on the sheets that before going overseas the children will have to pass a medical examination, which will probably be held in Weymouth. They will travel under suitable escorts and, on arrival, be boarded with private families and not institutions. They will receive as good an education as the children in the neighbourhood to which they are sent and their welfare afterwards will be carefully watched.

Extra clothes will be issued to them free, and when the war is won they will return home again.

Travel will be free. Parents will be expected to contribute for the maintenance of each child as much as they would have contributed had the child merely been evacuated to a receiving area in this country. If they offer to pay more than 6/- a week or more, no enquiry will be made; if not, they will be assessed according to their circumstances.[19]

It is interesting that the correspondent mentions *'forever contaminated by total warfare'*. Of course he was referring to total physical war, he had not considered, along with the vast majority of people at this time that children would be affected by the psychological effects of war and the trauma of being separated from their parents. It is also worth stressing that, with the benefit of hindsight, it is now known that the war finished in 1945, but when statements like these were issued, nobody would be aware of this and comments like *'face the pain of not seeing their own children, for perhaps years'*, would carry a greater poignancy.[20]

Today the language of these articles would seem to be rather fatalistic so it is really no wonder that parents were persuaded to apply. Worth considering that this was aimed at people in Weymouth, an area unlikely to be attacked, so imagine the effect such appeals would have had in areas which were known to be in danger.

The huge public response, which perhaps revealed to some extent the depth of public apprehension for the future state of the nation, was of great concern to the Government and is reflected in the minutes of the Cabinet meeting on 1st July;

---

19 Dorset County Chronicle & Swanage Times. 27 June. 1940.

20 In 1940, when asked how long he thought the war would last, Harold MacMillan replied, 'Twelve months if they win; five years if we do'.

> 'The Prime Minister drew attention to the scheme for evacuating children to North America. Many people were now expecting the scheme to develop on a considerable scale. A large movement of this kind encouraged a defeatist spirit, which was entirely contrary to the true facts of the position and should be sternly discouraged'.[21]

Shakespeare was instructed to issue a statement to calm things down and *'draw attention publicly to the dangers and difficulties involved in sending children overseas'.*[22]

Issued later on the same day it simply said.....

> 'The Government has no intention of shipping large numbers of children overseas. Any idea of mass migration is absolutely contrary to the wishes of the Government concerned. For scores of thousands of children to be transferred in a few weeks, as suggested in some quarters, is outside the bounds of any practical scheme and would be an extremely dangerous process'.[23]

This message was very similar to the one he had broadcast on the radio a few days earlier.

> *'Any notion of sending hundreds of thousands of children overseas in the space of a few weeks was both dangerous and stupid...The scheme could only operate subject to the limitation of shipping and offers made by each Dominion'.*[24]

Despite the Government's best intention, the statements did little to quell the rush and by the 4th July the total number of applicants was 211,448. Of these 11,702 were from Independent Schools and 199,746 from Grant Aided Schools. Almost 50% fulfilled all the criteria.[25] Overwhelmed by the numbers, the Cabinet decided to postpone the scheme *'without killing it to ensure that it was kept to quite small proportion'* and closed the lists stating that they had more names than they could cope with. Again Geoffrey Shakespeare was ordered to diffuse the situation.[26] As a result further pronouncements were placed in local and national newspapers.

> *'It has now been announced that in view of the adequate response already received from parents wishing to send their children overseas it will be impossible for any more applications to be entertained until further notice. No further applications from parents should therefore be made to either the local education authorities or the Children's Overseas Reception Board. Similarly, no further applications should be made for employment as escorts'.*[27]

So the scheme went ahead despite Churchill's reservations and its outright detractors, who were concerned that they had got tied up in a scheme driven by crisis and emotion rather than rational thought.

Shakespeare and his team now had to arrange the transport, and in collaboration with the Ministry of Shipping and the Admiralty future dates for sailings were worked out in enough time to allow for the selection of children, the process of informing parents and the signing of the requisite legal documents.

Schools were sent application forms and these were distributed to parents, in some cases after they had attended a meeting during which the whole process was explained. The forms were relatively simple to understand and complete, but out of necessity asked for a great deal of relevant information. This one was issued by Somerset Education Committee:

---

21 Gilbert. Churchill War Papers. Vol 2. op.cit p451
22 TNA.CAB. 65/7/174. Minutes. 21 June 1940. M.Gilbert. The Churchill War Papers. Vol.2 May 1940 - December 1940. Heinemann. 1994. p391
23 E.Stokes. Innocents Abroad. Allen and Unwin. 1994 p35
24 ibid. p36
25 TNA DO.131/39.
26 TNA.CAB.65/8/179 Minutes. 1 July. 1940
27 Dorset Daily Echo. 6 July 1940.

Somerset County Council

County Education Committee

PLEASE WRITE IN BLOCK CAPITALS

I desire that the following of my children should be evacuated overseas:-

My Child's/Children's name(s) is/are

1..Age................Sex

2...

Place and Date of Birth

1.......................

2.......................

Address

At present attending school at:-

1...................................

2...................................

Religion..........

Are they British?

Have you a preference for any of the following countries? If so, please state your preference(s) in order.

Canada/USA/Australia/New Zealand/South Africa

Have you any friends/relatives in the above countries with whom you would like your child/children to live? If so what is their

Name

Address

My name is...................

My address is..................

I understand that the above particulars are supplied for information only and do not bind me in any way.

Signed............................Mother/Father/Guardian

When completed this form should be returned to the Chief Education Officer. County Hall, Taunton or if your child has been evacuated under the Government Evacuation Scheme you may wish to send the form to the LEA of the area from which he/she was evacuated.

Somerset County Council
County Education Committee

This front side to be completed by Parent or Legal Guardian.

A separate form should be completed for each child.

OVERSEAS EVACUATION MEDICAL INSPECTION FORM

Name of child...Particulars copied from National Registration Card

Date of Birth

Name and address of parents

Normal Occupation of Father [28]

Religion

School Attended

LEA

Certificate of Parent or Legal Guardian I being the father/mother/legal guardian of................ hereby certify that there is no insanity, feeble-mindedness or epilepsy in the child's family, and that the child has never suffered from fits or epilepsy.[29]

Signature of Parent/Legal Guardian

Child's Signature
Date

2nd SIDE

For completion by Examining Medical Officer

Nutrition

Height

Weight

Disease of Skin

Cleanliness of Head........ Body..........

Teeth

Nose and Throat

Ear Disease

Hearing

Speech

External Eye Disease

Vision without glasses or with glasses if worn R.......L......

---

28 Interesting question! Perhaps there is a hint here of socio-economic manipulation. Begs the question why, if this was meant to be an egalitarian scheme, is the fathers occupation important.

29 On the one hand this was obviously screening out those who may simply not be fit for evacuation overseas, but on the other there could be a hint of a eugenics policy here.

Heart and Circulation

Lungs

Tuberculosis

Mental condition

Nervous System

Enuresis

Deformities etc

Other disease or defect[30]

Vaccinal State.......Number of marks

Medical officer's remarks......I consider this child suitable/unsuitable for evacuation overseas

MO Signature

Date

Children's Overseas Reception Scheme

Somerset Reception Area

Borough/Urban District or Rural District in which child is now residing..........................

Report of the Headmaster/Headmistress on the under-mentioned child who is attendance at the .... school, on his/her suitability for evacuation under the above scheme.

Name of Child....................................Date of Birth

Address

Regularity of Attendance

Conduct

Character

Educational Attainments

Ability

General Remarks

Date.................Signed Headmaster/Headmistress'

Each application was assessed jointly with the requisite school and medical reports and those who were considered to be unfit or unsuitable were rejected. Those who were accepted received this standard letter explaining what would happen next;

> *'.....In the accompanying letter you are informed that your child (children) has (have) been accepted for evacuation overseas. This does not necessarily mean that they will be sailing at an early date, but only that they have been placed on a waiting list from which children are selected as and when shipping accommodation becomes available. You should, therefore, make no special*

30 Again there are socio-economic implications underlying these questions.

preparations until you have had further notification.......When you receive notification you may conclude that the ship in which your child (children) is (are) to sail will be convoyed.....In the interest of security for your child (children) and others who will accompany them we ask you to regard this information as confidential.....'

The accompanying letter referred to above covered four main points;

'For retention by parents.

It is important that you should read the attached letter very carefully.

The main points are

That consent to the sending of the child must be given by persons having proper authority to give it.

That the child will be sent at the risk of the persons making the application.

That the government will do their best for the child but cannot accept responsibility for him or her.

That the parents or guardians will be liable to make payments mentioned in paragraph 4 of this letter.[31]

Interesting to note that the Government were not prepared to take responsibility for the children whilst in its care! In addition, although it was recognised that there might be problems getting the signatures of fathers in the services, the parents were asked to respond to this letter within 48 hours of receiving it The invitation to participate in the scheme was to be kept secret for security reasons and only the immediate family were to know. A few days later the family would receive a letter asking them to take their child for the compulsory medical examination at a School Clinic.

On the 2nd July, the CORB planning was brought to an abrupt halt when the former 15,500 ton Blue Star liner 'Arandora Star' carrying 1500 Italian and German internees and 86 prisoners of war, was sunk off the north coast of Ireland by U-47 while en route to Canada. A total of 714 lives were lost and although no children were involved it did convince the government to cancel the CORB scheme while at the same time allowing private travel to go ahead. This created a great deal of bitterness. The Labour MP for Llanelli, James Griffiths, informed the House of Commons about the resentment in his constituency because children of '*responsible public men*' had been sent overseas while '*poor children*' were left behind. He went on to say that '*.....common people did not ask for anything more than the ordinary protection which everyone else gets, but they resent it and feel indignant if rich people are looking after their own children and allowing the children of the poor to stand all the risks.'* His comments were reiterated in a Home Intelligence Report dated 16th July, which said that the postponement of plans for evacuating children to the Dominions was leading to '*sharp recrimination against the rich, whose children were enabled to sail*'. Another MP raised the question '*Was the scheme merely a camouflage to get out the well to do?*'[32]

The following day the Government reversed its decision.

However, on the 9th July the Admiralty warned the War Cabinet once again that the Navy could no longer provide adequate naval protection and on the 16th and 18th of July *both* Attlee and Churchill told Parliament that the evacuation had again been suspended.

In the Commons on the 18th July 1940 Frederick Cocks, Labour MP for Broxtowe, Nottinghamshire, asked the Prime Minister whether:-

---

31 Official communications sent to the parents of Patricia Johnston then living in Liverpool. Patricia went to Australia on the 6th August 1940 on the M.S. Batory. The ship was also transporting 1000 troops. I am indebted to the family for allowing me to use this now rare correspondence.

32 Parliamentary Debates. Commons 5th Series. Vol 363. 1939-40 col. 21.23,355-62

'...in view of the fact that the large scale evacuation of children overseas was an important factor in the military defence of Britain, will he reconsider the decision to postpone the scheme, bearing in mind that children can be evacuated in ships which are already convoyed?'

Churchill replied:-

'It is most undesirable that anything in the nature of a large scale exodus from this country should take place, and I do not believe that the military situation requires or justifies such a proceeding, having regard to the relative dangers of going and staying. Nor is it physically possible.... The scheme has been postponed, not abandoned, but any further emigration that may be possible, as opportunity serves, will be regulated, with a view to restoring the balance between classes, and not in pursuance of any policy of reducing the number of persons in this well-defended island. Furthermore, the scale of movement must necessarily be small in number and dependent in time upon naval facilities.'[33]

The Labour MP Benjamin Smith asked the Prime Minister whether he would, at some later date:-

'...reconsider the possibility of evacuation of children by neutral and American ships'.

Churchill replied;-

'Yes, of course; if a movement to send United States ships to these shores were set foot from the other side of the Atlantic, it would immediately engage the most earnest attention of His Majesty's Government'.[34]

Although his replies to specific questions are perhaps constrained by his need to maintain morale, reading through the debates of the time one can nonetheless sense Churchill's displeasure about the whole scheme. The concerns he expressed in the Press release of 1st July were reiterated in this debate on 18th July:-

'I must frankly admit that the full bearings of this question, (Overseas evacuation) were not appreciated by His Majesty's Government at the time when it was first raised. It was not foreseen that the mild countenance given to the plan would lead to a movement of such dimensions, and that a crop of alarmist and depressing rumours would follow at its tail, detrimental to the interests of National Defence...' [35]

Despite the official postponement, the scheme continued and Churchill must have been aware of the situation when he sent a memo to Sir John Anderson on the 18th July 1940 questioning the necessity of Geoffrey Shakespeare, leaving his post in London to see off 100 evacuees departing from Liverpool. The latter usually took the opportunity to say a few words to the children before their embarkation. In his memoirs he recalls....

'I usually told the children that they did not represent themselves when they were sent overseas, and therefore they could not behave as they liked. They were, in fact, like British ambassadors and consequently must behave even better than they knew how. If they behaved badly people would say 'What frightful children! Their parents in Britain really cannot be worth fighting for' on the other hand, 'What splendid children these are! We must do everything we can to help their parents win'. I said that when things go wrong, as they often will, remember you are British and grin and bear it....Be truthful, be brave, be kind and be grateful...' [36]

33 Martin Gilbert. Churchill War Papers. Vol 2 op.cit. p542
34 ibid
35 ibid
36 Shakespeare op.cit p256

Geoffrey Shakespeare with a group of CORB Evacuees prior to departure

However the whole question of elitism remained a matter of debate and undeniably there was a certain amount of substance to the claim.[37] On 1st July 1940, on the same day that the Cabinet had decided to close the overseas lists, Frank Aydelotte, American Secretary of the Rhodes Scholarships, had appealed to American Rhodes scholars throughout the USA to help house *'one or more children of Oxford and Cambridge dons, or those children of dons from other universities'*.[38] A few days later the suggestion that only the titled and wealthy were wanted by American hosts was played down by the 'American Committee in London for the Evacuation of Children', who explained that some sponsors were paying for the transportation costs of the poorer evacuees.

On the 9th July 1940, Eleanor Roosevelt established the 'National Child Refugee Committee' in New York[39], in order to raise $5m[40] to provide homes for '*refugee*' children, and in answer to a question from one of the welfare workers in the audience about whether or not the American Red Cross could send ships to collect the children, Mrs Roosevelt stated that:-

> *'...it would be a very grave responsibility, and might get us into the war. The USA, in all probability, would not feel that they could assume that responsibility'.*[41]

The Government had already recognised the concerns about exclusivity and in a debate to the House of Commons on 3rd July, Attlee pointed out that although the overseas evacuation scheme was part of the national defence, there was no intention of clearing out everybody from the country except fighting men and those engaged in war-related industries. Acknowledging that nothing would undermine public morale more than

---

37 This is still apparent today. At a conference on overseas evacuation held in 2009 at the English Speaking Union, some of the ex-evacuees who had been evacuated privately had no idea what CORB was?

38 Reuters. 1 July 1940

39 In this respect she was ahead of her husband who was treading a more careful political path.

40 At the time approximately £1m

41 Reuters. 10 July 1940.

granting such facilities to the privileged few, he went on to stress there was no class privilege in the scheme, a fact reiterated by Shakespeare in the same debate.[42]

Churchill was also keen to play down the possible perception of snobbery attached to the overseas evacuation. On the 18th July, after the scheme had been 'closed', he felt it necessary to address this question in the House of Commons.

> *'His Majesty's Government have been deeply touched by the kindly offers of hospitality received from the Dominions and the United States. They will take pains to make sure that in the use that is made of these offers there shall be no question of rich people having an advantage, if advantage there be, over poor'.* [43]

Although the decision to cancel CORB had been overturned, the question of shipping still remained a serious issue and of great concern to members of the Admiralty. They informed the evacuating authorities that there were three factors which would make it impossible to move all but a handful of children overseas:-

- Few ships were available capable of carrying large numbers of children.
- Most of the available passenger ships were needed to transport enemy aliens to Canada.
- U-boats were operating in the Atlantic and the Western Approaches and the Luftwaffe was also attacking shipping, resulting in a shortage of Convoy escort vessels.

Those selected for evacuation began to arrive in Liverpool where they were accommodated in schools, hostels and orphanages. The private evacuees were supposed to stay in the relative luxury of the Adelphi Hotel, but in reality spent their nights in the hotel's basement air-raid shelters as the city was being bombed. The late Margaret Wood, who was to sail on the Llanstephan Castle to South Africa on the 23rd August, stated that the only thing she can remember about her two days in Liverpool with her fellow evacuees was spending the time in a shelter and *'being dosed with Castor Oil...all 302 of us!'*. [44]

The longer the children waited for embarkation, the greater the danger of homesickness, which under the circumstances was not an uncommon occurrence. Shakespeare described homesickness '*....as a strange disease; it comes suddenly like a virulent germ, and such is its physical effect on the child that it lowers all power of resistance. But the same child within an hour is laughing and joking again'*.[45] Nonetheless, those with extreme homesickness were sent home[46], together with those children who, despite the initial medical examinations, were deemed unfit to travel. The total rejected at this stage was around 11%.

The remaining evacuees were seen by their ship-board escorts, who took over responsibility from the 'train' escorts, and each was given a metal identification disc with their CORB number inscribed on it. Those who lacked suitable clothing were kitted out by the WVS, and games and books were made available. Before departure, and while on board ship, the children were given lessons in etiquette and information about the country they were going to. In general terms it could be said that these children were facing a far more difficult time than their counterparts who had been evacuated within the country. Many of them were on their own, with no siblings, no school friends and no teachers who were known to them. Those from poorer areas who had probably never been outside their immediate locality before, now found themselves on board a ship travelling to a country whose culture was likely to be totally alien to them.

The escorts, many of whom were Salvation Army Officers, and others who were in their early 20s, took on the tremendous responsibility of making sure that the journey and the experience was as good as it could be, given

42 Reported in the Dorset Daily Echo. 3 July 1940.
43 Martin Gilbert. Churchill War Papers. Vol 2. op.cit. p543
44 Letter to the author and personal papers.
45 Shakespeare. op cit p259
46 Although there are no figures available it would be interesting to see how many of those sent home were from the working classes, as many of the middle and certainly the upper class children would have been sent away from school and had already coped with the problems of homesickness.

the circumstances. There was one escort for every fifteen children, one doctor and 2 nurses for every 100 and Ministers of leading denominations in every large group.

The Government was anxious to secure the help of the Salvation Army so an appeal went out in the June 1940 issue of the International War Cry asking for volunteers but stipulating certain criteria. They had to be:-

- Experienced in controlling children.
- Not more than 55 years of age unless possessed of exceptional health and other qualifications.
- Available at short notice.
- Good sailors.
- Persons with experience as leaders of Young People's Groups such as Life-saving Guards and Young People's Corps'.[47]

The total number of applications to become escorts, from all sources, reached more than 19,000.

These children are embarking on their journey to Australia

The first evacuees to Canada sailed on the 21st July 1940 on the 'Anselm' in convoy OB 189 and despite being attacked by U-boats on the 27th July during which time four other vessels sank, she survived.[48] Between July and mid-September 19 ships sailed with 90% of the 3119 evacuees leaving during August. By September, 16 ships had reached their destination. It is interesting to note that only 8 of the 19 ships could take more than 100 passengers. This was a calculated risk. Security of the children was a high priority and CORB had the choice of either sending them in unescorted fast passenger liners, or slower ships in a convoy Had they chosen the former the number of available ships would have been greater and the evacuation speeded up, but if torpedoed the casualties could have been higher. After the sinking of the Arandora Star, it was agreed that a small number of

47 International War Cry. 6 June 1940. Salvation Army Publications.
48 Stokes. Innocents Abroad. op.cit. p49

evacuees would be transported on each ship and these would then travel as part of a convoy. Although this would slow down the process, it would hopefully be safer. Three ships sailed for Australia. On the 5th August the 'M.S.Batory', a 16,000 ton luxury liner of the Polish Gydnia American Line and originally designed to carry only 300, sailed with Convoy WS2 with a complement of 1,340, including 477 children, 51 escorts and medical staff. The ship arrived at its destination on 16th October 1940 and in the New Year, Patricia Johnston's parents received the following letter from the CORB offices;

> 'January 1941
>
> Dear Sir
>
> I am glad to be able to tell you that Patricia is now living with Mrs William Fisher, 135 Bell St, Preston, Victoria. I hope that you will be receiving letters regularly and that Patricia is settling down happily.
>
> Yours faithfully
>
> Elspeth Davies.'

On the 24th August, the 'Nestor' of the Alfred Holts Blue Funnel Line, sailed with Convoy OB203 with 82 children and 8 escorts and medics and on the 17th September the 'Diomed' left with 18 children.[49]

Margaret Wood, was to travel from Liverpool to Gibraltar in convoy with some merchant vessels, together with an evacuee ship going to Australia. All the ships steamed east into the Mediterranean whilst the Llanstephan Castle struck out alone into the Atlantic, zigzagging its way to Cape Town hoping to avoid the U-boats. The journey lasted five weeks instead of two because of these evasive measures. In her diary Margaret described conditions and life on the ship.

> *'On Friday, 23rd August 1940, we boarded the ship Llanstephan Castle. We were very well looked after on the ship. Each morning for about an hour and a half, we had lectures on travel, South Africa and divinity. There was a church service every Sunday. There were two concerts, one was given by the escorts and the other by us. I sang duets with Olwyn Gibson, 'The Indian Love Call' and 'Somewhere over the Rainbow'. The voyage was quiet and the only port of call was Freetown in Sierra Leone. We all had to drink quinine, ugh! - and plaster ourselves with ointment if we went out after sunset because we were in a malaria infested area. When we crossed the line, the equator, we had a big party. It was very riotous and ended by putting bread and jam[50] down each other's backs'.*

The Llanstephan Castle had been converted into a troop ship so Margaret and her fellow travellers slept in three tiered bunks, bathed in hot sea-water and used a 'rough chunk' of soap which was supposed to lather. The food on board was described as very good and the restaurant, run on a pre-war style, even provided printed menus. Some were devised to make them fun. For example the tea provided on September 3rd 1940 comprised: 'Filleted Fitness, Soused Hasty Words with Toasted Tempers and Bright and Breezy salad'.

What the majority of parents did not know, or realise, was that when these ships and convoys travelled from Britain they only had a naval escort for a distance of circa 200 miles west of Liverpool. At that point the convoy scattered and the individual ships took their chance against the U-boats. There were two reasons for this action. First, as the USA remained neutral there was no provision for escort ships to refuel in ports on the east coast of America, and second, a shortage of Naval escort vessels in the Western Approaches, meant that they were compelled to leave outward bound convoys, carry out anti-submarine patrols and then wait to escort incoming convoys to either Liverpool or the Clyde.

In 'Children of the Benares' Ralph Barker describes the deployment pattern of the convoys:-

---

49 ibid p49
50 Interesting pastime when one considers the food shortages and rationing at home.

> *' They were arrayed on a broad front three miles across in eight columns of two vessels each, with an asymmetrical ninth column of three to vary the pattern, their generous spacing allowed them to zigzag in concert either side of their mean course to a prearranged schedule. This was their only defence, passive and ultimately unpredictable, against the submersible enemy.....'* [51]

An indication of how dangerous the journey could be can be found in the number of U-boat 'kills' confirmed during the summer of 1940; 58 in June, 38 in July and 56 in August as well as 15 other vessels sunk by the Luftwaffe.

On the 30th August 1940, the liner 'Volendam' carrying a total of 606 passengers, including 321 evacuee children, 26 escorts, 2 doctors and 3 nurses, was torpedoed, off the northern coast of Ireland, by U-60. Fortunately a second torpedo did not explode so she did not sink and was towed back to Scotland by tugs. The news was relayed to Shakespeare, who by coincidence was close to Glasgow where the survivors were to be taken. There were no casualties among the 321 children, but one did go missing. Robert, a boy of nine, was asleep in his bunk and among all the confusion had not been seen by the crew. Meanwhile, all the other children had moved into the lifeboats. At round midnight, Robert woke up to find he was alone. He went on deck, saw that the boats had gone and the ropes dangling from the davits so decided to go back to bed! In the morning Robert, along with a skeleton engineering crew, were taken aboard a destroyer. He arrived in Gourock clutching half the German torpedo. Had the news of this 'loss' got out it could have damaged the integrity of the whole scheme, but Shakespeare was able to persuade the Robert's father, and Robert himself not to reveal the true story. [52] Unfortunately, one of the Volendam survivors was to die on the Benares just three weeks later.

The escorts who had been travelling on the Volendam all received copies of the following letter from the CORB offices; (Note this postdates the sinking of the SS City of Benares)

> '23rd September 1940
>
> Dear Miss Close
>
> Although our experience in going with a party to Canada was so unfortunate, I am writing to ask whether there is any likelihood of your being able to help us in this way on another occasion. If so, will you please let me know when you will be free and which of the Dominions you would prefer. We will then let you know exactly what is being done with regard to a renewed exit permit....' [53]

Two had already volunteered again and sailed to Canada and others readily accepted the offer to travel on ships which in the event didn't sail.

The press and the Ministry of Information took the opportunity to use this narrow escape as positive propaganda commenting that *'the CORB children transferred to other ships in perfect order ...like guardsmen on parade, in high spirits...with pride in their adventure'.* [54]

However, little was learned from the experience. The 'Volendam' had been the leading ship in the centre column of the convoy and was therefore visible to other vessels, including the enemy. Surprisingly, as well as the evacuees she was also carrying a cargo of wheat to sell in North America, thus making it a legitimate target. [55]

Despite a great deal of work carried out by Shakespeare behind the scenes, an official CORB scheme to the USA never materialised. He had had discussions with Joseph Kennedy, the US Ambassador, and details had been worked out in Washington, but the inflexibility of the American immigration laws created barriers that were difficult to overcome. First and foremost, there was a quota system in place for each nationality and the arrival of

---

51 R. Barker. op.cit. p1
52 Shakespeare op cit p271
53 Fetheney. op cit p 132
54 The Times. 2nd September 1940
55 Barker. op cit. p43

too many from Britain would have upset the allocation of numbers. In addition, the medical tests for migrants were very stringent and could never have been applied to children in wartime. Finally, there was the fundamental problem of guardianship responsibilities and to what extent hosts could act *'in loco parentis'*. All these issues were not insurmountable and ironically were in the process of being finally resolved when in September 1940, the SS City of Benares was sunk and CORB was suspended again...this time permanently.

On Friday 13th September, the 11,000 ton S.S. City of Benares of the Ellerman's City Line, left Liverpool for Canada in Convoy OB213. She had been delayed by two days because of mines dropped in the Mersey, a delay which proved to be significant. The ship was carrying CORB and private evacuees, one of whom Tony Quinton (later Lord), aged 14 was travelling with his mother.

S.S. City of Benares

The fact that she was sailing in a prominent position similar to that of the Volendam, and in this case without any escort protection, possibly contributed to her loss. She was also the flagship of Rear-Admiral Mackinnon, the convoy commander, thereby making her a prize target.

The 'Benares' was torpedoed on the 17th September by U-48 under the command of Heinrich Bleichrodt,[56] with the loss of 77 children, 6 escorts and 173 adults and crew.

Heinrich Bleichrodt

56 Heinrich Bleichrodt. Korvettenkapitan was born October 1909 and was Captain of two U-boats U-48 and U-10. On his first venture at sea he sank eight ships which included the 11,081 ton City of Benares.

It is ironic that until 1am on the morning of the 17th the Convoy had been supported by the destroyer HMS Winchelsea which used her submarine detection echo sounders (ASDIC) to monitor U-boat activity in the vicinity of the convoy. At that time the Winchelsea was ordered to leave OB213 and pick up the inward bound HX (Halifax)71 convoy carrying ammunition and other supplies, but significantly, before going off station, the Commander of the Winchelsea had warned the Commodore of the Convoy that there was a U-boat operating in the area near to Longitude 20 degrees west.

There were other contributory factors to her demise. The ships were only making 6.5-7.5 knots into a headwind and although the Benares could go faster she was controlled by the given order of going as fast as the slowest ship in the convoy. Had she been allowed to travel on at her own speed she may have survived the attack. However, had she been originally permitted to sail on her own she would not have been allowed to have carried evacuees in the first place and it later came to light that the owners had requested convoy protection.

Thirty evacuees were killed almost immediately by the force of the explosion beneath their cabins. Those who survived did so primarily because they were thrown from their bunks. There was also a lot of confusion when the life boats were launched, one tipped over depositing all the children into the cold sea.

Lord Quinton who was 14 at the time described what happened to him;

> *'We were sitting in the lounge at about 10 at night and I was reading an historical novel about Napoleon. There was a terrific banging noise which sounded, where we were, more like a collision than an explosion, but it was in fact the explosion of a torpedo somewhere near the stern of the ship. Then the bells went and so on and so forth and we nipped down to our cabin and got our life jackets and put them on together with a heavy overcoat and went back to our boat station. Then absolutely nothing happened. Then a rather energetic man said 'I think we had better go to the boat'. So we all got up. Nobody came to call us. We headed off to where we knew our boat was going to be and indeed our boat was just waiting there for us, but it was a little on the full side. There were an enormous number of people in it. The crew began to lower it and then either a rope broke or somebody ran away from the winding thing, and it went. One end of it was held on by rope , the other end fell away and people fell down, and a lot of people just fell out and I fell out because there was an enormous weight of people falling on top of me, so I zoomed down quite a way. I must have hit my head in the course of it on some piece of tackle hanging off the side of the ship because I was not properly conscious for a while until I bobbed up...........and stayed up and then my mother saw me from 30 yards away I suppose, and yelled in an imperious way and I swam over to her and clambered in the boat. The boat was thoroughly water-logged but it was still buoyant because of the required buoyancy tanks and when we actually drifted away at that stage of the proceedings there were 23 people on the boat and I imagine there had been about 65 when we hit the water.'*[57].

To add to the problems weather conditions were bad, with gale force winds and high waves. Two of the escorts independently described the situation in their boats.

> *'….the little ones faded out, quite unable to stand up to the awful conditions….All we could do was to hold them above the water till they were gone….we gave them what comfort we could'* [58]

> *'….the children started to go into a coma one by one….We slapped their hands and faces, and then kept their heads above the water until we could tell it was no use'* [59]

Miss Day's boat was picked up by the crew of HMS Hurricane twenty hours after the event. John Collins a Cypher Officer on the Hurricane described the events:-

---

57 BBC Interview July 1999. Cited in Evacuation the True Story. Parsons and Starns. DSM 1999 p144
58 Miss Day. Escort on the Benares. ibid p138
59 Mrs Towns. Escort on the Benares. ibid.

'About midnight on 17th September I unscrambled a signal from the Admiralty commanding the Hurricane to go to a position in the North Atlantic where survivors had been reported. We hoped to lower the whaler to go off to pick them up. All the survivors we picked up were severely dehydrated, shocked and emotionally upset. Three little boys aged about 7 could not be revived. One little boy being shown around the ship saw his sister's dressing gown hanging up to dry and he thought she had been drowned, there was a monumental reunion.'[60]

Bess Cummings was in another of the boats;

'The water in my lifeboat came up to my chest, so you can imagine younger children, smaller children had no chance. The adults who had put themselves onto the side of the lifeboat like we had began to realise that for them there was no survival. It might be better just to let go and slip away, and they did. On board the whaler from the Hurricane I could see men jumping up and down, waving at us, calling us and shouting 'Hang on girls' To find two girls, alive, on an upturned lifeboat was just amazing for them, they were crying as well as laughing.[61]

Forty six of the survivors, including six children, spent eight days in an open lifeboat before eventually being rescued by HMS Anthony an 'A' Class destroyer.

The 'Anthony' left the convoy it was escorting because a Sunderland Flying Boat had spotted a lifeboat;

'The senior officer had to make the decision who would investigate and he decided he would liaise with the Sunderland. The weather was good and once the ship had been given a bearing from the Sunderland, it didn't take long for the Anthony to pick up the lifeboat, get it alongside get them all out and then sort them out. In the boat were a teacher, Miss Cornish, 6 children and 36 Lascars'.[62]

The fact that they survived was very much down to the determination of their escort, Miss Mary Cornish, who kept the children amused by telling stories and getting them to sing songs. She later received the British Empire Medal from George VI. Another escort of note was Michael Rennie, who dived into the sea on numerous occasions from the lifeboat to rescue children swimming in the water. Sadly, he was one of the casualties and died as the 'Hurricane' came into view. [63]

Mary Cornish

60 Evacuation the True Story. Op cit.p146

61 Bess Cummings. BBC Interview cited in Evacuation the True Story. Op cit.p145

62 Frank Bookshaw. AB on the Anthony. Ibid p147

63 There is a memorial to him in the Church of St Jude-on-the-Hill, Hampstead.

One interesting feature about the lifeboat that Mary Cornish was in may account for its survival. It had no oars....instead it was propelled by levers that turned a screw propeller in the stern. This meant that although many of them did not have the strength to pull an oar, they were able to pull a lever.

The Lascars who had been on the ship and rescued by the 'Anthony' were in poor shape as they were only dressed in pyjamas, overcoats and old fashioned life-jackets.

The ship that picked up Lord Quinton's boat had come from the West of Scotland and having collected the survivors returned to Greenock where the 'Anthony' also went. Here they were met by Shakespeare. Of 406 people on board, 256 died.

The parents of the children who died received a short letter from CORB headquarters simply stating;

> '.....I am very distressed to inform you that, in spite of all precautions taken, the ship carrying your child to Canada was torpedoed on Tuesday night, 17 September. I am afraid your child is not amongst those reported as rescued, and I informed that there is no chance of there being any further list of survivors.....'[64]

Twenty sets of parents were to lose more than one child and the Grimond family from South London lost five of their ten children in the disaster.[65]

The fact that some people remained in the sea for so long was partly due to an Admiralty order which forbade the crews in the Convoy and on Convoy escort duty to pick up survivors if it endangered the safety of their own ships. Any rescue by ships in the rear of the convoy would only be allowed to'*....when a local escort vessel was present. If such an escort is not present, a rescue ship should not act as such unless this can be done with undue risk'*. In the case of OB213 all the ships were in danger because of the U-boats still in the area so a later Board of Enquiry concluded that *'it would not have been proper to depart from these orders on account of the children.....as this would have endangered the ship'*.[66] Therefore, as soon as the 'Winchelsea' went off to meet the incoming convoy HX71 from Nova Scotia she had in effect neutralised the ability of any other ship to act as a rescue vessel. Had the convoy not been delayed, the Winchelsea would have been on station at the time of the attack.

At home, the Ministry of Information used the tragedy as anti-German propaganda and referred to it as *'a new Nazi outrage against all the rules of war'*. Cordell Hull, the US Secretary of State wrote *'I am sure there will be no division of opinion in this country that this was a most dastardly act.'* In Canada the Minister in charge of Evacuation described it as *'just another demonstration of Nazi frightfulness'*and the Robert Menzies, Australian Prime Minister stated that *'...this latest exhibition of savagery by the Nazis' will steel the British people to 'defeat the dark spirit for which the Nazi regime stands....'*

Shakespeare himself was widely quoted as speaking of his '*horror and indignation that any German submarine captain could be found to torpedo a ship over six hundred miles from land in a tempestuous sea....This deed will shock the world'*.[67]

Although without question it was a disaster this war of words was nonetheless useful in the British Government's attempt to influence USA neutrality. However, as American public opinion remained staunchly neutral it was to be another fourteen months before they entered the war,

Even Goebbels joined the argument, at first denying that a U-Boat had sunk a civilian ship then later, when the weight of visual evidence undermined his argument, laying the blame squarely on the shoulders of Churchill. *'If*

---

64 DO131/20 (CORB Files)
65 Fetheney op cit. p134
66 Fethney. op cit p149
67 Ibid p146

the ship was really torpedoed with the loss of 83 children, then the murderer's name is Churchill. Nothing is sacred to this monster'.[68]

It was acknowledged later that this tragedy took place in a time of war, and although some authors and contemporary journalists labelled it a war-crime, it is now important seventy years on, to look at the event from the U-boat commander's point of view. As far as he was concerned he was torpedoing an unlit ship in a convoy. He had no idea that there were children on the ship and as with other vessels carrying overseas evacuees, there were no signs or other recognition features on the boats to indicate that they were on board. Therefore, it could be argued that he was simply carrying out his orders to simply sink ships. The 'Benares' was only one of eight ships he sank on this, his first mission at sea. So he did not pick it out as a specific target. It is perhaps possible that had the British government declared in some way that the ship was carrying evacuees, the Germans, recognising the potential for anti-German propaganda, would not have attacked her. Especially as such an occurrence could have been seen as similar to the sinking of the Lusitania in May 1914 which eventually led to the USA's declaration of war in 1917.[69]

Mistakes were obviously made, and after the initial press response on both sides of the Atlantic with banner headlines such as '*Murder at Sea*'; '*Loathsome lawlessness of German conduct in war*', questions began to be asked. It soon transpired that some of the drain plugs in the lifeboats may not have been in position, that the handles used to propel the lifeboats were too stiff to operate and one lifeboat only had a single oar….which was broken. There were also some serious doubts cast on the Lascar crew's efficiency to perform well in a crisis as they were ill-equipped to deal with the sea conditions at the time. Later, Marjorie Day, the senior escort, commented that had there been a British crew on board the loss of life might not have been so bad.

At a subsequent enquiry it also transpired that when the Winchelsea was told to leave the convoy, the C-in-C Western Approaches had also sent a direct order to Rear Admiral Mackinnon to disperse the convoy ships at noon on the 17th. For some reason Mackinnon did not pass on this order until just after 10 pm so until that time all the ships were in convoy formation, not taking zig-zagging anti-submarine avoidance measures, and therefore making it an easy target for any U-boat in the area. As the Convoy Commander did not survive, the answer as to why he ignored the C-in-C's order for ten hours will never be known.

It was decided not to have a public enquiry into the event as it would have done little for morale and contributed nothing to the war effort and as most of the proceedings would have had to have been '*in camera*' to avoid the possibility of any information falling into German hands, the enquiry was unlikely to be public in the truest sense. One positive outcome of the disaster was the introduction of small fast vessels designed for the sole purpose of rescuing people from the sea. There were only 12 but over time they rescued more than 4000 seamen. It also meant that escort vessels did not have to endanger themselves in a rescue mission but instead concentrate on engaging the enemy. [70]

Shakespeare now found himself in somewhat of a dilemma. In the light of the recent events, should the 270 evacuees on the City of Paris be allowed to sail? A situation compounded by news received on the 21st September that the 10,000 ton 'City of Simla', coincidentally of the Ellerman Line, en route to Bombay via Capetown in the Convoy OB 216, had been sunk by U-138 off the Hebrides. Fortunately only three people had been killed in the explosion, all the life-boats had been launched, all the survivors, including 37 evacuees, rescued, and the Lascar crew proved to be very efficient. However, he felt it only right under the circumstances that the parents with children on the 'Paris' should be given the option of withdrawing them, so cancelled the sailing.

Throughout the rest of September there were a series of communications between CORB officials, Sir John Anderson and Churchill.

---

68 Barker op cit p 119
69 The Lusitania was torpedoed by a German U-Boat, 11 miles off the Southern coast of Ireland on May 7th 1914, , and sank in just 18 minutes with a loss of 1195 lives. The loss of 123 Americans among the dead resulted in a great deal of anti-German feelings in the USA.
70 Barker op cit p153.

On the 22nd, Shakespeare reported to CORB on future policy and while acknowledging that:

> *'On the one hand is the delightful welcome and home life awaiting the children, free from war atmosphere and particularly the nervous effects of discomfort of air raids,'* [71] *he conceded that the risks involved were increasing.*

The following day Churchill informed the Cabinet, that while recognising there was strong feeling against a complete discontinuation of the scheme, in view of the Benares disaster the future evacuation of children overseas must cease.[72] On the 25th Shakespeare sent a letter to the Home Secretary setting out CORBs recommendations;

1. Children should be sent on vessels crewed only by Europeans.
2. No more children should be sent overseas in a slow convoy during the winter months.
3. The policy of sending children to the other three Dominions should continue provided convoys were available.[73]

On the 30th Sir John Anderson, when supporting the proposal that the whole scheme should be suspended, raised the issue of whether or not parents should still be allowed to evacuate their children privately.

As a result the Cabinet decided that:

1. The CORB scheme should be suspended, but it would not be officially announced for two days in order to allow time to inform and discuss the matter with the relevant High Commissioners.
2. They should not refuse permits to those parents wishing to make private arrangements to evacuate their children overseas.

This latter decision went against the CORB philosophy of equality of opportunity and reopened the debate of elitism and the fact that money and privilege could still 'purchase' safety overseas.

The notion that there was a hidden political agenda behind this decision in that the British Government was intent on maintaining strong links with the USA in the hope that they would join the Allies, is debatable and raises the question as to whether or not the continuation of a scheme sending children to the USA would actually have influenced the latter to enter the war? Nonetheless, in hindsight, to an independent observer today this seems to have all the hallmarks of exclusive and selective decision making by a group of people looking after their own.

On the 2nd October 1940, the scheme was officially abandoned and the groups of CORB evacuees waiting in Liverpool to board the 'Largs Bay' bound for Australia and the 'Llandaff Castle' (South Africa) were sent home. The 'Rangitane' en route to New Zealand returned to disembark. Although the arguments of whether or not the scheme should be resurrected continued into March of the following year, nothing materialised.

After the evacuation of 2,670 CORB children; 1,535 to Canada, 576 to Australia, 355 to South Africa and 204 to New Zealand, the official scheme was now finished.

---

71 Ibid p143
72 TNA.CAB 79/6 folio 323 Gilbert Churchill War Papers. Vol 2 op cit. 23 September 1940. p862
73TNA CAB67/8. Letter to Home Secretary from G.Shakespeare. 25 September 1940

CORB Ships

Ship	Sailed	Convoy	Arrived	Evac Aboard		Escorts Aboard			Code	Dest.
				Boys	Girls	Dr.	Nurses	Escorts		
Anselm	21/7/40	OB189	3/8/40	39	43	1	2	7	D1	Canada
Hilary	6/8/40	OB194	?	70	84	1	2	12	D2	Canada
Batory	5/8/40	WS2(f/s)	16/10/40	477 Total		2	10	38	C1	Australia
Oronsay	10/8/40	ZA	21/8/40	187	166	2	4	29	D8	Canada
Antonia	10/8/40	ZA	21/8/40	145	139	1	3	21	D5	Canada
Duchess of York	10/8/40	ZA	21/8/40	256	238	2	5	36	D7	Canada
Bayano	16/8/40	OB199	28/8/40	45	44	1	2	7	D3	Canada
Ruahine	16/8/40	OB199	27/9/40	58	31	-	2	7	Z1	New Zealand
Llanstephan Castle	24/8/40	OB203	20/9/40	308 Total		2	6	23	U1	South Africa
Nestor	24/8/40	OB203	20/10/40	82 Total		-	2	8	C2	Australia
Volendam	28/8/40	OB205	Torpedoed	320 Total		2	3	26	D10	Canada
Rangitata	28/8/40	OB205	3/10/40	113 Total		1	2	12	Z2	New Zealand
Nerissa	8/9/40	OB210	?	16	18	-	1	3	D12	Canada
Newfoundland	8/9/40	OB210	?	4	7	-	1	-	D?	Canada
??	8/9/40	OB210	6/10/40	26	19		1	3	D?	Canada
City of Paris	10/9/40	?	13/10/40	45 Total		1	1	5	U2	South Africa
City of Benares	13/9/40	OB213	Torpedoed	47	43	1	1	6	D11	Canada
Diomed	17/9/40	OB215	?	18 Total		???			C3	Australia
Nova Scotia	21//9/40	OB217	3/10/40	29 Total		-	1	1	D?	Canada[74]

Although the CORB scheme finished, the second recommendation made by Cabinet on the 30th September meant that there was still nothing to stop private individuals or companies sending, or in the case of the USA hosts receiving, evacuees. If one looks at the progress of the overseas planning one can see a thread indicating that at all stages individuals in authority outside of CORB seemed intent on allowing private evacuation to go ahead. Back in July 1940 when Sir John Anderson had suggested that exit permits should be suspended to avoid any suggestion of class distinction and privilege, the Cabinet had opposed it stating; *'The proposal virtually to ban the sending abroad of any further children by private arrangements was considered unduly drastic'*[75]

The fact that CORB, set up to counter these criticisms of elitism, was now sidelined meant the field was left to those who wished to pursue their own agenda of providing safe havens for their own class. There was also a somewhat sinister aspect to some of this. Eugenicists[76] were keen to ensure the continuation of the British race by sending 'suitable stock abroad'. There had been a common belief before the overseas evacuation began that by sending children out of harm's way they would as the next generation return to reclaim Britain from Germany had the latter successfully invaded. According to the Canadian Liaison Officer involved in the programme the schemes participants were *'not just evacuees, transferred from the range of menace, but part of Britain's immortality, part of their greatness of her past and part of all the hope for the future'.* [77]

In the Eugenics Review April 1940-January 1941, it was stated that 'The function of the British Eugenics Society[78] was to select suitable emigrants under the age of 16 and arrange all the details of transport'.[79] At this

74 Appendix VIII. The Absurd and the Brave. Op cit. p 304
75 TNA.CAB 65/8WM (40) 199th Conclusions 10 July1940
76 The term eugenics was introduced by Francis Galton in 1907 and defined as 'questions bearing on what is termed in Greek, eugenics, namely good in stock, hereditarily endowed with noble qualities'. Ann Oakley Eugenics, Social Medicine and the Career of Richard Titmuss in Britain 1935-50 The British Journal of Sociology, Vol. 42, No. 2. (Jun., 1991), pp. 165-194.
77 TNA.DO 131/45
78'The aims of the Eugenic Education Society in 1907 included promoting the national importance of eugenics especially in relation to the domination of parenthood by eugenic ideals, the spreading of knowledge of the laws of heredity as applied to the improvement of the race, and the furthering of eugenic teaching in schools and Elsewhere'. Oakley op cit. Prominent members included John Maynard Keynes, Neville Chamberlain, Richard Titmuss Arthur Balfour, Julian Huxley.
79 Eugenics Review Vol 32 April 1940-January 1941

time a guarantee of homes had been received from the Eugenics Society of Canada and in response the British Society had established a 'Home in Canada Service Committee.' It was hoped that the cooperation of the two societies would create a situation whereby; 'provision will be made for certain eugenically important groups which do not come within the scope of the Government's evacuation scheme now being administered by the Children's Overseas Reception Board'.[80]

These groups were to include children who had won scholarships to non grant-aided schools and mothers with children under 5. It was apparent that the children would be selected by the committee in such a way that they would; *'represent a true cross-section of the British people as a whole.....the only qualification for the children selected are intelligence, good heredity and good health. The task of applying these fundamental eugenic safeguards has been entrusted to a panel of doctors who have been approved by the Homes for Canada Service Committee.'*

The Society was keen to stress that poverty would not stand in the way of any parent wishing to take part in the scheme. In fact, it created a fund from which parents could borrow money and pay back in a way to suit their own circumstances. But one wonders whether the Committee would consider 'poverty' and 'good heredity' as suitable bedfellows! This raises another important question; as this was not a scheme that was advertised widely and based entirely on detailed selection criteria how would the 'poor' in society get to hear of it? It would seem that the only ones privy to this scheme were subscribers to the Eugenics Review which would not, I suggest, be the reading choice of the majority of the population.

The article did intimate that all the planning was provisional and depended on many factors such as the provision of berths on ships, exit permits and medical examinations.

In the next issue of the Eugenics Review April 1941 – January 1942, it was reported that 41 mothers and 266 children had applied to go to Canada on the Society's scheme but only 5 mothers and 23 children were able to go, although it was hoped that the shipping situation would improve during the autumn of 1940 allowing others to travel. In the end all the planning and reassurances came to nought as in February 1941, the Society received a letter from Dr Hutton, President of the Eugenics Society of Canada, saying that *'.....the Government regulations and restrictions in Canada are so severe that the Eugenics Society of Canada can no longer carry on the work and was obliged to retire from the field'*. At the end of the same journal was a simple statement which in effect brought a halt to the Society's migrations to Canada; *'....We very much regret to learn that owing to circumstances, entirely beyond their control, the Eugenics Society of Canada no longer exists'*. There was no further explanation.

The Overseas Reception Board itself remained in existence, albeit with reduced personnel. They now had the responsibility or maintaining contact with those children who had already been evacuated abroad. Parents received somewhat cursory annual school reports as well as other updates via the CORB offices. As an example of the latter, parents who had children in Australia and were concerned that their children might now be in danger after Japan had entered the war, were sent a letter from CORB allaying any fears.

> *'....I should like you to know that the Board is in close touch with its representatives in Australia who reports that arrangements have been made by the authorities to evacuate school children from danger points if this should at any time be considered necessary......You may rest assured that should it be decided to evacuate the children from any district, the parents will be informed as soon as possible by the Board. In one or two instances private arrangements have been made by individual foster parents or schools, to move children inland, but there has yet been no official evacuation.....'*[81]

80 ibid
81 ibid 157

Face to face meetings between CORB representatives and the parents were also held to discuss various issues, such as education, training and employment.

Another way of keeping in contact with all overseas evacuees was by the wireless.

Children in an NBC Studio in the USA waiting to talk to their parents in the UK via a BBC radio link

One important broadcast made by Princess Elizabeth and Princess Margaret, and kept very secret by the BBC until the last minute, was transmitted to evacuees both at home and overseas on the 13th October 1940 via Children's Hour;

> '.....*In wishing you good evening, I feel that I am speaking to friends and companions who have shared with my sister and myself many a happy Children's Hour.*
>
> *Thousands of you in this country have had to leave your homes and be separated from your fathers and mothers. My sister, Margaret Rose, and I feel so much for you as we know from experience what it means to be away from those we love most of all...All of us children who are still at home think continually of our friends and relatives who have gone overseas, who have travelled thousands of miles to find a wartime home and a kindly welcome in Canada, Australia, New Zealand, South Africa and the United States of America...*'

It was also transcribed and appeared in many national and local newspapers across Britain:

'PRINCESS' RADIO TALK TO EMPIRE CHILDREN.

THOUGHT FOR THOSE WHO HAVE GONE OVERSEAS.

"WE KNOW IN THE END ALL WILL BE WELL"'[82]

Individuals were also able to take advantage of pre-recorded radio broadcasts. Parents were only given 30 seconds, about the time for 90 words, but they did provide a vital and necessary link between the child and home.

---

82 Dorset Daily Echo 14th October 1940

'BBC. 15th April 1943

Dear Mr and Mrs McGinty

We should be glad if you could come to the Art Gallery, Mosley Street, Manchester on the 21st April at 4pm to record a short message to your child overseas. It will be included in one of the programmes 'Hello Children' to be broadcast in our Overseas Service within the next few weeks. The children will be cabled about time and wavelength.......You joint message should last for thirty seconds only i.e. about 90 words'.[83]

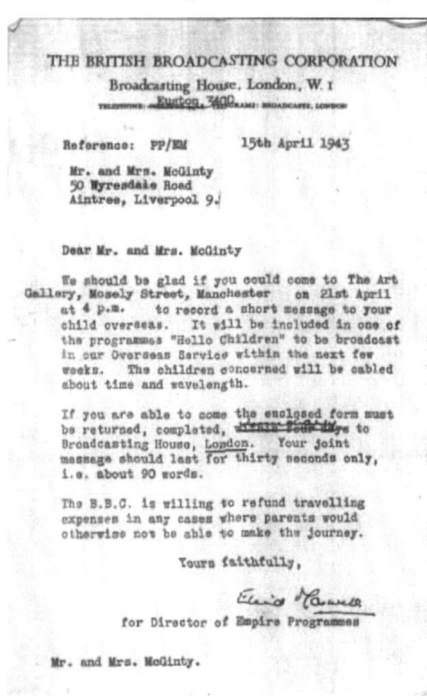

THE BRITISH BROADCASTING CORPORATION
Broadcasting House, London, W. 1
Euston 3400

Reference: PP/EM 15th April 1943

Mr. and Mrs. McGinty
50 Wyresdale Road
Aintree, Liverpool 9.

Dear Mr. and Mrs. McGinty

We should be glad if you could come to The Art Gallery, Mosely Street, Manchester on 21st April at 4 p.m. to record a short message to your child overseas. It will be included in one of the programmes "Hello Children" to be broadcast in our Overseas Service within the next few weeks. The children concerned will be cabled about time and wavelength.

If you are able to come the enclosed form must be returned, completed, ~~within four days~~ to Broadcasting House, London. Your joint message should last for thirty seconds only, i.e. about 90 words.

The B.B.C. is willing to refund travelling expenses in any cases where parents would otherwise not be able to make the journey.

Yours faithfully,

Enid Maxwell

for Director of Empire Programmes

Mr. and Mrs. McGinty.

There was an equivalent series of programmes from Australia called 'Hello Parents' which were sent to the BBC and transmitted on the Home Service.

Later in the war the main focus of CORB staff was getting the children back home. In August 1944, CORB officials informed parents that their children would be expected to return home with an official party unless they were remaining overseas to complete an apprenticeship or a course of exams and that the Board would only pay the transport costs of those coming back on prearranged vessels. In June 1945, after Germany had been defeated and the situation in Europe had become a little more stable, a general letter was sent to all parents notifying them that their children would soon be arriving home. Although there were significant amendments to the letter sent to those with children in Australia, where the Japanese threat of attack was still perceived to be real;

> '*....the passage accommodation for civilians is limited and there are many calls upon it; also as long as hostilities with Japan continue, military requirements must come first....*'[84]

When all the travel arrangements were confirmed parents were sent additional information about arrival times, and where they could meet their children. Few of the reunions actually took place at the port of entry as most children met their parents at Lime Street station in Liverpool, or if they travelled on, at railway stations near to their homes.

---

83 Letterfrom Enid Maxwell who was Director of Empire Programmes at the BBC.
84 Extract from letter from CORB to parents of evacuees in Australia and New Zealand. 20th June 1945

Some children found the return home just as traumatic, if not more so, that the journey out. Jean Cheyne, who came back from Canada in April 1945 on the SS Cavina wrote;

> *'I had wanted to go home so much. But, when the time came, I really did not want to go. I am afraid I cried a great deal, but, as so much was happening, I didn't have time to be sad'.*[85]

Some of the children, now in their teens and older, had been away from Britain for a long time and had developed strong relationships with their foster parents and had boyfriends and girlfriends who they now had to leave behind. It was also a wrench for some of the hosts now having to give up the children they had lovingly looked after as their own for five or six years. Rita Patterson, who returned from Sydney on the 'Andes' commented later that;

> *'......it was one of my saddest memories....my relatives took me onto the ship and insisted on seeing my cabin. I was inspecting everything excitedly, and when I turned round they had gone. I ran after them but wasn't allowed ashore. I know great-uncle had taken my aunt away because she was so distressed, and I think that was the only way he could do it'.*[86]

Her arrival at home was just as emotional;

> *'In the dusk we rolled across the Tyne Bridge. Through the window of the train, I saw Mum and Aunts start running alongside the train as they caught sight of me. As we stood there, embracing and crying, I looked over their heads and saw father at the gate. And as I write this, I'm crying again...I will never forget that meeting as long as I live'.*[87]

For some the homecoming was not always happy one. Some found that their parents had separated or divorced, some that they now had new siblings, and many were disappointed in their home environment and resented having to return to a drab, post-war austere Britain. It was all too easy to make comparisons between what they had left and what they had returned to and comments about their lives overseas and the families they lived with often led to resentment within their own families.[88]

Between May 1945 and February 1946, when CORB finally closed its offices, 2209 CORB children, had either returned home or were on their homeward journey.

At their last meeting Marjorie Maxse presented each member of the Advisory Committee with a statistical breakdown of the CORB scheme.

Position at 14/2/46[89]

Dominion	Evac from UK	Died	Withdrawn from Scheme			Returned to UK	Remaining Overseas			Serving in Dominion Forces
			Married	Joined by Parents	Parents making arrangements		Temp.to complete course or unfit for travel	Settling irrespective of parent plans	Settling if joined by parents	
Canada	1535	4 (*)	5	14	24	1326	18 (**)	34	54	56
Australia	576	2 (*)	3	3	11	416	15(***)	14	62	20
South Africa	355	-	1	9	3	284	16	4	14	24
New Zealand	204	1	1	2	3	153	3	10	29	2
Total	2670	7	10	28	41	2209	52	62	159	102

* 1 Killed in Action. 1 missing presumed killed.
** 2 for health reason
*** 1 for health reasons

85 Fethney op cit p230
86 ibid p233
87 Ibid p239
88 For further information about the problems of returning family members at the end of the war see Stranger in the House by Julie Summers. pub Simon and Schuster.
89 TNA.DO131/41

Some did not return until 1947.

After the war the Queen, recognising the help and support that families in the Dominions had given to British evacuees, sent a message to all who had taken part.

> *'I wish to mark by this personal message, my gratitude for the help and kindness which you have shown to the children who crossed the sea from the United Kingdom many months ago. Since the early days of the War you have opened your doors to strangers and offered to share your home with them. In the kindness of your heart you have accepted them as members of your own family, and I know that to this unselfish task you, and your entire household, have made many great sacrifices. By your generous sympathy you have earned the true and lasting gratitude of those to whom you have given this hospitality, and by your understanding you have shown how strong is the bond uniting all those who cherish the same ideals.*
>
> *Elizabeth.*[90]*'*

---

90 Queens letter of thanks sent to all host families in the Dominions.

The Return Home

'Perhaps the only solidly real place we ever know is the place in which we spent our childhood and youth. It's there that there are genuinely real streets, shops and houses, and their only fault is that they have a trick, like the queer cards that conjurers use, of appearing diminished every time we go back'.[1]

One important aspect of evacuation which is often overlooked is the return of the evacuees to their original homes. In some cases this was just as significant as leaving them in any of the previous evacuations.

As early as August and December 1943, a Departmental Committee in the Ministry of Health submitted a report on the eventual return of evacuees from the reception areas. Detailed planning took place in the Spring of 1944 but the V1 and V2 attacks on London, with the resultant damage, meant that the scheme would be first implemented in areas other than the capital.

Mothers and children leaving Marylebone Station in July 1944 as a result of the V1 and V2 attacks on London

By April, the Ministry had considered the arrangements that needed to be made for children returning to the Metropolitan areas, the Medway Towns and those situated along the Thames. However, even as late in the war as this, the Government still did not consider that the time was right for implementing a return, but nonetheless were concerned that local authorities should be in a position to respond immediately to any given order from central Government. On the 10th April 1945, the Ministry of Health distributed Circular 68/45 to all local authorities and County Councils which had taken part in evacuation.[2] This was the vehicle through which outline instructions were given. It was suggested that once the decision to return evacuees to their homes was put into operation, the

1 J.B.Priestley. Postscripts. Heinemann. London.1940
2 Duchy of Cornwall Archive. Duchy Office. St. Marys Isles of Scilly.

Minister would notify all areas by means of a telegram which would simply state 'Operate London Return Plans'. On receipt of the message local authorities were to adhere to the timetable appended to the Circular.[3]

The telegram was actually sent out on the 2nd May 1945.

The outline of the plan was to ensure the organised departure of all evacuees who had homes to go back to, and who were not prevented in any other way from returning. It was stressed that because of acute difficulties in the housing situation in parts of London, it was very important that evacuees who did not have adequate accommodation at home were to be given no assistance or encouragement to leave the reception areas. It was also pointed out that houses, or parts of houses, which had been damaged and were in need of repair to make them habitable, could not be regarded as being immediately available for occupation. As it was thought that many of this group would remain in the reception areas for a considerable time, the local authorities were to ensure that social and welfare services dealing with evacuees would remain in place. For instance, some pregnant women who had made arrangements to have their babies in the reception areas were to be billeted for up to four weeks after the birth, should they wish to stay. If, however, adult evacuees stated that their reason for not returning home was simply that there would be a shortage of bedding and equipment, or that nobody would be available to open the house, they were to be informed that they would return as normal but be accommodated for a few days in a Rest Centre while the problems were investigated.[4] A note of these was made on the registration card which the evacuees had to complete before departure from the reception areas. In the event, the WVS were prepared to make temporary loans of bedding to families in difficulty, and they also provided help in opening up houses and preparing them for occupation.[5]

The whole scheme involving the London areas was to be co-ordinated by the London County Council working with the senior regional officers in the Ministry of Health. They, in turn, appointed an officer in the reception area to take charge of the assembly, entraining and departure of the evacuees in their region. The LCC also appointed a 'train-marshal' for each train who was in charge of overseeing the actual journey. Both of these people were additionally responsible for making sure that the arrangements for any overnight stays of evacuees and escorts, movement of luggage and feeding, were in hand; although technically it was a 'Food Executive Officer' who was in charge of the latter. Food and luggage were very important considerations. On arrival in London all evacuees were to be given a meal, but for the journey they and their escorts were provided with just packed lunches, while drinks were to be distributed at stopping points along the route by members of the WVS and other voluntary organisations. Food and drink for unaccompanied children was loaded onto the relevant trains and handed out during the journey. Adult evacuees had been given notices about the movement of their luggage during the time leading up to the actual journey and also when they were asked to complete the registration cards. Once these cards had been returned to the Senior Regional Officer they were collated and specially coloured labels, representing the first dispersal centres in London to which the evacuees were to be taken, were returned to the evacuees' billets to be attached to their luggage. It was very important that the correct colour corresponded to the evacuees' home address.

As far as possible the plan was to move the evacuees in organised parties travelling by special trains, or alternatively in reserved seats on a regular service. The local authorities were informed of the stations where the evacuees in their areas were to travel from. Notification of these details, plus the times of departure and the names of those due to travel, were sent out a week prior to the journey. During these seven days, the local officers were to ensure that all persons were made aware of the travel arrangements and where they were to assemble. In some cases the stations were a considerable distance from the reception areas so private cars and other vehicles, including those belonging to the Civil Defence, were used for transportation. Where this was not possible, the Senior Regional Officers were able to organise transport as long as they had at least four days notice. Where the travelling distance to the dispersal centre was vast, it was necessary for the groups to stay in the area of the

3 See Appendix 12
4 Ministry of Health Circular. 185/44
5 Devon Record Office. ref.30584/19

stations, so suitable buildings in the immediate vicinity were requisitioned and the billeting authorities used the equipment and bedding previously provided in the evacuation scheme. Some were able to use the local rest centres which were staffed and supervised by existing personnel.

Alternative arrangements were made for those who, for various reasons, were unable to travel by rail. But free travel vouchers were to be given to those who wished to go independently only when they could not be included in any organised group, or where insufficient numbers in a specific area warranted an official organised party. Evacuees whose return had to be delayed were eligible for free travel. The vouchers could only be used on weekdays as the railway companies were not prepared to allow their use at the weekends. The parents, or designated guardians, of unaccompanied children who could not be included in the organised travel, could also apply for free vouchers in order to collect their children. This also applied to people acting as escorts to the blind, disabled and elderly. Authorities in the reception areas were asked to supply escorts for adults and accompanied children at a ratio of 1-40. Again the WVS provided many of them and they were usually co-ordinated by the local WVS centre organiser who liaised closely with the authorities. The ratio for unaccompanied children was 1-12, but in this case the escorts were only responsible for them up to the entraining stations, as supervision on the journey, and in London, was provided by the LCC.

Like its predecessors, the actual scheme was bound up in seemingly endless bureaucratic red-tape, but the plans were designed to avoid any disorganised evacuation from the reception areas. As it was, when evacuees did eventually arrive at the main-line termini in London, the sheer numbers of people and the luggage they brought with them, caused a great deal of dislocation to the day to day running of the stations.

This was the scene on Platform 1 of Euston Station on 11th September 1944. These prams had been sent on ahead by evacuees returning to London from the north of England. Italian Prisoners of War were used to help station staff deal with the problem of piles of luggage blocking the platforms.

It was a very difficult task to organise in advance the movement of a large group of people of indeterminate numbers from locations situated in a vast area of the United Kingdom. In March 1945, a census of the evacuees remaining in the reception areas showed that during the previous six months 600,000 had returned home independently. This was out of a known total of 1,040,200. In England and Wales, on the 31st March 1945, there were 175,000 mothers with children billeted in private houses, 68,000 in requisitioned houses, 109,000 unaccompanied children in billets, 23,000 in hostels, camps and residential nurseries, 36,000 old people, 3,000 invalids, 1,200 blind and 19,000 other adults.[6]

Most of these later returnees were Londoners so the overall plan was scaled down to account for the decline in numbers, which amounted to a total of 453,200, including 134,000 unaccompanied children. The LCC had to make arrangements to recover their children from around 1,000 different billeting areas, allocate them into travelling parties, take them back to London, sort them into the original eighty evacuation districts and accompany the individuals back to their homes.[7]

In order for this to happen relatively smoothly, specific measures had to be taken. During the week immediately after the delivery of the order to move, the billeting officers had to visit every adult evacuee in their area and get them to complete the record card giving personal information, including home address of any children in the adults care. Where the adult was *not* accompanying children the word 'priority' was to be written on the card where space had been left for the children's names. The card also included a code number for each of the reception areas so that the receiving authorities knew where the group had come from. These cards were returned to the Senior Regional Officer in the Ministry of Health, together with a full list of names of those able to travel. After 22 days from the original order, these cards were sent back to the reception areas with numbered lists of the evacuees and their home addresses.

Cards were also issued to hosts looking after unaccompanied evacuees. The same information was required and the same sequence of events took place, except that when the LCC received the cards from the SROs they ascertained whether or not individual domestic circumstances made it possible for the evacuees to return. Any important details concerning evacuees were included on the card to make the authorities in London aware of specific difficulties. As there had been previous correspondence between the authorities, some of these problems were already known to the relevant agencies. Registration cards were not issued to groups of special children, including those who were disabled or mentally ill, the under-five's in nurseries, and children in camp schools or self-contained secondary schools established by the education authority for the evacuation area. Instead, special arrangements were made for these categories. Some of this latter group of secondary age pupils were due to take their Higher School Certificate examinations and, because it was thought that the upheaval would jeopardise their chances of success, they were to remain billeted until the end of the summer term subject to the confirmation of the local Education Authority. However, if this child was part of a family group, then the mother and siblings were to travel in the organised party and the examinee was to be billeted unaccompanied.

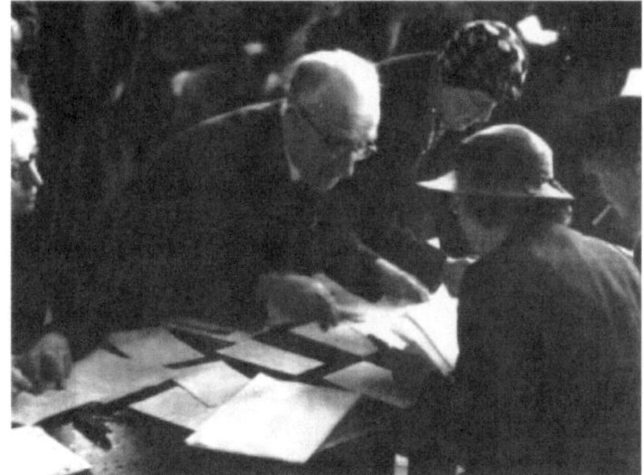

Evacuees returning to London in 1945 being 'processed'

6 Titmuss. op.cit. p433.
7 ibid. p431

The London scheme was completed and the evacuees returned home by 12th July 1945, three days later than originally scheduled. By then, 115 trains had taken a total of 54,317 evacuees back to the capital including 29,701 unaccompanied children, 21,127 mothers and children and 3,489 other adults.[8]

Still, despite all their good intentions, the Government had again not reckoned on people's independent thoughts and actions, and many of the 'organised' trains returned only half full because some evacuees had made their own arrangements without informing the authorities.

Those Remaining

All this was fine for those evacuees who had homes to go to, but it was different for those who had to remain behind in the reception areas, estimated in August 1945 to be around 76,000 people.[9] For reasons of Government planning, this group was divided into two separate units: Mothers with children and Unaccompanied children, and then into two further sub-divisions... those who wanted to remain in the reception areas, and those who wanted to return home.

The Government was concerned that householders in the reception areas should be relieved of the burden of housing evacuee mothers and children who wanted to stay and, where possible, the latter were encouraged to seek accommodation of their own through a local authority housing procedure. There were also emergency arrangements which could be used if:-

- The person had been rendered homeless as a result of enemy action,
- The re-housing after such an event was inadequate,
- They had given up their homes in the evacuated areas before being moved to the reception areas.

It was the responsibility of the authorities in the reception areas to check that those wishing to stay were in fact genuinely homeless, had not had previous housing, or had given theirs up at the beginning of the war.

The second group, those who wanted to return home, were also sub-divided into three distinct categories:-

a. Those that had been made homeless as a result of enemy action.

b. Families who had never had a home of their own.
This group consisted primarily of young mothers, often the wives of servicemen, who had lived with their parents before the war and had never had the opportunity to rent or buy a home of their own. If the parents or other relatives had lost their home, it rendered the people in this group homeless, and it was considered apposite that they should be given the same opportunity to gain accommodation as home owners who had lost their property. There was also the additional problem that families may have grown in numbers during the evacuation and would no longer fit into the pre-evacuation house.

c. Families who had given up their home in the evacuation area.
The number in this category was substantial. One reason why free accommodation had been provided under the Government evacuation scheme was to ensure that some of the expenses on housing would be avoided, and thus enable the evacuees to meet the demands arising from the retention of their home in the evacuated area so that they could return to it, as and when enemy action ceased. The Ministry of Health made it quite clear in Circular.No.69/45, that preference for accommodation should not be given, except under exceptional circumstances, to those families who voluntarily deprived themselves of any accommodation to return to. However, if these people genuinely were not able to re-house themselves, their names were to be added to the local authority list for housing.

8 ibid. p433
9 ibid. p434

In all three categories the authorities in the reception areas forwarded lists of families to the evacuated areas containing information which included:-

- The number of persons in each family and the ages and gender of the children.
- Their present address in the reception area.
- The address in the evacuation area to which the family state that they are unable to return.
- The reasons why the address in the evacuation area was now unavailable for reoccupation.[10]

There were problems in making these lists accurate, especially where families and evacuated groups had been billeted over a large area and, in some cases, in more than one official reception area. In the case of a mother and children being accommodated in one area and other unaccompanied members of the family in another, it was recommended that they should be listed as being with the mother, but with a note indicating that there were children elsewhere. It was thought that this would be enough information for both the reception areas and the authorities in London to make sure that families were eventually united. Nevertheless, administrative oversights made the plan very difficult to implement and a great deal of confusion resulted, especially where the billeting officer had not kept an accurate record of evacuee movements in the reception areas.

When the lists had been received and the 'homeless' situation had been verified, the local authorities in the evacuated areas were duty bound to either provide temporary accommodation, housing through normal authority channels, or use the emergency powers available to them.[11]

It was particularly important to find accommodation for those who had not had it before, or had lost their homes due to enemy action because, being in the reception areas, they had not had the chance to find any housing of their own in their home area.

Although these details concerned those who had been evacuated under the Government scheme, there were families who had made their own temporary arrangements within the reception areas in order to alleviate the pressure on the billets, thus taking themselves outside of the scheme, but who now wished either to return home or find more suitable housing within the reception areas. It was not the Government's intention to exclude people who had used their own initiative; therefore they were eligible to take part in the official scheme if they informed the relevant regional offices that they wished to do so. Unaccompanied children created other problems. The local authorities in the evacuated zones informed their counterparts in the reception areas of children who should remain in their districts because of lack of accommodation, or even room, in their homes. It was necessary that these children should be reunited with their families as soon as possible and, in order to do this, there was thought to be no alternative but to regard the *whole* family unit as 'inadequately housed'. This would then give the authorities just cause to re-house the family using the same powers as indicated previously. In many cases this was to be a last resort. Having received details of unaccompanied children awaiting return to their homes, the local officers re-visited the proposed accommodation to verify that it was unsuitable for their return. If there was no room, the family were actively encouraged to make alternative arrangements of their own but, at the same time, their names were added to the housing list. As soon as suitable accommodation had been found, the reception area was to be informed and the child sent home. If under exceptional circumstances the family had moved out of the original evacuated area, the local authority in the new area was to be responsible for the re-housing.

This scheme sounds idealistic, and in reality it was. There was a tremendous housing shortage, especially in previous target areas, and the early re-housing of evacuated families was virtually impossible. The Government and local authorities realised the situation but the scheme did demonstrate that they were at least making a start. They were concerned to ensure that billeting allowances should remain available until families were either re-

---

10 ibid.

11 Ministry of Health Circular 2845

housed or children were able to rejoin their parents, while at the same time encouraging as many people as possible to make their own arrangements. The Government tried to help those who simply did not have enough basic equipment to ensure that all the family could be accommodated. Some families, especially those who had been away for a long period, were supplied with beds and bedding, and with basic furniture, on loan or purchased from local authorities. This provision, implemented in December 1944, remained in effect until the 30th June 1947.

There were also some psychological and sociological problems which faced families after years of separation. Therefore, as well as providing the necessary physical help, the Ministry of Health advised local authorities in the previously evacuated areas to instigate follow-up visits to ensure that any problems or re-familiarisation with family and neighbourhood could be overcome swiftly. Some of these problems were caused simply by lack of physical space or the fact that the children had grown up significantly during their absence. This was particularly true of those who had been evacuated overseas and who had not seen their families for six years or more. Barbara Shawcroft found relationships with her family so difficult, and life in 'austerity drab' Britain so depressing, that within weeks of her repatriation from New England she had decided to return to the USA and become an American citizen.[12]

Quotes from evacuees returning from Australia indicate the same emotional stress felt by Barbara, which, in the following example was brought about by simple non-recognition:-

> *'Barbara Helical stood on Leeds station. There was a heavy mist swirling and everyone had gone. I'd passed this couple about three times. They didn't know it was their daughter, and I didn't know it was my parents. I felt so lonely, as if I was the only person left in the world....'* [13]

The possible problems faced by returning evacuees are unquantifiable. There were so many different individual experiences, both in the reception areas and in the home situation post-war, that it is only possible to view the ensuing problems in general terms, or to look at a vast number of individual case studies which, in isolation, would not necessarily have any bearing on the experience on another evacuee. One only has to interview ex-evacuees to realise that this is the case. Even child psychologists researching into the effects of evacuation immediately after the war, disagreed and contradicted each other's findings. How can one equate the experiences of a child who had returned from an excellent billet to a poor and sometimes abusive home background, with a child who had perhaps been abused or ill-treated in the reception area? In addition, there was the dilemma of the children who were returning home to parents who were finding it difficult coming to terms with the loss of their independence. There was also the problem of adolescents reverting to childish behaviour and seeking attention from their parents and just wanting some love and care. The experiences are wide and varied.

Another survey of evacuees still remaining in the scheme was taken in March 1946 to cover the period from July 1945. The number had dropped to 38,000, mostly mothers and children (c26,000), and families living in family groups, (3,000).[14]

The fact that they were now living in temporary accommodation did not necessarily distinguish them from any other person in the same situation across the country therefore, gradually, the label of evacuee was 'removed' and they became increasingly the responsibility of the local authority within the reception areas.

But one category of evacuees is rarely mentioned. What happened to those unaccompanied children who were unable to return to their original homes? What about those who, while in the reception areas, were orphaned?

When the 'official' evacuation scheme ended on 31st March 1946, there were 5,200 unaccompanied children left in the reception areas. These were either in billets with foster parents, residential nurseries or hostels.[15] Although this was below the estimated figure of 10,000, it still represented a significant social welfare problem for the

12 Interview with Barbara Shawcroft. San Francisco. op cit.
13 E.Stokes. Innocents Abroad. op.cit. p197
14 Titmuss op.cit. p435
15 ibid. p437

authorities. Although, if seen in relation to the total number involved in the whole evacuation scheme, one could argue, like Titmuss, that these numbers were in fact insignificant and could have been a lot worse.[16] The makeup of this group needs to be examined in context before any blame for their being overlooked can be apportioned to any authority or social group. For the majority, they remained in the reception areas because of the housing problems which still existed in the former target areas. Others had been orphaned and a very few, 29 out of a total of 9,000 in July 1945, had been deserted by their parents.[17]

It needs to be remembered that under any other circumstances, i.e. in peacetime, some of these children would have become the responsibility of the Poor Law authorities. Other institutions such as Dr. Barnardo's, and the National Children's Home and Orphanage took in children. According to Bob Holman, there was an increase in the interest of adoption in the 1930s, but the basic provision was in the area of residential care. The evacuation scheme, perhaps inadvertently, had taken over the responsibility for the social welfare and child care of some evacuee children who normally would have been taken from their home environment. There had been 32,700 children in Poor Law institutions in 1938-9.[18]

16 ibid
17 ibid. p437 footnote.
18 ibid.

The Evacuation of Belfast[1]

> *'…..Mass evacuation is an unnatural process justified only by the need for dispersing the civil population in war time. The transference of a large section of the populations, essentially industrial, to a completely different environment creates problems of a far reaching, economic, social and spiritual nature…..'*[2]

While the Government and Local Authorities on mainland Britain were planning Operation Pied Piper, the Northern Irish administration was trying to do the same.

However, in order to put the evacuation of school-children from Belfast into context, it is necessary to look at the history of education and some of the major political decisions leading up to the event. Unlike the scheme on the mainland, the Northern Ireland situation was introduced and controlled by Education legislation which had been drawn up after the partition of the country in the 1920s; policies which, to some extent, were determined and overshadowed by sectarian issues.

The Government of Ireland Act (1920) created two self-governing areas of Ireland; one comprising of six of Ulster's nine counties, the other, the remaining three counties of Ulster together with the twenty-three counties in the rest of Ireland. The mainly Protestant majority, in what was to become Northern Ireland, favoured the continuation of an Irish State, but decided to pursue the policy of Home Rule. Ironically, bearing in mind that the legislation had been intended to allow Home Rule for the rest of Ireland, it was these other 26 counties which objected to the proposal as being inadequate, and the situation was not resolved until the Anglo-Irish Treaty of 1921-22. In short, this gave the Irish Free State dominion status within the British Empire, while allowing Northern Ireland the opportunity to opt out: a decision it took. Although a boundary commission was set up to review the borders, it's report was never published as it was thought that even the minor adjustments of land-ownership that were being suggested, would bring about civil unrest. Instead, it established the border of Northern Ireland along the lines of County Antrim, County Armagh, County Down, Country Fermanagh, County Londonderry and County Tyrone.

The government in Northern Ireland was largely acceptable to the Protestant Unionists within the province, while those who found themselves on the wrong side of the divide gradually migrated to the six counties. However, the assembly was not accepted by the Catholic Nationalists. Over time, the manipulation of electoral boundaries also meant that the Catholics were unrepresented in local political bodies and, as a result, the Protestant majority was able to maintain control of local and provincial legislation; a situation which was to have a detrimental effect on the assimilation of the Catholic minority into Northern Ireland society as they suffered from discrimination in the workplace, education, housing and social services, thereby creating a disaffected and unrepresented community.

Before the division of Ireland, the Education system had been in urgent need of restructuring, especially in its administration which was carried out in six separate offices in Dublin, but both the Unionists and the Nationalists disagreed on what form this reform should take. On the one hand the former argued for a single Ministry of Education and financial support for Primary, Intermediate and Technical schools via the local rates, whereas the latter simply blocked the proposals.

From 1831[3] National Schools had been built across the whole of Ireland. This resulted in a basic, elementary education being made available to all children who followed a similar curriculum. Control over the National

---

1 I am indebted to the staff of the Public Record Office, Northern Ireland, particularly David Huddleston, who allowed me access to closed files and kept supplying me with documents they '*thought I might be interested in!*'.

2 From 'A Masterly Sermon' anon.

3 Before 1831, large numbers of children attended school, but they had to pay. In 1824 there were around 11,000 schools containing an estimated 500k children. Most were either fee paying or 'hedge-schools'. From 1695 there had been strict rules about the education of Catholics which forbade the establishment of Catholic Schools and the sending of children abroad to receive a Catholic education. So until 1831 these hedge-schools, or scoileanna scairte in Irish, were secret and illegal. Many provided a basic curriculum, but a significant number of others also delivered Greek and Latin. These hedge-schools provided education for a wide age group spanning anything from 4-19. Those who were employed during the day could have their lessons in the evenings.

Schools, the majority of which were managed by the Churches of all denominations, even though the scheme was, in theory, non-denominational, was vested in the Commissioners of National Education. It was they who paid staff salaries and provided the funds for building projects and expansion from State funds. Education beyond the basics was provided by Intermediate Schools (Secondary) which were mainly profit based institutions, and Technical Schools, controlled by local people, which came under the extended responsibility of the Department of Agriculture and Technical Instruction.

Religion played a big part in the control and establishment of schools within Ireland, and for many years this was a very serious issue and one which would later affect the evacuation of children from Belfast in the 1940s. From the very beginning, the Church of Ireland and the Presbyterian Church[4] had opposed the setting up of the National Schools but, by 1871, when the Church of Ireland had been disestablished[5], more of its schools came under the auspices of the National Scheme. The Presbyterians, having lobbied for a change in the rules which would allow school-managers greater control over who could attend and the type of religious education provided, eventually joined the National Schools in the late 1830s.

Once Northern Ireland was established, the Education department inherited all the schools within the six counties as well as St Mary's Teacher Training College, Queen's University and Magee College[6]. However, as all the administrative tasks had been previously carried out in Dublin there was no infrastructure in place to direct the transition, so the newly established Ministry of Education was given the task of overseeing the reconstruction and reorganization of the existing Dublin model. This created many problems, not least of which was the intransigence of Dublin over the Government of Ireland Act (1920)[7]. In addition, the inherited system was in administrative upheaval and the Dublin government refused to transfer the personnel files of teachers. In some areas, especially in the border regions, the teachers themselves did not help. Many of them, together with members of the Catholic Clergy, did not recognise the authority of the Northern Ireland ministry, a situation which was exacerbated by the fact that the salaries of Catholic teachers were paid from Dublin until the end of 1922 when, significantly, the Dublin authorities withdrew the funding and the campaign of non-cooperation ceased.

Perversely, what this confusion did allow was a free hand to establish a Ministry of Education in Northern Ireland with a sound, effective administration and on its own terms. Bringing all the factions under one management body meant that errors made by interaction between various groups were less likely to happen. As a result the Commissioners for all levels of schooling, including those previously administered by the Department of Agriculture and Technical Instruction, were brought under the one body. [8]

In 1923, within the Education Act, based on the report of the Lynn Committee 1921[9], the Minister of Education, Lord Londonderry[10], set out to establish a non-sectarian system of education, focused initially on improving elementary education in Northern Ireland. This scheme would be under local control, via local education committees, who would manage the schools within their area; a policy well supported by members of the Protestant Clergy and the Unionists. The Catholic Church played no part in the Lynn Committee, except for one administrator, Andrew Wyse. Cardinal Logue, then Archbishop of Armagh and Primate of All Ireland, refused to participate. According to Akenson; '*...in all probability, the refusal of the Roman Catholic Church to join the*

---

4 Irish Presbyterianism had its origins in the Scottish migrations to Ulster in the early seventeenth century. In spite of later Catholic uprisings and the hostility of the established Anglican Church, Presbyterianism grew in strength. In the eighteenth century, numbers declined because of the emigration to America and by internal division over subscription to the Westminster formularies and confessions, which encouraged Scottish Convenanters and Seceders to form congregations and presbyteries in Ulster. The restoration of subscription in 1835 led to a union with the Seceders to form the General Assembly of the Presbyterian Church in Ireland.

5 The Church of Ireland transcends the border between the Republic of Ireland and Northern Ireland. Despite its numerical minority the Church of Ireland remained the official state church until it was disestablished on 1 January 1871, by William Gladstone. The Church of Ireland is now, after the Roman Catholic Church, the second-largest church in Ireland.

6 Which included 2,040 National Schools, 75 Intermediates, 12 Modern and 45 technical. (PRONI. Education Archives)

7 This Act was also known as the Fourth Home Rule Bill.

8 PRONI ED/25 Reports of Ministry of Education 1922

9 The Committee had been set up in September 1921 under the Chairmanship of Robert Lynn. It is significant that of the 32 members only one, Andrew Wyse (later a permanent secretary) was Catholic.

10 Lord Londonderry (1878-1949) joined the first government of Northern Ireland in June 1921, as Leader of the Senate and Minister for Education. He left his post in 1926 and took up many roles within the administrations in Westminster. He was seen as encouraging Anglo-German friendship, and was not popular among some of his colleagues. He attempted to explain his position in a book call Ourselves and Germany which was published in 1938. He later became Chancellor of Durham University and Queens University Belfast.

Lynn Committee was the single most determinant of educational history in Northern Ireland from 1921 to the present...'[11]

One of the major issues was that of Religious Education. Lord Londonderry was vehemently opposed to segregation of children on religious grounds as he did not see that it was the State's responsibility to teach specific Christian beliefs. In contrast, the Lynn Committee had strongly recommended that any national education scheme should provide separate religious instruction. When published, the 1923 Act stated that *'Religious instruction was no longer to be part of the required curriculum except where it might impinge through moral education'*. Under the Act, this was forbidden in elementary schools and LEAs were not permitted to provide religious education to schools within their areas of responsibility. Neither were appointments of staff to be based on religious grounds. Not surprisingly this created a great deal of opposition from the Protestants, and in 1923 this part of the Act (Clause 26) was redrafted to state that moral education would be given in schools, but that this excluded *'bible teaching'*. This compromise failed to appease the opposition, and from 1923-29 the Protestant church campaigned for the inclusion of the original Lynn Committee's recommendations which would then allow religious education in elementary schools to be given by teachers within school time. The other contentious issue, that of school appointments, was also opposed on the lines that Catholic teachers could be appointed to Protestant schools and thereby influence the religious education of their pupils.

The debate continued. In 1928, the United Education Committee of the Protestant Churches, which was at the forefront of the opposition, made three significant demands: that there should be bible instruction in primary schools; that there should be no preferential treatment given to Catholics in the primary system; and members of the Clergy should be appointed to regional education committees. As a result the 1930 Education Act contained some of these suggestions: teachers could give simple bible instruction; schools would be allowed to check the religious background of applicants; Protestant clergy could share the control of elementary schools, although this remained under local political control. The Act also stated that the Ministry would pay for fifty percent of the building and equipping of new schools. A move which did not satisfy the Catholic minority which, under the National School system, had received 66% of costs incurred in building programmes.

Such was the state of Northern Ireland education when the evacuation scheme was being planned in 1938.

Evacuation Planning

The planning of the Belfast evacuation, as in other parts of the United Kingdom, began in early 1939 but specific questions needed to be asked before any such scheme could be developed and implemented. As with the rest of the UK, this had to be carried out with the background knowledge that the government in Westminster were stating that there was not going to be a war, and therefore all such planning had to be done in such a way as to avoid unnecessary panic and uncertainty among the general population.

In early 1939 a series of letters was sent out by various departments in Stormont specifically identifying various issues. In February 1939, the Minister of Education in Northern Ireland sent a memo outlining his initial concerns;

> *'....this Ministry is of the opinion that no real progress can be made in dealing with the problem of the protection of school children in time of air attack until a decision has been obtained on the following questions:-*
>
> 1. *Is it proposed to evacuate school children from Belfast in the event of war? It should be understood that 'school children' include ALL children, their mothers or female guardians, and the teachers. Evacuation would of course be on the English voluntary basis.*

11 D.H. Akenson. Education and Enmity. The control of schooling in Northern Ireland 1920-50. David and Charles 1973. p52

2. *Is it proposed to evacuate school children from any other area in Northern Ireland other than Belfast?'*[12]

These concerns were echoed in City Hall during the March meeting of the City Council:-

'.......questions of policy will have to be decided upon at a level higher than the Corporation. They are:-

1. *Is there to be an evacuation of the population? If so, by whom and to what extent?*
2. *Are trenches or shelters to be provided? If so, to what extent?*
3. *Is compulsory legislation to be introduced placing on employers the duty of providing for the safety of persons engaged in factories and workshops? If so, to what extent?*
4. *Are gas masks to be provided for infants and young children? If so, when?*
5. *To what extent will the Police Barracks and Police telephones be available to enable the corporation to carry out their duties?*

John Archer. Town Clerk.' [13]

This received a reply from the Ministry of Home Affairs:-

'.....The Ministry does not at present contemplate the necessity for any general evacuation of the city. A scheme will however be prepared for the children. As regards Gas Masks....There is no likelihood of supplies coming to Northern Ireland for some little time....'[14]

Two weeks later a meeting took place where the question of Evacuation was discussed in secret. A Mr Warnock explained that the Cabinet had approved of his proposal that a scheme for the evacuation of Belfast should be prepared and kept in readiness, even if it were never found necessary to put it into action. Initially the area of evacuation would be limited to within the Belfast County Borough boundary, and to children in elementary schools and of pre-school age. This would amount to around 65,300 of whom 46,800 would be Protestant and 18,500 Roman Catholic. As in England a further 10% would be added for teachers and helpers. The committee then discussed the designated 'Reception areas' within the six counties in the province and the means of transporting the children out of the city.

AREA 1 COUNTY DOWN	TRANSPORT	
Ballynahinch	Rail and road	BCDR
Downpatrick	Rail	BCDR
Newcastle	Rail	BCDR
Warrenpoint	Rail	GNR
Newry	Rail	GNR
Banbridge	Rail	GNR
Shrigley		
AREA 2 COUNTY ANTRIM	**TRANSPORT**	
Ballyclare	Rail and road	LMS
Antrim	Rail	GNR/LMS
Ballymena	Rail	LMS
Coast Rd villages: Glenarm	Rail to Larne or Ballymena	LMS
Carnlough		
Cushendall		
Cushendun		
Balleymoney		
Ballycastle		
Portrush		

12 PRONI MPS2/2/4 16th Feb. 1939
13 ibid 27th March 1939
14 ibid 14th April 1939

AREA 3 COUNTY LONDONDERRY	TRANSPORT	
Portstewart	Rail	LMS OR ROAD
Coleraine	Rail	LMS
Limavady	Rail	LMS OR ROAD
Castlerock		
AREA 4 COUNTY TYRONE	**TRANSPORT**	
Dungannon	Rail	GNR
Cookstown	Rail	GNR/LMS
Omagh	Rail	GNR
Strabane	Rail	GNR
Clogher Valley villages	Rail	GNR ROAD
AREA 5 COUNTY ARMAGH	**TRANSPORT**	
Bessbrook		
Tanderagee	Rail	TO PORTADOWN GNR THEN ROAD
Portadown	Rail	GNR
Armagh	Rail	GNR
Keady	Rail	GNR
AREA 6 COUNTY FERMANAGH	**TRANSPORT**	
Enniskillen	Rail	GNR

It was also pointed out that there was unused Union property in Ballymena with room for 300 people, and a roadhouse in Ballynahinch could be converted to accommodate a further 100. Other locations were discussed as possible reception areas but rejected for various reasons.

On grounds of *vulnerability*:- the triangle of land between Larne, Belfast and Donaghadee; the Lagan Valley comprising Belfast, Lisburn and possibly Lurgan and a strip 10 miles wide along the line; an area roughly within 10 miles radius of the Belfast boundary; the Ards peninsular on a possible line of approach and retreat of enemy aircraft; the city of Londonderry and its approaches.

On grounds of *inaccessibility*:- Most of Tyrone, Derry and Fermanagh

On grounds of *inhospitability* and lack of housing facilities:- The mountainous areas of County Antrim; the Sperrin Mountain area of County Londonderry and County Tyrone; the lake area of Country Fermanagh; the Mourne Mountains.[15]

It was decided that a small enquiry form should be sent to each householder in the designated reception areas asking what accommodation was available, how many children would they be prepared to take and of what sex and religion, and would they be prepared to accept young mothers. This accommodation survey was not as extensive as the scheme organised on mainland Britain in January 1939, and, in addition, the latter did not at any time question the sex or religion of the children they were prepared to house. It was suggested by one of the committee members, Commander Pim, that it would be useful if they could find out about the schemes being implemented in others areas, specifically West Yorkshire and Glasgow.

In May 1939 a confidential circular[16] was issued from the office of H.Conacher in Stormont to all 'Exchange managers' in the ARP sector. It was simply entitled 'The evacuation of schoolchildren' and contained all the information for the *initial* plans of moving personnel out of the city.

Unaccompanied school children and those under the age of five accompanied by their mothers or female relatives were to be evacuated with schools where there would be staff trained for this specific purpose. It was stated that the elementary school scheme was in the process of being planned, and arrangements for the Secondary and Preparatory schools were in hand. The transfer of the evacuees was to be arranged by the various transport organisations, and 'conductors' (equivalent to party leaders in England) would be responsible for the actual movement into the reception areas where they would hand over their charges to designated officials, in this case

15 According to Document MPS2/7/3 Ev.C133 all parts of Northern Ireland were to be regarded as Reception areas except:- Belfast and the country around it; the country bordering Belfast Lough as far as Larne and Donaghadee; Londonderry City; and the following towns and villages in the country between them.... Aghalee, Aldergrove, Ballinderry, Ballyclare, Ballynure, Bangor, Carrickfergus Comber, Crumlin, Donaghadee, Dromore (Co. Down), Dunadry, Hilsborough, Holywood, Islandmagee, Larne, Lisburn, Moira, Newtownards, Whiteabbey, Whitehead.
16 E.E.Circular 19/17 Stormont

simply called Clerks, (the same as the Billeting Officers on the mainland) who would make all the arrangements for the reception of children in consultation with the Ministry of Home Affairs. These Clerks would have already received the information about private and other suitable accommodation within their areas, the analysis of which had already been carried out by Ministry staff. The continuation of the children's education would be the responsibility of the Ministry of Education, and their general welfare would be overseen by officials in the local authorities. It was pointed out that the scheme would require a great number of volunteers, both in the evacuated and reception areas, and it was hoped that the National Services Committee would be able to help with the recruitment of suitable people.

At a subsequent meeting held in June 1939,[17] it was stated that 70,000 people had expressed a wish to be evacuated, and this was adopted by the evacuation planners as the basic figure to work with. Members also discussed the various accommodation options. Halls were rejected as they could only house limited numbers and would be needed for both communal purposes and overflows from schools. Camps were also dismissed as they were thought to be totally impractical and not an economically viable alternative. Not only would they take a long time to build, but the financial reserves would be exhausted in the process. Domestic billets were therefore seen as the most satisfactory means of housing evacuees, despite many objections from some residents in the receptions areas. It was suggested that local committees should be invited to arrange the billeting, and should also be empowered to transfer evacuees from one billet to another if temporary arrangements did not prove workable. Arrangements would also be made for the nursing and hospital services to be strengthened where necessary so that suitable provision could be given to the evacuees.

Further information was given in August when it was pointed out that the numbers of school children did not include Secondary School pupils, as most of these would have their billets arranged by their parents. [18] (Although in many instances this scheme was destined to break down as it was reported later that there were unspecified financial implications which could not be met, either by the local authorities or subsidised by the Government. As a result the costs were passed on to the parents)[19]. Therefore, the arrangements in Belfast would be made by the Ministry of Education with the help of the Public Elementary school teachers. These schools were to serve as assembly stations and the Head Teachers would act as evacuating officers. In the first instance they would receive applications from eligible persons for registration and the Director of Education would act as a 'clearing agent' to collect and transfer the information to the Ministry. A similar procedure, regarding the actual personal records of the participants, would come into effect once the scheme was in operation. Teachers, and selected volunteers would assist the Head Teachers and act as Marshalls in assembling and accompanying the children into the 25 designated reception areas, with Londonderry acting as a temporary one should the need arise. (Londonderry itself was classified as an Evacuation Area on 19th December 1941. See below) Other matters were discussed including the provision of food, both en route[20] and extra stores within the reception areas.

After much discussion the Ministry issued the Belfast Operation Plan which was divided into seven sections:-

Assembly

a. Each Public Elementary School was to be an assembly station. The head-teacher is the Chief Evacuation Officer for the assembly station. A senior teacher is the Chief Conductor for each assembly station. The class teachers are in charge of their rooms and act as a conductor. The assistant teachers act as conductors of squads. Additional Voluntary helpers act as squad conductors and as assistant conductors. Normally there are one Conductor and one assistant Conductor to each squad of 20.

17 Minutes of meeting D270. June 1939 (no specific date given)
18 Memo 4th August 1939
19 Minutes of meeting between Ministry of Home Affairs and Ministry of Education 4th September 1939.
20 For the train journey children were to be supplied with 0.5 pint of milk, a meat sandwich, a bun, an apple and 2 sticks of barley sugar.

b. Evacuees are of two classes: Stage I and Stage II. Stage I evacuees are the children of school age who will be evacuated in the charge of Conductors but without adult relatives. Stage II evacuees are young children accompanied by their mothers and other female relatives.

c. Normally all members of a family, whether Stage I or Stage II, will assemble on the appropriate day in the classroom of the eldest member of the family in the most senior school attended by any member of the family.

d. Evacuation from any given assembly station will be effected in 2 stages. The first will be the evacuation of Stage I, and the second will be on the second day thereafter and will comprise of Stage II.

e. Some conductors of Stage I evacuees will return to Belfast to act as Conductors for Stage II. These must include the Chief Conductor.

f. The Chief Evacuation Officer will remain in Belfast until both stages are complete.

Order of Evacuation

a. Belfast has been divided into 6 evacuation zones.

b. Zones 1/2/3 will be within a red line drawn on the record map retained by the Civil Defence Belfast, and the Ministry, and comprise the main congested districts of the city with exception of certain portions of Northern Belfast which are some distance from the specifically vulnerable Red area surrounding the port.

c. Zones 4/5/6 comprise the remainder of the city from the red line about to the city boundary.

d. Evacuation will be effected in 2 waves. The first will comprise of Zones 1/2/3 and will include both Stage I and II from each assembly station. The second will follow after an interval of days, determined by the transport arrangements and conditions in the receiving areas. As in the case of the first wave, the second will include both Stages I and II.

Transport

a. A transport plan will be prepared for each wave

b. The Chief Evacuation Officer of each assembly station will be notified in advance of;

- The railway station at which his party will entrain.
- The means of transport that will be available between the assembly station and the entraining point.
- The hour of entrainment and the hour at which the local transport will be available.

c. The Chief Evacuation Officer will determine, in the light of the above information, the hour of assembly at each Stage at his assembly station.

Food

a. An attempt is being made to prepare a practicable plan in regard to feeding of evacuees en route.

b. Pending further information on this subject it should be taken that evacuees will not carry travelling rations.

c. Special arrangements will be made in conjunction with the food control authorities, in regard to emergency rations in Reception Zones for the first few days of evacuation.

Reception Arrangements

a. Ultimately, all of the evacuees will be dispersed to billets in the Reception Zones on the basis of the result of a survey now in progress.

b. Normally, no attempt will be made to complete the dispersal to permanent billets of any parties on the day of evacuation, except in so far as it may be possible to place in their permanent billets those evacuees destined to remain in the towns.

c. The towns enumerated in Appendix II will act as Clearing Centres for the evacuees allocated to the Reception Zones in which the towns are situated.

d. Each of the clearing centres will be called upon, not only to accommodate permanently the number of evacuees allocated to the town, but also for a brief period of a few days, pending final dispersal, the evacuees destined to billets in the surrounding areas included in each Wave.

e. During the dispersal period there will be serious congestion and considerable discomfort for all concerned, but this is unavoidable. The period will be shortened and the discomfort lessened by energetic action on the part of the Zone-District Reception Officers and the Reception Committees in the matter of dispersal to permanent billets.

f. During the dispersal period abnormal use should be made of billets approved for permanent use rather than of unsatisfactory additional billets or improvised accommodation in halls etc. and, if emergency accommodation other than that provided in approved billets is necessary, improvised accommodation should be used rather than unsatisfactory billets.

g. The general principle to be adopted during the dispersal period will be to place in each approved billet those evacuees who will remain there, and roughly as many again for temporary accommodation. In the case of Londonderry City, all billets will be temporary. A room that will accommodate two children permanently should without undue difficulty accommodate four for a night or two. By dint of bed sharing, even if congested, and the provision of additional mattresses and blankets for use on the floor, it should be possible to give the whole number of evacuees present in each town during that period, sufficient shelter, rest and protection so as to avoid injury.

h. It will be necessary to supplement the bedding supplies in each of Clearing Centres. As there will be a general deficiency of bedding even in permanent billets, this supplementary bedding can be dispensed in due course within the country areas when the need for it in the town ceases. There will inevitably be a surplus of provided bedding since a large proportion of the evacuees ultimately dispersed to country billets will go to the billets where full bedding is available, but this surplus will easily be absorbed in war conditions for other purposes.

i. Bedding provided in advance in peace time, can, if no emergency arises for an extended period, be gradually absorbed by hospitals and unions so that the net cost should not in the end be very great.

j. It is unlikely that the reserve stock of RUC bedding will suffice and stocks in the hands of unions are very small, amounting in the aggregate to a relatively few hundred blankets. The purchase of blankets and mattresses must therefore be given urgent consideration. The voluntary survey revealed a deficiency in houses offering accommodation of around 12.5%. The deficiency, to be revealed by the survey now in progress, will probably be relatively higher. It would seem therefore that supplementary bedding for something like 10,000 evacuees will be required.

k. Instructions with regard to procedure as to billeting etc, in clearing centres and in Reception Zones will be prepared and issued.

l. Instructions as to the duties of Reception Committees will be prepared and issued.

m. An education scheme will be prepared on the basis of the final allocation of evacuees after complete dispersal.

Timetable

a. An interval must elapse between the order to evacuate and the actual evacuation. The minimum period required is 48 hours.

b. It is anticipated that preliminary instructions to prepare to evacuate will be issued by the Cabinet, to be followed by an executive order to evacuate.

c. In this event on receipt of the preliminary instructions the following procedure is proposed:-

1. A multiple telegram will be sent to the Chief Evacuation Officer at each assembly station reading for example:

   EVACUATION IMMINENT stop PREPARE TO EVACUATE AT 24 HOURS NOTICE. On receipt of this warning the Evacuation Officers will complete their machinery and teams of workers, and do all possible clerical work in advance.

2. A multiple telegram will be sent to each Zone and District Reception Officer reading for example:

   EVACUATION IMMINENT stop PREPARE RECEPTION ARRANGEMENTS TO RECEIVE EVACUEES AT 24 HOURS NOTICE.

3. On receipt of this warning Evacuation Officers will proceed in accordance with detailed instructions which will be furnished to them in advance.

4. The transport authorities and the food control authorities will be warned.

5. A suitable announcement to the public will be broadcast and published in the press.

d.

1. On receipt of the executive order to evacuate, a multiple wire will be sent to the Chief Evacuation Officer of each assembly station in Belfast Zones 1/2/3 reading for example: EVACUATE (day) (date) ACCORDING TO PLAN

2. A multiple wire will be sent to the Reception Officers in each of the clearing Centres for example: EVACUATION ON (day) (date) stop. ARRANGE RECEIVE ALLOTTED NUMBER FIRST WAVE EVACUEES

3. A multiple wire will be sent to all Zone Reception Officers reading for example: EVACUATION FIRST WAVE (day) (date) stop. CLEARING CENTRES ADVISED stop ARRANGE COMPLETE DISPERSAL SOONEST POSSIBLE.

4. The transport authorities will be informed

5. An appropriate announcement will be made by broadcast and in the press.

e.

1. Should instructions to evacuate immediately be issued by the Cabinet instead of a preliminary warning, it will not be possible to evacuate sooner than 48 hours from receipt of instructions.

2. In this event the multiple wires will read:

   To Evacuation Officers at Zone 1/2/3 Assembly Stations. EVACUATE ACCORDING TO PLAN (day) (date)

To Clearing Centres

FIRST WAVE EVACUATION (day) (date) stop PREPARE RECEIVE ALLOTTED NUMBERS

To Zone Reception Off

FIRST WAVE EVACUATION (day) (date) stop CLEARING CENTRES ADVISED stop ARRANGE COMPLETE DISPERSAL SOONEST POSSIBLE

3. Transport and food authorities will be informed as before.
4. Broadcast and press announcements will be issued.
5. Suitably modified procedure will be adopted for the Second Wave.
6. It is to be hope that sufficient preliminary warning will be given by the Cabinet to obviate the need for the fore-shortened procedure.
7. It is not practicable to evacuate within less than 48 hours of instructions if definite preliminary warning has not been issued. With preliminary warning this can be reduced to 24 hours by making full use of broadcasting and press publicity. No further reduction is physically possible.

Instructions to Evacuation and Reception Officers

1. It is proposed to issue instructions to Evacuation Officers and Reception Officers in regard to matters not yet dealt with in previous issues, as soon as possible.
2. It is also proposed that a parcel containing a complete outfit of all forms, literature, instruction sheets, etc., sufficient to meet the needs of the station and the district, shall be deposited with each officer, labelled with a list of contents and a Notice

   TO BE OPENED ON RECEIPT OF EVACUATION WARNING TELEGRAM.

   In this way every officer will be sure of starting off with all the material he needs, but

   will not be bothered by loose supplies of numerous forms and memos in his office with the risk of loss or mutilation.[21]

Despite the planning, some Secondary Schools were not prepared to take part in the scheme and had made other arrangements.

'14th July 1939

I am instructed by the Governors of Campbell College to inform you that in the event of war they propose to carry on the school at Campbell College and Cabin Hill as usual. The school already has a workable scheme in force for the evacuation of the buildings during an actual raid and this scheme will be revised during the summer holidays.

Claude Potter. Clerk to the Governors'.[22]

A memo issued by the Ministry of Education on the 21st July 1939, revealed the extent of the problem and the amount of disillusionment with the scheme. The Minister had met with the head teachers of the secondary schools on two occasions and as result sent a circular to all secondary establishments asking for their views. It was noted that there was a great deal of divergence of opinion amongst the schools as to the best course to pursue. Some schools such as Campbell College (above), the Methodist College, the Christian Brothers Secondary School and the Bloomfield Collegiate School for Girls, had decided not to evacuate at all. Others

21 Ref. File MPS2/2/22 (no date)
22 Letter to Ministry of Education. 14th July 1939. File MPS2/2/18

expressed themselves in favour of complete or partial evacuation and recommended various alternatives to suit their own needs.

The Richmond Lodge School for Girls proposed to keep going for those pupils who wished to continue their education under the present format, and to disperse the rest of the girls to other schools in safer areas. They suggested that if a sufficient number of their girls could be attached to one particular school, a member of their own staff might be sent to that school to act as liaison between the two establishments. They also referred to the possibility of additional accommodation in church halls being found for those who would attend country schools.

The Princess Gardens School for Girls had made tentative arrangements with the Countess of Clanwilliam for the use of part of Matalto, Ballynahinch, to which they would propose sending their pupils, giving boarders first refusal. If the actual accommodation at Matalto was insufficient for the numbers wishing to go, they would try to find accommodation for some of the older girls in Ballynahinch, and these would then attend Matalto as day boarders. With regard to equipment, they suggested that parents would provide both a bed and bedding for each of their children. With regard to the girls staying in Belfast, they recommended that if the numbers were sufficient, they would keep the school going with part of the staff; while the remainder would go to Matalto. Should the need arise they would ask the Government to provide transport for the girls from Belfast to Matalto, and perhaps help with the provision of bedding, although they would not ask specifically for any Government subsidy towards board.

The Governors of Victoria College had previously raised the issue of their liability in the event of any children being injured in an air raid while at school. A question, which it was agreed by the Ministry, raised a much wider problem which would have to be dealt with separately, if at all. With regard to their evacuation arrangements, they proposed trying to obtain, through Government help or otherwise, a building in the country capable of accommodating the pupils of both Victoria College and Strathearn, or at least such proportion of them whose parents wanted them to join in the school's evacuation scheme. However, the survey they had arranged among the parents seemed to indicate that only 30% of them were disposed to take part in any evacuation.

Ashleigh House School had made arrangements for the acquisition of Langford Lodge in the event of any emergency. They wanted the Government to arrange the transportation of equipment and for those pupils whose parents did not have a car, by providing financial help with fuel costs and a petrol permit for travelling between the two schools.

The Royal Academical Institution informed the Ministry that, if there was any possibility of a daylight raid on Belfast, they could not accept responsibility for allowing any large numbers of boys on the premises. They suggested two alternatives. First: to move the staff and pupils to the countryside where it would be possible to carry on as a boarding school. Second: To cooperate with other schools and obtain a number of premises convenient to all, but out of town. It was pointed out that neither would require government help.

The Mercantile College put forward a complete outline scheme with the idea of asking the Government to obtain or earmark a building, or buildings, in the vicinity of Antrim. They would then house their pupils with friends and relatives in the local area. They would require government help in transporting staff and pupils, but the regular boarding fee would be paid to those householders billeting pupils, thereby offsetting some of the costs.

It became evident that there was no way of dealing with the Secondary Schools as a whole. Because of their various idiosyncrasies the Government could not produce an evacuation scheme on the lines of that proposed for the Public Elementary Schools. However, it was apparent that there was sufficient demand on the part of the Secondary School parents and pupils to deem it essential that some form of evacuation should be devised. There was also an element of elitism inherent in the Secondary School requests, and it is obvious from some of the statements, that they considered themselves and their pupils superior to their Public Elementary School counterparts.

Mr Brierley, Head of the Academical Institute, regarded the problem of the Secondary Schools as a matter for the Government. His opinion, based on the premise that it was the duty of the schools to educate and train children, was that while the new school was being created it precluded the continuance of the education in its present format, and if that failed, the school would have to close down. Then, there being no school, the establishment would have no responsibility for the safety or even the continued education of the children who had formerly attended it. Mr Brierley's idea was that if the Government considered it desirable, in the public interest, that these children should be educated according to Secondary school standards in order that they become a *national asset of peculiar value (sic),* as distinct from the general run of the children whose education was limited to the Public Elementary standard, it was the Government's responsibility to create conditions in which the Secondary schools could provide this in such a way that no financial, or other burdens, should fall upon the School Governors.

The Minister agreed that although he could not concur entirely with the request from the schools, there was a consistent sub-text running through them all which persuaded him that the Government would have to provide assistance as quickly as possible, even though it would require a very substantial expenditure of public money. He tended to give more support for the Mercantile College scheme and suggested that this should be used as a basis for discussion. For their part the Government would help by ear-marking provisional acquisition of appropriate houses or buildings in the Reception Zones, providing free transport of equipment, staff and pupils from Belfast to the emergency school and applying the standard billeting allowance to secondary school pupils in evacuated areas in an approved scheme. It was pointed out that these allowances would be paid either to the householders taking in evacuees or to the school authorities for dispersal, but they would exclude all pupils who were already boarders at the school.

The Minister issued a formal statement on the 24th August 1939, saying that the position of the Ministry with regard to Secondary schools differed considerably with that of the Public Elementary Schools. In the case of the latter, it was pointed out that the Government had certain statutory obligations in the matter of providing an education and the parents of the children had a corresponding responsibility to ensure that their children took advantage of the facilities provided for them. Accordingly, the evacuation scheme for the PES pupils had to include provision for their continued education. However, in the case of the Secondary Schools, there were no statutory obligations on the part of either the Government or the parents, though the former recognised the importance of Secondary School education by making grants to those establishments which provided the most efficient service. Still, although the Minister did not accept that the Government had specific responsibility for ensuring the continued education of the Secondary School pupils in the reception areas, he did agree that it was desirable that opportunities should be afforded to the Secondary School schools, and their pupils, to continue the education in a safer area. As a result he was prepared to include Secondary Schools in the general evacuation scheme under five certain conditions. These were;

1. If a substantial proportion of the pupils of any Secondary School registered for evacuation, the Minister would endeavour to arrange, within physical limitations of the accommodation available, to evacuate the children as a body to a pre-selected area.
2. The selection of the area would be the matter for the school authorities and would presumably be one in which they either proposed establishing a branch of the existing school, or had made arrangements with another secondary school to take over the pupils. In the former contingency, the Ministry would be prepared, on the result of a survey being carried out at the time of the Memo, to suggest buildings which the school might consider suitable. However, the actual acquisition and furnishing of the premises would be the responsibility of the school authorities.
3. The Ministry would pay the transportation costs of the evacuated children and the accompanying staff, but would not provide free transport for any equipment or anything other than the pupils and their conductors.
4. The Ministry would pay the standard billeting allowances in respect of the evacuated children irrespective of the financial standing of their parents, and if the school cannot, or does not wish to deal with evacuated children as boarders, the Ministry would arrange private billets for them.

5. If the school authorities were prepared to undertake the board of the children communally as school boarders, the Ministry would pay the standard billeting allowances to the school on the understanding that such payments were used to make possible satisfactory financial arrangements with the parents of the children, which would enable the poorest of their pupils to take advantage of the scheme.[23]

A few days later a detailed plan of the evacuation arrangements for the Secondary Schools was released. It was agreed that as the Secondary Schools had chosen their place of refuge with quite different considerations in mind, it was conceivable that a school in Zone 1 may have arranged evacuation to a house in County Down. It was also decided that there would be no Stage II evacuees in the Secondary School schemes. When evacuation was necessary, Secondary Schools would move straight into their permanent billets and would consequently require transport door to door, as in many cases their billets were big country houses well away from railway stations. As the normal transport 'zone' arrangements would not apply to the Secondary Schools, the authorities would need to have detailed information about each school's destination and the numbers in the party in order to ascertain the most efficient way of getting them there. In view of the probable distance from the railheads, and to avoid a possible double movement via the central clearing centre, it was suggested that buses might be more suitable for the complete journey.

It was assumed that in many cases the whole number of pupils would be billeted within the new school building in the Reception area, but that a comparatively small number would be put into private billets. On arrival, the first task would be to check the 'travelling rolls' and summaries[24] to ensure that the contingent had arrived safely. If any pupils were to be billeted in private homes, it would be necessary to make billeting certificates (EvS21) available and dispatch them to their accommodation under the care of teachers and local Billeting Officers who would be allotted for the purpose. It would also be necessary to have a full billeting list *(....in triplicate on Form Sec. 3)* of the pupils housed in the new buildings so that allowances could be paid in bulk to the school. These allowances were fixed at 8/6d per week for all pupils for whom board and lodging was provided; 21/- per week for unpaid voluntary workers for whom board and lodging was provided; 5/- a week for teachers for lodging. Teachers were to be placed in the same category as a mother going with her children under school age, who was responsible for providing her own food. If the school undertook to give them full board, that had to be a private arrangement between the school and the teachers concerned.

In order to ascertain the final sum, a bureaucratic procedure was put in place. As soon as possible after the evacuation, the Billeting Officers attached to the Secondary Schools were to inspect the rolls, satisfy themselves that all was correct, and then complete a School Billeting Certificate Form EvS21, again in triplicate. One copy would be left with the Principal of the school, and two copies would be returned by the billeting officers to the Zone Officer, together with the EvS21 forms relating to pupils in private billets. A similar list was to be made out on Form Sec 4 for teachers and Form Sec 5 for unpaid voluntary helpers.

Once the payments were calculated, the allowances would be payable a week in advance, on presentation of the billeting certificates to the Post Office.

20/3/40

List of buildings in Reception areas earmarked for evacuation purposes by Secondary and Private Schools from Belfast

Building	Earmarked By
'Gorteen' Limavady. Co Londonderry	Richmond Lodge
'Montalto, Ballynahinch. Co Down	Princess Gardens
Shane's Castle, Randalstown, Co Antrim	Mercantile College
Castlewellan Castle,Castlewellan Co Down	Ashleigh House
Glenarm Castle, Glenarm, Co Antrim	Victoria College

23 Letter from J.A.McKeown. Ministry of Education. 24th August 1939
24 These were forms EvS8 and EvS11mm

Building	Earmarked By
Strathearn Evacuation School. The Argory, Dungannon, Co Tyrone	Strathearn
Dominican Convent, Portstewart Co Londonderry (Also Part Of Montague Arms Hotel And Perhaps Boarding Houses)	St Dominic's High School
Oldtown School Cookstown. Co Tyrone	Holyrood School
1. College View 3 Northland Place, Dungannon 2. House In Northland Row, Dungannon Lately Occupied By Mr John Mcadoo Irons Leased By The School For The Duration Of The War	R.B.A.I
Derrymoyd Lodge. Draperstown. Co Londonderry	Bloomfield Collegiate

By the 20 May 1940, the Ministry of Home Affairs had been informed of the number of Secondary School pupils who were to be evacuated:-

School	No. of Pupils
Victoria College (two parties of c40)	80
Princess Gardens	62
Ashley House Nursery School	88
Edenberry Nursery School	26
RBAI	136
Strathearn	32
Mercantile College & Royal Academy	57 (Royal Academy: 8 boys, 2 girls, 2 adults. 5 of these were Jews and the others Protestant) (Mercantile College 22 boys, 23 girls all Protestant)
Methodist College (to Magherafelt)	33 (A few from Bloomfield Collegiate)
Methodist College (to Coleraine)	20 (In the end only 12 registered....12 boys and 1 adult...1 RC)
College of Technology (to Lurgan)	77 (31 boys and 46 girls...1 Roman Catholic)
St Patricks Christian Brothers Junior Technical School. (to Lurgan)	12 (10 boys, 2 girls....all Roman Catholic)

In June 1940, the Ministry sent out further recommendations to the Secondary Schools. It was stressed that their evacuation schemes must be available during the school holidays for any pupils who are in Belfast and whose parents wish them to be evacuated. Children who may be out of Belfast on holiday when the scheme became operational were to be asked to remain at their holiday address and their parents should notify both the school and the Ministry as to their whereabouts. The children should then obey any instructions that were sent on to them. If the parents and pupils complied with this request they would be treated as coming within the scope of the scheme, but if they were non-compliant, or returned to Belfast and subsequently asked to be included in the evacuation planning, they would be regarded as having voluntarily withdrawn from the scheme and would not be allowed to take part. It was also pointed out that if any secondary school decided to suspend its evacuation for the holidays, it would be treated as '*final abandonment*' as far as the Government facilities and billeting allowances were concerned, and any future revival of the scheme after the holidays would have to be a private matter for the school and the parents. In the case of such abandonment the parents were to be informed by the Head-teacher that they were at liberty to either apply to the Ministry for individual registration, or to present the children as unregistered evacuees on the second evacuation day at '*some elementary school*'.

Again, it is quite astonishing that the Government were quite prepared *not* to allow children to be evacuated simply because of a bureaucratic oversight or intransigence on the part of the school. This obviously elicited some response from at least one school as this letter would indicate. One can only assume the content of the actual communication to necessitate this reply.

'10.6.40

Ref.D311

Dear Sir/Madam

In order to remove any misapprehension which may exist, I am directed by the Minister of Home Affairs to inform you that he is relying on the cooperation of the Governors and Staffs of the Secondary Schools to play their part in the operation, if necessary, of the evacuation plans during

> vacation as during term, and to request that you will be good enough to make arrangements to ensure that the operations Manager will reach you ,or a suitable department, and that a sufficient number of conductors remain within reach and available for recall should the need arise.......'

Although these accommodation arrangements had been made, there were notable conflicts of interest between some of the schools and other organisations requiring space outside the city. A brusque letter sent by William Duff in July 1940, illustrates the problem:-

> 3.7.40
>
> To Major Grant. Staff Captain. Northern Ireland District, Victoria Barracks. Belfast.
>
> Dear Grant,
>
> The lady Principal of the private school from whom you people stole the Castlewellan Castle after all the evacuation arrangements had been made, has succeeded after much toil and worry, in finding a house in County Londonderry which, by the expenditure of a considerable amount of money, can be made suitable for the school by about September, till which time other temporary arrangements for such of the pupils as not away on holiday will be made by her in Ballycastle.
>
> I note the address of the house (Learmont Park, nr Claudy. Co Derry) and I should be very grateful if you could see that the clutching hands of your accommodation branch are kept off it. We are formally notifying the earmarking of the house for evacuation purposes through the usual channels, but I am giving this personal notification because I hesitate to think what would happen if the house should also go. My decease at the hands of the irate lady would probably result'.
>
> William Duff.'

Some of the moves called for unforeseen expenditure...which raised the question of 'who pays?'. There was an interesting letter on file dated 12/12/40 concerning the Strathearn Evacuation School. The 'Argory' had been given over by Sir Walter Macgeouch Bond, but when the school returned, there was a request for reimbursement of expenses on behalf of the owner:-

> *'....Certain necessary expenses were incurred, one unavoidable, one being the provision of a pump to pump water for sanitary purposes – and on closing the accounts when the children returned to Belfast, there was a deficit of £53 7.10. Does the Ministry of Home Affairs make any grant towards losses incurred by Secondary Schools in carrying out the scheme of evacuation from Belfast, which at one time was considered to be imperative in the national interest?*
>
> *J.Milne Barbour'*

A reply, the next day, from William Duff at the Ministry was short and to the point:-

> *'No funds and no legal or implied liability in regard to the deficit. Deficit occurred because of withdrawal of support from the parents'.*

By September 1941 the Ministry of Home Affairs had a list of where the Secondary School pupils were receiving their education:-

School	Evacuation School
Ashleigh House School	Learmont. Nr Park Londonderry
Bloomfield Collegiate School	Waterfront,Glanariffe
Princess Gardens School	Carrowdore Castle. Co Down

School	Evacuation School
Richmond Lodge School	Portaballintrae
Victoria College and Strathearn School	Portaballintrae
Christian Brothers Junior Technical School	Cushendun & Branch Prep School
Mercantile College, Belfast	Jordanstown
Royal Academy Belfast	Portrush,Cookstown,Donaghadee,Ballygally, Arrangments For Instuction:- Coleraine Acad. Institution for Boys and Coleraine High School for Girls
Mercantile College	Lurgan College
Methodist College	Rainey School Magherafelt
Rbai	Dungannon Royal School
St Dominics	Dominican Convent. Portstewart

It is possible, by looking at the holistic figures for some of the individual schools, to map changes of pupil numbers and personnel in their establishment across the war years:-

Name of school	Address to which evac.	No. of pupils originally billeted	No. of teachers originally billeted	No. of pupils billeted 1942	No. of teachers billeted 1942	No. of pupils billeted 1944	No of teachers billeted 1944	No. of Voluntary Helpers
Ashleigh House	Learmont Castle	59	10	34	12	29	11	1
Princess Gardens	The Castle. Carrowdore	40	5	28	5	26	5	
Victoria College	The Red House. Port-ballantrae	55	5	53	7	20	6	
St. Dominics	The Dominican Convent	11		7		5		
Londonderry High	Greenfield Strabane	9	2	5		3		
RBAI	The Royal School. Dungannon	31		23		3		

One other issue of importance, which was dealt with in a confidential memo dated early August 1939, was the question of the training of elementary schoolteachers in Northern Ireland. At the outbreak of war, students were trained in three colleges; Stranmills in Belfast, St Mary's in Belfast, and St Mary's, Strawberry Hill in London, all of which were segregated on religious grounds. In the early 1920's, the Catholic authorities would not allow Catholic men to be trained alongside Protestants, and in April 1925 all Catholic, male, first-year students at Stranmills, were sent a letter informing them that they must leave and re-enrol at St Mary's Catholic College in Twickenham. If they did not, it would almost certainly debar them from finding employment in a Catholic Elementary school anywhere in Northern Ireland. As a result of this, after 1925 Stranmills was thought of as a Protestant institution simply because no Catholic men were trained there. Stranmills housed 200 students of both sexes, and it was understood that on the outbreak of war it would be taken over by the military authorities as a hospital. It was assumed that the training of women would continue, but it was not clear whether, as on the mainland, the training of men would be discontinued, or whether those who had already embarked on their training, would be allowed to complete it. In addition, it was unclear whether or not a temporary college should be established in Belfast for the duration of the war, or moved to a place of safety in line with the evacuation scheme.

St Mary's Belfast was a college for 75 Roman Catholic women run by the Dominican Order of Nuns. It was recommended that, as in the case of Stranmills, training should be continued, but again the question arose of whether if school children were to be evacuated, students should be summoned from the city to undergo classroom training, or whether arrangements should be made for the college to be moved outside the city. It was expected that the 20 Catholic men who were training in St Mary's, London would return to Belfast once their training was complete.

The Ministry of Home Affairs also had to consider the specific requirements of Jewish evacuees. In a letter from William Duff to Rabbi Schachter, it was pointed out that any Jewish school children, or those under five with their mothers, who wanted to be included in the scheme within the schools they normally attended, could be evacuated '*without distinction*' and '*without special provision.*' However, those parents who wanted 'special provision' could register with the Hebrew School at the Jaffe PES and they would be dealt with separately. The responsibility for housing these children was placed on the Rabbi who was asked to organise the billets within the Jewish community in Londonderry. Once these were sorted out, he was then to inform the Ministry of the numbers involved and their addresses. Having guided the Rabbi towards using Londonderry, there is evidence within the letter, of the Ministry then offering no guarantees for the safety of the children once they got there.

> '*.....You will understand that normally Londonderry is regarded as a Neutral Zone, that is, an area which is not sufficiently vulnerable to justify evacuation but is regarded as sufficiently free from risk of attack to be used as a Reception Area under the general evacuation scheme. In practice, my personal opinion is that the danger there to a relatively small number of Jewish evacuees is small, but it must be a matter for your organisation to decide....*'

For some reason the Ministry suggested that the evacuation of the Jews should not take place on the same day as the general evacuation.[25]

As well as the Jewish situation, it was quoted in a meeting held at the Ministry of Education on the 25th September 1939, that 'One of the troubles peculiar to Northern Ireland was that of religion. The Roman Catholic Church authorities had been very helpful, but in return they had exacted a promise that Protestant children should be sent only to Protestant homes and Roman Catholic children to Catholic homes. It was however easier to find Catholic homes in the provinces than Protestant in proportion to the number of each being evacuated.....With care it is hoped that the undertaking about religious segregation would be carried out....' [26]

Evidence of the willingness of some of the clergy to be accommodating comes in a letter from D. Mageean to William Duff dated 30th September 1939, although this attitude was not adopted by all.

> '*....I have to thank you for the trouble you have taken to arrange suitable reception areas for the children of the Convent and Monastery Schools. You mentioned a difficulty which might arise in the event of one of the evacuation days being a Friday; there will be no difficulty about granting the dispensation to which you referred, should evacuation take place*'.

The question of religion in relation to evacuation was one which was raised many times throughout the war, and one which had a significant bearing on the eventual placement of children within the reception areas. During an Education Committee meeting in October 1939, two members of the clergy voiced their opinions. The Reverend Quinn stated that many of the Belfast population had close ties with families in the country districts and suggested that, this being the case, evacuation by private arrangement should be encouraged. He was supported by the Rev. Smyth who declared that Ministers of Religion should be called upon to assist in arranging for the billeting of children within their denomination, since they would know the people who would be capable of taking in evacuees. In addition this would provide and maintain a pastoral oversight of the children and so inspire confidence in the parents at home[27].

Discussions relating to private evacuation took up a great deal of committee time as decisions had to be made and strategies put in place. When it was first examined in committee in November 1939,[28] members had to find answers to three basic questions:-

1. Whether or not the scheme would cover both relatives and friends.
2. Whether or not the private arrangements can be made with persons residing in the Pink Area (the zone immediately outside the city).

25 The Rabbi replied and asked for the children to be moved as a Unit on the 5th September 1939.
26 Minutes of meeting held at Ministry of Education. 25th September 1939
27 Education Committee Minutes. 26th October 1939
28 Memo. Private Arrangements for Billeting. 15th November 1939

3. Whether or not the householder on whom the children were to be billeted, would be entitled to payment of the Government billeting allowance, and, if so, would recovery be made on the same lines as under the terms of the existing Government scheme.

As to (1) it seemed reasonable for them to assume that not only would children be more likely to receive considerate treatment from friends of their family, but they would feel more at home and secure than they perhaps would with strangers. Therefore it was considered that the lesser of the two evils would be to make the scheme applicable to both relatives and friends, especially as it would be extremely difficult in a large number of cases to decide whether a person stated was indeed a relative, without first making extensive enquiries.

In the case of (2) it was a little more complicated. It was understood that any private arrangement should not apply to a district which was adjacent to the evacuation area, on the grounds that if it became necessary to evacuate school children from the city, the Pink Area might also then be considered to be in danger. As a result, the Government would not be justified in superimposing a scheme onto the present one which might, in some circumstances, result in children being transferred to an area of danger. However, this raised another question. If parents were willing and keen to send their children to friends and relatives in the Pink Area, would the Government be justified in placing an embargo on an area that they had not previously considered worthy of evacuation? A sort of compromise was reached. Although it was considered inadvisable to increase the number of children in the Pink Area it was agreed that if parents wanted to make private arrangements, they should be told that as the Government scheme did not cover evacuation to that area, they would be responsible for the travelling arrangements and the costs incurred.

With regard to (3), it was agreed that if the Government authorised the scheme, the billeting allowance should be paid to the relative or friend to whom the child was sent. However, the parents who were able to send their children to relatives should not be seen to be in any better financial situation than parents who were unable to do the same, therefore it was decided that the former should be required to contribute towards the cost of maintenance, if they were in a position to do so. The method by which this money would be collected would be explained to the parents when they applied.

The committee finally agreed on the basic procedures which needed to be followed:-

In the event of evacuation taking place the parents would be required to state whether or not they wished to have their children of school age evacuated, and if so, did they want them to go under the government scheme or to friends or relatives, and if the latter, to provide the names and addresses of where the children were going.

At the end of the meeting issues were raised about getting written consent from those friends and relatives designated by the parents, and ensuring that the children being evacuated under such a scheme were '*clean*'(*sic*). Both remained unresolved.

Three days later, after further consideration, the Committee drew up a modified scheme. Reference was made to the evacuation in England where parents were able to make private arrangements at their own expense, otherwise it was considered to be an undemocratic arrangement. With this in mind they listed the following recommendations:-

1. Publicity should be given in the press, by broadcasts and through schools. The public should be informed perfectly clearly and definitely, that at the backbone of the Government scheme there is provision for any children being sent under the Government Scheme to billets selected by the Government, the Government being responsible for the suitability of the billets and the areas in each case.

2. The Government will require endorsement of each of the private arrangements and reserves the right to disallow them.

3. They will be permitted only within the true Reception Areas.

4. Parents should be told under what circumstances evacuation will take place, namely when raiding has occurred in Great Britain, in areas where it would make it likely that Belfast would be raided.
5. If they wish to send their children for evacuation (non-privately) they would be required to register their children at the school for evacuation.
6. They should be informed of the financial implications of the scheme, the contribution parents would be expected to pay towards their child's upkeep.
7. Children's cleanliness would be inspected on arrival at the billets and it would have to be considered whether or not this would be extended to any private scheme.[29]

Item 7 was an issue which would be returned to on a regular basis.

At a meeting at the Ministry of Education in September 1939, it was announced that arrangements for the payment of billeting allowances would be made at Post Offices or Labour exchanges, and this would be fully explained on a card which would be issued to all householders in the Reception Areas. It was also agreed that, like their counterparts on the mainland, schools in the reception areas would operate on a double shift system, thereby allowing equal school time for evacuees and the resident population.

Alderman Lyle-Hall suggested that only children in the area adjacent to the Harland and Wolff shipyards and the Harland and Short aircraft factories should be evacuated, but this was rejected by William Duff who pointed out the inaccuracy of enemy bombers. Another Alderman, Dr Williamson, enquired as to whether any arrangements had been made to separate 'clean' children from the 'dirty'. It was estimated at the time that between 5-7% of Belfast children suffered from head-lice. He was told they would be examined on arrival which, in hindsight, may not have been good practice bearing in mind the close proximity of the children on the trains.

Despite all the meetings and discussions still no evacuation had taken place which was leading to a certain amount of frustration and confusion in some areas, as the following letter from the North Antrim Education Committee indicates:-

> '18th October 1939
>
> As yet I have received no official information from any quarter on the question of evacuation and it is impossible to carry out the Committee of Education's instructions unless I am given some idea as to the numbers of children likely to be evacuated and probable distributions'.
>
> Some even doubted that the measures put in place were actually workable; '....while recognising the necessity for plans for the evacuation of school children, the Education Committee (Belfast City Hall) are of the opinion that, in the light of the experience gained in England and Scotland, the proposed arrangements are open to grave objection in principle....' [30]

One significant group, which had been overlooked in the planning stages, was that containing children who were labelled as Deaf, Dumb and Blind. The scheme had not included any provision for the evacuation of these children as surprisingly perhaps, they were considered to be in Priority Class 4 and were therefore down the list. The planning had only really got to Priority Classes 1 and 2. However, the Ministry was keen to point out that there was a school for the Deaf and Blind run by the Ulster Society for Promoting Education for the Deaf, Dumb and Blind. Under the terms of the 1923 Education Act, this school was regarded as a PES establishment and as such would be placed in Priority Class 1 for evacuation. But in answer to an enquiry from a Miss Russell-Smith[31], the Minister adopted a rather perfunctory tone and stated that *'it is perfectly obvious that they cannot be*

29 Memo. Modified Scheme of Private Arrangements for Billeting. 18th November 1939
30 Letter to Minister of Home Affairs from City Hall Belfast. 6th October 1939
31 Although there is no evidence of her letter, nor her actual position, one can assume that she had something to do with the education of Deaf and Blind children.

broadcast into private billets like ordinary PES children and accordingly, if this school is evacuated at all, it will have to be evacuated specially'. As with some other previous enquiries he ignored the substance of the query and put the question back onto the questioner:

> *'There must be a considerable number of similar Institutions in England and Scotland , and I should be very grateful if you would tell me how they were treated in Great Britain in regard to the following points.*
>
> 1. *Were they evacuated specially as complete units into some building in a reception area and the pupils boarded therein?*
> 2. *If so, what arrangement was made about the billeting payments etc?*
> 3. *Did you give any contribution towards the capital cost of the removal or any other expenses of a like nature?*
> 4. *What are you doing about reclaiming contributions analogous to those now demanded from the parents of the unaccompanied children?*[32]

One wonders why his administrative staff could not find answers to these questions themselves, especially as they had inter-ministry communications with Whitehall?

As very little seemed to be happening, a Women's' Club in Belfast, chaired by Florence Davidson the only woman MP in the Ulster Parliament, came up with few suggestions as to how evacuation could be implemented. The children should be divided into four groups: Those under 3 evacuated with their mothers to private houses; those under 6 formed into nursery schools; under 11s billeted in private houses and sent to local schools; 11+ in mixed camps run by Scoutmasters and Guiders in collaboration with resident PSE teachers transferred from evacuated areas. The hutted camps could be used for workers post-war. Cheap fares would be made available for parents to visit their children, although they should take their own food. Finally, there should be a 'central receiving post' with bathing facilities and an emergency store of clean clothing.[33]

There is no evidence in the files of a reply to this letter, but it did prompt an updated report on the evacuation scheme to be sent to the Parliamentary Secretary in early December. It mentioned all those who had been involved and stores that had been ordered, such as felt pads to supplement the beds and blankets which had already been distributed. It indicated that a number of women were being trained as District Nurses as part of the Civil Nursing Reserve, and plans were in place for a domiciliary nursing and medical service in the reception areas under a Panel System. There had also been a survey of hospital provision. It pointed out that it had not been possible to put into effect any satisfactory arrangements for Secondary Schools which would combine evacuation with the continuation of the educational standards the parents expected their children to receive. No special arrangements had yet been made for children who were labelled as 'defective' (*sic*), tubercular, blind, deaf and crippled (*sic*). In addition the basic organisation of visiting, and the recreational and general welfare services in the Reception Areas, was incomplete.[34]

Considering the fact that evacuation had been discussed in committee since the beginning of 1939, the Government's plans for the overall scheme were woefully short of where they should have been by the time this report was written. Had any attack taken place in Belfast in the early months of the war the effects would have been unimaginable, as not enough of the infrastructure was in place to implement an effective evacuation of the city. By this time all categories of evacuees in the rest of Britain had already been in their reception areas for four months. In addition, no preparations whatsoever had been attempted for the evacuation of pregnant women, blind adults and the disabled. The committee shunned the responsibility somewhat by suggesting that it should be a matter for the Government to decide whether these classes should be included in the evacuation scheme

32 Letter from Stormont dated 16th November 1939. Ref. D270
33 Letter to the Minister of Home Affairs dated 20th November 1939
34 Memo to Parliamentary Secretary. 4th December 1939

'bearing in mind that no effective plans can be made in these cases without extensive preparations involving substantial preliminary expense'.

They did agree that they were way below the standard that their English counterparts had reached by September 1st, even in respect of the priority classes, and in an attempt to alleviate the situation they made three suggestions. But note these were again *suggestions* and not *actions* and one had already been discussed on a number of occasions.

The first was to allow Belfast parents to select billets in the reception areas with the help of friends and relatives. It was proposed that the plans should provide for the registration of such arrangements before evacuation took place, and the movement and billeting of the children should be carried out as an integral part of the transportation and billeting process. This had been discussed in November when different conclusions regarding transportation and costs had been reached.

The second proposal was to ensure the segregation and treatment of verminous children and those suffering from contagious skin diseases; again an issue which had previously been investigated. This was being done in Britain by examination in schools prior to departure, although it was far more successful in the evacuation of 1940 than in 1939. The idea in Belfast was to examine the children 'in the course of the evacuation' with follow up checks after dispersal. This would involve preparatory expense and details would have to be submitted when the plans were finalised. It was made clear that these inspections should not apply to those going to pre-arranged billets. It is interesting to note, that as with the plans to evacuate pregnant women and the blind, the economic considerations were very much at the heart of the prevarication. Nowhere in the report does it emphasise the possible need to get children to safety!

The final suggestion was to 'eliminate the mother or female relative from Class (ii) (Children with mothers). It was stated that *'the substantial failure of the Scheme in Great Britain for this class can be largely attributed to the influence and presence of the female figure and she is being excluded from the re-evacuation which is consequently necessary there'*. However, this was not the case. There is no evidence to suggest that mothers with their children caused the scheme to collapse. Some mothers with children were often difficult to house, and there is indication of some moving billets and eventually returning home, but not to extent that this statement would have us believe. In addition, there was no re-evacuation of people in England and Wales until June 1940, and this report was written in early December 1939! It goes on to say that the Ministry would want to *'ascertain precisely what their revised plans are and what they involve'*.....but there were not any revised plans at the level he is suggesting. Any changes of billets etc were usually on an ad hoc basis within the reception areas and carried out under the authority of the billeting officer, not a member of the Government.

Despite the overall lack of progress the report concludes that ' apart from the three suggestions, there does not appear to be any substantial improvement which can be suggested at present on the existing plan except to perfect the arrangements where we now fall short of British standards.....'

He goes on to list the deficiencies and the action needed to overcome them. All of which had been discussed before with the exception of the comments under 'Special Cases' which hinted that even children requiring special needs who were presently being catered for at home, would be housed in institutions in the reception areas. [35]

On the 8th December 1939, the Minister of Education received a deputation from the Association of Northern Ireland Education Committees[36] requesting that revisions be made to the planned evacuation scheme. They expressed both concern and disappointment that, as far as they were aware, no progress had been made. They were also worried that, as a result of them not being consulted during the initial planning stages, serious mistakes had been made in the assignment of schools and the movement of Belfast children to reception areas where there

35 The actual statement reads: These will require special plans for movement and institutional housing on reception, even those cases which do not necessarily require institutional treatment when in their home surroundings.

36 Minister of Education to Minister of Home Affairs. 12th December 1939. Ref. G332/5

was little surplus accommodation. They considered it would be most unfortunate if, owing to a sudden emergency, the scheme as presented had to be enforced without alteration. They felt that as a body they were able to supply a great deal of information which could be used to ensure the smooth running of the scheme.

The following week, on the 13th December, Sir Richard Dawson Bates[37], the Minister of Home Affairs, reported to the Cabinet on the progress of evacuation. He reiterated most of what had been said in the report to the Government, such as pre-selection of billets and medical provision for evacuees[38], but continued to address some of the more contentious issues from a bureaucratic rather than a humanitarian standpoint, without it would seem, supporting evidence. He reiterated the previous concerns about female relatives and how they had caused the failure of the scheme in England by returning home. As a result, he sought to reduce the numbers of women accompanying the evacuees into the reception areas. He realised that this would require the preparation of special arrangements for the care of the unaccompanied children, and make the role of the local committees even more important. He also recognised that it may not be possible to prevent all mothers going, but '*the fewer who go, the better the chance for the scheme*'.

The most controversial statement was that dealing with pregnant women, primarily because the argument is questionable and based it would seem, on conjecture rather than hard evidence. Bates stated there was more than 9000 births in Belfast every year, or 750 a month. According to him, this meant that there were always about 1500 women in the 8th or 9th month of pregnancy. If arrangements for them were to be made, it would be necessary to provide for at least 500 of these. He stated that no district in Northern Ireland could take them all, and they could not be put up in ordinary billets as householders could not be expected to accommodate women during childbirth. As a result he did *not* propose to make any provision for pregnant women in the evacuation scheme.

There had always been concerns about the evacuation of expectant mothers on the mainland, but after initial problems, including some of them being sent home, provisions were eventually made in the reception areas to house them, usually in hostels or nursing homes. They were not debarred from taking part in the scheme. In the light of policies elsewhere, and the fact that with some of the other measures the Ministry of Home Affairs had sought advice from their counterparts in Whitehall, this decision in Northern Ireland seems to be rather draconian.

On the 19th December, the Minister of Home Affairs sent a letter to the Minister of Education in which he outlined some of the main points of the evacuation discussion to that date:-

1. The Minister thinks it right to consult Cabinet before deciding upon the somewhat drastic revisions.
2. Subject to Cabinet approval, we accept the principle of adopting arrangements between friends where these can be organised.
3. When the billeting arrangements have been starred for 'private arrangements' and the allocation of numbers in the Reception Areas modified on account of these arrangements, we will expect the RAs and the Reception Committees to review the remaining billets available so as to arrive at a final allocation of the children whom we will have in place.
4. I do not know whether it would be possible to arrange that the billets for the children whom we will be responsible for placing should also be allocated individually before the move takes place. The idea has many attractions, but I understand that the number of transfers between schools, and the labour involved in keeping a satisfactory allocation up to date, would be prohibitive. Alternatively, it might be possible for the Principals of schools to be placed in direct touch with the Reception Area to which their schools are going so as to be able to assist in the allocation of billets.

---

37 Sir Richard Dawson Bates JP, DL, OBE, 1876 – 1949. Ulster Unionist Party member of the Northern Ireland House of Commons. Minister of Home Affairs June 1921-May 1943 and a member of the Privy Council of Northern Ireland. He introduced the Civil Authorities (Special Powers) Act, but opposed the Ulster Protestant Association. Under his administration, he was accused of gerrymandering, and of intervening to ensure that prison sentences were not imposed on Protestants who attacked Catholics.

38 Every child was to be attached to the 'panel' of a local doctor who would be paid 5 shillings per half-year for each child.

5. Comments on dealing with verminous children are inconclusive.
6. It is agreed that we work with all parties.....education/church etc.....[39]

On the 10th February 1940, three delegates from the Ministry visited a selection of six schools in the city to ascertain the level of commitment to the evacuation scheme. He reported that only 10% of the school rolls had registered. The main reason given for not registering was the disbelief among parents that Belfast would ever be bombed, and the fact that they had no idea what conditions would be like if raids did take place. A supplementary reason was the dislike of having to make contributions to the upkeep of their children while away. Three shillings per child (on the basic scale) was regarded by many as being more onerous than the cost of keeping a child at home. Many parents seemed to have taken the 6/- rate as fixed and were unable to see that the sliding scale could operate to their advantage. If this registration was projected across the city only 10,000 would take part. It was pointed out that the non-registration was in no way due to the failure of teachers to encourage evacuation as in some cases they had managed to get a 100% return of the forms; it was just that 90% of these said *no*.

However, it was realised that this would be a false assumption as it was hoped that more would want to go once any raids started. It was suggested that the government were in a worse situation than they had been at the initial planning stages, and there now seemed to be only three alternatives.

The first was to accept the 10% registration as representing the true demand, and to confine the scheme to registered children only.

The second was to assume that in the event many more, probably 40-50,000, would want to go and proceed with the scheme on that basis.

The third, and most contentious, was to abandon any attempt to provide for the safety of children of a population too firmly convinced of its immunity from danger to take basic precautions.

It was agreed that options 1 and 3 were not viable, which meant that 2 had to be adopted as the accepted format. It was hoped that further propaganda and announcements by the government might work and *'it might be possible to awaken the dreamers, at least some of them, but at best, a large number will dream on till the bombs awake them and for them we shall have to make provision'*.[40]

In a less formal memo, the registration scheme was referred to by 'ASD' as a '*complete fiasco*' and it was stated that even if 7,000 people in all categories registered, it would be a surprise. He suggested that although at first sight these figures represented failure, '*there is in fact a great deal to be thankful for*'. Had the registration been around the 20-25,000 figure there would have been grounds for accepting this as the real level of demand, and if the plans had gone ahead on this basis there may have been '*calamitous results*'. The '*very smallness of the registration frees our minds from the danger of accepting plausible but misleading information as truth, and we can now proceed to make our plans on the basis of the forecasts of probable events as intelligent thought suggests....*' It's rather extraordinary that he is using this lack of support for the scheme to put forward some tenuous arguments for future planning, without really looking in detail at the reasons why people were rejecting it.

As a basis for further discussion, he put forward his own opinions. First, they could not hope to add to the present registration information in advance of any evacuation scheme, as no more would go unless exact evacuation conditions developed. Second, as soon as evacuation conditions occurred, there would be panic demand from perhaps 30-40,000 more people. So, according to ASD the situation would resolve itself into that of providing the most effective method for a relatively small body of registered evacuees, including those who had pre-selected their billets, and the panic evacuation of larger numbers. A process which, according to him, could be

39 Letter from Minister of Home Affairs to Minister of Education Stormont 19th December 1939 in reply to a letter of the 12th December.
40 Report from 'ASD' dated 10th February 1940

done with comparative ease and without much alteration to the existing plans which a registration of 25k might have necessitated. It did not occur to him that these plans were based on the premise of panic and last minute implementation, rather than a planned distribution of evacuees before the event, similar to the rest of the UK. Had they sorted out the root causes for the lack of parental interest, they may have been able to have the children out of the city long before the eventual raids on the city.

As it is, the three proposals he presented seem unworkable if they had to be put into operation at the last minute. For example, he suggested that evacuation should be divided into three sections and the registered evacuees, of all categories, would be evacuated on *one day* immediately evacuation conditions arise. Surely these conditions would involve actual or expected enemy attacks; a little late to be moving children. Panic evacuation would first be *rigidly* restricted to evacuees in the inner zones, as in the first wave of registered evacuees and then in the outer zones of the Second Wave. But surely this presupposes that 'panic' can be controlled.

Bearing in mind that this was to take place when '*evacuation conditions arise'* this was the outline plan for those who Registered:-

Five main reception zones would be chosen for non-selected evacuees. Twenty-three assembly stations would be selected in Belfast. Of these, 15 would be used for non-selection evacuees and some of the pre-selection evacuees who were going to the 5 main reception areas. The other 8 stations would be used for miscellaneous pre-selection children. Teachers from all the schools concerned would accompany the children. One or two teachers would be on hand at the 8 pre-select stations to organise the proceedings. The pre-select parties would be sent out to the reception areas in the charge of volunteer conductors. All the reception areas would have a list of the names of the evacuees etc. and they would complete their own dispersal arrangements. According to the memo, this would only require 10 special trains and a small fleet of buses and not much interference would be caused to normal traffic.

With regard to the 'Panic' Scheme:-

The first 'panic' evacuation was to be timed about a week after the implementation of the registered scheme and the second several days later. All the remaining 22 reception areas would be used together with all assembly stations. All pre-registered evacuees would be discarded. Parents would be told to send their children to the school of the eldest child or any school attended by the child if they think fit. All mothers and children under 5 would be excluded completely. All the procedures previously used would be modified. They were to make arbitrary allocations to reception areas and make transport arrangements as required. They were to provide for a maximum of 40,000 with a reservation that this number may be less. Plenty of accommodation would be available with the elimination of the 20,000 Stage 2s. Cleansing filters were to be put in place and arrangements would be made regarding sick bays and medical treatment. This proposed action '*would eliminate the need for provision for those under 5 except where registered.'*

He then raised the question of publicity, and offered two alternatives. Either they could announce that provision would be made for a subsequent panic evacuation but that registered evacuees would receive preferential treatment and that panic evacuees would have to abide by the government's arrangements without the option to pre-select, or keep the panic arrangements confidential and announce them only when evacuation conditions have '*chastened the laggards with fear'*. It was thought that the second option would not be viable as it would be difficult to keep the plans a secret.

The overall figures were updated in March 1940 when the Parliamentary Secretary was informed that the total number of registrations had reached 17,500. This figure was made up of 9,000 pre-selected billets, and under the Government selections; 6,500 school children, 1,200 under school age and 800 mothers. So, in accordance with the plans to accommodate 40,000, preparations now had to be made for a further 22,500. For administrative purposes they could be divided up either as 17,500 registered and 22,500 unregistered or 9,000 selects and 31,000 unselected.[41]

There is an unsigned handwritten note in the files addressed to the 'Secretary' which raises some interesting issues. The writer says that he had been in contact with the Ministry of Home Security in London, A. Johnston, who had explained that the Secretary of State, in consultation with the Cabinet Committee, would decide on the times of evacuation in Great Britain and that evacuation will not be ordered generally but by areas as necessity arises and as transport is available, without prejudicing military needs. He had also pointed out that the Government in London would be seriously embarrassed if the authorities in Northern Ireland were to carry out an evacuation before they had decided to evacuate an equally or more vulnerable area.

This was followed up by an official communication from the Ministry of Home Security in London on the 4th June 1940, and labelled simply 'Agreement'.

> *Northern Ireland Evacuation Scheme: Arrangements for putting scheme into force.*
>
> *The Northern Ireland Government has made plans for the evacuation of children from Belfast which will be put into effect on a decision of the Northern Ireland Cabinet. We are anxious, however, that this decision should not be taken without prior consideration with the authorities responsible for evacuation in this country. It would be very embarrassing if the Belfast children were to be evacuated while the Government in this country were still refusing to evacuate children in Liverpool and Glasgow. The Northern Ireland Government also wish (sic) to be informed when a decision is in prospect to evacuate Liverpool or Glasgow. .....*

The reason why this communication is fascinating is quite simply that Liverpool and Glasgow had *already* been evacuated in the original scheme implemented in September 1939. Many children from the former were evacuated to North Wales and from the latter around 70,000 evacuees were moved into Kintyre, Dumfrieshire, Banton, Rothesay, Kilsyth, Govan, Inverary and other places. According to the Glasgow Herald dated 1st September 1939 there had been a last minute rush to join the scheme, especially in the Clydebank area where an estimated 80% of the population were moved. The authorities in Aberdeenshire had made provision for 40,000 evacuees (around 20,000 actually arrived) and Ayreshire a further 44,000 and, according to the report, plans were well advanced.

By the 2nd September, it had been reported that 65,000 had been successfully housed. The numbers were not as large as were expected on the first day, primarily because in some areas such as Broughty Ferry, many parents did not believe it was a danger zone and in some areas parents would not leave their children until they had received their public assistance or unemployment relief money. Some people misread the notices and turned up on the wrong day and simply too late. Some of the trains left half-empty and around 30,000 people in Glasgow failed to turn up. But, nonetheless, it was estimated that 60%-65% of those eligible actually left. By Monday 4th September, 171,787 people had been transferred to the designated reception areas, including 31,000 from Edinburgh.[42]

As regards to Liverpool, 85,000 children, mothers and teachers had been evacuated between the 1st and 6th of September, although at least 40% of these had returned by January 1940 during the Phoney War period.

Both areas reintroduced evacuation in 1941; 50,000 registered in Glasgow in March[43] following raids on Clydeside, and many left Liverpool in May following the Blitz on the city and docks.

---

41 Memo to Parliamentary Secretary. 5th March 1940

42 ED24/7 Second World War Files: Evacuation Scheme. Advisory Comm. on Evacuation. Minutes of Meetings 1939-40. HH50/104 Second World War files: Evacuation survey of sending and receiving areas.

43 26th and 29th March 1941

Neither of these plans was carried out on an ad hoc basis, so it is interesting that the communiqués between London and Belfast had made no mention of these schemes and the fact that 60% of the original evacuees remained in the reception areas.

A further message was sent from London on the 7th June 1940:-

> 'SECRET:
>
> ......I suggest that the signs of imminent danger which would justify a recommendation to the Cabinet that the evacuation of Belfast should be ordered might be:-
>
> Evacuation of Liverpool or Glasgow
>
> Enemy reconnaissance flights over Belfast
>
> Actual or attempted attack on Belfast.
>
> ......If there was any reason to expect landings or a ground attack on parts of the country to which the children go, evacuation should not be recommended even if Belfast is attacked...'[44]

The debate continued. In a telephone conversation with the Minister of Home Security in London on the 1st July, it was stated that the considered views of the Home Secretary were:- That if Belfast were a city situated in Great Britain, the UK Government would definitely not decide on evacuation at the present time. If the Government of Northern Ireland proceeds with its decision to evacuate Belfast it would unquestionably create embarrassment for London in regard to the evacuation of Liverpool and Glasgow.[45]

This is at odds with other policy as had Belfast been a city on the mainland, it would most certainly have been evacuated in September 1939 because it met all the criteria.....it was a major port and an important industrial area. Other ports, such as Plymouth, Southampton, Liverpool etc., had been evacuated, so it is interesting to see that Belfast was not considered to be a danger zone in the same way.

This was all to change on the following day, 2nd July 1940, as this copy of an encoded teleprinter message to the Home Secretary from the Northern Ireland Prime Minister indicates:-

> Anderson. Whitehall
>
> Following from Craigavon stop Cabinet have carefully considered voluntary evacuation of schoolchildren from Belfast and decided that it should proceed at early date in view of changed military situation, possible imminence of aerial attacks, desirability of carrying out evacuation unhindered by possible troop movements and having regard to congestion of children around vulnerable shipyard area stop understand you advise against this course stop further consideration in light of your representations does not affect our view stop military here realise difficulties and raise no objection stop don't wish to embarrass you but still feel that we should proceed. [46]

A supporting handwritten note was also placed on file:-

> *'The Cabinet has no information pointing to the fact that Belfast is in any greater or less danger than it was a week or month ago. But the beginning of the Battle of Britain may mean war becoming more imminent and as a precautionary step the Cabinet has decided to put into operation at an early date the scheme for evacuating those children whose parents have already expressed a*

---

44 Secret Memo from London to Belfast 7th June 1940

45 Part of a transcript of a telephone conversation between Minister of Home Security in London and authorities in Belfast. 1st July 1940.

46 Encoded message from Irish Prime Minister to Sir John Anderson. Saturday 2nd July 1940 at 4pm.

wish that their children should be sent out of the city. It is emphasised that the decision of the Cabinet is purely precautionary.....'

Sir John Anderson's Private Secretary telephoned on the 3rd July saying that;

'Sir John has been in consultation with a number of his colleagues and the conclusion they had reached was that if the Northern Ireland Government desired to put an evacuation scheme into force no objection would now be raised'.[47]

The Ministry then put together a statement, [48] to be released at a planned press conference, which included the following details:-

- The decision to evacuate was purely precautionary.
- The Port of Belfast was an area of national importance.
- The congested area around the harbour must be regarded as likely to suffer in the event of an attack.
- Timeliness of evacuation: In present circumstances may or may not be premature but it is obviously desirable in such a matter to be early rather than late.

Broad lines will be as follows:-

- On the first day only those children will be evacuated whose parents registered them for evacuation.
- Second and subsequent days, children attending schools within the area regarded as most vulnerable, namely the area surrounding the harbour, will be evacuated in so far as the parents express a wish to have them sent away.
- Under the registered scheme parents are already in possession of all the necessary instructions except the actual date. This will be notified to them via press announcements and by posters displayed outside schools.
- Children will assemble at the assembly point of which they have been informed. They will be taken in charge of a school teacher.
- They will be transported to a railway station for the journey to the dispersal point.
- They will be met at the dispersal point by members of the reception organisation.
- The scheme provides for the children to be under the care of a competent adult from the time they arrive at the assembly point until they reach their final destination.
- Provision has been made for their medical attendance in case of illness.
- The cost of the accommodation and feeding the children in the reception areas will be met in the first instance by the Government, and whilst a proportion will be recovered from parents, the contribution which will be demanded will be in accordance with the parent's capacity to pay.
- It will not be possible to tell parents on the day of evacuation the addresses of the homes to which the children are being sent. All these homes however, have been examined and passed as entirely suitable for reception purposes, and arrangements have been made for postcards to be sent by, or on behalf of, the child to its own parents notifying them of the address within approximately 48 hours of arrival.

47 Transcript of telephone conversation between PPS at Home Office London and Stormont. 3rd July 1940 at 12.30pm
48 The press release is undated but referenced as Ref.Evac 213.

- It is emphasised that the scheme is confined entirely to those children whose parents wish to have them sent away from the city. There is no element of compulsion in it, and it is also right to point out that in these times no guarantee of absolute safety can given, but the destinations to which the children are being sent are less likely to be damaged from aerial attack than the homes in which they are now living.

As will be noted from previous chapters, this document was similar to the statements made on mainland Britain in September 1939 with just two exceptions. First of all, the British Government was only responsible for getting the children into the reception areas. Once they arrived the accountability passed to the reception authorities. In some areas this caused a great deal of unrest as the costs of implementing the scheme were so high that in some instances the situation necessitated a rise in the local rates. Secondly, one of the unforeseen problems of the British scheme was that it was not compulsory and many 'unregistered' children turned up on the evacuation day. This resulted in accommodation problems within the reception areas on arrival[49], with all the attendant difficulties, both on the part of the authorities and the actual evacuees who in many cases felt they were unwanted. This situation was often made worse when the discussion between the billeting officer and the hosts about taking in extra evacuees took place in front of the children. The potential foster parents were understandably irritated by the situation, and evidence from oral testimony would suggest that in some cases they took out their frustration on the child verbally. The tone of voice was often enough to convince the evacuee that they were not wanted. Common sense would have suggested that these discussions should have taken place outside the reception locations or at least in another room.

There was also a certain amount of unease in the Northern Ireland reception areas. The Minister of the Presbyterian Church in Downpatrick, a designated reception area, wrote to the Ministry in February 1940 expressing concerns about the scheme and demanding answers to specific questions. Firstly, would a guarantee be given that no householder would have to accept a *mentally defective* (sic) evacuee where there are special institutions for such cases? (The Minister was basing this on his own knowledge of a situation in Glasgow.) Secondly, would the children be placed in an environment such as they are accustomed to, and would they be graded into the usual income groups and distributed in the reception areas as fully as possible within these groups? He pointed out that this would of course require the registration of householders with such a grouping in mind. Thirdly, would the Government relax compulsory billeting where the householders are aged, infirm, ill or otherwise unable to comply with the demands of the children in their care? [50] Fourthly, would precautions be taken that children should not be billeted in any house unsuitable by reason of living conditions, drainage, dirt, addiction of householders to drink, or overcrowding? Again, this should have been a matter for the billeting officer to have sorted out prior to any evacuation taking place. As far as possible in the original accommodation 'census', carried out in January 1939 on the mainland, account had been taken of the worthiness of the premises, but it has to be said that no checks were ever made on the suitability of the hosts. Finally, would there be an appeal tribunal with local knowledge not merely comprised of Government officials. These were in fact in place, but how effective they were depended largely on how the local officials fulfilled their responsibilities. [51]

There was no reply to this letter on file.

The question of the moral education of Belfast children was raised in the House of Commons on 14th March 1940. Captain Ramsay[52] a right wing politician and devout Christian, had previously introduced a Private Member's Bill entitled the 'Aliens Restriction (Blasphemy) Bill' on 28th June 1938. The main objective of which

49 Many areas received double the amount of evacuees they had been expecting.

50 This had been a provision of the original Anderson Committee recommendations on the mainland, but because of the numbers who turned up in some of the reception areas, those who were not expecting evacuees because they were either out at work all day, too old, or were not deemed fit enough for whatever reason, to look after them, suddenly found that they had 2 or 3 children foisted upon them.

51 Letter from J.Murray-Moore. Presbyterian Minister. 22nd February 1940

52 Captain Archibald Ramsay, 1894- 1955. Educated at Eton and Sandhurst Military College. A member of the Conservative Party, Ramsay was elected to the House of Commons in 1931. In May 1939 he founded a secret society called the Right Club. This was an attempt to unify all the different right-wing groups in Britain. In late 1940, after he had been implicated in a spying scandal, he was interned under Defence Regulation 18B. Although detained in Brixton Prison he was allowed to submit questions in the House of Commons which enabled him to continue to make racist comments. Ramsay was released from prison on 26th September, 1944. He was defeated in the 1945 General Election and in 1955 he published his book The Nameless War.

was "*to prevent the participation by aliens in assemblies for the purpose of propagating blasphemous or atheistic doctrines or in other activities calculated to interfere with the established religious institutions of Great Britain*". In this debate he had asked the Parliamentary Secretary at the Board of Education what steps the Belfast government had taken, or were planning to take, to ensure that children, particularly those who were to be evacuated, were not given moral instruction contrary to the principles held by their parents, and whether the Board will cause disciplinary action to be taken against teachers who *'offend this respect'*. Mr Lindsay, from the Board of Education, replied that he had no grounds for thinking that any such instruction was given in schools under Belfast's jurisdiction. This did not satisfy Ramsay who asked the same question in a different way: *'May I ask my honourable friend to answer my question and say whether or not he proposes to give the parents of children who have been evacuated the right to see that they are educated according to their wishes.'* A heated debate ensued....

Lindsay: *I think I should read the answer again....I should add that if my honourable and gallant friend* (Ramsay had seen service in France 1914-16 with the Coldstream Guards) *has any specific cases to bring to my notice, I shall be glad to look at them.*

Ramsay: *As the position stands, what rights have parents got to see that their children who are evacuated are taught according to their wishes. Have they any rights?*

Lindsay: *I shall be sending my honourable and gallant friend a copy of my answer. This is a serious charge and I think he should give me specific examples before I can possibly say more in answer to his question.*

Ramsay then asked the Secretary whether or not he was aware that a number of teachers with Marxist opinions were taking advantage of the evacuation scheme, and the consequent separation of children from their parents, to inculcate principles contrary to Christian teaching and morality, and to endeavour to destroy all respect the children have for their parents according to the tenets of Marxism. What steps was he proposing to take to prevent this?

Lindsay: *The answer to the first part is in the negative; the second part does not therefore arise. Any specific case which my hon. Friend can adduce will of course be investigated.*

Ramsay: *In view of the fact that a responsible organisation is prepared to give him details of complaints from five different counties, will my hon. Friend undertake to look into them and, if he finds the complaints substantiated, see that the wishes of the parents are respected and the children are protected from such teaching, whether it be Fascist or Marxist?*

This resulted in a barbed retort from Manny Shinwell, Labour, who commented: *Has the hon. Member any reason to believe that the hon. and gallant Member who asks the question is associated with any reasonable organisation.?*

(The significance in this comment being that a week later Shinwell, along with fellow Labour MP Ellen Wilkinson, made speeches in the House of Commons suggesting that Ramsay was a member of a right wing secret society, which indeed he was.[53])

While this debate was going on in London, a memo was sent out from William Duff in Stormont, confirming the arrangements for the closing of all schools in Northern Ireland for two weeks immediately an evacuation warning was given. This would be necessary because a large number of schools would be required for assembling evacuees, and the teaching staff would be involved in the scheme for an extended period. However, it was noted that if raids developed, then a widespread regrouping and consolidation of schools would be undertaken to deal with those children who had remained in the city. It was also pointed out that some schools in the reception areas would be required as dispersal stations. He stated that two weeks after the billeting arrangements had been

53 Extract from Parliamentary Debate. House of Commons Official Report. Vol 358. Thursday 14th March 1940

completed, the schools would then be used for enrolment purposes to absorb evacuees into existing or augmented local schools.

He then raised the question of the permanent allocation of Belfast teachers to country areas to supplement local staff. He agreed that it would be impracticable to plan this in advance because there was still a degree of uncertainty as to how many evacuees would actually take part. He suggested that teachers should remain in the Reception Areas to help with the volume of work expected in the immediate aftermath of evacuation, until such time as they received individual instructions to do otherwise. They would be informed that they should go to the reception areas with their school but that they would not necessarily remain there for their teaching duties. However, in order to avoid possible discontent among the profession, he felt that there should be a degree of personal choice by allowing teachers to select the area where they would wish to be posted. [54]

As has been pointed out previously, complaints relating to education were common although parents in some areas, notably Manchester[55], took it upon themselves to do something about it. It is often assumed, quite wrongly, that it was the evacuees who suffered most. As most of the state schooling across the country and Northern Ireland was being delivered on a half-day shift system, the majority of children in this whole generation suffered.

On the 22nd August 1940, William Duff visited some of the reception areas and reported on his findings which he listed under four distinct headings.

Materials: He established that many of the schools in the reception areas were having difficulty in providing school books and some of them had resorted to collecting second hand ones to make up the deficit. There was also some concern about poor parents who were unable to afford to clothe their children properly.

Transport: He found that some evacuees had to travel considerable distances to their nearest schools. Many of these journeys were by bus and in some cases the cost of the fares was excessive and unaffordable.

Scholarships: Concern was expressed about those children who had been awarded educational scholarships before evacuation but seemed to be losing the opportunity to make the most of them. He questioned whether transfer facilities were being considered, and what happened when the scholarships were related to private endowments? This situation was highlighted in an appeal sent to the Ministry in August 1940; *' A request for 2 boys who were evacuated to Stewartstown who had paid fees or won scholarships....as the local Public Elementary School would not offer the same, could they be moved to a school where they would receive a similar education...'*

Others: Some teachers had informed their pupils that they would only be away for the Summer holidays and that they would return to reopened schools at the end of the vacation. In addition, teachers in some Public Elementary schools in Belfast were telling parents of their former pupils, not in the reception areas, that if they did not return forthwith to take their places at the school they could not be held for them.

Some of the families were influenced by this and had brought their children back to the city. Duff was so concerned that he commented that this amounted to threats and harassment. Both of which were matters very close to the description of *'statements likely to cause confusion and dismay among His Majesty's Subjects'*. He was concerned that *'this sort of thing would sabotage any scheme ever designed'* and if he could get evidence which could stand the test of the law courts, he was inclined to think that prosecutions would probably result. [56]

While the Government scheme was being inspected and reported on, the evacuation of Private Schools was continuing, sometimes with unforeseen results. On the 3rd July 1940, the Acting Principal of the Royal Academical Institution in Belfast, Mr Harriman, sent a list of boys who wanted to be evacuated during the summer holidays to the education authorities. Once this was finalised the staff at the school were to send on the list of those who wished to be boarders at Dungannon. The Principal agreed to sort out the transport of

54 Memo from William Duff. 14th March 1940
55 See Parsons. The Manchester Evacuation. The Exception to the Rule. DSM 2004
56 Report from William Duff. 22nd August 1940. Visits to Reception Areas.

equipment with the Northern Irish Transport Board, but asked the Evacuating authorities to arrange transport for the boys. The numbers actually being evacuated were well below the original estimates. Two days later the Principal sent a letter home to all the parents informing them of the impending evacuation and to ensure that all their sons' luggage and bedding should be at the school no later than 4.00pm on the following day, Saturday. In addition, the boys were to take their ration book, National Identity Card and gas mask.

On the 6th August it was obvious that these private arrangements were unravelling. The Principal again wrote to the parents informing them that it was difficult for him to make arrangements for the Christmas term, as it had come to his attention that many parents did not intend to support the Dungannon scheme.

> *'I should be grateful if you would inform me, without any delay, if you wish your son(s) to remain at Dungannon in September. It now seems probable that the cost will amount to 30/- per week per boy in addition to the School Fees, and this may have some influence on your decision. As far as I can judge it seems improbable that only 30 boys will be at Dungannon from September......'*[57]

The scheme collapsed on the 19th August 1940, as this letter from Mr Thompson at the Ministry of Education would indicate:-

> *'It appears to me that it has become necessary for Mr Harriman to furnish us with a complete list of the parents whose children took part in the RAIB evacuation and who have been brought back through his representations or through other misunderstandings,....and that we shall have to write to them offering to re-evacuate the children on the 29th , and to billet them in houses in the vicinity of the Secondary Schools with which they can make their own arrangements for tuition. I do not think that Mr Harriman's statements and actions can be brought to a fine enough point to support his prosecution under Regulation 39B....'*[58]

The Belfast Blitz

The bombing of Belfast came as a surprise to many of its inhabitants who thought that it was out of range of German bombers. As a result, the evacuation scheme was largely ignored and few of the children who had been registered actually left the city. Therefore, when Belfast was attacked in two waves during April and May 1941, they created an almost panic reaction among the population.

The first attack occurred on the night of the 15-16th April 1941, when the city was part of a wider bombing campaign which included raids on Liverpool, Portland, Bristol, Plymouth, Sunderland and Tyneside. The Luftflotten groups 2 & 3 comprising of squadrons I/KG28/53/30 and II/KG30 combined to put 180 aircraft over the target and dropped 203 tonnes of high explosive and 29,000 incendiaries. Although the results were devastating, they could have been worse as the original plans involved 327 long-range bombers, but some of these were sent to the subsidiary targets. In addition, many of the aircraft destined for Belfast failed to reach the target areas as the weather closed in and they were diverted. Belfast had been free of cloud until 10pm, but conditions deteriorated resulting in complete cloud cover which gradually cleared again later. As a result, the early and later aircraft were able to bomb visually, but others relied on 'blind' bombing or were redirected to targets in the south-west of England where the weather was clearer. Flt Mechanic Heinrich Schmidt, who survived being shot down, recalled being held in the searchlights for much of the time once his aircraft had crossed the English coast. Such was their intensity that he was able to read his newspaper at 15,000 feet! [59]

There were three main areas of concentration; the north-western and eastern parts of the docks, Harland and Wolff shipyards and Harland and Short aircraft works, and the city centre.

57 Letter to parents from Principal of RAIB 6th August 1940
58 Letter from Mr Thompson to Minister of Education 19th August 1940
59 Blitz Then and Now. p529

The raids caused extensive damage and a considerable number of fires, some of which were still blazing the following day. There were so many that reinforcements were called in from the surrounding areas and 13 brigades were sent from the Republic, although these were withdrawn on the second night in case there were casualties which would have been very difficult for the Irish Republic to reconcile with its neutrality. The attacks also brought about a serious breakdown in communications and basic services. Both residential and commercial properties suffered damage resulting in around 20,000 people being made homeless. The initial estimate of casualties was 323 killed and 329 injured, but this rose significantly throughout the two days. The largest number of casualties outside Belfast was in Londonderry where 12 people were killed. The unidentified casualties, 123 in the April raid and 31 in May, were buried in the city cemetery. In addition a memorial was erected in Milltown Cemetery for the Roman Catholics who died.

The second raid occurred on the night of the 4-5th May, when 204 aircraft dropped 237 tonnes of high explosive and 96,000 incendiaries. It lasted from 9.22pm until 3.35 am. The main target area was north-east of the city where bombs, aimed visually, were dropped on the dock installations east of the Victoria Channel and the Harland and Wolff shipyard and the Harland and Short aircraft works. [60] As in the previous raid, there were extensive fires and public utilities were badly disrupted. An estimated 56 people were killed bringing the total casualties for the two raids to 955 killed and 2,436 injured. In addition, 885 houses were damaged and a further 3200 destroyed.[61] One aircraft didn't make it to the target. Robert Gotz wrote in his flight log dated 4th May 1941:

> *'......Take off from Villaroche 21.51. We are bound for Belfast in Ireland.......It only needs a very little light moonlight for us to be able to make out the coastline on the west coast, in both directions, and compare it with the map. But today there is only mist and clouds at all heights. After hours, we circle in to where we imagine the Isle of Man to be, in the Irish Sea; as the radio operator announces a message saying: 'Switch target to attack Liverpool harbour'. What's all this now? Shaking our heads we turn away; thinking that we were already seeing the Belfast flak flashing around us. The Liverpool flak welcomes us as usual, so then we at least know exactly where we are. We try to recognise the coastline and drop our bombs. We land at 04.45....'*[62]

Der Adler reported the raid as *'destroying 100,000 square metres, including silos, the Harland and Wolff shipyard completely destroyed along with 3 ships on slipway being severely damaged, extensive damage to the aircraft works and the oil depot at Conns Water'*[63].

As well as the shipyards, aircraft and engineering works, other reported areas of devastation included the Catholic Secondary schools of St Malachy's and Fitzwilliam both in the Antrim Road, St. Mary's in Barrack Street, St Dominic's in the Falls Road.

What the raids did do was create a new interest in the evacuation scheme and a desire to leave the city by whatever means possible. A report from Major Sean O'Sullivan on the 16th-17th April 1941, described the scenes in Belfast:-

> *'From the early morning on the 16th (April) and all throughout the day there was a continuous trek to the railway stations. The refugees looked dazed and horror-stricken and many were neglected to bring more than just a few belongings....I saw one man with just an extra pair of socks stuck in his pockets. Any and every means of exit from the city was availed of, and the final destination appeared to be a matter of indifference. Train after train and bus after bus were filled with those next in line. At nightfall the Northern Counties Station (in York St.) was packed from platform gates to entrance gates and still refugees were coming along in a steady stream from the surrounding streets.....open military lorries were finally put into service and even expectant mothers, and mothers with young children, were put into these in the rather heavy drizzle that lasted throughout*

60 ibid p585
61 ibid p529
62 ibid p585
63 ibid

the evening. On the 17th I heard that hundreds who either could not get away or could not leave for other reasons, simply went out into the fields and remained in the open all night with whatever they could take in the way of covering.....'[64]

In her diary entries of 18th April 1941, Moya Woodside described what was taking place around her:-

> *' Evacuation is taking place on panic proportions. Roads out of town are still one stream of cars, with mattresses and bedding tied on top. Everything on wheels is being pressed into service. People are leaving from all parts of town, and not only from the bombed areas. Where they are going, what they will find to eat when they get there, nobody knows. This business presents a problem of the first proportion to Stormont.....'*[65]

Later on the same day:-

> *'My mother telephoned to say that she took in 8 evacuees last night, 2 mothers and 6 children. Says one mother is about to have another baby at any minute. They are filthy and the smell in the room is terrible. They refuse all food except bread and tea; the children have made puddles all over the floor etc.*
>
> *She is terribly sorry for them and kindliness itself, but finds the revelation of how the other half live rather overpowering.....'*[66]

The day after, on April 19th, she wrote:-

> *'Belfast slum dwellers are pretty far down, and to those not used to seeing poverty and misery at close quarters, the effect is overwhelming. 'The smell is terrible', says my sister-in-law. 'They don't even use the lavatories. They just do it on the floor, grown-ups and children'. She said she had been given the job of finding private billets for the evacuees and she was ashamed to have to ask decent working people with clean houses to take in such guests. More a 'scared out' than a 'bombed out'.....'*[67]

(The Belfast Corporation was well aware of this social deprivation. In a survey commissioned by the authorities in December 1941 it stated that *' in bad working class areas people were living in indescribable filth and squalor....'* and with regard to housing policy, it went on to say,

> *'....political difficulties arose as some councillors were concerned that the provision of new permanent homes might upset the delicate sectarian balance in electoral areas, so enabling opponents to gain control of the council'.)*[68]

On the 6th May 1941, just a day after the second raid, an article in the Irish News mentioned that there was to be an extended evacuation scheme. This was a report of a meeting between the Prime Minister of Northern Ireland and a deputation from the Belfast District Trades Union Council, where he told them that the Government proposed to resume evacuation from Belfast and Derry at the earliest possible moment. Those to be evacuated were women and children, the aged, the infirm and the blind.

The statement continued in a rather critical manner pointing out that, on the one hand it was pleased to note that the authorities intended to evacuate other deserving cases other than just mothers and children, especially the old and infirm, who it said should be evacuated away from danger with the help of State Assistance. (The Irish News had in fact suggested this in an article published the previous week.) However, it was critical of the general lack of response to previous schemes, and called for more support stating that *'most people were content to live in a*

---

64 Report by Major Sean O'Sullivan on events of the 16/17th April 1941. NAD.D/T/S 14993. Cited in Northern Ireland in the Second World War. Brian Barton. Ulster Historical Foundation. 1995. p48

65 Moya Woodside. Diary MO.5462. Ref 16. 18th April 1941. Cited in Barton. Nothern Ireland in the Second World War.

66 ibid

67 Ibid 19th April 1941

68 Report to the Special Committee of the Belfast Corporation on the Municipal Health Services of the City. 24th December 1941, by Dr Thomas Carnwarth. Queens University Belfast.

fool's paradise where danger seemed remote'. But they did admit that publicity was not forthcoming and many did not know how the scheme would affect them. As a result it called upon the government to make sure that the regulations were clear and concise and that they should use the Press to '*take the message to those concerned'*. Hopefully, if such measures were used more people would be aware of what was going on and there would be little likelihood of the scheme collapsing when it resumed.

There was a flurry of evacuation activity after the May raids, but it is apparent that even at this late stage when it was necessary to evacuate as many people as possible, the scheme remained tied up in bureaucratic red-tape. It soon became obvious that difficulties were arising in the reception areas regarding specific evacuation forms (Form D) which were being presented to the local billeting officers when accommodation was not available. At the outset, the Ministry of Home Affairs and the Civil Defence Authorities (CDA) in Belfast had agreed that no such forms should be issued directly. As an alternative, lists of people who had applied for the Form, setting out the names of the persons with whom they wished to be billeted, were to be drawn up by the CDA and forwarded to the Clerks of the Unions concerned who were asked to return the lists, if possible within four days, indicating whether the persons who wished to be billeted could be accepted by the hosts. Initially, and perhaps surprisingly, considering the time scales involved and the fact that there was an expectation of further raids, the arrangement appeared to be an effective one. However, the number of applications soon became so great that it became unworkable. The authorities realised quickly that it would be impracticable for the billeting officers to complete the necessary enquiries within any reasonable time, even if a large staff could be employed for the purpose. In addition, the situation was made even more difficult by the lack of people applying for evacuation in the ordinary way, instead preferring to go to specific billets.

The authorities blamed the situation on the large numbers of people who were leaving the city at night and sleeping in the open. Although they were able, perhaps, to tolerate this practice for a while, it soon became evident to them that they could not sustain it for long, and therefore sought alternative accommodation. It was decided that the issuing of Form D should be abandoned altogether. Instead the CDA was to ask applicants to return in four days so that the Ministry would have the opportunity of keeping some sort of check on the number of people going to each area. This seems to be a remarkable decision when one considers the urgency of the situation, and the fact that many of the residents of Belfast would not be happy waiting in their homes for a further few days during which time raids might take place. It is another instance of the authorities not being prepared. This is now taking place 21 months after war was declared during which time mainland Britain had already instigated two major evacuations.

At this stage Billeting Officers were asked to *'billet very freely'* not only on houses of moderate size but also any large houses in their area. They were also instructed to make use of hotels, boarding houses and other such establishments and, if necessary, the Ministry was prepared to issue requisition orders to aid the process.[69] But a directive issued a few days later seems to be at odds with this billeting policy. On the one hand billeting officers are being asked to find as much accommodation as possible yet a directive issued to all Billeting Officers on the 15th May 1941by the Ministry, instructs them to send people home! This latter Circular is all to do with billeting allowances and is a further example of the bureaucracy involved.

> 'Circular Evacuation 41
>
> To all Billeting Officers
>
> As you are aware it is the policy of the Government that only persons belonging to one of the following priority classes should be billeted in the country.
>
> Children up to the age of 17
>
> Women between 18 and 60 accompanied by children

69 Letter from Ministry of Home Affairs to the Town Hall Belfast and Clerk of the Union. 9th May 1941

Expectant mothers

Aged and infirm persons, including the blind.

The Minister is aware that there are many persons billeted in the country at present in respect of whom billeting allowances are being paid, who do not come within these categories. These people are occupying billets urgently required for one of the priority classes and they should be given a travelling warrant, if necessary, and instructed to report to the Welfare Centre in Belfast nearest to the house in which they formerly lived. If they are eligible they will be accommodated with billets within the vicinity of Belfast......'

This raises a number of questions. What happened to those people who were not eligible? What would be the response of those now in safer areas, when they were told that they had to return to the city, back to their homes, report to a Welfare Centre and be redistributed when there was a possibility of further attacks? In addition, what happened to those who homes had been destroyed?

The Minister went on to inform billeting officers that:-

'.......No billeting allowances should in future be paid in respect of such persons. There must also be many cases in which the billets in your area are very overcrowded. You are therefore, as quickly as possible, to instruct the householder in each case that billeting allowances will only be paid in respect of that number of persons in each household for which you think there is adequate accommodation. As it is likely that some of these householders may attempt to retain some of the surplus number by agreeing to do without the billeting allowance and trying to make some private arrangement with the individuals concerned, they should also be instructed that no billeting allowance will be paid so long as there is a greater number than the number fixed by you accommodated in the house. If, after you have eliminated the adult males and females, you find that there are still persons entitled to be billeted in your area than the number for which you have adequate accommodation you should, if possible, billet these temporarily in halls and inform the Minister at once so that arrangements can be made to billet them elsewhere.....'

This was putting immense responsibility on the billeting officers and placing them in unenviable positions. Not only were they having to take the anger of those being relocated, they were also having to struggle with their consciences in regard to sending people back to a potential target area.

They were instructed that those individuals who were considered to be 'unbilletable' were to be housed in camps, still yet to be constructed!

'There are however, undoubtedly many persons who, because of their personal habits, must be considered 'unbilletable' and whom it would be most undesirable, and unfair, to billet them upon private householders. It is the intention of the Ministry to put these individuals either into camps or institutions under the care of wardens.....'[70]

On the 19th May 1941, a press statement released by the Ministry of Home Affairs appeared in the Irish News under the headline:

---

70 Circular Evacuation 41. Issued to all billeting officers on 15th May 1941

'Evacuation; Reopening of Registration'.

Persons belonging to the under-mentioned classes who wish to be evacuated from Belfast to the country AS OPPORTUNITY PRESENTS ITSELF (sic) should register.

Unaccompanied children of school age.

Mothers accompanied by children of school age or under.

Expectant mothers (applicants in this class should bring with them a Medical Certificate to the effect that they are in advanced pregnancy.)

Aged and infirm persons.

Blind persons.

The article also included the dates and times of the registration; 21st-24th May from 10.00am to 1.00 and then 2.00 – 4.00, and where they should register; Beechfield Public Elementary School in the city centre, Seaview PES in north-east Belfast, Hemsworth Square PES off Agnes St off the Shankhill Road, and Linfield Senior PES Blythe St., again in the city centre.

It was pointed out that *'Registration provides no guarantee of immediate evacuation, but it is a step which should be taken to secure evacuation as soon as appropriate accommodation becomes available'*.

This statement is interesting for a number of reasons. There had been a great deal of debate throughout 1940 about the evacuation of mothers and pregnant women and that it would be best if they didn't go. This document seems to reverse that policy, although it is apparent that they were only willing to take those women in *'an advanced state of pregnancy'*. Also, there seems to be little urgency about getting the scheme underway. This is only a couple of weeks after the second major raid on the city and yet the wording implies that accommodation had not yet been found in the reception areas, and applicants would only be moved 'as the opportunity presents itself'. It also goes against the statement in the report of 6th May, that the Government proposed to resume evacuation at the 'earliest possible moment'. This is two weeks later!

In addition, if one was planning to move a large number of people out of the city, one would have thought that the registration offices would have been manned all day and not closed for lunch. The timings would also have been very inconvenient for those mothers who were out at work and while their children were at school.

A notice was sent out to the Registration Centres informing them that it was not originally intended to take account of the pre-select billets in the registration of non-homeless belonging to one of the priority classes. However, so many pre-selects had applied that the Government had decided to include them in the scheme, as it seemed unfair to give preferential treatment to those without billets to go to. It was agreed that all pre-selects should register in the ordinary way for general evacuation but the letter 'P' should be written against their name so that the authorities would know that in their case they would need to refer to a pre-select registration form. In addition this 'P' form should also include the details of the billet they had chosen. The registrars were told to explain to the pre-selects that every endeavour would be made to send them to their own billet, but that it might not be possible to send them there in the first instance. Pre-selects who were unwilling to go anywhere except their own billet, should not register for General Evacuation but should register on a 'P' form only and these should be kept separate from the others and have the word 'Only' written after the P.

One of the registrars wrote back seeking clarification about some of the issues raised in the Ministry's original guidelines:-

- Blind persons should simply be registered on the supposition that an institute for these people will be set up in the country (Begs the question what happened when such institutions were not available?). That no provision should accordingly be made for guides or companions.

- In England, persons over 60 are considered to be 'aged'. In my opinion, infirmity of only very pronounced character for adults under 60 are held eligible for evacuation.
- By advanced pregnancy I understand the 7th month.
- Should an aged person present herself for evacuation with, let us say, grandchildren, the children should be registered as unaccompanied as clearly, if the person were recognised as aged and infirm, she would not be capable of attending to the maintenance of a family.....'

It was reported in the Irish News of the 24th May 1941, that '*....between 10,000-15,000 children, mothers and expectant mothers, blind, aged and infirm people have registered for evacuation from Belfast in the past three days....*'

In the letters page of the Irish News on the same day, there appeared a description of Belfast evacuees leaving Dublin on their journey north:

> *'Approximately 400 refugees from Belfast who had been in Dublin for some weeks past, left Amiens Street Station yesterday in a special train provided by the Northern Ireland Government. It was originally intended that they should be taken to Lisburn, but more suitable accommodation was found for them in the Newry district and they arrived there in the afternoon.*
>
> *Of the whole party 30 were men, the remainder being women and children. During their stay in Dublin six of the women gave birth to babies.*
>
> *Red Cross workers and local Security Force officers were on duty at Amiens St. A doctor, two nurses and six Red Cross officers accompanied the refugees to Northern Ireland'*[71]

In June 1941, the evacuating authorities in Belfast sent out a letter to those parents who had pre-selected billets for their unaccompanied children. It pointed out that the billeting allowance was dependant on a favourable report being given by the Local Reception Officer, after their child, or children, had been evacuated. The new home must not be overcrowded, be unhealthy or objectionable for any other circumstances. It was suggested that as the parents had given information to the authorised persons looking after their children, it would be useful for them to be acquainted with all aspects of the new home, specifically the number of people already in residence, the number of habitable rooms in the house, and the number of extra individuals the householder was able, or agreed, to take. It was seriously recommended that if they were not certain of any of these points it would be safer their children to take part in the General evacuation scheme and go to government billets. They were informed that they could make this change with the Registration official who would be at the school on the day of their child's medical inspection. They were advised that if the pre-selected billet was found to be unsuitable, or already occupied, it could result in a very serious delay before their child could be re-evacuated, and they needed to take into consideration that there was no guarantee that registration would re-open at a later date. [72]

By the end of May an estimated 220,000 people had fled from the city. Some had arrived in Fermanagh with little more than their nightshirts. A further 10,000 crossed the border into the Irish Republic. All available accommodation was stretched to the limit and resulted in the 'rack-renting' of barns. In some areas more than 30 people were crammed into very small cottages and houses.

This also had a knock on effect in those areas now receiving children into their schools. The following is a plea from the Cookstown Education Committee:-

> *'Sir....there are now of upward of 400 evacuee pupils enrolled in the schools directly controlled by this Committee and in consequence of this there is an urgent need for extra seating accommodation*

71 Irish News. 24th May 1941
72 Letter to parents dated simply June 1941 but would have been issued sometime between the 1st-5th

in certain schools, particularly Coagh, Cookstown and Orritor PE Schools where there are now respectfully 101, 35, and 40 evacuated pupils on roll. ...'[73]

This was a follow up letter to one the previous month which had requested extra desks and chairs, but to which the Committee had not received any reply.

(School equipment was not the only problem. In January 1942, a Miss Wilkinson wrote a letter to the Ministry pointing out the problems of non-attendance at school of evacuee children. Apparently, local attendance officers in some reception areas did not consider that the evacuees came under their remit. The problem was exacerbated by the fact that the Belfast authorities could do little about it because of the way in which the children '*had been scattered*'.)

In August 1941, 3 months after the May raids, Moya Woodside wrote in her diary:-

'A friend whose car broke down in a tiny seaside village found that the food situation was alarming. He could not find anywhere to stay the night and had to sleep out in the sandhills. He was unable to get anything to eat, even tea or bread. Village shops were completely sold out'.[74]

There was another air-raid alert on the 23rd July 1941 at 2.00am. As a result around 30000 people fled from the city in motor vehicles, bicycles and on foot. An eye-witness described it as being like 'a crowd from a football match. No aircraft arrived.' [75] This practise of leaving the city was not new. In fact even before the raids on Belfast had taken place Lord Craigavon had been quoted as saying '*If there is a Blitz on Belfast the people can take to the ditches*'. A newspaper report immediately after the April raids had reported the same phenomenon:

20,000 SLEEPING IN THE FIELDS.

NIGHTLY ORDEAL OF BELFAST FAMILIES

The nightly evacuation of Belfast by women and children who sought shelter in the fields and hillsides was raised in the Northern House of Commons yesterday following an announcement by the Premier (J.M.Andrews) to the effect that the Government had decided not to hold a secret session of Parliament. It was stated during the debate that in one district 20,000 people were sleeping out at night and the fear was expressed that if 40,000 family huts were not provided around the city before the winter there might be unspeakable calamity'.

Concern about the evacuation problems in Ulster were also expressed by the Trade Unions. A joint deputation from the Northern Ireland Labour Party, represented by Alderman Harry Midgley JP and Mr Dawson Gordon from the Belfast Trades Council, met the Parliamentary Secretary to the Ministry of Home Affairs, William Lowry on August 1941 on behalf of not only Trade Unionists, but also the working people of Belfast. They pointed out that in the evacuation scheme organised in July only 40% of the people registered took advantage of it and that only around 2,000 of the 5,000 mothers, expectant mothers, young children and the aged were in fact moved out. The representatives presented three key points to the Secretary in the hope that a more attractive scheme of evacuation could be arranged. These were that:-

'.......Aged and infirm people should be evacuated to hostels or to those mansions which had been promised to the Government for evacuation purposes.

Unaccompanied children should be evacuated to houses where the occupiers were willing to receive them. (However, they agreed there should be no compulsion to take them in.)

73 Letter to Ministry of Home Affairs from the Cookstown Education Committee. 15th May 1941
74 Woodside op cit. August 1941
75 O' Sullivan op cit. p50

> *Women with children should be evacuated to huts but not in a colony; the huts were to be within a reasonable distance of Belfast.....'*[76]

Mr Lowry pointed out that their reasoning behind the third proposal was affected by the fact that the concentration of huts in a particular area might not be safe because it might be taken as a military encampment and, as such, be seen as a legitimate target in any future air raids. The deputation wanted more '*intelligence shown'* in the evacuation scheme, and put forward the point that a '*woman with a young child should not be asked to sit in a corner of a strange house'* to which they had been evacuated. They quoted many examples of people who had met with indifference in their billets and receptions areas. Although they had nothing to suggest with regard to unaccompanied children, provided they were of school age, they did propose that children of one family should, as far as possible, be evacuated together. (The government response to the meeting is no longer available)

Despite the obvious concern, this was not to be revisited until November 1941 when it was reported that four evacuee camps were being constructed around Londonderry to accommodate 4,000 people. They were designed to provide initial rest and dispersal-centre accommodation in the event of severe air raids on Londonderry, but plans were in hand to ensure that in the event of a large proportion of the city being rendered homeless, the camps could be converted into hostels to be used for semi-permanent accommodation. There was also a policy to erect 1,200 huts in County Antrim on 16 sites and 300 huts on four sites in County Down. It was obvious from the official statements that *'Ditchers'* were still a problem and little had been done to alleviate the situation until six months after the last raid. Bearing in mind that the last raid had happened in May this statement, written on the 10th November 1941, indicates a certain lack of urgency:

> *'Approximately 110 (huts) have been erected for the accommodation of 'ditchers' and these are being equipped as soon as possible. Night Marshalls are being obtained for the supervision of these huts.*
>
> *Ditching is on the decrease and consequently fewer people are leaving their houses at night. The Ministry understands that at the moment the position is that people who formerly left the danger areas of the city immediately after darkness, are now staying in their own homes but are not going to bed until 2.am when they think the danger of a raid has passed. Efforts are being made to persuade those using ditcher's huts to be evacuated'.*[77]

One is left with the impression that the Government were not prepared to spend money on providing accommodation for the 'ditchers' if it proved to be unnecessary because of the lack of further raids. By leaving these plans for so long, the need for such accommodation did indeed become redundant, but it was a risky decision and one that could easily have had devastating effects had there been another Blitz.

On the 5th June 1941, the Secretary of the Ministry of Home Affairs, on behalf of the Minister of Labour, reported that as a result of the raids on Belfast, the Labour Exchanges in the city had registered a substantial number of skilled shipyard and engineering workers who had not been able to find local employment in other work, nor was there any likelihood of them being reemployed in their previous roles. There was employment on the mainland where they would be offering skills of 'urgent national importance', and there was also plenty of work for unskilled labourers, many of whom were sent to England each week. However, the bombing of the city had made Belfast men with wives and families unwilling to go overseas to find employment, as they were not prepared to leave their dependants at home in what they considered to be a dangerous location. The Ministry felt that under these circumstances men should not be asked to take up work which involved separation from their families and they should not have their benefit stopped if they refused the work offered, unless arrangements could be made for them to leave Ireland knowing that their families had been evacuated to safer areas. The

---

76' Government Hears Trade Union Views'. Belfast Trades Union News Letter 21st August 1941
77 Ministry of Home Affairs. Ref 324 10th November 1941

Minister asked if the Government would be prepared to arrange for the evacuation of the families of the men in this situation as a matter of priority.

The decision was that *no* priority was to be given, as those men leaving for the mainland would have left behind dependants in Class 2 (mothers and children), and as accommodation was delayed the children in this class were to be evacuated as normal.

A letter had been sent to various Church, Charity organisations and Ministers apprising them of the reopening of the registration, and that those who had taken the decision to send their children to friends in the countryside would be given certificates and vouchers to enable them to do so. However, not everybody was pleased with the arrangements.

> *'10th June 1941*
>
> *.....I am sorry we were unable to assist with the evacuation as hitherto.....Would it be possible to give us just a little more notice as I take it we would not have received your letter until the 7th and it would have been difficult to make arrangements for the following day.....*
>
> *St John Ambulance. Lady District Superintendent.'*

The Salvation Army could not help either as it was again too short notice. However, in a letter from the Brigade Divisional Commander they did offer to supply a canteen to dispense tea and sandwiches to evacuees at future evacuations.

There was also a complaint from the Womens' Voluntary Service that they were not receiving Government circulars and did not know what was going on. As a result, the WVS Evacuation officer, together with billeting and supply officers, was invited to attend a billeting meeting on the 21st July 1941 when final arrangements were going to be made.

As all these organisations had been at the heart of the evacuation dispersal in England and Scotland, it is rather strange that it was left to the very last minute to secure their support in Ireland.

In a similar way to the evacuation on the mainland, complaints started to come into the Education office about the state of the evacuees and their general behaviour. One situation necessitated an on-site inspection by a Mr Bing who then sent in a detailed report. The original complaint had been made by Mr Sam Wallace who said that his evacuees were 'impossible'. He had two cottages in which he had placed two families, in each case comprising of a mother and several children. He described the habits of the families as deplorable. The women made no attempt to keep the house in order; emptied ashes just outside the front door of the houses and the children 'satisfied the wants of nature' in the public road. According to his statement it was untrue that they 'wanted for anything'. They had used two hundredweight of coal in a week and although the house was spacious, they had used only the kitchen in which they both lived and slept, using the bed as seating. It had been his intention to make the families comfortable but had only a certain amount of furniture available and had therefore used onion boxes to supplement the chairs. He went on to say that at first the women had expressed pleasure in being placed in the houses, but almost at once it had become obvious that, as they had no intention of staying, they would take no care of anything given to them, and were 'idle, lazy and worthless'. If they had been otherwise he would have made the house comfortable for them 'by degrees'. Mr Wallace's statement was supported by his brother.

Mr Bing visited the premises and confirmed that the houses were very roomy, in very fair repair and seemed dry. However, there was no furniture at all beyond the beds supplied by the Ministry, one dilapidated washstand and a few pots and pans. He concluded that the house was inadequately furnished for the purpose of housing evacuees, but that its condition was not the real reason for their departure. Mr Wallace had stated openly that his houses would be more profitable to him to let to evacuees than to ordinary tenants. He was anxious to keep the families there but realised that the supplying of better furnishings would have no effect one way or another. Bing's opinions were confirmed by Mr White, the Billeting Officer, that Mr Wallace was anxious to make as much money as possible by letting out the houses to evacuees with the least possible expenditure on furniture and equipment and that his tenants resented this. He did concur that the families were unsatisfactory. [78] Mr Wallace, who was a prosperous businessman and head of the local LDV[79] was accused of profiteering.

The Irish Red Cross (IRC) were also expressing some concern about evacuees who had gone to Dublin. On 31st May 1941, the secretary of the Ballyshannon-Bundoran sub-branch of the Irish Red Cross, C.A.Stephens, wrote to the Evacuation Authority in Belfast saying that Samuel McConnell, late of 39 Meekon St, Belfast, had arrived in the area with his wife and two babies aged 15 months and 3 months. They had no friends and nobody to look after them. They had informed the authorities that their home had been demolished and that they had failed to be evacuated in the ordinary way from Belfast (although it was the opinion of the IRC that they had simply not registered at the correct time.) The IRC informed the Belfast authorities that they had neither the accommodation nor the means, for dealing with such a case. So, they had agreed to pay the train fare 31/2d to get the family back to Belfast, advising them to apply for official evacuation as an urgent case. The IRC hoped that the evacuating authorities in Belfast would refund the train fare as they had made no claim for housing and feeding the family for one night. They did point out that future cases could be arranged between the two parties rather than such families arriving on an ad hoc basis.

The IRC were reimbursed for the train fare and the Minister expressed his thanks for their action. However, in relation to the suggestion of collaboration, he did point out that it was impossible to prevent such persons leaving the city on their own initiative, but did suggest that '*any persons presenting themselves to the Society for assistance should be returned to Belfast with an intimation that they should report to the Welfare Centre in their district for the purpose of securing billets or of being evacuated. The Ministry would of course refund expenditure incurred by the Society in dealing with such cases....*'[80]

Between these two letters, the Fahan Branch of the IRC had also contacted Belfast enclosing details of some evacuees who had arrived 'practically destitute' and asking if their particulars were actually correct. The families were the Barnes of 93 Gracehill Street, and the Hunter/Creary of 49 Gracehill Street. In a reply sent on the 9th June, the Inspectors reported that 93 Gracehill St. had been demolished and that 49 had sustained only slight damage and was occupied at the time of the their visit by Mrs Hunter's husband and son. On the 17th June, they concluded that Mrs Barnes could be classified as a genuine evacuee but Mrs Hunter could not be classified as homeless.[81]

There were many other instances of evacuees making their own way to Dublin and creating problems. One was admitted to the Cork Fever Hospital with a suspected case of enteric fever (later unfounded)[82] and another to the Whiteabbey Sanatorium with tubercolosis.[83]

Some of the cases proved to be very costly. In January 1942, M.T.Killen, a Home Teacher and Visitor working for the National Council for the Blind of Ireland, wrote to the Belfast authorities expressing some concern about a 30 year old blind man named Joseph McGuinness who had left the city with his wife and child after the Belfast blitz. Formerly, he had been employed in the Belfast workshops as a basket maker and had earned had about £2.8.0 a week but was now reported as being '*absolutely destitute*' as he did not qualify for relief of Blind Assistance until he had fulfilled a two-year residency qualification. To make matters worse he adamantly refused to return to Belfast. The NCBI had hoped to find him work at the Richmond Institute, but there were no vacancies for 'out-door' workers, and he would not be accepted as in inmate unless the weekly maintenance grant of 17/6, which was normally paid by the Local Government or Corporation, was forthcoming. The authorities in the north had been informed and asked to take responsibility for the payment, but at the date of the letter nothing had been decided. It was also pointed out that the wife belonged to a clan of tinkers with whom the McGuinness family were now living. Conditions were described as being '*quite appalling*'. They already had a child of 11

78 Billet Inspection report. 10th August 1940
79 Local Defence Volunteers, the forerunner of the Home Guard.
80 Letter from Ministry of Home Affairs to Irish Red Cross 27th May 1941
81 Letter from IRC Fahan Branch to Evacuating Authorities in Belfast 13th May 1941
82 Letter from IRC Dublin. 24th May 1941
83 Ibid 18th June 1941

months old and another was expected very soon. The NCBI hoped that the relevant authorities in Belfast might be able to help what they considered to be a most deserving case.[84]

The Welfare Officer in Belfast followed this up and contacted the manager of the Workshops for the Blind, in Lawnbrook Ave. He confirmed that he knew McGuinness very well. He had indeed been employed at the workshops for a number of years and had, in addition to his wages, been given a weekly grant of 25/- from the Belfast Corporation, under the Blind Persons Act. He had left the workshops voluntarily after the Easter raids and nothing had been heard of him since. The Officer reported his findings to the Blind Persons Committee at City Hall and a decision about the McGuinness family was made.

The reply to the NCBI makes interesting reading:

> *'......the view of the committee is that this man should not be assisted unless he returns to Belfast where his work is still available to him. If they made a grant to help him live in the Free State they feel that they would be encouraging him to live a lazy, idle life. Mrs McGuinness is, as stated in your letter, of a clan of wandering tinkers and they are supposed to be living in a caravan. Reports state that they are very well able to fend for themselves, and that they usually live by begging. If McGuinness could be persuaded to return to Belfast he would be given employment again. The manager of the workshops states that he is a very decent man but his wife likes the roving life and may not wish him to return.....'* [85]

There is no indication of what eventually happened to the McGuinness family.

Another case had serious cost implications. Mrs Mary O'Connor and her family had gone to Dublin after the Belfast bombing and were housed by the Irish Red Cross until arrangements were made to join her husband in England. However, her daughter, also called Mary, had suffered shock and heart problems as a result of the bombing, and was admitted to the Mater Hospital on the Crumlin Road in Belfast, from where, on the 16th April 1941, she was eventually transferred to the Richmond Hospital in Dublin, where she stayed until she was discharged on the 15th June 1942. The Irish Red Cross informed the evacuation committee in Belfast that they had received an invoice of £64 5s 6d from the Richmond Hospital for 'maintenance from 16/4/41 to 15/6/42: 425 days @ £1.1.0 per week and an X-Ray @ 10/6, and asked whether they knew of any method by which the debt could be paid other than through the Red Cross.

This simple request led to a very intriguing and involved episode. Initially the committee were sympathetic and commented that they should get a full report from the Chief Administrator at the Mater Hospital, as it seemed unreasonable that the Irish Red Cross should have to pay the bills of someone sent to Dublin after the raids, with or without official sanction. They were then informed by telephone that personnel at the Mater Hospital had been through all their casualty records for the main hospital, in-patient and out-patient treatment and first aid, and they had been unable to trace the name of a Mary O'Connor as having been at the hospital. They also pointed out that it would have been very unlikely that any such patient would have been transferred to the Richmond Hospital in Dublin.

However, a little later, it transpired that Mary O'Connor had gone to Belfast with her mother from Manchester some months before the Easter Blitz and that they had lodged at 100 Spa Mount in the city. The Ministry of Home Affairs then sent an official letter to the Irish Red Cross asking specific questions:-

a. Did she receive medical treatment in Belfast before the 16th April 1941 and, if so, where did she receive such treatment, and the name of the doctor who attended her?

b. How long did she remain at the Mater Hospital, giving the dates of admission and discharge?

84 Letter to Belfast authorities from M.T.Killen on behalf of the National Council for the Blind of Ireland
85 Reply from Welfare Officer. 14th January 1942

c. Did she travel to Dublin by train or ambulance?

d. Who paid her fare and if she were issued with a travel voucher?

e. Was she accompanied by her mother when she travelled to Dublin?

f. Was she brought to Richmond Hospital from Amiens St. Station? Who brought her and by what means?

g. If the answer to (f) is negative, when did she go to Richmond Hospital and where did she live in Dublin prior to admission to hospital?

A simple one-line reply came from the Richmond Hospital not the Irish Red Cross:-

> Dear Madam
>
> In reply to you enquiry the above patient was admitted from the Mater Hospital, Belfast on the 16/4/41 and discharged on the 15/6/42.

This necessitated further phone calls to the staff at the Mater Hospital who, on the 2nd September 1942, were most emphatic that no person of that name appeared on the hospital records. However, a letter was received on the 4th September stating that she had in fact been a patient from the 1st March 1941 to the 17th April 1941 (interesting that much of this time predated the Belfast Blitz of the 15th/16th April). As a result of this conflict of opinion it was agreed that all future correspondence with the Mater Hospital should be carried out in writing.

On the 21st September a letter was received from the Richmond Hospital by the Irish Red Cross stating that the girl had received medical treatment at the Mater Hospital before the 16th April 1941 as she had been admitted on the 5th March, and she was seen by Dr McSorley. She remained there for 5 weeks and 6 days. She was discharged but became ill again and remained in hospital. She travelled to Dublin by train with her mother who paid her fare. She was taken straight from the station to the Richmond Hospital by a Red Cross ambulance.

After all the confusion and the time spent on dealing with the case, the Ministry issued a final statement in late September.

> *'....I am directed by the Minister of Home Affairs for Northern Ireland to refer to your letter of the 5th August last, regarding the account of the Richmond Hospital in respect of the treatment of Mary O'Connor....and to inform you that the Ministry is unable to suggest any source from which the cost of this girl's treatment could be met.*
>
> *The Ministry has been in communication with the Ministry of Health on the question of whether the account could be accepted as a charge to the Evacuation Funds, but it is advised that the Evacuation authorities cannot accept financial responsibility in this case and it accordingly regretted that this Ministry is unable to assist in this respect...'*

In short....she was not an official evacuee, therefore not the responsibility of the evacuation authorities. One wonders why this decision could not have been made earlier in the proceedings rather than have a protracted correspondence between the parties involved.

Others just turned up with nowhere to go and when returned to Belfast caused difficulties which took up valuable time at all levels of the administration. For example, a Mrs Hennessy and her three children were sent back on the 25th June, and instructed to report to the nearest Welfare Centre. The Irish Red Cross followed this up by asking the Evacuating Authorities if accommodation had been found for them. It transpired that the family had been billeted with a Patrick Gibbons in Wolfhill Lane by the District Billeting officer in Townsend St.....but this was in fact an evacuation area. The reply from the Evacuation authorities demonstrated a certain amount of frustration that this should have happened.[86]

> *' Update on Hennessy Family. 23th July 1941*
>
> *.....Surely these people should be billeted in a reception area? Gibbons has been drawing the allowance at the accompanied rate of 14/- a week. In other words we bring people back to the evacuation area and pay them to reside in such an area. It doesn't matter if their home has been blitzed or not, if they are covered by one of the priority classes we should find them accommodation in the reception areas.'*

Even Stormont became involved, and on the 14th August 1941, the Minister of Home Affairs felt it necessary to issue the following memo:

> *'.....to inform you that priority classes should not, under any circumstances, be billeted in an Evacuation Area and must be billeted in a Reception Area. If this family is not willing to go to either a billet of their own choice or to a government billet in the country, the Billeting Notice should be cancelled immediately.'*

Some people who had travelled to the Republic pleaded with the Belfast authorities to be allowed to return home. Mrs Margaret Christian, who had previously lived in Dock St, and had been sent to Ardlenagh in Donegal, wrote complaining about being ill and not having enough money or food. Her letter was passed onto the Evacuation Authorities who replied asking her for details about the ages of her family members, their names, religion and former addresses. Her own response was interesting and is perhaps a good example of mismatches which were often created by the scheme;

> *'I am a Protestant not working. Neil and wife, child. James, Margaret, Peter, Evelyn and Gerald previously lived in Falls Rd.....I know we will go to work. We want to get home to the North. Please let us come home. We will never want to come back here again. This is no place for Royal subjects....'*[87]

Other complaints concerned the perceived lack of education taking place in the reception areas. One correspondent wrote: 'When I agreed to the evacuation of my boys, they had been attending Belfort Model School and I understood that the teachers from the Model were also being evacuated, so that the education of the scholars would not be interrupted. I am now informed that not a single teacher has yet left the Model school for which, I think you will agree, is not very encouraging to the parents that have agreed to the evacuation of their children and I would be obliged if you would let me have particulars of the arrangements for continuing the education of the scholars evacuated which I consider only secondary to evacuation.....'

On the 7th August 1941, the Ministry of Home Affairs issued a Minute entitled *'Future Policy on Evacuation'* in which it outlined various strategies which in most cases had already been suggested before . All Billeting Officers would now be required to submit reports on a limited number of good billets. On receipt of these the Welfare Officer would be asked to visit a selection of these householders with the object of securing their cooperation. It was recommended that in the first instance the Welfare Officers should concentrate on householders in a single defined area. It was also suggested that the Women's Voluntary Service might be able to help. As soon as these billets had been pre-selected the Civil Defence Authority would then be asked to find suitable people to send to them. At this point it was strongly advised that those persons selected for evacuation should be given a clear understanding of their duties and liabilities *'as evacuees'*, and the statement implied that they should all attend a lecture on the topic!!

---

86 Ref 213
87 Series of communications dated 22nd July 1941

As well as suitable householders, the Billeting Officers would also be asked to submit lists of unoccupied houses in their areas, suitable for the accommodation of large families and 'special and difficult' cases. If necessary houses could be requisitioned by the Ministry of Finance and any repairs could be undertaken under its remit through district offices. It was pointed out that despite the lack of billets, prosecutions of recalcitrant householders would not change people's attitudes. However, it was accepted that the public should be aware that any refusal to billet might result in a '*sharp punishment*'. If prosecutions were necessary they should be selective rather than wholesale.

One other matter was that of a propaganda campaign aimed at breaking down the resistance of hosts to take in evacuees and also to promote activities, especially for mothers who had accompanied their children.

One area of concern, voiced by Billeting Officers, was the lack of support from many churches of all denominations. In some instances the local clergy helped in taking evacuees from their transports to the billets but did very little else. Some of them even refused to have evacuees in their own houses, which was not a good role model, especially in areas where it was difficult to find billets.[88]

A week later, a letter was sent from the Minister of Home Affairs to the Moderator of the General Assembly, President of the Methodist Church in Ireland, His Grace the Lord Archbishop of Armagh and Primate of all Ireland and His Eminence Cardinal MacRory, expressing his concerns:-

> '15th August 1941
>
> '.......from information at the disposal of the Minister, it is clear that the greatest difficulty is encountered in connection with the reception of accompanied families. It cannot be expected that the invasion of their home by mothers and their families from the cities will not cause considerable disturbance to the housewives in the reception areas, and in many cases there have been complaints of unjustifiable behaviour by evacuees. Nevertheless, it is necessary that every effort should be made to place all members of the same family in one billet and minimise the disruption of family life. The Minister is satisfied that essential elements of successful evacuation are:-
>
> a. Adequate reception arrangements
>
> b. Careful billeting
>
> c. Adequate Welfare arrangements
>
> The Ministry is actively engaged in modifying and improving arrangements under each of the headings, but it feels that a further and most important essential to success, is the creation of a good impression by a friendly householder on the arrival of the evacuees. In this connection the Minister is of the opinion that a vigorous and useful lead could be given in reception areas with the assistance of the Church and local church organisations, but particularly through the medium of the pulpit.....'[89]

This elicited a response from Cardinal MacRory;

> *'......may I say that Armagh is not a place to which Catholic families should be sent. Our people are poor with extremely little accommodation and, moreover, it is quite possible this will be a danger zone.'*[90]

On the 22nd August 1941, there was a meeting between representatives of the Churches, with the exception of the Church of Ireland, and the Ministry of Home Affairs where they discussed four proposals.

88 Ministry of Home Affairs. Minute 7th August 1941 Ref. RF 324 MHA
89 Letter from Ministry of Home Affairs to Church Leaders. 15th August 1941
90 Reply from Cardinal MacRory 20th August 1941

a. That the head of churches, through the medium of the Press, should address a joint communication to all householders in reception areas urging them to receive evacuees in a kindly manner, and to accept it as part of their neighbourly duty as Christians.

b. That the heads of churches, through the appropriate channels, should each address a communication to all local clergymen requesting them to make suitable pulpit references for securing the cooperation of the householders in offering willing and friendly accommodation to evacuees.

c. That local clergy should be urged to assist the Government by example, as well as by precept, and that for this purpose a scheme of the following nature should be adopted by each church. i.e. each of the Belfast Missions (Grosvenor Hall, North Belfast Mission and St Vincent de Paul etc) should select a number of suitable persons for evacuation. The persons so selected would be billeted in the houses of the clergymen in the reception areas, the usual billeting allowances being paid to the householders. It is felt that a scheme of this nature would set a magnificent example.

d. That the heads of the churches would arrange for local clergymen to display propaganda posters prominently on church notice boards.

The Clergy generally agreed with A and B. With D it was suggested that posters should not be put up until the scheme had developed further. There seems to have been no agreement on C.

There were additional comments. Adrian Robinson, of the MHA, explained that in the event of an invasion, the refugee problem might be acute and that refugees would be directed into certain country areas. In these areas dumps of food rations had been established by the Divisional Food Officers and the Ministry invited the Churches to undertake the establishment of small and informal local communities in these areas. The object being to form a nucleus of an organisation which, in the event of refugees arriving in any particular district, would be in a position to know where food had been stored, and to arrange for its distribution to the refugees.

It was also suggested that a prominent local resident could call together the local clergy of all denominations and have a preliminary discussion with the local, or area, representatives of the Divisional Food Office.

This anonymous letter was sent from someone who attended the churches conference. The title at the top simply says ‘A Masterly Sermon’ and is undated, but it seems to have been ‘established’ as the accepted statement as it is referred to in other correspondence.

Sir

‘.....Mass evacuation is an unnatural process justified only by the need for dispersing the civil population in war time. The transference of a large section of the populations, essentially industrial, to a completely different environment creates problems of a far reaching, economic, social and spiritual nature. There is a wide gulf between the sentiment, habits and outlook of town people and country folk. The crowded streets and shops, the diversions, which form the normal background of daily life in the city, are suddenly swept away, and the evacuee finds herself in a country district where the environment is altogether different from that to which she has become accustomed. It cannot be expected therefore, that a scheme for billeting women and children in country households can be carried without friction. Nevertheless, it is essential that every effort should be made to encourage women with their children to transfer to country areas. At the same time, it is imperative that the disruption of family life, thus caused, should be reduced to a minimum by ensuring that mothers and their families wherever possible, are kept united in the country.

The desired result can be achieved only with the full cooperation of householders in country areas, and we desire therefore to address ourselves to all householders in country areas who have accommodation in their homes which is suitable, or which can be made suitable, for the reception of mothers and their families.

In the first instance, we would point out that householders whose homes are situated in areas less vulnerable to air attack and who have not experienced the horror of night bombing, are apt to forget the strain under which the evacuated family has been living, and very often the intrusion on private life by strangers of different outlooks and habits is resented. A friendly welcome is lacking and the absence of a friendly welcome, coupled with the fact that the mother of the family which has been evacuated may arrive in a condition of mental distress full of anxiety for her husband and her home, renders impossible any real chance of successful cooperation between householder and evacuee. The guest feels the strangeness of the new surroundings, and time hangs heavily on her hands. If in these circumstances an unfriendly atmosphere is created and she is made to feel that she and her family are not wanted, the urge to return home, even at the risk of further bombing, becomes overwhelming.

We are conscious of the fact that, in a number of instances, kindly householders who went to considerable trouble to make their guests comfortable, found that their efforts were negative because of the personal habits and lack of cleanliness of certain classes of evacuated persons. We understand that every possible step is being taken by the appropriate authorities to ensure that unfortunate experiences of the nature referred to will be reduced to a minimum. At the same time, we feel that the community as a whole cannot divest itself of a measure of responsibility for the conditions which have never resulted in this experience.

Nevertheless, we are of the opinion that out of evil good may come, and it is certain that evacuation, in itself a thing to be deplored, offers a golden opportunity to demonstrate that the principle 'Thou shalt love thy neighbour as thyself' is a living reality in the hearts of Christian people. Who would place a limit on the good which must result from a warm Christian welcome given in a thousand homes to distressed and anxious mothers and children of impressionable ages. We are appealing therefore to all householders in country districts to cooperate with the billeting authorities by accepting with patience and friendliness the Christian duty of neighbourly treatment of the homeless and distressed......'

Not everyone agreed. The Archbishop of Armagh did not send a representative to the meeting but commented on the outcome. He felt that too much had been placed on the friendliness issue. Although he thought he should, he was not prepared to associate himself with the public statement until changes had been made to the report.[91]

The Cardinal, although agreeing with the statement, insisted on protocol being followed:-

'Parochial House Armagh

His Eminence has asked me to state that he is in fullest accord with the sentiments expressed in the draft of your proposed letter. In the case of a joint letter however, the question of precedence arises and much as he would deprecate any such difference of opinion or discussion, his Eminence, as a Cardinal, would have to insist on his name being placed first. ......He also points out that a letter of this kind, signed by heads of other religious bodies, though suitable for the Press, could not be used in the pulpits...'[92]

The question of precedence of signatories resulted in a number of memos suggesting various orders. One simply stated: '*.....I don't know how we are going to get over this matter since the Cardinal will feel that he should head the signatories, but I would suggest that we allow him to sign first and get the others to sign in this order.....Primate/Moderator/President of the Methodist Council.....*'[93]

---

91 Letter from the Bishop's Palace to the Ministry of Home Affairs. 3rd September 1941
92 Letter from Cardinal MacRory to the Ministry of Home Affairs. 29th September 1941
93 MHA Ref. 324

There was still some disquiet expressed in some of the designated reception areas after the May raids. In October 1941, the ARP Services Committee in Coleraine, protested to the Ministry of Home Affairs and raised six important reasons why the area should not be used: It as a dangerous area; it was a port authority; it was an important rail junction; the bridge of the River Bann was an important military objective; there was extensive military occupation; and there was insufficient water supply. The council also expressed concern about 'the waste of public money in connection with the evacuation scheme as at present being operated'. They highlighted the numerous cases where considerable expense was incurred in sending evacuees into the reception areas, only for them to return within a few days.

The Ministry noted the arguments, but pointed out that they could apply equally to other areas of the province. It went on to say that *'at the present time no large scale evacuation is contemplated from Belfast, but certain numbers of evacuees are being sent to reception areas daily'*. Since Coleraine was only expected to receive 30 evacuees it was felt that the committee need not be overly perturbed about the possibility of large numbers being located in the town.

By November 1941, the evacuation scheme had virtually been abandoned on the grounds that many were no longer interested in the scheme. Experience in Belfast and Londonderry had shown that while many were still content to register, they were unwilling to be sent to the reception areas when the Ministry decided to put any scheme in force. As evidence of this, it was reported that of the 5,000 who had registered for evacuation from Belfast earlier in the year, only 20 had turned up.

Instead the authorities introduced a 'trickle' evacuation whereby batches of 50 women and children who were willing to be evacuated, were sent to Reception Areas on a daily basis. From August, 94 families had been admitted to hostels in Newcastle. These included 90 mothers, 4 guardians and 27 children. As a result a nursery centre had been established for children under 5 and the Public Elementary School had been expanded. A further 300 women and children were also being housed in Stuart Hall.

Even so, there were still complaints from the Reception areas about expected evacuees not turning up. This letter was obviously in reply to a complaint made by the Women's Voluntary Service in a reception area:-

> '12th December 1941
>
> To WVS
>
> ......when we send anyone out from Belfast we try to ensure as far as possible that the persons who have expressed their wish to go will go. The persons are interviewed, the position explained to them and when they have given all the necessary assurances they are told to report at a certain time....but in several cases nobody has turned up.'

Eventually even the trickle evacuation was curtailed.

In July 1943, the Minister of Home Affairs issued the following statement:-

> *'The Minister has decided that Trickle evacuation shall be suspended until further notice. It is proposed not to make any public pronouncement to this effect as any such announcement might increase an erroneous impression in the public mind that the danger of further raids had ceased'.*[94]

And in November 1944 to Secondary School teachers in the evacuated areas from the Secretary to the Minister of Home Affairs:-

> *'.....I am directed by the Minister of Home Affairs and Local Government to inform you that it has been decided that arrangements should now be made for the return of evacuated persons to their home areas. This decision will affect the pupils who have been evacuated with your school and I*

94 Ministry of Home Affairs. Memo. 24th July 1943

> *am to suggest that the date for commencement of the Christmas vacation as a suitable date on which the billeting allowances should be withdrawn.....'*

To all intents and purposes, the evacuation, such as it was, was over. It would seem that the scheme amounted to too little, too late and that policy was dictated by a series of related issues. Evidence would suggest that the Government at Stormont prevaricated and procrastinated to such an extent over their decision - making that the actual evacuation of people from the city was almost a non-event. In addition, the fact that many people simply fled the city and took to the ditches, both during the raids in April and May 1941 and for months afterwards, demonstrates both the lack of evacuation possibilities and shelter provision eighteen months after the war had started. Possibly most surprising of all, was the fact that during this time the population was being misled by authoritative comments from Stormont and other bodies based on spurious evidence. In some cases, as in the statement about pregnant women and mothers going with their children causing the downfall of the scheme in England, they were being lied to. On the positive side, although one would expect maybe that the scheme might have been undermined by sectarian issues, this would seem not to be the case. There is evidence of minor disagreements between the churches but not to the extent that one might have imagined.

Therefore, the lack of enthusiasm for the evacuation scheme comes down to three simple factors:-First, the strongly held belief that the city would not be bombed; second, the Government's unwillingness to make firm decisions; third, many judgements being made on economic rather than social grounds.

Evacuation: Success or Failure?

'....The whole experience marked me for life. Until fairly recent years I suffered bad bouts of homesickness if I was away from home for any time.....I am angry that the whole scheme was so ill thought out and put into operation. They were messing about with children's lives, for God's sake. How dare they give it so little thought.'[1]

The question that most people ask relating to the evacuation scheme is whether or not it was successful. This really does depend on how one measures success. If it comes down to saving lives, then it had to have been successful, because one can assume that many of the children remaining in the target areas would have become casualties. But one has to add a supplementary statement *...at what cost*?

The evacuation scheme of September 1939 was perhaps not as successful in its original aim as it should have been because of three major factors:-

First, there was a certain element of panic in the original implementation of evacuation measures before there had been any evidence of a bombing campaign being waged against the country. This was to some extent influenced by the over estimation of potential bomb damage and resultant casualties.

In 1937, the Imperial Defence Committee calculated the cost of compensation rates for expected casualties in any future war where the main thrust of the attack would be from the air. Working on the assumption that there would be 1,800,000 casualties, 600,000 in the first two months, the cost would be £120,000,000 and for the first two years between 1 million and 2,800,000 hospital beds would be needed, depending on the length of stay. The Committee continued in this statistical vein and worked out that 20 million square feet of timber would be needed for coffins each month at a cost of £300,000, a figure so unacceptable that they were resigned to using lime pits and mass graves.[2]

Revised costing resulted in the stockpiling of thousands of collapsible papier-mâché and cardboard coffins. The committee concluded that the cost of damage would work out at £35,000 per bomb and 5% of all British property, valued at £550,000,000 would be destroyed in the first three weeks of the war. Finally, in 1938, they stated that 3,500 tons of high explosive would fall on London in the first 24 hours and then 700 tons every day after that for the first fortnight.[3]

Titmuss intimated that, if useful for nothing else, these figures show why war-time emergency services put their energies overwhelmingly into aiding the effects of death, destruction or crippling hurt, and had little consideration for the less obvious and possibly greater side effects on humanity such as confusion, anxiety, dislocation and distress.

There was also some belief that schools would make easy targets and provide a morale sapping coup for the enemy should they hit any. In 1938, civil servants started collecting information and press cuttings about the bombing of a school in Getalfe, in Madrid, in October 1936 when 70 children were killed. They were concerned as to what the effect on civilian life would be should a similar result occur.[4]

In the event, any such situation had the opposite effect and strengthened people's resolve to secure a victory. Such a raid did take place on the 20th January 1943, when fighter bombers from Jabo Staffel Jagdgesschader 26 carried out a daylight raid on London and a diversionary attack on Maidstone. The main force dropped bombs on the Sandhurst Road School in Catford, south-east London, killing 38 pupils aged 5-12, and 6 teachers. The photographs taken at the time showing bodies of children covered in tarpaulin were not released until 1983,

---

1 Freda Costa (née Risely) cited in No Time to Wave Goodbye. Ben Wicks. Bloomsbury.1989 p207.
2 Titmuss op.cit. p13
3 ibid. p15
4 Memo. SRO.ED.24/1. cited in War and Social Change. ed. Harold L.Smith. Manchester University Press. 1986. p11

although the raid was widely reported in the press and a great deal of anti-German propaganda resulted from the raid which some believed was intentional.

Instead of having a negative effect on morale, this particular raid seemed to increase the bitterness and hatred towards the Germans. Although there had been other hit and run raids which had resulted in the deaths of children, for example 31 had been killed in Petworth in September 1942, the media coverage in Britain and abroad, maintaining that the school had been hit deliberately, continued to increase the propaganda effect. The idea that this school had been a designated target may have arisen from a misinterpretation of an interview with one of the pilots of the raid in a broadcast on German radio on 21st January and reported in the British press on the 22nd. A phrase *'we dropped our bombs where they were to be dropped'* was considered to be an admission that the school had been bombed deliberately. However, if one looks at the transcript of the broadcast other targets are mentioned but the school is not, although it could of course be intimated in the last phrase! It really depends on how you want to read it, an excellent example of interpreting or misinterpreting information for propaganda purposes.[5]

Second, Britain wanted to maintain peace, or be seen to be doing so, in the period before 1939. Thus most of the Government and local organisation was carried out in secret with the result that, in many cases, neither side knew what the other was doing or planning. In July 1934, Stanley Baldwin, commented:-

> *'We feel with regard to the protection of the civil population that our plans have been carried as far as possible without the wider publicity that has hitherto been deemed to be in the public interest. The next stage involves communications with local authorities, with public utilities and so forth, and with all those on whom responsibilities for action would fall in the emergency contemplated, and before long, steps will be taken to communicate the necessary instructions to the public generally'.*[6]

Any pre-planning could be seen as anticipating war, and panic could have ensued. In 1931, the first committee dealing with evacuation saw it as a problem not of getting people away from London, but as a way of preventing a disorderly and panic-induced exodus. So paranoid were they about panic flight, that in 1931 it was suggested by the Sub-Committee on Evacuation that the Police Force should be increased and a cordon should be put around London. Also, between December 1937 and the Munich Crisis in September 1938, there were a number of discussions between the Army and the civilian authorities, notably the Commissioner of Police, for the use of 17,000 troops. On 29th April 1939, orders from the War Office to Commanders in Chief explained in some detail the role the army would play in preventing panic and restoring civilian order.[7]

These, together with an extra 20,000 reserve constables, would prevent problems occurring at Tube and mainline stations.[8]

These concerns about panic had been strengthened by the reaction of some members of the public during the Munich crisis in September 1938 when 150,000 people moved into Wales. There was a mass exodus of cars leaving London and panic buying in the shops. It has to be said that in this instance Government secrecy about what was going on certainly did not help the situation, and the hasty digging of one million feet of trenches in London and the distribution of 38 million gas-masks, did little to allay the fears of the population. The Government did not mention anything publicly about any evacuation scheme until 29th September, by which time the crisis was over, although there is evidence to suggest that some schools [9] took the initiative to make their own arrangements[10]

---

5 The Blitz. After the Battle. Vol 3.p 214. See Appendix 13.
6 House of Commons Debates. 30 July 1934. vol 292.cols.2335-6
7 Titmuss op.cit. p19
8 ibid.
9 SEE PAGE....ON TOTTENHAM SCHOOL PLANS
10 .ibid. p31

On 26th September 1938, there was a meeting of parents with pupils at the Becontree Infants School, Dagenham, where they were told what evacuation would entail should war be declared. Teachers were instructed to keep their rucksacks packed with essential items and their gas masks at school in case the order for evacuation was given[11].

It was a fact that during the planning stages more attention was given to the evacuation than to the reception, a situation which inevitably heightened the frustration of those people trying to organise the social service infrastructure within the reception areas. Ineffective communications between central, local and district government also added to the confusion, especially with regard to the billeting of evacuees which, in many cases, became the responsibility of small Rural District Councils which, until the outbreak of war, had spent most of their time discussing road sweeping, planning applications and very localised issues. These were usually chaired by a local dignitary or solicitor with limited experience of anything beyond their immediate community, and they were ill-prepared for taking on such a responsible part in a national scheme. Examples from the Minutes of these councils can give an interesting insight into their priorities. The following is taken from the East Retford Rural District Council, in Nottinghamshire. (this council no longer exists) and is a reply to a memo sent by the Ministry of Health to all Rural District Councils asking for help with the reception of evacuees:-

> *'The Parish Council wish me to acknowledge the receipt of your letter but regrets it cannot help because the Rector has left'.*

Presumably the war needed to be delayed until they could find another incumbent![12]

As late as the 23rd August 1939, the Billeting Officer in Edeyrnion wrote to the Clerk at *Bala Urban District Council asking:-*

> *'I wonder whether you would be kind enough to let me have a copy of your scheme 'Evacuation'. I know you have made a very thorough job of it and it would help me greatly and give me a good idea as to what ought to be done'.*[13]

Under the circumstances it is perhaps surprising that more mistakes were not made. However, some errors, not necessarily the fault of the local and district councils, were made with potentially devastating results. The following list from the Berkshire County Council Minutes, September 1939, indicates the great differences between the numbers of evacuees expected and those which actually arrived in the County. It also demonstrates that even the local councils who were well advanced and organised in their planning, had to respond on an *ad hoc* basis when the scheme was actually implemented. One can just imagine the panic measures which had to be enforced in order to house all the evacuees who eventually turned up. Especially the Billeting Officer in Hungerford, who probably thought he was going to have an easy time! When confronted with such evidence of bureaucratic confusion one can sympathise with the billeting officer in the Ministry of Information propaganda film 'Living with Strangers' who, when interrupted during dinner, says *'Who'd be a billeting Officer?'*[14]

It is no wonder that many evacuees returned immediately to London, or found the reception areas unwelcoming. From such a simple occurrence myths about unwelcoming hosts can be created and remain in the memory.

Number of Expected Evacuees and Actual Numbers Arriving in Berkshire September 1939

Region	Numbers Received	Numbers Expected
EAST BERKSHIRE		
Maidenhead Borough	4,040	3,958
Cookham Rural District	2,160	1,408
Wokingham Borough	1,800	1,004
Wokingham Rural District	6,498	3,056
Easthampstead Rural District	5,000	1,687

11 Letter to the author from Win Lewis and Sylvia Elliott. April 1998. MERL Archive
12 James Roffey. op.cit. Personal Archive.
13 Penllyn RDC File. Evac. Arrangements. 1939. Letter 23 August 1939. Dolgellau R.O.
14 'Living With Strangers. MoI Film. 1941. op.cit.

Number of Expected Evacuees and Actual Numbers Arriving in Berkshire September 1939		
Windsor Borough	4,000	2,004
Windsor Rural District	3,200	1,726
Total	**26,698**	**14,843**
SOUTH BERKSHIRE		
Bradfield Rural District	3,200	1,436
Newbury Borough	2,400	1,310
Newbury Rural District	2,424	483
Hungerford Rural District	800	Nil
Total	**8,824**	**3,229**
NORTH BERKSHIRE		
Abingdon Borough	1,400	381
Abingdon Rural District	2,600	1,341
Faringdon Rural District	2,400	1,234
Wallingford Borough	500	557
Wallingford Rural District	1,900	1,346
Wantage Urban District	480	279
Wantage Rural District	1,920	705
Total	**11,200**	**5,843**
GRAND TOTAL	**46,772**	**23,915** [15]

This vagueness in communication resulted in both central and local Government being able to accuse the other of ineptitude. Central Government seemed intent on issuing memos and circulars to the reception areas with little thought for the implementation of the recommendations contained in them. For example, the Board of Education had thought that local authorities had been warned of the possibility of evacuees having head-lice and that they could overcome the problem by giving the children steam baths.[16]

They had successfully shifted the responsibilities to the local authorities without, seemingly, any comeback. Central Government adopted a complacent attitude which was to make the success of evacuation questionable from a very early stage. After receiving evidence of the problems inherent in the evacuation 'rehearsals' which had taken place in some areas in September 1938, Ben Smith, a Labour MP wrote to the Board of Education in December of the same year stating that:-

> *'...there would be enough ill-clad and poorly shod children to hinder the successful operation of any evacuation scheme'.*[17]

In reply, Earl de la Warr, President of the Board of Education, denied that this would happen...and let the matter rest.[18]

One could suggest that the evacuation in 1938 was far more significant than a mere rehearsal. During the Munich Crisis the London County Council drew up a very basic plan to move 637,000 children from London, and other plans were instigated in cities such as Birmingham. The LCC actually evacuated 1,200 nursery school children and 3,100 children whom they labelled as 'physically defective'.[19]

All these were brought back from the reception areas immediately after the conclusion of the Munich conference. What this mini-evacuation demonstrated was that improvised schemes introduced by the local authorities on an ad hoc basis would be detrimental to the success of any scheme, which is what the planners had been saying from as early as 1933. Titmuss highlights a few examples.

Children were to be evacuated from the East End of London to Essex at the same time as Essex County Council were evacuating children to other areas. And, after pupils from King's School, Canterbury were to be moved to Scotland, children from London were to take over their school. Such occurrences continued into the war. Detailed investigations into the unwitting testimony continued in the Ministry of Information propaganda film 'Living

15 Berkshire County Council. Minutes. September 1939.
16 TNA.ED.10/245
17 Ben Smith to Earl de la Warr. 21 December 1938. TNA.ED 50/204.
18 ibid. Earl de la Warr to Ben Smith. 13 January 1939.
19 Titmuss op.cit. p29

with Strangers' shows that the people in the film had been moved out of London to Essex. The evacuees are shown getting off a bus with a destination board saying 'Chingford'.[20]

Samuel Hoare, in a censure debate in the House of Commons on 3rd November 1938, defended the Government's actions against those MPs who criticised it for not having an overall evacuation policy when the country was near to war by stating:-

> *'...On the broad question of evacuation I claim that the plans were laid on sound foundation, and further that if we had been compelled to bring them into operation, they would have worked satisfactorily'.*[21]

This may have been true, but it should be noted that the correspondence to Local Authorities indicating the number of evacuees to expect, together with a memo 'Instructions to Billeting Officers', were not sent out until the last week of September 1938 and after these had been processed by the Clerks of the Council, were not distributed to the Parish and Rural District Councils until the 30th September, after the Munich crisis was over. This was true in Dorset. A letter in the correspondence file of the County Council dated 30th September 1938, indicates that the County was to expect 30,000 children from Croydon and these were to be billeted in rural areas. The tone of the letter indicates the rapidity of the implementation and also the fact that they were somewhat unprepared. For instance, Billeting Officers had yet to be appointed, although it has to be said that they did have transport arrangements in place for those coming from London in the first wave.[22]

Plans had been instigated in other areas. In September 1938, Ellen Davis, WVS Organiser for Caernarfon and Anglesey, reported to the Penmaenmawr Urban District Council:-

> *'In the event of hostilities, on Monday next about 500 children with their teachers, with day rations, 1 blanket and gas mask will arrive. The children of local schools are to be given a holiday, and those from further away will occupy the rooms temporarily. They will lie on straw in schools and, at the expiration of three days, arrangements are to be made for billeting'.*[23]

These examples are an indication that the Munich evacuation in 1938 was not as ad hoc as some historians have previously been led to believe. A document in the Dorset Record Office, again dated 30th September 1938, lists the stations of arrival, the name of the reception schools, the evacuated schools and the estimated number of evacuees expected at each venue. It had obviously been well-planned and required the co-operation of a number of parties.

Dorset stations for arrival of Croydon schools.

Air Raid Precaution: Disposition of Secondary School Children from Croydon				
Railway Zone	**Railhead**	**Dorsetshire Secondary School**	**Croydon School**	**Estimated No. of Croydon Children**
1st	1. Semley Jn. Shaftesbury	Shaftesbury Grammar	Tennison Boys	150
	2. Gillingham	Gillingham Grammar School. (Mixed)	St. Michael's	200
	3. Sherborne	Sherborne Fosters (boys)	Selhurst Boys	400
		Sherborne Lord Digby's (girls) Also public schools	Selhurst Girls	400
	4. Lyme Regis	Lyme Regis Grammar	Heath Clark	350
2nd	1. Poole	Poole Grammar (Boys)	St. Joseph's College	350
	2. Swanage	Swanage Grammar (Mixed)	Ruskin	350
	3. Dorchester	Dorchester High School (Girls)	Girls High School	750
	4. Weymouth	Weymouth Grammar (Mixed)	Old Palace	350
		Weymouth Technical (Boys)	Stanley Technical	250
3rd	1. Blandford	Blandford Grammar (Mixed)	Lady Eldridge	250 [24]

20 Living With Strangers. op.cit.
21 House of Commons Debates. vol.340 col.446
22 Dorset County Council. Correspondence File. Letter dated 30 September 1938.
23 Penmaenmawr.UDC. ARP Evac.File No1. Caernarfon RO. cited Wallis op.cit. p16
24 Source Dorset County Council. DC/SYR/E3

From C.P.Bruton. Clerk of the County Council of Dorset;

To the Clerks of the Borough, Urban and Rural District Councils in the County of Dorset.

30 September. 1938

Dear Sir,

I am informed by the Home Office that they have authorised the evacuation of 30,000 children from the Borough of Croydon to Dorsetshire and I am requested, in consultation with the Clerks to the Rural and Urban Districts in the County, to make arrangements as soon as possible for the accommodation of this number of refugees. I shall therefore be glad if you will let me have the names and addresses of persons to be appointed as billeting officers, which should be about 1 officer for every 100 refugees, for your area when I will issue to them a form of authority to act.

I enclose a copy of instructions to billeting officers for your information and assistance and will also forward a copy to each billeting officer with his authority.

I also enclose a list of the Croydon Secondary and Elementary school children which you would be expected to accommodate in your area and shall be glad if you would instruct the billeting officers to make provisional arrangements for billets immediately pending the receipt of official authority.[25]

These evacuees were to be allocated without any previous detailed accommodation survey therefore had the scheme been implemented there would have been severe problems.

Air Raid Precautions County of Dorset: Schedule of Accommodation for Refugees			
Area	ACCOMMODATION		
	Total	Allocated (Croydon)	Balance
Boroughs			
Blandford	2,325	1,250	1,075
Bridport	3,500	-	3,500
Dorchester	4,600	3,750	850
Lyme Regis	2,000	2,000	-
Poole	7,300	5,700	1,600
Shaftesbury	875	850	25
Wareham	1,070	-	1,070
Weymouth	20,000	10,600	9,400
Urban Districts			
Portland	No figures yet available		
Sherbourne	1,370	1,300	70
Swanage	5,995	5,850	145
Wimborne	5,471	-	5,471
Rural Districts			
Beaminster	3,079	-	3,079
Blandford	3,498	-	3,498
Bridport	4,221	-	4,221
Dorchester	6,037	-	6,037
Shaftesbury	5,391	200 (Gillingham)	5,191
Sherbourne	2,693	-	2,693
Sturminster	4,613	-	4,613
Wareham	7,013	-	7,013
Wimbourne	5,995	-	5,995
TOTAL	**97,046**	**31,500**	**65,546**

25 ibid.

Disposition of Secondary and Elementary School Children from Croydon			
Town	**Secondary**	**Elementary**	**Total**
Poole	350	5350	5700
Weymouth	600	10,000	10,600
Blandford	250	1000	1250
Dorchester	750	3000	3750
Gillingham	200	-	200
Swanage	350	5500	5850
Lyme Regis	350	1650	2000
Shaftesbury	150	700	850
Sherbourne	800	500	1300
TOTAL	**3800**	**27,700**	**31,500** [26]

What is significant is that the information sent out to Billeting Officers did contain a great many of the details which would be reissued in 1939.

Third, there was a certain amount of ignorance on the part of the planners and administrators of the incredible social impact that the scheme would have, both in the evacuated and the reception areas.

The vast majority of evacuees and hosts alike were not prepared in any way for the culture shock that awaited them. It is true that evidence of poorly clad and under-nourished children, although not all were in this state, was a shock to many of the people in the reception areas. However, instead of seeing this as an opportunity to help the 'less fortunate' many tended to blame the parents for lacking care, or were concerned about the effects such children would have on local health provision. Numerous letters were sent to local newspapers expressing concern about the topic. The following is just one example:-

> *'Sir,*
>
> *May I plead through your columns that the Medical Officers of Health for the County and the Borough will pay the closest attention to the health of the evacuees in our county. I am seriously concerned that these evacuees from London may lower our bill of health. In the first place it is obvious that in some cases our visitor's standard of hygiene is far removed from our standard, possibly through environment....the facts are disturbing.*
>
> *Signed 'Anxious Parent'.*[27]

It is important to remember that many parents of evacuees were not told how long their children would be away for and so only sent them with clothing to last for a few days. In fact they were encouraged to do so in order to cut down on children's luggage. Also, pay-day for many of the working classes at this time was Friday which, for some, coincided with the first day of evacuation, therefore household funds would be at their lowest, and although this cannot be used as evidence to account for the plight of the majority of evacuees it is nonetheless a consideration. One could argue that parents, realising that evacuation could have been a possibility at the outbreak of war, should have been better organised but, as the Government had effectively maintained the secrecy surrounding evacuation, many parents were actually given short notice and were not in a position to react favourably to the situation.[28]

> 18th Oct 1940 circ 2178
> MoH Whitehall
>
> '.....the initial responsibility for finding accom for persons who arrive in the district and are unable to find accom. for themselves rests with the Public Assistance Authority'.

26 ibid.
27 Bedfordshire Times and Standard. September 1939.
28 Titmuss. op.cit. p122

> 'The billeting authority should, when requested by the public assistance authority, undertake the provision of accom. for mothers and children even if they have arrived in the area without certificates from the evacuating authority.'
>
> Women arriving with children should be billeted
>
> Other women who are not normally in employment should also be billeted, but warned that if the need arose as a result of the need for making provision for members of the priority groups, they might have to give up their accom.
>
> Women without children who are normally in employment should be urged to return to work but if persuasion fails they should, as a last resort, be temporarily billeted and instructed to apply for new work at the Employment Exchange.
>
> Men arriving in the district should NOT be billeted but be instructed to return to their work or go to the Employment Exchange.....
>
> 'Full use should be made of existing services and organisations, both official and voluntary, both county and district, to provide for the needs of evacuated persons and to absorb them as rapidly and fully as possible into the life of the Community.
>
> 'The release of some of the mothers for employment will be facilitated by the making of arrangements for the care of the children during the day and the establishment of nursery centres and communal meals......mothers could help in the centres...'
>
> 'Making and mending of clothes.....' The women concerned are not generally accustomed to making garments, their habit being to purchase cheap ready made clothing when required.....'

Many children experienced the embarrassing complaint of Enuresis which, like other psycho-neurotic symptoms, is considered to be an expression of mental protest. Bed-wetting by a number of evacuees during the first few weeks of the war, estimated at anywhere between, 1% - 33% of evacuees, depending on reports by local reception committees, was caused by an acute sense of insecurity.

The evidence of head lice and bed wetting is not indicative of domestic child abuse, although many Government officials and volunteers, usually from the middle-classes, resorted to this explanation when confronted with the problems and with ill-disciplined evacuees. In fact a lot of research had been carried out by the London County Council in 1919, and again in 1934, about the incidence of enuresis in residential and camp schools[29], and a report entitled 'Our Towns', produced in 1943 by the Women's Group on Public Welfare, identified widespread incidence in 'public schools, poor law homes, charitable institutions, approved schools, holiday camps, Ministry of Labour training centres and shipping companies.' [30] However, although this report indicated that the most important cause of enuresis in evacuees was poor or absent toilet/habit training by parents and bad home conditions, later research into the domestic environment of enuretic evacuee children did not confirm this assumption.

J.J.Kempton[31] defined enuresis in the Postgraduate Medical Journal published in October 1951, as 'the involuntary and usually unconscious voiding of urine, predominantly during sleep, in the absence of organic disease of the urinary or nervous systems'. Estimates of the frequency with which it occurred in children varied; W.Sheldon reported an incidence of 5% in 5,000 children living in institutions, 60% of whom were boys,[32]

29 London County Council. Annual Report. 1915-19. Vol.III. p95 and LCC Memo 'Enuresis in Residential Schools. 28 November 1934 cited in Titmuss op.cit.p123.
30 Report. Our Towns. Women's Group on Public Welfare 1943..
31 J. J. Kempton, M.D., M.R.C.P., D.C.H.
32 W.Sheldon. Proceedings of the Royal Society of Medicine, 37,344. pub. 1944

whereas S.Gill estimated an incidence of around 5% in 14,000 children evacuated from London to the Brighton area.[33]

This phenomenon of enuresis was not restricted to young evacuees. An interesting comparison can be found in an article in 'The Lancet' where the three authors state:-

> *'In a proportion of the soldiers evacuated from Dunkirk in 1940, enuresis was noted as a response to feelings of stress and insecurity'.*[34] *There was also evidence of increased enuresis in prisoner of war camps.*[35]

The Ministry of Health had actually recognised there could be a possible problem with enuresis and in May 1939 ordered the provision of rubber underlays for an estimated 60% of those evacuees below 5 years of age. By the beginning of the war few had been delivered to the reception areas and no account had been taken of older children who might have suffered from the same complaint.[36]

What is often overlooked is the fact that some evacuees were affected by the bed-wetting of a third party. Lyn Mendlson, (née Blacker) describes how she and her brother had to share a bed with a persistent bed-wetter:-

> *'When we returned to London I was able to sleep in a dry bed again. Most nights our bed at Kettering was wet because Tony, the other evacuee who slept with us, had a weak bladder and couldn't help wetting it, so we all had to sleep in soggy sheets and blankets. The wetness always made me feel cold'*[37]

As well as bed-wetting, the other serious complaint from the reception areas was the number of evacuees who many officials and hosts in the reception areas considered to be 'verminous'. The summer of 1939 had been a very hot one in which head lice would have thrived and, as evacuation took place at the end of the long holiday, many had not been checked by the School Medical Service for some time. This is an important factor when one considers how many of the evacuees from the poorer areas of the cities relied on this Service for all their medical needs. It is also a known fact that head lice can be transferred from people in close proximity and, as many of the evacuees were crammed into railway carriages, it is obvious that many of them could have picked up the infestation during the journey to the reception areas. What was unfortunate, and possibly one of the reasons for the outcry in some areas, was that the Minister of Health had assured the House of Commons in March 1939 when outlining the evacuation scheme that:-

> *'Any householder who raises a question as to the cleanliness of the children may be assured that schoolchildren are subject to regular medical inspection, that there is no greater danger of dirt or infection from these children than from any other representative group in the country, and that the best possible arrangements will be made for their medical supervision'.*[38]

In May 1939, H.W. Lowe, announced to an evacuee planning conference in Caernarfon that:-

> *'...the people of Liverpool would go to Caernarvonshire in good order and the children, in properly organised parties in the charge of their teachers, would be clean and free from infectious diseases'.*[39]

Unfortunately, this was not to be the case and there were serious problems between hosts and evacuees over their state of well-being on arrival. As early as 1938 the Senior Medical Officer in Liverpool found that the number of

33 S.Gill British Medical Journal. ii. 199. Pub 1944
34 C. Anderson, M. Jeffrey & M.N.Pai. The Lancet 12 August 1944 ii.p218
35 J.J.Kempton. op cit
36 Titmuss op.cit.p121
37 .Lyn Mendlson. Letter to the author 29 January 1997. MERL Archive
38 House of Commons Debates. 2 March 1939 Vol 344 col 1524
39 North Wales Chronicle. 12 May 1939.

children in the city's schools found to be verminous was 24,130, or 20.8% of the total school population. This was the highest in the country.[40]

It would seem from accounts and complaints in the North Wales reception areas that little had been done between the time of the report and the evacuation of Liverpool children to control the situation. Some authorities did ask for assurances regarding the general health of expected evacuees. In May 1939, members of the Ruthin Borough Council attempted to find out from the Liverpool evacuation authorities what steps they were taking with regard to the immunisation of children being sent to their area. The Medical Officer stated that there was:-

> *'...danger of serious disturbances of the epidemiological balances of the districts into which these town dwellers are introduced arising from the differences between the immunity values of town and country populations'.*[41]

But, as Titmuss stated, this fear, whatever its scientific basis in the light of contemporary knowledge of immunity, never reached the point of materially influencing official policy.[42]

The question of immunising Liverpool evacuees continued to be an issue during the early part of the war. Although some progress was made, the problem of funding the scheme made this slow. Immunisation could only be carried out if the money was available and if parents gave their consent. In March 1941, the authorities in Liverpool agreed to pay 3/6 for every evacuee immunised if parental consent was forthcoming.[43]

Although only a small percentage of evacuees was considered to be in a 'deplorable state', adverse publicity and a plethora of complaints created the impression that this was the whole story.

As early in the scheme as 6th September 1939, the Clerk of Buckley Urban District Council in Flintshire wrote to the County Council and Welsh Board of Health:-

> *'I regret to inform you that serious difficulties have arisen in connection with some of the evacuees who have come to this Urban District from the County Borough of Birkenhead. They arrived here on Friday and Saturday last. Several occupiers of Buckley houses have called at my office to complain of the verminous condition of the children and that the children are suffering from skin diseases. In addition many of the children are apparently, according to the report, filthy and they are not observing the ordinary decencies in the houses where they are billeted. Regarding the adult women, more than one complaint has come that they are not merely offensive in their behaviour, but also that they are guilty of excessive drinking. In addition, a certain number of women are as filthy as the children who have come with them'.*[44]

The Clerk of the Rural District Council revealed he was:-

> *'...daily receiving complaints of their (evacuees) verminous condition. Several householders complain that they have already had to burn their bedding and the unanimous opinion in the district is that it is time to call a halt to the evacuation scheme.'*[45].

The WVS organiser in Llanrwst reported on 4th September 1939, that:-

> *'Unless steps are taken to remove these people I am afraid that we shall have rioting here'.*[46]

In the October issue of the 'Welsh Nationalist' the correspondent used the opportunity to reinforce their party's concern about the general effect the evacuation English mothers and children would have, and had already had, on the population of Wales.

---

40 Our Towns a Close OUP. 1939-42. Women's Group on Public Welfare Oxford. 1943 p7.
41 Epidemiological Aspects of ARP Evac. Scheme. p174. cited Titmuss p15.
42 Titmuss. op.cit p15.
43 Denbigh Borough Council Letter book. May 1942 - March 1943. Ruthin RO. BD/A/412.
44 Flintshire County Council.Clerk Evac. Minutes. Letter from Llewellyn Jones to Welsh Board of Health. 6 September 1939 Flintshire R.O. FC/C/4/2/50.
45 ibid. Letter F. Grimley to J.Harvey Davies. 13 September 1939
46 Denbighshire County Council File 8/9 Llanwrst UDC. Letter to clerk Llanwrst UDC from N.Jones and J.M. Parry Jones. WVS 4 September 1939. Ruthin R.O Z1348.

'Welsh people will never forget the English evacuees. Some of the diseases they brought with them are well-known....diphtheria, whooping cough, measles, TB, chicken pox. Congenital syphilis is not so well-known in Wales, neither are bugs and body lice. One wonders whether the English Government will compensate the families of Llyn for the destruction of bedding and furniture. One cannot but pity the evacuees, but we are left in frank amazement at the inhumanness of a Government which allows such a condition of affairs to exist in its country, while preparing a war of many years in order to teach the German people about the inestimable benefits of English civilisation'.[47]

In Anglesey some schools were used as Cleansing Stations. In March 1940, the Merionethshire Medical Officer *'inspected every mother and infant from Liverpool and found the large majority being unfit for admission to billets mostly because of a verminous condition'.*[48]

This could account for the traumatic physical experiences that Lillian Evans, and her classmates went through when arriving at their billets 'clean'.

The problem of apportioning blame on their visitors was not confined to Wales. In one particular village in North Oxfordshire it was the local nurse who blamed the incidence of head lice on evacuees! When this nurse went on her rounds checking hair and heads of all the school children she stated that:-

'...if any of the village children were found to be verminous it would be due to London children'.[49]

One evacuee recalls that the first thing that happened to him and his siblings was a *'hair inspection by a nurse wielding a comb dripping in disinfectant.'*[50]

Scabies was also a problem, but one that was around in the reception areas before evacuation took place. The scabies mite is small and burrows beneath the skin, therefore the sufferer could not have been segregated from fellow passengers on the trains and other transport had they picked up the complaint before leaving for the reception areas. Close personal contact with infected others would lead to the contraction of the disease which thrived in the warm atmosphere which would have been found in overcrowded train carriages. A Ministry of Health Circular 2517 issued on the 14th November 1941, and known as the Scabies Order, increased the power of Local Authorities to combat the spread of the disease. A report from the Holywell Rural District Council stated that:-

'The treatment of scabies is, from the point of view of this department unsatisfactory in that many children sometimes within a few days of discharge, break out again and have to be sent back again to the sick bay for further treatment. Some children have been sent back several times and a report in one case was sent to the Ministry Inspector'.[51]

One particular council, Cricklade and Wootten Bassett RDC, expressed concern in March 1940 about the cleanliness of evacuees in general but specifically adolescent girls:-

'The Council appreciate what is being done with regard to medical examination and improvement in the health of children, but something more is needed, i.e. education in how to be clean, particularly girls of over 13 years of age, who in many instances appear to have no knowledge of nature and how to be clean. This was a cause of a number of soiled beds and of considerable annoyance'.[52]

---

47 cited Wallis. op.cit. p87.
48 Menai Bridge UDC. File GES 39-40. Letter to Liverpool medical officer from Medical officer Menai Bridge 2 March 1940. Llangefri RO cited Wallis.p85.
49 Letter to Author from John William O'Connor. March 28 1998. MERL Archive
50 Letter to author from J.Roffey 9 June 1998. MERL Archive
51 Holywell RDC Council Minutes. No 36. April 1942-3. Meeting of Evacuation.Committee. 10 June 1942. Flint R.O. Cited Wallis.p120
52 WRO/F2/850/1-12.

In Circular Ev.10 issued to parents in the Portsmouth area in 1940, instructions were given about cleanliness, a rather patronising hint that not all parents knew how to keep their children clean:-

> **'What must a parent do in preparation for evacuation?......**
>
> Make sure the child is CLEAN and ready to go at any time......
>
> After evacuation had taken place last September complaints were made by Householders in the Receiving Areas that some children were not clean. You will wish to be sure that this cannot be said about your own child and do everything possible to make sure that he goes away with clean clothes, clean hair, clean body. Children from the cleanest homes have sometimes had the misfortune to get lice in the head which they pick up from other children.......'[53].

Similarly, the Liverpool Public Health Authority issued a leaflet in February 1940, entitled 'Advice to Householders on the Care of Children's Hair' and the WVS printed one called 'The Cleansing and Care of Children's Heads...Be Thorough'.

It should also be remembered that the problems of head lice was not confined to evacuees, nor indeed children. During April 1942, a number of letters were sent to 'The Times' complaining about the prevalence of head lice especially among women workers living in close proximity in industrial areas and women refugees living in hostels. Many remedies were suggested such as:-

> *'The Department of Entomology in the London School of Hygiene and Tropical Medicine has evolved a simple and effective means of delousing by the rubbing with the fingers into the roots of the hair a suitably medicated cream, and not washing the hair for eight to nine days so as to allow time for the lice to be killed'.*[54]

This correspondent also suggested that the 'Permanent Wave' fashion be prohibited because it was a waste of time and electricity and did nothing to alleviate the problem of head lice.[55]

Another correspondent writing a few days later supported the use of the 'Perm' and cited the example of the many high-ranking officers in the Women's Services who had their hair 'permed' regularly.[56]

The letters also give an interesting indication of how some people thought that head lice could lead to an outbreak of Typhus.

> *'It is imperative that the louse be got rid of when there is a danger of typhus reaching this country'.*[57]

There is absolutely no evidence whatsoever that head lice was, or ever could be, a source of Typhoid.[58]

Any such suggestion would seem to be rather irresponsible and inflammatory, but one concerned correspondent suggests that evidence of a link was supported by both the Ministries of Labour and Health. If this statement had been made public it is no wonder that many people were concerned that lice should be eradicated, but one has to say that there is no evidence that the Ministries were involved in spreading such misinformation.

However, in the light of other evidence cited earlier, it is interesting to note that none of the letters refers to head lice as a symptom of poverty. Also, although many authorities were quick to lay the blame for bringing various diseases into the reception areas on the evacuees, little mention is ever made of the risk some of the latter were exposed to in the choice of hosts. There was serious concern in Wales about the high incidence of Tuberculosis.

---

53 ibid
54 British Medical Association Journal. 11 April. 1942
55 Sir Leonard Hill to 'The Times' 15 April 1942. cited Livesey op.cit. p142
56 W.Neville to 'The Times' 24 April 1942 ibid. p143
57 Sir Leonard Hill. op.cit
58 Interview with Dr. Robin Borthwick. Theale Medical Centre. 9 January 1997.

A report by the Anti-Tuberculosis service in Wales and Monmouth expressed concern, and in the light of this the Ministry of Health sent a letter to the Deudraeth Rural District Council on the 28th August 1939, notifying them that the Housing Inspector would make an early visit to ascertain the nature and extent of the problem. Before this visit could take place Deudraeth took in 800 evacuee children and no account was taken of the high incidence of TB.[59]

There are no general records of how the hosts dealt with the problems they faced when dealing with their evacuees, although accounts from some evacuees would suggest that some were rather draconian.[60]

Although local authorities reacted to overcome some of the physical ailments such as delousing, the extra burdens of finding new clothes and cleaning became the responsibilities of the hosts,[61] and this was partly responsible for the resentment shown by some who felt they had been misinformed as to their role and responsibilities. The problem of bed-wetting and body and head lice, although still apparent in the later evacuations in 1940 and again in the 'Doodle-bug' raids of 1944, never reached the same level of recrimination as it had in 1939. This was due to a combination of three factors:-

First, after 1939 the Government abandoned the principle of mass-evacuation which meant that it was easier to conduct medical checks on evacuees. One needs to remember that although the initial evacuation scheme had been worked out in the summer of 1939, when it came to putting it into practice there was no time for each individual child to be medically examined, and so some children suffering from various complaints and illnesses, were taken into the reception areas through nothing more than bureaucratic oversights. When faced with this criticism of inaction, the Government's defence had been to state that to search for lice while bombs were falling would not have been possible. However, as early as 10th March 1939, the Board of Education and Ministry of Health had concluded that all routine medical inspections of schoolchildren in all areas would have to be suspended in the event of war.[62]

A memo. from Sir George Chrystal to Sir Maurice Holmes, the Permanent Secretary at the Ministry of Health, dated 10th March 1939, admitted that medical checks would be impossible and other routine medicals would have to be abandoned.

> *'It is quite impossible to arrange for the inspection of 1.5 million children so that it could be said that the children were handed over to the reception areas certified as healthy. At least one of the three routine medical inspections normally carried out during a child's school career would be dispensed with altogether'.*[63]

But, in some areas, it could have been possible to have included a medical examination in the evacuation practices which had taken place in August 1939. Also, checks could have been carried out by the reception authorities at the time of arrival. Although again this happened in some areas, others were too understaffed to carry them out effectively, if at all. The later evacuation schemes, carried out in perhaps a more relaxed way, enabled the administrators to introduce a scheme of medical screening. In March 1940, the Ministry of Health sent out a general letter to local newspapers stating:-

> *'It is an unfortunate fact that the lamentable condition of some of the children who were received in clean and bright country houses has caused many rural householders to dread a repetition of the scheme. As a matter of fact we now have the assurance of the minister that the examination of children will take place prior to their leaving London and also on arrival in the reception areas before the billeting officer allocates them to different homes'.*[64]

---

59 Deudraeth RDC Minute Book. 1937-40. 28 August 1939. Dolgellau R.O. cited Wallis p49
60 See Yesterday's Children. L.Evans
61 Titmuss. op.cit.p133
62 ibid. Footnote p145.
63 TNA HO/186/128/643/3.
64 North Berkshire and Oxfordshire Advertiser. March 1940

There were problems because according to a newspaper article on 4th April 1940, there were conflicting reports. Although the Minister of Health had given this assurance, the evacuating authorities told the local authority in Dorchester, Dorset, that they would only have time to check those children who had been registered for evacuation. This proportion would be very small as in the event of an air raid, parents would wish their children to be evacuated, whether they were registered or not. [65]

However, after May 1940, children were all examined and their details entered onto cards in a coded form. These codes, a series of symbols, were transferred to the labels worn by the children so that they could be easily identified on arrival in the reception areas as requiring special help.[66]

From evidence of the time, it is noticeable that the number of pupils suffering from specific conditions and complaints was in fact quite low, which tends to refute the myth that all pupils from the evacuated areas were suffering from something.[67]

Studies carried out at the time by teachers, members of His Majesty's Inspectorate, social workers, and schools medical officers emphasised the remarkable ability of most children in the target areas to maintain an emotional equilibrium as long as they were able to remain with their parents or relatives who were generally cheerful in their outlook and were not too depressed by the war situation. [68]

A school medical officer reported:-

> *'I have had the opportunity to see several hundred children during the last month. On several occasions I saw them and watched them while bombs were falling in the neighbourhood and air raids were overhead and asked them questions relating to the war, sirens etc...Children have adapted themselves to present condition of life surprisingly well...Even children who were bombed out of their homes did not seem to suffer in any way...There is no question of shock'.* [69]

This was supported by work done by Anna Freud in Hampstead. She found that evacuation and the break-up of family units did induce an emotional response where the family stability was lacking. This was heightened when the evacuees were under stress during air raids. [70]

Second, during the evacuation of 1940, a number of hostels had been established to house evacuees and any others suffering from enuresis so that they could be removed from potentially unsympathetic householders. It has to be said that in some areas staff in these houses were just as unsympathetic. A survey of hostels carried out by Liverpool University in 1939-40 found that:-

> *'...there were widespread misconceptions regarding enuresis, for a visit to one such institute gave the feeling that we still live in the Middle Ages. In this clinic the children were treated like little criminals and threat and punishment were the means of teaching them cleaner habits. The results can easily be imagined; no progress was made at all'.*[71]

Early in 1939 the Ministry of Health had requested the sum of £405,000 to cover the estimated cost of adapting existing premises as hostels and maternity homes and for providing extra toilets at rural railway stations and in city dispersal centres. The Treasury questioned the need for such expenditure and by August only £22,500 had been sanctioned. [72]

---

65 Dorset County Council & Swanage Times. 4 April 1940.
66 Ministry of Health Circular 2027 & Board of Education Circular 1509. 21 May 1940.
67 J.Macnicol. The effect of the evacuation of schoolchildren on official attitudes to State intervention. in War and Social Change. ed. Harold L.Smith op.cit.p17
68 ibid.p5
69 Testimony by Dr. J.Gavronsky. Board of Education Memo. 'Nervous Strain in Children' 1941. TNA. ED.50/206.
69 Ministry of Health Circular 2027 & Board of Education Circular 1509. 21 May 1940.
69 J.Macnicol. The effect of the evacuation of schoolchildren on official attitudes to State intervention. in War and Social Change. ed. Harold L.Smith op.cit.p17
69 ibid.p5
69 Testimony by Dr. J.Gavronsky. Board of Education Memo. 'Nervous Strain in Children' 1941. TNA. ED.50/206.
70Macnicol op.cit. p5
71 Our wartime guests. Opportunity or Menace? University Press Liverpool 1940 p 20.
72 ibid. p92

The toilets provided for evacuees on the stations comprised of wooden seats on top of galvanised buckets inside a canvas construction with the back and the roof covered but the front open to view. One of the reasons why so many children were in a bad state when they reached their destinations on the outward journeys, was that the vast majority travelled in third class carriages with no corridors and no toilets. At every station where the trains stopped, the members of the Women's Voluntary Service and the Women's Institute and other bodies, provided them with free drinks and, in consequence, the children had nowhere to relieve themselves[73].

Some of the boys resorted to urinating from the windows [74] but many, including the girls, for basic physical reasons, simply wet themselves because they either did not have time to use the station toilets during a stopover or, as some evacuees have said in interviews, refused to suffer the indignity of using toilets which were open to view.

'We may have been busting to go but we were not using those with everyone gawking at us'. One evacuee described the outcome of such a situation rather poetically...*'One small boy in our compartment wet himself and it ran in a little stream along the floor, changing direction as the train went around bends or braked'*. [75]

It is no wonder that when they reached their destination and were lined up to be chosen, some of the children would not have looked very suitable for fostering! There is little evidence of the same sort of problems occurring on the return journeys in 1945, although the circumstances under which the physical travelling took place were similar and drinks, again provided by the Voluntary Services, were readily available.

As late as the 31st August 1939, no hostels had been completed in the reception areas. Equipment allocated for these establishments had either been sent to the wrong place or had not been ordered. [76] This created a problem for some reception authorities who needed to find accommodation for those children who were difficult to billet, usually because of health or behavioural problems. Some such placements were available early in 1940 in Buckinghamshire as this entry from a school log-book would indicate.

> *'18th April 1940. Paul ***** was removed today to a school for Difficult Children at Bourne End. This has been approved of by the Billeting Officer since the boy has been difficult in four billets'.*[77]

An earlier entry in the same log-book shows that Paul had been admitted to the Sick bay for Children at Aylesbury for observation because of his 'nerves', which might suggest that these might have been the cause of his actions rather than just plain misbehaviour.

In other areas the Government ordered that makeshift hostels, where available, were to be opened, and as early as 12th September, they authorised the payment of compensation to those householders who had had damage caused by evacuees[78]. This order was reinforced in October when specific compensation guidelines were issued.[79]

In the same month an article appeared in the British Journal of Nursing under the title of Hostels, Sick Bays and Nurseries, commenting on the special residential arrangements required for dealing with specific classes of children or mothers, who under normal circumstances would be difficult to billet with a householder in the ordinary way. There was a suggestion that separate accommodation might be provided for children suffering from minor ailments or convalescing from more serious illnesses who could not be cared for in a usual billet. A trained nurse could then be in attendance and regular visits from the local doctor could be arranged. Another concern was the difficulty in providing suitable billets for women immediately prior to, or discharge from, an emergency maternity home and there was a suggestion from the Minister of Health, that local authorities should consider establishing specific pre and post-natal hostels within easy reach of the maternity homes. In line with

---

73 See film 'Westward Ho!' Ministry of Information 1940.
74 Oral testimony from a number of ex-evacuees.
75 J.Roffey. Letter to the author. 9 June 1998. MERL Archive
76 Titmuss op.cit. p111
77 E/LB/8/1 op.cit. 18 April 1940.
78 Ministry of Health Circular 1871.12 September 1939.
79 Ministry of Health Circular 1897. 24 October 1939

this, it was thought necessary to provide short-stay, fully staffed nursery accommodation for young children who would have to be temporarily separated from their mothers during an illness or confinement. The Minister also proposed the setting up of long-term residential nurseries for children separated for a longer period, and day nurseries in the more densely populated areas. The author of the article commented on the fact that such plans would take years to implement and cost millions of pounds.[80]

The Treasury did not give full approval for the hostel scheme until May 1940 as it was cheaper to keep evacuees in home billets rather than provide full board, lodging and social welfare on a 24 hour basis. It was as a result of unease in the reception areas that the Government made plans to give more active encouragement to local authorities to construct, or adapt existing buildings, for use as hostels. These were to be made available in the reception areas for those unaccompanied children who, on arrival, were thought to require special help. The Government estimated that this would amount to 5% of the evacuee population. [81]

By July 1941 there were 660 hostels in England and Wales housing 10,000 children[82] and by January 1942, 30 special hostels had been established for children of secondary school age. [83]

These hostels were also to be used as 'Clearing houses' for 'normal children' who had to be removed from their billets because of illness or any other reasonable cause. However, they were to return to their billets as soon as possible after the emergency so that places in the hostels could be freed for newcomers. In this way it was hoped that temporary relief could be given to a large number of householders, while if children remained for prolonged periods, the effect would have been to simply relieve a small number of householders of an obligation they perhaps ought to have shared with neighbours or other organisations.

Brian Maystone recalled his stay in the Lismore Hostel in Woking which at the time was run by an ex-jockey and his wife. They were helped by assistant wardens, one of whom was dismissed for 'having a small boy in bed with him'. The hostel was a large house in its own grounds. The boys were housed in two large dormitories and three smaller ones, which were on the first floor. On the ground floor was the warden's office, the front room, the games room and the dining room. There was also the servants' wing which contained the kitchen and showers. The boys spent their time playing sports, making model aircraft out of balsa wood and building crystal sets. They were taken to swim at the local open-air pool which could be extremely cold. Brian is not sure what type of hostel it was but remembers that the Warden would often be at the Magistrates Court pleading for one of the boys. He remembers one of them climbing up the drainpipe of the hostel entering the storeroom window and stealing blankets which he then posted home! [84]

In a circular entitled 'Notes for Billeting Officers' produced in 1940, they were instructed to say, in answer to the question:-

> *'Why can't all evacuated children be housed in Hostels and Camps?' that ...'it was all a question of arithmetic. Over 400,000 children were already in the reception areas and plans were in hand to send another 500,000 should more attacks take place'.* [85]

However, there were problems with organisations competing for the same accommodation. Whole factories and Government departments had also been evacuated, and some owners did not want their buildings used as hostels at all, especially by evacuees, and preferred instead to allow their use as convalescence homes for servicemen. This was not only a local issue. The following example, quoted by Titmuss, is an indication of the infighting between individual Government departments.

---

80 British Journal of Nursing. Oct 1939 p258
81 Titmuss op.cit. p165
82 Government Evacuation Scheme. Notes for Billeting Officers. 1940. Exeter Blitz Box 5. Devon Record Office.
83 Titmuss op.cit. p372
84 Brian Maystone. Letter to the author. February 1997.
85 Exeter Blitz Box. 5 op.cit.

'One MP with three mansions and at least six servants voluntarily offered his houses for the reception of evacuees at a time when the military seemed about to take possession. When the danger was past, attempts were made by the military to recover the premises and eject the evacuated children. The Ministry of Health resisted these attempts'. [86]

Some areas found the billeting of extra evacuees to be particularly problematic. In response to the government Circular 1968 15th February 1940, requesting that reception areas take in more evacuees, the Rural District Councils of Cricklade and Wootton Bassett, and Marlborough and Ramsey, and the Warminster Urban District Council, all complained independently that there were too many service personnel in their areas to take any more. In fact the Warminster Council hinted that they would request that one of the three large schools billeted in their area should be removed because of pressure of finding accommodation for servicemen. They also pointed out that they were concerned about the pressure placed on the Public Health services in the area. The Council at Marlborough laid the blame for an outbreak of Spotted Fever, Scarlet Fever and an epidemic of Measles on the influx of so many new people. They also had a public health problem which resulted in the military having to bury their rubbish and waste water from the cook houses. Wootten Bassett already housed 500 soldiers and a new airfield was under construction at nearby Lyneham.[87]

The same problems arose in September of the same year when Circular 2140 was sent out, again requesting more billets to be made available. Many more letters were sent to the Wiltshire County Council from various Urban District, Borough and Rural District councils complaining that there was just no space left because areas of Wiltshire had become an armed camp. Calne and Chippenham RDC wrote on 30th September 1940 that:-

1. *Unofficial evacuees are flowing into this area at the rate of 50 a day.*
2. *We already have 1500 persons billeted under the evacuation scheme.*
3. *Our allocation under Plan VI.B is 500 unaccompanied children.*
4. *In response to the urgent appeal of the Ministry of Health we offered to accept not more than 100 mothers and children. The Ministry advised us that they were sending a party of 82 and actually 140 arrived on Sunday last.*
5. *There are four large Aerodromes, two RAF Training Camps, and one large Ammunition Dump in the area of this Council and large numbers of the personnel attached to these places are billeted in our area and I estimate that there has been an increase of approximately 5000 persons in this area since the outbreak of war'. Clerk. Calne and Chippenham RDC. 30 September 1940.* [88]

Pewsey RDC....30th September 1940

About 1200 women and children have come into this area during the past 3 weeks and 900 of these are from London. We are dealing with them as fast as we can but the work of issuing billeting notices is in arrears.

In addition to this, the Military Authorities have requisitioned all empty houses, village halls etc. and have many soldiers and Airmen in private billets.

During today the Air Ministry has taken 57 of my billets and filled them with airmen!'[89]

86 Titmuss op.cit. p372
87 WRO/F2/850/1-12
88WRO/F2/580/1-12
89 Clerk. Pewsey RDC. 30 September 1940. WRO op.cit.

Borough of Devizes 30 September 1940

'.....I informed the Ministry of Health it would be impossible for us to take further Mothers and Children....As you are aware Devizes is the Depot Town of the Wiltshire Regiment and in addition we have Camps around the Town and wives and relatives of soldiers are arriving daily to take up accommodation....As far as I can ascertain any available house which might be used for billeting has been requisitioned by the military Authorities'. [90]

Borough of Wilton 30th September 1940.

'...The Ministry do not seem to appreciate, although it has been impressed on them, not only by me but also I understand by the War Office, that we now have in Wilton a very large Army establishment and a great portion of the Staff, both Military and Clerical are living in the town. Therefore billets are limited'. [91]

Borough of Marlborough 28th September 1940

'.....Since the arrival of evacuees from Bexhill we are continually being asked to provide accommodation for stragglers from London. The provision of this has entailed the use of all Condemned Houses and the point has been reached when no further accommodation is available.

At the moment we have four mothers and babies in the Rest Room waiting for billets'.[92]

Even after taking possession of such premises, the local authorities were faced with the problem of furnishing them during a period of extreme hardship. It was estimated that for a residential home housing 40 children over 4,000 items of equipment were needed. [93]

They also had to pay for the upkeep. There was a great deal of discussion at the Dorchester Rural District Council in June 1942, which had received a report from the Billeting Committee about the cost of running a hostel for evacuated families at 'The Hollies', Buckland Newton, which housed seven mothers and twenty children. It was reported that the revenue received from the families living at the hostel was not sufficient to cover the cost of basic maintenance. The Council had already asked the Ministry of Health for permission to make up any financial shortfall from the 'Evacuation Account', but they were denied permission and told that the deficit had to be made up from local rates. The Council recommended that:-

'...the Ministry should be informed that they were no longer prepared to accept any financial responsibility and, unless the Ministry allowed them to charge for the costs of past and future maintenance, the Council would close the Hostel down and de-requisition the premises. By doing the latter the property would revert back to the original owner and no further compensation would have to be paid'.

There were a few dissenting voices who felt that having spent a great deal of money getting the building into good order they should not be too hasty in agreeing to close it down. The discussion went on at some length until it was decided to do nothing about the recommendation and pass the matter back to the Billeting Committee for further thought! [94]

---

90 Clerk. Borough of Devizes. 30 September 1940. WRO op.cit.
91 Clerk. Borough of Wilton. 30 September 1940. WRO op.cit.
92 Clerk. Borough of Marlborough. 30 September 1940. WRO op.cit.
93 Titmuss. op.cit. p372
94 Dorchester Rural District Council. Minutes. June 1942.

What this does illustrate however, is how much financial burden was placed on the reception areas and it can be seen as another reason why some local rate payers were not keen to have evacuees. Problems such as these could only have heightened tension between the evacuees and the hosts.

Third, having learned from the experience of the first evacuation, both the reception areas and the Ministry of Health knew what to expect and the distribution of rubber sheeting for the protection of beds was better organised. Also the Ministry of Health agreed, somewhat reluctantly, to authorise extra payments to hosts to cover the costs of extra bedding where any evacuee was suffering from enuresis.

This scheme turned out to be costly. According to Titmuss, in one Welsh village a host was paid 3s 6d extra allowance for one week in October 1940. The other villagers got to know about this and a total of £350 was paid out to the village by the end of the financial year March 1942, despite a reduction in the number of evacuees.[95]

Much has been said in books and in the media about the poor state of evacuees reaching the reception areas. Poverty in the cities was common place in the 1920s and 1930s and was not confined to specific geographical areas. Any district containing a majority of the working classes experienced at some time the three-phase 'poverty cycle' which had been identified by social researchers long before the 1914-18 war. These phases included;-

a. The ages between birth and 15.

b. In the first years of marriage and bringing up young children.

c. Old Age.

Social Welfare legislation in the early part of the century and immediately post-(Great) war had alleviated some of the problems, but there were still some sectors of the community who existed below the poverty level. At this point people could experience anything from total destitution to a precarious existence where the economies involved in attaining the basics of life... housing, clothes, food and health provision was a continual struggle, and, according to Stevenson became 'life on the knife edge'.[96]

But, it must also be remembered that there was a great deal of rural poverty which, in a number of cases, was a contributory factor in the decision of some evacuees to return home. Although, in the 'Our Towns: A Close Up' report published by the OUP in 1943, members of the Women's Group on Public Welfare stated that:-

> *'...although poverty and low incomes were also found in the country such areas did not suffer the special town conditions of overcrowding, lack of open space, smoke and noise'.*[97]

Even the BBC ignored the fact when it reported that evacuation had *'brought home to the British public and Government alike the disturbing widespread poverty throughout much of Britain'.*[98] Presumably this referred to both rural and urban poor. At the outbreak of war 3,432 parishes in England and Wales had no piped water and 5,186 had no sewage systems. It was estimated that 30% of the population living in rural houses were not connected to a water main.[99]

A survey conducted by the Women's Institute in 1944, found that in 21 counties 50% of the villages schools investigated had earth or bucket toilets. In many schools in Wales using this form of sanitation, no toilet paper was available, and in one school in Wantage the situation was so bad that playtime had to be staggered in order to allow children, including evacuees, access to the toilets.[100]

---

95 Titmuss op.cit. p125
96 John Stevenson. British Society 1914-45. Penguin. 1990. p138 & 140-141.
97Holman. The Evacuation. op.cit. p144.
98 Sian Nicholas 'The Echo of War'. Manchester University Press. 1996. p75
99 House of Commons Debates. 10 May 1944. vol.399 cols 1930-1 and Cmd. 6515. 1944.
100 Titmuss. op.cit. p178

Also, contrary to popular belief, the health of city children did not suddenly improve because they were now breathing fresh air and eating 'natural' food. Some teachers did in fact report that children's height and weight were improving, but when the Government tried to substantiate the claims in order to keep the children in the reception areas, they could not prove it because there were so many variables to consider. These included the type of food available to them, the general care taken by the hosts, and simple things such as whether or not the evacuees were living on a farm with daily fresh milk.

The patronising attitudes of many people in the reception areas did little to break down the social barriers between city and country, if anything they reinforced them. One can see that to view evacuation as the key to initiating universal social awareness and change, as some contemporary politicians did, and many people today still do, is not necessarily valid. What it did do however, was to make more people aware of the need for social policies which would alleviate some of the plight of the poor but not, as some school text books would have us believe, that which existed purely in the inner cities, but also among the rural poor.

Without the evacuation scheme one could argue that this basic awareness would have taken longer to come into the wider public domain, and some of the social welfare services would have been established long after their original dates of inception.

Establishing Social Welfare

Where does the media and text books and other material leave us with Evacuation? According to the majority of school text books the children were sent away, some returned and were caught up in the bombing and, in some books, some children were re-evacuated. There is little more than a cursory reference to Overseas Evacuation and the Second and Third Government schemes, and usually nothing at all about the problems faced in 1945 when evacuees came home. To all intents and purposes Evacuation was just another simple event which took place during the war.

More recently some authors, such as Julie Summers, author of When the Children Came Home and Stranger in the House, have illustrated the significance of the Evacuation process in the wider social history of the time, especially in the development of the Social Services, services which have been significant in the lives of pupils in today's classrooms. This is certainly one area which was a positive development amidst some of the administrative problems of the evacuation scheme and should not be dealt with lightly. The care of those in society who required help, had its foundation in the Elizabethan Poor Law Act of 1597 and the Relief Act of 1601. The former contained little that had not been tried before. In 1563 the need for a compulsory poor-rate had been recognised and in 1572 the method of collection of dues had been introduced. 'Houses of Correction' were introduced under the Act of 1576 and reinforced the apprenticeship of paupers which had been implemented in 1536.

In 1834, the Poor Law Amendment Act introduced social welfare practices which were to have an effect for the next one hundred years. By introducing Workhouses for the 'able-bodied' destitute who required help, the Act created a social stigma of social failure which was to affect many of the needy up to the end of World War Two.

In 1939 the Workhouses, or Public Assistance Institutions, as they were then called, still contained 100,000 people.[101]

Some MPs, including the Christian socialist George Lansbury, wanted the Poor Law abolished, but Parliamentary lobbying only resulted in the responsibility for the administration and implementation of the Poor Law being taken from the Guardians and placed with the Public Assistance Committees of the local authorities, which in turn were under the overall control of the Ministry of Health.

---

101 Holman. The Evacuation. op.cit. p113

During 1939 and 1940, little had been done to improve the social welfare of unaccompanied evacuees and those who went as families. But it needs to be borne in mind that despite the seeming lack of social care in general, the social service provision was worse in the rural areas than in the major cities. However, if social welfare was to be improved it would have been expensive and the local authorities were disinclined to spend their money and, it has to be said, where they were willing to do so, they were restricted by Government legislation until a plethora of Government circulars were sent out from Central Government from October 1940 which removed many of the restrictions imposed on local spending. However, the contents of the Circulars encouraging local authorities to introduce feeding centres, nurseries and hostels, created a great deal of administrative work. It was very difficult to put some of the schemes into practice because many of the major building projects came at a time when materials were in short supply. [102]

Many Women's groups took responsibility for investigating the social welfare provision in the early 1940s. One in particular, the Women's Group on Public Welfare, made an important and significant contribution to the whole debate and influenced even the most conservative of the middle and upper classes. This group concerned themselves primarily with the social problems highlighted in the evacuation scheme. It established a committee of eight women who called witnesses, including health visitors, social workers and members of local authorities. In 1943, the group's report 'Poverty; Our Towns: A Close Up', highlighted the deplorable home conditions of many of the poor in the city areas which resulted in high infant and child mortality rates. They estimated that between 22-30% of children were in dire poverty.[103]

This report is significant because for the first time the blame for such conditions was not apportioned to the town councils controlling the areas from where the evacuees had come, but on the national situation. The evacuees, and those in what we would refer to today as the poverty trap, were not an underclass which could be ignored.

Having reached their conclusions, the committee suggested social reforms which at the time were considered radical and which, in some cases, have still not been implemented today. Some of their recommendations included:-

1. Nursery Education for all children.
2. Education.

   No classes with over 30 pupils.

   Secondary Education to be available to all.

   School Leaving Age to be raised to 16.

   Committed teachers with the time off for courses every 7 years.

   No bar for married women teachers.
3. Good Housekeeping. To be promoted as key to a good family life.

   Landlords to provide bathrooms and inside toilets.
4. Better health provision for all.
5. Measures to be taken against poverty to include:

   Payment of child allowances.

   Abolition of low wages

   Food price control

---

102 Titmuss. op.cit. p370
103 Holman op.cit. p144.

It is also worth noticing that one or two suggestions hint at the conservative and upper-class make-up of the committee, for instance it makes the assumption that working class girls needed an education which was best suited to train them for being mothers. [104]

Though some of the social measures had been suggested pre-war, according to Macnicol, evacuation itself had little specific effect, and he suggests that it is difficult to find evidence that brought absolute fundamental ideological shifts, notably in Whitehall.[105]

However, evacuation was in fact the catalyst which helped bring the social service plans into reality. Without evacuation and its attendant problems the inclusive school meals service, nursery provision and other measures would probably not have developed as quickly as they did. In the same way that aircraft and weapon technology grew out of necessity, so did the social welfare schemes. One needs to consider that those evacuees who had been evacuated to homes better than their own saw how the 'other half lived' and wanted the same for themselves. Many were no longer prepared to put up with life in below standard housing in areas of economic decline and were resolved, as Holman states, to 'vote for the politicians who would make their demands a reality'.[106]

---

104 ibid. p 146
105 Macnicol. The Evacuation of Schoolchildren. op.cit. p27
106 Holman. op.cit. p147

European War Children[1]

Germany

'I hereby give my permission for my son/daughter to be sent away on the programme of the Extended Kinderlandverschickung by the NSDAP. I agree to him/her being sent away for a period of at least six months, and appreciate that he/she cannot return before this period has elapsed. I also give my consent for him/her being vaccinated prior to departure.....

Signed Father or legal guardian'[2]

Operation Pied Piper was not the only official evacuation scheme planned during the war. Both Germany and Finland had authorized plans to move children. However, there were few similarities. The former was organised and carried out by the State, whereas the latter was initiated by two Swedish women, Maja Sandler and Hannah Rydh.

The official German policy regarding the protection of children, was to implement a gradual dispersal of the population away from the towns and cities, in order to cut down the possibility of panic which could obstruct vital communication networks, whereas the Finnish scheme was instigated against the background of a possible invasion from the USSR from the East, both in the Winter War of 1939-40 and the Continuation War 1941-45. Primarily the latter was concerned with the advance of ground forces, although there were air raids on Helsinki, whereas the former was worried about possible attacks from the air. In 1936 [3] Colonel Teacher[4], stated that the practicality of evacuation would depend on three considerations:-

a. The number of people to be moved something which was impossible to predict because of the number of people recruited to the German ARP (all those over 15 not in the services). Some would already have been called up, and children under 10 would stay with their families.

b. The time the movement was to take place.

c. The means of transport involved in the movement.

He recommended that some people should be allowed to find their own accommodation but people would have to satisfy the police that they had made arrangements for the care of their own homes before they left and significantly, bearing in mind the hidden agenda of Operation Pied Piper was to control panic, they would also need to get written permission from the police as it was felt that too much voluntary evacuation would turn into an uncontrolled exodus.[5]

However, it was not until the beginning of 1938 that the German Government developed specific plans for the evacuation of children under the age of 15 to the countryside.

In a secret directive to the leaders of the local Nazi party branches, Hitler set out their responsibilities during any evacuation:-

'..........This evacuation is a precautionary measure which is made necessary due to the proximity of the enemy's frontier. The task of the local branch leader is to convince the population of the

1 For a more detailed explanation of German/Finnish and Children of Collaborators. See Parsons. M. War Child. Children Caught in Conflict. History Press. 2008
2 Jeremy Noakes (ed) Nazism. Vol 4. Exeter University Press. 1998 p429
3 A series of articles appeared in 'Gasschutz & Luftschutz,' ('Gas Protection and Air Protection') the official magazine of the Reich Air Protection League in 1935-6, discussing the difficulties of evacuation.
4 An official at the Air Protection Department of the German Air Ministry,
5 TNA HO45/17636

necessity of these evacuation measures, to urge them to remain calm and to prevent any movement of refugees'.[6]

To pre-empt any disruption caused by possible raids, the Federal minister gave instructions to local 'air-raid protection leaders' and local school administrators on September 5th 1939 to prepare the evacuation of school aged children.

As the air war against Germany intensified the German evacuation scheme, known as 'Ewertite Kinderlandverschickung'[7] (KLV) was, according to Gerhardt Brook, instigated in September 1940 primarily for psychological reasons and used for the pacification of the population, who were shocked by experiencing the first bombs.[8]

On the 26th September Baldur von Schirach,[9] the former leader of the Hitler Youth was put in charge of the scheme and one of this first acts was to increase the influence of the Hitler Youth at the expense of the education authorities, particularly the 'National Socialist Teachers League'.[10] Hitler insisted that evacuation should be voluntary and as they were no longer needed, the teaching profession should be cut by half.

He was not concerned that such a measure would affect the education of German children[11] and ordered that the word 'Verschickung' should not be used and it should have the appearance of simply moving the children into the country. However, those teachers remaining in the profession were still expected to take a lot of responsibility for ensuring that some semblance of an education continued.

On the 27th September Martin Boorman issued a circular to party members in which he explained that young people who lived in areas which were subjected to repeated air raid warnings, particularly those who lived in areas with inadequate shelter provision, should be given the option of being moved to other areas of the Reich on a purely voluntary basis. Their teachers were to go with them in order to make sure that lessons continued. The children were to be dispatched in two group to reception areas which would include: Bavarian Eastern March, Brandenburg, Upper Danube, Saxony, Silesia, Sudetenland, Thuringia, Wartheland and Ostland. Those aged between 6-10 were to be housed with families and those 10-14 in Camps, youth hostels, inns or similar accommodation to enable the schools to maintain its identity. For those in their 5th year at school and above, the housing would be organised by the Hitler Youth while the NSV (Nationalsozialistische Volkswohlfahrt)[12] would be responsible for sending away pre-school children and children in school years 1-4. The NSLB (National-Socialist Teacher Association) would also be involved in the scheme which would come into effect on October 4th 1940.

Gauleiters in the evacuation areas were given responsibility for persuading parents to send their children away by sending them all letters explaining the details, and although there would be no propaganda or announcements in the press, there could be press releases in local papers in the reception areas advising the population of what was about to happen.

Using a Reich Law[13] introduced on September 1st 1939, Gauleiters and KLV representatives in the reception areas were able to start requisitioning hotels, hostels, and other suitable buildings. Initially they tried to place children of a specific social and economic background with equivalent hosts so the domestic circumstances of the children were listed on their register. However, as more children arrived in the reception areas this became virtually impossible.

---

6 Noakes op cit p60

7 'Sending children to the countryside'.

8 Gerhard Debit Brock. KLV Essay. Children in War Journal No 3. 2005

9 Baldur von Schirach was the former Reich Youth Leader. In June 1940 he was appointed Gauleiter of Vienna while retaining the title of 'Delegate for the Inspection of the Whole of the Hitler Youth'.

10 Nationalsozialistische Lehrerbund'

11'In reply to my question whether or not the evacuation of young people should be compulsory or voluntary the Fuhrer replied that the whole action should be on a voluntary basis. The number of teachers should if necessary be halved. I pointed out that in these circumstances regular instruction could not be absolutely guaranteed. The Fuhrer said that one would have to put up with that...' Notes from a meeting held between Shirach and Hitler 27th September 1940

12. National Socialist Welfare Organisation.

13 'Reichsleistungsgesetz'

All central government directives were cascaded down to local level via neighbourhood administrators, as this memo would indicate.

'In accordance with the Fuhrer's instructions.....Please begin at once with the recruitment of host families, since the children are expected to arrive in January. You should take note of the fact that the number allocated to you by the Gau Headquarters of the NSV in the enclosed letter must be adhered without fail...'

A great deal of pressure was applied to parents to send their children away and on a simple level warnings like these were common;

'While the children who are sent will have the best possible education from their own teachers, those who remain behind will have to expect to be transferred to a class containing a collection of children from other classes or to another school'[14]

The first batch of children left Berlin on 3rd October 1940 and travelled to Saxony.

At first only Berlin and Hamburg were involved,[15] and by the beginning of December

189,543 [16] children had been moved to either KLV camps or private homes. Although the reception areas were mainly in the north and east of the Greater Reich, there were also KLV camps in regions that had been annexed, including Hungary and Poland.[17] By November 1942, a total of 1,198,377 people had been transported by 1,654 trains and 78 ships on the Rhine and Weser rivers.[18] Of these, 335,409 were aged between 10-14, who were destined for KLV camps and 862,968 mothers and children who were being cared for by the Nazi Welfare Agency.[19]

While the schemes were being planned and implemented the German High Command were trying to assure the German population that they were not in any danger. In Hamburg the reasons for the children going away were given as the need to protect them during the winter. Nothing is said about the possibility of air-raids.

Hamburg 7th November 1942.

'.....It is the Gauleiter's strongly held wish that as many Hamburg children as possible should be protected against risks to health this winter. As is well known, up to now over 150,000 boys and girls from our city have spent six months at a time in southern Gaus and have had many happy experiences in the KLV camps. Experience has shown that their education can best be assured if they are sent away together as classmates.......Carefully selected efficient Hitler Youth and League of German Girls leaders support the teachers in their work and ensure that Hitler Youth duties are carried out in an exemplary manner.....'[20]

There was often a great deal of tension generated by the respective roles of the Hitler Youth and the teachers. Primarily the former dealt with the extra-curricular activities while the latter looked after the classroom, although it was often the case that the Hitler Youth over-exerted its authority in all matters relating to the evacuation.

'.........In response to a remark made by the district leader concerning our responsibility for the dispatch of the children, one of the BDM[21] *leaders declared that they were not teachers' skivvies*

14 G. Dabel, KLV. Die erweiterte Kinder-Land-Verschickung. KLV Lager 1940-45. Freiburg 1981 p 32. cited in Noakes op cit p428
15 Later other areas such as Dusseldorf, Koln and Hanover were involved in the scheme.
16 G.Hock 'Der Fuhrer sorgt fur unsere Kinder....' Die Kinderlandesverschickung im Zweiten Weltkrieg. Paderborn. 1996 p136
17 Gerhard Brock. Essay Notes.
18 Earl R.Beck. Under the Bombs. The German Home Front. 1942-45. University Press of Kentucky. p24
19 These 'evacuees' were issued with 127,000 tubes of toothpaste, 7,500 first aid kits, 9,900 musical instruments, 140,000 suits for boys, 130,000 suits for girls and 110,000 pairs of wooden shoes. This was in total contrast to the British scheme where no evacuees were given such official help with clothes and basic necessities. Although, a series of Ministry of Health circulars which arrived in the reception areas only six days before evacuation took place, did give permission to those authorities responsible for evacuating people from their areas, to buy boots, clothing and knapsacks up to the value of £1 for every 200 children, on the strict understanding that no publicity was given to such help.
20 The management structure in the KLV camps consisted of the following: Camp Head, Camp Team Leader, Deputy Camp Head, Camp teacher, Camp boys/girls section leader, Camp boys/girls group leader, Camp Matron, Personnel for maternal care, Bursar. Noakes. op.cit p433
21 League of German Girls (Maidens)

and that they received their instructions from the BDM alone. This negative attitude led to various tensions during the journey.........The BDM girls announced that they had the decisive authority in the KLV programme and the teachers were responsible for the school work....' [22]

The Hitler Youth appointed officials with specific responsibility for making sure that the reception of the children was problem free and unlike his British counterpart, the German equivalent to the billeting officer had the responsibility of not only visiting the children on a regular basis in order to make sure that all was going well, but also of organising at least two games sessions a week, or excursions, in order to take the pressure of the hosts. For their part, the hosts also had to make sure that the children kept in contact with their own families.

There was a special section in the *'Guidelines for the Reception of Children in Host Families on the Basis of Special Action',*[23] on how to deal with enuresis. No chronic bed-wetters were to be sent to host families but dispatched instead to unspecified *'alternative accommodation'*. Only those who wet the bed as a result of insecurity and changes in routine were to be tolerated, and then hosts would be given help on how to deal with the situation.

There were some problems relating to class divisions with some Berliners complaining that there was too much official concern for the welfare and safety of the middle classes. There was some truth in this as those people working in offices had priority over those working in the factories, and statistics show that more people were evacuated from the middle class areas to the west of Berlin than from the more working class north.[24] From the hosts point of view there were also complaints that their 'guests' sat around and did nothing except '*...while away their time in gossip, pram-pushing and raids on the meagrely stocked shops.*'[25] (Not dissimilar to the comments made by residents in some of the reception areas in Britain.) Complaints were also received in some reception areas where hosts were forced to take in people from towns further afield, yet were unable to take in those nearer to them geographically. This was evident in the Allgau district where residents were asked to take in evacuees from the Ruhr instead of Munich, an area where many of them had relatives.

As in Britain, there was a drift back of evacuees to their homes causing a great deal of concern. The numbers coming back from South Westphalia were so large that the 'home' authorities cancelled the returnees ration cards resulting in food riots! Some people were tempted back by the knowledge that those who had remained in the danger areas were given privileged treatment when food and rare consumer products were allocated.

Food rationing was another issue which created a certain degree of disquiet, especially when evacuees were hosted by farming families who, being registered as 'self-suppliers,' were excluded from rationing. Such evacuees not only ate better than their counterparts, but the food itself was often of a higher standard.[26]

Religion was often a problem within reception areas. In a situation similar to that of the Catholic evacuees from Liverpool being sent to non-conformist 'Chapel' areas of Wales, some evacuees from the Rhineland, who had been used to the National Socialist neo-paganism, were sent to villages in the Alpine regions still practising fundamental Catholicism. Even though the Hitler Youth was an anti-religious organisation children in the KLV scheme were allowed to attend church if they wished to in order to appease some of the parents. However in practice this was not always possible as the teachers, who as members of the NSLB would have nothing to do with church or religious groups, made it very difficult for the children to attend them. For example, Hamburg issued the following directive to teachers:

'....The KLV camps should be made to exercise the strictest possible reserve in confessional matters. On no account should there be any instruction by clergy, members of religious orders or

---

22 Noakes op cit p434-5
23 Issued on the 20th April 1940 by the NSV headquarters in Wurttemberg,
24 From July 1943 - October 1944 the child population in West Berlin was reduced by 66.9% compared to only 40.4% in North Berlin. Berlin. Kurt Pritzkoleit. Dusseldorf. 1962 p55
25 A Social History of the Third Reich. Richard Grunberger. Pelican. 1971 p56
26 In the beginning children were to be boarded free of charge but this proved to be difficult and on March 28th 1941, the rates ranging from 2 – 5.5 Reichsmarks per week were introduced depending on classification.
26 Claus Larass, Der Zug der Kinder. KLV-Die Evakuierung 5 Millionen deutscher Kinder im 2 Weltkrieg. Munich 1983. p102. cited Nazism. Noakes. Op.cit. p430

church representatives. On the other hand, there should of course be the closest possible cooperation with official agencies of the NSDAP' [27]

In September 1943, the author of a report on the progress of the KLV, commented: *'Churchgoers express the view that the whole point of evacuation is to separate the young people from their parents in order to teach them to become heretics in the camps'*.[28]

In February 1939, the Hitler Youth introduced the Youth Service Day, first implemented in 1940 it set out to challenge the position of the Churches by creating an elaborate induction ceremony for its 14 year old members. This was calculated to compete with Confirmation and First Communion services in the Protestant and Catholic churches. One girl described the event in her diary[29]:-

'......The ceremony took place in the market square. A huge platform covered in a shining swastika was erected in the middle and we recruits were lined up in rows of four in front of it. ....The swearing-in flag was carried in and then four of us had to step forward in helmets and rifles at the ready......We were then inspected by the Mayor...then came the swearing in. I have sworn loyalty to the German Flag and to Adolf Hitler'.[30]

As the allies bombing became more intense in the west, more evacuees and refugees, most of whom were children, were moved east into Saxony in the hope that they would be beyond the range of the bombers. In July 1943, Martin Mutschmann, the Gauleiter of the area, issued a secret communiqué to Burgomeisters of the major cities in the region, ordering them to assimilate individual evacuated children and whole schools and their teachers within existing establishments.

Basically there were two reasons for doing this. First; as the 1940 edict stated, it was easier to absorb whole schools because they would be with their friends and teachers Second, it made the implementation of National Socialist policies by the Hitler Youth and BDM, easier to carry out.

As in the Britain, many school buildings had already been taken over for other purposes so it meant that as the school populations increased in size,[31] teachers and pupils alike had to cope with extremely difficult and overcrowded conditions. As a result the authorities had to introduce double shift schooling in some areas with the effect that the education of both evacuee and indigenous pupils was affected, similar to the situation in Britain.

There was also another issue which had not been thought through. As many of the schools had been taken over for industrial and military use there was little in the way of shelter accommodation for the evacuees, a situation which was to become extremely serious in February 1945.

As a result of more intense bombing, especially around Hamburg and Bremen, more evacuees arrived, and by the end of 1943 the area was so saturated with incomers that the authorities could not take any more, and as a result the area became known as the Reichsluftschultzkeller, (The Reich's air raid shelter). This was a situation not dissimilar to many reception areas in the UK and the following comment, made by a local party official in Northern Bavaria in April 1944, could also have been said by some billeting officers in the Britain.

'.....It is always the people who've been bombed out who are responsible for the general mood. There are always some of them who have something to grumble about and are continually discontented. Big city people and country people simply don't suit each other. One woman says: 'we're left to starve here in the sticks'. Another complains that there's no entertainment here;

27 National Socialist German Worker's Party.
28 ibid p431
29 Anon diary account cited in Noakes op cit p410.
30 'I swear that I will serve the Fuhrer Adolf Hitler faithfully and selflessly in the Hitler Youth. I swear that I will always strive for the unity and comradeship of German Youth. I swear obedience to the Reich Youth Leader and to all leaders of the HJ. I swear on our holy flag that I will always be worthy of it. So help me God'.
31 As an example. The annual school intake in Dresden in 1940 was around 5,500 in 1943 it fluctuated between 8,500 and 9,000. (ref. Dresden. Frederick Taylor. pub. Bloomsbury. p139)

> *another says to the shopkeeper: 'I'll buy anything off you but not your Bavarian stupidity'. One often has to step in and sort things out.'* [32]

During the latter months of 1943, the authorities in this designated 'safe area' were becoming increasingly concerned about the closeness of the allied air raids,[33] and had been making secret preparations to evacuate the children again, so by November arrangements had been made to move them into the surrounding countryside.

In order to avoid unnecessary panic the general population was not informed [34] but secret documents were sent out to Head Teachers outlining the plans for dispersal. A few days later, the city of Leipzig, only sixty miles away from Dresden, was bombed and as a result, on December 6th , Head Teachers were given permission to inform their staff of the arrangements but ordered specifically not to use the word 'Evacuation', but 'Country Vacation' instead.

On the 9th the Gauleiter's office issued an 'Address to Dresden Parents' which stated:

> *'The danger exists that after his attack on Leipzig, the enemy will extend his aerial terror to other cities. In order to keep the losses as low as possible, it is planned to transfer school children from the most at risk cities to less threatened places.'* [35]

On December 11th and 12th meetings were held in schools to assure parents that this would be a voluntary measure and would only take place after the Christmas holidays, and encourage them to either send their children to friends or relatives in the countryside, or join the Government Scheme. Meanwhile newspapers were forbidden to mention the scheme so as not to incite any panic or unnecessary unease.

However, only 30% of the children in Dresden took up either option.

This lack of parental interest was not new. Although the movement of children from the Ruhr started in January 1941 it was met, as in other areas, with strong parental resistance. According to Gerhard Brock, only 40% of the school children eligible in the industrial city of Bochum were evacuated and only around 16,000 school children were moved on their parents' initiative to relatives and friends.[36] In the summer of 1943, the evacuee numbers increased in response to the four months continual bombing of the Ruhr and the fact that the schools in areas which were in particular danger had to be closed, and eviction orders had already been issued. However, parents were guaranteed that schooling would continue on the same lines in the KLV camps[37].

Despite the dangers, it was obvious that some parents were keeping their children at home and 20% of the total remained in the area throughout the war, even though Bochum was very heavily bombed[38]. Bochum was not the only city to demonstrate parental resistance as in the neighbouring city of Herne 41% of those eligible for evacuation remained. Quite simply, some parents did not wish to be separated from their children.

A report from the SD[39] issued on September 30th 1943, had already stated that the success of persuading parents to send their children away depended very much on the skill of the speakers involved. The fact that some of them, especially in Berlin, could not provide specific details about when and where the children would be relocated was affecting the numbers signing up. Even Goebbels praised the KLV scheme, and in order to allay parental fears the Propaganda Ministry produced films such as '*Hands Up*' which showed a rather romanticised view of camp-life.

The situation was not helped by the issuing of an order in the Saxony area forbidding mothers to travel with their children. The reasons given were that there would not be enough accommodation for the mothers, but the hidden

---

32 Noakes op cit p359

33 During 1943 the number of air raid alerts had totalled 52, by 1944 this had increased to 151. Taylor. op cit. p143

34 Very similar to concern that the working classes would panic in the UK if they thought there was a war coming. An issue which necessitated the Anderson Committee decisions being kept out of the public domain for as long as possible.

35 Martha Heinrich Acht: Dresden 1944/45. ed. Matthias Neutzner. Pub Dresden 2000 p23

36 Ibid

37 Circular from the Federal Minister for Science and Education 4th June 1943.

38 The first intensive raid began on the 14th May 1943 when 394 houses were destroyed and 302 people killed and the second, more devastating because of the ensuing fire-storm, occurred on the 13th June, resulting in widespread destruction and the deaths of 312 inhabitants.

39 Sicherheitdienst.

agenda was that as these children were to be the future of the Reich, the Party wanted control of them without undue interference from parents.

'Control' had always been the *not so hidden* agenda of German evacuation. Even the official policy of evacuating whole schools under the KLV scheme had a dual role; removing the children to safer areas and taking the children away from parental and, in some cases, religious influences.

Perversely, for this to work the State still needed support from the parents, and there was a genuine concern that some parents did not quite believe the humanitarian intentions of the authorities and were beginning to question their motives.

The State reacted to this by issuing a Directive in 1943 telling parents that what some of them were hearing about the scheme was simply a result of rumour-mongering and allied propaganda.

> *'Rumours have been spread in various Gaus in the Reich that the sending away of young people of school age is not purely a war-time measure but intended to remove from parents the education of their children and to place the boys and girls under the exclusive influence of the State and the Party. These rumours must be vigorously refuted. They are spread by enemy propaganda to disturb parents and are gladly passed on by negative elements among our people. The extended Kinderlandverschickung is of course a measure designed purely for the protection of the lives of German youth as a result of the air war.*[40] *After the war Kinderlandverschickung will be returned to its original purpose and will have the sole task of providing children with impaired health with the opportunity to recover'.*[41]

By mid January 1944, continued parental indifference was becoming a serious issue and the authorities issued a statement through the local press saying that if children remained in the cities, they would not be entitled to schooling. An order was sent to individual parents who had to acknowledge receipt of it and then make a decision to send their children away or not. In Bochum, all children between the ages of 9-13 who were still in the city, had to report to the Hitler Youth and then be sent on to a KLV camp. Non-compliance resulted in the parents being informed that they were deemed to have removed their children from compulsory education and would be subject to the legal consequences. But these threats did little to increase the numbers of children sent away, in fact rather the opposite. By February there were many reports of children already in the country now experiencing home sickness and expressing a desire to return to their families and despite the authorities closing down the city schools while keeping the ones in the country open, a gradual drift back to the cities began.

After the USAAF had bombed Freital to the south west of Dresden on August 24th 1944, more school meetings were called and the Ministry of Education compiled lists of those children who still remained in or had returned to the cities. These were now to be put to useful work through the Hitler Youth networks while at the same time teachers were ordered to make home visits to parents to 'persuade' them to send the children away.

A few weeks later everything changed. The National Socialist People's Welfare organisation in Berlin sent out a message to Dresden and other areas informing them that the concept of 'Total War' had been redefined and there were no longer any available resources to help in the protection of the civilian population. All financial and human assets were to be redirected towards the military war effort.

Consequently, all civilians would now have to fend for themselves in a country where civil authority was becoming more disrupted and disorganised as the months went on. Unfortunately, thousands of children still continued to pour into Saxony in search of safety, and many were in Dresden on the night of the 13/14th February when the heavy bombing and subsequent fire-storm resulted in thousands of deaths.

---

40 The desire for State control still resulted in those teachers in the KLV camp schools, who either disagreed with the policies or tried to dilute the National Socialist side of the curriculum being called up into the Wehrmacht and sent to the Eastern Front!
41 Hoch op.cit p308

Lack of actual numbers makes it difficult to be specific about how many children were involved in the whole evacuation process, but according to the estimates of Gerhard Dabel, the last leader of the KLV scheme, 2.8 million girls and boys between the ages of 10-18 were sent to 9,000 KLV camps. In addition, around another 3 million infants and mothers, and children between 6 –10 were evacuated under the KLV scheme. A most recent study suggests a lower total, but nonetheless the figure is around 2 million.[42]

The immediate result of the KLV scheme was that several hundred thousand of young children and adolescents were taken out of the cities considered to be targets, to areas of perceived safety. It was intended that in the designated reception areas they would live a relatively quiet life away from the psychological and physical impact of the air-raids. For some it was an adventure. However, as in any scheme of this kind, there was a down-side. There was the pain of homesickness, bed-wetting brought on by insecurity, the lack of facilities, the unfriendliness of some hosts, the lack of education, the neglect and the often brutal treatment meted out by the Hitler Youth and BDM leaders in the KLV camps.

Within all this state planning and control, there is a contradiction which has to be addressed by all historians investigating war children in Germany. They were at an impressionable age and had little experience of a pre-Nazi state and therefore, by necessity, were unable to adapt to the changes in their own lives and to those around them caused by the social, ideological, political and geo-political environment. Therefore, as in the case of the British and war-children in other parts of Europe, it is very difficult to generalise about the nature of their experiences. However, what can be said is that all their lives were intrinsically linked to the power of the totalitarian state. As Stargardt says in 'Witnesses of War':

> *'It was precisely what was irreconcilably different about their individual experiences that linked them together within the same system of rule in which officials badgered some parents to let them be evacuated to the safety of the countryside, while at the same time logging the transports that took others to be killed…'*[43]

Finland 'The Sotalapsi'

> *'The initial aims had been to save the human resources of Finland during a very difficult time and eventually have the children return in a good physical and mental condition so that they could re-build the country. So was it basically a question of population policy?'*[44]

Evacuation from Finland took place amid the backdrop of the Winter and Continuation wars against the USSR; wars which were to result in the movement of more than 80,000 children and have sociological and psychological effects for decades afterwards.

During the latter months of 1939, when it was thought that Germany would attack the USSR through Finland, the former suggested that the latter should accept military assistance from the Soviets. The Finns however, not wishing to negate their position of neutrality or lose their independent sovereignty by becoming part of the USSR sphere of influence, refused, stating that they would defend themselves against any enemy.

However, the Molotov-Ribbentrop, non-aggression pact between the USSR and Germany signed in Moscow on 23 August 1939 contained a secret protocol which declared that when spheres of German and Soviet influence were decided, Finland was to belong to the USSR.

> *'Secret Additional Protocol.*
>
> *Article I. In the event of a territorial and political rearrangement in the areas belonging to the Baltic States (Finland, Estonia, Latvia, Lithuania), the northern boundary of Lithuania shall*

42 Gerhard Brock. KLV Essay 2005
43 Stargardt. Witnesses of War. p381
44 Dr Martin Parsons. In conversation with Pertti Kaven. University of Helsinki and ex-war child.

represent the boundary of the spheres of influence of Germany and the U.S.S.R. In this connection the interest of Lithuania in the Vilna area is recognized by each party.'

In October 1939, at a meeting in Moscow between the USSR and a Finnish delegation, Stalin proposed a pact of mutual assistance, but again this was refused by the Finns. The Soviets were particularly interested in the Hanko Peninsular, the western part of the Karelian Isthmus and some of the outer islands in the eastern Gulf of Finland as a defensive 'buffer' for Leningrad from any attack from the west. As a result the Finnish military forces on the Karelian Isthmus were reinforced and the Finnish army was fully mobilised in October 1939.

By 30th November the USSR had lost patience, cancelled a non-aggression pact with Finland, broke off diplomatic negotiations and initiated a broad attack involving 460,000 men and 2,000 tanks, along the whole of the Finnish eastern border.[45] Simultaneously, bombers attacked Finnish cities including Helsinki, resulting in the deaths of 161 civilians.[46] The Soviet plan was to overcome Finland in two weeks, install a 'puppet' government in Helsinki called the 'Terijoki Government' and then establish the 'Democratic Republic of Finland'.

Field Marshal C.G.E. Mannerheim[47] was appointed C-in-C of the Finnish Defence Forces at a time when there was a shortage of everything, especially weapons and equipment. However, this was more than compensated by a strong sense of national unity known in Finland even today, as 'The Spirit of the Winter War'. The Finnish defence was very successful. Its full field army of 200,000 men (rising to 340,000 in February 1940) was deployed to defensive positions along the border. In December 1939, the Finns destroyed a large number of Soviet battalions and captured useful war material at the battles of Suomussalmi and Raate.

By February 1940 the Russians forces had increased to 1 million men with 3,000 tanks and 2,500 aeroplanes. In the same month the USSR started an attack on the Karelian Isthmus where their forces, concentrated on Summa, managed to break through the Finnish positions, forcing them to withdraw from the western part of the Isthmus. The situation became worse as the Russians attacked over the frozen Bay of Viipuri and advanced as far as the Viipuri-Hamina road, an area around which fierce battles continued until the end of the Winter War.

In response to a Finnish appeal to the League of Nations for war materiel and diplomatic and political support, the Soviet Union was expelled from the League and Finland received a great deal of support, including aid from the UK and the USA (despite the latter being neutral). This assistance was not entirely altruistic as the British government was concerned about Swedish iron ore falling into German hands. However, despite intense discussions in the British War Cabinet about sending an armed force to help the Finns, and the French commenting that '*the loss of Finland would be equivalent to the loss of a great campaign*'[48], little actually happened[49]. So, with military losses increasing and promises of Allied reinforcements and aid not forthcoming,[50] the Government in Helsinki had little choice but to sue for peace. On March 12th 1940, the Russo-Finnish Treaty was signed in Moscow.

The 105 day Winter War cost Finland a great deal as 20,000 soldiers died, 1,500 were declared missing and 45,000 were wounded. In addition, almost 500,000 Karelians had to be repatriated from the area ceded to the USSR, and Finland lost the cities of Viipuri, Kakisalmi and Sortavala. The Russians also took part of Kalastajasaarento, an island near Petsamo, to provide them with access to the Arctic Sea, and they leased Hanko as a military base for 50 years.

This was an uneasy peace and there was always a threat of a new war. Having accepted defeat in the Winter War and now geographically isolated from Britain by Germany's successes in the west, the Finns sought to counter

45 A total of 1200 km

46 Churchill War Papers. 'At the Admiralty' Vol 1 September 1939 – May 1940. Martin Gilbert Heinemann 1993. Footnote p445.

47 Baron Carl Gustaf Emil Mannerheim (June 4, 1867 – January 28, 1951) was the Commander-in-Chief of Finland's Defence Forces, Marshal of Finland, an astute politician and a successful military commander. He was the sixth President of Finland (1944–1946).

48 War Cabinet. Confidential Annex . Cabinet Papers 65/12. 12th March 1940

49 The Winter War actually attracted 11,000 volunteers, mostly from Sweden (although officially neutral).

50 Neville Chamberlain had proposed sending 3 armed divisions (15000 men) to Scandinavia to help the Finns, landing at Narvik (Operation Avonmouth) and at Trondheim, Stavanger and Bergen (Operation Stratford), proceeding overland through Norway and Sweden to Finland, occupying the Gallivare Iron-Ore mines on the way. He informed the war cabinet that the expedition should take place by 20 March 1940 'if we are to be sure of forestalling the Germans'.

further Soviet pressure by looking to Berlin for diplomatic and military support, and in June 1941 German troops were granted access to the country in advance of Operation Barbarossa, making Finland a co-belligerent with the Axis Powers.[51] Even so, the Finns were unwilling to be the aggressors so waited for the Soviets to declare war on them, which they did on 25th June 1941[52]. The Continuation War had begun.[53]

Throughout both conflicts, the movement of the children to safer areas in Sweden, Denmark and Norway was taking place.

The initiative for the evacuation came not from the Government but Maja Sandler, the wife of the Swedish Minister of Foreign Affairs Richard Sandler, and Hannah Rydh, the head of the Fredrika Bremer Association[54]. They established an organisation called *Centrala Finlandshjälpen* (The Central Help Organization for Finland) and contacted the Finnish authorities about the possibility of evacuating children to Sweden. The response from the Finnish Ministry of the Interior was not encouraging as rather than the Swedes providing support for children, they would have preferred war materiel instead.

Despite being rebuffed, the *Centrala Finlandshjälpen* held a press conference in Finland in December 1939 outlining their plans and inviting children to Sweden. As a result of this appeal, the *Pohjoismaiden Avun Suomen Keskus* (The Finnish Centre of Nordic Help), was established in Helsinki[55] with a remit from the Ministry of the Interior to organise the transfer of people from Finland to Sweden. The upper age at which the children could be transferred was set at 12, and mothers would be allowed to accompany their children if they were 3 years of age or under. Pregnant women and elderly people would also be included in the scheme.

It was significant that approval for the evacuation was given by the *Mannerheimin Lastensuojeluliitto* (The Mannerheim League for Child Welfare) and its founder, Marshal Mannerheim.

The first official 'child transports'[56] from Finland to Sweden left on December 15th, 1939. About 9,000 children, plus an additional 3,000 under the age of three were evacuated either with their mothers, or with the *Lotta*, a member of the Finnish voluntary women's organisation, as well as an estimated 3,000 children who were sent privately to hosts known to their parents. A few were also sent to Denmark and Norway, but the majority of these returned when both countries were later occupied by the Germans.

When the Winter War ended on March 13th 1940, and all but a thousand children (who were to remain in Sweden) returned to Finland.

There were political factors involved in the Finnish-Swedish evacuations and the Swedish Prime Minister, Hansson, was criticised for not doing anything to help the Finns, especially as the child transports had been the result of a personal rather than a government initiative. As a result of intense pressure, he nationalised the private committee which resulted in members of the Royal Family taking over the responsibility for the transports, and the Swedish government paying all the administrative costs. This humanitarian help suited Hansson very well as there was no risk of getting involved in the war, something which the government were greatly concerned about.

When the Continuation War began in June 1941, the official Finnish reaction towards continuing the transfers was again unenthusiastic. As in 1939, they would have much preferred to have received war materiel instead. Later, in September 1941 the Swedes not only offered to look after Finnish children but also promised to pay all the costs of transportation. The very pro-Swedish Finnish Minister of Social Affairs, Karl August Fagerholm[57]

---

51 The Winter War caused Hitler to begin to attack Norway and Denmark earlier than he had planned. In addition the performance of Russian forces during the winter war made Hitler critically underestimate their capabilities. A mistake which was to result in the heavy defeat during the invasion of Russia..

52 General Mannerheim called upon the people of Finland to take part in a Holy War against communism.

53 For details of the Continuation War see Appendix.14

54 Since 1884, the Fredrika-Bremer-Association (FBF) has led the debate on equality between men and women in Sweden.

55 Pertti Kaven 70 000 Precious Commodities. Keuruu: Otava, 1985 p41-45

56 This was the name given to the scheme by the Swedes.

57 Karl-August Fagerholm (31 December 1901 - 22 May 1984) was Speaker of Parliament and three times Prime Minister of Finland (1948–50, 1956–57, and 1958–58). Fagerholm became chairman of the Social Democrats after the armistice in the Continuation War. As a Scandinavia-oriented Swedish-speaking Finn, he was believed to be more in favour of the Soviet Union's leadership than his predecessor Väinö Tanner. However, during Fagerholm's post-war career he was opposed by both the Kremlin and domestic communists.

accepted the offer and the *Lastensiirtokomitea* ('The Committee for Transporting Finnish children to Sweden')[58] was established and given responsibility for organising the transportation of children out of the country. This was not an entirely altruistic gesture on the part of the Finns as they were concerned that had they had not allowed the child transfers, they might not have received any other war-related help from Sweden.

In the first instance only those children who were Karelian or the children of mothers who had gone back to Karelia to start rebuilding the area after the Winter War were allowed to go overseas. Others included those from areas where there was a shortage of food, children of war-invalids, children whose homes had been destroyed during the bombing raids, and war orphans. In 1942 the criteria were relaxed even further, and more children were allowed to go.

In December 1941, the Swedish relief organisations wanted to provide further help to those Finnish children considered to be in particular need. Nothin, leader of the organisation and a very influential political figure in Sweden, made an appeal to the Swedish Government asking for help to deliver food and clothes to children in Finland via the International Red Cross, but because of serious concerns regarding the possible contravention of Sweden's neutrality the Government did nothing and there are no notes in the files of the International Red Cross relating to any such activities by the Swedish authorities.[59] Hansson was not prepared to take any risks that would contravene the country's neutral status, an attitude supported to some extent by the Swedish Foreign Minister, Gunther, who stated that the country was ready to give Finland all the help possible '*within the limits of their resources and political interests*'. Yet in spite of the statement, humanitarian aid to Finland from relief organisations did not materialise.[60]

The evacuation of children during the Continuation War can be divided into two distinct phases. First, between September 1941 to June 1943, when approximately 22,000 children were sent to Sweden to ensure both the physical and mental health of young Finns and that future generations returning to Finland would be strong and in good health. Second in early 1944, when Helsinki was heavily bombed and there was the threat of a possible Russian occupation, 31,000 children, together with an estimated total of 15,000 who were evacuated privately, left the country. In total approximately 67,000 of whom around 5,000 children were sick, many suffering from tuberculosis and the effects of malnourishment. Additionally, 3,759 children went to Denmark; 850 in 1941, 2,606 in 1942 (580 returned during the same year) and 303 in 1943 (when 2,000 returned). During 1945, a further 364 children came home from Denmark.

Children went either by train, ship, or in some cases by aeroplane. But, as with the British children going overseas, their safety could not always be guaranteed. In January 1940, one of the ships carrying children was attacked by a Soviet submarine, but fortunately there were no child casualties, although one of the escort ships was destroyed and many sailors died.[61] Consequently transfer by ship ended, very soon to be followed by the cessation of air travel and trains as even the remaining rail transportation was not entirely safe. In March 1940, a train travelling north to Haparanda in Sweden collided with another one and as a result 15 children were killed.[62]

The journeys were also often arduous and traumatic for young children. In some cases it took ten days for them to get to their destinations as often they only travelled by night because of the possibility of air-raids, and once they arrived at the dispersal centres some, especially those who had been allocated to hosts in the countryside, had another long journey within Sweden itself. This also raised health issues as it was very easy for disease to spread among children in confined spaces. According to the Swedish National Board of Health in March 1944, some children died of diphtheria and other infectious diseases contracted *during* the transfer, and about 20% of the

58 The committee was to remain in place until 1948.
59 The reason for this could have been a fear of the rescinding of the so-called 'Gothenburg Traffic', whereby the Swedish marine fleet was guaranteed safe-conduct during World War Two by both the British and German navies. In addition, they may have been concerned about the possibility of British counter-measures had great amounts of food and other help been delivered to a co-belligerent of Germany. As Sweden got vital supplies via 'Gothenburg Traffic', including all her oil for her air-force and navy, it was vital that she was seen to be an independent nonaligned country.
60 The Swedish National Archive. The Committee to help Finnish children. The letter of Nothin. Signug B:1. Rockberger, Nicolaus: Göteborgs trafiken. 1973. Rockberger, Nicolaus: The Gothenburg Traffic. 1973.Pages 286-291)
61 Kaven op cit p22
62 ibid p22

children, who at the outset had been perfectly healthy, had to be hospitalised once they reached their destinations.[63] It is interesting to note that the Finnish National Board of Health did not have a regular member on the Committee for Transporting Finnish Children to Sweden, which could be regarded as a crucial absence in the planning of the whole operation.

These are found at all the stations where evacuees left to go to Sweden

By 1942, the Continuation War had become one of entrenchment and as a result the number of child transfers decreased. By 1943 about 9,000 children had already returned home, although even after the armistice was negotiated in September 1944, the majority of children remained in Sweden.

Although the evacuation of the children sounded good in theory, in practice it was not without its problems. They travelled in groups and were not separated until they got to their destinations. Those who arrived in Denmark already had their billets allocated, but as the pressure increased on the Swedish fostering authorities, the hosts went to distribution centres to collect their children, very similar to the situation in Britain. Again, not dissimilar to the UK, their stay in these centres was often upsetting. It was frequently the case that hosts took the small children and the fair-haired girls first, while the older dark-haired boys were left until last. The plan had also been that siblings would be billeted together, and where this was physically impossible they would go to foster homes which were close to each other. In reality, this was hardly ever the case and many were separated, not to see each other until after the war; a particular long term dilemma for those where one or more siblings had decided to remain in Sweden and the others return to Finland.

Throughout both the 'Winter' and 'Continuation' Wars, approximately 80,000 children, representing 2.1% of the Finnish population, left the country. It is worth noting that 8.6% of the total Finnish population comprised of children, and those below 14 years of age, 928,100, made up 25% of the whole population. Thus any movement of children within this age group was certain to have had some sort of effect on Finnish culture and way of life.

63 ibid p24

What was the final result of this 'Sotalapsi' operation? The initial aims had been to save the human resources of Finland during a very difficult time and eventually have the children return in a good physical and mental condition so that they could re-build the country. [64] So was it basically a question of population policy? It is now recognised that the medical treatment and improved nutritional programmes put in place in Sweden at the time, saved the lives of around 8,000 war-children. These included those suffering from tuberculosis who could not have been treated in Finland. As 7,000 children remained permanently in Sweden, either through continued fostering or adoptions, one could argue that Sweden also benefitted from the scheme at a time when their own population was declining.[65]

The War Child statue on the Border of Finland/Sweden.
The insert is the logo of the Finnish/Swedish war child organisation.

Other European Children

Leningrad

Little is written about the Russian children who were caught up in the siege of Leningrad. Recent research carried out by Professor Marina Gulina concentrated on the blockade exclusively through the eyes of children and adolescents. An estimated 641,000[66] people out of a total of 2.8 million[67] died during the siege which began on 8th September 1941 and lasted 900 days. There was little food[68], very little power, no heating and no water

64 As regards their general well-being, it has been found that the standard of health of Finnish war children raised in Sweden was more or less the same as that of their peers who grew up in Finland, but over the years the former have suffered more from psychosomatic symptoms. Interestingly the mortality rate of those who remained in the country was higher than among those who had gone to Sweden.

65. Dr Elgenmark, Olle: 'The treatment of sick Finnish children in Sweden'. Finnish Journal Huoltaja,1943 pp 439-444. and Dr Sourander, Bertil: 'Experiences of the evacuation of Finnish children to Sweden 1941-42'. Finnish Medical Journal Duodecim, 1942. pp 269-273.

66 Recent estimates have put this nearer 800000

67 Including c400k children

68 When food rationing was introduced in November 1941 an 'essential worker' received 250 grams of bread per day and non-essential and dependants 125 grams. Two months later this had been reduced to 125 grams for everybody.

except that collected from the River Neva and canals. Around 200,000 died of starvation and cold during the freezing winter of January-February 1942 when temperatures reached minus 40C.

When the siege was lifted on 27th January 1944, only 560,000 inhabitants had survived and remained in the city. As many of these were children, the trauma they experienced at the time has remained with them throughout their lives, and some are only now beginning to come to terms with it. According to Prof. Gulina the children experienced at least two traumas of such severity that few children of a similar age in different circumstances would be able to cope with them. First they included those relating specifically to the individuals themselves such as: pain, hunger, cold, loneliness, dependence, isolation, and danger from other adults; Second, a fear that the mother, or any other person responsible for the child's welfare might not return from work or an errand. According to her findings 'fear for the other' takes precedence over 'fear for one's self'.

It is impossible for the vast majority of people today to empathise with the emotional problems that these children and their mothers went through at the time. Since the war many of the 'siege children', like their contemporaries in other war zones, have been affected by severe depression, lack of self-worth and restricted personal development and some are only able to cope with the effects, and certainly the acute depression, by reverting to various forms of aggression.

The research shows that siege survivors see self-reliance as an important factor in their survival. As a result they now demonstrate a sense of responsibility, are more strongly drawn into contemporary social life, and are able to adapt to the changing conditions in the society around them.

The Netherlands

The Children of Collaborators[69]

Another group of war-children, largely ignored in war-time social histories, are those who suffered, and continue to suffer, because of the beliefs and behaviour of their parents; the offspring of collaborators. To what level parental collaboration actually took place was very much up to the specific circumstances and individual involvement, but generally they were members of the population who were deemed to have worked with, slept with, or gained financial, social and political benefit from the occupying forces. However, one needs to recognise the fact that the Germans could not have administered the Greater Reich without local support. After the war, even the head of German security in Amsterdam claimed that, *'the main support of the German forces in the police sector and beyond was the Dutch police. Without it, not ten per cent of the German occupation tasks would have been fulfilled'*[70].

One area of occupied Europe which to some extent has now come to terms with its 'collaborative' past, is The Netherlands, largely through the work of the Herkenning ('Recognition') group[71]. At the end of the war over 200,000 Dutch people were investigated as collaborators, 50% of these were imprisoned, some for as little as being seen to give the Nazi salute. 17,500 civil servants lost their jobs and 40 people were executed. What this has led to is a generation of Dutch people, many of whom have now retired, who have had to live their lives under the shadow of being a 'child of a collaborator'. Many of their present problems can be traced back directly to their parents either being members of the Dutch National-Socialist Party (NSB)[72] or expressing a sympathy for German National Socialist policies. When the war ended, and non-party members needed a focus for their anger, the collaborators and their families became the obvious group on which to project all the resentment for the negative experiences that they had gone through.[73] Gonda Scheffel-Baars, herself the daughter of a collaborator,

69 For a more detailed account of Children of Colloborators see War Child. Parsons op cit.

70 Tony Judt. Postwar. A History of Europe since 1945. Pimlico 2007 p39

71 Herkenning was founded in 1981 by a journalist, a member of the clergy working on radio, a psychologist and a psychiatrist.

72Nationaal Socialistische Beweging

73 The German occupying forces surrendered on May 6th 1945, the NSB was outlawed and Mussert and other members of the NSB were arrested. Only a few were convicted, including Mussert, who was executed on May 7th 1946. Most of those who were eventually convicted were given a 3-year or a 5-year sentence and all the collaborators lost their Dutch nationality and their right to vote for a period of ten years.

states that by transferring and projecting guilt onto this group '....*(the Dutch) could prevent themselves from seeing their own lack of courage during the war, their accommodation to the occupiers and turning a blind eye to the dramatic decrees that led to the elimination of the Dutch Jews'.* [74]

When the allies liberated the southern provinces of the Netherlands, many Party members and their relatives were arrested and taken to internment camps. Small children often accompanied their mothers but many of the older children were left behind. Some were looked after, by relatives, neighbours or friends, somewhat reluctantly as they did not want to be stigmatised for providing help. Some of these children had to express their gratitude by doing domestic chores, or in some cases providing sexual 'services'.

Many children found no shelter at all and had to be found temporary respite in children's homes[75] which were often in schools, barracks or vacant houses where there was little in the way of personal and material comfort, food, clothes or beds.

An additional problem was that many of the women who agreed to help in these homes were ill-equipped to deal with the emotional problems of their charges[76] and few provided anything resembling tender loving care[77] but instead took revenge on the children for the years of suffering under the occupation. As a result, many of the children felt abandoned and alone and were left to fend for themselves.[78]

During the war, hundreds of Dutch children had stayed in Germany, Austria and Czechoslovakia, some as part of the KLV scheme and others employed on the land. However, when they tried to return to the Netherlands at the end of the war, often on foot, they were prevented from entering at the borders and were subjected to intense interrogation about their possible Nazi sympathies. When some eventually reached their homes they found them either closed up or other people living in them, and it was often very difficult for them to discover the whereabouts of their parents and family.

A split became apparent in Dutch society between the estimated 5% of the population who had been collaborators and the other 95%, comprised of the 5% who had been active in the resistance and the 90% who had just attempted to survive the war. This divide was to have a significant effect on the lives of collaborator's children for many years. Gonda recalled what happened when she and her family were forced to walk to a provisional internment camp in April 1945;

> '.......*The inhabitants of the village stood alongside the road shouting 'traitors' and spitting at us.........They did not ask themselves whether the women and children were guilty or not. That is the moment that they threw us out; we were 'expelled' by our own people. Over the years I have overcome my feelings of guilt and shame, but never managed to feel Dutch. I resented them becoming our oppressors...'* [79]

It is interesting to note that the Dutch label of 'Bad' or 'Wrong' goes beyond the normal recognised meaning. The 'good' did not consider the 'bad' to have made the wrong choice of political allegiance, but they were simply 'wrong'. Even those who had been members of the original NSB and had then resigned their membership in protest of the party policies were still labelled as wrong. According to Gonda if one's membership of the party becomes known, even today, one is labelled with 'Wrong' - which amounts to a life sentence. Although now in retirement, she has come to terms with her own feelings by reflecting that

---

74 Gonda Scheffel-B aars. The Role of Dutch Society in the victimisation of collaborators children. Children in War Journal. Vol 1 No.4 p106. DSM December 2006

75 The Bureau Bijzondere Jeugdzorg had the responsibility for looking after the children of NSB families and it supervised many children's homes from its headquarters in Den Bosch.

76 Paul Mantel and Gonda Scheffel-Baars, N.S.B.-kinderen in tehuizen, (Collaborators' Children in Children's Homes), MA dissertation

77 Some of the homes did provide a semblance of support for the children. One in particular 'Huize Lievenshove', a converted large villa, is remembered by one former war-child:-
'The leaders tried to do something special, even though food was scarce, especially if one of the children had a birthday. There was always a nurse in the room during the night and the Matron tried to maintain a personal relationship with us all. The majority of children and staff were Roman Catholic, but one of the Protestant nurses used to tell stories and sing songs to the Protestant children on Sunday mornings.....'

78 As in post-war Germany children over the age of 10, i.e. those who may have been tainted by the political allegiance of their parents, were forced to take part in a re-education programme in democracy. However, it was delivered in such an authoritarian way, that it defeated the object.

79 Personal conversation with the author September 2009.

> '*...as soon as I started coping with my war-related problems, I knew that my feelings of guilt were not well founded, because I was not responsible for my father's guilt.....but knowing and feeling are two different phenomena*',

She nonetheless commented on the opinions of a Dutch journalist, who stated that a collaborator is never able to disassociate himself from his former ideals and past. *"Once a collaborator, once 'wrong', always 'wrong'"*; unfortunately, according to Gonda the opinion of many Dutch people today.[80]

Many never found any escape from the stigma, and even those who moved to townships where their past could be hidden, lived in permanent fear of the inhabitants finding out about their background. For many, the simple solution was to remain silent. Previous 'official' isolation now became self-isolation simply for pragmatic reasons and although some of the children gradually became physically integrated into a community they rarely did so emotionally. Instead they simply internalised the rejection of the Dutch people to themselves, or even their parents and in consequence remained outsiders and 'different'.

Although there are no accurate figures it can be assumed that there were between 200,000-300,000 children of Dutch collaborators who were to be socially abused, denigrated, harassed and dehumanised for something that was neither their own fault nor of their own making. Few would remain unscathed.

Norway[81]

One other country which felt the full impact of German occupation, and consequently the long term effects of collaboration is Norway. According to Professor Baard Borge[82], there are at least 100,000 people in Norway today who are children of parents who belonged to the Nasjonal Samling (NS)[83] party during the war, the collaborationist movement led by Vidkun Quisling, a name now synonymous with 'collaboration' and 'traitor'. Pre-war, other established political groups saw it as an offshoot of German National Socialism and refused to have anything to do with it and by the time war broke out the party was little more than a sect on the fringes of Norwegian politics. However, during the German occupation the NS became the official party and formed a 'puppet' government. In a Hitler Decree of 24th April 1940, Reichskommissar Josef Terboven [84] was entrusted with the executive power in Norway, relating to civilian affairs, and was answerable only to the Fuhrer, General von Falkenhorst [85] exercised military control over all the other German institutions in the country. Quisling was not given a formal political position until 1st February 1942, when he became Minister President in a NS government.[86]

Many of the children who were brought up in NS households were labelled 'NS-barn' (NS-child) and, as such, experienced problems growing up in post-war Norway because their parents were considered to be 'Quislings' or traitors. Today, many of the NS-barn still remain silent about their past for fear retribution or ostracism, a dilemma which has been recognised by some social scientists within Norway; '*....there can be no doubt that the NS-children got an unfair and painful childhood.*'[87] One such 'child' Kari Berle stated; '*We still fear being condemned and rejected because of our parents, just like many of us have experienced throughout childhood*'.[88]

---

80 Gonda Scheffel-Baars. The Role of Dutch Soc. op.cit

81 Again...for a more detailed account of the children of collaborators in Norway and of those who were the result of war-time liaisons between German soldiers and Norwegian women, see Parsons. M. War Child. History Press. op.cit.

82 Prof Baard Borge. Harstad University. Norway.

83 Norwegian for "National Gathering" or "National Unity" the NS was a fascist party in Norway, between 1933-45. It was founded by former Defence Minister Vidkun Quisling and a group of sympathisers such as Johan Bernhard Hjort, who was to lead the party's paramilitary wing the Hird for a short time before leaving the party in 1937.

84 Josef Terboven. 1898-1945 was basically dictator of Norway during the war years. Although he had no authority over the occupying forces, he did have control over 6000 'militia' which included 800 members of the secret police. He committed suicide by blowing himself up on 8th May 1945.

85 Von Falkenhorst 1885-1968 was dismissed from his command in Norway on December 18, 1944 for opposing the policies of Josef Terboven. After the war he was tried by a joint British-Norwegian military tribunal for violating the rules of war. He had passed on the Führerbefehl known as the Commando Order which required captured saboteurs to be shot. He was convicted and sentenced to death in 1946 but the sentence was later commuted to 20 years' imprisonment. He was released on July 23, 1953 due to bad health and died in 1968.

86 Other important ministers were Jonas Lie who as Minister of Police was head of the Norwegian wing of the SS from 1941, Dr. Gulbrand Lunde Minister of "popular enlightenment and propaganda", Albert Viljam Hagelin Minister Domestic Affairs.

87 Jarl Eik and Stein U. Larsen ed The Aftermath of War. Oslo 1999. p259

88 NS Child. Kari Berle. Dagbladet 3. June 1996. Cited in The Norwegian NS-Children. Baard Borge.

As in the Netherlands, a great deal of stigma is still attached to being on the '*Wrong*' side during the war and there are a number of people in the country who feel that concentrating research on the predicament of the children on the 'wrong' side, is disrespectful to those on the 'good' side who fought in the resistance. In response to such comments, Borge states that one of the reasons why research *should* be focused on NS-children is actually for their own well-being. As many of them have remained silent over the years they may have grown up feeling that they were the only ones tainted with the sins of their fathers, whereas in truth, there are many thousands in the same situation. In a similar situation to their peers in the Netherlands, some became and remain the scapegoats in order to moderate some of the guilt felt by those who perhaps consider that more should have been done in terms of resistance. For others the act of attaching blame has become something of a cathartic reaction.

As Borge points out, many older Norwegians who lived through the war still hold negative feelings towards the Quislings and their children. One correspondent stated that; *'...regrettably, my generation, whenever we encounter, or read of individuals who were on the wrong side, we 'ignite' right instantly. This can also be the case as far as their children are concerned, I am sorry to say'*.[89]

Many NS-children have suffered discrimination over the years in areas such as employment and housing, a situation which is slightly baffling when one considers that in relative terms the German occupation of Norway and the imposed NS regime was not as repressive as in other parts of the Reich.[90]

According to new research[91], one reason for this could be that civil resistance against the Nasjonal Samling manifested itself in the form of a social boycott by those who were not members of the party, resulting in known NS members in local communities being ostracised. This not only included the adults, but their children as well, as 'non-party' children were forbidden to play and associate with 'party' children. In addition, at the end of the war it was deemed a criminal offence just to have been a member of the NS, even if an individual's role had been a passive one. As a result many thousands of children grew up in post-war Norway with parents who were now legally convicted traitors. There was also a need for a post-war social identity which meant that those who had sided with the enemy were no longer considered part of a country which had stood up to the invader. The opposite of *'loyalty'* was therefore considered to be '*treason*'....hence the discrimination.

According to a recent survey[92], almost 66% of former NS-children believe that their lives had been made more difficult by the fact that their parents had been members of the NS although 21% said that it had had no effect at all. Also, 53% had been regularly bullied at school, whereas 38% had not.[93] Although most of them rated their education as 'good', many NS children did explain that they had been concerned whenever the topic of the war or the NS was raised in class. Significantly the research indicates that the effect of the NS on their lives depends very much on when the child was born. Only 10% of those children born after 1955 complained that their lives had been seriously affected because of parental links to the party, against 86% of those born between1930 and 1939. [94]

One of the common concerns among children born after the war is discovering in later life that their parents had been members of the NS and then unwittingly being drawn into a political and sociological debate which they now find difficult to cope with.

In recent years there has been a willingness in Norwegian political circles to put 'right' a number of historical 'wrongs'. For the past 20 years, media investigations, television and press interviews and the search by some of the children for their German fathers, have kept the topic in the public domain.

---

89 Terje Herrem. 9th April 2001 cited Borge. op cit.

90 To a degree, the German leniency may have resulted from the Norwegians' high standing within the racial hierarchy of National Socialism. In a written instruction carried by Wehrmacht soldiers during the 1940 campaign in Norway, residents were to be seen on a par with the farmers of Friesland (Friessen) in Germany. Like elsewhere in occupied Europe, food was sometimes scarce and frequently of lesser quality than in normal times. But, unlike the situation in many other occupied areas, civilians never starved, even though the country was dependent on import of food and other vital commodities from Germany and occupied Denmark.

91 By Baard Borge

92 The following figures are taken from a recent pilot study carried out in Norway by Baard Borge. I am indebted to him for allowing me access to this material.

93 As with UK, Finnish and Dutch war children one has to take into account what they would recognise as bullying or harassment. As this would depend very much on their individual circumstances and experience it is very difficult to generalise. Another factor is quite simply what criteria are used for such behaviour. What might well be considered bullying and harassment today would have been common place in the 1930s and 1940s, so any action has to be seen within its historical and sociological context.

94 However, the figures show that even up to 1949, 77% of the children had been affected 'absolutely' or 'partially' by the association with the NS.

However, one particular incident created a great deal of interest and resulted ultimately in pro-war-child legislation being passed in the Norwegian Parliament. On 15th March 1998, it was reported in many of the national newspapers that West Germany had given Norway a reparation payment in 1956 to the equivalent of £10 million which was to be shared among those people who had suffered as a direct result of the war, including the children of German/Norwegian liaisons. It then transpired that the latter had never received any of this compensation because it had been confiscated by the government at the time.

In 1998, an enquiry led by Kare Olsen found that over a period of time, state and local officials had systematically discriminated against war children and their mothers, and a more comprehensive investigation carried out during 2001-5, reached the same conclusion and laid the blame squarely on the government. The children were now seen by many Norwegians as victims and seven of the war-children sued the State of Norway for contravening their human rights. Although the case failed on the grounds that it was 'outdated', the reporting of it raised public awareness and it became a serious political issue. In January 2000 in his Millennium address, Prime Minister Kjell Magne Bondevik, made an unreserved apology to the war children on behalf of the State. This was followed up by one from the Parliamentary Justice committee in December 2002 and in April 2005, after a heated debate on *how much* rather than *if* compensation should be paid, a Reparation Law was passed by the Norwegian Parliament....almost 60 years to the day that World War II ended.

France

From previous experience, the French government had realised the possible vulnerability of Paris from an air attack in the case of any future war and had organised a civilian evacuation of the city as early as February 1931[95]. Marshal Petain, as Inspector General of Aerial Defence for France, established a plan which was based on the premise that 1 million citizens would leave voluntarily. The information about evacuation was to be contained in 1.5 million leaflets which were to be distributed throughout Paris.

The Scheme was to take 2 forms:-

LONG RANGE: Those persons who did not have public or private duties to fulfil or whose presence in the city was not essential were to be removed to areas as far away as possible from the vulnerable centre. Their departure was to be implemented at the first threat of war and they were to remain in their reception areas throughout the duration of hostilities. It was estimated that two days' mobilisation would be enough to remove 200,000 citizens from the area, although the actual numbers were to be decided by the Mayor of each district. Billeting arrangements were to be organised by the Prefects of the Departments in the reception areas approximately 150 kilometres to the South-West of Paris.

Each person who was to be permanently evacuated would be issued with a card which doubled as a rail ticket. On it would be marked the name of the billeting area, entraining and detraining stations, the day and time of departure and the number of trains. Transport was also arranged in the reception areas to take evacuees from the train stations to their billets.

SHORT RANGE: This evacuation was to be either permanent or on a daily basis. However, it was not to be implemented during an air-raid warning. This daily evacuation, affecting 250,000 Parisians,[96]was primarily concerned with the officials, shopkeepers, tradesmen and other workers who had to work in a vulnerable area during the day but who could leave at night to join their families.

Unlike residents in the UK who had been given Anderson or Morrison shelters, or access to adjacent street shelters, Parisians were advised to construct their own air-raid shelters in their gardens or where possible to take shelter in the Metro, should the need arise.

95 British document dated the 17th December 1937 headed ARP Intelligence Branch.
96 Exeter Blitz. Box 16 Group O 188. Devon Record Office.

The French evacuation scheme was tested briefly during the Munich crisis and it became obvious to the organisers that it needed to be greatly improved.

In line with the original plans of earlier years, the idea was to send the non-combatant population of the 25 Departments closest to Germany and those in the cities of Paris, Lyon and Marseilles to those areas which the planners presumed would be well away from any military operations. This movement was to be done entirely by rail, which as it turned out, was to cause a great deal of congestion.

On the 31st August 1939, the same day that 'stand-by' orders for evacuation were issued in London, 16,313 Parisian school-children were evacuated from the city on 27 trains. [97] The main evacuation took place on Friday September 1st.

Notices and leaflets informed the French population in the designated areas that they could only take 30 kilos of belongings per person, but this had to include bedding, a cooking pot and food for three days. Rather than the paper and cardboard luggage labels draped round the necks of British and Finnish evacuees, French children under the age of 7 were to have their labels containing personal information sewn into their clothes.

As evacuation was to be by train only, many people who lived some way from the designated assembly points were required to travel long distances to reach them which meant that roads became congested with tractors and trailers and walkers, some pulling handcarts. Over time, the routes became littered with abandoned carts, bicycles, excess baggage and pets. Once they arrived at the stations the sheer enormity of moving so many people meant that there were long waits for overcrowded trains.

Not all evacuees were welcomed in the reception areas. According to Lynn Nicholas, 250,000 inhabitants of Strasbourg were evacuated to the then primitive region of the Dordogne. Speaking their Alsatian/German language they were referred to by the locals as '*boche*'[98]. Their designated lodgings lacked the basic services such as electricity and running water and amenities like beds and cooking stoves, and they were expected to cook on tripods with stew pots hanging over open fires. [99]

Food distribution became a problem, especially butter and milk, and finding a job in the area was almost impossible. While the threat of invasion existed people were willing to accept the hardships, but as time went on and nothing happened, the locals became less tolerant of the incomers who seemed to spend their time sitting in cafes and on benches.

The situation in the capital was slightly different, especially for those who had been moved only a short distance away. Rather than put up with the privations in the reception areas it was easier to return home. However, 520,000 of those who did leave the city did not return and remained in the country.

After a short time, with nothing happening on the war front apart from a few air-raid warnings, the Parisians were becoming less inclined to take precautions[100]. The Paris blackout was not implemented fully and restaurants began to reopen, although sometimes just in the basement. Although there was a semblance of rationing, it was rather odd as one visiting Cabinet Minister, on a designated 'meatless day' had to 'make do' with oysters and grilled sole. [101]

Life in France returned to an air of normality, some schools were reopened and horse racing and dancing was now permitted, although events with the potential of attracting large crowds in confined stadia were banned because of the potential loss of life in an air raid. Ski resorts remained open in the mountains and hotels on the

---

97 The process was not without its problems. The Mayor of Chartres was expecting children from two schools but eighteen schools arrived causing serious logistical problems for the local authorities.

98 This was a term of abuse that had originated in World War I, and was aimed collectively at German soldiers.

99 Lynn Nicholas. Cruel World. The Children of the Europe in the Nazi Web. Vintage. 2005 p174

100 It is interesting to note that although it was reported in January 1940 that France was way ahead of Britain in terms of home front organisation, Colonel Baldwin-Webb the Conservative MP for Wrekin, Shropshire returned from a fact-finding tour of the country where he found there was virtually no blackout, no evacuation and no rationing. As a result of his trip he questioned whether Britain was justified in applying stringent home-front controls thought necessary for safety Reported in Dorset Daily Echo 12 January.1940

101 ibid p175

south coast were preparing for an influx of overseas holiday makers. All of which was to come to an abrupt end when the German infantry crossed the Meuse River on 13th May 1940.

The occupation of France for the next four years by an enemy force comprising somewhere between 400,000 and 1,000,000 of men between the ages 20 and 40, was to have some long-term consequences. Although sexual relations between the German soldiers and French women were forbidden, because the latter were considered to be of 'inferior race', they did of course take place. Many of the women became pregnant by such liaisons and were left to fend for themselves when their German lovers were deployed elsewhere[102]. Some sought abortions and many simply 'disappeared' for a while until after the baby was born.

In December 1941, Vichy brought in legislation which allowed women to have their children anonymously. This meant that it has been difficult to calculate the actual numbers of German/French children, as not only were there serious consequences for anyone violating the confidentiality of the woman, but after the birth the babies were usually put up for adoption. As a result it has been impossible for some of these children to find out who their birth mothers were.

Some women kept their babies and in some areas special facilities were established to deal with them. In October 1941, the Prefect in Cozzèze reported the development of *'a secret maternity hospital for pregnant prisoners-of-war wives'* and estimated that there were 300 such pregnant women in his area.[103]

Fabrice Virgili interviewed a small number of children of German soldiers (*enfants de Boches*) and has estimated that there were 120,000 – 200,000 German/French children born during the occupation.[104] These children were of great concern to Vichy, and to some extent the German authorities. However, little was done to provide for them.

Life could be hard for children with German fathers, both within their families where some children were abused by their own parents because they were a living reminder of the mother's guilt, and were often disowned by their grandparents who had lived through the First World War and now found themselves with a German grand-child, and in their local communities where their background was known and where they often called '*boche*' or '*fritzouille*'. Many suffered from serious depression and some attempted suicide. Some of Virgili's interviewees described themselves as *'....guilty for being born'* another *'....the teacher really emphasised the brutality of the Germans, the monstrousness (sic) of these barbarians, and she kept reiterating it throughout the entire lesson, so that I felt she was speaking to me, singling me out'*.[105]

In '*Enfants Maudits'*, (Cursed Children), Jean-Paul Picaper provides a number of examples of how the *'fils de boche'* were treated by people in their neighbourhood. One interviewee, Daniel Rouxel, who was forced to sleep in a locked chicken coop because his grandmother was so ashamed of his birth, described a situation where a local official forced him to stand up at Mass and asked him, *'Do you know the difference between the son of a boche and a swallow? I'll tell you: The swallow takes its babies with it when it leaves France. But the boche leaves them behind.*'[106]

Although there has been some assimilation, France, unlike Norway and the Netherlands, has yet to really address the problems of its war children. It is a delicate subject and as such is affected by individual experiences, personal reactions and, in some cases, guilt. Few speak out and remain silent, usually out of respect for the mother and, in some cases, for the original father who may still be alive.

At the Liberation it was relatively easy to purge the memory of the so called *'collaborateurs horizontales'* by the ritualistic shaving of the women's heads,[107] but at the very time that this was happening, the government and

---

102 In some cases these encounters had taken place while their husbands were being held by the Germans as Prisoners of War therefore, these women not only had to live with the moral condemnation of having slept with the enemy, but at the end of the war they were also labelled as traitors of France.

103 Virgili, Fabrice (2005) "Enfants de Boches: The war children of France" in Ericsson, Kjersti and Simonsen, Eva (eds.) Children of World War II. The Hidden Enemy Legacy. Oxford and New York: Berg Publishers, p.142

104 ibid p144

105 ibid p147

106 ibid p144 reported in Reuters 1st June 2004.

107 Although in some places it went beyond that. Some were tortured, one woman was kicked to death in Paris and others were stripped, tarred and forced to walk through the streets. Unfortunately, some of these incidents involving these women were simply a way of 'settling old scores' and had nothing to do with collaboration at all.

French society as a whole were condemning the children of such 'collaboration' to the shadows. Fathered by the enemy and ignored by their country, these children, now in their 70s, are still very much the invisible victims of war.

BBC Schools Broadcasts and Children's Hour

The Impact of the BBC

' Schools Broadcasts: The reason why so many adults were listening to the programmes was because; they really enjoyed them...for instruction...and to keep abreast of the children because they listen at school. As a consequence there was a suggestion that they should be repeated in the evening.' [1]

'......I understand from our Education Officer that school inspectors consider that Children's Hour can play a valuable part in bringing children in off the streets during the early black-out hours of the winter months. This should be a strong point in pressing for an extension of time....'[2]

' It may never have been realised just how vital and fulfilling Children's Hour was during the war years. Children had the permanence of a regular programme which assumed higher status than ever before in the listening habits of the nation. One writer in the Listener referred to Children's Hour as an 'abiding consolation' Derek McCulloch [3]

The two most important personal radio communications in wartime Britain, aimed specifically at children in the cities, the reception areas, and in schools were Children's Hour and those broadcast for educational purposes.

First introduced in April 1924 with the belief that *'broadcasting could bring great teachers to permeate the elementary school with the standards of the Universities,'* [4] Schools programmes, described by one head-teacher as *'lifebuoys in a queer, turbulent, scholastic sea'*,[5] continued to be broadcast throughout the war to an increasing number of schools, despite the problems of evacuation. Notwithstanding the obvious problems of maintaining continuity in education the BBC tried, as much as possible, to keep broadcasting programmes specifically for schoolchildren, including some foreign language lessons which were later abandoned.

By the late 1930s many schools in the London County Council area were being encouraged to make use of the radio. A report on broadcast lessons in London Elementary Schools in 1937 stated that *'.....they should be unique, fascinating, dramatic, coloured and new, coming as it were from a world which teachers and pupils without their help cannot enter. The broadcaster should not be concerned primarily with teaching the facts; rather he should use all the resources at his disposal in order to provide stimulating educational experiences for his listeners'*.[6]

Immediately prior to the war, when emergency broadcasting arrangements were considered in greater detail, the BBC decided that two hours each day should be allowed for Schools Broadcasts. As a result, arrangements were made in advance for an emergency programme which was designed to meet the conditions likely to be apparent in the first few weeks of a war. This programme was brought into operation on the 6th September 1939 and continued until the 22nd. The broadcasts were simpler and contained more entertainment than the normal fare. Moreover, many were specifically aimed at helping town children who had been evacuated to the countryside, understand and respect their new environment.

---

1 ADVISORY COMMITTEES SBC Exec Comm. Minute Book Appendix File1A 1939-40 R6/104/1 Adults and Schools Broadcasting. Confidential Report. BBC Archive. Caversham. Reading.
2 Nan Macdonald. Children's Hour North. Letter to Derek McCulloch, 'Mac', 12th November 1939
3 BBC Children's Hour. Wallace Grevatt. Book Guild 1988 p111
4 Ian Hartley. Goodnight Children Everywhere. Midas Books 1983. p74
5 ibid
6 ibid p76

Reports sent to the BBC from various interested parties indicated that, taking into account the changed conditions[7] both in the schools and in the studio, schools would be sufficiently settled by 25th September to justify the introduction of a schedule as near to the normal pre-war programming as possible. The line-up was planned to meet the needs of the many schools that were at the time working in shifts. In addition, because of the emphasis which the Board of Education had now placed on speech and the power to use and understand words, more time than usual was given to the study of English. In view of the change to a single broadcasting programme, it was not possible to include certain subjects which were considered to be of minority appeal, with the result that Modern Languages and Welsh broadcasts were not in the Autumn Term timetable.[8]

The changes made to the programmes from September to December 1939 were designed to create a high degree of familiarity, and the evidence received from schools[9] suggested that the more 'normal' they became, in terms of routines, timetabling etc., the more likely they were to use Schools Broadcasts of the sort to which they were accustomed in peace time.

However, at a meeting in November 1939[10], it was reported that in England and Wales many secondary schools had been *very* disorganised and were devoting their time to making up lost ground on subjects in the examination syllabus and, as a result, were not using broadcasts as much as they had pre-war. In non-secondary schools the position varied considerably from areas such as the Home Counties where schools broadcasting, in common with all other aspects of education, had suffered as a result of Air Raids, to those where conditions were practically normal and transmissions were being used to the same extent as peace time. Although in Scotland they were particularly disappointed at the response from Secondary Schools.

It was generally agreed that the changes due to air raids were so variable that they might be ignored in planning future programmes, and that the changes due to the late morning blackout would not affect the normal schedule for schools, with the possible exception of the timing of the morning religious service.[11]

The Secretary also reported that the Board of Education proposed to issue a Circular on *'Education in Air-Raid shelters'* and that he had arranged for a paragraph to be inserted calling attention to the service that Schools Broadcasting might render in this connection and saying that the Council would give advice on the installation of sets[12]. With regards the shelters, there was also a discussion about the desirability of introducing talks on shelter hygiene and the danger of epidemics during the coming winter.[13]

As the Autumn Term progressed two main points emerged from the reports coming in from schools and Central Government. First, that there was a steady and general decline in the number of schools working in shifts and second, the need for special help in evacuation areas. These points were taken into consideration when planning the 1940 Spring Term programmes which, because of the reduction in the number of broadcasts arranged for shift schools, was very near to the normal pre-war schedules. There were one or two exceptions; the inclusion of a series designed specifically to help children in the evacuation areas called *'For Home Listening*[14]*: Mr Cobbett and the Indians'*; and one which dealt with Current Affairs. The latter had already been discussed in March 1939 when it was felt that the difficulties in presenting Current Affairs talks

---

7 The war-time system of transmission had improved the standard of reception for schools in some areas, but others were adversely affected In 1941, in answer to a question related to reception of broadcasts the Advisory Council stated: 'Wartime difficulties in receiving the BBC Home Service are due to two facts (1) Radio transmissions can in certain circumstances help enemy aircraft in finding their way to the targets they want to attack (2)The BBCs system of transmission and the methods that it follows are designed to avoid giving this helpful guidance to enemy aircraft'

8 Communications Council Schools Broadcasting Executive 22nd Jan 1940. Schools Broadcasting in Wartime. Confidential Report.

9 Some schools, as part of a 'Consumer Body', were asked to send reports to the BBC about various aspects of the service.

10 November 7th 1939. Meeting of Broadcasting Executive

11 At the November meeting, there had been discussions with the BBC Director of Religious Broadcasting on the suggestion that there should be a weekly service for children in Elementary schools between 9.00 and 10.00am. The idea was to have service lasting around 20minutes including 5 minutes devoted to an explanation of something in the act of worship (eg a hymn, a prayer or some words of the Scripture read in the service). At the meeting held on the 8th April 1940, it was decided that this should not be part of Schools Broadcasting, however, it was agreed to introduce the programme at the meeting in November 1941.

12 The question of the supply of sets was a point of discussion throughout the war. At a meeting on the 7th April 1941, a letter was sent to the Board of Education noting the increasing difficulty of supplying radios for school use. The President agreed to approach the Board of Trade with a view to having radio valves released for the manufacture of the standard set. Under a new scheme radios would still be issued to schools even when none were available for domestic use. The rationale behind this was that schools were often used as centres for community activities such as feeding, and it would be possible for the general public to listen to broadcasts of national importance on the school set.

13 Board of Education. Memo No 22. Schools in War Time: Use of Schools Broadcasts.

14 By the Spring of 1941 few people were listening to the 'For Home Listening' series. As a result it was removed from the schedules and the 'slot' offered to the Scottish Council for a series for Scottish Schools on Speech Training.

in war-time might be so great as to render them impossible to produce. However, these problems had not materialised. In addition, as a result of strong representation from the Welsh authorities, the BBC agreed to provide programmes in the Welsh language on Friday afternoons. In the Spring of 1940 this would comprise of two alternating series, one for Juniors and the other for Seniors.

One of the main changes brought about by the war and paper shortages was the discontinuance of children's pamphlets[15] and all broadcasts would have to be planned accordingly. It was agreed that for the Spring Term the detailed schedules would be supplemented by leaflets providing suggestions to teachers, the publication of which was simply an extension of the policy which had been approved pre-war in relation to Geography and English.

From the beginning of the war, the BBC maintained a close contact with the Board of Education and the latter had referred to the possibilities of Schools Broadcasting in a number of Memos sent out to schools.[16] An example of practical help was the issuing of a reply-paid card to every school asking questions about their use of the schools broadcasts. By January 1940, 10,872 schools had returned the cards, indicating that 5,327 of them had used the programmes in the Autumn Term of 1939, 1,332 intended to use them in the Spring of 1940, and 3,780 were not intending to use them at all. The remaining 433 gave an indefinite response.[17]

One of the main problems during the first weeks of the war was simply making contact with schools. Although it was not the only one; at the Advisory Committee on Schools Broadcasting 22 January 1940, Item 66 dealt specifically with School Broadcasting in Wartime, and the Director of Schools Broadcasts commented on programme and productions problems in war-time referring particularly to: (a) The practical difficulties especially in the early days of the war, of a producing a programme at the emergency studio centre. (b) The special educational problems (e.g. Music and Biology) that had arisen as a result of the discontinuance of children's pamphlets and the reduction of the time available for certain subjects. (c) The fact that whenever possible interest in the War is used to illustrate and drive home points in the broadcasts (d) The experiments with broadcasts for children under 7 and for Home Listening.

Local Education Authorities were informed about all stages of the planning and many of them cooperated by sending out schedules to schools in their areas, and further announcements were made on the radio, and in the national and local Press. However, it became clear that many teachers anxious to use the programmes were not getting any information. As a consequence, at the end of September 1939 a letter was sent to all schools on the *pre-war* register enclosing a timetable. In addition, to make sure that the opinions of teachers were 'heard', a modified panel of reporting-schools was re-established and set up on similar lines to the pre-war model.

One aspect of Schools Broadcasting provision across war-time Britain, which is often forgotten, is that it had to take account of the fundamental differences between the Scottish and the English & Welsh education systems, resulting in completely separate broadcasts in certain subjects.

	No of Separate Series Broadcasts	No of series in the English Programme	No of series in the Scottish Programme.
1936-37	34	23	20
1937-38	36	24	26
1938-39	35	25	27
1939-40	33	25	27

The following table summarises the differential position of the systems immediately pre-war and how it was expected to look after September 1939 when the regulations of the Day Schools (Scotland) Code Minute 1939 should have come into force.

15 11th Oct 1945. The Advisory Council discussed the Restoration of Pamphlets and stated that there 'was no evidence to suggest that there was serious danger that the provision of a pamphlet would cause either children or teachers to rest content with what was provided and so lose the value gained from hunting for information and visual supplements themselves....'

16 Schools Broadcasting in War Time. Memos 4, 6 & 8

17 It was hoped that these replies could be used to establish a war-time register of listening schools.

England		England Post 1939	Scotland Post 1939
Elementary	**Primary**	**Elementary**	
Infants aged 3 or 5-7	Infants 5-7	Infants 3 or 5-7	Infants 5-7
Juniors 7-11	Juniors 7-9	Juniors 7-11	Primary 7-12
Seniors 11-14	Seniors 9-12	Seniors 11-15	
Secondary	**Secondary**	**Secondary**	**Secondary**
Secondary Age from 11+	Advanced Division 12-14/15	Secondary Age from 11+	Junior 12-15
	Secondary Age 12-14/15+		Senior 12-17/18

One basic reason for the differences in curriculum input can be found in the dissimilarity in the age-ranges within the educational structures. In addition, and perhaps more importantly, one has to contrast the strictly integrated nature of the Scottish system with the greater flexibility within the English. When a child in England and Wales completed his Primary School courses, he went on either to the Senior Elementary School or to the Secondary School, depending on his level of attainment. These two forms of post-primary education were not linked in any way and were therefore free to develop on entirely individual lines. Whereas in Scotland, the child passed from Primary school to a 2, 3 or 5 year post-primary or secondary course.

In both systems there was a tendency, even in war-time, to make examination success the main benchmark of a schools effort. However, because the situation varied so much from area to area, no generalisation can be made on the effect exams had on primary and post-primary education. In England, the need to obtain scholarships for secondary school certainly created pressure on some pupils in their last year of Junior Elementary school, and there were equivalent demands in Scotland where there was pressure to pass the Control exams.

Both examination systems had a significant bearing on Schools Broadcasts in so far as they determined the amount of exam 'strain' on a class and the age at which such pressure became operative. Basically, teachers were not prepared to make extensive use of the programmes if an examination was imminent. In addition, variation between the two countries in terms of the years that exams were actually taken, created difficulties when planning joint courses. For example, the 11-14/15 year group in the Senior Elementary School had no examination to face, while the 3-year course for the 12-15 age range in Scotland was terminated by the Day School Higher. The fact that very few Scottish pupils took this exam did not help the situation, as in many cases the course of study, even for those pupils who left school at 14 without this Certificate, had previously been designed with reference to the assessment.[18]

Despite the possible organisational difficulties, many of those concerned with Education in Scotland at the time agreed that Schools Broadcasts acted as a stimulus to both teachers and pupils; the former using them to learn different classroom strategies and for widening their own subject knowledge.

England		Scotland		Scotland Post 1939	
AGE	**EXAM**	**AGE**	**EXAM**	**AGE**	**EXAM**
11+	Annual Schools Exam for Scholarship entrance into Secondary School	12	Control (to determine type of Post-Primary Education)	12	Control (to determine type of Post-Primary Education)
13+	Occasionally a second opportunity for unsuccessful candidates in the above exam	14	Day School Cert. (Lower). Set locally and taken after 2 year course.	15	Junior Leaving Cert.
15/16	School Cert.	15	Day School Cert. (Higher) taken on completion of 3 yr. Course	17/18	Senior Leaving Cert
18	Higher School Cert.	17/18	Higher Leaving Cert. Taken on completion of 5/6 yr course		

18 When comparing the 2 systems, it has to be remembered that the conception of Education for the general population developed earlier in Scotland. Education was regarded as the best way of escaping the drudgery of the land and the most rapid means of increasing both economic and social status. In such circumstances the approach to education was bound to be more intellectual and the first thought was generally for the more gifted pupil. Historically, it was an education system in which the fittest survived. These same traditions were apparent during the war. As a result the Scottish child saw his school life as a self-contained period of time during which he had to acquire certain skills for later use. In comparison, the English system in its best aspects was more ready to regard the school years in relation to, and as part of, the development of the child's whole life.

In order, to some extent, to cater for the new influx of children into the countryside, two 'Rural Schools' series had been provided for the Autumn Term of 1939, one in the morning and one in the afternoon, to meet the needs of schools working in shared buildings. But, information coming back to the BBC indicating that there had been a decline in the number of schools in this situation, resulted in there being only one Rural Schools course in the Spring and Summer terms of 1940, and throughout the rest of the war.[19]

The rationale for this single series was 'to provide a special course for rural schools that will encourage children to take a new interest in their environment and to undertake project work related to it.'[20]

As part of the planning, evidence was gathered about the type of audience this would be aimed at, the distribution of rural schools across the country and to what extent children in such establishments were restricted in support material which provided a basis for visualising things outside of their direct experience and environments, such as illustrated books, posters, films etc.

The title proposed for the 1940-41 series was '*New Lamps for Old*' and it was suggested that in order to demonstrate that the countryside was constantly changing, the broadcasts should present a picture of contemporary rural conditions and the changes that had taken place over the previous 100 years.

Looking at the proposed course structure, there did seem to be a very strong focus on 'Change'. Not only in terms of *perceived* changes, but also how they had come about through economic, social, scientific, aesthetic and other factors. Pupils were asked to calculate how far such 'change' had been of benefit to the rural community and to suggest the direction this should take in the future. In hindsight one could argue that such a series might have been of benefit to children who had spent all their lives in the countryside, but one wonders to what extent the majority of evacuees, to whom of course it was also aimed and whose arrival had actually brought about the shared school system, would profit.

The choice of topics in the series was governed by a number of considerations, but primarily they had to be of significance to rural life as it was in 1939, and provide a striking contrast between old and new. One example considered under the subject of Dairy Farming, and to be covered in three programmes, was the simple topic of Milk, and the following chart was drawn up to assist the planners:[21]

Old	New	Factors Affecting Change	Community Value	Future Direction
Just Cows	Scientifically selected herd (Friesians and Jerseys). Hygienically cared-for herd	Increased knowledge of scientific breeding in relation to quantity and quality of yield. Increased concern for hygiene	Better general health resulting from improved diet	Common high standard of production throughout the country
Byres and Milkmaids	Cowsheds specially designed with cleaner gear in situ. Sterilised milking machines	Economic advantage. (Milk keeps longer with modern methods)		Enough milk for all
Stone-Flagged Dairy with shallow cream pans, hand churn etc	Separators, coolers, large scale containers and glass bottles. Factory more often than farm as dairy. Butter machines	Publicity and Advertising		

It was also suggested that a BBC Special reporter for rural schools should be found whose role would be to go out, sometimes with a recording van, and visit places that illustrated the subjects of the broadcasts. He would then go into the studio each week to talk about what he had seen and what he had been told. In addition, it was proposed that, now and then, he would bring with him *'interesting people'* with special knowledge to talk to

19 Advisory Committees. Schools Broadcasting Council. Rural Programmes Sub-Committee Minute Book. 1936-46 R6/158/2 BBC Written Archive. Caversham
20 Course For Rural Schools 1940-41....Draft Analysis (Central Council Schools Broadcasting and Scottish Council for Schools Broadcasting. R6/158/2)
21 ibid

the schools, and he could occasionally introduce a dramatisation of what had happened in the past or what was happening in the present.

A detailed sample outline was provided for the first programme in the 'Milk' series called 'The Herd' .

a) *'The special reporter tells how he went to see an exciting modern dairy farm where there is a rather famous scientifically selected herd...not just cows*

b) *Reconstruction: Farmer takes the Special Reporter around, talking to him about his herd and showing him all his modern gadgets. The reporter asks him why he became interested in scientific farming and the farmer tells him he was sent by his father to an Agricultural College which specialises in dairying. ....While going around the farm they meet a retired cowman , a sceptic, who says that he doesn't think the milk tastes any better for all this fuss and 'anyhow old Daisy, she gave far more milk that any of them there....'*

c) *Reconstruction 2....Interview with, for example, Mr Boutfleur of Cirencester, an ex-Dairy Commissioner, who would build up a picture of change in the principles of herd selecting and at the same time would give the rationale of the changes in milk producing legislation in his own time.*

d) *In summarising his experiences, the Reporter tells how he has a friend who sells milking machines and next week he is going with this friend to see what all this hygienic dairying looks like.'*[22]

The teachers' leaflets sent out to the rural schools were to contain; notes on the broadcasts, suggestions for appropriate project work in the form of model making, local surveys etc , suggestions for sources of illustrations, and questions based on the broadcasts for class discussion e.g. *Has the improvement in roads been a good or bad thing for our village?*

Having discussed the proposals, the Advisory Council resolved that each broadcast should aim at the middle of the age range, i.e. 9-11, but should contain something that could be followed up with both older and younger children. They were not sure about the title and suggested, '*The Changing Village*' or '*Our Changing Countryside*' as alternatives. In order to make it accessible to all schools, it recommended that there should be examples of old and new methods from different parts of the country, including remote areas such as the Orkneys where it was felt little change had taken place, and also from those communities nearer the coast which might be influenced by the sea. Although the Council was in favour of the proposal of using a Special Reporter, it felt that he should not be bound to interview real rural characters at the microphone where this might '*mean speech of a kind difficult for most children to follow*', and that instead it might occasionally be better to have dramatised dialogues based on actual interviews that had taken place prior to the broadcasts. Strangely, the Committee suggested that the programmes should not contain too much Science!

In May 1941, the Rural Schools Programme Sub-Committee met to evaluate the series and the response it had received from schools. The Autumn Term broadcasts appeared to have been more successful than those in the Spring Term. This was primarily because in the latter Mr Mais (the Special Reporter) was thought to have been too condescending in his manner, had not spoken in a way which appealed to the children, and had dealt too much with agricultural technicalities; whereas in the former, the dramatic presentation had had a greater appeal for the children, who had gained from the variety of characters who had been introduced. However, some teachers had stated that this would have been even better had the children been given specific points to listen to during the programme. Based on this success the committee suggested that there might be an ever-

22 ibid

present character running through subsequent series who might take some children out with him on his search for *interesting things*.[23]

There were some surprising critical comments, especially about dialect and the fact that the programme on 'Sowing' was thought to be too agricultural! With regards the former, the most criticised programme had been the one set in Scotland, because schools in Lancashire, Yorkshire, and the Isle of Man found the Scottish Dialect more troublesome than schools in Wales, Norfolk and Surrey.

It is perhaps significant to note that there were very few comments in the programme surveys from evacuated teachers and schools.

It was proposed that the Rural Series for 1941-42 should simply be called '*Living in the Country*' and should not only contain interviews with country characters and the work that they did, but also the influence of the rural areas on artists and literary figures both past and contemporary. The format was changed again in 1942-43[24] when it was called *'Exploring Our Village'* and the programmes were made similar to those in the 'Our Village' series broadcast in 1937-38, but with the addition that changes in village life brought about by the war should be reflected. However, Programme VI, entitled 'The Blackout'.... '*too big a topic*', and Programme VII 'The Homeguard'..... '*packed with too much interesting material*', were both dropped from the schedules!

Throughout the meetings, regular comments were made on children finding problems going from narration to dramatisation within the programmes, but nothing was said about the difficulties some children had with socialisation and simply interacting within the classroom. It was as if no war was taking place and there were no evacuees in the countryside.

Such external pressures were largely ignored. At a meeting of the Advisory Council on the 31st March 1944, it was stated that '*.....on the questions of War strain on children and the disorganisation in schools, the Committee did not feel there was a strong enough prima facie case for considering changes in the policy of broadcasts to schools*.'

It is not until the meeting of 27th February 1945[25] that one finds any mention of the pressure put on the teachers to maintain an accessible curriculum.

> *'Some teachers may not be taking the broadcasts because their value depended largely on follow-up activities which with this series in particular included. It required very hard and strenuous work on the part of the teacher, who was in any case feeling the strain of teaching under wartime conditions.'*[26]

At the same meeting it was stated that the number of rural schools registered for schools broadcasts had increased by over 1000 (nearly 50%) since the beginning of the war.[27]

	Elementary Rural Small	Elementary Rural Unreorganised	Elementary Rural Junior	Elementary Rural Senior	Total
June 1939	835	1229	293	110	2467
June 1944	786	1748	822	162	3518

The line-up for the Spring Term of 1940, which commenced on 8th January, ostensibly continued the pre-war diet. Mondays were devoted to Herbert Wiseman's 'Singing Together', world history, book talks for the Senior English course, the practice and science of gardening, preparatory concert broadcasts and English for the under-nines. Tuesdays included Physical Education, Science and the Community, and a programme called

23 20th May 1941 Rural Schools Programme Sub-Committee Meeting Minutes. BBC Written Archive

24 At a meeting of the Advisory Council on 30th March 1942, programme planners recognised that in some towns some schools would remain open throughout the summer months for the benefit of children whose parents were engaged in war work.

25 On 10th July 1945 the BBC received a letter from Lady Simon suggesting that broadcasts for teachers should be aired on Sat. Mornings.....Exceedingly difficult to provide facilities for a minority audience The diplomatic reply was that 'It was doubtful that programmes could be addressed to teachers about their own work.

26 Senior Education Assistants Report (Miss D Foulger).27th February 1945 BBC Written Archive.

27 Advisory Council op cit. 27th February 1945

'The River' designed especially for the rural schools. There was also Senior English with play-writing and drama productions. On Wednesday the children heard Current Affairs from 'Alf' a 'lorry driver'. There was also a programme called 'Home Listening' which was designed specifically for those children who, because of the war conditions, were working at home, either alone or in groups of not more than ten, with or without the supervision of a teacher. These programmes were centred on the exploits of a milkman from Northern Canada, who told stories about his life with the Native Americans and the lumberjacks and trappers of Canada. 'Music Making' also appeared on Wednesdays along with Biology and Junior English. On Thursdays the children could listen to 'Music for Every Day', the Senior Geography course, and British History, and on Friday they received a diet of Senior English called 'Rhyme and Reason' and topical talks for sixth formers. There were also broadcasts in the Welsh Language for both juniors and seniors.[28] By 1944, thirty-one weekly series, a daily news bulletin and twice weekly religious services were available and the number of schools using them rose from 10,000 to 12,000 throughout the war.[29]

However, Schools Broadcasts, like many other productions, were subjected to war-time policy and editorial directives. On the 27th December 1940, a document was issued by R.H.Eckersley[30], which basically defined what practice had already been taking place in the first year of the war. It was noted that Schools Broadcasts had *'lived up in wartime to their excellent peacetime level'* and had not been subjected to any criticism. However, Mary Somerville, the Director of Schools Broadcasts (DSB)[31] needed to use her judgement when a proposed subject, or passage in a script, called for reference to Home Division policy. This did not mean that every programme draft had to be seen, but that any last minute reference to sensitive matters was to be avoided. There were three areas which could be dealt with as separate issues; those broadcasts dealing with Daily News/Commentary, those with Current Affairs and those which came under 'Other items', and procedures were in place to with deal with all of them.

In respect of Daily News and Commentary, the subject was to be agreed between the competent Schools Officer in London and the speaker after the 9.00 pm news on the evening before the broadcast. The Officer of the Schools Department would then consult the Programme Controller the same night as to whether the subject proposed was suitable. Next morning the text, having been passed by the Schools Officer, would be seen by the Shift Leader in the Home News department. His responsibility was only to ensure that nothing in the script conflicted with current news and news points. He was not expected to go beyond the policy parameters. Reference could be made to the Programme Controller the next morning if any point of doubt arose. It was pointed out that the function of these talks was to make the day's news interesting and intelligible to school children, and that they were to *'stick to being a school-room gloss and avoid speculation or personal expressions of opinion'*

The ten minute News Commentary programmes for the 11-15 age groups were broadcast every day of the week and they had very comprehensive aims and guidelines, the most important of which was to give a clear and objective explanation of the latest news. Writers were instructed to include facts and not opinions, and there was to be no hate propaganda. In addition, children were to be given frank instructions and praise regarding their own behaviour as *'citizens of a country at war'*. Producers were also instructed to explain all difficult words and geographical locations and, where possible, references were to be made to past historical events. In addition, they were to reassure children about issues that they might be particularly concerned about, with the proviso that such statements were not to sound like belligerence or crude optimism.

As 'Other Items' were ostensibly a mixed bag, how much they were referred to the Home Division rested entirely with the Director of Schools Broadcasting. If she was satisfied that no policy point arose then she

---

28 Dorset Daily Echo 22nd December 1939

29 Tom Hickman. What did you do in the war Auntie? BBC. 1995. p79.

30 Roger Eckersley chaired the first meeting of the London Children's Hour Programme Board on the 12th November 1926.

31 Mary Somerville was the first Director of School Broadcasting. Appointed in 1929 she held the post until 1947.

would allow it to go ahead. If she was doubtful, or if she wanted an opinion, or help, in dealing with the Ministry of Information or other Departments, then she would refer to the Controller of programmes.[32]

In the final year of the war, a meeting of rural teachers[33] was convened in Lewes, Sussex by the Schools Broadcasting Council in order to consider past programmes and future developments. Seventy teachers attended and they raised some important issues and made some recommendations, the first of which was to put Schools Broadcasts into the afternoon, from 13.30 – 15.30 so that teachers could do their '*real work*' (sic) in the mornings. In addition, they questioned whether rural schools actually wanted to study 'rural subjects' and if they did, to what extent could the broadcasts help them? They also queried the value of broadcasts as a stimulus to activity in their own right, and how far they were, or could be, an aid to *serious work* (sic). [34]*

There were no written answers to these questions, but the fact that they were actually raised perhaps demonstrates the extent to which the planners were unaware of the needs of the teachers in the classroom. The fact that the latter used phrases such as '*real work*' and '*serious work*' begs the question to what extent were the broadcasts an aid to education or simply a method of entertainment.

Children's Hour

The other stalwart of the air-waves was Children's Hour. In response to the belief that Britain would be subjected to '*an immediate blitzkrieg*' followed by invasion, the BBC had honed down its' scheduling to all but the most important programmes. These included the News, the Daily Service and surprisingly Children's Hour (although cut to 30 minutes). [35] The Blue Peter of its day, organising via the air-waves such things as salvage competitions[36], it broadcast patriotic programmes based on stories of bravery and 'daring do' and talks by guest speakers and fictional series written by such luminaries as L.Du Garde Peach. In 1945 Derek McCulloch (Uncle Mac)[37] summarised Children's Hour's wartime policy as '*giving children a sense of stability and continuity in a world of chaos and change*'. [38]

However, the programme did not escape political intervention and like all broadcasts on the BBC, was subject to censorship. Personnel in the control room were given written scripts of the programmes and although there was an acknowledgement that some improvisation could take place, this was very much left to the discretion of the producer and if it was considered that a character had gone too far beyond the bounds of the script the broadcast was stopped. [39]

Children's Hour closed down in London at 6.00pm on Friday 1st September 1939 and reopened on the 6th from Bristol, where it was to remain until late 1943. Although the programme had originally been Regional, cut backs meant that the Midland team was disbanded with the Director, Enid Maxwell, deployed to Scotland to work for the Ministry of Information. She returned in November 1940 to run overseas broadcasting for the SeaVacs, originally just to the USA but later to Australia, New Zealand and South Africa.

32 This was also to apply to Children's Hour:-
DMcC to RHE 10th February 1941 '.......I think the only talks which would require watching are; News Talks (which have always been vetted since war began), Once a Month (certain items), and isolated topical talks on for example Greece, Malta etc......5th March 1941 Policy Direction in CH'.......There are two quite different questions involved ....(1) Political vetting of talks in CH....(2) The production of these talks in London As regards (1) I should like to have early information as to (a) the idea and object of the talk or talks you have in mind. (b) Speaker and (c) any points that you wish me to put to the speaker on your behalf before he gets to work on these broadcasts. I think this preliminary discussion of this kind is most important, as it saves a great deal of 'censoring' later. ......'

33 A similar Conference, but for all teachers, had been previously held in Salisbury between the 21st-24th July 1944. It had been organised by Board of Education as part of research into the use of SB. (40 selected teachers attended).

34 Minutes of the Meeting of Rural Teachers. 20th January 1945. Lewes Sussex

35 The Radio Times 4th September 1939 under the heading 'Broadcasting carries on'......'.....From next Wednesday, of all goes well, all 'live' entertainment will begin.....There will even be a Children's Hour and regular broadcasts to schools.....'

36There was a suggestion in August 1940 that money could be raised for a Spitfire, which elicited this response from the Controller of Programmes. B.Nicholls. 13th August 1940 ' Children's Hour Spitfire: '....We are not in favour of a Children's Hour Spitfire Fund, as we do not like the principle of appealing to children for money to purchase weapons of war...' On the 26th Aug. it was agreed to raise money for a Mobile Ambulance Unit or Mobile X-Ray apparatus van instead.

37 Derek McCulloch OBE 1897-1967 joined the team organising Children's Hour on 1st January 1930. He had been severely wounded in the First World War and was often in a great deal of pain.

38 File R11/51/2. BBC Written Archive.

39 Memo. Censorship in Wartime. 17th June 1938.R34/266 BBC Written Archive

Programmes during the first weeks of the war were presented by Derek McCollough ('Mac'), May Jenkin ('Elizabeth'), Eileen Maloney in the West, David Davies and Rex Tucker (Bristol), and Ursula Eason, who was responsible for all output in Northern Ireland[40]. It was at this time that 'Mac' introduced his signing off message of '*Goodnight Children Everywhere*', a phrase which was to become an important memory of childhood in the 1940's and 50s, and one which also provided hope and courage for those children in occupied Europe listening secretly to Children's Hour.

At the end of the war Mac received a letter from Elizabeth Knudsen in Denmark.

> *'Now at last we are allowed to send cards to England so I can write to you. I have been wanting to do so for a long time. I am fifteen years old and have listened to Children's Hour almost from the beginning of the war. I want to thank you very much for everything I have heard and especially to your 'Goodnight Children everywhere', for then I knew it meant me too'.* [41]

During the opening weeks great reliance was placed on the familiar pre-war favourites such as Winnie the Pooh, Wind in the Willows, Toy-town and Zoo Man (David Seth-Smith[42]), tried and tested programming brought about, to some extent, by wartime restrictions, especially in terms of personnel. In response to a memo from Christine Orr, Controller of Children's Hour, Scotland, Mac pointed out the need to check the artists working on the programmes.

> *' 7th September 1939*
>
> *CH from Scotland*
>
> *It is not immediately possible to name the day for you to put out your first emergency programme, particularly as there is the important factor of authorisation of use of artists who must be specifically approved for broadcasting by the MoI......*
>
> *DMcC'*[43]

Not to be put off, Christine Orr replied on the 11th September 1939;

> *'Provided that the necessary artists are approved, my details for programming from 30th September 1939 include:*
>
> *Songs.....The Tale of the Pig/Bonny Blue Handkercher/Blow, my bully boys, blow.*
>
> *Story for younger listeners; 'The Door Mat rebels'*
>
> *The Musical House (a guessing game) played with gramophone records, for listeners of all ages. Answers to be given at the end of the programme*
>
> *Additional items by Douglas Morrice, Whistler and Bird Imitator.*
>
> *If there is any delay in getting the artists approved, the only alteration in the above would be the substitution of another story or Xylophone solos for the Whistling Items.'*[44]

The appointment of performers remained a problem throughout the month. As part of a longer internal memo 'Mac' wrote on the 20th September;

> *'......There have been innumerable difficulties to overcome, the largest of all being the question of actors. With all our resources and number of artists on the 'required list' there has been delay for permission in every case so far, almost up to the date of output.*[45]

---

40 Very occasionally the whole Children's Hour was broadcast from there.
41BBC Children's Hour. Wallace Grevatt. Book Guild 1988 p82
42 David Seth-Smith began his animal talks in 1934.
43 Children's Hour Policy File. 1 1939 – May 1940. R11/51/1 BBC Written Archives. Caversham (No individual ref. numbers)
44 Ibid

It would seem that Mac, at the behest of his superiors, also wanted to keep the programme as 'National' as possible with little attempt at 'regionalisation'.

'14th September 1939

DMcC

It must be apparent that our Children's Hour as at present constituted must remain for some time on a National Basis.

I am certain that I can rely on you, and I in turn can be relied upon, by the Director General[46] *and the Controller (Programmes) to maintain the highest possible standard in Children's Hour material. I feel also it is essential that our programmes reflect far more a National flavour than a regional one, aiming so far as is possible at entertainment. In seeking for an exception to the rule, the Zoo Man may be cited as an example'.*

This was a decision which did not please everyone.

'18th Sept. 1939 M.A.MacDonald. CHO North

When we discussed future programmes informally on the phone the other day, you mentioned that three programmes a week were to come from Bristol and the other three divided between Scotland and North, so that we would probably have alternate weeks. Three weeks programmes have now been planned, in which only one half-hour each week is coming from the North. I notice also from the projected arrangements that there is to be a Children's Hour on Sunday as well, and am wondering whether it would be possible therefore for both Scotland and North to supply 2 programmes each week'[47]

To add to the overall discontent it soon became apparent that because of the social situation regarding the war, the BBC hierarchy wanted 'Mac' and 'Elizabeth' to be heard more than their regional counterparts because of their familiar voices; a decision which was to bring about a certain amount of conflict between the regions and London/Bristol.[48]

'DMcC

20th September 1939

....despite my disability, I was asked to take charge of CH at this base (Bristol) and was told it was essential that I should be heard as much as possible. My voice has been known to listeners for nearly 14 years, and that of Miss Jenkin for a considerable time. It has been my desire to get Children's (half) Hour well planted before we gradually merge again into a pooled concern. That will come and, if it is possible, two regions outside mine must share one of the six days...in addition to the two 30mins already allocated.....'

The war-time situation did bring about changes in the programming schedules as some Regional Controllers required guidance on programmes which could be considered of a sensitive nature. On the 29th September, Christine Orr sought clarification regarding the policy concerning thrillers, spy stories or anything to do with the secret services; eliciting this reply from Mac.

---

45 R/11/51/1
46 F.W. Ogilvie (1938-1942)
47 ibid
48 The Regional Controllers of Children's Hour were Christine Orr/Kathleen Garscadden (took over 1940) /Peter Moyes in Scotland; Nan Macdonald in the North, Gwen Parry-Jones/Nan Davies (Enid) 1941/Morfudd Mason Lewis/Lorraine Jameson in Wales.

'4th Oct. 1939
DMcC: Re Policy

I think we must be very careful about thriller serials, stories or plays, in the light of the present emergency. For our own part we are not hastening on a new serial written for us by Sidney Horler, although it has no naval, military or Air Force element in its general theme. On the other hand we have closed down on an excellent, authentic play series dealing with aircraft, warships etc.

It is of course apparent to you that this type of entertainment fairly bristles with difficulties. Spies, Secret service etc. I think you will agree must therefore be left out of our plans. The difficulty is, or are, those listeners who tune in at the wrong moment and get hold of an imaginary spy situation.....'[49]

This meant of course that some playwrights had their source of income curtailed.

'M.A MacDonald.
CH North 6th Oct. 1939

Thank you for your memo. We note what you say about thriller serials, stories or plays. As you may know we have a schoolboy thriller called the Secret Agent which was originally in our programmes for September but on the outbreak of war we wrote to the author and told her there was now no real chance of our putting it on......'

They even had to be careful about the sound effects that were being used.

'10th September 1940 WIND EFFECTS

There has been some outside criticism about 'eerie noises, resembling air raid sirens' in Children's Hour Productions. Specific references have been made to one production recently in which there was a preponderance of Valkyrie music.

There is a directive about wind noises etc. but I think we must make a joint effort to keep an even closer watch against employing the kind of effects likely to upset certain types of listeners. DMcC'

And even the Children's Hour competitions were postponed, although alternative activities were provided.

'Hullo Children Everywhere

We have decided after careful consideration to suspend our normal competitions during war-time. These are the silver pencil and Certificate competitions.

The postcards and letters which you send us normally and which you might continue to send us, would make heavy calls upon the postal services at this time. Additional difficulties would be the sorting out and correcting of competition entries now that there is only one programme and your entries might swell considerably AND we cannot hold regional competitions just now.

We hope you will not only understand our difficulties, but also that you will at any rate join in the occasional Children's Hour Puzzle Corners, Pencil and Paper items, etc. just for the fun of the thing from the loudspeaker end.

Good luck to you all.
DMcC'

---

49 This could have been a reference to the radio drama of H.G.Wells' War of the Worlds, directed and narrated by Orson Welles, which was broadcast on the 30th October 1938 by CBS. Much of it was presented as a series of 'news bulletins' which led many listeners in the USA to believe that an actual alien invasion was taking place.

There was also unease, and a certain amount of entrenchment, regarding the timing schedules of programmes, resulting in Mac expressing serious concerns about the proposed items in the Welsh Language. On the 13th October 1939, Tudor Jones wrote to Mac explaining that programmes in Welsh were to be broadcast for children on another wavelength on a weekly basis. The latter was not impressed, replying by Memo;

> '.......*I have now only 30mins per diem and an hour of which per week comes from North and Scot. As you will be catering in Welsh for your listeners, I feel strongly that I should be left to provide entertainment for English Speaking children.....*
>
> *It is true that we are to cater in Welsh for our listeners, but only for half of them. Moreover, material from Wales is not necessarily for Wales is it? The regions entertain the rest just as much as they entertain themselves from all accounts. We would gladly let you have access to some of our English material, but out experience is that the authentic Regional accent and atmosphere can be produced only in the Region itself. Welsh stuff produced elsewhere has generally been a bit of a fiasco.....*'[50]

Mac issued a further memo on the 14th November 1939, regarding the programming and times allocated to the regions, and he was adamant that Children's Hour should be based fundamentally on Head Office material.[51] Correspondence in February 1940 would suggest that Mac was not too impressed by the work of some of his colleagues, nor the standards of some of the programmes.

> '......*With one or two exceptions (notably Scotland) it is my belief that the standard of appointment of CH Organisers has not been high enough in relation to the success which, without boasting, I believe Regional (London) has achieved. By this I mean that Regions enjoy a certain amount of what one might term reflected glory, while at the same time, probably for reasons of regional pride and certain desire to participate in the programmes, a great deal of what I would consider to be 'below standard' material has undoubtedly been broadcast....*' [52]

From the 19th February 1940 until the 28th July 1945, Children's Hour could be heard from 5.20-6.00 pm although there was a slight variation on Tuesday to incorporate the 20 minutes of programmes in Welsh. Much to the delight of some parents Sunday Children's Hour was introduced in 1939[53], with a large biographical input and on 9th July 1942 a short Epilogue was broadcast which became '*Prayers*' from the 30th. These were focused on children who had been killed in the war. However, although this became part of the official planning in 1942, there is evidence of it occurring earlier. On the 23rd September 1940, an epilogue finished with the following words, '*We should like for the next moments quietly to remember all the children, and all those who were taking care of them, who went down in the torpedoed ship last week*', a reference to the sinking of the SS. City of Benares which had been carrying evacuees to North America.

The public response to the Overseas Evacuation Scheme had taken the Government by surprise to the extent that they had to issue a directive to Children's Hour and Schools broadcasters on the 4th July 1940, entitled '*The Voyage of the Children*'[54] stating that 'microphone publicity' would encourage more to people to apply, many of whom would be disappointed. The Dominions Office was particularly concerned with the content of a Schools Broadcast involving Bob Bowman and an Australian which was reassuring children about the life they would live if they were to be evacuated to Australia.

From 18th October 1939 a Methodist Minister, the Rev George Bramwell Evens, whose pseudonym was Romany[55] or The Tramp, had a regular 'First Tuesday of the Month' slot when he ' travelled' in his caravan

---

50 R11/51/1 op cit
51 ibid
52 Memo from Mac to Regions 6th Feb 1940 entitled Staff and Economic Wartime Organisation. R11/51/1
53 6th November 1939 Dear Mac'.....I would like to say how glad I was that you have at last got a Sunday CH programme. It is a thing that, as a father of a family, I often felt the need of while sitting at the fire on Sunday afternoon about teatime, particularly in the winter.....' Letter from Parent File R11/51/1 op cit.
54 Memo from S.J de Lolbiniere, Dominions Office. 4th July 1940. 'The Voyage of the Children' FILE R11/51/2 June 1940 – 1946 4th July 1940. BBC Written Archive.
55 Evens' grandfather, Cornelius Smith, had in fact been gypsy. He became a Christian after attending a revivalist meeting and subsequently introduced other gypsies to the faith.

with Comma the horse, Raq the spaniel, and his young friends Muriel and Doris. A pleasant and innocent pastime one would have thought, especially as the whole sequence of events was pre-scripted and performed in the studio. However, on the 7th October 1941, he fell afoul of the censors for being too descriptive about weather conditions, and, while supposedly watching some Grey-Lag geese, stating that the birds would have '*passed over Spitzbergen and seen what our Navy did to it*'.

In response to the criticisms levelled at the programme Mac sent a memo to the producers....

> *'Ref. Out with Romany 7th October*
>
> *You must think I am always wanting to interfere, but I feel bound to bring certain points to your notice in connection with the above programme.*
>
> *The other day the DG was here and while endorsing, also stressed the importance of policy he considered I was adopting. i.e to keep war and direct references or jokes about war out of the CH programmes . He said further that I ought really to be responsible for all content matter in the CH programmes.*
>
> *I pointed out the difficulties but said I could always reserve the right to see certain manuscripts, while I must obviously leave the censorship control in the hands of the responsible authority in your region.*
>
> *Subsequently, C(P) held a meeting here, and stressed with extreme emphasis the necessity for and the meaning of the word censorship.*
>
> *I do not suggest for one moment that either Romany or his aides were deliberately padding a censored manuscript, but it was quite apparent to me that padding was going on and that certain things in the menu might have been left out, while other things, not shown in his script, ought not to have gone in.*[56]
>
> *....Surely it cannot be in order to let a script be broadcast uncensored? Every programme and every announcement we put out is passed by me personally and subsequently censored by the proper authority......*
>
> *I think the whole question comes down to one issue: do head Office instructions operate throughout the whole of our existing services? If so, then Miss MacDonald ought not to place me in the position or feeling of unhappy uncertainty, which is my lot in this case.*
>
> *DMcC'*

After the war Eunice Evens (Romany's Wife) wrote[57]:-

> *'There came the war censorship of the Romany Scripts. What was worse, not a word had to be added after it had been typed. To be cramped in this manner was heart breaking; it took away so much of the naturalness of the walk if he could not extemporise as he stood before the microphone. Apart from a reference to the weather, what could he tell the enemy about the birds and animals that would help them, he wondered?.......'* [58]

There were other programmes related to the countryside and animals including the 'Zoo Man' and 'The Farmer' in England, and, in Scotland, occasional talks on the war-time aspects of the countryside north of the border given by John R. Allan. Although the Zoo Man's broadcast of 2nd December 1940 about the bombing of London Zoo was criticised by the censors, his programmes were used for positive propaganda purposes.

---

56 This was commented on by Miss MacDonald the producer who stated that Mac's statement was not accurate as the scripts in these programmes were treated mainly as guides and there was a good deal of gagging and alteration in the course of the broadcast.
57 Grevatt op cit p101
58 Romany died suddenly on 20th November 1943. As a tribute, a special programme about the countryside was broadcast on the 7th December.

This occurred after the 22 March 1942, when the Ministry of Agriculture had suggested waging war against the '*destructive house - sparrow*' by destroying nests and leaving traps!! In a letter to the Times, F. Howard Lancum, the Press Officer to the Ministry, stated that;

> '*the Minister of Agriculture....never invoked the aid of school children in its campaign and does not encourage the use of Sparrow Clubs.....and it makes sure that all its announcements include a warning not to molest beneficial birds...such as the hedge sparrow etc.*'

The letter went on to suggest that parents and teachers should make it clear to children that they ought not to destroy nests or eggs of any birds, and that the 'Zoo Man' should re-iterate this on Children's Hour.

Another one of these series '*Walks with Wilfred*' (Wilfred Pickles) was aimed specifically at the evacuees now resident in their rural billets. The producers chose a young boy who had been evacuated from London to Cheshire and got Wilfred to take him around the area of the country in which he was now living.[59]

There were other programmes that also focused on the evacuation and the evacuee. In 1939, L.du Garde Peach wrote a special series of plays called *'Safe in the Country'* about three children from the city evacuated to a farm, the idea being to give the child listeners who were evacuees a sense of identity with the characters. Another, *Town Folk and Country Folk*, broadcast in July 1941 and produced by Eileen Maloney,[60] looked at the way in which children from the evacuated areas were being accommodated in the countryside. Although it touched on relevant issues such as homesickness and possible conflicts between rural and urban children and created an image of the hardworking evacuee, its' prime *raison d'être* seemed to be simply to reassure adults that their children were being well looked after.[61] The programme was produced as a quasi-documentary and contained interviews with evacuees interspersed with obvious fictitious sequences. It was publicised as a programme with no prior agenda and one which used the opinions of actual evacuees in the West to support the evacuation scheme. [62] On the 18th July 1941 Eileen Maloney introduced the sequence of programmes in the following way:-

> '*Hullo, children! And especially evacuated children.*
>
> *We've just returned from a tour in the West Country with our recording van where we've been talking and listening to all sorts of children and people trying to find out what they think about evacuation. How are they enjoying themselves? Are they fitting in well in their new surroundings? What, if anything, are they doing to help the National Effort?*
>
> *It isn't easy to answer all these questions at once, and so I think the best thing we can do in this programme is to try and reconstruct some of our adventures for you so that you can hear all that we heard on our tour – and then we'll leave you to draw your own conclusions. Listen, then to "Town Folk and Country Folk" – a programme for and about evacuees!*'[63]

However, although the programme created an image of the industrious evacuee clearing plots of land to plant vegetables, collecting salvage, and 'doing their bit' in other ways, one needs to question to what extent the opinions heard are those of genuine evacuees, especially as many of the characters, including the '*evacuees*', were actually adult actors.

Nonetheless, Maloney was at pains to fashion a positive picture of the evacuee's role within the rural community; a propaganda image which to some extent created a somewhat romantic notion of the scheme as a whole; one which has remained to this day.

---

59 Produced in 1942
60 Children's Hour organiser in the Western Region.
61 By the late thirties Children's Hour was attracting a large adult audience, see Radio Times 'Children's Hour' 26 February, 1937, p.3. cited in Simon Flynn. op cit. This is supported in the report September to December sent to the Home Service Board on 13th December 1939 '.......Listener research has revealed that quite a large adult audience habitually listens to the CH, a fact that strengthens the claim put forward to a daily prog, of a least 45mins....' R11/51/1 op cit
62 According to Simon Flynn these were often transcriptions from original interviews made into scripts which could be recited in the studio.
63 Eileen Maloney, Town Folk and Country Folk, BBC 18 July 1941

> *'.......In every village we went into we seemed to hear of fresh ways in which the children were learning either to make themselves useful to the local people and help the war effort, or else to help themselves and take some of the burden of the work and expense of evacuation on their own shoulders'.* [64]

Children's Hour was under great pressure from the BBC management not to mention the war in any of its output, but despite Mac's assurances to comply with such directives [65] it was impossible for the political situation not to impinge on the schedules. On the 24th August 1940, Mac received a memo. from BBC Management asking....

> *'....Have you any plans for safety in the blackout programmes towards the end of September? MoI are keen about this ...'*

To which he replied

> *'We will watch this and will include something suitable, probably on dramatic lines. DMcC'*

In addition, public service announcements such as '*How to use your gasmask*' and '*Safety in the Blackout*' were broadcast at the request of the Ministry of Information, and the use of Children's Hour was even raised in Parliament in May 1943 during a debate on the dangers to children of unexploded bombs and incendiary devices;

> *'Sir J. Grigg.....In conjunction with my Rt Hon Friend the President of the Board of Education, steps are being taken to bring these dangers to the notice of all concerned by means of posters and warnings issued to schools and on the wireless'.* [66] *(Mac instructed the regions to broadcast the warning on the 28th May 1943)*

Some Children's Hour productions were simply cut, or censored, although in somewhat of an arbitrary way. For example, the wartime exploits of Gwynedd Rae's talking bear '*Mary Plain*' was cut, whereas the drama '*Out of the Clouds*' , an adventure story by J. Robert Evans about two boys who thwart a scheme by the Germans to steal an RAF plane, was not censored at all.[67] According to the BBC Yearbook 1945[68], Mac had been keen to review the policy of 'war evasion' at various times and in May 1940, asked the BBC's head of listener research, R.J.Silvey, whether children, if polled at some point in the future, could be asked if they did want *'real war material in their programmes'*.[69]

Mac was also keen to promote the war-time efforts of children, and on the 7th August 1940 sent a memo to this effect to all Regional organisers asking them to send any examples of outstanding and interesting juvenile activities such as Clubs, Welfare, Salvage, Message Carrying etc. which could be included in a new serial entitled '*Children in War-Time*'. He hoped that such a programme could be launched with a 'biggish bang'.[70]

However, by the 27th August 1940 he had received no replies although some of the regions did request further information. They were informed on the 4th September that the definitive date for the first inter-regional programme would be the 3rd October. It would be compeered by Mac in Bristol and a script would be sent to all the regional organisers, who in the meantime should send him suggestions for their regional contributions, lasting about eight minutes.[71]

---

64 Ibid.

65 On 31st May 1940 he wrote in an Internal Memo on Programme Planning'.....I hope that from now onwards you will take great care to review details of your programmes in the light of the general war situation. AC(P) and DPP and I look at the days programme every morning from the point of view of general incongruities, and some adjustments have already been made to suit the gravity of the news, without making it look graver than it is or making a present to Lord Haw Haw for his exploitation.....' R11/51/1 BBC Written Archive

66 Extract from Hansard 25th May 1943. Col. 1391 British Army Explosives. Accidents to Children.

67 Simon Flynn. 'Those Billets':constructions of evacuation& evacuees in the BBC radio programme Children's Hour. Children in War Journal Vol 4 DSM 2004)

68 Grevatt op cit. p67

69 R11/51/1 op cit

70 File R11/35 7. Aug. 1940 Memo from Mac to West Region. Propaganda and Juvenile War-Time Efforts

71 It was not thought possible to link up with Northern Ireland in the same way as the other regions, but if they felt that they had anything to include they might be given the last few minutes of the programme.

The 'biggish bang' was in fact the Children's Hour broadcast made by the then Princess Elizabeth on the 13th October 1940, but because of security issues, Mac was not able to inform the regions of her input. In her message she referred to children in wartime and it was following on from this message that Mac had wanted to launch what he hoped would be a successful series of programmes[72].

However, this proved not to be the case. On the 30th October, Mac sent a rather angry communication to all regions outlining the sequence of previous memos and criticising them for their lack of input and their overall lethargy in getting suggestions to him.

> '*.......it will be seen that it took fully two months before any detailed scripts reached us. I am quite aware that Scotland made the suggestion about the Glasgow children and a similar sort of programme when they wrote on the 31st July, It was however, decided to treat this in a separate programme.......finally a script was sent on the 11th October. From the North Memos were sent on the 2/17th September offering suggestions. On the 27th came a suggested billing for their part of the programme and on the 1st October the script in its final form. Wales wrote with their first suggestion on the 3rd Sept., followed by an apology on the 26th September for delay owing to air-raid casualties. The completed script arrived on the 10th October........ I feel quite certain you will agree this is not very satisfactory state of affairs or of general cooperation, making full allowances for wartime difficulties of every kind. I do realise we are rather more isolated, although I have made attempts, handicapped as I am , to get to regions, and have in fact succeeded in visiting both Cardiff and Manchester. I am shortly visiting Glasgow. It is however, team work that counts at a time like this..... Whether or not we can go on with this series is problematical, but I feel that we have got to do better than on the last occasion. So far as the next programme is concerned, on the 27th November.....material and suggestions must be sent in at once.......*'[73]

Children's Hour also encouraged children to raise money for good causes, either as individuals, with friends or with their schools. There had been concerns in August 1940 about asking for funds to buy a Spitfire, and the fundraising was to come under further scrutiny in November 1942, when the Journal of Education criticised the BBC for praising the efforts of school-children who raised money by means of raffles.[74] However, having checked with all the regions, it was found that no reference to, or indeed encouragement of, raffles had been made in any Children's Hour broadcasts. Nonetheless, Children's Hour did continue to raise money. The Christmas Appeal of 1944 for 'Invalid and Crippled Children' amounted to £18,600, a record sum, and throughout the war the average of the Children's Hour annual appeals was £10,000.[75]

In July 1942, Mac reviewed the status of Children's Hour in a confidential document entitled *Children's Hour Policy Report*. In it he stated that the objectives of the programmes, designed primarily for children in Elementary and Secondary education between the ages of 7-13, were; to encourage the best development of the listening tastes of the future generation of adult listener, to interest children in contemporary life and in their own part of the country, and to help them contribute towards their moral and religious education. Implicit in this was the desire to help '*train children to become good citizens and loyal subjects of the Empire*'. In order to achieve this it was important that under no circumstances should anyone involved with Children's Hour talk down to the listener. He commented that the average child was quick to spot and resent this form of insult and thought it better '*to speak at chin level, or just above the child's head rather than risk going one step in the other direction*'.

He expressed concern about the living conditions under which some children were coping; as many poorer class children were living in such crowded conditions that they could not really listen in the proper sense of the

---

72 See Appendix 15
73 File R11/35 Letter from Mac. 30th October 1940
74 Raffles and lotteries of any kind were illegal and the BBC would therefore have been committing an offence by broadcasting information about them.
75 The Christmas Appeal in 1939 raised £3,333 for Children's Hospitals, and in 1940 £15,000 for a mobile X-Ray Unit called 'The Children's Hour'. (Radio Times 24th January 1941)

word and instead spent their time running errands, minding the baby or, most frequently, playing in the street. He hoped that the *'Children's Hour net is spread pretty wide and catches the better majority'*. He emphasised the fact that only the best is good enough for child listeners. He concluded by saying that Children's Hour was really a self-contained miniature of broadcasting as a whole, and that the staff working on the programmes was privileged to entertain the adult listeners of the future and, consequently, the work they were doing was of vital importance and deserved every encouragement. At the time this report was written, Children's Hour was listed as the third most popular activity for children after 'playing outdoors' and 'going to the cinema'.[76]

Children's Hour was to continue until the mid-sixties. New programmes were devised throughout the late 40s and 50s to cope with different tastes, but the high standards of programming, especially in drama, were maintained. In 1958, even with the advent of wider television reception and the introduction of ITV in 1955, Children's Hour received 31,000 letters in its Request Week.[77] However, by 1960 there were more adults than children listening to Children's Hour and as a result its name was changed to *'Home at Five'* then to be called *'For the Young'*. After the broadcast of *'The Selfish Giant'* on March 27th 1964, it went into the annals of radio history. There were many reasons given for its eventual demise: Had children changed so much that the format was out of date? Was it interfering with the arrangements for other programmes? Primarily it was a combination of these, plus the fact that more children were watching the television. However, Norman Shelley[78] stated that the decision to close-down broadcasting aimed specifically at children as *'nothing but assassination'*.[79]

Despite a Policy Statement from the BBC made as early as 1940, that 'there were many approaches to the issue of evacuation other than a sentimental one across a variety of programmes both factual and fictional'[80], Children's Hour had nonetheless offered a diversion for children during the war years, and often provided a necessary link with those who had been displaced. Uncle Mac's phrase 'Goodnight Children Everywhere' somehow became synonymous with a feeling of relaxation and safety and, for forty minutes each day, children were transported to fictional locations far removed from the horrors and pressures of wartime.

---

76 Hartley op cit. p63
77 ibid
78 Norman Shelley was probably best known as the voice of Winnie-the-Pooh. He was also Dr Watson in the Sherlock Holmes adaptations, Toad in the 'Wind in the Willows' and Dennis the Daschund in 'Toytown'. He was also well known in his role of Colonel Danby in 'The Archers'.
79 Ibid p66
80 R11/51/1 CHILDRENS HOUR. Policy File 1. 1939-May 1940

The Long-Term Effects

> *'Even now, I could cry when I think about it, but why, because it did not affect me at the time. But looking back it does now. You sort of feel sorry for yourself you know, it was quite a big gap in your life. No it never really affected me until years and years and years onwards. They asked us to go to this local school, they was doing this play on evacuation. And I went to it, and it affected me for about two weeks, I don't know why, but it did. I could have cried all the while. I thought well, it didn't affect me at the time, so perhaps it never sunk in. I don't know'.*[1]

It is too easy to view the evacuees and war children in World War Two holistically because the media and text books force us down that route. Today, children in conflict areas are often shown in the newspapers and in news bulletins; the images used deliberately to grasp our attention and attack our emotions in the same way as some of the posters used in World War Two. Seeing a figure of a vulnerable child makes us want to help, and the same applied then. However, one would suggest that by using children in this way, at whatever stage in history, the media is forcing us to pay attention to the situation as a whole, rather than the plight of the individual child who has their own story to tell and recall[2].

A group of evacuees waiting patiently at a London station.
Read the faces and one can see that each individual is coping with the situation in their own way.

The psychological long term effects that evacuation had on the British children who were sent away, either within the country or overseas played a significant part in the lives of many of them post-war. Many of the children returned from the reception areas, sometimes after five years away, with little or no support either for themselves as individuals, as a national group or for their families, both hosts and parents. As a result many had to deal with the situation as best they could and often resorted to behaviour and insularism which would allow them some sort

1 Betty Rose. Children on the move. Op cit. p166
2 A photographic-media experiment I do with my university students would suggest the children are still invisible.

of mental protection. Some found themselves completely isolated within their communities and the family unit. In a situation where not all the siblings had been evacuated, those who had been away now had no common experience to share with their families, and in some cases were even criticised for having escaped from the bombings. James Roffey recalls that his elder brother, who had not been evacuated, once said to him:-

> '*...when you came back from Sussex it was like having a stranger in the house, we didn't speak the same language and had little in common*'.[3]

For James himself, he felt as if he was an outsider looking on:-

> '*...The family seemed to talk about things and people that I knew nothing about and they took little interest when I tried to talk about Sussex*'. [4]

The English children had no language problems to the same degree as the Finnish evacuees returning from Sweden. Although some had gone to Welsh-speaking Wales, they all had sufficient knowledge and basics of English to revert back to it when they got home. Neither did the vast majority have to deal with the issues of feeling guilty for their fathers like some of their German counterparts; but nonetheless there were psychological and social difficulties. As these were very much dependant on the experience of the individual children, both in the billets and at home, these problems are unquantifiable. It is only possible to view them in general terms or to investigate vast numbers of specific case studies which, in isolation, would not necessarily have any bearing on the experience of a fellow evacuee.

The fact that while some had been away their houses had been destroyed and they now found themselves living in temporary accommodation, did not help the domestic situation. For some it was simply a lack of space, as the children had grown up during their time away. This was particularly true of those who had been evacuated overseas and had not seen their parents for six or more years. In addition, as the 'label' of evacuee was removed (officially in March 1946) they just became another '*ordinary*' child and treated as such. There was no counselling, no account was taken of their lack of schooling, or possible difficulties within the home, which in some instances were so serious that it resulted in a complete breakdown of the family unit, especially where the children were returning from evacuation and the husband from the forces[5]. Although the Ministry of Health had advised local authorities in the previously evacuated areas to instigate follow up visits for the returning evacuees to ensure that any problems relating to the re-familiarisation with the family or neighbourhood could be overcome swiftly, research would suggest that few evacuees knew that this was taking place. In my own extensive research with evacuees, involving many interviews, the general consensus was that little was done to ensure that their return home was trouble free.[6] The majority were left to get on with their lives. Such was the pressure on some, that those who were near to leaving school took the opportunity to go away from home to get jobs in the areas where they had previously been as evacuees, in a few cases even living with their ex-hosts as paying guests.

Some of those British children coming back from the USA and the Empire countries also found the return difficult to cope with. As they had been away for a considerable length of time in a totally different environment, they were often affected more in sociological and psychological terms than their peers who had been evacuated within the UK. One of the reasons being that they had left the country for an unknown period of time, to live in a culture which to some extent must have seemed alien to them, and were now returning to war-affected areas which were now equally as unfamiliar. In addition, having been sent out of the country for their formative years, they returned, some not until 1947, to find themselves having to renew relationships with parents, brothers and sisters they no longer knew, or deal with new siblings born during their absence. Some were now adults. But despite all of this, little was done to help them.

---

3 Interview with author. James Roffey is founder and Chief Executive of the Evacuees Reunion Association in the UK.
4 James Roffey. Big Boys Don't Cry. unpub manuscript. p164
5 See Julie Summers 'Stranger in the House'.
6 Taped interviews carried out by Author. Now available at Evacuee Archive, University of Reading.

Two sisters, who had been forced to return to the UK against their will by the courts, found family life in London very difficult. *'We resented having to come back to England and didn't like our parents, especially our mother'.* [7] They were forbidden to receive or send any communications to their former hosts and were not allowed to have anything to do with Canada. Totally disenchanted with being at home, they decided to return to Canada as soon as they were old enough to do so, and when they were older considered the years in between as a painful stage in their lives. One sister commented;

> *'The evacuation scheme separated us from my mother for the rest of her life. We could not discuss the subject with her. I believe it was her greatest sorrow that she did separate from us for this long period of time'.* [8]

On the other hand there were children who wished to return from overseas, but were prevented from doing so because of family circumstances. Michael Fethney recalls one poignant example where four sisters stayed in Canada and although they enjoyed their lives there, one in particular still finds the original experience difficult to cope with;

> *'The experience led to the total fracture of our family. I have three sisters whom I do not know. My father died alone in England without ever seeing his four daughters evacuated to Canada. And I have never returned to the city of my birth. But some day I will! You ask how long was I homesick? The answer is: I still am!'* [9]

However, it would be wrong to dwell entirely on negativity. To see the positive side of the British overseas evacuee plans, it is worth quoting a statement made by Michael Henderson in a recent journal article:-

> *'.....There may be social scientists who regard the whole overseas evacuation as a big mistake. Many accounts tend to dwell on the trauma of separation and cite examples where it didn't work out well. All I can add, as would many others with whom I have been in touch, we would not have missed the experience for anything. It has enriched our lives and the links with the United States and Canada it opened up to us are a blessing. The final sentence of the report of the US Committee for the Care of European Children reads, 'In the long run, the 861 British children in the Committee's program turned into nearly that many emissaries of good will, who through the personal feelings they developed and provoked added solid substance to the friendliness of British-American relations.' The report described the evacuation as 'an applied lesson in international understanding'.* [10]

Today in Britain, where some people still assume that the children did not suffer any psychological problems, there is evidence to suggest that a few ex-evacuees still have no sense of belonging;

> *'All the time I was evacuated I used to tell myself that one day the war would be over and I could go back home. After the war we were living in a different part of London and I made my way back to where I used to live. The whole area had been completely obliterated during the first few days of the Blitz and I was quite unable to find the spot where my house once stood. This happened more than 50 years ago. I have lived in many other places. I now have a grown-up family of my own and I am a grandfather. I now have a lovely house, but somehow I'm still waiting to go home!'* [11]

> *'I hate it, I hate it.....Oh you're a vaccie'. That's it. I've got six children, worked away from home, worked every county in the country and abroad yet I am just a loner'* [12]

---

7 Michael Fethney 'Absurd and the Brave'. op cit. p247
8 ibid
9 ibid p 249
10Michael Henderson. The evacuation of British children to North America in World War II. Children in War. Vol.1 No 3. 2005
11 Jim Bartley. Parsons. I'll Take That One. Becket Karlson. 1998.
12 Pete Mirams. Children on the Move. op cit p169

It is easy to forget now that the ex-evacuees are adults, that at the time many of them were very young children. Depending on their circumstances, some of them were forced to take on roles well above their age and as a result some have never really experienced a childhood. Few realise now and at the time, that in the British evacuation, some children just over the age of 5 were given responsibility for siblings under the age of 5. Although this was not common, it occurred more frequently than one might imagine, and for some of the children involved it has had an effect on all the parties ever since. As an example in a research project carried out in 2004, where the interviews were being filmed rather than just recorded on sound tape, two sisters who had been 7 and 4 at the time of their evacuation were sitting side by side in the studio. As the older one (A) was recalling her experiences as an evacuee, the younger of the two (B) started to swivel round and ended up with her back to her sister. When questioned about this after the session, B denied that she had done it and was therefore very surprised to see her response when the tape was replayed. Further questioning revealed that all her life B had considered her sister to have been an '*interfering busybody*', questioning her fashion sense, her choice of boyfriends her life in general etc., so much so that B had refused to allow her own children to stay with her. However, during the filming she had realised for the first time that for five years of her life, her older sister had in fact been her mother, a role which the latter had found hard to give up on their return home. [13]

Many children grew up both during the war and afterwards, without a male role model. Not only creating problems for some children in relating to male figures, but in a situation where the mother was left on her own and took on the role of both father and mother, causing a breakdown in the traditional mother-child relationship. In some cases, as in the example above, children were forced into taking on the adult roles themselves and not only had to look after their siblings, but in some cases even their own parents who been affected by the war or, in the case of the mothers, by their own separation from their husbands.

> *'I think I matured very rapidly during the war. I was the sole, male member of a household and I had to take a leading part in some respects. I'm not saying that my mother was weak in any sense, because she wasn't, but I think she leaned on me and I leaned on her and we made a good team.'.*[14]

Some parents were so emotionally scarred by their own experiences that they were unable to raise their children in a loving, caring family unit. In interviews, many evacuees refer to the difficulties in establishing and maintaining a relationship with their fathers who had returned from the war[15]. One woman described her father as ....*'the man who returned after the war was the biological shell of a father whose mind and spirit had been darkened by the war years and captivity. After coming home, he suffered from depression for years. His life melted away while he was lying on his bed'*. [16]

Heinl refers to this as '*emotional fatherlessness*', a situation where the father is so psychologically damaged that although physically alive he is unable to provide support and a 'healthy psychological growth structure' for his children. [17]

In some examples the mothers also found such relations difficult because for the previous five years they had had the responsibility of having to run both a home and maintain a job for themselves, and now they were required by convention to transfer their family responsibilities back onto men who perhaps were unable to cope because of their own war experiences. Under such circumstances, the children were the least of their concerns.

Inadvertently, some of the external pressure was actually placed on the children by their fathers, especially when they were called up, and seemingly throw away comments such as *'You are the man of the house now'* or '*Make sure you look after your mother and sisters'* only added to the child's anxiety to do right.

For some war children a desperate need for a father figure became very debilitating and affected the upbringing of their own children. It has also meant that those evacuees and children remaining in the evacuation areas who

13 Parsons and Sandelin-Benko. Joint (pilot) research project into the long term effects of war child separation. Universities of Reading and Helsinki. 2004
14 Children on the move. op cit p161
15 For a detailed examination of this topic see Julie Summers 'Stranger in the House'
16 Heinl op cit p67
17Ibid p75

had to take on the quasi-parental roles so early in life, were denied a childhood of their own, including all its inherent features such as play, socialisation and in some cases, education.

In the psyche of many war children there is an element of distrust. As children they had no say in what was going on at the time, nor indeed their future, and consequently they relied on adults to make decisions for them, some of which turned out to be detrimental to their well being. They became aware that relations, friends, schoolteachers and adults in general could not necessarily be trusted and also that life could be unpredictable. As a result, some have found it difficult to enter into any sort of relationship, and when they have there is often an unnecessary willingness to end it *'before it happens to them'*; they can have a fear of rejection, and habitually find it difficult to express their emotions and anger. Barbara Shawcroft has been married and divorced a number of times, and blames her inability to forge long-lasting relationships entirely on her evacuee experience. In a way the need for a relationship is offset by her uncertainty that it is genuine and there is an ever-present underlying fear that it will inevitably be snatched away from her. [18] Sometimes this difficulty in familial bonding can be witnessed between parents and their children. Some evacuees who have found it difficult to talk about their experiences have distanced themselves from their own offspring physically as well as emotionally, so as not to have to confront difficult questions or situations. Some suffer from psychosomatic disorders, and others, at a simple level, are incapable of saying goodbye to friends and relations, and will make any excuse not to be at a point of departure. Others have created separate identities and alter egos to enable them to cope with their memories.

However, one needs to be aware that these symptoms are not only found it British children. For all war children, no matter what country they came from or which country their parents fought for, the traits and anxieties are the same, and few, if any, received support or counselling post-war; an oversight which to some extent exacerbated an already critical situation with regard to war-child welfare.

Britain has yet to confront the long-term effects of war-child separation. Even today, little attention is paid to Operation Pied Piper, which was a massive undertaking, and it is one of the few aspects of the war which not only goes unrecognised, but which does not have its own tangible memorial. The armed services are recognised, so are women in war and even animals....but not the evacuees themselves or those who took part in any of the four evacuation schemes. As an indication of the general lack of awareness at high levels, a senior politician and one-time Cabinet minister when hearing of my work once told me quite categorically that the evacuees would receive no financial compensation; totally missing the point of the research. Nobody has ever mentioned compensation, the evacuees just want to be heard and the truth to be told. They want to be recognised as participants in a Government initiative which although carried out with the best of intentions never considered the impact it would have on the lives of those taking part. Many people were involved and all have been affected in one way or another, either as evacuees, hosts, children in the reception areas, or mothers sending them away. Add to the list those who were involved in the administration and transportation, the teachers, the billeting officers, the escorts, local government officials, the medical services, train drivers, bus drivers etc., and one begins to see how extensive and all encompassing the scheme was. It just cannot be ignored and swept away. It will be remembered and its effects will still be apparent long after the 'evacuee generation' has gone.

It can be very difficult for those born post-1945 and who have not experienced conflict elsewhere to empathise with those who witnessed death, destruction and disruption on a scale never witnessed before. It is also very important to keep in mind that such memories know no geographical or national boundaries and although this book has dealt primarily with the evacuees in Britain, one can only imagine the effect that scenes like these described by Helen Schneider had on the children in immediate post-war Berlin:

> *'We are vegetating in a ghost town, without electricity or gas, without water; we are forced to think personal hygiene as a luxury and or hot meals as abstract concepts. We are living like ghosts in a vast field of ruins, where the few remaining buses and trams cart us circumspectly around like animals for the slaughter, where the schools have no pupils, the shops have no goods, the theatres*

18 Interview with author. California 1992

no actors and the churches no congregations...and where the few hospitals still standing are without water, electricity, medicines and doctors.....If we want to fetch water, we have to go to the fountains or pumps, where terrified queues form, presenting far too easy a target for the enemy. Often the queues are mown down by shells or mortar-fire, or by lightning artillery attacks'.

'Nothing works any more: there are no postmen, no milkmen, not a single doctor to be found, and the emergency services, which had until recently been clearing the streets of corpses, have stopped answering the phone. A city once organised and functioning has abandoned its citizens to their own devices: there are no rights anymore; and no duties either'. [19]

For German children the end of World War Two did not represent salvation, and for some not even liberation. For many it was a tragedy on both a personal and grand scale. They had been led to believe that they were part of a Thousand Year Reich, and those born post-1933 had grown up knowing only the controlling influence of a totalitarian Nazi regime during which time many young children and adolescents had been manipulated by the Hitler Jugend and the Bund Deutscher Mädel. In May 1945, the State was literally in ruins and for many the hitherto consistent parts of their life, the ideals and philosophies of National Socialism, the camaraderie of the youth organisations were gone. Their physical and figurative world had disintegrated and they now found themselves in a country devastated by war and controlled by foreign powers. There were severe housing shortages and basic accommodation was lacking in many of the cities where vital services were deficient, the black market was rife, the infrastructure was non-existent and the economy was in ruins. Lack of essential foods and amenities meant that some were not equipped to survive the extreme winters of 1945-6 and 1946-7, and many died as a result.

It is easy to forget that as well as the Hitler Youth who had been sent to 'colonise' eastern areas, there were thousands of other children living within the Greater Reich with their parents, who in 1945 were expelled and forced to return to Germany; some in cattle trucks, some forced to walk, and some in front of the advancing Russians. They were caught up in a maelstrom of humanity wandering around Europe at the end of the war, desperately trying to find a refuge or simply get home. One of Ulla Roberts interviewees remembers at the age of 4 crossing the River Weichsel in Poland;

'The panic stricken face of my mother as we fled across the frozen river. Would the ice hold us? The expression in her eyes warned me 'be quiet, don't speak'. I was struck dumb with fear. I felt completely helpless and unprotected. When I look back I can relate the expression of fear on my mother's face with my own problem of looking somebody in the eyes when I talk to them today'. [20]

One woman recalled fleeing from East Prussia at the age of five. By this time she had already been raped, seen her grandfather shot, and in the chaotic scenes of escaping she and her younger brother had been separated from her sister. They were now on their own. She recounts that '*....during a train journey her brother died in the icy cold. His stiff frozen corpse was thrown out of the train window as they crossed a bridge over a river. There was no grave, no prayer, and no memory as to where this happened'. But the memory of what happened lived with her for the rest of her life'.* [21]

Although there may be a temptation to think that more than seventy years should have provided a sufficient time to mourn such loss, evidence would suggest that in some cases the mourning has not yet even started. [22]

'Ashes and shifting sands have covered the footprints of war'......(However) despite the progress of time, and against a tide of forgetting, childhood war trauma, which had been buried for decades,

---

19 The Bonfire of Berlin. Helga Schneider. Vintage 2006 p5
20 Roberts op cit.
21 Heinl op cit p5
22 ibid p85

suddenly surfaced, entering the light of consciousness with an immediacy as if these traumas had occurred only yesterday'[23]

The actual number of these post-war refugees is unknown but estimates fluctuate between 12 and 15 million, of whom only 9 million survived. It is difficult to envisage what it must have been like for the hundreds of thousands of children caught up in this exodus, and what effect these experiences and memories had on their later lives.

Some authors, such as James Bacque, have attempted to show that the fate of the post-war Germans was not helped by allied obduracy and neglect. He quotes more than 1 million being starved and abandoned, statements which have been refuted by John S. Conway, of the University of British Columbia, who claims that Bacque's figures are based on records of perhaps questionable authenticity, mainly from the KGB archive in Moscow. Nonetheless, Bacque declares that 9.3 million German civilians died needlessly and asserts that the silence about their fate amounts to a vast international conspiracy maintained for fifty years.[24],

'Sometimes the Allies have lied in co-operation with the Soviets, sometimes they have lied to foment hatred against them, sometimes they have lied to cover up their own crimes. They are still at it'.[25]

He claims that the suffering resulted from the Allies somewhat vindictive policy of dismantling the industrial infrastructure, which he says was a determined plot on the part of those people who instigated the policy of unconditional surrender.

Whether one agrees with Bacque or Conway, it is true that German children were starving. Immediately after the war finished, the Allies had either confiscated, or had refused permission to unload, numerous consignments of food sent by various pacifist religious organisations. To some extent this was eased in January 1946, when the ban on private help was less rigidly enforced and the Allies established 'CARE' (Cooperative for American Remittances to Europe) which covered 22 American charities supplying aid; followed closely a few weeks later by CRALOG (Council of Relief Agencies Licensed for Operation in Germany) which supervised a further 16. According to Bacque it was Herbert Hoover and Victor Gollancz who pressurised governments into relaxing the ban on private aid to the German population, thus easing the plight of the civilians. Yet, despite these initiatives, no aid was sent by either organisation until October 1946. In 1945-46, the number of calories per adult per day was 900 in the British and American zones of occupation, and in 1947 the situation remained so critical that appeals were published in Canadian newspapers on behalf of Canadian Lutheran World Relief, entitled '*At Christmas remember the starving children in the British Zone of Germany*'.[26]

For those children who had been members of the Hitler Youth, life was even more difficult, especially when it came to finding gainful employment. As it had been virtually compulsory to be members of the organisation, this situation affected more than 90% of the now adolescent population. Most of the young people claimed to be victims of the system as they had known nothing else. The comradeship which was very much part of the Hitler Youth ideal was by its very nature, dehumanising and destroyed the need to be an individual. Within the organisation food, shelter and clothes were provided, routines were enforced and dictated by the State, and the daily rigours of existence and personal worries were removed. As a result, the camaraderie within the Hitler Youth was itself a source of 'decivilisation' which for some made it all the more difficult to cope with life 'outside' the organisation.

Over time, re-socialisation was gradually introduced, first of all in the Allied internment camps and then outside where youth and social clubs were initiated for leisure activities and democratisation purposes. This policy was not accepted by everybody as some of the young people had been so immersed in National Socialism that they found it difficult to accept any other doctrine. What's more, although there were some classes such as farming,

---

23 Heinl op cit px
24 James Bacque. 'Crimes and Mercies. The fate of German civilians under Allied Occupation 1944-1950', Toronto: Little, Brown and Co., 1997 288 pp.
25 ibid p.88
26 In July 1946 around 400 German children were sent to Ireland for three years to get over the rigours of war and these were followed by a further 100 in 1948. ibid p165

horticulture, commerce and trades, aimed specifically at getting people back into the work place, some of the teaching and instructional methods employed by the occupying forces were less than subtle, resulting in abject rejection by many participants.

In August 1946, there was a political amnesty in the American and British sectors, an offer that was not fully accepted by the die-hard ex-members of the Hitler Youth. Having grown up in a one-party system they had to be taught the merits of multi-party politics. At the Nuremburg Trial in 1946, Baldur von Schirach stressed; *'It is my fault to have educated the youth in the service of a man who was a murderer of millions. I believed in this man. This is all I can say in my defence, or to explain my actions. I bore the responsibility for youth. I held it in my charge, and hence I alone bear the guilt for these juveniles. The young generation is guiltless'.*[27]

According to Michael Kater, despite von Schirach's confession the Hitler Youth had to be answerable on its own behalf. In only being marginally complicit in what happened in the broader spectrum of war, they nonetheless had become part of the system and as such helped guarantee its functionality.[28] However, the question of moral guilt is much more difficult to define and depended very much on the position of the individual within the organisation and their related functions.

Ulla Roberts, herself a German refugee expelled from Czechoslovakia in June 1945, has been researching the effects of war and memory and agrees that the suffering of the children must be seen within the context of the pain caused by the Nazi regime in occupied Europe.[29]

One could argue that *all* children who lived through World War Two were affected in one way or another, especially those who had experienced separation, loneliness, fear and other emotional stress. Dr Hans Keilson, a Dutch psychologist who studied the long-term effects of the persecution of Jewish child survivors separated from their parents and who had then spent much of their lives in hiding, introduced a term called *'sequential traumatisation'* whereby in a situation where a child has been subjected to more than one traumatic event, the latter one confirms the former and thereby increases the impact. Where the child received support from parents, siblings and others, the trauma was lessened, but where no such support was available, the later traumatic experiences became more intense. Although this research was focused on Jewish children, the results can be seen just as strongly within other war child groups, certainly those, like the children of Dutch collaborators, who spent some time in internment camps. One needs to consider the fact that '*hiding*' can also be a relative term. It does not have to mean 'physical' seclusion, but also 'hiding' in terms of an emotional response. Many collaborators children remained, and in some cases remain 'in hiding' trying to keep their own and their family's past a secret.

The same effect is apparent in Germany where children have not only had to live 'with a past', but in some cases have had to contend with the 'sins of their fathers'. When interviewed a son of a leading member of the Nazi party commented;

> *'I am something like a connecting link between the guilty and the guiltless, the son of the guilty and the father of the guiltless. I feel obliged to give the guiltless a chance. My generation is the generation of bad conscience'.*[30]

In some instances it transcends more than one generation;

> *'...while those who came of age during that time complain that when they were young they were told next to nothing about the Nazi era, today's youth complain that all they hear is that they were, and perhaps still are, a nation of murderers and accomplices'.*[31]

Some of the later 'grandchildren' found the realisation of what had gone on in their parents and grandparents generations, difficult to accept.

---

27 Michael Kater. Hitler Youth Harvard. 2004 p261
28 ibid
29 Ulla Roberts. War and Memory: the long shadows of childhood in Nazi Germany. Conference Paper. April 2005. Frankfurt.
30 'Werner' in Peter Sichrovsky. Born Guilty. New York 1988 p147
31 ibid p165

> *'…of course I knew that there had been concentration camps and that 6 million Jews had been murdered. We'd been told about it in school. But I also learned about the Crusades and later, when I was older, about the French Revolution. And later still about World War Two and gas chambers. But who, for God's sake, had ever told us that our own parents had been there?'* [32]

In Finland the situation was perhaps worse because thousands never returned to the country after the war was over, and it was not until the mid-1950s that legal proceedings to get some of the remaining children back from Sweden were stopped. As in Britain, returning home for some of the children was problematic and, again as in the UK, they often came back to families and siblings they did not know and speaking a language many of them no longer understood. Over the years, many children forgot their Finnish roots and biological parents, and their relationships with their Swedish foster parents grew stronger. This especially affected those children who were separated from their mothers for long periods of time, while many of those under the age of three, with few or any memories of home, forgot all about their families.

As a result, unless the parents could speak Swedish, or in some cases Danish, basic communications within the family broke down. In addition, they were often bullied and ostracised in schools, in some cases even by the teachers and this may also have affected their academic progress as studies have indicated that war children coming back from their evacuation did less well in school than those children who had remained in Finland for the duration of the war.

Such has been the response to the long term effects of this separation, that in modern day Finland the media has shown dramatic reconstructions of the evacuation on Finnish children's television in an attempt to illustrate the difficulties that their grandparents might have faced. The programmes were so popular when they were first broadcast that they were repeated on prime-time television for adults. In addition there was also an award winning feature film called 'Mother of Mine', which dealt with the problems of not only the evacuation, but also the effect it had on the mothers, in this case the foster mother.

Research carried out by Dr Pertti Kaven and the late Professor Singa Sandelin-Benko (both Finnish war-children), show that guilt was a common factor among the Finnish families, particularly the mothers who had sent their children away. Many also felt jealous of the fact that in some instances their children had been better looked after and enjoyed a higher standard of living than they could have provided in Finland.

There were also serious problems with some parents simply not wishing to have their children back.[33] The main reasons given were parental willingness to shed their economic and educational responsibilities and an alienation and indifference regarding the future prospects of their children. This is one of the saddest, and unexpected, results of the evacuation of Finnish children to Sweden.

In addition, some of the Finnish evacuees themselves did not want to go back home, or if they did so, to stay for any length of time. As many of the children, some from very poor rural backgrounds, had enjoyed a much better standard of living in Sweden, their eventual return to an impoverished Finland was one of the most difficult experiences they had ever faced.[34] A lot of the homes in the country, especially those in the previous conflict zones, were in a serious state of decline after the war so some of the children came back to a life of poverty and deprivation.

Sirpa Kaukinen returned to Turku and found herself *'missing paradise: her room in Sweden, the spaciousness of it all, the fields, the food….the certainty of it all'*. She remembers the return to Finland as the greatest trauma she suffered, far worse than leaving on the outward journey.[35]

---

32 'Anna' ibid p165
33 At the end of the war an enquiry was set up and 600 families in Helsinki were asked about their children still resident in Sweden. Surprisingly, only 33% wanted them home
34 Räsänen, Eila: The effect of the Separation Experiences during Childhood on the Mental and Physical Health and social Well-being in Adulthood. A psychosocial study of the later effects of war-child separation experiences. University of Kuopio. 1988. pp 121-123.
35 Sue Saffle. Children War and the rhetoric of remembrance. The Stories of Finland's war children. Children in War Journal. DSM. Dec.2006 p101.

The majority of Finnish war children recall their time in Sweden as a positive experience and once they became adults and able to make their own choices, many of them returned to Sweden in the emigration wave of the 1960s. One Swedish study by Eric de Geer found that 16% of the Finns who had settled in the Gothenburg region in the 1960s were former war children.[36]

But there were some who had suffered during their evacuation. Marja Bell, sent to Sweden when 8 years old, was fostered by a dentist who insisted on showing off her good teeth. The new clothes she had been sent away in had been burned in case they harboured lice and she was forced to wear outfits which were too small for her. Eventually, after many letters home, she returned to Finland.[37] There are other examples. Soila Ilveskola who lived in Sweden for two years with an elderly couple was abused and forced to weed complete fields of sugar beet. Anita Lof, called *'Finnish Brat'* by her hosts, had to sleep in the kitchen and was not allowed to go anywhere else in the house.[38]

Finland had lost a significant percentage of its young people to Sweden, and thereby its next generation and as such the return of the children became a political 'hot potato' for the next decade with some political parties demanding immediate repatriation and others exercising caution. Problems stemmed from one of the hidden agendas of the evacuation to Sweden which was that the arrival of the Finnish children helped fill the population gap that had been created within the country when the birth rate declined in the 1930s[39].

There were long-term implications. In 1942, the Finnish Parliament thought there was a serious risk of losing children to Sweden if the child transports continued and the Conservative parties suggested that Finland should resign from the 1931 Scandinavian Treaty regarding marriage and adoption and they wanted an amendment making adoption of a Finnish child always dependent of the permission of the Finnish Minister of Justice. It is thought by modern researchers[40] that this could perhaps be seen as one of the underlying motives to the whole of the Parliamentary treatment of child transports to Sweden. In addition, the Swedes may well have objected to the fact that the number of adoptions taking place in the country was being closely monitored by the Finnish authorities.

In Finland, the criticism levelled against the child transports was started by IKL, The Patriotic Movement of Finnish People, a party aligned to German politics. According to Fagerholm, a social-democrat and well known for his anti-German feeling, child transports *'were a living symbol of the solidarity between Finland and Sweden'* and he believed that the hidden agenda behind the IKL's policy was to alienate the two Nordic countries from each other, and by so doing, increase German influence. Risto Ryti , the President of Finland, and other political leaders did not accept Fagerholm's interpretation of events. Nonetheless, there was a serious concern that the valuable political relationship between Finland and Sweden should not be jeopardised in any way. As a result from February 1942, all negative criticism of the child transports to Sweden was censored and replaced by a policy of positive propaganda in favour of them. To add weight to the party-line, the Finnish Aid Bureau urged parents to write thank-you letters to their child's host in Sweden so that they could be published in Swedish newspapers.

When one evaluates the effectiveness of the measures introduced by the Finnish Government in 1942, one can see that they did not introduce, or even consider, any legislation which would have actually prevented the adoption, and thereby permanent residence in Sweden, of Finnish children. In addition, the written agreement signed by parents stating that the child would 'under no circumstances' be left in Sweden permanently, had no authority after the war. Had the country withdrawn from the 1931 Treaty on Adoption, which required that all legal procedures relating to adoption were carried out according to the legislation in the host country, it would have harmed the political relationship between the two countries. In fact it was still legally possible to prevent

36 De Geer, Eric. The Finnish war-children in Sweden 1941. Special edition of the book 'The Finnish language in Sweden nr 39'. Stockholm 1986.

37 Saffle. op cit p101

38 ibid p101

39 Two Swedish demographers, Alva and Gunnar Myrdal, had written a startling book in 1935 called 'Crisis in the population', and a committee had been set by the Government to find ways to solve this problem, mainly by giving economic support to families.

40 Pertti Kaven, the late Prof. Benko

adoptions of Finnish children by Swedish parents, but under some circumstances such actions would have been harmful to the child who had wanted to stay with their Swedish hosts, and were not considered to be part of the family.

The fears about the delay in the repatriation of some children after the war proved to be well founded and continued into the 1990s.[41] There was a lot of discussion in the Finnish Parliament about the problems of the children remaining in Sweden and in some cases it became a very difficult process to get them home.[42] Although the 'Committee for transporting Finnish Children to Sweden' wanted to repatriate them all, the Finns compromised and on the 28th March 1946 made the decision that certain categories of children could remain in Sweden if they wished to. The list included:

- Orphans.
- Those in a situation where there was either sickness in the Finnish homes or where the domestic situation was not conducive to their return.
- Those where the economic circumstances of the Finnish family was poor.
- Those where there was no suitable residence for the child to return to.
- Those for whom a return would interrupt occupational and vocational training in Sweden.

A private passport was to be arranged for the children meeting these criteria, and the Committee was given the authority to make a foster-child agreement with both the Swedish and Finnish parents to ensure the legal status of the children remaining in Sweden.

The list of those eligible for residency meant that almost all the children could stay in Sweden. But the committee was in a difficult position. If they made a formal request that the children should return home, there was a possibility that general Swedish humanitarian aid to post-war Finland would be affected. Throughout the war there always seemed to be some sort of economic concern underlying the war-child situation and the Finnish Government's motives cannot always be seen as being entirely philanthropic. One gets the impression that the children became pawns in a bigger political game where the maintenance of good relations with Sweden was a major factor.

In 1949, a new committee was established called '*lastenkotiuttamiskomitea*', 'The Committee for the Repatriation of Finnish children'. Its brief was to look at the legal issues surrounding the return of the children remaining overseas but it was too late to have any effect. By this time very little could be done, and the requirement of the Committee that Finnish legislation should be used to bring about the return of children had little or no significance.

While passive legal attempts were made to bring the Finnish evacuees home from Sweden other children were in a state of abject turmoil.

One can only commiserate with those children, who as part of the migrant horde of collaborator families moving from Germany back to the Netherlands at the closing stages of the war, found themselves at the end of their

---

41 Finland ratified the Hague Convention on the Civil Aspects of International Child Abduction in 1994. The most important features of these national arrangements are the following:
– The Hague Convention rules on the return of an abducted child have been made retroactive.
– Only one court, the Court of Appeal of Helsinki, is competent to receive applications and make orders for the return of children. Besides, an order for the return is always immediately enforceable, unless the Supreme Court, upon appeal, orders the stay of enforcement.
– The `fundamental principles" exception in Article 20 of the Convention cannot be invoked against the application in Finnish return proceedings. According to Article 20 the return of the child can be refused where the return would not be permitted by the fundamental principles relating to the protection of human rights and fundamental freedoms of the requested State.
The first cases indicate that the retroactive application of the Convention provided by the Finnish Act has been less successful. The courts have shown obvious reluctance towards the ordering of the return in these cases whereas in the `new" cases the Court of Appeal as well as the Supreme Court have generally followed the spirit of the Convention in a loyal manner. The Hague Convention on Child Abduction of 1980 and its implementation in Finland. Nordic Journal of International Law. Vol 66 No 1. January 1997. Abstract.

42 Initially, according to the Suomi-bureau in Stockholm, it was estimated that 15,000 children remained in Sweden and a further 500 in Denmark. However, these figures for Sweden are now considered to be inflated as Estonian social scientist and demographer, Alur Reinans, together with Pertti Kaven, have calculated that the real figure was about 7000. Their research was based on the Swedish population registers compiled by the Swedish church. The number of children staying in Denmark is correct because under the German occupation there was a strict registration of anyone entering or leaving the country.

journey confined to internment camps where there was little in the way of comfort and where the overriding concern was daily survival. Peter Heinl makes a very poignant comment when recalling a child's experience in a Danish camp. She had been in a group of German refugees who had been evacuated via the Baltic Sea from Eastern Prussia. However, instead of ending up in Germany, they were dropped off in a Danish port and ended up in an internment camp. *'....she and her family were forced to spend several years in the camp where there was neither warmth nor lightheartedness. Even a teddy bear*[43]*, which might have given her some comfort and company, was unobtainable behind the fence....'* [44]

(This was almost 70 years ago, but the description could equally apply to similar scenes being replicated in the world today.)

Many children in such circumstances, not only in Germany, were conditioned to repress their fears in order to cope with everyday living. In so doing, some entered adolescence and adulthood believing that there was neither a place to call home, nor a relationship they could consider secure.

> *'I don't have a sense of belonging to a place, a town or a region. I lost my home and became a refugee, a fate shared by millions of other children. I have always grasped at the sense of collective identity, the sense of community, in painful experiences and in the sense of consolation. I believe this was important to me as a child'.*[45]

Such concerns have led to low self-esteem and lack of identity on the part of the war-child; traits which are very apparent in collaborators children who continue to question who they really are, will they make the same mistakes as their parents, will they ever become a 'person' in their own right?

Some children were not even given the chance to escape and were again interned within their adopted countries, very much a feature of post-war Czechoslovakia, where German-Czech families found themselves subjected to arrest and imprisonment.

In some cases parental fears overrode the desire to gain safety. Peter Heinl recalls an example where a woman, living on her own and fearing the advance of the Red Army, instructed her eldest son to shoot her first, then his younger brother, and then himself. He obeyed and a whole family was wiped out, consigned to the pages of history as a simple statistic.

As well as the effects of the tangible aspects of war such as air-raids, death, destruction and devastation, one must remember that many of these war-children across post-war Europe (and indeed in parts of the world today), who were concerned primarily with survival, have memories of environmental and personal experiences which manifest themselves in their later lives as psychological triggers. Their need for food, warmth, and a sense of belonging occur many times within their stories.

As a child this woman had left Danzig and remembers the snow on the road leading to the railway station;

> *'Whenever I recall the time when we fled, I always experience a cold sensation. I always feel cold. My feet turn as cold as ice. Nothing helps me to keep warm. My nice woollen socks make no difference to this feeling I get. When I look outside, the summer landscape which is filled with illuminating green trees and vibrant flowers,....suddenly turns white'.*[46]

Another woman, now suffering from depression, had been taken into a children's home and recalled how desperately cold it was in the winter of 1944-5. This '*coldness*' and memory of '*cold*' has affected her ever since and her depressive state is not only more intense during the winter months, but she is almost in a suicidal state if the heating in her house fails.[47]

---

43 Interesting to note that some UK evacuees had their dolls and teddy bears confiscated because they took up too much room in their luggage!!
44 Peter Heinl. op cit p71
45 Roberts op cit
46 Heinl op cit. p53
47 ibid p15

What present day research[48] shows is that trans-generational transmission of war trauma does not fit in neatly with historical dates or periods and does not stop when wars or conflicts end, so it is important that such data is considered by those dealing with children in present day war zones, such as the civil conflicts in Africa and the so called drug wars in parts of South America. The examples mentioned above are not confined to children of World War Two and the post-war years of the late 40s and early 50s. The same issues are being witnessed today and significantly not only with children in areas of conflict. Psychological and social problems brought on by separation are now apparent in some children whose fathers have been deployed to war zones. (see Postscript).

So much evidence of war-related trauma in children is now available that it simply cannot be ignored. Authorities can no longer bury their heads in the sand and repeat the same adage that *'they are only children they will grow out of it'* which we now know not to be true. It should be the responsibility of governments and child-welfare organisations around the world, especially those in present day war zones, to make sure that the cycle of trauma is broken at some point.

One has to acknowledge that some countries, unlike Britain, have recognised the importance of confronting the issues and are now dealing with the problems that ex-war children have had within their own countries. In the Netherlands there is now a greater awareness of the discrimination levelled at the children of collaborators, largely as a result of the work done by the Herkenning group. Although as children they were not the guilty ones, the title of a recent autobiography '*Not Guilty. All the same punished*' would indicate that the scars still run deep. For the past 20 years there has also been a significant change in the way in which Germany has been addressing the question of the Nazi era. Rather than simply ignoring it, teachers and psychologists now recognise that in order to inform future generations, there is an obligation to record the memories of all of those who took part in the rise and fall of the Reich, both the victims and the perpetrators,. Uniquely, the Norwegian government has offered financial compensation to the children of so called 'Quislings' in recognition of the state's harsh treatment of them both during and after the war.

For some adults who have lived through various conflicts as children, the long term effects are very similar in nature. The work that Dr Peter Heinl and Dr Helga Spranger and have been doing in Germany, the late Prof Sandelin Benko's and Dr Pertti Kaven's research into the Finnish/Swedish scheme, Prof. Marina Gulina in Leningrad/St Petersburg, and my own investigation into evacuees in Britain, have exposed the similarities in the symptoms of war-child separation. One positive result from the Leningrad research is that deprivation of even the most basic necessities, even in very early childhood, and for a very long time, does not stop the child's personal development if there is psychological support within the family. In addition, the child in such circumstances can often transform traumatic experience into something positive and creative. The important thing to consider is that some of the children mentioned in this book, did not have, and still do not have, the security of a family structure. Many have had to cope on their own with little support from familial and external sources.

The past 70 years have witnessed the removal of many of the physical reminders of the Second World War. The bomb-sites and buildings have been renovated and restored, cities have been rebuilt, public air-raid shelters have been removed, and personal effects and ephemera have been dispatched to museums. The War has now been consigned to a time in history which present generations are able to witness on various television channels, read about it books and tactically reconstruct on their I-pads. Unfortunately those who participated in the war, including the children and evacuees, are included in this 'media package' and little attention is paid to their present situation and state of mind.

Although there seems to be an increasing concern within society for the welfare of children in war-torn areas, the long term effects are still largely ignored and for some 'children' the attempt to create and maintain some air of post-war normality has been hindered by trials, tribulations and intrusive memories. Those of us working with war children now have a responsibility to study these long-term effects so that present and future governments can be informed and advised on how to provide support, both short and long term, to children in war zones and to

48 Peter Heinl Maikäfer flieg, dein Vater ist im Krieg Seelische Wunden aus der Kriegskindheit Kösel-Verlag, 1994 and Splintered Innocence op cit

make the results of our research known in order to stop the present cycle of War Child abuse continuing. This will be a difficult task, but one which, with dedication, will hopefully have a positive effect on future generations of children. If this does *not* happen, then we are not learning from the past, however if it does then there might be some hope that the mistakes of the past will not be repeated in the future.

Graça Machel is correct when she states that the International Community must address the plight of war-affected children and women with new urgency. Their protection is not a matter of negotiation. Those who wage war, or legitimise and support wars must be condemned and held to account as surely the children must be cherished and protected. Children cannot afford to wait.

In conclusion, this is why our research is important. The psychological and sociological problems being experienced by children in present day war zones is almost exactly the same as those in World War Two. Many are robbed of a childhood, miss out on their education, suffer from the lack of family relationships, feel guilty, lack security and have an indeterminate future.

A former child migrant received the following advice from her employer:

> *'You are the hardest working, most reliable, punctual girl I have ever had the pleasure to employ, but your insecurity stands in the way of promotion with this company. If you want my advice, girl, go out there and find out who you are and come back and see me when you find yourself.'* [49].

The final comment should be left to Peter Heinl who in a few simple words encapsulates the reason why we continue to research and work with war children:-

> *'....sadly, there is no end in sight for wars on this planet. The childhood sufferers of today will be the suffering adults of tomorrow. Peace stands by helplessly. There is one conclusion, which can be drawn firmly with respect to children in war time, be it victory or defeat: children tend to be the great losers overlooked by history'.* [50]

---

49 Alan Gill op.cit p29
50 Heinl op cit p.x

Postscript

'Many authors over time have referred to the rationale of war as something which is politically determined. To put it simply, attack to destroy, capture, raid or defend.

But a better suggestion is that the purpose of war must be to establish a better peace. If this is the case we have to comprehend the full (generational) consequences of warfare. The research reflected in this book goes some way to understanding the long-term costs for a society at war; costs which should be weighed up before politicians are determined to fight again.'[1]

Surprisingly, despite extensive research and the opening up of previously closed files, it is still very difficult to get a totally balanced view of what happened during the British evacuations of 1939, 1940 and 1944. While countries such as Norway and the Netherlands have recognised that the children of collaborators have been treated badly by the authorities, and Sweden and Finland have made a conscious effort to tell the story of their war children through various media channels, and some Scandinavian countries hold a War Child Memorial day, little has been done in the UK; so why the reticence?

First, there is always the problem that the emotional factors inherent in this period of history will sometimes influence the objective and rational views of those people who lived through it.

Second, a general ignorance of the complex nature of evacuation and the effects the experience had on those taking part; not only the children but the families, teachers, billeting officers, hosts and all those in the administration and support services. Many of the present day opinions are still based on the effective, sometimes misleading, propaganda surrounding Operation Pied Piper and although the objective evidence is available, it takes a great deal of time, patience and determination to trawl through the relevant documents to find it. As a result many simply rely on their own memories, second or third hand stories and the myths and prejudices which have come from the time. As an example; at a commemorative parade and reunion in Weymouth in July 1998, an ex-evacuee was persistently verbally harangued by a wartime member of the Women's Land Army who stated that the evacuees had no right to march in the procession because they had not been bombed or machine-gunned,[2]

There is a great deal of evidence to show that the wartime experience of many evacuees was just as traumatic as others affected by the war, and one only needs to look at the evidence of the bombing of the Sandhurst Road School and the sinking of the SS.City of Benares to see that many were subjected to direct enemy attacks. The problem is that such facts are not reaching the general public, and although one would suggest that some people might be aware of the tragedy of the Benares, few would know about Sandhurst Road. This is not altogether their fault as there is still an element of 'selection' in the material allowed in text books and other media as some publishers and producers are more interested in the bigger picture rather than specific elements within it. Unfortunately, as 'evacuation' is not seen as directly contributing to the war effort, it often comes a long way down the list of priorities.

However, what has happened over the past few years, albeit slowly, is an acknowledgement in some quarters that the research into the long-term effects of exposure to war and separation carried out on 'children' of the 1940s, can now be applied to behavioural and psychological problems exhibited by some modern day service children and those in present war zones.

Many welfare officers in the armed forces now recognise the effect that the deployment of parents, usually fathers, has on children, and there is a greater awareness of what anxiety and emotional turmoil these children may be going through.

---

1 Lt. Col. C.S.MacGregor
2 Correspondent to 'The Evacuee'. August 1998.

In-service training being carried out in schools which have a high percentage of service children has resulted in not only some curriculum and pastoral materials being developed to make all pupils aware of potential signs of stress in their peers,[3] but also developa better understanding by staff of the effects that separation, and the frequent relocation to different schools has on the child's relationships with family and friends, and their educational achievement. Moreover, new school transfer records are being trialled which not only provide details of the number of schools a service-child has attended, but also include a list of where the father has been deployed during the child's school career, because the latter can be of great significance when assessing the impact on the child's education and life in general.

In addition, as part of the overall 'package' Service organisations are attempting to maintain a closer link between children and parents on deployment through support networks[4] and initiatives such as 'Reading Forces'[5,] 'Emotional First Aid', the 'Big White Wall', and books such as *'My Daddy's Going Away'*[6] and '*Service Children: A Guide for Education and Welfare Professionals'*.[7]

Despite the detractors, it is encouraging to see that research related to European war-children of the 1940s is now having a positive effect on the lives of the present and future generation of children.

Finally.....

It is important to remember that many of the war children referred to in this book came from a generation and a time when one just didn't talk about personal fears, anxieties and emotional problems, but just got on with life.

Fortunately, a cry for help is not seen now as a sign of weakness, and there is no longer any need to suffer in silence or have to confront the past alone.

If you have read this book and are an ex-war child yourself, or you know of someone who perhaps needs help and support, the following organisations will be able to provide information about their services and membership.

The Evacuees Reunion Association. era@evacueesreunion.co.uk

The Finnish War Child Association. www.sotalapset.fi

Service Children's Support Network. www.servicechildrensupportnetwork.com

The Swedish War Child Association. www.krigsbarn.se

The Herkenning (Children of Dutch Collaborators). www.werkgroepherkenning.nl

German War Children. www.kriegskinder.de

Norway. www.nkbf.no

---

3 Much of this classroom work has been carried out by Pippa Bleach. Head of Humanities at Connaught School Aldershot.
4. Joy O'Neill See www.servicechildrensupportnetwork.com
5 Initiated by Dr Alison Baverstock.
6 Author. Lt. Col C.S. MacGregor (Christopher)
7 Author. Joy O'Neill

Appendices

Appendix 1

Letter to All Householders in Shaftesbury, Dorset relating to Government Survey. January 1939

Shaftesbury Rural District Council.

16th January 1939.

Dear Sir or Madam

GOVERNMENT EVACUATION SCHEME

The Council have been requested by the Government to co-operate in plans which are being made for the protection of civil life in the event of war.

Recent experience in other countries has shown that under the conditions of modern warfare the greatest loss of life is caused by bombardment from the air. This danger is most acute in crowded cities. It is to lessen this danger in case our own country were involved in war, that arrangements are being made now to enable children to leave the crowded cities and be received in homes elsewhere. This protection can only be given with the co-operation of those like ourselves who live in the less congested towns or villages. We shall all agree that it is necessary for all of us to help in this plan for saving human life.

We are aware that some arrangements were made last September as a matter of emergency which had perforce to be improvised, but we are sure that, in the light of the experience gained, we shall be able to improve on these. The plans for this, as for other branches of civil defence, must be made in time of peace. We hope that it will never be necessary to put them into operation, but we shall all be all the happier to know that the plans have been made and that if ever they do have to be put into operation, the work will be done in an ordered manner, and that all will know their parts.

The Government has asked each local authority in the country to find out what housing accommodation would be available in case of emergency, and what homes would be suitable for those children who would be given the means of leaving the great cities. It is particularly important to know in which houses homes could be provided for the children, where they could be lodged, boarded and cared for. Payment would be made by the Government at the following rate:-

Evacuees:allowances
For Unaccompanied School children lodged and boarded:

10s 6d per week where one child is taken.
8s 6d per week per child where more than one child is taken.

For Children under School age accompanied by their mothers, or some other person who will be responsible for looking after them:

For lodging only:

5s per week for each adult.

3s per week per child

For lodging for a Teacher or Helper only:

5s per week.

School children would be moved school by school, accompanied by their teachers, and arrangements would be made for the children to attend school in the districts to which they were taken.

A visitor, representing the local authority, will call upon you in the near future to find out how far you will be able to assist in this matter, and will produce to you a card showing that he or she is authorised to make these inquiries.

This note is sent to you now in order that you may be aware, in advance, of this enquiry, and why it is being made.

We give you an assurance that the information supplied by you will not be used for any other purpose than that which we have described, and that it will not involve you in any work or responsibility unless and until an emergency arises. We feel that we can rely on the people of the district to offer all the help they possibly can in this important branch of civil defence. It needs no words of ours to convey to you what that help will mean to children of the big cities.

Yours faithfully.

F.S.Miller, Chairman of the Council

C.E.G.Vesey Lt-Col. Chairman of the A.R.P. Committee.

Appendix 2

Average school attendance across Bristol. October 1939-April 1942.

BRO 21131/EC/Adm/M/12/1 Evacuation Committee.

Date	Average no. on registers
1939- October	50009.2
November	50265.8
December	50350.7
1940- January	49287.7
February	49712.1
March	49885.3
April	49690.9
May	49913.7
June	50327.5
July	44956.7
August	47969.1
September	46766.4
October	47512.7
November	45304.7
December	46934.4
1941 January	43815.1
February	40813.8
March	36689.9
April	34376.8
May	31079.0
June	28137.7
July	29278.2
August	30217.8
September	31668.8
October	33177.3
November	33569.7
December	33701.9
1942 January	34003.3
February	35906.5
Mar	37743.0
April	38185.1

Appendix 3

Women's Organisations

Women's Organisations which became directly concerned with social poverty during the latter stages of the war and afterwards.

This list does not include the Women's Institute and the Women's Voluntary Service which are mentioned in the text.

National Council of Women

13,000 'Educated' women. They spent a great deal of their time planning for post-war Britain.

National Union of Townswomen's Guild

This comprised of 554 branches containing between 10 and 20 members.

Soroptimist Clubs

3,500 professional women.

Women's Mutual Service Club

12,000 working class women.

Source: Holman. p142-3

Appendix 4

Evacuees Remaining in Reception Areas in January 1940

	From Evac areas in England		From Evac areas in Scotland			
	Number Remaining	%	Number Remaining	%	Total Remaining	%
Unaccompanied Children	420,000	55	37,600	61	457,600	55
Mothers & Accompanied Children	56,000	13	8,900	9	64,900	12
Expectant Mothers	1,100	9	40	10	1,140	9
Blind Persons, Cripples & Special Cases	2,280	43	160	9	2,440	35
Teachers & Helpers	43,400	49	3,100	23	46,500	45
Total	522,780	40	49,800	28	572,580	39

Source. Problems of Social Policy. HMSO 1950 p172

Appendix 5

School Attendance;Statistics December 1940-December 1941

(Average attendance pre-war. 87%)

Year/Month	Estimated No of Children of School Age in London	Number on Roll	Number on Half-time	% of Attendance
1st Nov 1939	70,000	—	—	—
31st Dec 1939	192,000	—	—	—
May 1940	240,000	—	—	—
July 1940	181,000	—	—	—
December 1940	80,400	44,400	—	—
January 1941	81,200	56,600	—	—
February 1941	89,200	75,125	2,246	—
March 1941	95,200	86,662	6,070	—
April 1941	103,300	94,445	7,228	—
May 1941	104,400	93,282	6,802	—
June 1941	105,500	98,470	4,070	—
July 1941	112,700	109,983	2,954	82.7
August 1941	120,400	117,355	2,212	76.6*
September 1941	128,500	125,145	2,546	79.9*
October 1941	135,800	132,858	1,866	83.5*
November 1941	141,100	138,793	1,192	83.1
December 1941	149,934	148,430	695	82.8

* These figures were affected by the number of children hop-picking in Kent.

School Attendance;Statistics: 1942-1945

Year/Month	Number Of Schools	Estimated No. of Children of School Age in London	Number on Roll (4)	Under 5s on Roll	Number on Half-time	% of Attendance
March 1942	579	178,200	175,974	2,703	1,645	84.1
June 1942	630	202,800	200,915	4,315	1,741	85.1
September 1942	657	213,700	211,613	5,462	1,081	78.8
December 1942	674	222,500	220,887	5,523	454	82.8
June 1943	724	235,400	234,354	6,369	348	85.3
December 1943	741	243,100	241,419	8,858	39	77.9
February 1944*	—	245,000	—	—	—	—
June 1944	705	237,200	235,670	8,673	788	32.0
September 1944	661	128,994	127,273	4,116	174	79.8
October 1944*	—	136,500	—	—	—	—
December 1944*	668	173,178	172,418	5,227	347	84.7
March 1945	692	191,960	190,445	5,820	nil	82.1
May 1945*	—	213,500	—	—	—	—

* Taken from statistics showing only estimated number of children of school age in London.

Source: Samways op.cit. p34.

Appendix 6

Mr Walter Elliott's Broadcast on the 6th January 1939.

'Transfer of Population in Time of War'

There are many big tasks we want to forward in the coming year. We want to press on with housing, with health, to make sure that in the schools, in the homes, in the factories, in the shops, in the countryside, the possibilities which our times open out, for a happier life for all, are secured. But there are possibilities of emergency ahead, as well as possibilities of peace.

One of the biggest problems is, undoubtedly, what is called evacuation, that is to say many people would leave, many people ought to leave, crowded or dangerous areas in time of war. Who are they to be? Where are they to go?

Well, first, I do not want you to think that the policy is to *empty* our big cities. Nothing of the sort. Most people will and should stay where they are, carrying on with their ordinary duties; for most of us, in fact, are engaged on work of real service to our country. There will, however, be many who should go to places where they will be relatively safer.

Of these, children must come first. There are many children in Great Britain, eight million of them. Many of them, of course, are in places of relative safety. But there are a million of these children in London alone. Without doubt there would be, in time of trouble, and even when trouble was feared, a widespread rush to get children away from dangerous areas. Unless that is organised beforehand there will not only be widespread distress amongst the families in exposed areas, there will be enormous disorganisation in areas into which people might flock. Take shops in these areas, for instance. they would be sold out of supplies in twenty-four hours if nothing was done.

To organise this, it is clear that we have to look for homes for the children mainly in houses where people already *are*. Empty houses and camps will be used as far as possible; but the mere numbers make it impossible to rely on these alone. We cannot always rely on summer weather. We may have wintry weather like tonight. In the recent storms many camps where children *were*, had to be cleared into surrounding houses.

What will the method be? Schools will be moved as units, with their teachers who will continue with their education. These school children will need both board and lodging. But when children have their mother or someone else to look after them the householder will be asked to provide lodging only. But it is not only the householder; we have all got a part to play.

The Local Authorities will arrange for reception.

The Government will provide transport, will put money in the householder's purse, and will see that there is food in the shops, at reasonable prices, for that purse to buy. *Detailed* arrangements for these matters are well advanced.

I know that money does not settle everything. So the Government and the Local Authorities are doing their best to make allowances for the thousand and one individual differences. We have to see not only that the houses for instance are suitable for the children, but that the children are suitable for the homes. We want this to be a matter of real human relationship and affection, a willing host and a willing guest. The whole nation will have to feel itself as one if such a crisis really comes. And remember, no one can say 'My house will never be destroyed'. It may be for any of us to ask, as well as to give, this national hospitality.

Is anything going to be done about it immediately?

Yes. That is why I am talking to you tonight. Amongst other things, Mr. Colville and I are asking the Local Authorities in England, Scotland and Wales to make a survey of housing accommodation by the end of next month.

What do we want to know? We want information about the number of rooms and the people already in the house. We want to estimate how many people could be properly accommodated, for we don't want either the guests or the hosts to be overcrowded. We also want to know about existing responsibilities of the household, whether, for example, the householder is aged or infirm, or out all day, or perhaps himself or herself expecting relatives. Whether a farmer, for instance, needs his spare rooms for extra workers; whether the householder needs extra bedding.

Obviously the more information we can get the better it will be for everybody.

So householders will shortly be visited and asked for this information. It will be confidential, collected for this emergency purpose alone, and will be used for no other purpose. I hope therefore, that every householder, whatever his or her personal circumstances, will give all possible help to the visitors.

Finally, this work differs from most of our work, the real tasks of which I spoke to you when I began. Here our great hope and prayer about this is that it may never be needed at all. But the foundations of our work must be sound if our life is to be happy; and one of the foundation stones of any nation is that it has thought of danger, faced danger, and decided on action so that in danger it may be secure.

Appendix 7

Ashley Green School

In order to put the effect on a small school of a migrant evacuee population into perspective it is worth listing the schools where evacuees came from to join the two-roomed village school at Ashley Green in Buckinghamshire, the subject of the film 'Village School'. The information is taken from the school registers 1939 - 45 found in the Bucks. Record Office in Aylesbury. Not all the pupils remained for a long time, in fact some only stayed for a few days and there is no indication as to which evacuees were privately evacuated or those which were sent under the Government Scheme.

Year	School
1939	St. Thomas More's Roman Catholic School, London St.
	Crayford Council School, Kent.
	St. Sepulchres, London EC1
	Central Street School, London EC1
1940	Mile End Senior School
	Mile End Central School
	St. Lawrence School, Ramsgate
	Ellington Rd. School, Ramsgate
	All Souls School, London NW6
	Methodist School, Canterbury.
	Mount Pleasant School. London E5
	Detmold Rd. School. London E5
	Downspark Grocers School
	Scarthoe School, Grimsby
	Sigdon Road School
	North Hackney Central
	Wilberforce School Paddington
	Coventry Road School, Nottingham.
	Ennersdale School, Lewisham.
	Greenham School, Uxbridge.
1941	Tottenham Road School, London N1
	Totworth School, Bristol.
1944	Culver School, Tottenham
	Headstone School, Pinner
	St. Joseph's Convent School, Sidcup
	Downhills School, London N15
	Haberdashers School, West Acton
	Chesterfield Road School, Enfield
	Chater School, Watford

Appendix 8

Barnett House Group

A précis of the recommendations for the development of education provision made by the Barnett House Study Group in the light of their research into a group of Evacuee children billeted in war-time Oxford.

1. Extension of the scope of education. Provision should be extended to include:-

   '...a lively environment in which, by pursuit of a variety of interests and activities, both boys and girls alike may bring to fruition the character and capacities with which they are severally endowed.'

2. Extension of Day-school activities: The scope of non-academic education in day schools should be extended.
3. Provision of Rooms for Private Reading and Study: They suggested that if children are to have a fair chance of developing their individual 'gifts and abilities' they must be provided with the opportunity for private study. As many pupils do not have access to this provision at home the school should provide it.
4. Residential Country terms for Urban Schools: Evacuation had created a greater awareness of life in the country and as an extension of this it was suggested that schools maintain a 'country department' which would be a residential facility where town children could spend at least three terms and provide the opportunity of studying all aspects of rural life.

Finally it was thought, surprisingly, that there should be more facilities for boarding education: 35 from 185 of London parents questioned by the group were in favour of some form of boarding provision. Although they did suggest that the sample was too small to reach any significant conclusion.

Source. Barnett House Study Group. A Study of War-time Oxford. OUP. p110-113

Appendix 9

Letter from Clerk of the Bradford-on-Avon RDC. 15th February 1941 concerning Expectant Mothers

Dear Dr. Tangye,

Government Evacuation Scheme.

I confirm my conversation with you on the telephone this morning, with regard to the difficulty which has unfortunately arisen in connection with the Billeting of Expectant Mothers.

The position is that my Billeting Officer found that one of the Expectant Mothers received in this district yesterday appeared, to use his own words, to be 'a lady of a very superior type', and he felt, in order to conscientiously carry out his duty, she should be billeted in a superior type of billet. He therefore billeted her in a fairly large house containing seven rooms, of which, he tells me, four are bedrooms. The Occupier was not at home, but the servant employed there informed the Billeting Officer that not more than three persons would be sleeping there that night, although friends were expected sometime. The Billeting Notice was duly served, and the Expectant Mother billeted, and I have been informed this morning that the Occupier last evening conveyed the Evacuee in her own car to Berryfield House, informed the Matron that the latter could not stay in the House, and she was, therefore, admitted to the Maternity Home, where she is now accommodated. My information with regard to this came from the Maternity Home, and I have had no communication whatsoever from the Occupier concerned, who still retains the Billeting Notice, so far as I am aware.

As you know, upon the facts shown above there would appear to have been an infringement of Defence Regulations on the part of the Occupier by reason of failure to comply with a Billeting Notice, but, apart from this, if the Occupier of a better-class type of house can be so easily relieved of the obligation to provide accommodation as required by a Billeting Notice, what will be the position of Occupiers of smaller houses who do not desire Evacuees and who may do the same thing? It seems to me that the present difficulties with regard to billeting will be increased, and that it will only be possible to Billet upon people who are willing to carry out their obligations, which will mean that certain sections of the community will be imposed upon, and that the authority of the Billeting Officers will count for nothing.

Unfortunately, there has been difficulty before in connection with Billeting Expectant Mothers upon this Occupier. Two expectant mothers were billeted at this house in January, and the next morning the lady who resides at this address called at this Office and to say the least, was far from courteous in her protest, that she should not be expected to co-operate in connection with the operation of the evacuation scheme. A few days later, this lady again called and stated that she had informed the Evacuees that they must leave the house each morning and stay out until the evening, and she was informed that, in my view, this arrangement was contrary to the requirements of the Billeting Notice. The evacuees later called to say that they had been forced to leave the house that morning at short notice, and without being given an opportunity to wash.

I gather that the Occupier contends that no notice was given of the intention to Billet, but, as you are aware, there is no legal necessity to give any notice, and in many cases it is not always practicable to do so. On many occasions I have arranged billets for expectant mothers, given notice of their time of arrival to the occupiers concerned, then at the last moment have found that the persons have not arrived. The results have been that the Occupiers to whom the notice has been given have been very resentful at being put to unnecessary trouble. In other cases Occupiers have deliberately left their homes and remained away during the period of Billeting, in an attempt to avoid having to provide accommodation. It is, therefore, difficult to know what to do for the best, and whatever is done does not meet with the wishes or views of everybody.

At the time of the complaint with regard to the billeting of the two expectant mothers in January, I gathered that one grievance was that certain large houses in the Parish of Westwood were not being used for the provision of accommodation for evacuees, but, as I pointed out, that was a matter for the Rural District Council.

I am sorry to trouble you with this matter, but I do feel that something should be done to prevent a repetition of action such as has now occurred, as, after all, the Occupier has a right of appeal to the Billeting Tribunal if she feels aggrieved, and if the matter is dealt with through the regular channels, no objection can be raised by anybody. On the hand, if the practice is allowed to continue, there is bound to be trouble as Billeting will be practically impossible, except in those cases where the co-operation of the Occupier can be secured. Any help or advice which you can, therefore, kindly give to me in connection with the settling of this unfortunate matter, will be very much appreciated.

Yours truly.

Robert Trace.

Appendix 10

List of Camp School Sites as at the 26th of June 1939

ED/10/236. (sub file number G672/3)

County	Evacuated Area	Site
	LONDON (15)	
Beds		Heath and Reach.
Berks		Cockpole Green.
Bucks		Horseleys Green.
		Penley Hollies, Nr Stokenchurch.
		Moor End
Herts		Nettleden
Oxford		Kennylands
		Bishopswood Farm, Peppard.
		Uxmore Farm, Nr Henley.
Surrey		Merstham.
		Tilford.
		Sayers Croft, Ewhurst.
		Elmbridge, Cranleigh.
Sussex		Coopers Farm, Itchingfield.
		Wrens Warren, Hartfield.
	BIRMINGHAM (3)	
Staffs		Pipe Wood, Rugeley.
		Shooting Butts, Nr Rugeley.
Worcester		Warton's Park Estate, Bewdley.
	MANCHESTER AND LIVERPOOL (6)	
Cheshire		Somerford Hall
		Marton Newchurch.
Denbigh		Colomendy Hall (1)
		Ditto (2)
Lancs.		Moreton Hall, Whalley
	LEEDS & BRADFORD (3)	
Yorks W.R.		Pateley Bridge
		Linton
		Grassington
	NEWCASTLE (2)	
Northumberland		Dukeshouse Wood, Hexham.
		Bellingham.
	SHEFFIELD (1)	
Derby		Woolley Bridge or Kelstedge.
	HULL (1)	
Yorks. E.R		Etton.
	PORTSMOUTH (1)	
Hants		Laverstock. Wisewell.

Appendix 11

RETURN OF EVACUEES TIMETABLE.

Day	Adults And Accompanying Children	Unaccompanied Children
0	(2nd May 1945) Date of Circ informing local authorities that the return plans are to be operated	
3	Complete Delivery of Notices	
6		Complete delivery of notices to householders
10	Complete Cards	
11	Send Completed Cards to SRO	
18		Complete Cards
19		Send Complete Cards to SRO
20	Cards received back from SRO	
22	SRO give first notice of trains	
25	Complete delivery of notices	
29	First Trains run	
35		Cards received back from SRO
37		SRO gives notices of first trains
40		Complete delivery of notices
41		First trains run

(Ref. Devon Record Office. Exeter Box 5)

Appendix 12

Transcript of the broadcast made by HauptmannStuhman relating to the attack on Sandhurst Rd. School. 20th January 1943:-

"We have recently been harassing the English quite a lot on their southern coast. The low-level attack on London in daylight will probably remain for all our airmen an experience which they will remember for a long time. We reached our objectives and dropped our bombs where they were to be dropped. The British flak was active but bad, and the Spitfires which were in the air took no notice of us. While flying away we saw the barrage balloons slowly going up and used the moment to make a diving attack on them.

Interviewer: 'I understand you also attacked industrial buildings with machine-gun fire?'

Stuhman: 'Quite right. We shot, in London, two gas reservoirs into flames and at a railway station an engine was under fire. We also attacked some other things as well".

After the Battle. Vol 3 p214.

(Hauptmann Stuhman was later shot down near Charleroi in August 1943)

For a detailed account of the raid and its aftermath see 'After the Battle'. Vol 3 pp 204 - 214.

Appendix 13

The Continuation War in Finland

25th June 1941 – 4th September 1944

The Finns attacked in July and attempted to occupy the Ladoga region of Karelia. The old border was reached in two months. This was then followed by a long period of trench warfare. Hitler proposed that the Finns should help in the attack on Leningrad or take part in the cutting of the Murmansk railway, but both suggestions were rejected by the Finnish authorities. They were fighting their own war as their goal was to regain the Finnish areas lost in 1940.

With Finland a *de facto* ally of Germany and the British now allied to the Soviet Union, Churchill had no doubts as to where Britain's loyalties should lie. But, well aware of Finland's dilemma, Churchill was reluctant to see the Finns put *'in the dock with the guilty Axis powers'*[1], and hoped that Helsinki could be persuaded to halt its offensive against the USSR. On 10th July 1941, Mannerheim issued a declaration stating that the Finns were determined to cross their 1918 borders and invade Eastern Karelia, held at the time by Russia. As a result, Churchill commented that the Finns should be informed that if they went over the borders, Britain would declare war.[2].....which they did from midday on December 7th 1941

After the German defeat at Stalingrad, the Finns held secret talks with the USSR and Paasikivi again travelled to Moscow. (Paasikivi had been the intermediary before the Winter War and led the Finnish-Russian negotiations in Moscow. When ambassador to Moscow 1940-1941 he was, by necessity, isolated from the most secret decision making initiatives held by the government in Helsinki, and when he found out that they were contemplating entering the conflict on Germany's side, he resigned and retired for a second time).[3] Having seen that Stalin did not intend to change his policies, he supported compliance with some of the Russian demands. After this unsuccessful diplomatic mission, Paasikivi was cast aside from political activities until September 1944, when the peace treaty was finally negotiated and Mannerheim, now President of Finland, asked him to be Prime Minister.[4] (He later became Finnish President from 1946-56).

At the talks, Stalin's terms were harsh and he insisted that Finland should break off relations with Germany, return to the 1940 borders and pay reparations of around £450,000 they were all rejected.

In 1944, the Russians started a huge attack on the Karelian Isthmus and succeeded in breaking through the Finnish lines. The Finns were forced to retreat and abandon Viipuri. Although the defence lines remained intact, Mannerheim had to order the evacuation of Eastern Karelia.

Germany was concerned that the Finns were negotiating a peace and offered to supply weapons and food in order to keep them in the war. As a result, President Ryti wrote to Hitler promising that they would not accept a separate peace. This was called the 'Ribbentrop Agreement' and the new supplies resulting from it enabled the Finns to reinforce their front line and halt the Soviet advance. Stalin was in a hurry to get to Berlin first, and as further attacks by Russian forces failed in the Karelian Isthmus and Eastern Karelia, an Armistice was agreed. President Ryti resigned and Mannerheim was elected President under a special law of 4th August 1944. The Soviet-Finnish Armistice was signed on 4th September 1944 resulting in loss of land and the requirement that Finnish forces should remove the German army from the country.

On the 15th September the 'Lapland War' began. The Germans were taken by surprise and sought revenge. They used the tactic of 'scorched earth', burning almost every building within the whole Lapland area, and laid mines

1 Winston Churchill to Joseph Stalin. Churchill Papers 20/45 21 November 1941
2 Anthony Eden to Sir Stafford Cripps. Foreign Office Papers. 954/24 September 4 1941
3 Paasikivi: Toimintani Moskovassa ja Suomessa 1939-1941. 1986. Paasikivi: My activity in Moscow and Finland 1939-1941. 1986
4 J.K. Paasikiven päiväkirjat 1944-1956. Ensimmäinen osa. !985. The diaries of J.K. Paasikivi from 1944-56. Part one. 1985.

in order to slow down the advance of Finnish troops. The area was virtually destroyed. On 23rd September 1944, actually during the conflict, the evacuation of the population of northern Finland took place. A total of 127,000 Finns and Laplanders were moved, out of which 56, 000 went to northern Sweden with the help of the Swedish Army and the Swedish Red Cross. Many of those who were displaced never returned to their homes again, but resettled in Sweden. The 'Lapland War' ended on 25th April 1945, but the last battle between Finnish and German forces did not take place until two days later on the 27th.[5]

Although Finland was never occupied, and was the only country that had achieved independence at the end of World War One to remain an independent sovereign state in 1945, it lost approximately 96,000 people, around 2.6% of the total population which at this time was around 3.7 million. Of these, almost 2,000 were civilian deaths caused as a direct result of bombing.

[5] The USSR no longer demanded absolute surrender of the Finnish forces and an Armistice was agreed under the 1947 Treaty of Paris:-

- Defined the 1940 Finnish Border.
- Reparations of £200,000 to be paid by 1952. (They were paid in full)
- the Porkkala Peninsular was to be leased to the USSR as a military base.
- The Finnish authorities were to punish war criminals and to suppress Anti-Soviet organisations. (Ryti was sentenced to 10 years in prison...although he was released very soon because of ill health).

Appendix 14

Full Text of Princess Elizabeth and Princess Margaret's Broadcast to Evacuees. BBC Radio, 13th October, 1940.

'In wishing you all 'Good evening' I feel that I am speaking to friends and companions who have shared with my sister and myself many a happy Children's Hour.

Thousands of you in this country have had to leave your homes and be separated from your fathers and mothers. My sister, Margaret Rose, and I feel so much for you, as we know from experience what it means to be away from those we love most of all. To you, living in new surroundings, we send a message of true sympathy, and at the same time we would like to thank the kind people who have welcomed you to their homes in the country.

All of us children who are still at home think continually of our friends and relations who have gone overseas, who have travelled thousands of miles to find a wartime home and a kindly welcome in Canada, Australia, New Zealand, South Africa and the United States of AmericaUnited States of America.

My sister and I feel we know quite a lot about these countries. Our father and mother have so often talked to us of their visits to different parts of the world. So it is not difficult for us to picture the sort of life you are all leading, and to think of all the new sights you must be seeing and the adventures you must be having.

But I am sure that you too are often thinking about the Old Country. I know you won't forget us; it is just because we are not forgetting you that I want, on behalf of all the children at home, to send you our love and best wishes, to you and to your kind hosts as well.

Before I finish, I can truthfully say to you all that we children at home are full of cheerfulness and courage. We are trying to do all we can to help our gallant sailors, soldiers and air-men and we are trying too, to bear our own share of the danger and sadness of war. We know, everyone of us, that in the end all will be well; for God will care for us and give us victory and peace. And when peace comes, remember it will be for us, the children of today, to make the world of tomorrow a better and happier place.

My sister is here by my side and we are both going to say goodnight to you.

Come on Margaret.

Goodnight

Goodnight to you all.'

Appendix 15

SECRET
RAILWAY EXECUTIVE COMMITTEE
ARP CIVILIAN EVACUATION SCHEME.

LIST OF RAILWAY OFFICERS who will deal with the arrangements for civilian evacuation in an emergency from the areas below:-

BIRMINGHAM AND SMETHWICK	(All Mr) * Takes Initiative	
GWR	W.E.HART.	BIRMINGHAM
LMSR	S.E.PARKHOUSE	CREWE
LIVERPOOL,BOOTLE,BIRKENHEAD		
LMSR	S.E.PARKHOUSE	CREWE
MANCHESTER AND SALFORD		
LNER	J.A.JENKINSON*	MANCHESTER
LMSR	J.H.ROBINSON	MANCHESTER
LEEDS AND BRADFORD		
LMSR	H.RUDYARD *	DERBY
LNER	W.E.GREEN	LEEDS
SHEFFIELD		
LMSR	H.RUDYARD *	DERBY
LNER	J.A.JENKINSON	MANCHESTER
HULL		
LNER	J.S.HARPER	HULL
NEWCASTLE AND GATESHEAD		
LNER	W.A.FIDDIAN	NEWCASTLE
CHATHAM,GILLINGHAM AND ROCHESTER		
SO.RAILWAY	H.E.O.WHEELER	WATERLOO STATION
PORSTMOUTH,GOSPORT,SOUTHAMPTON		
SO.RAILWAY	H.E.O.WHEELER	WATERLOO STATION

Appendix 16

TOP SECRET List of Evacuation, Reception and Neutral Areas

REF D 89475-1-250 D/d 5034 3/39 (Somerset Ref. C/CD 1/61)

Evacuation Areas	Reception Areas (Excluding in Each County any Evacuation and Neutral Areas				Neutral Areas Within Each County or Part of County
London Together With. Middlesex. Acton, Edmonton, Hornsey, Tottenham Willesden Essex East Ham West Ham Barking Ilford Leyton Walthamstow	County	Borough	Urban	Rural	
	Bedford				
	Berks				
	Bucks				
	Cambs				
	Cornwall				
	Devon				Saltash B. Torpoint UD, Plymouth CB
	Dorset				
	Isle of Ely				
	Essex				Southend On Sea CB Chingford B Dagenham B Harwich B Romford B Wanstead And Woodford B Benfleet UD Billericay UD Canvey Island UD Chigwell UD Hornchurch UD Rayleigh UD Thurrock UD Waltham Holy Cross UD
London	Part Of Glos		Cirencester	Cirencester North Cotswold Northleach Tetbury	
	Herts				Watford B Barnet UD Bushey UD Cheshunt UD East Barnet UD Barnet RD
	Hunts				
	Part of Kent	Folkestone Hythe Lydd Maidstone New Romney Tenterden Tunbridge Wells	Ashford Sevenoaks Southborough Tonbridge	Cranbrook Dartford East Ashford Hollingbourne Maidstone Malling Romney Marsh Sevenoaks Tenterden Tonbridge West Ashford	Beckenham B Bexley B Bromley B Dartford B Erith B Chislehurst&Sidcup Crayford UD Northfleet Orpington UD Penge UD Sheerness UD Swanscombe UD
	Part of Leics		Market Harborough Cadby Wigston	Billesden Blaby Lutterworth Market	Leicester CB

Evacuation Areas	Reception Areas (Excluding in Each County any Evacuation and Neutral Areas				Neutral Areas Within Each County or Part of County
London				Harborough	
	Part of Lincs		Spalding	East Elloe Spalding	
	Norfolk				Norwich CB Gt Yarmouth CB
	Northants				
	Oxford				
	Soke of Peterborough				
	Rutland				
	Somerset				
	Part of Southampton		Petersfield	Petersfield	
	Suffolk East				
	Suffolk West				
	Surrey				Croydon CB Barnes B Beddington & Wallington B Epsom & Ewell B Kingston-0n-Thames B Maldon & Coombe B Coulsden &Purley UD Esher UD Merton & Morden UD Walton & Weybridge UD
	Sussex East				
	Sussex West				
	Part Of Wark	Rugby		Rugby Shipston On Stour	
	Part Of Wilts	Calne Chippenham Devizes Malmesbury Marlborough Swindon	Bradford On Avon Melksham Trowbridge Warminster Westbury	Bradford & Melksham Calne & Chippenham Cricklade & Wooton Bassett Devizes Highworth Malmesbury Marlborough& Ramsbury Mere & Tisbury Pewsey Warminster & Westbury	
Newcastle & Gateshead	Cumberland				
	Durham				Darlington CB South Shields CB Sunderland CB W.Hartlepool Durham B Hartlepool B Jarrow Stockton-0n-Teesb Bellingham UD Blaydon UD Bolden UD Chester-Le-Street Consett UD Felling UD Hebburn UD Hetton UD

Evacuation Areas	Reception Areas (Excluding in Each County any Evacuation and Neutral Areas				Neutral Areas Within Each County or Part of County
Newcastle & Gateshead					Houghton-Le-Spring UD Ryton UD Seaham UD Stanley UD Washington UD Whickham
	Northumberland				Tynemouth CB Blyth Borough Wallsend Ashington UD Bedlingtonshire UD Gosforth UD Longbenton UD Newbigging UD Newburn Pruhoe Seaton Valley Whitley & Monkseaton
	Westmoreland				
	Part Of Yorks North Riding	Richmond	Northallerton Pickering	Bedale Croft Easingwold Helmsley Kirkby Moorside Leyburn Masham Northallerton Pickering Richmond Startforth Stokesly Thirsk Wath	Middlesborough CB Redcar B Thornaby-On-Tees Eston UD
Kingston-Nn Hull	Part Of Lincs (Lindsey)	Scunthorpe	Brigg	Glanford Brigg Isle of Axholme	Barton Upon Humber
	East Riding (Except York CB)				Haltemprice UD
	North Riding	Scarborough	Guiseborough Loftus Malton Saltburn & Marske Scalby Skelton & Brotton Whitby	Flertor Malton Scarborough Whitby	
	Part of Yorks (West Riding)	Goole	Selby	Goole Selby Thorne	
Liverpool, Bootle, Wallasey (Part) Crosby (Part)	Part of Cheshire	Chester	Alsager Hoole Hoylake Middlewitch Nantwich Neston Northwich Sandbach Winsford Wirral	Chester Nantwich Northwich Runcorn Tarvin	Bebington B Crewe Ellesmere Port Runcorn UD
	Part of Herefordshire	Leonminster	Kington	Dore & Bredwardine Kington Leominster &	

Evacuation Areas	Reception Areas (Excluding in Each County any Evacuation and Neutral Areas				Neutral Areas Within Each County or Part of County
Liverpool, Bootle, Wallasey (Part) Crosby (Part)				Wigmore Weobley	
	Part Of Lancs.	Southport	Formby Ormskirk Slekmersdale	Warrington West. Lancs	St Helens CB Warrington CB Widnes CB Abram CB Ashton In Makerfield UD Billinge & Winstanley Haydock UD Huyton With Roby UD Litherland UD Prescot Rainford UD Whiston UD
	Part of Shropshire	Bishops Castle Bridgnorth Ludlow Oswestry Shrewsbury Wenlock	Church Stretton Ellesmere Wem Whitchurch	Atcham Bridgnorth Clun Ellesmere Ludlow Oswestry Wem	
	Anglesey				
	Brecknock				
	Carnarvon				
	Cardigan				
	Carmarthen				
	Denbigh				
	Flintshire				
	Part of Glamorgan	Llwchwr UD		Gower RD Pontardawe RD	
	Merioneth				
	Montgomery				
	Pembroke				
	Radnor				
Manchester Salford Stretford (Part)	Part of Cheshire	Altrincham Congelton Maccelsfield	Alderley Edge Bollington Bowden] Cheadle & Gatley Hale Hazelgrove & Bromhall Knutsford Longendale Lymm Marple Wilmslow	Bucklow Congelton Disley Macclesfield Tintwhistle	Stockport CB Dukinfield B Hyde Sale Stalybridge B Bredbury & Romiley Ud
	Part of Derby	Buxton Glossop	Ashbourne Bakewell Matlock New Mills Whaley Bridge Wirksworth	Ashbourne Bakewell Chapel-En-Le Firth	
	Part of Lancs	Blackpool CB Accrington Bacup Clitheroe Darwen Fleetwood Haslingden Lancaster Lytham St Annes Morecombe &	Carnforth Church Clayton-Le-Moors Dalton-In-Furness Fulwood Grange Great Harwood Kirkham Leyland Littleborough	Blackburn Chorley Clitheroe Fylde Garstang Lancaster Lunesdale Preston Ulverston Wigan	Barrow In Furness CB Blackburn CB Bolton CB Bury CB Oldham CB Preston CB Rochdale CB Wigan CB Ashton Under Lyme B Chorley B

Evacuation Areas	Reception Areas (Excluding in Each County any Evacuation and Neutral Areas				Neutral Areas Within Each County or Part of County
Manchester Salford Stretford (Part)		Heysham Rawtenstall	Oswaldtwistle Poulton Le Fylde Preesall Ramsbottom Rishton Thornton Cleveleys Tottington Turton Ulverston Walton-Le-Dale Wardle Whitworth Withnell		Eccles B Heywood B Leigh B Middleton B Mossley B Redcliffe B Swinton & Pendlebury B Adlington UD Aspull Ud Atherton UD Audenshaw UD Blackrod UD Chadderton UD Crompton Ud Denton UD Droylsden UD Failsworth UD Farnworth UD Golborne UD Hindley UD Horwich Ud Ince In Makerfield Irlam UD Kearsley UD Lees UD Little Lever UD Milnrow UD Newton In Makerfield UD Orrell UD Prestwich UD Royton UD Standish With Langtree UD Tyldesley UD Upholland UD Urmston UD Westhoughton UD Whitefield UD Worsely UD Limehurst RD
	Part of Shropshire		Market Drayton UD	Drayton RD	
	Part of Staffs.		Leek Uttoxeter	Cheadle Leek Newcastle Under Lyme Uttoxeter	Stoke On Trent CB Newcastle Under Lyme B Biddulph UD Kidsgrove UD
Bradford	Part of Lancs.	Colne Nelson	Barrowfield Brierfield Padiham Trawden	Burnley	Burnley CB
	Part of Yorks North Riding			Aysgarth RD Reeth RD	
	West Riding	Keighley Todmorden	Barnoldswick Bingley Colne Valley Denby Dale Denholme Earby Hebden Royd Holmfirth Kirkburton Meltham Midgley Ripponden	Bowland Sedbergh Settle Skipton Todmorden	Halifax CB Huddersfield CB Brighouse B Aireborough UD Baildon UD Elland UD Heckmondwike UD Queensbury & Shelf UD Shipley UD Spenborough

Evacuation Areas	Reception Areas (Excluding in Each County any Evacuation and Neutral Areas				Neutral Areas Within Each County or Part of County
Bradford			Saddleworth Silsden Skipton Sowerby Bridge		
Leeds	Part of Lincs. (Kesteven)			North Kesteven Rd	
	Part of Lincs. (Lindsey)	Lincoln CB Louth	Alford Gainsborough Horncastle Mablethorpe & Sutton Market Rasen Skegness Woodhall Spa	Caistor Gainsborough Grimsby Horncastle Louth Spilsbury Wilton	Grimsby CB Cleethorpes
	Part of Notts.	East Retford Worksop		East Retford Worksop	
	Part of Yorks (East Riding)	York			
	West Riding	Harrogate Ripon	Garforth Ilkley Knaresborough Otley	Doncaster Hemsworth Nidderdale Osgoldcross Ripon & Pateley Bridge Tadcaster Wakefield Wetherby Wharfedale	Barnsley CB Dewsbury CB Doncaster CB Wakefield CB Batley B Morley B Ossett B Pontefract B Pudsey B Adwick-Le-Street UD Bentley With Arksey UD Castleford UD Conisborough UD Cudworth UD Darfield UD Darton UD Dearne UD Dodworth UD Featherstone UD Hemsworth UD Horbury UD Horsforth UD Hoyland Netherud UD Knottingley UD Maltby UD Mexborough UD Mirfield UD Normanton UD Rawmarsh UD Rothwell UD Royston UD Stanley UD Swinton UD Tickhill UD Wath Upon Dearne UD Wombwell UD Warsborough UD
Sheffield	Part of Derbyshire	Chesterfield Ilkeston	Alfreton Belper Bolsover Clay Cross Dronfield Heanor Long Eaton	Belper Blackwell Chesterfield Clown Shardlow	Derby CB

Evacuation Areas	Reception Areas (Excluding in Each County any Evacuation and Neutral Areas				Neutral Areas Within Each County or Part of County
Sheffield			Ripley Staveley		
	Part of Leics.	Loughborough	Melton Mowbray Shepshed	Barrow Upon Stour Castle Donnington Melton & Belvoir	
	Part of Lincoln (Holland)	Boston		Boston Rd	
	Part of Lincoln (Kesteven)	Grantham Stamford	Bourne Sleaford	East Kesteven South Kesteven West Kesteven	
	Part of Notts.	Mansfield Newark	Kirby In Ashfield Mansfield Woodhouse Sutton In Ashfield Warsop	Basford Bingham Newark Southwell	Nottingham CB Arnold UD Beeston & Stapleford UD Carlton UD Eastwood UD Hucknell UD West Bridgford UD
	Part ofYorks. (West Riding)		Penistone Stockbridge	Kiveton Park Penistone Rotherham Wortley	Rotherham CB
Birmingham & Smethwick	Part of Derbyshire		Swadlincote	Repton RD	
	Part of Glos.	Gloucester CB Cheltenham Tewkesbury	Charlton Kings Nailsworth Stroud	Cheltenham Dursley Gloucester East Dean Lydney Newent Sodbury Stroud Thornbury Warmley West Dean	Bristol CB Kingswood UD Mangotsfield UD
	Part of Hereford	Hereford	Bromyard Ledbury Ross-On-Wye	Bromyard Hereford Ledbury Ross & Whitchurch	
	Part of Leics.		Ashby De La Zouch Ashby Woulds Coalville Hinckley	Ashby De La Zouch Market Bosworth	
	Part of Salop		Dawley Newport Oakengates Wellington	Shifnall Wellington	
	Part of Staffs.	Burton On Trent CB Lichfield Stafford Tamworth	Brownhills Cannock Rugeley Stone	Cannock Lichfield Seisdon Stafford Stone Tutbury	Walsall CB W.Bromwich CB Wolverhampton CB Bilston CB Rowley Regis B Tipton B Wednesbury B Aldridge UD Amblecote UD Brierley Hill UD Coseley B Darlaston UD Sedgley UD Tettenhall Wednesfield UD

Evacuation Areas	Reception Areas (Excluding in Each County any Evacuation and Neutral Areas				Neutral Areas Within Each County or Part of County
Birmingham & Smethwick					Willenhall UD
	Part of Warwicks	Royal Leamington Spa Stratford Upon Avon Warwick	Kenilworth Solihull	Alcester Atherstone Meriden Southam Stratford Upon Avon Tamworth Warwick	Coventry CB Nuneaton B Sutton Coldfield B Bedworth UD
	Worcs				Dudley CB Halesowen B Oldbury B Stourbridge B
	Part of Glamorgan	Merthyr Tydfil CB Cowbridge	Aberdare Caerphilly Gelligaer Glyncorrwg Maesteg Mountain Ash Ogmore & Garw Pontypridd Porthcawl Rhondda	Cardiff Cowbridge Llantrisant & Llantwrt Fardre Neath Penybont	Cardiff CB Swansea CB Neath B Port Talbot B Barry UD Bridgend UD Penarth UD
	Monmouthshire				Newport CB
Portsmouth, Gosport, S' Hampton	Part of Dorset	Poole	Wimborne Minster	Wimborne And Cranbourne	
	Part ofSouthampton	Bournemouth CB Andover Basingstoke Christchurch Eastleigh Lymington Romsey Winchester		Andover Basingstoke Droxford Kingsclere & Whitchurch New Forest Ringwood & Fordingbridge Romsey & Stockbridge Winchester	Fareham UD Havant & Waterloo UD
	Isle of Wight				
	Part of Wilts.	Salisbury Wilton		Amesbury Salisbury & Wilton	
Chatham, Gillingham Rochester	Part of Kent	Canterbury CB Deal Dover Faversham Sandwich	Herne Bay Sittingbourne & Milton Whitstable	Bridge Blean Dover Eastrey Elham Sheppey Strood Swale	Gravesend B Margate B Queensborough B Ramsgate B Broadstairs & St Peters UD Sheerness UD

Appendix 17

Selected Extracts from the Report on Conditions in the Reception Areas - 14th March 1941.

The Nature of the Problem

5. In seeking to estimate the measure of success of this experiment it must frankly be admitted at the outset that evacuation on this large scale is neither a natural nor a popular process. In a country like ours, predominantly industrial, a wide gulf is fixed between the sentiments, habits and outlook of town and country. The London woman is gregarious. The busy multitudes, the crowded streets and shops, the cinemas and similar diversions for the background of her life. She is not overburdened by domesticity. She has a partiality for tinned foods and readily resorts to the fish and chip shop.

6. The life of the sister in the country parish or provincial town is more often centred in her home. She is more house proud and a better cook. Outside her home the social activities of the Churches and the Women's Institute occupy her leisure hours. The outlook of the London mother is hard for her to understand and she does not make allowance for habits so often due to bad housing conditions. These are broad generalisations to which there are many exceptions, especially in the larger towns, but we believe that many of the causes of friction in the scheme of evacuation are traceable to these differences of habit and outlook.

7. It cannot be expected that the invasion of the home of the housewife in the reception areas by the London mother will be achieved without friction. Even if friction be avoided, it is not a desirable process that the family life in London should be disrupted, that wives should be separated from their husbands or children from their parents. We desire to emphasise these fundamental facts which are sometimes forgotten. Furthermore, the evacuated mother so often arrives in a state of mental distress. She, too has her pride. For weeks she has borne the brunt of the night bombing with unconquerable spirit and under conditions that might well have impaired the strongest nerves. She feels the strangeness of her new surroundings. She is full of anxiety for her husband and her home. Time hangs heavily on her hands. If then an unfriendly atmosphere is suspected the urge to return becomes overwhelming. Evacuation on this large scale has no intrinsic merit; it can only be the lesser of the two evils, and justified by the necessity for the dispersal of population in wartime.

Success of Experiment

8. For all these reasons this great migration should have been doomed to failure. We were surprised to find that in the great majority of cases it is succeeding. The tremendous efforts made by the local authorities, by devoted members of the voluntary organisations and by the warm-hearted householders themselves, cannot be adequately realised without a personal visit to the reception areas. In many districts it has even become a matter of local pride to retain evacuees and it is considered a reflection on the hospitality offered in the district if they return. The standard of achievement is not everywhere uniform and much still remains to be done, but by and large great progress is being made. The hard lessons learnt in the 1939 evacuation have not been forgotten. Nor is it generally realised what careful prevision has been shown by the Ministry of Health, both centrally and in the Regions, to ensure that all necessary powers are made available.

9. Broadly speaking, it can be stated that the most careful study of problems likely to arise has been continuously made and the procedure has been modified in the light of experience. The suggestions we make, therefore, are not of an iconoclastic or revolutionary nature but rather tend to emphasise certain features essential to the continued success of the scheme, so that the public conscience may be quickened and action taken immediately for the provision of further welfare arrangements and for the overhauling of machinery where this has proved deficient.

12. The work done by hostesses in looking after unaccompanied children is worthy of the highest praise and more recognition should be given to it. Very often the hostess is unable to join one of the uniformed or more spectacular war services because she is looking after children in her home.

Reception of Mothers and Children

13. It is in the reception of mothers with their children that problems mainly arise. We heard many accounts of unjustifiable behaviour by London women. When traced to their source, most of these related to the earlier evacuation in September 1939, when the process was a novelty and less adequate arrangements had been made for their reception and welfare. But experience has now been gained. The sufferings of evacuees have created widespread feelings of sympathy and good will from housewives in the reception areas, which has evoked a better response in the conduct of London mothers themselves. Host and guest are making an effort to understand each other's point of view and there is a noticeable spirit of give and take. Where this is not forthcoming it is due perhaps in part to the too rosy picture of country life painted by canvassers in London in their efforts to induce mothers to leave their homes. Their disappointment on arrival leads to bad feeling and a display of ingratitude which is resented. But these we believe are now exceptional cases. It is abundantly clear from our investigations that where there is an atmosphere of friendliness and adequate welfare arrangements are made, London women are full of gratitude and are settling down with resignation but not with enthusiasm in their new surroundings.

Appendix 18

The following notice was printed in all London newspapers during August 1939:-

EVACUATION

A message to all Londoners concerned from Herbert Morrison, M.P.

His Majesty's Government has now decided on the evacuation of the priority classes from London and the other areas regarded as vulnerable in case of air raids. In this great task of organisation the London County Council has played, and will continue to play, its full part. We all hope that sanity will prevail, that war will not come. Precautions are however, necessary. We must be prepared.

Now a word of appeal and advice to those concerned:-

To the Children

With your teachers and friendly helpers you are going to the country, where the Government considers you will be safer than in London if war should come. London children are cheerful. I want you to be cheerful and friendly on your journey and when you get to the other end. It is a big task to move you all; so please do all you can to help make things run smoothly. Above all, be kind to each other. Help each other in any little difficulties that may arise.

To the Parents.

I know you will have your anxieties at this trying time. I understand your feeling. You will be cheered, however, by the knowledge that it is better for the children to be out of London as things are. More-over you are, I know, assured that the great organisation of the London County Councils' teaching staff will do all that is humanly possible to make the journey a success. Please help your children to go away in a cheerful mood. See that they bring with them all that their teachers asked them to bring and no more.

Arrangements at the other end are in the hands of other authorities. We are grateful to them for their work and we know they will have done all they can to ensure success.

About Difficulties and Snags

However good the organisation some difficulties and snags are bound to arise. If and when they do I beg you all to take them as easily as you can. Don't get 'nervy', above all don't get on the nerves of those who are organising the evacuation. Take your troubles as lightly and cheerfully as you can. Remember, there are others, actively engaged in the service of our country, whose troubles may be much graver. As many of your fathers used to sing 'Pack up your troubles in your old kit bag and smile, smile, smile'. To all the evacuated and to those going with them...Good Luck. And a safe return to dear old London.

Herbert Morrison.

County Hall. London.

Appendix 19

Area Billeting Officers

Area Number	Name and Address of Area Inspector of Billeting Records	Area Covered. (Admin Counties and Authorities Therein)
London	F.J.Laycock. County Hall	London
1	W.Foord.Carlisle	Cumberland. Durham. Northumberland. Westmoreland
2	E.J.Miller-Williams. Preston	Lancaster (Except County Boroughs of Bootle/Liverpool/Manchester/Oldham/St Helens/Salford/Warrington)
3	E.M.Tuke.Leeds	York And West Riding (Except County Boroughs of Doncaster/Rotherham/Sheffield
4	L.P.Walker. Birmingham	Gloucester. Warwick. Stafford. Worcester
5	J.W.Crowe.Chester	Chester. Salop. Anglesea. Caernarvon. Denbigh. Flint. Merioneth. Montgomery. (County Boroughs of Bootle. Liverpool .St Helens. Warrington)
6	R.K.Cowperthwaite. Cardiff	Hereford. Monmouth. Brecon. Cardigan. Carmarthen. Glamorgan. Pembroke. Radnor
7	O.E.Brigden. Exeter	Cornwall. Devon. Dorset. Somerset. Wiltshire. County Borough of Bournemouth
8	E.F.Davis. Broadway. London	Berks. Buckingham. Hertford. Isle of Wight. Middlesex. Oxford. Southampton. (Except County Borough of Bournemouth)
9	E.H.V.Weigall. Tonbridge	Kent. Surrey. Sussex East. Sussex West
10	W.E.Pitcairn. Chelmsford	Essex. Norfolk. Suffolk East. Suffolk West
11	D.F.Belchamber. York	Derby. Nottingham. York. East Riding and York North Riding (County Boroughs of Doncaster. Manchester. Oldham. Rotherham. Salford. Sheffield.
12	A.E.M.Coles Northampton	Bedford. Cambridge. Huntingdon. Isle of Ely. Leicester. Lincoln Parts of Holland. Lincoln Parts of Kesteven. Lincoln Parts of Lindsey. Northampton. Rutland. Soke of Peterborough.

Appendix 20

Detraining Schedule

This is an example of a Detraining Schedule. These were sent to the reception areas before the war. This one deals with the movement of evacuees from London to Buckinghamshire. The figures in the second column under each of the headings are the amended numbers to be moved by train updated to 20th June 1939. Note the vast disparities in numbers expected and numbers received in some areas.

Detraining Stations	Total Capacity for Reception Districts Allocated		Districts Served
	BUCKINGHAMSHIRE L.N.E.R.		
Aylesbury 4,400 Metro or L.N.E.R	10,000	1,600	Aylesbury Borough
Amersham 7,400/6,000 Metro or L.N.E.R	10,400	6,000	Amersham R.D Chesham R.D.
High Wycombe 7,000/6,600 G.W.R or L.N.E.R	7,000	6,600	Chepping Wycombe
Beaconsfield 1,600/1,200 G.W.R or L.N.E.R	1,600	1,200	Beaconsfield U.D
Princes Risborough 6,000/4,800 G.W.R & L.N.E.R	6,000	4,800	Wycombe R.D
Total	**35,000**	**22,800**	
	BUCKINGHAMSHIRE G.W.R.		
Slough G.W.R 5,000/3000	5,000	3,000	Slough Borough
Windsor & Eton	8,800		Eton U.D, 800 Eton R.D, 8,000
Maidenhead Berks. G.W.R	1,600		Marlow, 1,600
Total	**15,400**	**13,600**	
	BUCKINGHAMSHIRE L.M.S.		
Bletchley L.M.S 2,000/2,466	4,500	1,096 1,370	Bletchley U.D Winslow R.D, 2,500
Wolverton L.M.S	9,200	3,895 950 2,385	Wolverton U.D, 5,000 Newport Pagnell U.D, 1,200 Newport Pagnell R.D, 3,000
Total		7,230	
Leighton Buzzard	2,200	600	Linslade U.D, 600
L.M.S (Beds.) Excluding Nos. For Beds, 1,600/1,460		1,460	Wing R.D
Total	**15,900**	**11,756**	
	NORTHAMPTONSHIRE L.N.E.R.		
Brackley. L.N.E.R 1,000/580	2,800	580 1,100	Buckingham Borough Buckingham R.D, 1,600/1,000
GRAND TOTAL	**69,100**	**49,836**	

(Source. Bucks Record Office. AR 177/81, no.356.)

Appendix 21

SPECIAL TRAIN TIMETABLE. GWR Sept. 1st 1939

Day 1

Paddington	Acton	Ealing Broadway	Destination	Approx Arrival
		8.30	Maidenhead	9.00
		8.39	Oxford	10.10
8.30			St Austell	3.55pm
		8.48	Chippenham	11.05
		8.57	Henley-on-Thames	9.45
		9.07	Frome	11.40
		9.16	Highbridge	12.50pm
		9.25	Dorchester	1.10pm
		9.34	Bath	12.10pm
		9.43	Devizes	11.45
		9.52	Weston-Super-Mare	1.05pm
		10.02	Oxford	11.35
		10.11	Taunton	1.40pm
		10.20	Bridgwater	2.00pm
		10.29	Swindon	12.35pm
	10.30		Totnes	3.45pm
			Kingsbridge	4.45pm
		10.38	Slough	11.05am
		10.47	Trowbridge	1.00pm
		10.56	Weston-Super-Mare	2.10
		11.06	Watchet	3.35
			Minehead	4.00
		11.15	Axbridge	2.30
		11.24	Maidenhead	11.55
		11.33	Bath	2.10
		11.42	Malmesbury	2.00
		11.51	Oxford	1.30
		12.01pm	Swindon	1.55
		12.10	Wellington	3.55
		12.19	Wantage Rd	1.45
		12.28	Banbury	2.05
	12.30		Teignmouth	5.20
			Newton Abbot	5.40
		12.37	Weston – S-M	3.50
		12.46	Taunton	4.15
		12.55	Chipping Norton	3.30
		1.05	Langport East	4.30
		1.14	Uffington	2.50
		1.23	Weymouth	5.20
		1.32	Oxford	3.05
		1.41	Newbury Town	3.00
		1.50	Bath	4.25
		1.59	Culham	3.15
		2.09	Warminster	5.10
		2.18	Weston-S-M	5.35
		2.27	Witney	4.40
	2.30		Dorchester	6.10
		2.36	Bicester	3.55
		2.45	Cirencester	5.15
				5.50 *Train split into batches of 400

Paddington	Acton	Ealing Broadway	Destination	Approx Arrival
		2.54	Bruton	5.50
		3.04	Bath	5.40
		3.13	Andoversford	6.10
		3.22	Wells	7.00
		3.31	Swindon	5.25
		3.40	Savernake	5.20
		3.49	Bridgwater	7.30
		3.58	Oxford	5.35
		4.08	Weston-S-M	7.25
		4.17	Shepton Mallet	7.50
		4.24	Bath	7.00
		4.33	Henley	5.20
	4.30		Weymouth	8.25
		4.42	Swindon	6.35
		4.51	Devizes	6.55
		5.00	Maidenhead	5.30
		5.09	Theale	6.10
		5.18	Swindon	7.15

Appendix 22

DRAFT OF DAILY NUMBERS TO BE ENTRAINED. GWR Sept 1st -4th 1939

Entraining Station	Exchange Stations	Day 1	2	3	4	Balance (if any)
Paddington		773	773	773	773	Nil
Acton		3251	3251	3251	3251	Nil
Ealing Broadway GW	Ealing Broadway LPTB	46453	46453	46453	46453	Nil
		50477	50477	50477	50481	
				TOTAL	201912	

Detraining Station	Day 1	2	3	4	Total	Total Cap. of Reception Areas
			DETRAINED. GWR			
			BERKSHIRE			
Maidenhead	2400	1600	1600	1600	7200	10000
Culham	800	1600	800	800	4000	6000
Cholsey & Moulsford	-	800	800	800	2400	3200
Wantage Rd	800	-	800	800	2400	4000
Uffington	800	800	-	800	2400	3000
Newbury Town	800	800	800	-	2400	3500
Newbury Racecourse	-	800	800	800	2400	3300
Hungerford	-	-	800	-	800	1500
Theale	800	800	800	800	3200	4000
			BUCKS			
Slough	800	800	800	800	3200	5000
Maidenhead						1600
			CORNWALL			
St Austell	800	-	-	-	800	8200
Camborne	-	800	800	-	1600	15700
Truro	-	-	800	-	800	9500
Falmouth	-	-	-	400	400	5000
St Ives	-	-	-	400	400	8100
Penzance	-	-	-	400	400	6000
Liskeard	-	-	-	400	400	5500
			DEVON			
Tiverton	-	-	-	400	400	8000
South Molton	-	-	-	400	400	3600
Barnstaple	-	-	-	400	400	12700
Plymouth	-	800	-	-	800	8000
Kingsbridge	400	-	-	-	400	6900
Torquay	-	-	400	-	400	8000
Paignton	-	-	400	-	400	8200
Totnes	400	-	-	-	400	5200
Newton Abbot	400	-	-	-	400	9900
Teignmouth	400	-	-	-	400	4800
			DORSET			
Bridport	-	800	800	-	1600	3700
Dorchester	1600	800	800	1600	4800	7400
Weymouth	1600	1600	1600	1600	6400	11000
			GLOUCS			
Andoversford	800	800	800	800	3200	7000
Circencester	800	-	800	800	2400	4000
Kemble	-	800	-	-	800	1800

Detraining Station	Day 1	2	3	4	Total	Total Cap. of Reception Areas
			DETRAINED. GWR			
			OXON			
Witney	800	800	800	800	3200	5400
Oxford	4000	4000	4000	4000	16000	25500
Chipping Norton	800	800	-	800	2400	3700
Banbury	800	1600	1600	800	4800	6900
Bloxham	-	-	-	-	-	900
Henley on Th	1600	800	800	1600	4800	7000
Bicester	800	800	800	-	2400	3800
			SOMERSET			
Bath	4000	4000	4000	4000	16000	20000
Frome	800	800	800	800	3200	5000
Radstock	-	800	800	-	1600	2500
Langport East	800	-	-	800	1600	2900
Wells	800	800	800	800	3200	4800
Shepton Mallet	800	800	800	800	3200	4500
Chard	-	800	800	800	2400	5700
Bridgwater	1600	1600	1600	1600	6400	8000
Highbridge	800	-	-	-	800	1500
Bruton	800	-	800	800	2400	4000
Weston-S-M	4000	3200	3200	4000	14400	20000
Clevedon	-	800	800	-	1600	3000
Axbridge	800	800	800	800	3200	7000
Taunton	1600	1600	1600	1600	6400	9300
Wellington	800	800	-	400	2000	4300
Minehead	400	800	800	800	2800	4700
Watchet	400	-	-	-	400	500
Dulverton	-	-	-	800	800	1800
			WARWICK			
Shipston on Stour	-	-	-	-	-	600
			WILTSHIRE			
Swindon	4000	4000	4000	3200	15200	19500
Wooton Bassett	-	800	800	800	2400	3400
Malmesbury	800	-	800	-	1600	2800
Chippenham	800	1600	1600	800	4800	6400
Melksham	-	800	800	800	2400	4400
Trowbridge	800	800	800	800	3200	4900
Savernake	800	-	-	800	1600	2400
Pewsey	-	800	-	-	800	2000
Devizes	1600	800	800	1600	4800	6400
Westbury	-	800	800	800	2400	3900
Warminster	800	-	-	-	800	1300

Appendix 23

NORTHERN IRELAND. Ref. MPS2/2/39

Evacuation of Unaccompanied. Children 8th June 1941

Destination	Assembly Station	Time of Assembly	No of Children			Train Depart	Train Arrives	Other Transport
			Total	P	C			
Ballymena	Montcollyer P.E.S	9.30	101	101	-	10.50	11.35	
Cushendall	"	"	80	20	60	"	"	By bus from Ballymena Train
Kells	"	"	80	80		"	"	"
Broughshane	"	"	82	82		"	"	"
Cullybackey	"	"	84	84		"	"	"
Ahoghill	"	"	79	79		"	"	"
Portglenone	"	"	81	81		"	"	"
Ballymoney	Grove	11.00	497	378	119	12.20	1.30	
Coleraine	Montcollyer P.E.S	11.30	196	196		12.55	2.30	
Ballycastle	"	"	272	224	48	"	3.00	
Armoy	"	"	50	50		"		

Appendix 24

NORTHERN IRELAND.

Sunday 27th July 1941 EVACUATION of Accompanied Families. Programme

(P.E.S…Public Elementary School)

Destination	Assembly Point	Time of Assembly	Nos of Evacuees			Time of Dep.	Time of Arrival	No of conductors in addition to one i/c	Buses Req	Period Hrs	Railway
			P	RC	Total						
Newry	Technical College	6.30 am	700	-	700	8.30am	9.52am	24 +1	12	4	GNR
Omagh	R.B.A. Institute	9.20 am	300	200	500	11.20	1.10pm	16+1	4	3	GNR
Armagh	T/C	9.30 am	201	79	280	11.30	12.25pm	11+1	5	2	GNR
Enniskillen	Queen Victoria PES	9.45 am	310	25	335	11.45	2.35pm	1+1	3	2	GNR
Portadown	RBA	12.30 am	214	94	308	2.30	3.20pm	13+1	5	2	GNR
Dungannon	T/C	1.00 pm	222	363	585	3.00	3.50pm	25+1	8	4	GNR
Cookstown	T/C	1.00 pm	82	75	157	3.00	4.45pm	6+1	3	2	GNR
Magherafelt	Mountcoll yer PES	7.30 am	300	-	300	9.30	10.46am	5+1	2	2	LMS
"	"	10.00am	-	100	100	12.00	1.00pm	3+1	1	1	LMS
Newcastle	"	6.45 am	400	-	400	9.15am	10.25pm	13+1	10 to Rail	-	BCDR
TUESDAY 29th JULY 1941											
Omagh	Queen V	9.15 am	500	-	500	11.15	1.00pm	19+1	4	3	GNR
Newry	T/C	9.55 am	-	700	700	11.55	1.10pm	24+1	12	4	GNR

RBA = Royal Belfast Academical Institute

APPENDIX 25

NORTHERN IRELAND

Evacuee figures from Red Cross Dublin. Early May 1941

Date	On Hand	Departures	Arrivals	Total
3.5.41	259	20	0	239
4.5.41	239	0	2	241
5.5.41	241	0	45	286
6.5.41	286	7	52	331
7.5.41	331	24	25	332
8.5.41	332	13	7	326
9.5.41	326	8	13	331
10.5.41	331	0	9	340
11.5.41	340	0	6	346
12.5.41	346	4	10	352
13.5.41	352	7	6	351
14.5.41	351			

Appendix 26

NORTHERN IRELAND.

List of Families scheduled to be billeted in various reception areas.

The List is not dated but is sometime in August 1941

Area	No of Families and Religion	Schedule of Billets Composition of Families (M=Mother)								
		M+1	M+2	M+3	M+4	M+5	M+6	M+7	No of persons	Date
MAGHERAFELT	10P	9	-	-	-	1	-	-	24	
	10P	-	10	-	-	-	-	-	30	
	7P	-	-	7	-	-	-	-	28	
	7P				7				35	
	8RC	5				1	2		30	
	8RC		4	3		1			30	
	6RC				5	1			31	
	2RC 9P	 9				2			12 18	
	6P				6				30	
	7P			7					28	
	10P		10						30	
									TOTAL P223 RC 103	
BANBRIDGE	11P	6	3	1			1		32	
	9RC	2	3	2				2	37	
	9P		2	3	4				38	
BALLYMENA	10P	6				4			36	
	12P	2	10						34	
	10P	4		5			1		35	
	6P				5		1		32	
	12P		10	2					38	
	3P			3					12	
	7RC	3	2	1	1				21	
LISNASKEA	12P	2	3	4	2				39	
	13P	4	10	1					38	
	3P		2				1		13	
	7RC	1	3	1	1	1			26	
DOWNPATRICK	6P				6				30	
	10P		5	5					35	
	3P	1	2						8	
	13RC	13							26	
	6RC			3			3		33	
	11RC		9		2				37	
PORTADOWN	10P		10						30	
	10P		10						30	
	3RC	3							3	
ARMAGH	10P	2	3	2	2	1			37	
	4P		4						12	
	7RC	2	3	2					21	
	11P		7	2	1	1			40	
	2P	2							4	
	7RC		2		4		1		33	
CLOGHER	6P				5	1			31	
	12P	4	6	2					34	
	10RC	1	6	1	2				34	

Area	No of Families and Religion	Schedule of Billets Composition of Families (M=Mother)								
		M+1	M+2	M+3	M+4	M+5	M+6	M+7	No of persons	Date
	5RC		5						15	
	4P				4				20	
	12P	3	6	2	1				37	
BALLYCASTLE	8P	1	5	1	1				26	
	8RC		2	3	3				33	
	7P		5		2				25	
	7RC		1	2	3		1		33	
LURGAN	10P		8		1	1			35	
	2RC	1	1						5	

Appendix 27

The London underground network 1939/40.

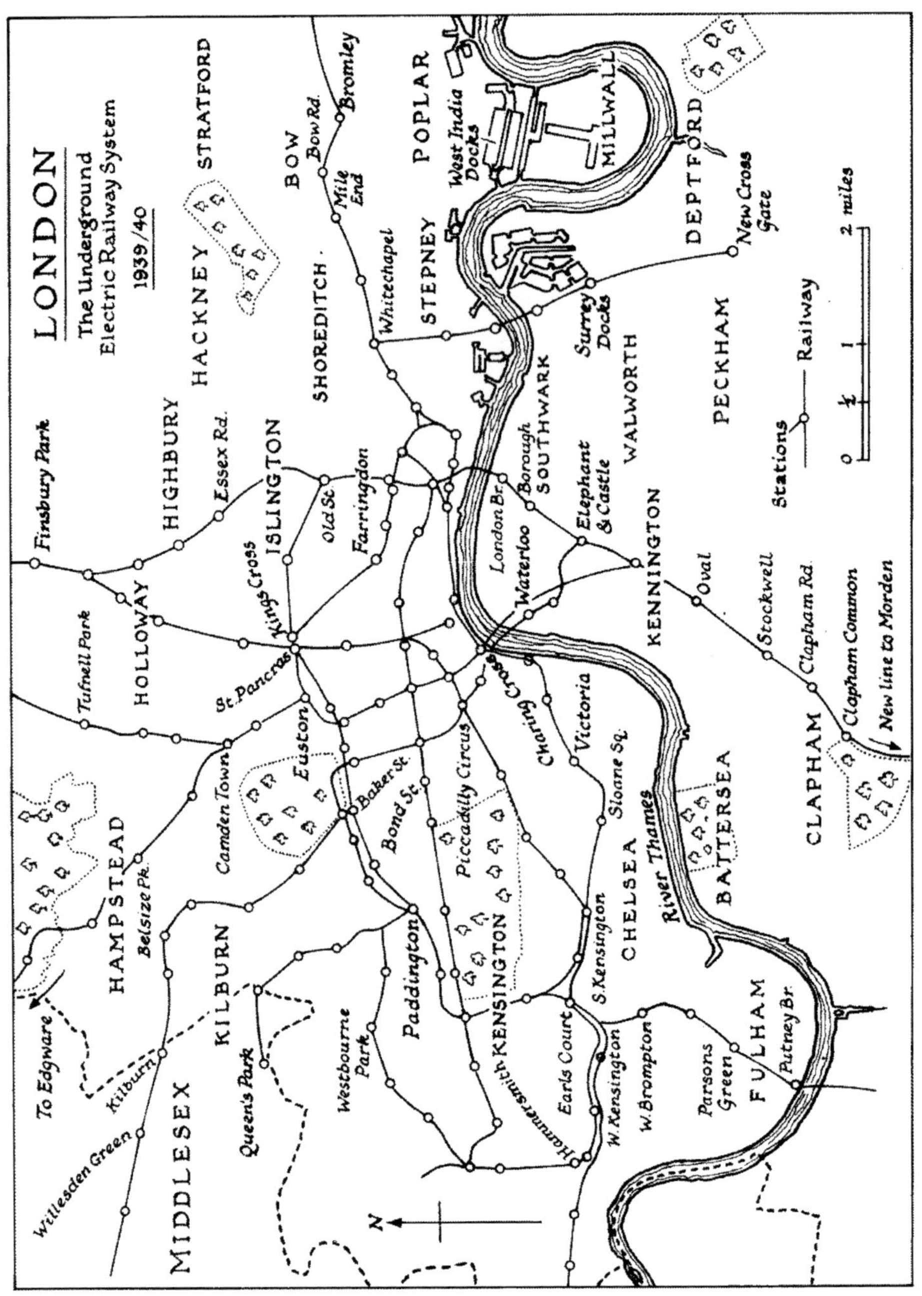

Appendix 28

Principal rail routes in Great Britain 1939/40.

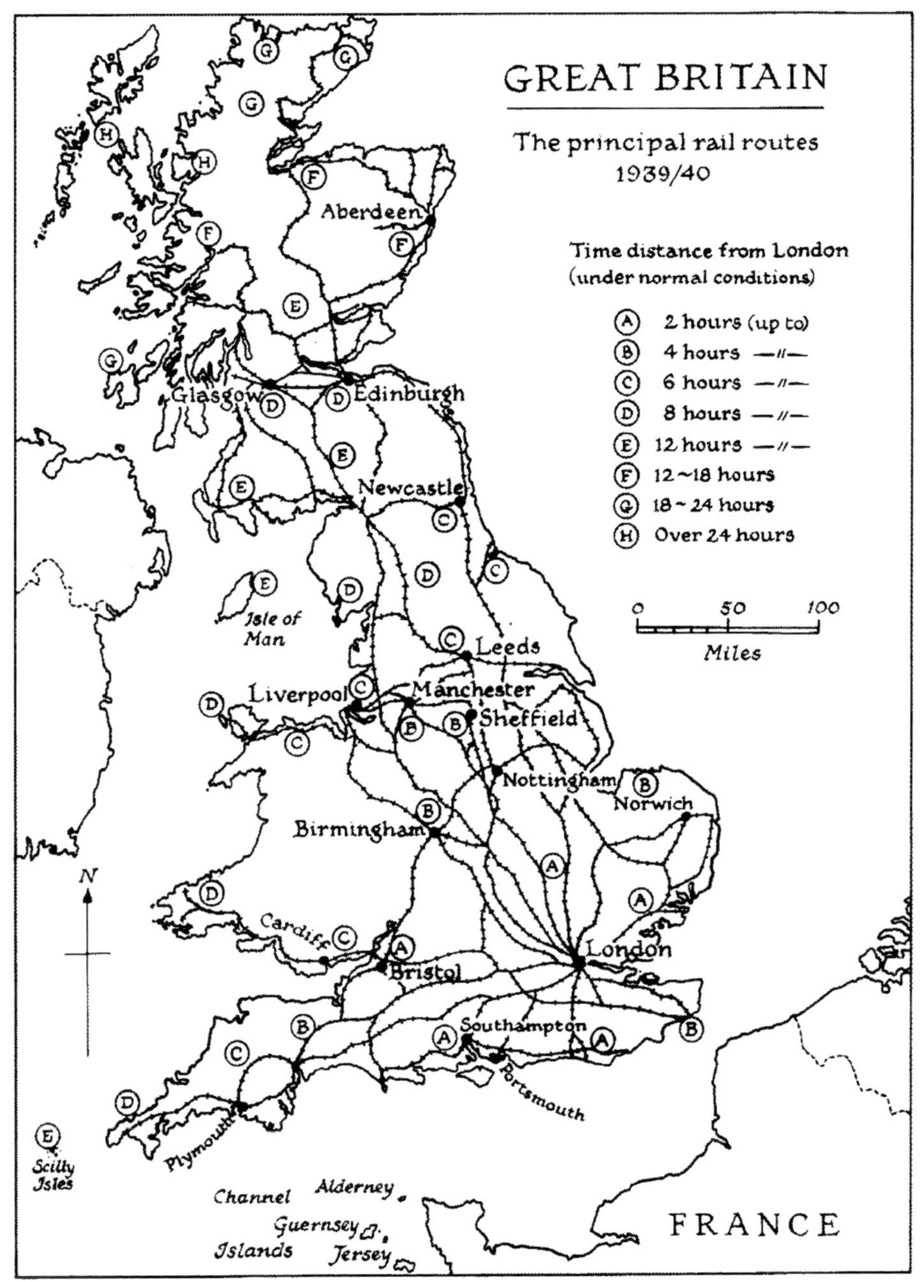

Appendix 29

Principal rail routes in north Wales and north west England 1939/40.

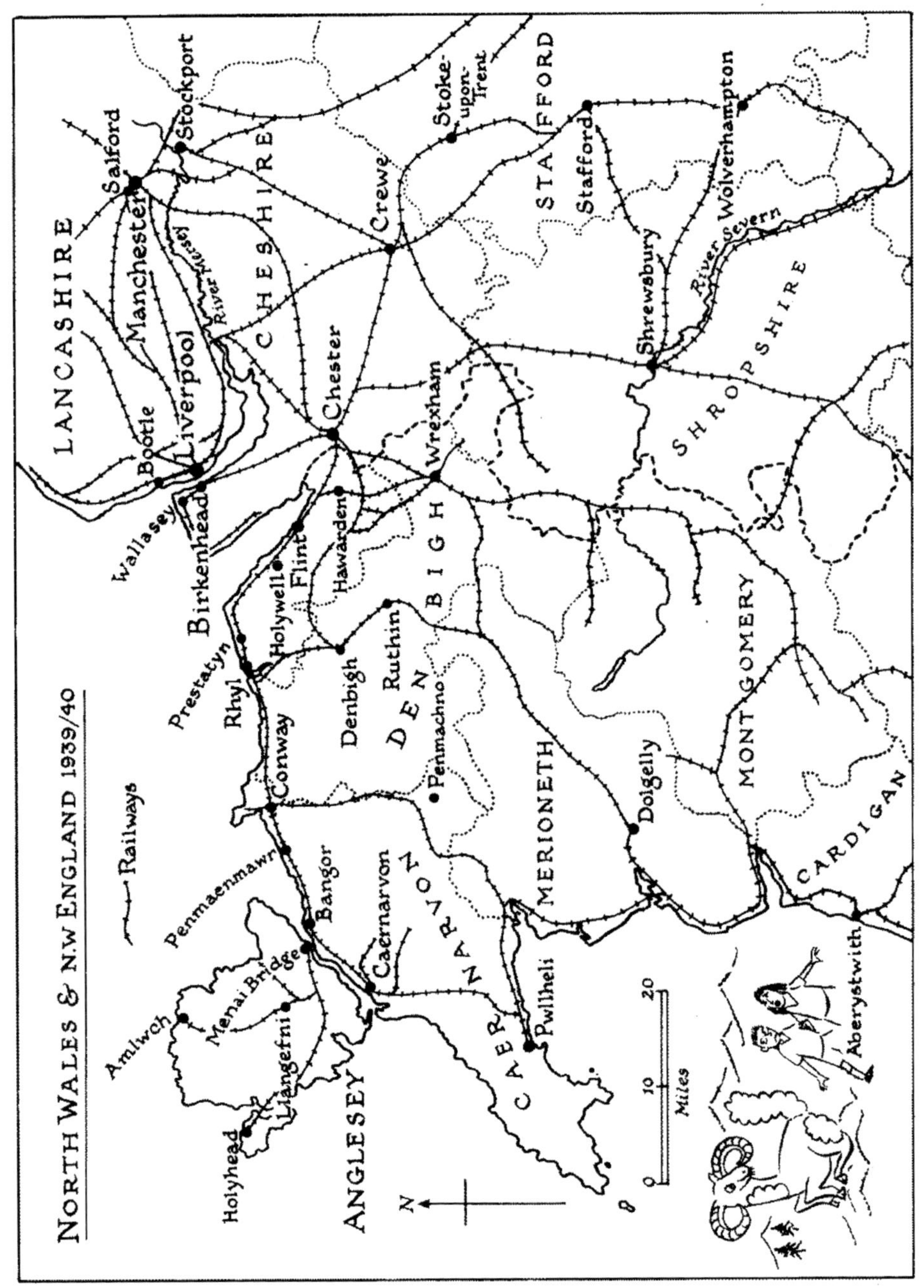

Bibliography

ARCHIVE

Centre for Evacuee and War Child Studies. Museum of English Rural Life. (MERL) University of Reading.
Times on Line
'CORB' and 'SEAVAC' interview recordings. MERL

University of Reading. Media-site.

Children: The invisible victims of War. International Conferences. September 2009 & 2011
(Film recordings of delivered papers)

JOURNALS et al.

- British Journal of Nursing 1939 - 1940
- Children in War. Vols. 1-8. DSM. Evacuee Archive. MERL Reading Room.
- Education Journals 1934 – 1945
- Eugenics Review 1938-40
- Farmers Weekly 1938-1941 MERL
- Herkenning' International Bulletin. MERL
- International War Cry. 21/1/39 – 6/7/40
- Our Towns. A Close up. A study made in 1939-42. (1943) OUP
- Radio Times 1939 - 41

PRIMARY SOURCES

BBC ARCHIVE. CAVERSHAM

- Advisory Committees SBC Exec Comm. Minute Book Appendix File1A 1939-40 R6/104/1
- Adults and Schools Broadcasting. Confidential Report.
- Advisory Council Minutes
- Advisory Committees. Schools Broadcasting Council. Rural Programmes Sub-Committee Minute Book. 1936-46 R6/158/2
- Board of Education. Memo No 22. Schools in War Time: Use of Schools Broadcasts.
- Children's Hour Policy File. 1 1939 – May 1940. R11/51/1
- Communications Council Schools Broadcasting Executive 22nd Jan 1940. Schools Broadcasting in Wartime. Confidential Report.
- Course for Rural Schools 1940-41....Draft Analysis (Central Council Schools Broadcasting and Scottish Council for Schools Broadcasting. R6/158/2)
- Memo from S.J de Lolbiniere, Dominions Office. 4th July 1940. 'The Voyage of the Children' FILE R11/51/2 June 1940 – 1946 4th July 1940
- File R11/51/2. General
- File R11/35 7. Aug. 1940. Memo from Mac to West Region. Propaganda and Juvenile War-Time Efforts
- London Children's Hour Programme Board
- Minutes of the Meeting of Rural Teachers. 20th January 1945
- R34/266 Memo. Censorship in Wartime. 17th June 1938.
- Schools Broadcasting in War Time. Memos 4, 6 & 8

BERKSHIRE COUNTY RECORDS OFFICE. READING

- County Council Minutes 1939 C/CL/C1/1/42
- County Council Minutes 1940 C/CL/C1/1/43
- Alfred Sutton Primary School Log Book 1934-62 89/SCH/37/1
- Bradfield C.of.E Primary School Log Book 1934-51 D/P 22/28/3

- Purley (on-Thames) Parish Council Minutes. 1939-41

BRISTOL RECORDS OFFICE

- BRO 11757/1, 'Evacuation correspondence r.e. 1941-1942'
- BRO 21131/EC/Adm/M/12/1, 'Minute Book'
- BRO 33779/8, 'Plan of bombs dropped, ranging from 50 kilos to 1,000 kilos, with fractures to gas, electricity, water and sewer mains, during 1939-45 War'

BUCKINGHAMSHIRE COUNTY RECORD OFFICE. AYLESBURY

- Aston Clinton Evacuee School Diary 1939-43
- Ashley Green C.of.E School Log Book.1931 – 73
- E/LB/6/3 Commercial Street. LCC School. Log Book.

CAERNARVONSHIRE RECORD OFFICE. CAERNARFON

- Amlwch RDC. Evacuation File 1939-41
- Caernarfon British School. Log Book 1910-1942. 19th February. 1940.
- Evacuation Group. Prince Rupert School. Liverpool. Log Book 1941
- Evacuation File
- Nant Conway RDC. Evacuation File
- Nant Conway RDC. Evacuation 1939-45 Letters File
- Penmaenmawr. UDC ARP Evacuation File No 1

CERIDIGION RECORD OFFICE. ABERYSTWYTH

- Tregaron Rural District Council. TGR SE/15/9 + TGR SE/15/1 & 2
- Evacuation Records:-

1. Government Evacuation Scheme. Evacuee Cards 1940-44
2. Private Evac. Scheme. Evacuee Cards 1940-44
3. Liverpool Evac Scheme; School medical officers recommendations; and Government Evac Scheme, householders cards 1940-47
4. Billeting of civilian population, payment slips
5. GES register of billets 1940-47
6. National Registration and Census. 1941-43
7. Nat. Registration and Transcript book (unused) 1941
8. Nat Reg. correspondence 1939-43
9. Record of people billeted in the Tregaron area contained in water rate book 1940-41
10. Circulars concerning compensation scheme for war damage to property 1941-50
11. Circulars concerning billeting under the GES 1941-45
12. 12/13 List of applications relating to billeted persons under the GES
13. 1939-43
14. 1940-47
15. GES; proposed distribution of registered schoolchildren from Liverpool (by school) 1940
16. Requisitioning of Abbey View Pontrhydfendigaid 1942-47
17. Circulars concerning premises requisitioned for housing purposes and war damage repairs, 1945-50
18. Correspondence relating to the purchase of Corner House, Tregaron and a list of evacuees 1943-46
19. Receipts for camp beds and blankets 1941-46
20. Gift Food distribution scheme 1941-48
21. 1948-52
22. Evacuation circulars 1950-54
23. Evacuation reception and billeting 1956-65
24. Correspondence concerning the County Council C.Def. scheme 1951-57
25. (ex SRD/1/618-640)
26. 24. Circulars etc. re civilian deaths due to war operations 1942-44 (ex SRD/1/668)

- CRO. Evac. File 10
- CRO. TGR/SE/15/
- CRO.TGR/SE/11
- POL9/6/17 Police Records
- CRO.TGR/SE/15/9
- CRO.TGR/SE/15/1 & 2
- CRO.TGR. SE/15/3 Evacuees from Liverpool to Tregaron

SCHOOL REGISTERS

- DYC/ED/1/21
- DYC/ED/2/12
- DYC/ED/1/9
- DYC/ED/2/15
- DYC/ED/1/18

(separate files) 109b/110/114b/117Ab/117Dd/120Aa/120Ac/123A/124a/126B/128C/129A/13 0AII/130D/133a/136A/136b/136D/137ab/137B/137C/137Eb138A/138B/

CORNISH RECORD OFFICE. TRURO

- CRO/SRU/SAM/1/77
- CRO/S.SAM1/4/77
- CRO/SAUS2 Trethurgy School Log Book
- CRO/AD792/3 Wartime Evac. Record of Palmer family. Fowey
- CRO/P/244/28/12/2/(CD15) Diary. Miss Bennett
- CRO/DC/RESTORMEL/580 Medical

COVENTRY ARCHIVES. COVENTRY HISTORY CENTRE

- CCA/CD/1/58., Evacuation of schoolchildren: correspondence and other papers of the Education Department
- CCA/CD/1/59/4/Folio 9-10., Letter from head teacher, regarding evacuation of Coventry Children.
- JN352., Coventry Archives, City Council Minutes, October 1938 – March 1945

DENBIGHSHIRE RECORD OFFICE. RUTHIN

- Denbighshire County Council. File 3/4
- Denbigh Borough Council. Letter Book. May 1942 – March 1943 BD/A/412
- Denbigh County Council. File 8/9 OZ1348
- Denbighshire County Council File 36.Z1352

DEVON RECORD OFFICE. EXETER

- Box 4. GES
- Box 12. ARP Evacuation. Nos. 117 – 135
- Ref. 39584/1 (9) WVS Loans to enable mothers to purchase bedding or open up homes
- Ref.441E (WVS) Arrival of Evacuees
- Form EV 60 Returns of Unaccompanied Children
- Form EV 61 Returns of Evacuees and Homeless persons. March 1943
- Ref. 30584/19 Return of Evacuees

DORSET RECORD OFFICE. DORCHESTER

Beaminster DC/BE

- A1/1/10
- A1/1/11

Blandford DC/BFB

- Evacuation Scheme Register and Accommodation

- Civil Defence Papers
- Council Minutes 1933 – 40 & 1940 – 45
- Civil Defence. Reception. Billeting and Schools

Bournemouth DC/BH

- Box 9 Acc. 5157/3 Loc. 5L 78 -86

Bridport DC/BTB

- Corporation Minutes 1906-45
- A.CC 1019/DC8 Contribution for Evacuation. 1941-45 Accounts
- A/1/1/8
- A/1/1/9

Dorchester DC/DOR.
Minute Books

- November 1936 – March 1940
- April 1940 – February 1943
- March 1943 – July 1945
- A/1/5/2
- A/1/5/3

Lyme Regis

- Council Minutes 1934 – 1940
- Council Minutes 1940 – 1947

Shaftesbury DC/SYR

- Evacuation 1930-45
- Correspondence. 1938 – 47 Evacuation (2 boxes)
- Registers. Evacuation 1939-45 (2 files)
- Council Minutes 1936 – 1940
- Council Minutes 1941 – 1944
- Council Minutes 1944 – 1946
- Evacuation (4 files) 1938 – 1942
- Parish War Books
- Register of Accommodation c1939
- Register of requisitioned properties
- File E3 Evacuation of Refugees. General File. 16th Sept 1939 -16th March 1939

Sherborne

- Committee Minutes (4 vols)

Sturminster.

- Annual Minute Books 1939 – 1946

Wareham.

- ARP Committee. 1938 – 1939

Weymouth.

- DC/WYB

Wimborne

- Committee Reports 1939 – 1947 (3 vols)
- Clerk. War Emergency Information
- A/1/3/8
- A/1/3/9

DORSET REFERENCE LIBRARY

- Dorset County Chronicle & Swanage Times 1938 - 1946
- Dorset Daily Echo 1938 - 1946

FLINTSHIRE RECORD OFFICE. HAWARDEN

- E/LB/11/5. St Mathew's Infant School. Buckley
- E/LB/11/12 Lane End School. Buckley
- E/X/50/2 Prestatyn British Council School. 1891-1946
- E/X/50/5 Board of Education Returns. 1902 – 1940
- E/X/56/6 Board of Education Returns. 1898 – 1950
- FC/C/4/2/50 Evacuation Minutes

MASS-OBSERVATION ARCHIVE. UNIVERSITY OF SUSSEX

- TC. Air Raids 9/B2
- TC.Transport 4/C
- Evacuation Box 1 File E

MERIONETH RECORD OFFICE. DOLGELLAU

- Dendraeth RDC. Minute Book. 1937-1940
- Penllyn RDC. File. Evacuation Arrangements.1939

NATIONAL ARCHIVE. KEW

- Minutes 21/389
- Minutes 23/79 31st July 1934
- Air Ministry 8/238
- TNA. CAB/24/279
- TNA.HO45/17636.
  79/6 Folio 323
- TNA. HO186/128/643/3
- TNA.CAB 67/9 (41) 44
  81/82
- TNA.CAB 67/7/172
- TNA.CAB 67/7/170
- TNA.CAB 65/8/179
- TNA.CAB 65/7/174
- TNA.CAB 65/9/244
- TNA.DO.131/29
- TNA.DO.131/39
- TNA.DO. 35/259/B277/4
- TNA.DO. 35/259/B305/4
- TNA.DO.35/259/B305/8
- TNA.DO.131/43
- PREMIER PAPERS 3/22/3 Folio 199
  3/314/2 Folio 64-5
  120/300
- TNA.S.7248 [AIR 2/5238]
- AIR.20/1627
- WAR CABINET 246.1940
  65/9
- TNA.ED 136/205 (13th November 1939)

- TNA.ED 138/34
- TNA.ED 134/74
- TNA.ED 50/207 (26th October 1939)
- TNA.ED 136/125
- TNA.ED 50/204
- GLRO EO/WAR/1/83

CIRCULARS

- 2882 Ministry of Health. Evacuation
- 2539E Ministry of Health. Evacuation
- 2592/2592A/2592B Ministry of Health. Furniture Allocation
- 2592C Ministry of Health. Furniture for Homeless
- 2754 Ministry of Health. Utility Furniture
- 1857/2273 Ministry of Health. Evacuation. Billeting
- 1640 Board of Education. 5th November 1943. Evacuation
- 185/44 Ministry of Health. Temporary Accommodation
- 68/45 Ministry of Health
- 2845 Ministry of Health
- 69/45 Ministry of Health
- 2027 Ministry of Health
- 1871 Ministry of Health

PUBLIC RECORD OFFICE. NORTHERN IRELAND. BELFAST

- Ministry of Home Affairs Ref. RF324. 7/8/41 Future Plans
- MPS2/2/18 Letters
- MPS2/2/4
- MPS2/7/3 Ev C133
- MPS2/2/22 Belfast Operational Plan 1941
- MPS2/2/39 Evacuees. Unaccompanied Children 8/6/41
- MPS2/7/10 Arrival & Departure to and from Dublin. April 1941
- E.E.Circ. 19/17 STORMONT
- E.E.Circ. STORMONT
- D270 Minutes
- G.332/5 Ministry of Education
- ED/25 1922
- Evac.213 Press Conferences
- ED24/7 Second World War Files: Evacuation Scheme. Advisory Comm. on Evacuation. Minutes of Meetings 1939-40.
- HH50/104 Second World War files: Evacuation survey of sending and receiving areas.

SOMERSET RECORDS OFFICE. TAUNTON

- A\AOE/3, 'Memoirs of Somerset evacuees during Second World War: EARLE-FOSTER'.
- A\AOE/4, 'Memoirs of Somerset evacuees during Second World War: GODFREY-KINGWELL'.
- A\AOE/5, 'Memoirs of Somerset evacuees during Second World War: LANHAM-PUGSLEY'.
- C/CD/1/1, 'Committee Minutes and Reports
- C/CD/1/6/1, 'General Correspondence on the government evacuation scheme concerning Somerset: 1938-1939'
- C/CD/1/6/2 GES.Plan V & VI 10th July 1940
- C/CD/1/6/3, 'General correspondence on the government evacuation scheme concerning Somerset:

1939-40'

- C/CD/1/6/3, 'General correspondence on the government evacuation scheme concerning Somerset: 1940-1941'
- C/CD/1/6/4, 'General Correspondence on the government evacuation scheme concerning Somerset, including Women's Land Army documents: 1941-43'
- C/CD/1/6/8 Wartime Nurseries. July 1941
- C/CD/2/4/2 SCC. CD General Services
- C/CD/2/5/3, 'Correspondence concerning evacuation arrangements in the Chard area'.
- E/4 Bx80 2631-3 East Chinnock Log Book
- ED.Comm. E288. Air Raid Precautions in Schools
- FD 1839/38 Food (Defence Plans) Dept.
- MOH 17832/2/42
- MOH Circular E391 1939. Unaccompanied Evacs.
- MOH Circular 1882 2nd Oct 1939.....generally the provision of services for members of the priority classes of Evacs.
- MOH Circular 2212 Nov. !939.....Xmas Festivities
- MOH Circular 1953 19th Jan 1940......treatment of the evacuees with TB
- MOH Circular 2307 14th March 1940....Welfare in Reception Areas
- MOH Circular 2300 14th March 1940....Free Travel Vouchers
- MOH Circular 1979 March 1940....Medical Examination of Evacuees
- MOH Circular 1978 March 1940....Return of Evacs. in Easter Holidays
- MOH Circular 1500 March 1940...Welsh Dept. Holidays in Reception Areas.
- MOH Circular 1998 19th April 1940....Maternity and Child welfare services
- MOH Circular 2095 13th July 1940...Provision of services for persons evac. from certain East and SE coast towns.
- MOH Circular 2422 14th July 1940...War Orphans
- MOH Circular 2178 Oct. 1940 Accommodation in Reception Areas
- MOH Bristol. SW5/5201/13/1
- SCC County Ed. Committee. Circular E287 Nature Study in School
- SCC County Ed. Committee. Circular E281 School Accommodation
- THZ.37/16 Evacuation of Bristol
- WARS/CMW 5th May 1941. Official Notification of Evac. of Bristol

WILTSHIRE RECORD OFFICE. TROWBRIDGE

- WRO/F2/850/1-12 Wartime Correspondence Files Sept. 1938 – March 1946
- Ministry of Health Circular 2140

OTHERS

- Cambridgeshire County Record Office. Council of the Isle of Ely Minutes of the Proceedings of the County Council for the Year 1939-40
- Children on the Move. (2012) Staffordshire Archives & Heritage
- Didcot Parish Council Minutes. 19th January 1939.
- Didcot Parish Council Minutes 21st October 1938
- Duchy of Cornwall Archive. Duchy Office. St. Marys Isles of Scilly
- Oxfordshire Record Office. Chipping Norton. Doc. 10
- Oxfordshire Record Office Idbury and Fifield C.of E. Primary School. Log Book
- Peter Farley-Rutter. Personal Family Papers.
- John Rawlins. Personal Family Papers.

BOOKS

Kate Agnew and Geoff Fox (2001), Children at War: from the First World War to the Gulf. London: Continuum
D.H. Akenson. (1973) Education and Enmity. The control of schooling in Northern Ireland 1920-50. David and Charles
James Bacque. (1997) Crimes and Mercies. The fate of German civilians under Allied Occupation 1944-1950. Little, Brown and Co. Toronto
Daniel Bate. (2010) Coventry's Evacuation Scheme. Unpub. dissertation.
Ralph Barker. (1987) Children of the Benares. A War Crime and its victims.
Barnett House Study Group.(1947) London Children in Wartime Oxford. OUP
Brian Barton (1995) Northern Ireland in the Second World War. Ulster Historical Foundation.
R. Batho et.al. (n.d.)War and Peace in Children's Books.
George Beardmore. Civilians at War. Journals. 1938-46. OUP
Earl R. Beck. (1986) Under the Bombs. German Home Front 1942-45 Univ. Press of Kentucky
Antony Beevor (2003) Berlin. Weidenfeld and Nicolson
Richard Bessel. (2001) Life in the Third Reich. OUP
Geoffrey Bilson. (1988) The Guest Children. Fifth House.
Vera Brittain. (1981) England's Hour. An Autobiography 1939-41. Doubleday
Sidney Brown (2010) Coping with classes during conflict; Education during World War II. Unpub. Paper.
Tim Bryan. (1995) Great Western Railway at War. pub. Patrick Stephens Ltd.
Patricia Cave. (1995) War Guest. Recollections of being evacuated to Canada in 1940. Adept Services
Angus Calder. (1991) The Myth of the Blitz. Jonathan Cape
G.L.Carpenter. (1944) On the Way Home. Salvation Army
James Chapman. (2000) The British at War. Cinema, State & Propaganda, 1939-1945.I.B. Taurus
A.S.Clifton. (1988) Salvation Army. Actions and Attitudes in Wartime 1899-1945 (unpub. PhD)
Travis L. Crosby. (1986) The Impact of Civilian Evacuation in the Second World War. Croom Helm.
John Colville (1985) The Fringes of Power. Downing Street Diaries 1939 – 55 Hodder & Stoughton
Nicholas Cull (1995) Selling War. Oxford.
Eric De Geer (1986) The Finnish war-children in Sweden 1941. Stockholm 1986.
Charlotte Dormer. (2010) Evacuation to Cornwall. Unpublished dissertation.
Oliver Edwards The USA and the Cold War. 1945-63. Access to History.
Kjersti Ericsson & Eva Simonsen (ed) (2005) Children of World War II. Berg
Lillian Evans. (1997) Yesterdays Children 1939-45. Evacuees True Stories. Personal Pub.
Michael Fethney. (2000) Absurd and the Brave. Book Guild Sussex.
Simon R.D. Flynn. (2004) 'Those Billets': constructions of evacuation and evacuees in the BBC radio programme. Children's Hour. Children in War Journal .Vol 4
Carol Fox et al (eds.) In Times of War: An Anthology of War and Peace in Children's Literature
Carol Fox et al (2000), War and Peace in Children's Books. Brighton: University of Brighton
Anna Freud and Dorothy T. Burlingham. (1942) War and Children.
Juliet Gardiner. (2004) Britain at War. Review
Martin Gilbert. Winston.S. Churchill. Hutchinson
Biography Vols.
V 1922 – 1939 (pub 1979)
VI 1939 -1941 'Their Finest Hour' (pub 1983)
VII 1941 – 1945 'Road to Victory' (pub 1986)
Documents Vols.

V 1929 – 1935. The Wilderness Years. (pub 1981)
VI 1936 – 1939. The Coming of War (pub 1982)
Churchill War Papers.
Vol 1 September 1939 – May 1940 (pub 1993)
Vol 2 May 1940 – December 1940 (pub 1994)
Vol 3 1941. (pub 2000)
Wallace Grevatt, (1988) Children's Hour. A Celebration of Those Magical Years. BBC
Richard Grunberger. (1971) Social History of the Third Reich. Penguin
Haffner. Defying Hitler Phoenix: London 2003
Tom Harrisson. (1978) Living Through the Blitz. Penguin.
Ian Hartley. (1983) Goodnight Children Everywhere. Midas Books
Peter Hayward. (1999) For the Sake of the Children. Buckland
Peter Heinl. (2001) Splintered Innocence. Brunner Routledge.
Michael Henderson. (2004) See You After the Duration. The Story of British Evacuees to North America in World War II. Britannica.
Tom Hickman. (1995) What did you do in the war Auntie? The BBC at War. BBC
Laurel Holliday. (1995) Children's Wartime Diaries. Piatkus. .
Bob Holman. (1995) Evacuation. A very British Revolution. Lion
Alistair Horne (1993). Bundles from Britain. Macmillan
Stephen Howarth (1989) August 1939. The last weeks of peace in Europe. Hodder & Stoughton.
E.O.Humphreys. (1940) The Education of Evacuated Children. University College of North Wales.
Margaret Humphreys. (1994) Empty Cradles. Doubleday.
Ruth Inglis. (1986) The Children's War. Fontana.
Max Irving. (2011) To what extent did the designation of Bristol as a 'Neutral' evacuation zone damage the lives of its children? Unpublished dissertation.
Tony Judt. (2007) Postwar. A History of Europe since 1945. Pimlico
Michael Kater. (2004) Hitler Youth. Harvard University Press
Martin Kitchen. (1995) Nazi Germany at War. Longman
Caroline Lang. (1989) Keep Smiling Through. Women in World War Two. Cambridge Educational
Anthony Livesey ed. (1989) Are we at War? Letters to the Times 1939-45
Norman Longmate. (1976) Air Raid. Hutchinson
Roy Lowe. ed. (1992) Education and the Second World War. Studies on schooling and social change. Falmer Press
Graca Machel (2001) The Impact of War on Children. Hurst
Jessica Mann. (2005) Out of Harms Way
James Marten (ed) (2002). Children and War. A Historical Anthology. New York University Press.
Arthur Marwick. (1988) Total War and Social Change. Macmillan
Ross McKibbin.(1991) The Ideologies of Class. Social Relations in Britain 1880-1950. OUP.
Tom Mathews. (2005) Our father's war. Growing up in the Shadow of the Greatest Generation. Broadway
W.E.R. Mons (1941) 'Air Raids and the child'. British Medical Journal Vol 2. No 4217
Elinor Mordaunt. (1944) Here is to Valour. Salvation Army
David Morgan and Mary Evans. (1993) The Battle for Britain. Citizenship and Ideology in the Second World War. Routledge
Leonard Mosley. (1971) Backs to the Wall. Weidenfeld & Nicolson
John Murphy. (1979) Dorset at War DForest Pub. Co.
Lynn Nicholas. (2005) Cruel World Vintage

Bibliography

Sian Nicholas. The Echo of War. Home Front Propaganda and the Wartime BBC 1939-45. Manchester University Press.
Harold Nicolson. (1966) Diaries & Letters 1930-1939 ed. Nigel Nicolson. Collins
Harold Nicolson. (1967) Diaries & Letters 1939-1945 ed. Nigel Nicolson. Collins
Noakes. ed (1998). The German Home Front in World War Two. Vol 4. Exeter University Press.
P.E.Owen. (1961) The Development of the Bilateral System of Education in Caernarvonshire 1903- to date University College of North Wales.
Martin Parsons and Penny Starns. (1999) Evacuation. The True Story. DSM
Martin L. Parsons. (1998) I'll Take That One. Dispelling the Myths of Civilian Evacuation 1939-45. Beckett Karlson.
Martin L. Parsons. (2004) The Manchester Evacuation. The Exception to the Rule. DSM
Martin L. Parsons.(1999) Waiting to go home. DSM
Martin Parsons ed. (2009) Children the Invisible Victims of War. DSM
Martin Parsons. (2008) War Child. Children caught in conflict. Tempus
Padley & Cole.1940 Evacuation Survey. London.
John Penny (2000) Bristol at War, Breedon Books Publishing Company LTD
John Penny (2007) 'The Bristol & District War Memorial'
Clive Ponting. (1990) 1940. Myth or Reality. Hamish Hamilton.
J.B.Priestley. (1940) Postscripts. Heinemann.
W.Ramsey (ed) (1992) The Blitz: Then and Now. Vols 1-3. After the Battle
Eila Räsänen 1988 The effect of the Separation Experiences during Childhood on the Mental and Physical Health and social Well-being in Adulthood. A psychosocial study of the later effects of war-child separation experiences. University of Kuopio.
Charles Ritchie. 1974 The Siren Years. Macmillan.
James Roffey. (1990) Big Boys Don't Cry. Unpublished manuscript.
Niall Rothnie. (1992) The Baedeker Blitz. Ian Allan
Sue Saffle (2006) Children in War and the rhetoric of remembrance. The Stories of Finland's war children. Children in War Journal. DSM.
Raphael Samuel & Paul Thompson. The Myths We Live By.
Raphael Samuel. (1994) Theatres of Memory. Verson
Samways. 1995 We think you ought to go!. GLRO.
Helga Schneider 2006 The Bonfire of Berlin Vintage
Pam Schweitzer. ed. (1990) Goodnight Children Everywhere. Exchange Theatre Trust.
J.E.O. Screen. (2000) Mannerheim. The Finnish Years. Hurst
Sir Geoffrey Shakespeare. (1949) Let Candles Be Brought. MacDonald and Co.
Dorothy Sheridan. ed. (1991) Wartime Women. Mandarin
Peter Sichrovsky. (1988) Born Guilty. Basic Books. New York.
Brian Simon (1991) Education and the Social Order 1940-1990. Lawrence and Wishart
K.R.M. Short (ed.), (1983) Film and Radio Propaganda in World War II.
Harold L. Smith ed (1986) War and Social Change. British Society in the Second World War. Manchester University Press.
Susan Soyinka (2010) From East End to Land's End. Derby Books
Edward Stokes (1994) Innocents Abroad The Story of Child Evacuees to Australia 1940-45. Allen & Unwin
Paul Swain. (1989) The British Documentary Film Unit. 1926-46 Cambridge Univ.Press
Ann Spokes Symonds .ed.(1990) Havens Across the Sea. Mulberry Books.
Nicholas Stargardt. (2005) Witnesses of War. Jonathan Cape.

St.Loe Strachey (1940) Borrowed Children. John Murray.
J.Stevenson. (1990) British Society 1914-45. Penguin
Edward Stokes. (1994) Innocents Abroad. The Story of child evacuees in Australia 1940-45. Unwin.
Julie Summers. (2008)Stranger in the House. Simon and Schuster
Julie Summers. (2011) When the Children Came Home. Simon and Schuster
Richard Titmuss. (1950) Problems of Social Policy. HMSO
Ursula von Kardoff. (1965) Diary of a Nightmare. Berlin 1942-1945 Hart-Davis
Waller & Vaughan-Rees (1990) Blitz: The Civilian War 1940-45 Optima
Jill Wallis. (2000) A Welcome in the Hillsides? The Merseyside and North Wales Experience of Evacuation 1939-45. Avid Publications.
Miriam Ward. Evacuation. A Reception Area in Berkshire. unpublished account. Undated
Sadie Ward. 1988 War in the Countryside. David and Charles.
G.Wasley. (1991) The Attacks on Plymouth. Devon Books
Frank Wintle. (1981) The Plymouth Blitz Bossiney Books
Ben Wicks. (1990) No Time to Wave Goodbye. Bloomsbury.
Philip Ziegler. (1995) London at War. Sinclair-Stevenson.

FILMS

ARCHIVE/PROPAGANDA (Imperial War Museum)

Westward Ho 1940

Living with Strangers 1941

The Village School. 1941

(All 3 on a DVD compilation called. *'Keep The Wheels Turning'*)

Spring Offensive 1942

FEATURE: Mother of Mine (Äideistä parhain) 2005.

Index

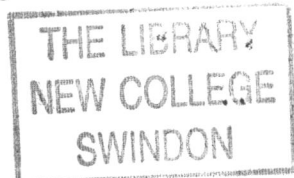

About the Author

Martin Parsons, PhD FRHistS, is considered by many of his peers to be one of the leading academics in the field of War Child research, and his personal papers and ephemera now form the basis of the publicly accessible Evacuee and War Child Archive located in the Museum of English Rural Life at the University of Reading. His first book on Evacuation 'I'll Take That One' and published in 1998, examined the myths surrounding the scheme and was regarded as the first definitive history of evacuation in the UK and overseas. His other academic books on the topic include; 'Waiting to Go Home', 'Evacuation the True Story', 'Manchester Evacuation. The Exception to the Rule', 'War Child. Children in Conflict', and an interdisciplinary book entitled 'Children: The Invisible Victims of War'. In addition he has written a series of four books on the topic for school-children and also edits the international 'Children in War' journal, which has attracted contributions from academics and colleagues world-wide.

Martin has given lectures to various national bodies and conferences around the world including the English Speaking Union, the Cabinet War Rooms, Westminster Central Hall, the German Embassy, the Imperial War Museums in both London and Manchester, and a number of Universities in the UK, USA, Scandinavia and Central Europe.

He was a consultant and contributor on the BAFTA-winning 'Britain at War in Colour' documentary for Channel 4, the BBC2 programme 'Evacuees' in The Lost Decade series (2005), and many other TV and radio programmes. In 2008 he was historical advisor for a TV documentary in Germany and completed a series of programmes (Evacuees Reunited) for ITV. In 2000, with Dr Penny Starns (Cambridge and Bristol), he co-researched and co-wrote the Radio 4 series on Evacuation that won the Sony Gold Award for 'Best Documentary'.

At present he is working with the Armed forces applying his research to the plight of present-day 'service' children whose parents have been deployed to conflict zones.

When not writing or researching, Martin makes stained glass windows and attempts to play golf.